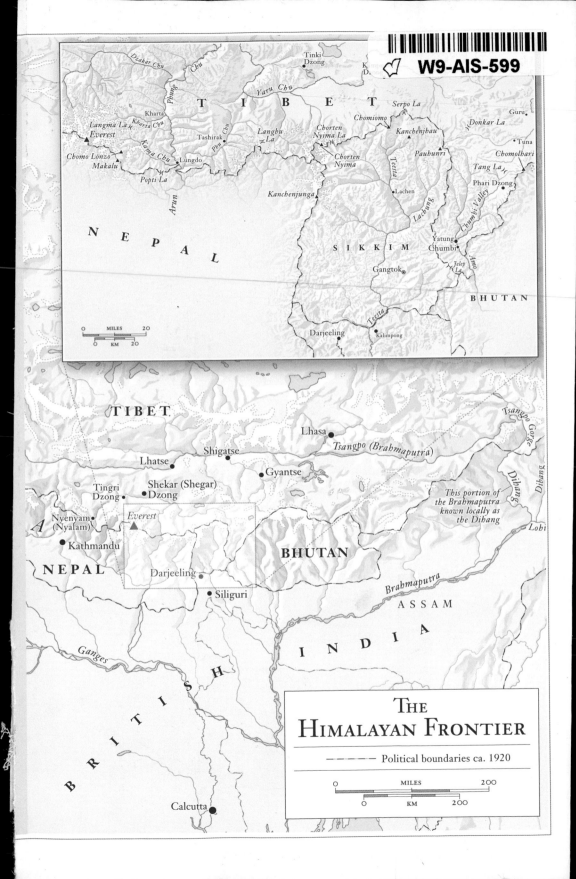

Dzakar Chu
Phung Chu
Yaru Chu
Tinki Dzong
K

T I B E T

Serpo La

Guru

Kharta
Chomiomo
Donkar La

Langma La
Everest
Kharta Chu
Tashirak
Phu Chu
Langbu La
Chorten Nyima La
Kanchenjhau
Tuna

Chomo Lonzo
Makalu
Kama Chu
Lungdo
Chorten Nyima
Pauhunri
Chomolhari

Popti La
Tang La

Arun
Kanchenjunga
Teesta
Lachen
Phari Dzong

Chumbi Valley

N E P A L
Lachung
Yatung
Chumbi
Amo

S I K K I M

Gangtok
Jelep La

MILES   20

KM   20

B H U T A N

Teesta

Darjeeling
Kalimpong

T I B E T

Lhasa

Tsangpo (Brahmaputra)

Tsangpo Gorge

Shigatse

Lhatse
Gyantse

Dibang

Tingri Dzong
Shekar (Shegar) Dzong

This portion of
the Brahmaputra
known locally as
the Dihang

Dibang

Nyenyam (Nyalam)
Everest
Lohi

A
Kathmandu
BHUTAN

N E P A L
Darjeeling

Brahmaputra

Siliguri
ASSAM

I N D I A

Ganges

B R I T I S H

Calcutta

THE
HIMALAYAN FRONTIER

—·——·—— Political boundaries ca. 1920

0   MILES   200

0   KM   200

INTO THE
SILENCE

INTO THE SILENCE

The Great War, Mallory, and the Conquest of Everest

WADE DAVIS

ALFRED A. KNOPF   NEW YORK   TORONTO   2011

THIS IS A BORZOI BOOK
PUBLISHED BY ALFRED A. KNOPF

All photographs courtesy of Royal Geographical Society except
p. 1 (top): Pitt Rivers Museum, University of Oxford; p. 7 (top): Fell
and Rock Climbing Club; p. 7 (middle and bottom): Alpine Club;
p. 10 (top) and p. 16 (top and middle): Ed Webster.

Library of Congress Cataloging-in-Publication Data
Davis, Wade.
Into the silence : the Great War, Mallory, and the conquest of
Everest / by Wade Davis.—1st ed.
p.   cm.
"A Borzoi book."
ISBN 978-0-375-40889-2
1. Mallory, George, 1886–1924.   2. Mountaineers—
Great Britain—Biography.   3. Mount Everest Expedition
(1924).   4. World War, 1914–1918—Great Britain—
Influence.   I. Title.
GV199.92.M356D38 2011
796.522092—dc22
[B]   2011013888

Library and Archives Canada Cataloguing in Publication
Davis, Wade
Into the silence : the Great War, Mallory, and the conquest of
Everest / Wade Davis.
Includes bibliographical references and index.
Also issued in electronic format.
ISBN 978-0-676-97919-0
1. Mallory, George, 1886–1924.   2. Mountaineering expeditions—
Everest, Mount (China and Nepal).   3. Mountaineers—
Great Britain—Biography.   4. Soldiers—Great Britain—
Biography.   5. Everest, Mount (China and Nepal).   6. World War,
1914–1918—Great Britain.   I. Title.

GV199.92.M34D39 2011   796.522092   C2011-901741-5

Maps by David Lindroth, Inc.
Jacket image: *Mount Everest from the North East*
by L. V. Bryant, 1935 © Royal Geographical Society
Jacket design by Barbara de Wilde

Manufactured in the United States of America
First Edition

To my grandfather Captain Daniel Wade Davis,
who served as a medical officer in France with the Royal Army
Medical Corps, 80th Field Ambulance, 32nd Division Train,
1915–1916, and in England with the Canadian Army
Medical Corps, 1916–1918

Contents

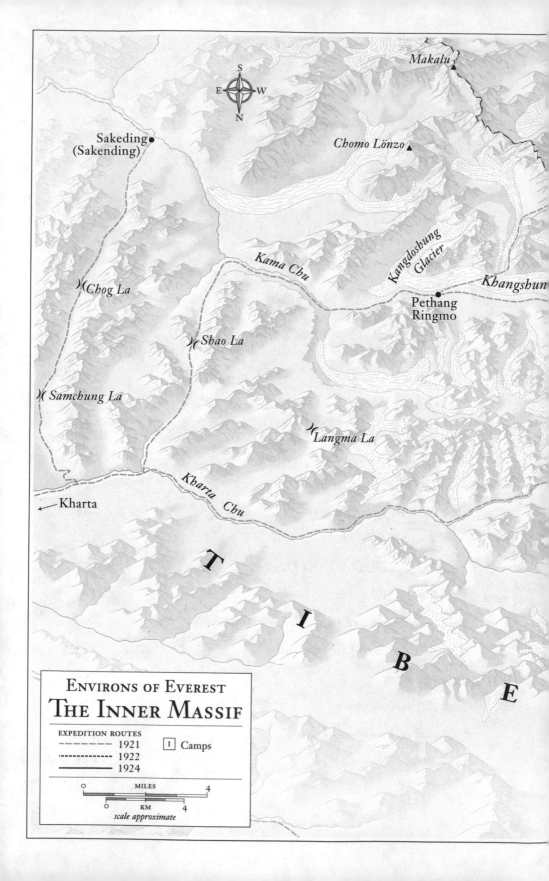

Makalu ▲

Chomo Lönzo ▲

Sakeding
(Sakending) ●

Kama Chu

Kangdoshung Glacier

Khangshun

)(Chog La

Pethang
Ringmo ●

)(Shao La

)(Samchung La

)(Langma La

Kharta Chu

← Kharta

T

I

B

E

S
E ✦ W
N

ENVIRONS OF EVEREST
THE INNER MASSIF

EXPEDITION ROUTES
– – – 1921   I Camps
------------ 1922
———— 1924

0   MILES   4
0   KM   4
scale approximate

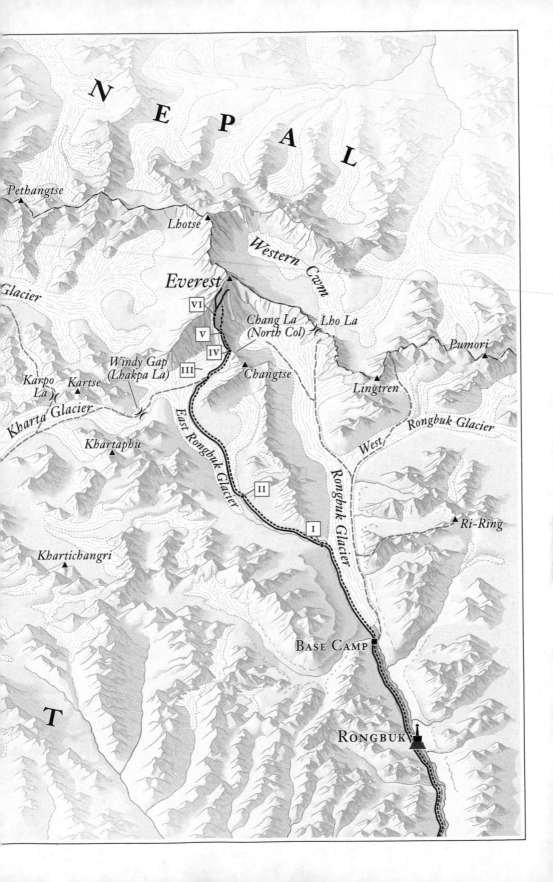

N E P A L

Pethangtse

Lhotse

Western Cwm

Glacier

Everest

VI

Chang La
(North Col)

Lho La

Pumori

V

IV

*Windy Gap
(Lhakpa La)*

III

Changtse

Lingtren

*Karpo
La*

Kartse

East Rongbuk Glacier

Kharta Glacier

Rongbuk Glacier

West

Khartaphu

II

Ri-Ring

I

Khartichangri

BASE CAMP

RONGBUK

T

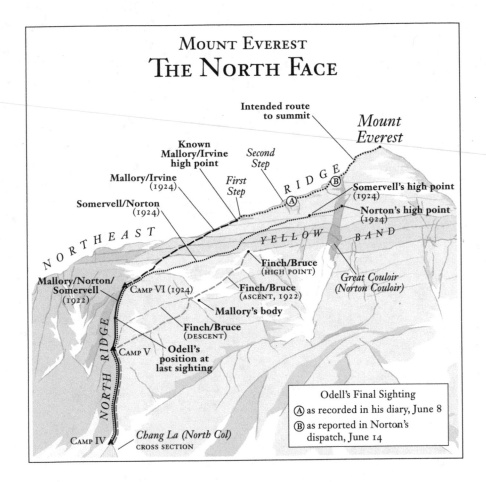

MOUNT EVEREST
THE NORTH FACE

Intended route to summit

Mount Everest

Known Mallory/Irvine high point

Second Step

Mallory/Irvine (1924)

First Step

RIDGE

Ⓑ

Somervell's high point (1924)

Somervell/Norton (1924)

Ⓐ

Norton's high point (1924)

NORTHEAST

YELLOW BAND

Finch/Bruce (HIGH POINT)

Great Couloir (Norton Couloir)

Mallory/Norton/ Somervell (1922)

CAMP VI (1924)

Finch/Bruce (ASCENT, 1922)

Mallory's body

Finch/Bruce (DESCENT)

CAMP V

Odell's position at last sighting

NORTH RIDGE

CAMP IV

Chang La (North Col)
CROSS SECTION

Odell's Final Sighting
Ⓐ as recorded in his diary, June 8
Ⓑ as reported in Norton's dispatch, June 14

Preface

O N T H E M O R N I N G O F J U N E 6, 1 9 2 4, at a camp perched at
23,000 feet on an ice ledge high above the East Rongbuk Glacier and just below the lip of Everest's North Col, expedition
leader Lieutenant Colonel Edward Norton said farewell to two men
about to make a final desperate attempt for the summit. At thirty-seven,
George Leigh Mallory was Britain's most illustrious climber. Sandy
Irvine was a young scholar of twenty-two from Oxford with little previous mountaineering experience. Time was of the essence. Though
the day was clear, in the southern skies great rolling banks of clouds
revealed that the monsoon had reached Bengal and would soon sweep
over the Himalaya and, as one of the climbers put it, "obliterate everything." Mallory remained characteristically optimistic. In a letter
home, he wrote, "We are going to sail to the top this time and God
with us, or stamp to the top with the wind in our teeth."

Norton was less sanguine. "There is no doubt," he confided to John
Noel, a veteran Himalayan explorer and the expedition's photographer,
"Mallory knows he is leading a forlorn hope." Perhaps the memory of
previous losses weighed on Norton's mind: seven Sherpas left dead on
the mountain in 1922, two more this season, the Scottish physician
Alexander Kellas buried at Kampa Dzong during the approach march
and reconnaissance of 1921. Not to mention the near misses. Mallory himself, a climber of stunning grace and power, had, on Everest,
already come close to death on three occasions.

Norton knew the cruel face of the mountain. From the North Col,
the route to the summit follows the North Ridge, which rises dramatically in several thousand feet to fuse with the Northeast Ridge, which,
in turn, leads to the peak. Just the day before, he and Howard Somervell
had set out from an advanced camp on the North Ridge at 26,800 feet.
Staying away from the bitter winds that sweep the Northeast Ridge,
they had made an ascending traverse to reach the great couloir that

clefts the North Face and falls away from the base of the summit pyramid to the Rongbuk Glacier, ten thousand feet below. Somervell gave out at 28,000 feet. Norton pushed on, shaking with cold, shivering so drastically he thought he had succumbed to malaria. Earlier that morning, climbing on black rock, he had foolishly removed his goggles. By the time he reached the couloir, he was seeing double, and it was all he could do to remain standing. Forced to turn back at 28,126 feet, less than 900 feet below the summit, he was saved by Somervell, who led him across the ice-covered slabs. On the retreat to the North Col, Somervell himself suddenly collapsed, unable to breathe. He pounded his own chest, dislodged the obstruction, and coughed up the entire lining of his throat.

By morning Norton had lost his sight, temporarily blinded by the sunlight. In excruciating pain, he contemplated Mallory's plan of attack. Instead of traversing the face to the couloir, Mallory and Irvine would make for the Northeast Ridge, where only two obstacles barred the way to the summit pyramid: a distinctive tower of black rock dubbed the First Step, and, farther along, the Second Step, a 100-foot bluff that would have to be scaled. Though concerned about Irvine's lack of experience, Norton had done nothing to alter the composition of the team. Mallory was a man possessed. A veteran of all three British expeditions, he knew Everest better than anyone alive.

Two days later, on the morning of June 8, Mallory and Irvine set out from their high camp for the summit. The bright light of dawn gave way to soft shadows as luminous banks of clouds passed over the mountain. Noel Odell, a brilliant climber in support, last saw them alive at 12:50 p.m., faintly from a rocky crag: two small objects moving up the ridge. As the mist rolled in, enveloping their memory in myth, he was the only witness. Mallory and Irvine would not be seen or heard from again. Their disappearance would haunt a nation and give rise to the greatest mystery in the history of mountaineering.

Never did Odell doubt that they reached the summit before meeting their end. Nor did he question the sublime purpose that had led them all to cross hundreds of miles on foot, from India and across Tibet, just to reach the base of the mountain. Odell wrote of his two lost friends: "My final glimpse of one, whose personality was of that charming character that endeared him to all and whose natural gifts seemed to indicate such possibilities of both mind and body, was that he was 'going strong,' sharing with that other fine character who accompanied him such a vision of sublimity that it has been the lot of few mortals to behold; few while beholding have become merged into such a scene of transcendence."

INTO THE
SILENCE

CHAPTER I

Great Gable

ON THE VERY DAY that George Mallory and Sandy Irvine dis-appeared on Everest, another party of British climbers slowly made their way to the summit of a quite different mountain and in very different circumstances. At 2,949 feet, Great Gable was not a serious or difficult climb, but it was said to be "the most completely beautiful of English mountains." It anchored the fells of Cumbria, and from its summit could be seen a dozen or more of the rounded hills and rocky crags of the Lake District, where so many English climbers had first discovered the freedom of open space and the feel of wind and rain and sleet on cold hands jammed into cracks of granite and slate.

There were some eighty men and women in this solemn party, most of them members of the Fell and Rock Climbing Club, a loose association founded in 1906 and dedicated exclusively to the celebra-tion of the English hills. Among them was the club secretary, Leslie Somervell, whose brother Howard was then with the Everest expedi-tion, and Arthur Wakefield, club president since 1923. Wakefield had served as medical officer on the 1922 Everest expedition and had been the first to rush to the relief of the climbers swept away by the ava-lanche on the North Col that buried alive seven Sherpa porters. Death was something he knew well.

The most prominent figure on Great Gable this day was Geof-frey Winthrop Young, who brought up the rear, supported by his wife, Len, as he struggled over boulders and wet stones in rain so fierce it swept the cape from his back. Considered by many to be the greatest English mountaineer of his era, Young was the mentor of Mallory, and had been responsible for both Mallory and Wakefield securing invita-tions to join the Everest expeditions. This was his first climb since losing his left leg to an Austrian shell on the night of August 31, 1917, at Monte San Gabriele while serving on the Isonzo Front, in Italy. In time he would summit the Matterhorn with a prosthetic limb of his own design, but for the moment it was all he could do to keep his balance and move steadily up the slope toward the others. A gifted Georgian poet and a fine orator, he was here at Wakefield's invitation to help dedicate a bronze plaque inscribed with the names of those members of the FRCC who had been lost in the war, and to consecrate in their memory a tract of some three thousand acres purchased by the survivors and gifted by them to the nation as a living memorial. The actual deeds to the land had been presented by Wakefield to a representative of the National Trust several months before, on October 13, 1923, at the annual FRCC dinner at the Sun Hotel in the nearby village of Coniston.

"These title deeds," he had told his audience that night, "represent the lives of those of our members who died for their country, men with whom in many cases we have walked over these fells, and whose friendship we treasured. The cost is great indeed. Sir, we hand these deeds over to you in the hope and belief that future generations will be inspired with the same sense of self-sacrifice and devotion to great ends, even at the cost of self-obliteration, that were shown by those who died and whose monument this is." The names of the dead were then read, as those present stood in silence.

Now many of the same company of men and women gathered around a boulder at the summit of Great Gable. Covering the memorial plaque was a rain-soaked Union Jack, the very flag that had flown at Jutland from the bridge of the battleship *Barham* of the 5th Battle Squadron of the Royal Navy. Before drawing back the flag to reveal the bronze, Arthur Wakefield stepped forward and began to speak of the land, the breath of the moors, the spirit of freedom that had impelled them all to march to war. It was an inspiring address, wrote a reporter for the *Manchester Guardian* who was present, one that brought all thoughts back to those years of strain and trial and sacrifice.

Wakefield's rhetoric was moving, heartfelt, and sincere, but his appearance shocked Young, who had not seen him since before the war. Both were scions of the British elite. Born six months apart in 1876, they'd gone to college together, attending Trinity at a time when no fewer than 195 members of Parliament, fully a third of the House, were Cambridge men, and of these 68 were from Trinity. Young remembered Wakefield as a short, broad-shouldered, curly-haired, good-looking northern lad with an attractive smile, well liked by all. But it was Wakefield's prodigious strength that had led Young to recommend him to Captain Percy Farrar of the Alpine Club and the Mount Everest Committee as a candidate for the Everest expeditions. Wakefield, known to his friends as Waker, was a man who liked to walk. In 1905 he had set a record in the Lake District, traversing Scafell Pike, Helvellyn, Skiddaw, Green Gable, Kirk Fell, Steeple, Red Pike, and a score of other summits, covering some fifty-nine miles with a total vertical ascent and descent of some 23,500 feet in twenty-two hours, seven minutes. He had climbed in Switzerland in 1893, and in the spring of 1894 had encountered for the first time the rock of the Lake District, the Central Gully of Great End. Powerful, cautious, methodical, he never fell.

But this was not the man who appeared at Young's side ready to pull back the flag to reveal the names of the dead. What stepped forward was a shadow of the man he had once known, with eyes that appeared to be focused into some distant past, as if on a memory that could not be embraced, a thought impossible to distill. Then, unexpectedly, the weather cleared; as Young recalled, "The sun broke through the clouds as he made his address under the highest rocks, and in the rather silvery gleam, with its faint halo of mist, I saw him for a few moments again as he had been in his very vital and sunnily serene youth." Other witnesses remember Wakefield hesitating and then slowly beginning to sob as the flag drew back to reveal the names of those who had perished: caught on the barbed wire, drowned in mud, choked by the oily slime of gas, reduced to a spray of red mist, quartered limbs hanging from shattered branches of burnt trees, bodies swollen and blackened with flies, skulls gnawed by rats, corpses stuck in the sides of trenches that aged with each day into the colors of the dead. It was, according to Wakefield's son, the last time his father ever displayed human emotion. He would go to his end never speaking of the war, consumed only by abiding hatred of all things German.

A Mr. Herbert Cain began slowly to read the names of the deceased: S. Bainbridge, J. E. Benn, H. S. P. Blair, A. J. Clay, J. N. Fletcher . . . There were twenty in all, from a club with a membership of 450, men and women, young and very old. Such rosters had become all too familiar. Young had dedicated his recent book, *On Mountain Craft*, published in 1920, to fifty friends who had died— some on mountains, but most in the trenches. In another of his books, *The Mountains of Snowdonia*, he recalled innocent times before the war when climbing had the freshness of the dawn and some of the best minds and certainly the finest climbers of a generation—George Mallory, Siegfried Herford, John Maynard and Geoffrey Keynes, Cottie Sanders, Duncan Grant, Robert Graves, George Trevelyan, and many others—came together in Wales at the top of Llanberis Pass, at a place called Pen y Pass. By day they would climb and by night they would sing, recite poetry, debate, and argue. In ways impossibly innocent to the contemporary eye, they explored dreams of purity and purpose in a new century where all that mattered was authenticity and beauty, loyalty and friendship. Young was the inspiration for these gatherings, the maître d' and impresario, and from the first in 1903 he recorded each event in a photographic album, which he called the Pen y Pass diary. Of the honed and beautiful faces, the innocent glances—no fewer than twenty-three of the men would be killed in the war, another eleven so severely wounded that to climb again they would have to overcome immense physical impediments, just as Young himself had done.

But of the names read with such intense emotion from this memorial bronze on this cold and windswept day, there were two that especially haunted Young. One was that of Hilton Laurence Slingsby, the brother of his wife, Len, who stood stiffly by his side. Geoffrey was twenty years older than she, and as he looked over the rocks and into the mist, he could see the face of Hilton as a young boy of nine when he had first led the lad up this very mountain. He recalled the day— August 20, 1917—when a letter had reached him in Italy with word that Hilton, after three years at the front, and having already survived a grievous wound, had been "killed in action," a term, of course, that could mean anything.

The second name was that of Siegfried Herford, killed at Ypres in 1915. A friend of Mallory's and arguably the finest rock climber of his generation, he was, as Young recalled, "a poet at heart," a youth who came and went with the "spontaneity of the wind, so near to the light and wonder of the hills in spirit that his feats upon the cliffs only seemed natural." As much as anyone who came to Pen y Pass, Herford had inspired Young to dream. "With our coming together," he would write, "in that high air all cares seemed to drop from us, like clouds sinking below on that two way view down the pass."

The litany of the dead had done much to quell such sentiments. In August 1917, when it seemed to everyone that the war might go on forever, Young recorded in his diary a list of good friends who had died, no fewer than twenty-five, and this left room for those he termed acquaintances; of these there were another twenty-five. Writing from Ypres in 1915, he'd spoken of the dead in more intimate phrases, as noted in his book *The Grace of Forgetting*.

In the new army around us I knew that there were many younger friends, those who would have become the leaders in mountaineering and in our country. I saw in passing Twiggy Anderson, the perfect hurdler and lively scholar, again an Eton pupil; Terrence Hickman of Kings, good friend of so many mountaineers; and J. Raphael the football player, whom I took to Wales to climb, and who ran hard up the steep slopes of all his mountains, springing on his toes, and explaining to me that that really was the correct way to climb.

They were killed very near to us, and the news came slowly and fatally. The toll of tragic loss, and not only among climbing friends, kept mounting. Dearest of all, Wilbert Spencer at La Bassée, Kenneth Powell the classic athlete, Nigel Madan a close friend, Werner of Kings, cousins John and Horas Kennedy. On other fronts, C. K. Carfrae, Guy Butlin, the brothers Rupert and Basil Brooke, Julian and Billy Grenfell . . . Gilbert Hosegood, very fair and tall, came to me in excitement because he had met his brother by chance as he marched with his company through Ypres; and he walked beside him in talk all down the Menin road. Not long after, I drove him south down the front to visit his brother's grave, a lovely spot, and Guy du Maurier, his brother's colonel, was more than kind to us. We were hardly returned to Ypres when news of du Maurier's death also reached us. Hosegood joined up soon after, to take his brother's place he said; he too fell.

Young had been at Zermatt climbing with Herford during the soft summer of 1914, when all of Europe glowed with weather so beautiful and fine that it would be remembered for a generation, invoked by all those who sought to recall a time before the world became a place of mud and sky, with only the zenith sun to remind the living that they had not already been buried and left for dead. Stunned by a mix of emotions—horror, incredulity, morbid anticipation, fear, and confusion—Young returned to London to find "the writing of madmen already on the wall." He recalled, "I attended the peace meeting in Trafalgar Square, the last protest of those who had grown up in the age of civilized peace: and then the dogs of war were off in full cry." Forty years later, near the end of his days, he would write, "After the hardening effects of two wars it is difficult to recall the devastating collapse of the structure of life, and all its standards, which the recrudescence of barbarous warfare denoted for our generation."

He had been born to a privileged life, the second son of Sir George

Young of Formosa Place, a stately eighteenth-century house of gardens and roses perched on the banks of the river Thames. His mother was Irish, a splendid storyteller and a great hostess, and their home regularly welcomed such luminaries as Robert Baden-Powell, founder of the Boy Scouts and the hero of Mafikeng; the poet laureate Alfred, Lord Tennyson; and Roger Casement, the Irish nationalist and enigmatic champion of human rights who would be knighted in 1911 for exposing the atrocities in the Belgian Congo, only to be hanged for treason in 1916. Of his three siblings, he was closest to his younger brother, Hilton, who would lose an arm in the war. His childhood was one of action and fantasy, endless days outside in all weather and all seasons, among the bitter cherries and silver beeches, the weeping willows and ancient yews of a country setting that inspired within him a love of color and nature, rivers and the wind, mountains and rain. He never practiced religion in an orthodox sense, but all of his life was infused with a celebratory quest for the wonder of beauty and friendship, the sheer vitality of being human and alive.

At Marlborough, a school that would send 733 boys to die in the trenches, he was known for his good looks, his poetry, and his remarkable athletic abilities. At Cambridge he became a climber, of both mountains and the Gothic rooftops of the university colleges. His impish side penned anonymously *The Roof Climber's Guide to Trinity*, thus beginning a long tradition of illicit midnight scrambles over slate and lead and gargoyles. Following graduation in 1898, he went abroad, living for three years in France and Germany and becoming fluent in both languages. His true affection was for Germany; he translated the ballads of Schiller and the devotional poems of Dietrich Bonhoeffer. In 1902, he returned to England to take a teaching position at Eton; there he met the young John Maynard Keynes, who would later join him on climbing trips to the Alps.

Young first encountered George Mallory in 1909, at a Cambridge dinner. At Easter he invited Mallory to Pen y Pass, and the following summer the two went off, at Young's expense, to the Alps, where they were joined by Donald Robertson, a close friend and peer of Hilton Young's. They climbed a number of peaks, none more dramatic than the southeast ridge of the Nesthorn, where Mallory nearly died. He was leading at the time, inching his way across fluted ice, seeking a route around the third of the four great towers that blocked the way up the ridge. Young would later recall his sudden astonishment: "I saw the boots flash from the wall without even a scrape; and, equally soundlessly, a grey streak flickered downward, and past me, and out of sight. So much did the wall, to which he had clung so long, overhang that from the instant he lost hold he touched nothing until the rope stopped him in mid-air over the glacier. I had had time to think, as I flung my body forward on to the belayed rope, grinding it and my hands against the slab, that no rope could stand such a jerk; and even to think out what our next action must be—so instantaneous is thought." Miraculously, the rope held and Mallory was uninjured.

In another book, *On High Hills*, Young would remember and praise his companions on that dramatic climb: "To both of them life was a treasure of value; but it was also a talent to be reinvested for the profit of others. Neither hesitated to risk the loss of his share in it, if by doing so he could help to keep the great spirit of human adventure alive in the world." Robertson would die a year later, on a rock face in Wales. A chapel would be built in his memory, and a monument erected within sight of the cliffs where he fell, and a trust established to bring English youths to the hills. Such were the sensibilities in the years immediately before the war, a time when powerful and virile men could speak of love and beauty without shame, and sunsets and sunrises had yet to become, as the painter Paul Nash would write, "mockeries to man," blasphemous moments, preludes to death.

AT THIRTY-EIGHT, Geoffrey Young was too old for active service in 1914. But within a week of returning from Switzerland on July 28, and two days before Britain formally entered the war on August 4, he was on his way to France as a war correspondent for the *Daily News*. By then five German armies, more than a million men, had advanced into northern France and begun a broad enveloping sweep through Belgium, with Paris as the goal. To the south the French had fallen into a German trap, launching their armies east toward the Ardennes and Alsace, hundreds of thousands of troops dressed in bright red trousers and electric-blue coats moving boldly over open ground as if on parade. The result was a slaughter unlike anything previously known in the history of warfare. In the Battle of the Frontiers, France suffered the loss of more than 300,000 men in a fortnight. In three days beginning on August 20, while Young reported from Namur, on the Belgian Front, some 40,000 French would die, 27,000 on August 22 alone. By Christmas, after but four months of war, with four years to go, France would suffer nearly a million casualties.

While the Germans attacked with 87 divisions, and the French countered with 62, the British Expeditionary Force mustered only 4, which were hastily flung into the line at Mons, in Belgium. There, amid the slag heaps and pit heads of the coalfields, 100,000 British regulars, outnumbered three to one, took on the entire German First Army. Obliged to retreat, the men walked blood-shod, their feet so swollen that boots once removed could not be put back on, fighting constantly as they retreated 170 miles with scarcely a rest.

As the British fell back, fighting an epic rear-guard action at Le Cateau, the German commander, Helmut von Moltke, lost his nerve and ordered his three northern armies to turn south, abandoning the effort to envelop Paris from the west, and thus exposing his flank to the French before the Marne River. The French attack on September 5 brought more than two million men into battle. Each side would suffer over half a million casualties. The German assault was stopped but not shattered, and thus began the so-called race for the sea as the armies moved north and west, each constantly trying to outflank its enemy and turn the battle line, which, with each passing day, became more deeply inscribed into the body and soil of France. A final desperate German bid to reach the channel ports of Dunkirk, Boulogne, and Calais was thwarted by the British at the medieval town of Ypres, in a battle that the Germans would remember as Kindermord zu Ypren— the Massacre of the Innocents.

The frontal assaults on the British began on October 20 and did not stop until the third week of November. The line held, but at a tremendous cost. By the time the rains of winter, the wettest in forty years, drowned out the guns, the British Expeditionary Force, virtually the entire regular army of the empire, had ceased to exist. A third of its 160,000 men were dead. Battalions that had embarked for France in August with 40 officers and 1,000 men had, on average, been reduced to 1 officer and 30 men. The 7th Division, which arrived in France in October with 400 officers and 12,000 men, would lose 9,000 soldiers in eighteen days.

In a strategic and tactical move that would seal the fate of many tens of thousands, the British at Ypres took up defensive positions on a series of low, gentle hills that enveloped the town to the east, thus creating a bulge in the line, a salient that would be dominated throughout the war by German artillery securely positioned on higher ground on three sides. Defending the Ypres Salient, never larger than four miles deep and twelve wide, would over the course of the war cost the British 90,000 men killed and 410,000 wounded. Another 89,880 simply vanished, swallowed by the mud or vaporized by shell fire. German losses were comparable. In four years, an area of shattered ground one could walk around in a day would see no fewer than 1.7 million casualties. Cradled within this cauldron of death, the old medieval center of Ypres, with its noble buildings and great Cloth Hall, would vanish, blackened by fire, battered by artillery, reduced to crumbing ruins and shell-shattered streets; there civilians and soldiers alike lived a subterranean existence in cellars where rain, oil, and blood ran together to dampen any memory of peace.

Thus over the last weeks of 1914 came into being the topography of Armageddon. The trenches ran some 460 miles from the Swiss border to the English Channel. The British sector contained some of the worst and most indefensible terrain. The low fields of Flanders were flat, water-soaked, with no feature rising more than two hundred feet above sea level. The slightest hill took on strategic importance, and thousands would bleed and die for a height of land that in Surrey, with its rolling downs, would go unnoticed. The actual British trench line was astonishingly short. From Ypres to the channel was held by Belgian forces. To the south, the French controlled the front from Picardy and the Somme all the way to the Swiss frontier. The British sector, anchored by the towns of Armentières, Arras, and Albert, ran from Ypres south and slightly east into northern France, through the mines of Lens, past Vimy Ridge, across the Scarpe River near Arras and down to the Somme. For much of the war it was a mere 85 miles in length, and at no time did it exceed 125 miles.

Indeed, the entire British zone of operations, in which millions of men lived, trained, and died, measured but 50 by 60 miles, roughly the size of the English county of Lincolnshire. To the west was the sea, never more than 50 miles to the rear, and the great staging ports and bases of Étaples, Le Havre, and Rouen. To the east were the Germans. To supply and defend roughly 100 miles of war front, the British would dig more than 6,000 miles of trenches. The normal wartime provision of shovels for the army was 2,500; in the mud of Flanders, more than 10 million would be needed. No fewer than 25,000 British coal miners would be engaged around the clock to tunnel beneath the enemy and set charges, which detonated with blasts that could be heard in London.

"The stories of madness are frequent," Young confided to his diary in February 1915. "The strain no man seems able to support, under accurate shell fire. In one British trench all the men were dead when at last relieved after four days. One surviving subaltern had made himself drunk on the men's brandy, to endure it, after having pegged out his senior, who was mad, with bayonets to prevent him shooting himself."

Young lived in Ypres from November 1914 through the end of July 1915. His dispatches, collected in the book *From the Trenches*, were among the first and finest eyewitness accounts of a conflict unlike anything that had ever been known. This was not war, he wrote; it was the monstrous inversion of civilization. To call it war was to imply that something of the sun remained, when in fact all that existed was a bruised sky in a bitter night of cobalt rains. He recalled, "Time and again in the blackness ahead the votive candles on the wayside shrines fell dazzlingly across the road. Once I stopped the car and through the sudden silence, a woman's voice called unemotionally, 'Is that death?' "

Streams of human misery, refugees fleeing the German terror, flooded the roads of Belgium. In the remnants of the town wandered wounded and stunned British soldiers, caked in mud, crawling and choking through the shell-blistered streets. Beyond the front the leprous earth was scattered with the swollen and blackened corpses of hundreds of young men, and hovering over everything was the appalling stench of rotten carrion.

"In the half-exposed remnant of what may have been a vestry," Young wrote, "a young RAMC surgeon was working alone, at hurricane speed, on the wounded being carried or led in, or lying on the bloodstained, shattered floor. His face was a mask, his blue eyes like hard steel. The precision with which he cut garments, dressed wounds, bandaged limbs and passed silently on to the next was as remarkable as his speed. All inside was a jostle and a carnage; the noise outside was distracting; the hot dust covered us from the shrapnel bursting above the ruined walls. The bearers bringing or supporting the wounded had been often wounded themselves as they came. I marveled—how could any man stand it, and for hours, and alone?"

Overwhelmed by the suffering, shamed into action by the desperate need for more medical support for the troops, Young abandoned journalism to serve in an ambulance unit of his own creation, flaunting his social connections shamelessly to keep his men close to the front, where lives could be saved. First in Flanders, and later in Italy, Young and his colleagues would rescue more than 100,000 wounded soldiers before he himself would be cut down. Ypres was the inspiration. He was there still on April 22, 1915, when the Germans attacked using poison gas for the first time.

"The bombardment," he wrote,

seemed heavier and more menacing . . . I walked uneasily through our wards and offices. A wounded soldier, in the half coma we knew later as shell shock, was being tended and was muttering continuously 'White faces . . . the moonlight . . . white faces' . . . I went out. I could see figures running back, the yellow pale of cloud was higher, and again dots of figures in khaki were hurrying forward across the fields out to the northeast of us . . . The wounded began to pour in . . . the first poison gas sufferers. This horror was too monstrous to believe at first . . . But when it came, far as we had traveled from our civilized world of a few months back, the savagery of it, of the sight of men choking to death with yellow froth, lying on the floor and out on the fields, made me rage with an anger which no later cruelty of man, not even the degradation of our kind by the hideous concentration camps in later Germany, ever quite rekindled; for then we still thought all men were human.

ARTHUR WAKEFIELD had followed his own path through agony and despair. He began the war a man of deep religious faith, a devout Anglican who never drank and never failed to attend Sunday service. As Geoffrey Young remembered, at five foot eight, 160 pounds, with a thirty-one-inch chest, he was ferociously strong, a champion boxer and rower at university, with brilliant blue eyes and a penchant for adventure that led him, in 1900, to suspend his medical studies and sign up as a cavalry trooper and sharpshooter with the 70th Company 1st Imperial Yeomanry, destined for service in the Boer War. A year on the South African veldt fired his imagination with the glory of empire, and the duties and obligations of a Christian man and nation. Upon completion of his medical training at Edinburgh and Heidelberg, he joined the Royal National Mission to Deep Sea Fishermen, which led to his meeting Sir Wilfred Grenfell, who had established a series of remote missions along the rocky shores of Newfoundland and Labrador, the first and oldest British possession in an empire upon which the sun famously never set.

Wakefield arrived in Newfoundland in 1908, a time when cod still blackened the sea and the capelin runs were so abundant that their spawn softened the rocks and greased every shoreline with roe. For six years he lived a life of considerable hardship: intense cold in winter, clouds of mosquitoes in summer, a diet of little but flour and grease, molasses, tea, caribou meat, and salted fish. Traveling sometimes by dog team, sometimes by horse or reindeer, on foot or by skiff, he patrolled the entire length of Labrador, a broken coastline of nearly five thousand miles. One of only two qualified doctors in the entire land, Wakefield treated everything from beriberi and tuberculosis to bear maulings and bullet wounds. On one memorable day he extracted no fewer than 149 teeth. Dedicated to God and king, impervious to physical suffering, possessed of medical skills that seemed wizardly to the scores of people he saved, Wakefield became one of those stalwart colonial figures that loomed over the wild frontiers of the British Empire. A photograph from the Wakefield family album shows him perched on an iceberg in his skivvies, about to leap into the dark ocean for his morning constitutional.

The war came to Newfoundland in the summer, as the entire country was at sea fishing for cod. When word of the hostilities reached Labrador, Wakefield left immediately for St. John's, the capital, sailing in a small rig named the *Amber Jack*. He was present on August 10 for a high-level government meeting. Wakefield, who retained the rank of captain, had a place at the table because he had been active in the creation of a Newfoundland arm of the Legion of Frontiersmen, an empire-wide militia that had originated during the Boer War. Using family money, he had personally equipped the entire local force.

Rifles were in short supply in Newfoundland in 1914, and when the government, on August 21, issued a call for 500 volunteers, with pay equal to that of the Canadians and free transport to St. John's from any corner of the colony, it was inevitable that the first to respond would be those already recruited and armed by Wakefield. These were boys and young men he had known since their birth, teachers, trappers, farmers, and fishermen from a hundred coves and draws and compact towns and mission posts. Thus out of Arthur Wakefield's personal sense of mission and duty came the legendary First Five Hundred, the core of the Newfoundland Regiment, which in time would send well over 7,000 men to war, of whom one in two would be wounded or killed.

Such casualties were unimaginable to Wakefield and his men as they marched past the throngs lining the streets of St. John's on the fateful day of October 3, 1914. At the pier was HMS *Florizel*, the troopship that would carry them to England. The boys eagerly clung to their rifles, fixed with bayonets, as they marched the Regimental Colours on board. The crowds cheered, and everyone present, including the troops, broke out in a rousing rendition of "Auld Lang Syne."

The *Florizel* sailed the following night, heading through the Narrows and south to a rendezvous in the darkness with a flotilla of thirty-one ships, escorted by the 26,000-ton battle cruiser *Princess Royal*, transporting to England the first Canadian troops, together with nearly 7,000 horses. The Atlantic crossing took eleven days. On Sunday, as the men gathered for prayer, it was Wakefield who was chosen to deliver the sermon. Following disembarkation at Plymouth, the force was transported to a training camp at Salisbury Plain. There they remained through a long fall and wet winter, soaked by two feet of rain in four months, twice the normal precipitation, as they drilled and marched and practiced all the skills deemed essential in the military training manuals, few of which would serve any purpose in France.

BRITAIN HAD NOT FOUGHT a major continental war in a century, and the high command exhibited a stubborn disconnection from reality so complete as to merge at times with the criminal. A survey conducted in the three years before the war found that 95 percent of officers had never read a military book of any kind. This cult of the amateur, militantly anti-intellectual, resulted in a leadership that, with noted exceptions, was obtuse, willfully intolerant of change, and incapable for the most part of innovative thought or action. Thus men who had fought in 1898 at Omdurman—a colonial battle in which the British, at a cost of just 48 dead, had mowed down with Maxim guns 11,000 Sudanese, wounding another 15,000—nevertheless in 1914 rejected the machine gun as a useful weapon of war. As late as March 1916, after twenty months of fighting, Douglas Haig, the British commander in chief, who had been at Omdurman as a staff officer to Kitchener, sought to limit the number of machine guns per battalion, concerned that their presence might dampen the men's offensive spirit. For a similar reason, he resisted the introduction of the steel helmet, which had been shown to reduce head injuries by 75 percent. In the summer of 1914 he dismissed the airplane as an overrated contraption, and he had little use for light mortars, which in time would become the most effective of all trench weapons. Even the rifle was suspect. What counted was the horse and saber.

"It must be accepted as a principle," read the *Cavalry Training* manual of 1907, "that the rifle, effective as it is, cannot replace the effect produced by the speed of the horse, the magnetism of the charge and the terror of cold steel."

Throughout the war, Haig would insist on holding in reserve three full divisions of mounted troops, 50,000 men, ready at all hours to exploit the breakthrough at the front that would never come. As late as 1926, as the nation mourned the death of nearly 1 million men, Haig would write on the future of war, "I believe that the value of the horse and the opportunity of the horse in the future are likely to be as great as ever. Aeroplanes and tanks are only accessories to the men and the horse, and I feel sure that as time goes on you will find just as much use for the horse—the well bred horse—as you have ever done in the past." The frontline soldiers knew better. Of the cavalry reserve one remarked, "They might as well be mounted on bloody rocking-horses for all the good they are going to do."

None of this, of course, was known or anticipated by the men of the Newfoundland Regiment diligently training on the sodden fields of Salisbury Plain. A solid body of troops prepared to accept moderate casualties, they were instructed, could with "grit, determination and the qualities of a stalker" readily overcome a machine gun emplacement. The essential precondition for success, noted the official training manual of 1909, was that the men maintain throughout the attack the "sporting spirit inherent in every individual of the British race" and that they cheer as loudly as possible throughout their charge, "so as to effect, by vibration, the enemies' nerves." The key weapon would be the bayonet, the point of which "should be directed against an opponent's throat, as the point will enter easily and make a fatal wound on entering a few inches, and, being near the eyes, makes an opponent flinch. Other vulnerable, and usually exposed parts are the face, chest, lower abdomen and thighs, and the region of the kidneys when the back is turned. Four to six inches penetration is sufficient to incapacitate and allow for a quick withdrawal, whereas if a bayonet is driven home too far it is often impossible to withdraw it. In such cases a round should be fired to break up the obstruction." In point of fact, bayonet wounds caused but a fraction of 1 percent of casualties during the war. Rifle and machine gun fire brought down a third of the dead and wounded; high-explosive shells accounted for the rest. Most who died awaited their fate helplessly, clinging to the mud of a trench wall, as a storm of steel and fire rained from the sky.

As MEDICAL OFFICER, Arthur Wakefield ran a strict camp, and insisted on cleanliness and order as a prerequisite for good health and morale. He was known to his men as "Droppings" because of his obsession with litter, and each morning they would stand aghast as he stepped into a metal pan, naked to the winter, and poured buckets of cold water over his body. Old enough to be the father of most of the troops, and a veteran of another distant war, he took a strong personal interest in their well-being, which made it all the more peculiar when, on August 17, 1915, he submitted an urgent request for a transfer to the Royal Army Medical Corps.

While Wakefield's reasons for leaving the regiment are unclear, it was certainly not fear of action that forced his hand, for within a week he was attached to the 29th Casualty Clearing Station, destined for some of the worst fighting in France. He arrived at a time when the British were just coming to terms with the extent of the medical challenge. In the first months of the war, with the numbers of dead and wounded reaching levels never before contemplated, and with men suffering injuries of a kind and severity never before experienced, with new conditions of morbidity overwhelming everything that had been taught in medical schools, the RAMC scrambled to provide even a modicum of care. Initially those brought back from the fighting broken but still alive lay on stretchers on bare floors as their wounds festered with mysterious pathogens derived from the rich organic soils of Flanders. The sterile sands of South Africa were but a memory to army surgeons who now had to deal with gas gangrene, rampant infections that soured the atmosphere of every improvised ward with a scent of death that caused even the most stoic young nurses to vomit in repulsion.

Amputation and radical surgery became the norm as doctors raced against time to defeat the infectious spread of rot. There were, of course, no antibiotics, and they had little knowledge of germ theory. X-ray technology was primitive; locating iron in a body riddled with shrapnel was often problematic. Blood transfusions would be pioneered during the war, with Mallory's close friend Geoffrey Keynes playing a vital role, but in the opening campaigns thousands simply bled to death. Medical officers such as Wakefield and his Everest colleague Howard Somervell were a short generation away from a medical orthodoxy that employed leeches to treat disease, rhubarb purgatives for typhus, and mosquitoes to address syphilis.

The first challenge was to get the wounded away from the front. Those who could still walk or crawl found their way to the regimental aid post, generally located in a front line or reserve trench. There a medical officer sorted the casualties, tagging each soldier with a label identifying his unit and the nature of the injury, marking each man's forehead with indelible ink to distinguish those who might live from those certain to die, then dressing wounds, administering morphine, and severing the tangled remnants of limbs whenever necessary, often with a simple knife. Those left stranded and helpless between the lines waited stoically for darkness to fall, with the hope that they would be found by the stretcher bearers. Often they were not, for each battalion of a thousand men had only thirty-two assigned to carry the wounded and the dead, sixteen teams in all, charged with the impossible task of evacuating battlefields that frequently saw casualty rates of 50 percent. Struggling at night through mud and across collapsed trenches dense with corpses, stumbling upon the rotten flesh of horses and men killed in previous battles, in mortal danger at all times, the stretcher bearers had to carry the men, for often an hour or more, to reach the regimental aid post or a road head where the wounded might be taken by ambulance to the nearest casualty clearing station, the key link in the chain of medical rescue.

Located out of immediate threat of shell fire, yet as close to the front as possible, the CCS was both a hospital and a clearinghouse. There the medical teams, generally eight surgeons working around the clock, two to a six-hour shift, separated by triage those strong enough to be immediately evacuated by rail to the base hospitals from those whose injuries necessitated emergency surgery. A third cohort comprised those so severely wounded that there was no hope. These were tagged in red and placed in a moribund ward where they might be sedated and bathed, and comforted by nurses who did what they could to shield the lads from the inevitability of their fate. In the morning, burial details sewed their mangled remains into blankets and carted them off to the mass graves that only long after the war acquired the dignity of individual crosses placed in neat rows—an illusion that pleased the living but offered little comfort to the dead.

The stress on the medical officers at a casualty clearing station was intense and unrelenting. They were encouraged by social convention, decency, and military orders to do all that was possible to maintain good cheer. At the same time, as surgeons they had to deal with an endless flow of carnage, working through the night as guns roared and flares and star shells lit up the sky, silhouetting the ghostly figures in khaki, wrapped in bloody blankets, labels dangling from limp bodies carried into tents where the flicker of acetylene torches cast barely enough light for the doctors to determine the nature of the wounds.

Their smocks drenched in blood, with the nauseating scent of sepsis and cordite and human excrement fouling the operating theater, they cut and sliced and sawed and cauterized wounds of a sort they never would have known in ordinary practice. High-velocity bullets traveling at two thousand miles per hour could splinter the base of an oak tree, or slice the legs from a human. Shrapnel did the most damage, jagged splinters of steel, red-hot, driving debris and bits of uniform and the flesh of battlefield cadavers deep into wounds. Shell blasts could rupture the lungs, collapse organs, and drown the brain in blood such that men with no external signs of injury would lie dead beside others whose bodies had been mutilated beyond recognition. Limbs severed by steel, skulls dripping with brain tissue, genitalia simply gone, displaced by a hole in the lower gut oozing intestines. Facial injuries were the most difficult to bear; young boys with lip-less mouths, bloody orifices in place of the nostrils, a shock of blond hair on a shell-skinned skull. Plastic surgery was born of the war and the need to repair, to the extent possible, faces so violated that for the rest of their lives those who survived lived behind masks, and gathered together at special rural camps where they might feel the wind on their gargoyle features without fear of mockery or pity. In addition to 108 million bandages and battle dressings, the RAMC by the end of the conflict would require 22,386 artificial eyes.

In response to the strain, the surgeons attempted to find their own peace in the midst of the madness. Some simply blanked out the war and focused exclusively on their duty, as if everything beyond the shadow of their flickering lamps and the reach of their scalpels had no intrinsic meaning or reality. One night late in the war, Mallory's friend Geoffrey Keynes was operating in a dungeon of a citadel at Doullens on a young soldier whose genitals had been mutilated by a shell frag-ment. He paused for an instant to rub the sweat from his brow and looked up to see King George V standing at his side, observing the procedure. Without a word or a gesture, Keynes turned back to con-centrate on his work, utterly ignoring his sovereign.

Howard Somervell, Mallory's closest friend on Everest, was attached during the war to the 34th Casualty Clearing Station, located at Vecquemont, between Amiens and Albert on the Somme front. Like Wakefield, Somervell was a religious lad of the Lake District. He was born in 1890 in Kendal, Westmoreland, to a devout Presbyterian and evangelical family that owned a prosperous bootmaking company. Physically tough but artistically inclined, he grew up in a world of nature, music, and fine art, and as a young man thought nothing of riding his bicycle from Rye, in Sussex, to Queen's Hall in London to hear classical performances of Beethoven, Chopin, and Schumann at the Promenade Concerts, a round-trip journey of some 150 miles.

After leaving Rugby School, he received a science scholarship to Caius College, Cambridge, and for a time flirted with atheism, joining the Heretics, a society in which, as he recalled, "all my cherished reli-gious beliefs were dashed to the ground. For two years I strenuously refused to believe in God." But then, toward the end of his second year, he slipped by chance into a prayer meeting at a local church in Cambridge. There he experienced a revelation and emerged to become an ardent and passionate evangelical. "It was not long," he noted, "before I was preaching, with shaking knees and beating heart, at open aired meetings in the Cambridge marketplace." In time, however, he came to see this period of his life as representing, as he put it, "the sowing of a kind of spiritual wild oats, an alternative to the more usual sexual variety, but a natural expression of youthful energies transferred or sublimated into spiritual channels." His evangelical zeal mellowed, but he remained nevertheless a man of intense religious faith, convinced of the power of prayer, which he took as a visceral reality.

A medical student at the outbreak of the war, Somervell had been tempted to sign up immediately. Wise counsel from his mentor, Sir Frederick Treves, who recognized that the need for surgeons would be great, led him to continue his studies at the Royal College of Surgeons. Commissioned a captain with the West Lancs, he finally joined the RAMC in 1915. His surgical records, among the very few not to have been destroyed by fire during the German Blitz of 1940, reveal in precise detail every procedure and operation performed during the war. On August 18, 1918, for example, he treated one Lance Corporal G. A. Dickenson of the 1st Lincolns, a strong lad in his early twenties who had suffered multiple shell wounds to the eyes, face, hands, arms, shoulders, chest, and abdominal wall. The right eye Somervell excised, and several fingers were amputated.

Two subsequent days, selected from the records at random, find Somervell first in Ward 8 treating a shell wound to a shoulder, then in Ward 5 for a gunshot wound to a left arm, and immediately thence to the litter of a Private A. Griffiths of the 2nd Royal Welsh Fusiliers, whose leg required a "supracondylar amputation for shattered knee joint." Then it is back to Ward 8 to treat a gunshot wound to the head of a Private Read of the 6th Dorsets, before returning to Ward 5 to amputate the left leg of Lance Corporal F. Thornton of the 10th West Yorks, shot in the ankle.

The following morning the routine continues. A gunshot wound has shattered the left arm of Private Russell of the 7th Lincs. In Ward 5, W. D. Smith of the 10th West Yorks has had both thighs fractured by a shell. Somervell moves to Ward 6 to remove bone fragments from the lungs of a subaltern of the 1st Lincolns. Several other gunshot wounds are treated before he rushes to Ward 5 to try to do something to save the face of Private W. R. Filton of the 15th Welsh

Regiment, who has suffered a gunshot wound that has fractured both jaws and severed the facial arteries. After Filton awaits a Private Gunn of the 10th West Yorks, with a shell wound to the right buttock that has driven cloth and dirt deep into the wound. Then he moves on to Ward 9 to deal with a gaping chest wound, and the shattered ribs of Private J. Mann, also of the 1st Lincolns. From there it is on to another enlisted man with a gunshot wound; this one, to the back, has destroyed the scapula and third rib. Finally, Somervell returns to Ward 5 to deal with a gunshot wound to the left buttock of a Private Richards. Twelve major operations in two days, two amputations, a severe facial wound, fractured bones, and blasted buttocks. Every conceivable indignation and this, in but forty-eight hours of a wartime career that lasted with similar intensity for nearly four years.

Somervell appears to have coped with the war by maintaining a precise and highly disciplined focus on the abstract possibilities of the academic moment. He became a surgeon's surgeon, a young intern who by the age of twenty-eight had seen and dealt with virtually every possible medical trauma. In his free moments he would go out sketching, his eyes attracted, as he would later write, to the most humble objects of nature, with his heart yearning to treat every animate being as worthy of respect. His faith remained strong, but tempered by a new understanding of and patience for the fragility of the human spirit. In one moment, while on duty, he would enter a building or a tent and find it strewn with corpses or piled high with amputated legs and arms. In a ward at night he would hear the groans and curses of the wounded, young men crying out in delirium, a boy shouting "Charge!" at the top of his lungs. Then, by dawn, the constant stream of dying and mutilated men might be forgotten, at least for a morning, when the sun rose and butterflies alighted on the burnt snags and chards of a landscape seared to darkness by the war. With his fellow officers he would picnic in the copses of oaks and maples behind the line, beyond the range of shells, where larks and robins sang, and the dread and anxiety and physical pain of exhaustion could be for a moment forgotten. Thus the war became a dream, an inversion of reality that left open the possibility of faith.

ARTHUR WAKEFIELD HAD BEEN STATIONED behind the lines at the Somme since the last days of 1915. In the weeks before the battle he was attached to the 29th Casualty Clearing Station, encamped at Gézaincourt, a village southwest of Doullens and less than a day's walk from Somervell at Vecquemont. The stark simplicity of his diary entries suggests the values of a generation of men not yet prepared to yield their emotions to analysis or reflection. He describes his daily routine: a cross-country run in the early morning, followed by a hot bath and "breaker," as he called breakfast. He visits the wards, attends sick parade, processes the wounded, and oversees as he can the religious rites that attempt to give meaning to the incessant burial parties that dampen each afternoon. In the evening he reads and writes, or "yarns" with his fellow officers in the mess. And, like Somervell, he slips away whenever possible to seek color and life behind the desolation and bleakness of the front. He plants a garden, sets snares for rabbits, enjoys the wildflowers of a Picardy spring, while all the time hovering over everything are the sounds of distant and not so distant bombardments. Each day he writes a single page in the diary, and each entry concludes with a description of the weather.

Of his work and the wounded he speaks little, and it is only the official war diary of the 29th CCS that reveals the extent of the casualties brought in every morning and night, fifty to a hundred a day, and this at a time—the early spring of 1916—of relative calm on the front. This constant attrition, what the high commanders in their distant châteaus termed wastage, can only be understood in the context of a war that went on for four years and four months and saw among the British forces alone, on average, some 600 deaths a day, with 1,700 additional daily casualties.

On April 4 Wakefield recorded the arrival of the 29th Division, which, to his surprise and delight, included the ranks of the Newfoundland Regiment. He had had no direct contact with his boys of Labrador since the previous summer, when he'd remained in France as the regiment, swollen to battalion strength, embarked for Egypt and the Gallipoli campaign. He knew from the scuttlebutt that they had landed at Suvla Bay and for six months, afflicted with cholera, dysentery, typhus, and trench foot, had faced a bloody trial until finally being evacuated from the Dardanelles in the first days of 1916. Now, having landed at Marseille on March 22, they were back with him. By remarkable coincidence, Wakefield's casualty clearing station was positioned in the very sector of the front where his boys would fight. With considerable pride, Wakefield stood by the roadside in Gézaincourt and searched for familiar faces. It was an ominous sight: 12,000 men, 6,000 horses, along with heavy and light artillery, supply wagons, ambulances, and field kitchens, spread along fifteen miles of road. On a day of constant drizzle and cold rain, it took the division five hours merely to pass through the town. "There is an air of expectancy and rumours of our going are rife," Wakefield noted in his diary that night. "Leave has been stopped and those on leave have been recalled."

On Tuesday, May 16, Wakefield slipped away from his work and bicycled through Beauquesne and Marieux to visit the regiment at Louvencourt. It was a splendid day, he later wrote: lunch with the senior staff, followed by a tour of the company headquarters, where he caught up with the junior officers and "yarned with the enlisted men." After tea at battalion headquarters, he left at 6:00 p.m. and pedaled home in an hour, a "perfectly glorious ride" on a cloudless day with a soft wind blowing from the south. He had no idea that he would never see any of the men again. A month later the roads everywhere were clogged with guns and ammunition. On June 21, Wakefield wrote: "All preparations are ready for dealing with patients expected from the great advance. There is a universal atmosphere of growing expectations in the air. Wind SW, moderate, fine and sunny. Warmer."

THE ATTACK ON THE SOMME had been six months in the planning. After all the debacles of 1915, the failed effort to break through at Neuve Chapelle in March, the disappointment of the Dardanelles, the suicidal resistance of the Canadians at Ypres in April, the collapse at Aubers Ridge and the disaster at Loos, the September battle known to the Germans as Der Leichenfeld von Loos (the Corpse Field of Loos), every British hope lay upon one great massive offensive that would finally break the German line and open the coastal plain to a war of movement, thus relieving the French and freeing commander and soldier alike from the degradation and agony of the trenches. This was the promise that ran like a wave through the men of the Fourth Army, half a million strong, poised for the assault.

With the outcome of the war—indeed, the fate of the empire—seemingly in the balance, nothing could be left to chance. The battle orders for the Marne in 1914, the massive confrontation that had saved France, had been outlined in six paragraphs. For the Somme, the British General Staff, some three hundred officers working under Haig's command at his luxurious château far behind the lines at Montreuil, devised a document of fifty-seven pages that outlined precise timetables with exactitude, considering every detail, prescribing every action, anticipating every outcome. It was a masterful plan on paper, certain to succeed. The British armies had since 1914 increased from four to fifty-eight divisions. At the Somme they would outnumber the Germans seven to one. For the preliminary bombardment, Haig planned on having nearly three million shells available. More guns would be fired in a week than had been discharged by the British thus far in the entire war. In the first seven days alone some twenty thousand tons of steel would blast the German lines. Then the men would attack, 13 divisions in the initial assault, 66,000 men in the first wave, rising out of the trenches along a fourteen-mile front. Victory would be assured, though, as a staff document cautioned, "All must be prepared for heavy casualties." As more than one historian has suggested, the British in the end guaranteed such casualties by their tactics.

The generals did not trust their men as soldiers, or their ability to control the field once the battle broke. The war, though industrial in scale and firepower, remained primitive in terms of communications. Radio was only beginning, and phone lines and cables rarely survived bombardments. Once the artillery barrage had lifted and the men went over the top, they were essentially on their own, with communication with the British line limited to signals and flares, and messages hastily scrawled in lead pencil and carried back by runners or courier pigeons. A plan to identify units from the air by sewing diamond-shaped pieces of reflective tin on the backs of the men collapsed in the chaos of the battle and succeeded only in making individual soldiers more effective targets. An order from headquarters to a frontline battalion could take as long as six hours. Frequently such messages, disconnected from the immediate reality of the scene, did more harm than good, and when possible were best ignored—unless, of course, they mercifully ordered a withdrawal.

For Haig and the General Staff, the biggest uncertainty was the quality of the troops under their command. The regular army, the men with whom these generals had known glory in South Africa and the Sudan, on the North-West Frontier and at a hundred other distant imperial postings from Gibraltar to Barbados, lay dead in the mud of Flanders. Territorial units, derived from various local militias, volunteers, and yeomanry, had by late 1914 been hastily forged into 14 infantry divisions, along with 14 cavalry brigades. Initially dispatched oversees to free garrison troops for service in France, they would almost all end up doing time in the trenches. Death was such a constant that the physical criteria for joining the army shifted by the month. At the outbreak a man had to stand five foot eight to join up; by November 1914, those as short as five-three were eagerly recruited.

Lord Kitchener, British minister for war, alone among British leaders had from the start of the conflict predicted a long, impossibly brutal industrial war that would consume the wealth of nations. He placed little faith in the Territorial units, dismissing them as a "town clerk's army." His mission was to forge from the two million volunteers who flocked to the colors during the first eighteen months of the war a "New Army" in his own image, prepared to win victory and enforce the peace. By 1916 Kitchener himself was dead, drowned at sea while on a mission to Russia, but his army was ready, the largest, best-equipped, and most thoroughly trained force in the history of the country. His recruits of 1914, boys and men from every hamlet and valley and street corner, drawn from every guild and club and voluntary civic association, had become the foundation of British arms. Of the 143 battalions scheduled for the attack at the Somme, fully 97 were New Army. Many had signed up together, drawn by Kitchener's promise that those who enlisted together would fight together. They shared an almost mystical patriotism, and a sense of duty and honor difficult to imagine today. They were indeed, as was often said, the flower of British youth and manhood.

But Commander in Chief Douglas Haig had his doubts. None of these Kitchener soldiers had been tested in combat, and he was about to send them against a German army at the height of its power. The officers of the New Army were young and inexperienced, or drawn from the ranks of the old, "keen amateurs," as Haig put it, retired commanders of the Indian Army, pensioners, and militia colonels. In 1916, virtually any British gentleman could secure a commission, but this was no guarantee that he would know how to fight. Veterans of the prewar army and units of that army were dispersed among the attacking force, but no battalion destined for the Somme had more than a quarter of its complement drawn from survivors of the regular army. Of the eleven divisions of the Fourth Army listed for battle, six had never seen combat.

Haig's solution was to treat the entire battle as if it were a complex training exercise, a military parade under live fire. The Fourth Army's orders made this injunction explicit: "The men must learn to obey by instinct without thinking. The whole advance must be carried out as a drill." There would be no attempt at surprise. Following a preliminary bombardment, unprecedented in scale and destructive power, the army would advance in ranks in regular waves. Two battalions of a thousand men each would leave the trench by scaling ladders, extend their soldiers in four lines, a company to each, with each man separated from the next by two yards, and with each line of advance separated from the next by twenty yards. Each soldier would carry, in addition to rifle and bayonet, sixty-six pounds of gear; wire cutters, 220 rounds of ammunition, mess kits, empty sandbags, flares, an entrenching shovel, battle dressings, two gas masks, and two grenades. Given these loads, the ranks of the attackers would be formed slowly and deliberately, with order maintained by officers equipped only with swagger sticks to overcome the noise: polished blackthorn for the Irish regiments, malacca cane and ash wood for the rest. These were as useful in combat as a conductor's baton. It was an officer's duty to lead, not to kill, and save for a service revolver, none carried arms into battle. To guarantee discipline and order, Haig insisted that the advance on the German line be done at a deliberate walking pace. The distance between the lines varied up and down the front and in places was as much as 1.5 miles. To the British high command this was of no concern, for the artillery bombardment would assure that the enemy wire would be cut and that no German would be left alive to resist the advance.

On Sunday, June 25, Wakefield's diary has a single brief entry. "The big Strafe began last night. We couldn't hear much, but late at night we could see the flashes of the guns in the sky almost continuously. Wind W, light. Fine except for a few light showers. Hot."

For the following seven days, the sky by night and day rained steel upon the Germans. In London the air throbbed above Hampstead Heath, and the sound of the war was felt throughout the south of England. At the front the British troops stumbled as the ground shook through their boots. A Canadian private wrote, "One's whole body seemed to be in a mad macabre dance . . . I felt that if I lifted a finger I should touch a solid ceiling of sound, it now had the attribute of solidity."

The bombardment grew to a sustained crescendo, a hurricane of piercing screams that hovered over the entire length of the front. Nothing like this had been seen in the history of war. Napoleon at Waterloo had fired 20,000 shells; the British at the Somme had in place 1,537 batteries, each capable of firing 1,000 rounds a day. An NCO of the 22nd Manchester Rifles described the bombardment: "The sound was different, not only in magnitude but in quality, from anything known to me . . . It hung over us. It seemed as though the air were full of vast and agonized passion, bursting now with groans and sighs, now into shrill screaming and pitiful whimpering, shuddering beneath terrible blows, torn by unearthly whips, vibrating with the solemn pulses of enormous wings. And the supernatural tumult did not pass in this direction or in that. It did not begin, intensify, decline and end. It was poised in the air, a stationary panorama of sound, a condition of the atmosphere, not the creation of man."

The frontline troops pitied their enemy, for they knew what it was to lie defenseless before such an assault: the horrible nightmare of bursting shells, the noise that shatters the nerves, the waiting for the ugliest of deaths, obliteration in a whistle. To lie helpless in a trench in the midst of a bombardment was, as one soldier recalled, like being tied to a post and attacked by an enemy wielding a sledgehammer. The hammer swings back for the blow, whirls forward, till, "just missing your skull, it sends the splinters flying from the post once more. This is exactly what it feels like to be exposed to heavy shelling." The blood rises to the head, fever burns the body, nerves, stretched to their limit, break. Men lose control, whimper and moan, and their eyes sink deep into sockets that will never again know the light.

The thunder of the shells filled the British with a hope that would be cruelly betrayed. Haig had chosen the Somme for the attack in part because it allowed his troops to escape the sodden fields and muddy slime of Flanders and promised the possibility of breakthrough. But the very conditions of Picardy that had drawn his attention also allowed the Germans to dig, and they did, establishing dugouts and shelters in the chalk forty and sixty feet below the torn surface of the earth, impervious even to the shells of the relatively few heavy howitzers the British brought to bear. And here was another problem: the vast majority of the British guns fired shrapnel, which made an impressive sight as it tossed skyward the German wire and burst with sprays of soil. But it did not cut the wire, and most certainly did not penetrate the ground. What's more, a third of the projectiles were duds. Unbeknownst to the British, the German troops, stunned and afraid, often bleeding from the ears and nose due to the concussive pressure of the shells, quaking in fear of death but quite unprepared to die, waited deep beneath the ground, anticipating the onslaught.

Their commanders had had two years to prepare their defense. Haig was not a man of impulse or instinct, but he did have the unfailing ability to select for attack the strongest conceivable point in his enemy's defenses. The Germans had established three successive lines of defense that followed the high ground. They had transformed the gently undulating farmland into thickets of wire, interlocking zones of fire with a depth of more than four thousand yards, well beyond the range of the heaviest of British artillery. For the British to advance they would have to penetrate not simply the front line and reserve trenches but fully twelve lines of defense before open country might be embraced. On an eighteen-mile front the Germans had fortified as unassailable redoubts nine villages, the names of which would echo in history: Montauban, Mametz, Fricourt, La Boisselle, Ovillers, Thiepval, Beaumont-Hamel, Serre, and Gommecourt. The German line wound across and over every point of high ground and each promontory was fortified. More than a thousand machine guns were in place. Attacking troops confronted an impossible choice of assaulting the strong points directly in the face of fire or attempting a flanking movement exposed to fire from all sides.

Unlike the British, the Germans fully understood the power of the machine gun. Even the finest soldier with a rifle must pick his own targets, struggle with distractions, and ignore the cries of the wounded to get off perhaps fifteen rounds a minute, if highly trained. The machine gun was, by contrast, the concentrated essence of war. The operators did not aim, or even fire the weapon. They simply fed the belts of ammunition into the breech, monitored the level of coolant, and with precise two-inch taps traversed the barrel across the field of fire, unleashing a stream of bullets so dense that a mile out no one could walk upright without being shot. The weapon mechanized death; properly calibrated, it could be ready to sweep a parapet with a maelstrom within moments of being anchored in place. And this is precisely what the Germans accomplished.

On the night of June 30, 1916, the eve of the attack, Arthur Wakefield wrote, "The sky was alight with gun flashes, but we could scarcely hear any reports. One of my patients tells me we have been using large quantities of an exceedingly poisonous gas. One single breath of it had gassed him. He says a raiding party that had gone over reported the German trenches full of dead. Wind SW, light, showering a.m., dull p.m. then clearing to a beautiful night." The previous day Wakefield had picked up other news from a pair of old friends, Green and Strong, both young officers of the Newfoundland Regiment, who had been badly wounded in their own raid on the German lines. Green had personally killed six of the enemy. Wakefield noted, "Yarned with them a bit and then walked back to the station and stayed with them till they were put on the train. Then I did my ward rounds. After lunch I saw new cases and did a little gardening. Wind NW mod—strong, cloudy but fine all day." The new cases in fact numbered 135, twice a typical dispatch. This gave Wakefield pause, for he knew what was coming. What he did not know at the time, of course, was that these fortunate young Newfoundland subalterns, Green and Strong, would be, aside from the commanding officer and his adjutant, the only officers of the Newfoundland Regiment to survive the first day of the Somme.

On the afternoon of June 30, General Haig cut a fine figure, escorted by his Lancers—horses groomed, saddles and tack waxed to a perfect sheen—as he led them at a quick trot between the avenue of soaring plane trees that ran away from his château headquarters at Montreuil. With everything in place, there was no need to break his daily routine, and his afternoon constitutional was one of the highlights of his day. Riding a favorite horse with his polished staff at his side, not a button or buckle amiss, allowed him to maintain the illusion that the world was still a place of gentlemen and order, and that war as an exercise had not lost its luster or glory. In four years at the head of the largest army the British Empire had ever placed in the field, a force that would suffer 2,568,834 casualties in France and Belgium alone, Haig never once saw the front; nor did he visit the wounded. Long after the war Haig's son attempted an explanation: "The suffering of his men during the Great War caused him great anguish. I believe that he felt that it was his duty to refrain from visiting the casualty clearing stations because these visits made him physically ill."

On the eve of the Somme, Haig was convinced that Providence held the key to the battle and that God walked at his side. "I feel every step of the plan," he confided to his wife, "has been taken with Divine help. The men are in splendid spirits . . . The wire has never been so well cut, nor the artillery preparation so thorough." The morale after months of training and expectation was indeed high among the British troops. But the wire most assuredly had not been well cut. Indeed, for twenty-seven miles, the length of the immediate German front, it had hardly been cut at all.

In the final hour before the attack, over a quarter million shells fell on the German line. Then came silence—of a sort and only for an instant. A hollow, stunned moment, as if the ground itself had been given a reprieve. Time stood suspended. The British troops crowded at the base of the scaling ladders could hear the plaintive moaning of the wounded in what remained of the enemy trench, the buzzing of great swarms of flies, the high-pitched screaming of rats, even the sublime singing of birds, larks and mourning doves on this misty day, which the poet-warrior Siegfried Sassoon would later describe as "of the kind commonly called heavenly." Ashen faces, watches synchronized, a tot of navy rum, a last letter to a loved one pegged to the trench with a knife, a muted prayer and a glance at a mate, a half smile certain to be one's last. The smell in the trench was of fear, and of sweat, blood, vomit, excrement, cordite, and the putrescence of cadavers. At precisely 7:30 a.m. shrill, piercing whistles signaled the attack. Eighty-four battalions, 66,000 men jammed as a single throng in trenches along a fourteen-mile front, struggled to climb out onto the field of battle. At the same moment, from the depths of dugouts of a scale and complexity unknown and unimaginable to the British, the survivors of six German frontline divisions raced to the sunlight. In the minute it took them to reach the parapet, the battle was decided.

The Germans, of course, had known that the assault was coming. For weeks their agents in London had heard open talk of the Big Push. The buildup behind the Somme front, the construction of hundreds of miles of track and road and communication trenches, the accumulation of millions of shells, the increased traffic in the air and on land, the concentration of some two thousand guns and the tens of thousands of men of General Henry Rawlinson's Fourth Army had been impossible to conceal. The bombardment heralded the assault, which the Germans knew would end precisely before the men went over the top. Haig always attacked at 7:30 in the morning following the cessation of a cannonade. Anything cleverer, such as suspending the guns just long enough to fool the Germans into reoccupying their trenches so that they might be killed in a final bombardment, was beyond the reach of his imagination. What's more, Rawlinson's message at 2:45 a.m. to the 34th Division had been picked up by the Germans. They knew the attack was on, and they knew the time to the minute.

What astonished them were the British tactics. Karl Blenk, a German machine gunner of the 169th Regiment, wrote; "When the English started advancing we were very worried; they looked as though they must overrun our trenches. We were very surprised to see them walking, we had never seen that before. I could see them everywhere; there were hundreds. The officers were in front. I noticed one of them walking calmly, carrying a walking stick. When we started firing we just had to load and reload. They went down in their hundreds. You didn't have to aim. We just fired into them. If only they had run they would have overwhelmed us."

Siegfried Sassoon was a witness to the advance, as the men went over the top, formed up, and then, shoulder to shoulder, burdened by in some cases a hundred pounds of gear, with bayonets fixed, leaned forward to walk into a storm of lead. At 7:45 he saw in a reserve trench men cheering their mates onward as if watching a football match. Two hours later, he wrote, "The birds seem bewildered; a lark begins to go up and then flies feebly along, thinking better of it. Others flutter above the trench with querulous cries, weak on the wing." At 10:05, he noted, "I am staring at a sunlit picture of Hell, and still the breeze shakes the yellow weeds, and the poppies glow under Crawley Ridge where some shells fell a few minutes ago." At 2:30 that afternoon: "I could see one man moving his arms up and down as he lay on his side; his face was a crimson patch."

Of the battalions in the first wave, twenty were utterly destroyed in no-man's-land. Within the first hour, perhaps the first minutes, there were more than 30,000 dead and wounded. By the end of the day, there was not a British soldier alive within the German wire. Not a village had been taken, nor a single major objective achieved. Machine guns cut the men down like scythes slicing through grass. Those few who reached the German front line were incinerated with flamethrowers, blown up by bombs, or riddled with bullets and left condemned to hang on the wire "like crows shot on a dyke," until their flesh fell from their bones.

It was the biggest disaster in the history of British arms. The army lacked the "clerk power," it was said, even to record the names of the dead, 19,240 altogether, which in time would fill 212 pages of a log. Of the wounded there were more than 35,000, a figure that would double by the end of the third day of a battle that would rage for four months. Regiments up and down the line suffered casualty rates of 75 percent. By the end of the morning of July 1, 1916, Kitchener's New Army was no more. Its soldiers lay in rows, their tunics red with blood. "We were two years in the making," wrote Private A. V. Pearson of the Leeds Pals, "and ten minutes in the destroying."

BEHIND THE LINES at the casualty clearing stations, medical officers such as Howard Somervell and Arthur Wakefield waited for the deluge. July 1 was the only day of the war that Wakefield neglected his diary. Writing on July 2, he recalled the hours of anticipation: "We felt there was something in the air, everything seemed to be alive with an electrified undercurrent of excitement. We knew that only a few miles away men were killing and being killed in thousands and possibly the ultimate history of the war and the Empire was being decided, though we could hear and see nothing."

The first trainloads of wounded arrived about 2:30 p.m., and kept coming until more than 2,000 wounded and dying men surrounded the medical marquees. "It was very hard to ignore their cries for help," wrote a medical orderly, "but we had to concentrate on those who might live."

"I was dressing as hard as I could go," wrote Wakefield, "only stopping two or three minutes to gulp some food down . . . We never got through. They seemed an endless stream . . . New convoys came about 9:30 [p.m.] and I dressed them until 2:30, then, as more MOs and orderlies had arrived, we changed shifts. It was after 3 a.m. when I turned in. Called about 4 for a new crush and by 5:30 all was clear and I turned in again and slept till 10:30 a.m. Wind variable, light, warm, sunny. Very cold at night."

At the 34th Casualty Clearing Station, at Vecquemont, Somervell had been told to expect no more than a thousand casualties on the first day of the battle. Instead, he and one other surgeon found themselves surrounded by a charnel ground of suffering, hundreds upon hundreds of limp figures bandaged in blood, boys and men, white, cold, and still:

> Never in the whole war did we see such a terrible sight. Streams of motor ambulances a mile long waited to be unloaded . . . The wounded had to lie not merely in our tents and shelters and in the adjacent farm buildings, but the whole area of the camp, a field of five or six acres, was completely covered in stretchers placed side by side, each with its suffering or dying man on it. Orderlies went about giving drinks and food, and dressing wounds where possible. We surgeons were hard at it in the operating theatre, a good hut, holding four tables. Occasionally we made a brief look around to select from the thousands of patients those few fortunate ones whose lives or limbs we had time to save. It was a terrible business. Even now I am haunted by the touching look of the young, bright anxious eyes, as we passed along the rows of sufferers.
>
> Hardly ever did any of them say a word, except to ask for water or relief from pain. I don't remember any single man who even suggested that we should save him and not the fellow next to him. Silently beseeching they lay, as we rapidly surveyed them to see who was most worthwhile saving. Abdominal cases and others requiring long operations simply had to be left to die. Saving of life by amputation, which can be done in a few minutes, or saving of limbs by the wide opening of wounds, had to be thought of first. There, all around us, lying maimed and battered and dying, was the flower of Britain's youth—a terrible sight if ever there was one.

Throughout the night, as the guns flashed and sheets of yellow light illuminated the glare, Somervell and his colleagues toiled, their arms and frocks drenched in the blood of the 12,000 wounded who reached the fields of Vecquemont that day. On the first day of the Somme, the

Fourth Army alone suffered 32,000 men wounded. The total capacity of all medical facilities behind the front was only 9,500. And so the bodies arrived, some standing, some on stretchers, others in carts or perched on sheets of corrugated tin, carried by the lightly wounded. The injured and dying lay on the ground—like cordwood, as one soldier remembered—left to their fate, stifling their agony, open wounds untended, hoping that it would not rain.

FROM WAKEFIELD'S DIARY it appears that the full extent of the catastrophe took weeks to register. The London newspapers, which reached the front within a day, simply echoed official military bulletins, which had little connection to reality. "Sir Douglas Haig telephoned last night," the *Times* noted on July 3, "to report that the general situation was favourable . . . Everything has gone well . . . effective progress, nay substantial progress . . . We got our first thrust well home, and there is every reason to be sanguine as to the result . . . Our troops have successfully carried out their missions, all counter-attacks have been repulsed and large numbers of prisoners taken." Enhancing the tenor of the lie, the *Observer* stated, "The New Armies, fighting with a valour and fibre never surpassed by any people, have excelled our best hopes."

The *Daily Mail* was one of many papers to personify the dead in florid language, as if mendacious rhetoric might resurrect their lives. "The very attitudes of the dead," it claimed, "fallen eagerly forwards, have a look of expectant hope. You would say that they died with the light of expectant victory in their eyes." On July 4 the *Times* declared the battle a complete success, noting that the wounded were "extraordinarily cheery and brave." Most wounds were slight, the report noted, and the proportion of permanent disablements very small. Artillery fire had been highly effective, the account continued, though "there were places where individual bits of trench and stretches of the protecting barbed wire had miraculously escaped. Some of the latter caused our attacking infantry considerable losses."

Evidence of these losses lay all around Arthur Wakefield at the 29th Casualty Clearing Station. Yet as he walked through the fields of wounded, deciding who might live and who was destined to die, not a boy or a man spoke with the lilt he knew so well. None wore blue puttees, unique to the Newfoundland Regiment, and not a single soldier's cap bore its insignia, the head of a caribou wreathed in gold. It was as if the regiment had simply vanished.

Not until July 6, nearly a week after the battle began, did he first hear an eyewitness account of the fate of even one of his Newfound-landers. In a heavy rain, wearing his mackintosh and gum boots, he had walked to Doullens, desperately seeking information. "The cinema show was on 6–8," he wrote that night, "but I did not go. Lt. Baillie came in, told about Capt. Duff's death and the cutting up of his Bat-talion. Duff was leading the charge, was wounded in the arm as soon as he got over the parapet but got up and went on. Was wounded again in the chest, but picked himself up and went on again. He reached the Boche trench with only a very few of his men. He had previously loaded himself with bombs, and with these bombs he killed 30 Huns, before his head was blown off by a shell. Wind SW, light, fair a.m., shower 5:30, then dull but fair."

Two days later Wakefield encountered in his ward another friend from home, an officer named Summers, mute and catatonic with shell shock. He then treated two victims of gas gangrene, and recognized one as a lad named Gandiner, also from the regiment. "I had a long yarn with him and wrote a letter for him. Then went for a short walk and had a bath before mess. Wind N, light, fine, sunny and warm." It was not until July 21, as evident in his diary, that Wakefield learned the full truth about what had happened to his beloved Newfoundland Reg-iment on the first day of the Somme. It was this story that broke his spirit and maddened him with a rage that would haunt him for the rest of his life. It led to his retreat after the war to the forests of Canada, his desperate yet forlorn efforts on Everest in 1922, and his agonized cries from the summit of Great Gable on the very day that George Mallory and Sandy Irvine walked to their doom on Everest. He had brought into the world each of the dead of Beaumont-Hamel.

ON THE MORNING of the Somme attack, the Newfoundland Regi-ment was attached to the British 29th Division, one of four divi-sions that made up VIII Corps, scheduled to assault the German lines on a three-mile front at the extreme northern end of the bat-tlefield. Anchoring the center of the German defenses was a fortress at Beaumont-Hamel, which commanded the valley across which the British attack would be launched. No-man's-land here varied in width from two hundred yards in the north to five hundred at the south-ern end of the assault, and all of it was open and bare, completely exposed. The battlefield, in fact, was in the shape of an amphitheater, with high ground flanking the fort on both sides. In these heights the Germans had had two years to build dugouts, establish bunkers, and position machine gun nests that dominated every inch of the field. Due to the lay of the land, the British fought partially blind, unable even to observe sections of the German front to ascertain the extent of the damage from the preliminary bombardment.

In the weeks before the battle, English sappers had tunneled to within thirty yards of the German front line. At 2:00 a.m. on July 1, these saps were unveiled as emplacements for Stokes mortars. The Royal Engineers had also planted forty thousand pounds of ammonal explosives directly beneath the German line at the crest of Hawthorn Redoubt, immediately opposite Beaumont village, which dominated the head of the valley. Rather than detonating this mine either well in advance or at the precise moment of attack, the British General Staff insisted on blowing it up at precisely 7:20 a.m., a timetable perfectly conceived to alert the Germans of the coming assault.

A German regimental account recorded: "The ground all round was white with the debris of chalk as if it had been snowing, and a gigantic crater, over fifty yards in diameter gaped like an open wound in the side of the hill. This explosion was a signal for the infantry attack, and everybody got ready and stood on the lower steps of the dugouts, rifles in hand, waiting for the bombardment to lift. In a few minutes the shelling ceased, and we rushed up the steps and out into the crater positions. Ahead of us wave after wave of British troops were crawling out of their trenches, and coming forward towards us at a walk, their bayonets glistening in the sun."

The mine blast lifted dirt four thousand feet in the air. The German guns responded. Sixty-six artillery batteries, undetected and undamaged, laid down a withering fire on the British infantry massed in the trenches, ready to attack. The lanes cut through the British wire for the assaulting troops were too few and too narrow. German machine guns ranged across each gap, butchering the men as they emerged from the trench, until the passage through the wire became so choked with their own dead that the following troops had to clamber over mounds of the corpses simply to reach no-man's-land. Physical movement along the trench became impossible. Men writhing with wounds, whimpering and crying like children. Headless torsos, faces on fire, blood shooting out of helmets in three-foot streams, bodies cleft like the quartered carcasses in a butcher's shop, splinters of steel in brains, shattered backbones and spinal cords worming and flapping about in the mud.

In the noise and chaos and horror of the battle, all communications collapsed. A false report of a glorious victory resulted in even more men being fed to the slaughter. At 9:15 a.m. the Newfoundland Regiment was ordered to advance. Its right flank hung in the air because the 1st Battalion, Essex Regiment, the next unit in line, had been delayed reaching the starting point by the sheer volume of dead. Shells landed on corpses, and flying fragments of flesh and bone blinded the living. Men enveloped in flames went mad and fought each other as they died. The soldiers of Wakefield's beloved Newfoundland Regiment barely got out of their own trench, and when they did they floundered and died at their own parapet, their ranks swept by German machine gun fire. Those few who advanced slowed and faltered, burdened by their loads, leaning and bowing into the storm as if to limit their exposure to the lead. The British artillery barrage, timed to the second, had long since moved ahead and away from the immediate battlefield. Men dropped dead at every yard, and still the regiment pressed on. A few miraculously reached the German line only to be shot down in the mud or skewered on the wire, which was not cut. Indeed, the last thought of many of these brave men, breathless with exhaustion, blood-whipped and deranged with fear, was the horrid realization that the German line was utterly unscathed. Nothing had been damaged at all. The preliminary bombardment had missed. In fury they spun into the wire, tossing grenades, their screams baffled by the throaty gurgle men sound when hit in the brain.

Altogether 810 men of the Newfoundland Regiment went over the top that morning. Only sixty-eight emerged from the battle physically unscathed. Every officer was lost, including three who should not have been in the attack at all. Only the commander and his adjutant survived to hear the praise of the General Staff. "It was a magnificent display of trained and disciplined valour," one of Haig's staff officers told the Newfoundland prime minister, "and its assault only failed of success because dead men can advance no further."

After the disaster of July 1, 1916, Haig could not call off the Somme attack without admitting failure on a scale so vast as to be murderous. Thus he redefined the goals of the campaign and declared that attrition rather than military breakthrough had always been his intent. The Battle of the Somme would go on for 140 days, and at a cost of 600,000 wounded and dead, the British line would advance six miles, leaving the Allies four miles short of Bapaume, which Haig had planned to take on the opening day of the campaign. Thirty million shells would be fired, 600,000 Germans would be killed or wounded, and after four months the battlefield, a few score square miles, would be covered in layers upon layers of corpses, three and four deep, bodies bloated, bones sticking up randomly from the ground, faces black with blue-bottle flies.

ON OCTOBER 12, 1916, while the Battle of the Somme still raged, Wakefield's time was up, and after two years in service he was decommissioned to return to Canada. At Boulogne on October 21 he slept in a bed for the first time in a year, and after a week in London, he sailed on SS *Ionian*, a battered vessel with decks still stained with blood from its service in Gallipoli, arriving in Montreal after a stormy passage on November 13. He did not stay home for long. Two days before Christmas, he enlisted in the Canadian army, and for the next year he served first on the hospital ship *Letitia*, and later on the *Araguaya*, sailing back and forth across the Atlantic, from Liverpool to Halifax. Wakefield's letters from 1917 have been lost, and are believed by his family to have been burned. But the official accounts of these voyages tell of hundreds of young men, stacked in cots, suffering from grievous wounds. Wakefield was in charge of the most severely injured: stretcher cases, amputees, men with shattered minds and broken spirits bound down by necessity with leather straps in wards reserved for the mentally insane. The routine was numbing, endless rounds of the wards, examining men without memory, blinded by gas, maimed beyond recognition. Breakfast at 8:00 with the ward officers, a noontime meeting followed by luncheon, return to the wards until tea, deck exercises before dressing formally for dinner at 6:00.

With each transatlantic passage, Wakefield suffered some erosion of the spirit. He was still capable of great deeds; he personally orchestrated the rescue of the wounded on August 1, 1917, when, ten days out of Liverpool and only ten miles from the safety of Halifax harbour, the *Letitia* ran aground in the fog. But what haunted him were incidents that went largely unnoticed, such as when, on the afternoon of September 19, one of his patients, an invalid driven mad by the war, jumped overboard. "The sea was very rough," Wakefield recalled, "with waves coming over the boat. Two life buoys were at once flung over by the aft lookout man, one of which fell beside him, but he sank and did not appear again."

Wakefield remained in service on the *Araguaya* until December 12, 1917. Two weeks later, he was in England and on December 29 traveled to Kent to visit the home of a good friend, a lad named Leggett, who was the only survivor of four sons. Three had died in France. As the year turned, Wakefield was forty-two years old. He had served since the beginning of the war and was free at any time to return home. Instead he joined up again and by February 1918 was back in France with the Canadian Field Hospital, first at its reserve base by the sea, and later at Outreau, close to the front. By 1918 his hatred of Germans was evident in his letters. In his diary he wrote of children shot while helping a starving prisoner, of a doctor's wife tied to her house by her hair, of dozens of deeds real and imagined of a people he condemned as the "bestial boches." He looked forward to victory as a chance to make accountable all those he held responsible for the war: the German nation, every man and woman untouched, as he saw it, by the pain and consequences of their deeds. No amount of vengeance would be enough. On December 4, 1918, he wrote from Thounnen, on German soil, "The Boche does not know what war means. It's up to us to teach him. I assure you that I'm doing my best."

SIX YEARS LATER found Wakefield on the top of Great Gable as the mist lifted and, in the words of a local reporter, "yielded to golden rays," prompting the assembled congregation to slip out of their rain slickers and lift their eyes to the sun. Geoffrey Young stepped onto a rock above the commemorative bronze and, at Wakefield's cue, slowly began to speak. His voice was deep and strong, and in the spacious silence it carried far. Climbers who had reached only the top of Green Gable, across Windy Gap, said afterward that they heard every word, ringing as clear as the trumpet that attended in the memorial service. "They had asked for verse," Young later recalled, "but I knew it must be prose. Of course I had Gettysburg in mind. As I spoke it, I felt the inspiration of the words welling up."

> Upon this mountain summit we are met today to dedicate this space of hills to freedom. Upon this rock are set the names of men—our brothers, and our comrades upon these cliffs—who held, with us, that there is no freedom of the soil where the spirit of man is in bondage; and who surrendered their part in the fellowship of hill and wind and sunshine, that the freedom of this land, the freedom of our spirit, should endure . . .
>
> By this symbol we affirm a twofold trust: That which hills alone can give their children, the disciplining of strength in freedom, the freeing of the spirit through generous service, these free hills shall give again, and for all time.
>
> The memory of all that these children of hills have given,

service, and inspiration, fulfilled, and perpetual, this free heart
of our hills shall guard.

Following the oration, a party of cadets from the St. Bees School
led the hymns "Lead, Kindly Light" and "O God Our Help in Ages
Past." The weather came in once more, and "in the swirling mist,"
reported the local correspondent of the *Advertiser,* "the singing was
most impressive. Mr. Godfrey Solly read the psalm 'I will lift up mine
eyes to the hills, from when cometh my help' and the Rev. J. H. Smith
read the dedicatory prayers."

All the time clouds moved over the mountains, and cast shadows
across the faces of the host. Wakefield did not pray or bow his head.
Never again would he speak of God or attend religious service. His
children would never in his presence know the inside of a church.

The ceremony on Great Gable ended with the singing of "God
Save the King."

CHAPTER 2

Everest Imagined

GEORGE NATHANIEL CURZON, 11th Viceroy of India, suffered from a congenital curvature of the spine that in time would condemn him to an iron corset and bring pain to his every step. But this did not stop him from traveling on foot and horseback halfway across Asia on several occasions. He began in 1887 with a slow circumnavigation of the world, by sea and rail, west to Canada and beyond to Japan, Hong Kong, India, Aden, and home. A year later he penetrated the khanates of central Asia, traveling overland from Moscow, crossing the Caspian Sea, moving by rail to Bukhara and Samarkand, and thence by horse-drawn cart to Tashkent and the Black Sea. In 1889 he traversed Persia, riding as much as seventy-five miles a day through searing desert sands, his precise observations filling hundreds of pages of notebooks that in time would yield a definitive two-volume account, *Persia and the Persian Question*, published to acclaim in 1892. His eye was that of a spy. Nothing, it seemed, escaped his notice.

In 1894, following a second journey around the world, Curzon traveled alone to India and, after a stubborn effort, secured permission from the Raj to embark on a diplomatic mission to visit the newly instated emir of Afghanistan. His route of approach was deliberately circuitous. He marched north from Gilgit to the Pamirs, beheld the savage beauty of Hunza, and continued northward to become the first Westerner to trace the Oxus River to its source in Russian Turkistan, a feat of exploration for which he would be later awarded the coveted Gold Medal of the Royal Geographical Society. When finally he entered Kabul, he did so in style, having arranged with a theatrical costume designer in London to outfit him with a dazzling uniform, complete with massive gold epaulets, a row of glittering medals and decorations, and a giant curved sword. The entire getup was a purely constructed fantasy, given meaning and power by the audacity of the man.

Moving through life with cold certainty, his awkward gait concealed by what one peer described as an "enameled self assurance," Lord Curzon in many ways embodied the essence and contradictions of British rule in India. The scion of a seven-hundred-year-old aristocratic dynasty, he was the son of a distant father and the product of a sadistic nanny who once forced him to write the family butler to order a cane to be made with which he might be properly thrashed. At Eton and Oxford he acquired an air of "ineffable superiority." In London society his libido was said to rival his intellect. He inherited lands and titles, but found wealth in marriage to a beautiful American heiress, Mary Leiter. His family seat in Derbyshire, Kedleston Hall, had inspired the architecture of the regal palace in Calcutta, and thus he slipped readily into the role when finally, in 1899, just short of his fortieth birthday, he achieved his political dream and became viceroy of India.

Like the entire British adventure in India, Curzon was at once pompous and vain, earnest, ruthlessly enterprising, and rigidly devoted to a mission of moral superiority. He wrote books on Indian carpets, restored the glory of the Taj Mahal, and preserved the Pearl Mosque of Lahore, the Mandalay Palace, and the temples at Khajuraho. He sought justice in the abstract and demanded accountability from the army, punishing entire regiments for the violation of a single Indian woman, even as his government stood idle while famines swept the land and the cadavers of children fed growing packs of jackals and wild dogs. Like his queen, whose only knowledge of India was derived from her dispatch box and the behavior of her servants—Victoria, empress of India, never visited the jewel of her realm—Curzon believed that he had a special feel for the real Indians, the colorful and quaint villagers, who were so unlike the educated classes he disdained. "There were no Indian natives in the Government of India," he once observed, "because among all 300 million people of the subcontinent, there was not a single man capable of the job." It was the idea of India, not its reality, that fired his imperial imagination.

As viceroy he sat alone at the pinnacle of a cadre of a mere 1,300 British men of the Indian Civil Service that ruled fully a fifth of humanity. The Indian Army was strong and well trained, but it numbered only 200,000, and only a third were British regiments, and these were dispersed from Siam to Persia. In much of the subcontinent, British authority resided solely in a single district officer, who spent each day in the saddle, moving from village to village, adjudicating disputes, levying taxes, enforcing the rule of law, and maintaining order across thousands of square miles with populations sometimes measuring in the millions. Mercantile zeal, severe military reprisals, and the subversion of local elites all played a role in the maintenance of the Raj. But what really held it together was the very audacity of the venture, the sheer gall of a small island nation that had never set out to rule the world, and yet did so with such flair.

The entire British presence in India, as Curzon fully understood, depended on the presumption of power, which in turn was reinforced on a daily basis by ten thousand acts of domination and will intended to inculcate in the Indian people a sense of their own inherent inferiority. This was the essence of colonialism. Image counted for everything. The summer palace at Simla employed three hundred domestic servants and no fewer than a hundred cooks. In a typical season, the viceroy would hold court at a dozen grand dinners for fifty, in addition to twenty-nine somewhat smaller affairs, which flanked the summer's truly important events: the state ball, a second, equally sumptuous fancy dress ball, a children's ball, two evening parties, two afternoon garden parties for a thousand, and six dances with 250 invited guests. A stickler for ritual detail and protocol, Curzon insisted that his servants dress in livery, white breeches and silk stockings, and he took precise measure of the length of the red carpets unrolled before him on ceremonial occasions.

Victoria's Diamond Jubilee, in 1898, was the most expensive event ever staged in the history of humanity, but for color and exotic opulence it was no match for the 1902 Durbar orchestrated by Curzon in celebration of the coronation of her son Edward VII. With the new king unable to attend and represented in Delhi by his brother, the Duke of Connaught, the entire two-week extravaganza became, in fact, a tribute to the viceroy, just as Curzon had anticipated. His moment came on New Year's Day as a million Indians lined the streets of Delhi to behold the imperial procession as it moved from the city to the plain above, where five miles of railroad had been laid simply to handle the flow of the invited guests, who numbered 173,000. A great amphitheater had been constructed, and along the axis of the approach were magnificent pavilions containing the largest displays of Indian art ever assembled—acres of carpets and silks, pottery and enamels, priceless antiquities. Every region of India had its camp, identified with glorious silk banners that shone in the sun through the dust of the parade.

Flanked by a peacock array of ambassadors from some fifty princely states, the viceroy received all the native rulers of India, as prayers and hymns celebrated the investiture of scores of men and women being honored for their fidelity and service to the Raj. A yellow haze spread over the fields as the first of some sixty-seven squadrons of cavalry and thirty-five battalions of infantry, artillery, and engineers trotted or marched past in a military review that lasted for three hours. Finally a mounted herald approached the dais and throne and, with appropriate flourishes, proclaimed the coronation of the new king. The imperial salute of 101 guns still resounded as Curzon moved front and center to summon the multitudes in their loyalty to the unchallenged supremacy of the British Crown. "There has never been anything," he would later write, "so great in the world's history as the British Empire, so great an instrument for the good of humanity."

THE BRITISH had indeed transformed the face of India, building thousands of miles of canals and railroads, bringing into being entire cities. But at a deeper level, the British presence was but an ephemeral veil over the body of a land that was more a state of mind than a national state, a civilization that had endured for four thousand years as an empire of ideas rather than territorial boundaries. India had yielded time and again to the onslaught of invaders, but had always won in the end, absorbing foreign impulses and, through the sheer weight of its history, prompting mutations that inevitably transformed every novel influence into something indelibly Indian.

At the same time, India was itself a British invention, an imagined place defined by the ever-changing and expanding boundaries of political and commercial interests, which, in turn, were woven into reality by the mathematicians and technicians of the Survey of India. Maps were the key to the very notion of India. They codified in two dimensions the geographic and cultural features of a subcontinent, even as they created the rationale for occupation. India the imagined landscape became concrete and meaningful when reduced to a map sheet. Thus it was not by chance that the greatest scientific undertaking of the nineteenth century was the literal measurement of India, or that through this endeavor would be discovered the highest mountain in the world.

GEOGRAPHERS HAD LONG SUSPECTED that the earth, flattened at the poles, was not a perfect sphere. But the extent of the distortion, of critical importance to science and cartography, was unknown. The Great Trigonometrical Survey set out in 1806 to solve the mystery by calibrating with a precision previously unimagined the true shape of the planet, the curvature of the globe, by measuring an arc of longitude across the face of India. The basic idea was rather straightforward: if one can establish three visible points in a landscape, and if one knows the distance between two, one can measure at each of these the angle to the third, unknown point and, with trigonometry, determine its distance and position. Once the third point has been thus established, it can form with one of the known points the base of a new triangle from which the coordinates of a new reference point on the horizon, often a mountain or other prominent landmark, can be established. Thus, over time, a chain of triangles was created, a Great Arc that ran sixteen hundred miles south to north over the length of the subcontinent.

Distance was determined with calibrated chains and measuring rods, which implied teams of men hacking through jungles, crossing swamps, climbing across the face of glaciers. To measure the angles with the requisite precision required the finest of instruments, enormous brass theodolites that weighed as much as a thousand pounds and needed a dozen men to be carried. Essentially elaborate telescopes that could pivot both vertically and horizontally to measure all angles in a plane, these theodolites had to be mounted, erect and perfectly immobile, on a circular platform bolted to the top of a thirteen-yard-long spar, which itself was dug into the ground and secured by long stays. A second platform, complete with scaffolding, had to be built alongside so that the observer might take the measurements. The slightest movement of the theodolite would render the calculations useless.

For more than forty years, the intrepid members of the Survey of India, supported by armies of laborers who suffered and died by the score, marched these exquisite instruments across the length of the subcontinent. Their seasons were short and desperate, for only with the monsoon did the haze clear and the dust settle from the air. Tormented with fevers, perched in the ice on the summits of mountains, or in empty deserts where thirty-foot platforms had to be built of stones, they meticulously recorded their observations. Quite literally nothing stood in their way. If necessary to establish a point of triangulation and properly position a theodolite, they razed entire villages, leveled sacred hills, and crushed into fragments the façades of ancient temples.

By the 1830s the Great Arc had reached the foothills of the Himalaya, the highest and youngest mountains on earth, a wall of white peaks a hundred miles deep, stretching in a gentle curve for fifteen hundred miles, from the Brahmaputra to the Indus, a distance, the British would discover, equal to that of London to the Urals of Russia. Here the members of the survey would hesitate before branching east and west, through the foothills and the malarial forests of the Terai, where a new series of baselines would be established, marked by observation posts built of mud bricks, also thirty feet high, from which they would look up and stare into the hidden heights of a mountain range that fired their imaginations. Above the heat and dust of the Indian plain, rising out of the forests of Burma, were more than a thousand mountains that soared beyond 20,000 feet, elevations scarcely comprehensible to the European mind.

The mathematical elegance of the survey's methods made it possible to calculate the height of these summits from extraordinary distances. In 1846 a party led by John Armstrong took note of a rugged knot of mountains some 140 miles west of Kangchenjunga, then considered the highest point on earth. Compared with the stunningly beautiful massif of Kangchenjunga, which dominates the sky beyond Darjeeling, these distant summits were unassuming, mere fragments of white on a dark horizon. Armstrong designated the highest simply Peak B. During subsequent seasons it remained hidden in cloud, and it was not until November 1849 that another officer of the survey, James Nicolson, was able to make a series of observations from six different stations, the closest being some 108 miles from the mountain, by then known as Peak XV. Only in 1854, at the headquarters of the Survey of India in Dehra Dun and in Calcutta, did work begin on Nicolson's computations.

Andrew Waugh, surveyor general of India, assigned the task to a brilliant Indian, Chief Computer Radhanath Sikhdar. Given the distance of the sightings and the problem of atmospheric refraction, the challenge was enormous. It took two years for Sikhdar to determine that this unknown summit was, at 29,002 feet, fully a thousand feet higher than any other known mountain on earth. It was a most impressive feat of computation. The actual elevation of the mountain, measured today by satellite technology, is 29,035 feet. But the mountain itself has been rising at a rate of a centimeter a year for the last several centuries. In the 1850s, when Sikhdar did his calculations, the summit of the mountain in all likelihood would have been some five feet lower. Thus, with pencil, paper, and mathematical wizardry, Sikhdar was off by only twenty-eight feet.

The subsequent naming of the mountain provoked controversy. The Survey of India by tradition adopted local names whenever possible. But in a letter dated March 1, 1856, addressed to Sir Roderick Murchison, then president of the Royal Geographical Society, Waugh proposed naming the mountain after his predecessor. Sir George

Everest was not pleased. He was a remarkable geographer and largely responsible for the success of the Great Trigonometrical Survey, which he led from 1829. But he was a miserable man, venomous and cantankerous, and he had made few friends in India, in part because of his disregard for ancient religious monuments, which he considered temples of idle and pagan superstitions, mere impediments to his work. His family name was actually pronounced Eave-rest, and it is ironic that his legacy was to have a mountain named in his honor yet mispronounced for all time. Though the discovery of the mountain's height was published in 1858, it was not until 1865, a year before his death, that the Royal Geographical Society officially adopted the name.

The naming controversy, however, was hardly of great significance to the Raj, which had just endured the fires of the Indian Mutiny. Nor did the mountain itself spark immediate interest. It would be nearly twenty years before a British climber, W. W. Graham, traveled to the Himalaya strictly for sport, and another ten before, in 1893, a subaltern of the 5th Gurkha Rifles, Charles Bruce, and a young explorer and political officer, Francis Younghusband, already famous for his traverse of the Gobi Desert, came together on the polo grounds at Chitral, on the Afghan frontier, and first resolved to scale the mountain. Everest itself was a "singularly shy and retiring mountain," Younghusband wrote, that "hides itself away behind other mountains." From the Indian side, the only vantage then available to the British, "its tip appears amongst a mighty array of peaks which being nearer look higher." For the British rulers of the Raj, it was the land that lay beyond Everest that mattered most, a place of mystery and danger, where the great rivers had been born long before the mountains arose, and the impenetrable canyons were the refuge for all that was sacred to Buddhist and Sikh, Hindu and Jain.

IF MAPS WERE THE METAPHOR by which the Raj came into being, knowledge provided a foundation upon which the entire imperial adventure rested. The botanical explorer and archaeologist, along with the trader, surveyor, and missionary, were the forward scouts of empire. Anthropology was born of the need to understand peoples and cultures that they might be properly administered and controlled. Commercial and military imperatives aside, noted Curzon, "it is equally our duty to dig and discover, to classify, reproduce and describe, to copy and decipher, and to cherish and conserve."

In just the decade before Curzon became viceroy, the British acquired new territories equivalent to fifty times the size of Great Britain. The overseas empire, a quarter of the land surface of the world, six times the size of the Roman Empire at its height, was nearly a hundred times larger than the home islands. Victoria, as sovereign, ruled one in four human beings, altogether some 500 million people, and her navy commanded the sea. What the British did not rule, they influenced to the point of domination. The world measured time and longitude from Greenwich. British telegraph wires and cables encircled and entwined the planet. English stamps bore only the queen's profile, as no other national identification was deemed necessary. "In the Empire," wrote Curzon, "we have found not merely the key to glory and wealth, but the call to duty, and the means of service to mankind."

India was the crown jewel, the "peacock bird in the gilded cage," and for the British it was intolerable that the empire's most prized possession was surrounded and potentially threatened by mountainous lands of which so little was known. If the British obsession throughout the early part of the nineteenth century had been Afghanistan and the North-West Frontier, increasingly the strategic concern shifted to include the ring of nations and kingdoms that contained the Raj on the north. In the 1850s, Britain secured Ladakh as a dependency of Kashmir. A decade later, the Raj absorbed the southern districts of Sikkim, intervened in a civil war in Bhutan, and fomented intrigue in the palaces of Kathmandu. Looming over all, however, remained Tibet.

"Frontiers are the razor's edge," Curzon famously wrote, "on which hang suspended the issue of war or peace and the life of nations." The frustration for the British was the fact that beyond the visual reach of the Great Trigonometrical Survey, much of the map of central Asia was blank. Boundaries and borders were rumors. No one knew where the Himalaya ended and the Hindu Kush began. The Karakoram and Pamirs had scarcely been penetrated. The hidden ranges of Tibet lay uncharted and unknown. Between 1750 and 1900, only three Westerners had reached the Tibetan capital of Lhasa. At the end of the century, the British still had no diplomatic presence there. Curzon, as viceroy, had no certain way even of opening a channel of communication with Tibetan authorities, though Lhasa lay but 250 miles from Darjeeling, a major British commercial and agricultural enclave in northern India that exported tea to every hamlet in England.

Tibet, united in the seventh century, conquered by the Mongols in the thirteenth, and then subjugated by native dynasties from 1368, had since 1642 been ruled by the leaders of the Gelugpa Buddhist order, the Dalai Lamas, believed by Tibetans to be the successive incarna-

tions of Chenrezi, the bodhisattva of compassion. The first to dominate and codify the entire nation was the Great Fifth, who gave his
spiritual teacher, the abbot of the monastery at Shigatse, the honorific
title Panchen Lama, the Great Scholar. From that point onward, these
two great complementary spiritual figures were the institutional pillars
of the nation.

In 1720 the Manchu Ch'ing dynasty began to take an active interest in Tibetan and Mongolian politics and established an ambassado-
rial presence in Lhasa, with a titular but impotent figure, the *amban*,
in permanent residence. The British acknowledged and exploited for
their own purposes the fiction of Chinese rule, even as the Ch'ing
dynasty faded toward its final destruction in the Sun Yat-sen revolution of 1911. In the infamous Chefoo Convention of 1876, Britain formally recognized Manchu authority over Tibet in exchange for China
accepting the British right to invade and colonize Burma. Tibet was
not party to the agreement.

With the decline of Chinese influence, power in Lhasa was in fact
concentrated in the hands of a Tibetan aristocratic elite, dominated
in good measure by the high lamas of the great Gelugpa monasteries,
Ganden, Sera, and Drepung. The regents who served between Dalai
Lamas were appointed by the Tsong-du, the National Assembly, and
bore the honorific title Sikyong Rinpoche, Precious Protector of the
State. The other anchor of government was the Kashag, the Council
of Four, made up of three laymen and a monk, which exercised control
over the civil administration of the nation in all matters political, judi-
cial, and financial. Beneath the Kashag was an ecclesiastical council, a
body of four monks responsible for all the monasteries in the land. The
country itself was divided into five districts, each headed by a commissioner who oversaw two district officers, or *dzongpens*, one a monk and
the other a layperson. The *dzongpens* were directly responsible for local
governance. They maintained order, collected taxes, adjudicated disputes, and pronounced justice, harsh as it might be.

Tibet in the late nineteenth century certainly possessed an aura of
mystery and intrigue, but it had yet fully to acquire the mystique that
in time would temper all foreign perceptions of the land, secular and
metaphysical. Few in diplomatic circles thought of it as a cosmic meri-
tocracy, let alone an isolated earthly paradise straddling the roof of the
world. It was simply a nation. The streets of Lhasa, though empty of
Europeans, bustled with Tatars, Muscovites, Kashmiris, Han Chinese,
and Nepalese, merchants and traders who came from all parts of central Asia. Monasteries drew monks and pilgrims from as far away as the

Black Sea. For a thousand years, Tibetan influence had been felt from the capital of China throughout the steppes of Mongolia to the courts of Persia.

Like any complex society, Tibet had great inequalities. The ebb and flow of warfare had swept the land for centuries. Punishments were severe and by contemporary standards out of all proportion to the crimes. But if the country was not a perfect society, its failures, complexities, and contradictions were its own. Fending off invasions, struggling with civil strife, Tibetans engaged like any other people the sordid realities of nationhood. As the officials of the Tibetan government looked south toward India, they saw in the British Raj a new player on their geopolitical stage, a formidable power that consistently allied itself with Nepal, a bitter enemy with whom Tibet had repeatedly gone to war, most recently in 1855. The Tibetan government, deeply suspicious of British motives, was especially incensed by territorial incursions and the persistent and irritating presence of British spies in its midst.

In a dance of espionage famously celebrated by Kipling in the novel *Kim*, the British had since 1851 trained Indian cadres as surveyors, disguised them as pilgrims, holy men, or peasants, and sent them on foot across the high passes of the Himalaya to find out what lay beyond the wall of mountains that defied their every diplomatic initiative. The goal could be Lhasa and a chance to ferret out information as to the nature of the Tibetan government, the strength of its armies, the bounty of harvests, the possibility of hunger and famine. More typically, these pundits were ordered to explore the borderlands in search of raw geographical information, the height and orientation of mountain chains, the location and accessibility of major passes, the character and extent of the rivers that drained the Tibetan Plateau and flowed into the foothills of India. For survey instruments they had only what could be disguised and carried as the religious icons of a monk. Trained to walk at precisely two thousand paces to the mile, they were given rosaries with one hundred beads rather than the traditional 108, and instructed to drop a single bead into their prayer wheels for every one hundred steps taken. The scroll hidden within the prayer wheel that spun mantras of compassion to the universe was replaced by a blank roll of paper upon which data could be surreptitiously recorded. The pundit Nain Singh, the first surveyor to fix the location of the Tibetan capital, traveled on foot from Sikkim to Lhasa and then all over central Tibet, walking 1,580 miles, or 3,160,000 paces, each counted. To establish the horizon, that he might ascertain longitude and latitude, he used quicksilver, which he carried across the Himalaya in cowrie shells sealed with wax.

The most astonishing caper of all was that of Pundit Kinthup, dispatched into the mountains to solve the single most bewildering enigma of Himalayan geography. It was known that the Tsangpo River, born in western Tibet on the flanks of Kailash, the mountain most sacred to Hindu, Buddhist, and Jain, flowed east for a thousand miles and disappeared into the Himalaya from the north at a place known as Dhemu Chamnak. On the other side of the range, the Brahmaputra, one of the greatest rivers of India, flowed out of the mountains at Sadiya, a mere 120 miles from Dhemu Chamnak. The elevation drop was an astonishing 12,000 feet, and the question lingered as to whether the two rivers were in fact one. If so, what was the nature of the gorge through which such a massive river fell so precipitously? Rumors of mystic waterfalls, higher than any known on earth, captivated British and European imaginations.

In 1880 Kinthup was given the assignment to enter Tibet in disguise and find his way down the Tsangpo to a point where he might cast into the river marked logs, which, if found by spotters assigned to the task on the upper Brahmaputra, would prove that the two rivers were a single artery. It took him seven months just to reach the village of Gyala, perched at 8,000 feet at the head of Tsangpo Gorge, whereupon he was betrayed by a companion and sold into slavery for fifteen months. It would be four years before he was finally able to trace the Tsangpo down to the Marpung monastery on the Dihang and, beyond that, to the country of the Abor, a mere thirty-five miles from the plains of Assam. He prepared five hundred logs, casting into the river fifty a day. But by then his mission had been forgotten, and there was no one waiting to watch for the logs.

When Kinthup finally returned to Darjeeling, in September 1884, those who had sent him into the mountains had either left India or died. No one of significance believed his account. His accomplishment was not acknowledged until 1913, when F. M. Bailey and Henry Morshead validated his claims, even as they nearly perished while exploring the Tsangpo from the south. Bailey will return to this narrative, as will Morshead, who mapped the route to Everest, climbed with Mallory in 1921 and 1922, and was later murdered in the forests of Burma. Thanks to Morshead and Bailey, Kinthup in old age would be celebrated in Simla and decorated personally by the viceroy.

. . .

Espionage and intrigue aside, the British in fact had no territorial ambitions in Tibet. What they wanted was for Tibet to remain a neutral buffer, insulating the Raj from the one great rival that truly did pose a threat to the entire British position in South Asia. The Russian Empire, as dominant on land as the English had been at sea, had throughout the late nineteenth century expanded south and east from the Aral Sea toward the Afghan border at an astonishing rate of fifty-five square miles a day. By the summer of 1902, Russian agents were penetrating the Hindu Kush and Pamir Mountains from the north, even as the English probed from the south. This thrust and parry, a bitter rivalry known to the British as the Great Game and to the Russians as the Tournament of Shadows, had twice since Crimea brought the nations to the brink of war, with hostilities in 1885 becoming so imminent that the British Stationery Office had actually printed documents declaring a state of war to exist between the two empires.

War was narrowly averted by a territorial compromise, the 1885 Anglo-Russian Boundary Commission, which created a buffer zone, ceding to Afghanistan a narrow panhandle of land along the cusp of the Hindu Kush. The crisis, however, prompted a shift in British strategy. In less than a century Russia had expanded over two thousand miles, reaching literally to the gates of the Raj. By all accounts, the czar's ministers had further designs on Chinese Turkistan and points beyond. The British, no longer content to control the valleys at the base of the mountains, adopted an aggressive forward policy, establishing military outposts, constructing roads, and launching incursions into the uncharted reaches of the North-West Frontier, from the Karakorum and Pamirs in the north to Baluchistan in the south.

If the ultimate foe was Russia, the actual enemy for the British became almost immediately the people of the frontier provinces. To control the passes leading to India meant maintaining remote garrisons in hostile territory where some 200,000 fiercely independent tribal peoples, Afridis, Mahsuds, Pathans, and Wazirs, armed with modern rifles that could kill at a thousand yards, lived by a blood code that demanded that a man avenge any harm or insult to his clan's honor. In the six years Curzon served as viceroy there were more than six hundred raids and clashes, and more than one British soldier would be found dead, the flesh flayed from his bones. For the Indian Army, stationed at Gilgit and Chitral, the only way to stay alive was to retaliate with equal ferocity, with raiding parties that took as a motto the phrase "Butcher and bolt." Britain's goal was to keep the Russians out, whatever the cost.

On the Tibetan frontier tensions also remained high, with border clashes between Tibetan and British troops leading to open conflict in March 1888 as two thousand British troops were dispatched to repel a Tibetan military intrusion into Sikkim, the second in as many years. In 1890 Britain moved to annex Sikkim, and by the terms of the Anglo-Chinese Treaty, which fixed the boundaries, and the subsequent trade regulations, negotiated in 1893, it was granted the right to establish a trade mart and install a permanent agent at Yatung, in the Chumbi Valley, a verdant sliver of Tibetan territory that runs between Sikkim and Bhutan and had long been the traditional trade route between India and Tibet. Lhasa was party to neither agreement and actively intervened to impede commerce, imposing custom duties on the Chinese at Phari, at the head of the valley, and physically barricading the valley beyond Yatung to keep out the British.

Curzon inherited the standoff when he became viceroy in 1899 and was not about to accept such an affront to British prestige. Recognizing the futility of dealing with Peking, he sought to open direct relations with Lhasa. Trade was a concern, but by far the greater worry were rumors of growing Russian influence in the Tibetan capital. On May 24, 1899, Curzon wrote to the secretary of state for India at Whitehall in London and stated unequivocally that Russian agents were present in the inner circles of Tibetan government. He had in mind a shadowy figure, Agvan Dorzhiev, a monk from the Buriat region of Mongolia, formally a Russian citizen and an attendant to His Holiness the Thirteenth Dalai Lama. Known to Tibetans as Tsenshab Ngawang Lobzang, Dorzhiev was, in fact, one of seven revered instructors, or *tsenshabs*, to His Holiness, and highly regarded as a master of dialectics. The British, however, believed that Dorzhiev was dealing arms and engaged in treaty negotiations on behalf of the czar.

In the autumn of 1899, Curzon sent two official letters to His Holiness the Thirteenth Dalai Lama, but neither one was opened or acknowledged. The Tibetans had no interest in affirming British trading rights granted by the Chinese in a treaty to which they had not been privy. Curzon took this diplomatic rebuff as an insult to the Crown and vowed in a third and final note to take whatever measures he deemed necessary to secure British commercial interests in Tibet. This direct threat again provoked only silence, which led to further suspicion. A Japanese monk, Ekai Kawaguchi, reported to the British— inaccurately, as it turned out—that the Tibetans were receiving small arms from Russia, and that over two hundred Buriat Mongolian students, presumed acolytes of Dorzhiev's, were living at monasteries in Tibet, a perfect cover for Russian espionage.

On October 22, 1900, a telegram reached the Foreign Office in London from St. Petersburg, reporting that Dorzhiev had carried a letter of greeting to the czar from the Dalai Lama. Count Vladimir Lamsdorf, the Russian foreign minister, denied that the monk had any formal diplomatic appointment. The Russian newspapers nevertheless celebrated his arrival, referred to him as an envoy extraordinaire, and reported the manner in which he had charmed the Russian court. Less than a year later, in June 1901, Dorzhiev was back in Russia as the head of a mission of eight prominent Tibetans and was heralded a second time by the press and lavished with gifts from the czar. It appeared to all, most especially the British, that the Dalai Lama was actively seeking Russian support as a foil to the Raj. Rumors were rife of a secret agreement between Russia, China, and Tibet. There was talk of a Russian railroad to Lhasa, of camel caravans delivering Russian rifles by the score to an arsenal in the Tibetan capital rebuilt and garrisoned by Russian Cossacks. It was even said that Dorzhiev's influence was such that he could personally muster Tibetan armies and order them into battle.

How much of this was true was uncertain; but any Russian influence in Lhasa was unacceptable to the British. Curzon took it as his duty to "frustrate this little game while there is still time." The only solution would be an Anglo-Tibetan accord, signed in Lhasa, guaranteeing if not British domination, then at the very least an ongoing neutrality that would deny Tibet to both English and Russian alike.

In the spring of 1903, Curzon dispatched a representative to London to seek approval for an advance on Lhasa with a military force of twelve hundred rifles. The home government, unwilling to antagonize the Chinese or openly threaten the Russians, sanctioned only a secret trade mission to treat with the Tibetans at Kampa Dzong, a fort and crossroads located less than a day's ride from the summit of the Serpo La, the 16,900-foot pass that marks Sikkim's northernmost frontier with Tibet. To lead the diplomatic foray, a chastened Curzon chose an old friend, Francis Younghusband, whom he felt he could trust both to promote his aggressive forward policies and to overcome the dangers and challenges inherent in such an initiative launched into hostile and unknown country.

SOLDIER, PHILOSOPHER, mystic visionary, and spy, Younghusband was a man of firm will and gentle nature, yet an adventurer and imperialist to the core. Born in 1863 in the foothills of the Himalaya and later schooled in Britain at Clifton, he attended the Royal Military

College at Sandhurst, returning to India in 1882 as a young officer in the King's Dragoon Guards. In 1886, after several probing expeditions to the Himalaya and reconnaissance work along the Indus and Afghan frontier, he joined a research party destined for Manchuria, intent on rediscovering the Long White Mountain, a sacred peak that had been described two centuries earlier by an itinerant Jesuit priest. After seven months in the field, Younghusband, then aged twenty-five, found himself alone in Peking, obliged to return to India. He elected to walk, becoming the first European to traverse the Gobi Desert, then passed through Kashgar and Yarkand and plunged into the unknown ranges of the Aghil and Karakoram. Crossing the perilous 18,000-foot Muztagh Pass, seeking a route home to Baltistan and Kashmir, he discovered glaciers the size of small countries, and wild rivers running through mountains unlike anything ever before seen by an Englishman, including the fluted northern flank of K2, the second-highest mountain on earth.

Little more than a year later, promoted to the rank of captain, Younghusband returned to the Karakoram, ostensibly to investigate attacks on trade caravans by Kanjut raiders from Hunza. His real purpose was to explore the passes and rivers leading beyond the mountains, in both the Karakoram and the Pamirs, and track the presence of Russian agents in these most inaccessible border regions of the Raj. His escort included a small party of the 5th Gurkhas commanded by Charles Bruce, who would, like Younghusband himself, figure large in the Everest saga of 1921–24. Their friendship, forged in the strain of the Great Game, would be the driving force that would draw the British to the mountain.

In the summer of 1891, Younghusband was taken captive by a Cossack patrol and ordered back to India. The confrontation prompted a major diplomatic incident and seared in Younghusband a deep and lasting impression of the seriousness of the Russian menace, a conviction he shared with Curzon, whom he first met in Chitral two years later while serving as political agent. Curzon was then a young member of Parliament, engaged in his own remarkable explorations in India, writing dispatches for the *Times* of London even as he scouted the defenses of the Raj for any evidence of weakness.

By the time Curzon, as viceroy, would tap his friend for service in Tibet in 1903, Younghusband was well on his way to becoming the most famous geographer of his age. The youngest person ever elected a fellow of the Royal Geographical Society, recipient of its coveted Founder's Medal for his explorations in the Pamirs and Karakoram, author already of three of the twenty-six books he would produce over a long and distinguished career, he was described by the press as a "hero of dazzling adventures in hazardous exploration, a writer of noble English, a daring soldier and a great gentleman." Not to mention a record holder in the hundred-yard dash, a fact not lost on his many young schoolboy admirers.

ON JUNE 19, 1903, Francis Younghusband, dressed in breeches and gaiters, brown boots, a khaki coat, and a forage cap, left Darjeeling for the sweltering heat and driving monsoon rains of the Teesta Valley, the first stage in the approach march to Tibet. With him as translator was Captain Frederick O'Connor, one of the only Tibetan speakers in the British Army. Escorting the party was a force of five hundred sepoys of the 32nd Sikh Pioneers, all veterans of the ferocious fighting that had marked the Relief of Chitral in 1895. At Gangtok, Claude White, political officer of Sikkim, joined the expedition as Chinese translator. Arrogant, opinionated, and deeply resentful of Younghusband's authority, White ran Sikkim as a personal fiefdom. In his presence, local people removed their hats and prostrated themselves on the ground, foreheads in the mud. Younghusband was not impressed.

On July 4 Younghusband sent his main force over the Serpo La and into Tibet, while he remained behind, botanizing in the meadows of the Tangu Plain, reading Tennyson, deliberately delaying his arrival until the force was fully established at Kampa Dzong, so that he might arrive with appropriate diplomatic aplomb. He did so on July 18. Flanked by a mounted and armed escort, his oilskins black with rain, he crossed the pass and rode down the side of the Himalaya and onto the open barren plain of Tibet toward Kampa Dzong. There the British encampment, dotted rows of white tents surrounded by barbed wire and entrenchments, lay on a brilliant windswept flat in the shadow of a massive Tibetan fort that dominated the valley.

Kampa Dzong would be his base for five frustrating months as he waited in vain for Tibetans to send to the table officials of sufficient rank for meaningful negotiations. "Never have I met so obdurate and obstructive a people," Younghusband confessed. The Tibetans, in fact, had no interest in dialogue, most especially on their own soil. Nothing could occur, they insisted, until the British force retired to the frontier. Under the circumstances, a protracted diplomatic standoff was inevitable: His Holiness the Thirteenth Dalai Lama had entered into a three-year spiritual retreat, and with his isolation no major decision of state could be made. It was a clash of cultures for which the British were quite unprepared. After weeks of boredom interspersed with flashes of diversion—gazelle hunts and duck shoots, plant collecting and horse races—Younghusband and his men retreated to Sikkim. For the Tibetans it was a Pyrrhic victory: the humiliating loss of face virtually guaranteed that the British would be back in force, and not under the guise of a diplomatic mission.

When it came, the excuse for war did not do honor to the British. On November 3, 1903, Lord Curzon, the queen's viceroy, ruler of 300 million men and women on the subcontinent that was India, sent a cable to London alerting Whitehall to an overt act of hostility. A small group of Tibetan soldiers had attacked Nepalese yaks on the frontier and carried them away. The Younghusband Mission, which began with an attempt to oblige Tibetans to accept trade regulations the British had negotiated exclusively with the Chinese, was transformed into a full-out military invasion because of the poaching of a few animals.

The British force gathered in early December at Darjeeling and Gangtok, altogether some 5,000 soldiers, Gurkhas and Sikhs for the most part, but also sappers, engineers, artillery and machine gun units of regular British Army, as well as military police, cooks, medical staffs, telegraph and postal specialists, diplomats, and a handful of journalists dispatched from Britain to cover the adventure for the London papers. In support were no fewer than 10,000 porters and 20,000 yaks, which each day would carry some 40,000 pounds of food, ammunition, and equipment over a tenuous supply line eventually reaching from Lhasa to Darjeeling.

In weather so cold that white rainbows spread across the sky, the army headed not north to the Serpo La and Kampa Dzong, but east to the Jelep La, the 14,390-foot pass that led to the Chumbi Valley and the main trading route from Sikkim to Tibet. This was the direct approach to Gyantse, the immediate goal, and Lhasa, the ultimate quest. Younghusband himself went through the Jelep La on December 13, a Sunday. In terrible winds, with thermometers recording thirty degrees of frost, he surely must have reflected on the audacity of marching an army across the Himalaya in the heart of winter along narrow tracks that had never seen the passage of a European.

The invasion met no resistance at the frontier, and after three weeks in the Chumbi, Younghusband continued toward Gyantse, crossing the Tang La at the head of the valley and dropping at last onto the vast Tibetan Plateau. He established his advance camp at Tuna, an insignificant place brutally exposed to the fierce winds of winter. The cold was merciless. Old soldiers woke to find their dentures frozen in ice. Breath cracked in the wind. Damp clothing froze and could be broken like a stick.

Younghusband elected to remain for the winter at Tuna, a site that his military commander, General James MacDonald of the Royal Engineers, considered far too barren and exposed for his army. MacDonald retreated to the Chumbi, leaving the diplomatic party with a skeletal security force on the plateau to endure three months of bitter winds and limited forage, with only frozen yak dung for fuel. Younghusband himself presumably remained warm, for his personal kit alone filled some twenty-nine cases, including two large steel trunks and a container exclusively for hats. As an English gentleman, he naturally had proper dress for every occasion. His clothes at Tuna included, among other things, eighteen pairs of boots and shoes, twenty-eight pairs of socks, thirty-two collars, and sixty-seven shirts, some flannel, others white, twilled, or colored, along with studs and any number of ties. He had a dozen suits with matching waistcoats. His twelve winter overcoats included a Chinese fur, a chesterfield, an old ulster, a posteen long coat, two Jaegers, and a waterproof. For headgear he had a white helmet and a khaki, a brown felt hat, two forage caps, a white Panama, a cocked hat, both a thick and a thin solar topi, and, finally, a shikar, intended only to be used when shooting partridges in the Chumbi Valley. With such baggage to carry, it was no wonder that eighty-eight porters died of exhaustion on the march.

Unfortunately for Younghusband, opportunities at Tuna to display sartorial preparedness were limited. Three months of fruitless negotiations climaxed with an encounter on March 3, 1904, at which time the Tibetans insisted that Dorzhiev, the imagined nemesis, was nothing more than a simple Buriat monk, and that Russia and Tibet had no diplomatic engagement, let alone an alliance. The British, at this point, were far too committed even to ponder such a possibility. At Kampa Dzong they had learned of a phonograph delivered by Dorzhiev to His Holiness the Dalai Lama. To restore British prestige and prove their superiority in all things technical, they had labored through the night, scraping flat a disk to improvise a device that, to the delight of all, faithfully recorded and played back the voice of a monk. There was to be no quarter in this struggle with Russia. The British had decided that Dorzhiev was an agent. It was the only way to rationalize the extreme measures that Curzon had pressed upon the expedition.

Cold, indignant, bored, and anxious for resolution, Younghusband decided to march on toward Lhasa, even in the face of certain Tibetan resistance. At the end of March they crossed a flat and barren expanse of stone and at Guru came upon a wall roughly the height of a man, spanning much of the valley. Grassless hills climbed away to the west, and to the east the receding remnants of a lake shimmered with ice. Beyond the stone wall were several thousand Tibetan soldiers, dressed in the colors of the rainbow. Some were perched as infantry, with ancient flintlocks, slings, axes, swords, and spears, arms unlike anything seen in Europe in a thousand years. Others were mounted on Tibetan ponies, whose short stature provoked the scorn of the English. No one initially wanted bloodshed. The British dispersed into the tactical formations that had won an empire: infantry in front, artillery to the rear, and Maxim guns to the flanks, which controlled the high ground. With admirable constraint and at some considerable risk, the infantry advanced, assuming that the obvious evidence of superiority would cause the enemy to capitulate or flee the field. To their astonishment, not a Tibetan wavered. They came so close their breath mingled. All was calm, an empty impasse, until the British demanded that the Tibetans disarm. Language was lost, and the tension shattered as a Sikh enlisted man grabbed the bridle of a Tibetan general's horse. In outrage, the general drew his pistol and shot the Indian in the face. There was a moment of stunned silence, followed by the crack of a single rifle bullet. And then all hell broke loose.

The Tibetans barely had time to draw their swords before the Maxim guns opened up. A people whose knowledge of firearms was limited to muzzle-loading muskets encountered for the first time the murderous efficiency of the machine gun. It was another Omdurman, an effortless colonial victory. More than six hundred Tibetans were killed, countless wounded. The British losses were nine wounded: seven sepoys, one officer, and one journalist, Edmund Chandler of the *Daily Mail*, who suffered seventeen sword cuts and lost his hand. The Tibetans did not surrender. They simply turned away and, as if impervious to the bullets that cut them down, began to lean north toward Lhasa. "It was an awful sight," wrote a British officer to his mother, "and I hope I shall never again have to shoot down men who are walking away." Younghusband himself called it a "terrible and ghastly business." A British correspondent, Henry Savage Landor, well known in England for his own graphic exploits in Tibet, indignantly described Guru as the "butchering of thousands of helpless and defenseless natives in a manner most repulsive to any man who is a man."

In the wake of the debacle at Guru, the Tibetans retreated north and the British pushed on, fighting a series of skirmishes that climaxed in a two-month siege at Gyantse, where they endured tens of casualties while inflicting on the Tibetans some five thousand. With such a ratio of suffering, it is not surprising that the British generals had come by 1914 to view war as something glorious. Their military strategy, successful in countless colonial encounters, was distilled in two short lines of Victorian verse, poet Hilaire Belloc's famous ditty: "Whatever happens, we have got / The Maxim gun and they have not." By the time Younghusband saw the glittering roof of the Potala Palace and passed with his soldiers through the West Gate of the holy city, more than twenty-six hundred Tibetans had been killed, against British losses in all ranks of just forty dead.

Still, Lhasa had been achieved. Perceval Landon, a correspondent for the *Times*, recalled the moment in hushed tones: "Here at last it was, the never-reached goal of so many weary wanderers, the home of all the occult mysticism that still remains on Earth. The light waves of mirage dissolving impalpably just shook the far outlines of the golden roofs and dimly seen white terraces. I do not think any one of us said much."

Such reverie was short-lived. Within a few days Landon came upon the part of the city where dwelt the Ragyabas, the breakers of the dead, those destined to devote their lives to carving up the remains of the deceased, to feed the vultures and to remind the living, through the drama of the event, that all things material in the end must decay. The British who witnessed a sky burial had no idea what they were seeing, but of the lives of the Ragyabas, Landon had no doubts. "It is difficult," he wrote, "to imagine a more repulsive occupation, a more brutalized type of humanity, and, above all, a more abominable and foul sort of hovel than those, which are characteristic of these men. Filthy in appearance, half naked, half clothed in obscene rags, these nasty folk live in houses which a respectable pig would refuse to occupy."

Lhasa would prove a disappointment. Heeding the counsel of the Nechung Oracle, His Holiness the Thirteenth Dalai Lama had broken his retreat and fled toward exile in Mongolia four days before the British reached the city. He would not return for five years. In his absence, Younghusband struggled to find an appropriate authority with whom to negotiate. The Chinese were powerless. A British attempt to replace the Dalai Lama with the Panchen Lama went nowhere. With the help of the Tongsa Penlop, later maharaja of Bhutan, Younghusband eventually dictated terms to the four members of the Kashag, or Cabinet. The convention, forced upon them and signed on September 7, 1904, gave the British control of the Chumbi Valley for seventy-five years, allowed free access to Lhasa for a British trade representative, and forbade the Tibetans from having any dealings with any foreign power without British consent. The third and final clause was, in the circumstances, an afterthought. Younghusband found no evidence of Russian influence in Lhasa, no arsenal or railroad, no diplomatic or military mission. Dorzhiev, whom he met, appeared indeed to be a simple monk. The very thought of Russia threatening India through Tibet, as Edmund Chandler reminded his readers of the *Daily Mail*, was rendered absurd by the impossible geography they had struggled through to get their modest force to Lhasa.

The holy city itself, stripped of the radiance of the Potala and the Jokhang Temple, appeared to the invaders as decrepit, medieval in aspect. In the streets hungry dogs lay abandoned as children in rags smoked wild rhubarb and tobacco. In the shops were bundles of scented soaps that had been on the shelves for decades. The people bathed once a year. They had prayer wheels but no wheeled transport. They called guns "fire arrows." They took it as a given that the world was flat. They allowed women to marry more than one man, and men to embrace in matrimony any number of women. Refusing to kill an insect or harm a blade of grass, they enforced the most ruthless of sanctions, the gouging of eyes, the severance of limbs for petty theft. In religious services, they played music with trumpets carved from human thighbones, and drank offerings from chalices made of human skulls. Religious devotees lived in the darkness of caves and sealed chambers for their entire lives. It was all too much for English sensibilities. Even the notion of reincarnation, a sliver of the complexity of the Buddhist science of the mind, was seen by them as abject tyranny, a sleight of hand intended and devised to hold the spirit in ransom for eternity.

Within a fortnight of the signing of the treaty, the British, fearing the onset of winter, abandoned Lhasa and retreated across the Tsangpo River and over the harsh, sweeping uplands that led to the Tang La and the slow descent into the Chumbi Valley. Two weeks in the Tibetan capital had been enough to dispel for some, most especially Perceval Landon of the *Times*, any romantic illusions. The Tibetans, he wrote, were a "stunted and dirty little people," their religion nothing but a "disastrous parasitic disease," while their government was a theocratic regime, oppressive, inefficient, bizarre, tyrannical, and corrupt. This sense of good riddance, distilled in journalistic dispatches fired over the telegraph wires that the British had laid in the wake of their advance on Lhasa, defined English perceptions of a Tibet that remained a political adversary. Only in subsequent years, when the diplomatic ground shifted, did it serve British interests to cultivate an image of Tibet as the place of innocence and mystic fantasy it has since occupied in the Western imagination.

For Younghusband the political and military success in Lhasa was short-lived. The expedition had been widely praised in the British press. Congratulatory telegrams arrived from King Edward VII, and from Curzon and Lord Ampthill, who had taken over as acting viceroy in the months the army had been in the field. Younghusband could with confidence look forward to a hero's welcome in London, complete with an audience at Buckingham Palace. But praise was far from universal. Indian and European papers condemned the negotiations as a farce, the treaty as a "useless scroll of paper," the invasion itself as a murderous imperial adventure, anachronistic, vainglorious, and self-serving on the part of its leader. There were reports of the plundering of monasteries, of caravans of loot strung out over the tracks leading back to the Raj. For Younghusband the cruelest blow came from Whitehall, which disavowed key elements of the treaty even before the mission departed from Lhasa. A telegram arrived just days before he left, ordering him to reopen the negotiations and modify the terms, reducing the size of the indemnity charged to the Tibetans and eliminating the demand that a British trade agent be stationed in Lhasa. Younghusband simply ignored the request as impractical, given the advance of the season.

MANY OF THOSE who had accompanied the expedition left Lhasa disenchanted. There was a sense that something very special had been violated—not a country but the idea of a place, a forbidden land, one of the last blank spots on the map. On the eve of their entry into the city for the first time, Chandler had sent a dispatch to his paper saying that after Lhasa, "there are no more forbidden cities, no real mysteries, no unknown land of dreams." The Younghusband expedition, wrote Curzon to the famed Swedish explorer Sven Hedin, has "destroyed the virginity of the bride to whom you aspired." In London John Buchan, later Lord Tweedsmuir, reflected, "It was impossible to avoid a certain regret for the drawing back of the curtain which had meant so much to the imagination of mankind. With the unveiling of Lhasa fell the last stronghold of the older romance."

Younghusband, by contrast, despite setbacks and disappointments, left Lhasa on September 23 positively elated, his spirit liberated from the tensions and pressures of the campaign. A day before his departure, a high lama, Ti Rinpoche, gave him an image of the Buddha as a gesture of peace. He would carry the icon with him for the rest of his life, and his daughter would place it reverently on his coffin when finally, having witnessed two world wars, he would pass away in 1942. His headstone would be a relief of Lhasa with a simple inscription: "Blessed are the pure in heart, for they shall see God." Clearly something powerful had touched the man during his weeks in Lhasa. He would leave the city transformed, a mystic warrior drawn thereafter to the spiritual life. As founder of the World Congress of Faiths, he would devote all his energy to shattering barriers between the great religious traditions of the world. His heart and mind would remain remarkably open. At a time when the English in India spoke openly of their disdain for the "wogs," and visionary men such as Mahatma Gandhi provoked only scorn, Younghusband was asked by a group of officers seated around a campfire to name the historical figure he most admired. Younghusband selected Ramakrishna, a Hindu religious leader much derided and mocked by the British as a wild fakir. After Lhasa, his eyes were focused on another realm, another reality.

As the mission departed the sacred city, Younghusband slipped away from his retinue at the first opportunity to take a walk alone in the mountains. The sky was radiant blue, and on the ridges, he recalled, the light was violet. He looked back at the distant outline of Lhasa and felt the intention of the lama's parting words of peace, coming over him as a wave of compassion. "And with all the warmth still on me," he later wrote, "and bathed in the insinuating influences of the dreamy autumn evening, I was insensibly suffused with an almost intoxicating sense of elation and good will. The exhilaration of the moment grew and grew till it thrilled through me with overpowering intensity. Never again could I think evil, or ever again be at enmity with any man.

"Such experiences are all too rare," he continued, "and they but too soon become blurred in the actualities of daily intercourse and practical existence. Yet it is these few fleeting moments, which are reality. In these only we see real life. The rest is ephemeral, the unsubstantial. And that single hour on leaving Lhasa was worth all the rest of my lifetime."

Younghusband had entered the holy city a man in pursuit of enemies, both real and imagined, only to emerge with his mind intent on the sky, the stars, and the mountains that soared on all sides. The unveiling of Lhasa had provoked in him a new set of mysteries, both of the heart and of the spirit. His convictions robust, his idealism not swayed, he swept the horizon for a new possibility upon which to anchor his dreams. The place of innocence once occupied by Lhasa both in his and the British imagination, sullied and emptied by the reality of conquest, would not remain vacant for long.

As Younghusband made his way back to India, his soldiers describing narrow tracks through the snow, his officers tripping lightly through his mess in the cold evenings, he charted the last adventures of the mission. Free of political obligations, looking south toward a side of the Himalaya utterly unknown to the British, he conceived two great thrusts of exploration. One would be a move on the upper gorge of the Tsangpo, where the Pundit Kinthrup had suffered, to see if a way might not be found through the mountains, along the river to Assam. This would be led by Claude White and supported by Captain Charles Ryder as survey officer. The second expedition would be under the command of Captain Cecil Rawling, an intrepid explorer who only weeks before the beginning of the Younghusband Mission had returned from a clandestine journey of a thousand miles in which he had crossed into western Tibet from Kashmir and Ladakh to survey some thirty-five thousand square miles of unknown country. His duty now, as conceived by Younghusband, would be even more ambitious. Rawling's orders were to head west on horse, tracking the Tsangpo, as the upper Brahmaputra is called, to its source, wherever it might be, and then find a way through the Himalaya from the north to return to India, all before the onset of winter. In the end the government of India vetoed the exploration of the Tsangpo Gorge, fearing that White and Ryder and their men might be slaughtered by the "truculent, independent tribes between the border of Tibet and Assam." The result was the reinforcement of Rawling's expedition to the headwaters by two remarkable men, Lieutenant F. M. Bailey, a soldier who as a spy would make history, and Captain Ryder, who in later years as surveyor general of India would do much to facilitate the Everest expeditions of 1921–24.

What especially excited Younghusband was the trajectory he had proposed for the journey to the headwaters, an uncharted route of nearly a thousand miles that would take the party, though at a distance, along the northern flank of a destination far more difficult of access than Lhasa, a place purer in nature, more dangerous in character and disposition, which had been in his sights as an explorer for nearly twenty years. Younghusband had first seen Mount Everest from Darjeeling, and from there it appears a modest mountain, a white fang on the horizon, dwarfed by the magnificence of Kangchenjunga. At Chitral in 1893, he and Charles Bruce had spoken of attempting Everest from the south with an approach through Nepal. But until Younghusband's first diplomatic foray to Kampa Dzong, in 1903, a year before the invasion, no Englishman had ventured beyond the Himalayan divide into Tibet. With the possible exception of the Pundit Hari Ram, who in

1871 completed a secret traverse from Shigatse to Nyelam and may well have glimpsed Everest from the Tingri Plain, no agent of the British had ever seen the mountain from the north.

Younghusband had been among the first to do so when, on the morning of July 19, 1903, he woke to an early frost and a perfect sky in the shadow of the fortress at Kampa Dzong. His tent was pitched on a bare stretch of earth in the midst of stiff patches of grass and wormwood. There had been rain the previous day, and upon his arrival the entire camp had been enshrouded in mist. But now the air was clear. Looking out into the spectral light he saw, far to the southwest, "the first streaks of dawn gilding the snowy summits of Mount Everest, poised high in heaven as the spotless pinnacle of the world." In that instant, he later recalled, the mountain became fused with his destiny, its summit a symbol of all that was vital in the heart and spirit of man.

The irascible Claude White, also at Kampa Dzong that day, photographed the mountain with his large-format camera. The image is preserved in the Curzon Collection in the India Office in London. In the foreground are rolling hills, in shadow, without discernible evidence of vegetation. Above the hills is a ring of clouds marking the horizon. Beyond the horizon, reaching to heights incomprehensible to the ordinary man, are the summits of Makalu, Chomo Lonzo, and Everest, a ridge of white scoring the skyline.

THE RAWLING EXPEDITION left Gyantse on October 10, 1904, and headed northwest, away from the height of the Himalaya, to reach the Tsangpo River at Shigatse, Tibet's second city and the site of the great monastery of Tashi Lhumpo, the religious seat of the Panchen Lama and the home, at the time, of some forty-five hundred monks. After an official audience with the high lama, and a few days spent provisioning the men with fur coats and hats and thick woolen blankets, as well as securing new transport, the expedition, altogether thirty-five men and forty-four ponies, along with a hundred hired horses and the requisite drivers, left Shigatse on October 16.

In four days they reached Lhatse, a fort and monastery perched on a rocky outcrop dominating a wide plain and guarding the approaches to the heart of central Tibet from the west. There the expedition divided. Bailey and another officer, Captain Wood of the Royal Engineers, taking all the heavy baggage and most of the transport animals, followed the traditional trade route, which ran overland, parallel to the river but well north of it for some 160 miles. Rawling and Ryder, lightly equipped, elected to continue west along the right bank of the Tsangpo, a perilous track perched at times 200 feet above the water on rock ledges too narrow to permit the movement of a loaded pony. For three days they traversed the bluffs, a dangerous passage relieved only by the discovery of verdant valleys, isolated between the long stretches of rock and ice. At the monastery of Rujé, balanced on the edge of a steep precipice rising sheer from the riverbank, the way was finally blocked by cliffs impossible to turn, and their party headed south into richer country, a low-lying district of grassy meadows and fens, abundant in herds of yaks and sheep, and dominated by the ruins of towers and fortresses shattered by the invading Gurkha army during the war with Nepal a half century before.

On the morning of October 27, having spent the night some 2,000 feet above the river, exposed to relentless and bitterly cold winds, Rawling and Ryder broke camp early and made their way through deep snow to the summit of the Kura La, a 17,900-foot pass that overlooked the Tingri Plain to the north and marked the divide between the drainage of the Tsangpo and that of the sacred Ganges. They paused at the divide and on a whim decided to climb higher, up the steep slope of a conical hill that offered the promise of an unimpeded view to the south from its summit. The morning was cold, crisp, and clear, and from the top of the rise, at a distance of perhaps sixty miles, could be seen fully exposed the wildest heart of the Himalayan range. Dominating the skyline, instantly putting to rest the notion that it might anywhere have a rival, was the northern face of Everest, never before seen by a European from this vantage, a sheer precipice so daunting that even at such a distance it caused Rawling to shudder in anticipation.

"Towering up thousands of feet, a glittering pinnacle of snow," he wrote, rose Everest, "a giant amongst pigmies [*sic*], and remarkable not only on account of its height, but for its perfect form. No other peaks lie near or threaten its supremacy. From its foot a rolling mass of hills stretch away in all directions, to the north dropping to the Dingri [Tingri] Plain, 15,000 feet below. To the east and west, but nowhere in its immediate vicinity, rise other great mountains of rock and snow, each beautiful in itself, but in no other way comparing with the famous peak in solemn grandeur. It is difficult to give an idea of its stupendous height, its dazzling whiteness and overpowering size, for there is nothing in the world to compare it with."

The wind was too bitter for Rawling and Ryder to remain long at the height of the Kura La and they soon descended, ultimately reaching a narrow gorge, a mere slit in the rocks that ran for miles before finally opening onto the Tingri Plain, which they did not reach until after dusk. The following day Rawling's cook fell ill and the expedition was obliged to lay over for twenty-four hours. Captain Ryder took advantage of the opportunity to head south, across the vast and open expanses of grass stretching all the way to the flanks of the mountains that formed the wall of the Himalaya. That afternoon, he saw Everest again, and in the rarefied air the mountain seemed nearer than it actually was. He probably came within fifty miles, close enough to glass the ridges leading to the summit and report back to Rawling that the mountain might be climbed, should it prove possible to penetrate and force a line up its lower slopes, hidden as they were from his view. From that moment Rawling vowed to return and find a way to the mountain's inner sanctum, where an assault on the summit might be staged.

For the time being, however, Rawling's route would carry him away from Everest. Winter was upon them. The temperature dropped with each frost, and the river flowed with great blocks of ice. The grass was dead, the horses hungry, the men weakened by the cold and the westerly winds, which rose to gale force virtually every morning. Such was their haste that when finally, on December 1, they reached the source of the Tsangpo, the marshes northeast of Mount Kailash, and, beyond, the sacred lakes Manasarowar and Rakas Tal, they had but a few days to explore a faint height of land that gives rise to three of the greatest rivers of India: the Indus, Brahmaputra (Tsangpo), and Sutlej.

Like many Europeans who would eventually follow in their wake, they tried, even as they charted the outlines of the major geographical features, to make sense of a place considered holy by millions of people, Buddhist and Hindu alike, a sacred landscape anchored by Kailash, a mountain so revered that to tread on its slopes would condemn the trespasser not only for this life but for a thousand to come. For Hindus, Mount Kailash is the divine seat of the god Shiva and his wife, the goddess Parvati. It is the point where the sacred form of the Ganges, the holiest of all rivers, spills from the heavens and runs invisibly through the silk of Shiva's hair before slipping into the earth to emerge from the mouth of a glacier, found some 140 miles to the west. For Buddhists, Kailash is the site in legend of the Buddha Chakrasamvara, who sweeps up Shiva and his circle into the embrace of a gentle mandala of bliss. It is famed in history as the place of the great victory of the Tibetan yogi Milarepa, a mystic wanderer of the twelfth century who, through the magical powers that accrue to supreme spiritual purity, flew effortlessly to the summit of the sacred mountain, thus vanquishing his great rival, Naro Bhun Chon, a priest and shaman of the pre-Buddhist Bon religion, and securing forever the Buddhist path in Tibet. It was Milarepa who established homes in the mountains encircling Kailash for the five hundred Buddhist saints who had achieved enlightenment, and whose prayers are still heard by the pilgrims who gain spiritual merit by circumambulating the mountain, through prostrations, one body length at a time.

Rawling knew nothing of this history, but he nevertheless recognized the grandeur and resonance of the mountain. "It is indeed difficult to place before the mental vision a true picture of this most beautiful mountain," he wrote. "In shape it resembles a cathedral, the roof of which, rising to a ridge in the centre, is otherwise regular in outline and covered in eternal snow . . . No wonder that this spot is believed to be the home of all the gods, that of the waters of its lake they drink, and that in its unexplored caverns they dwell."

The expedition moved away from Kailash on December 3 and continued to the northwest, traversing the headwaters of the Sutlej and entering the drainage of the Indus to reach Gartok, where they had been charged by Younghusband with the task of establishing a trading depot. Gartok, a miserable and desolate outpost, did not hold them long. With winter threatening to close the passes to the south, they moved quickly to complete their survey and return to India, crossing back into the basin of the Sutlej by way of the 18,700-foot Ayi La and thence to the Shipki La and the slow descent to Simla, the summer capital of the Raj, which was reached on January 11, 1905, three months and a day from when they'd left Gyantse. The expedition was heralded as a great success. In conditions of extraordinary cold and exposure, with temperatures often as low as sixty degrees of frost, Ryder had surveyed more than forty thousand square miles, a feat of exploration that would win him the Patron's Medal from the Royal Geographical Society. Rawling's prize, by contrast, lay waiting in a landscape yet to be achieved. South of the bank of the Brahmaputra, beyond the reach of the Ryder survey, remained one large blank on the map, an area of some thirteen thousand square miles between the river and the northern face of the Himalaya. At the center of this uncharted land, defining the divide between Tibet and Nepal, stood Everest, the sentinel of a rugged knot of mountains that Rawling, by the end of his expedition, knew for certain to be the highest in the world.

HAVING DISPATCHED Rawling's party from Gyantse, Younghusband and the invasion force hastened south toward India, following the old trade route that his sappers and engineers had transformed into a main trunk road. In a race against winter, the army lost. The blizzards struck savagely on the heights of the Tang La, and then blanketed the advanced columns as they trudged through Phari, at the head of the Chumbi Valley. Snow and glare blinded hundreds of soldiers, and the chaos and disarray reminded at least one officer of Napoleon's retreat from Moscow. It was a sad ending to the last of the great imperial adventures, a military campaign a year in duration and for the British essentially bloodless. When Younghusband reached Darjeeling, on October 28, and presented his casualty list, the British wounded numbered but thirty officers and men, the dead just five. The enlisted ranks of native sepoys suffered a total of 145 casualties, killed and wounded, against Tibetan losses in excess of three thousand dead alone.

After nearly a month on sick leave, Younghusband returned to Britain, eager both to silence his critics and to assist those supporters and family members demanding that he be knighted, an honor he would in fact achieve before the end of the year. His ship, SS *Mongolia*, reached Port Said in the last days of November 1904, where by chance he encountered Lord Curzon, who was heading out to India to begin his second term as viceroy. Curzon was effusive in his praise of the Lhasa adventure, offering his unfailing support with an "overpowering" authority that Younghusband later described in a letter to his wife as "one of the experiences of my lifetime." Younghusband, for his part, debriefed his friend and mentor not only about the Tibetan mission and its consequences but also about his dream of Everest.

Like Younghusband, Curzon had long had his sights on the mountain. As early as July 9, 1899, just six months after becoming viceroy, he had written Douglas Freshfield, a former president of the Alpine Club, and mentioned his intention to seek permission for an expedition to Everest from the maharaja of Nepal during an upcoming state visit to Kathmandu. Nothing, evidently, came of the effort. But some years later, even as Younghusband was marshaling his force for the invasion, Curzon sent to the Royal Geographical Society and the Alpine Club thirteen photographs taken in the summer of 1903 at Kampa Dzong by J. Hayden, a geologist attached to Younghusband's party. These were, if anything, more revealing than the images taken by Claude White, for they presented a panorama of the entire northern flank of the Himalaya, from Kangchenjunga through Everest and beyond. Freshfield immediately recognized the significance of Hayden's photographs, which appeared in the *Alpine Journal*. The land was treeless, with low ridges rounded off by ice, and across the landscape, he wrote, the "horizontal prevails over the vertical. It is open country."

The photographs left no doubt that Everest could be approached from the north.

Freshfield's enthusiasm was significant, for at fifty-nine he was one of the most respected geographers in Britain. As a young man he had explored the Caucasus, making the first ascents of Kazbek and Elbrus and later writing the definitive book on the region, *Exploration of the Caucasus*. Editor of the *Alpine Journal* from 1872 to 1880, he served both as president of the Alpine Club (1893–95) and, later, as president of the Royal Geographical Society (1914–17), where he broke tradition and, over considerable opposition, insisted that women be accepted as fellows. He was the first explorer to complete a circuit of the base of Kangchenjunga, an expedition that electrified the British public and resulted in a highly regarded book, *Round Kangchenjunga*, which appeared in 1903, the same year he was awarded the Founder's Medal by the RGS. His influence in London extended well beyond the mountaineering community, a fact not lost on Curzon.

Frustrated in Tibet, his initiatives increasingly restrained both by public sentiment and government officials in Whitehall, Curzon, like Younghusband, saw in Everest an opportunity for a grand imperial gesture. As early as 1885 an English surgeon, Clinton Dent, had published *Above the Snowline*, in which he compared an assault on the mountain with the quest to reach the poles, a notion certain to appeal to Curzon. A few years later Dent, in an October 1892 article in the journal *Nineteenth Century*, became the first in print to suggest an attempt on Everest. Having studied the physiology of high-altitude exposure, he was confident that climbers could adapt to oxygen deprivation through acclimatization. "I do not for a moment say that it would be wise to ascend Mount Everest," Dent cautioned, "but I believe most firmly that it is humanly possible to do so; and, further, I feel sure that even in our time, perhaps, the truth of these views will receive material corroboration."

Even before Rawling and Ryder reached Simla, Curzon laid down the challenge. Everest could and must be scaled and by an exclusively British climbing party. In the spring of 1905, inspired by Rawling's account of seeing Everest at close quarters, Curzon reached out again to Freshfield: "It has always seemed to me a reproach that with the second highest mountain in the world for the most part in British territory and with the highest in a neighbouring and friendly state, we, the mountaineers and pioneers par excellence of the universe, make no sustained and scientific attempt to climb to the top of either of them." He was speaking, of course, of Kangchenjunga and Everest. But he went on, cautioning Freshfield that it was now or never:

My time in India will not in any case be very much longer and my successor may not care for such matters. I would be prepared to lend every aid the Government can give to a thoroughly well appointed climbing party, comprised of trained experts with Swiss Guides, that should come out with the set object of climbing one of these mountains. I should not mind asking the Maharaja of Nepal for permission for a party to climb Everest but the Nepalese are very suspicious and he might refuse. Again I do not see how the coolies and supplies could be obtained in such a region. Would you care to interest yourself at all in such an expedition? It occurs to me that it might be done by the Alpine Club and the R.G.S. in combination and you are at liberty to pass on what I have written to the President of either society. I suppose that the months from August to October would be the time. It occurs to me that two years, or possibly three, might be required.

Camps would be instituted and gradually pushed forward until one day the advance camp would be placed on a spot from which a dash could be made for the summit. Coolies could be trained, attempts made on the mountain from different sides, everything leading up to the final denouement. I do not know what such expeditions cost. But it is possible that the Home Societies might pay half if the Government of India paid the other. I have not consulted my colleagues. But I think I could promise this assent to a moiety of 2,500 to 3,000 pounds, i.e., to half of the total expenditure of 5,000–6,000 pounds. Ought we not be able to do this?

Freshfield took this letter to the Alpine Club, which appointed a subcommittee to address the viceroy's proposal. Serving on that committee, in addition to Freshfield, was Martin Conway, one of the seminal figures in British mountaineering. An art historian and gifted writer drawn to the hills by the sheer beauty and freedom of the heights, he would, more than any other climber, save possibly the Duke of Abruzzi, set the precedent for the large-scale, military-style expeditions infused with national identity that would define Himalayan climbing throughout much of the twentieth century. In 1892 he had traveled into the unknown Karakorum, recognized the impossibility of an assault on K2, and instead scaled a subsidiary ridge of Baltoro Kangri, establishing a height record of 22,600 feet on a feature he named Pioneer Peak.

Conway recognized the immensity of the Himalayan problem for the mountaineer. He was the first to bring Whymper and Mummery tents to the region, the first to use crampons, the first to consider the importance of diet, the threat imposed by altitude, the need for adequate hydration in the searing light and heat of Himalayan exposures. And if he invoked military rhetoric to describe the expeditions—mountains to be assaulted, heights to be conquered, flanks to be attacked—it was, in part, because he was quite literally advancing in the wake of the military. He was able to approach the Karakorum only because the 1891 Hunza-Nagar campaign had brought peace to the region, at least for the moment. His escort included soldiers of the 5th Gurkha Rifles, under the command of the same extraordinary young officer, Charles Bruce, who had protected and guided Younghusband in 1888 during his perilous explorations of the Karakoram. Military pacification of the frontier opened the way for the climbers, and the mountaineers, in turn, elevated their soldier escorts into the rarefied world of the climber.

No INDIVIDUAL more perfectly personified this symbiosis than Charles Bruce, a man born to be a British soldier, destined to be a climber. His family home was in the hills of Glamorgan, in the Aberdare Valley of South Wales. The land of open moors and rocky crags had been transformed by the industrial revolution into a place of coal pits and iron foundries populated by wiry men who dug from the ground two million tons of coal a year and drank away their earnings in the local public houses. Bruce lumbered into the world in 1866, the last of fourteen children sired by a father who had lived during the reign of George III, the monarch responsible for the loss of the American colonies. As a boy Charlie met Lord Albemarle, who had served under the Duke of Wellington at Waterloo, and was regaled with tales of war by his grandfather Sir William Napier, the official historian of the Peninsular Campaign against Napoleon.

A child of privilege, Bruce was sent away to school at five. At Harrow he was revered for establishing a school record by having been thrashed by the headmaster more often and in a shorter period of time than any student in the school's history. His final transgression involved throwing a pot of geraniums at a highly respected lawyer from the roof of the headmaster's house. Among other skills acquired at school was his ability to balance a peacock's feather on the end of his nose, blow it up into the air, and catch it on the tip of the same prow, a trick he earnestly but unsuccessfully attempted to teach a family friend, the archbishop of York.

By family tradition Bruce ought to have attended Sandhurst, but having twice failed to submit his examination papers on time—another record—he ended up in the militia, stationed at York, where for two years he did, as he recalled in his memoir, "minimum work, maximum sports." In the summer of 1887 he first went to the Alps, where his climbing style and ambitions earned him the nickname MMM, for Mad Mountain Maniac. That same summer he joined the 1st Battalion of the Oxford and Buckinghamshire Light Infantry, the unit in which his grandfather had served in the Napoleonic Wars. A year later he was ordered to India, where he would make his mark with the 5th Gurkha Rifles, stationed at Abbottabad, on the North-West Frontier.

Service in the Indian Army, Bruce soon discovered, was a far cry from the life of ease enjoyed by the patrician officers of the regular home army and militias. The Indian Army was a truly professional force, its officer corps composed of upper-middle-class British men for whom military service was a serious career, its ranks drawn from the finest fighters of a subcontinent, Muslims and Sikhs, Rajputs, Pathans, and Marathas, all volunteers for whom soldiering was a highly honorable calling. Unlike the home army, which by the late nineteenth century had not seen combat since Crimea, the forces in India were well honed by the endless skirmishes and campaigns of the North-West Frontier. These were not trivial encounters. In the Afghan border campaigns of 1897, hundreds were killed, scores of villages put to the torch, and prisoners on both sides slaughtered without mercy. "There is no doubt that we are a very cruel people," Winston Churchill wrote home from the front. "Severity always," went the British motto, "justice when possible."

Warfare suited Bruce. He was a man of action and deed, as subtle in movement as an ox. Given to horseplay and crude practical jokes, a brilliant mimic with a voice like a bass drum and a great hissing laugh, he was a figure cut to inspire Kipling: a British officer fiercely loyal to his regiment, paternally protective of his men, fluent in a dozen native tongues, with a limitless appetite for drink, sport, food, and anything Indian. Martin Conway described Bruce's energy as that "of a steam engine plus a goods train." As a young man he was so strong that he could, with his arm extended, lift a grown man seated in a chair off the ground to ear level. To keep fit he regularly ran up and down the flanks of the Khyber Pass, carrying his orderly on his back. As a middle-aged colonel he would wrestle six of his men at once. It was said by some that he had slept with the wife of every enlisted man in the force. To his friends he was known as "Bruiser" Bruce; the men of the regiment called him simply Bhalu, the bear, or Burra Sahib, the Big Sahib.

Like all field officers, Bruce watched his troops carefully and had strong opinions about the fighting abilities of the various tribal and ethnic groups that made up the army. Neither Brahmans nor untouchables, the highest and lowest castes of India, were any good at war, he maintained. The ethnic Tibetans, by contrast, were too good at it. They stood up to the British, defied authority, and refused to submit to the cardinal rule of the Raj, which forbade any native from hitting a white man, whatever the circumstances of the affront. Tibetans could never be cowed. Pathans and Punjabis made the best soldiers, tough, obedient, subservient, yet never obsequious. But for serious mountain work no one could touch the Gurkhas, the soldiers of Nepal, a polyglot of men and boys recruited from a half-dozen peoples, Gurung, Magar, Tamang, Rai, Limbu, and Sherpa. Bruce had created a unique military unit, the Frontier Scouts, a prototypic counterinsurgency force that specialized in infiltration, ambush, and assassination. The Gurkhas excelled as guerrilla fighters, and Bruce trained them to be mountain soldiers prepared to take the fight aggressively to the enemies of the Raj, the Wazirs, Orakzais, Afridis, and a host of frontier tribes whose villages were to be razed, elders killed, and younger men and women cowed into submission. Younghusband himself had witnessed their prowess in 1888 in the Karakoram, and when, later, talk turned to Everest, both Younghusband and Bruce knew the men to recruit. Their skills in the mountains, nurtured since birth, had been tested in actual battle, in circumstances comparable to if not more perilous than what they might expect to confront on the unexplored flanks of Everest.

CHARLES BRUCE, by chance, was in London on leave in late 1906 just as events came to a head on the first serious proposal for an attempt on the mountain. The Alpine Club had enthusiastically embraced Lord Curzon's Everest initiative but had authorized a meager £100 toward its support. Curzon had suggested a budget of £6,000, half of which might be provided by the government of India. Upon hearing of the shortfall, an affluent member of the Alpine Club, the publisher A. L. Mumm, offered to make up the difference, provided he was allowed to become a member of the expeditionary party. The tradition of wealthy individuals purchasing a place on Everest climbs began from the inception of the dream.

But Mumm was not simply a wealthy patron. He was a real climber and an entrepreneur who in a very modern sense grasped the symbolic power and economic potential of the mountain. He was the owner of Edward Arnold & Co., the literary firm that would publish all the seminal early works on Everest, including the official reports of the 1921, 1922, and 1924 expeditions, and the subsequent personal accounts of several of the climbers. In 1907 he saw an assault on the mountain as a proper and honorable way of celebrating the Golden Jubilee of the Alpine Club, which had been founded in 1857. The first party on Everest was to be Mumm himself, he hoped, accompanied by the highly regarded British climber Tom Longstaff, a team of Swiss guides, and Charles Bruce with nine of his Gurkha soldiers in support.

The immediate problem lay in access. Nepal was out. Despite Lord Curzon's efforts the maharaja would not budge, and British political interests recoiled against too severe a push. The only other route of approach lay through Tibet, across the very passes traversed by the Younghusband Mission. Sir George Goldie, president of the Royal Geographical Society, endorsed the campaign, and hopes ran high when Lord Minto, another climber and a member of the Alpine Club, was selected to succeed Curzon as viceroy in 1905.

Unfortunately for the Everest initiative, the Liberal government that came to power in 1905 sought to distance itself as far as possible from both the aggressive forward policies of Curzon and the legacy of the Younghusband Mission, which it viewed as an embarrassing and futile imperial folly. The point person for the government was the secretary of state for India, John Morley, an austere, joyless, empty shirt of a man known to his own cabinet colleagues as "Aunt Priscilla" or, with equal affection, the "petulant spinster." Reluctant to do anything that might offend the Chinese or the Russians, particularly in the wake of the signing of the 1907 Anglo-Russian Convention, Morley decided to forbid all nonessential travel to Tibet, which in his mind most assuredly included mountaineering expeditions. When Goldie, on January 23, 1907, wrote on behalf of both the Alpine Club and the RGS to seek cooperation from the government of India for a climbing party to enter Tibet, Morley categorically withheld consent, citing issues of national interest and security.

Morley's stubborn refusal to cooperate provoked public scorn. At a general meeting of the Alpine Club on March 3, 1908, Curzon, an honorary member, was called upon to address the government's recalcitrance. His scathing criticism of Morley was followed by acid remarks by Douglas Freshfield. "With regard to Dr. Longstaff's expedition, Lord Curzon and I stood to it somewhat in the position of godfathers; he, as Viceroy, started the idea, and I found the men. At the last moment, however, as so often happens in stories, there appeared a malignant fairy who was not invited to the christening. His Majesty's government discovered reasons why no British expedition could be allowed to approach Mount Everest. It is not a little vexatious to see a Swede, Dr. Sven Hedin, even though he is one of our honorary members, wandering at will in territory forbidden to Englishmen."

In truth, the government of India had far greater concerns than a mountain climb in Tibet, even of Everest. Not the least of these was a full-out Chinese military invasion of Tibet, under way by 1908, orchestrated by a murderous warlord and prompted by the power vacuum created in Lhasa by Younghusband's destruction of the Tibetan army and subsequent and immediate abandonment of the country. Such geopolitical realities, oddly disregarded by Curzon, mattered little to most members of the Alpine Club, whose interest in getting to the top of Everest was heightened only by the failure of Britain to win the race to either pole.

In 1908 Bruce made another attempt to secure permission to attack the mountain through Nepal. A year later the Duke of Abruzzi tried unsuccessfully as an Italian to obtain permission for an approach through Tibet. In October 1911 Curzon once again, and to no avail, sought the intervention of the maharaja of Nepal. Two years later Cecil Rawling and Tom Longstaff secured the formal backing of both the RGS and the Alpine Club for a major two-year effort, an initial exploration and reconnaissance to be followed by a second climbing expedition, during which the mountain would be assaulted. The team would include, as naturalist, A. F. R. Wollaston, with whom Rawling had traveled in New Guinea, as well as Henry Morshead of the Survey of India, who had explored the lower reaches of the Tsangpo Gorge with F. M. Bailey, who, in turn, had been with Rawling on the survey expedition to the headwaters of the Brahmaputra. Also included in the roster were two remarkable men, one a medical scholar, Dr. Alexander Kellas, the other a maverick visual artist, a photographer and filmmaker with a flair for the dramatic, army subaltern John Noel. The expedition was scheduled for 1915, with the attempt on the summit to occur the following season, in what turned out to be the summer of the Somme. Needless to say, the proposal, never endorsed by the government of India, was overtaken by events.

IN THE ABSENCE of any immediate possibility of a legally sanctioned expedition to Tibet, the challenge of Everest, in what would turn out to be the last months of peace, was taken up by Kellas and Noel. Both were prepared to slip alone into the mountains, Kellas with the invisibility that comes to those for whom recognition and fame mean little, Noel with a cloak of intrigue carefully cultivated to enhance his personal narrative. Noel was stopped short of his goal, but still managed to get to within forty miles of the mountain, closer than Rawling, Ryder, or Younghusband himself. Kellas was never seen by anyone, and no one knew precisely where he had gone, or how he managed to achieve what he did. He came back with photographs composed in the Kama Valley on the eastern approaches to the mountain, images taken within ten miles of the glaciers that guard the Kangshung Face. One of these men would die, quietly, without fanfare, on the first expedition to Everest, in 1921. The other would outlive every other participant in the saga of 1921–24, and through his work leave a legacy that would forever seed the challenge of Everest in the public mind.

Alexander Kellas was born in Aberdeen in 1868 and as a young boy came of age rambling alone over the summits of Ben Macdhui and the blue ridges and mountains of the Cairngorms in the Grampian Range of central Scotland. A wanderer perpetually drawn to the unknown, he had by 1913 spent more time at extreme altitude than any man alive. What made him unique was the lens through which he experienced the world. He had no interest in records or first ascents. A solitary scholar, he considered himself less a climber than a scientist who frequently found himself on the summits of mountains. Trained at Edinburgh, University College London, and Heidelberg, he served as lecturer in chemistry at Middlesex Hospital Medical School from 1900 till 1919. His specialty was human physiology and the effect of altitude on the body. His classroom was in London, but his research laboratory lay on the highest flanks of the Himalaya. Between 1907 and 1921, with a hiatus for the war, he embarked on eight major expeditions to Asia, almost always traveling alone, save for a small party of dedicated Nepalese porters. In 1910 he spent four months in the field, rarely below 14,000 feet, and in a single season climbed no fewer than nine peaks 20,000 feet or higher. Kellas was the first to reach the summits of Chomiomo (22,430 feet), Pauhunri (23,186 feet), and Kanchenjhau (22,700 feet), all dramatic mountains marking the Sikkim-Tibet frontier. He did not simply climb these peaks; he traversed them, heading up one unknown face or ridge only to descend by yet another route never before trampled by a mountaineer. For a slight, modest little man, with spectacles and an academic's stoop to his back, it was no mean achievement.

Kellas's research had a direct bearing on the prospects of any assault on Everest. It had been long known through experience in the Alps that at altitude climbers could become severely debilitated, incapacitated to the point of death. The symptoms of mountain sickness were well known: malaise; cyanosis, or the bluing of the extremities; lassitude; loss of memory and mental acuity; nausea; loss of appetite; and acute, paralyzing headaches. It was also recognized that the syndrome affected different people at different times and in different ways. Though it was evident that local people suffered less, there was no certain correlation between fitness and strength and resistance to the affliction. There was no specific elevation beyond which the body succumbed. The botanist Joseph Hooker, one of the preeminent scientists of the nineteenth century, described the ailment in simple but graphic terms. Above 14,000 feet, he wrote, it was as if he had "a pound of lead on each knee cap, two pounds in the pit of the stomach, and a hoop of iron around the head."

For centuries, causation remained a mystery. The Jesuits who reached the Himalaya in the 1600s blamed poisonous weeds, strange minerals, a miasma of gases seeping from the earth. Others claimed that the syndrome was merely the result of indigestion from bad food, a disorientation sparked by electrical disturbances from lightning, or the psychic effects of nervous tension and stress, an affliction said to be common among cardplayers and miners in the gold towns of the American West. Astonishingly, it was not until 1878 that the actual culprit was identified: a lack of oxygen due to reduced atmospheric pressure at altitude. Despite this discovery, wild theories continued to gain notice. Some claimed the ailment was caused by the intensity of the sun's rays. Others at the RGS and Alpine Club laid the blame on stagnant air inhaled by climbers as they traversed hollows and draws, away from ridgelines invigorated by the wind.

Kellas, by contrast, was the voice of scientific reason, drawing his conclusions from precise calculations based on empirical measurements and observations. Fatigue, cold, inadequate sleep, and diet, he argued, were contributing factors, but without doubt mountain sickness was precipitated by oxygen deprivation. The body through respiration draws air into the lungs twelve to eighteen times per minute. Air is basically oxygen and nitrogen. Pure nitrogen is highly toxic, and if inhaled alone causes unconsciousness within seconds, death within minutes. Oxygen is the gas of life. As elevation is gained, air pressure is reduced. At 29,000 feet, the summit of Everest, atmospheric pressure would be a third of that at sea level; thus, if a climber breathed normally, he would absorb only a third of the normal requirement of oxygen.

Would this be enough to survive? Many had their doubts. Kellas argued, however, that the body possesses astonishing adaptive capabilities. Tibetans thrived at 14,000 feet, he noted, the very height of Pike's Peak, in Colorado, where unfit tourists regularly collapsed on trains carrying them to the summit. His studies of arterial oxygen saturation suggested that an ascent of Everest could be possible, but that two critical factors would be in play. First there would be an elevation—no higher than 22,000 feet, he predicted—beyond which acclimatization would be ineffective. One could keep climbing—in 1909, for example, the Duke of Abruzzi had set a height record by reaching 25,110 feet on Chogolisa, or Bride Peak, in the Karakoram—but for every moment spent above the limit of acclimatization, the body would be in decline. This was the second critical factor. A climber would have to get up and down the mountain as quickly as possible.

On Everest this promised to be difficult. Kellas ascertained from studies of oxygen consumption and energy expenditure that an individual's maximum rate of ascent would drop dramatically the higher one climbed, from roughly 600 feet per hour at 23,000 feet on a moderate incline, to perhaps 360 feet per hour above 25,000 feet. This implied that, at the very least, an Everest expedition would have to establish one camp, if not two, at an altitude where no man had ever slept, at ominous heights that would become known to later generations as the death zone. More than anything, this inexorable reality distinguished the challenge of Everest from the quest for the poles. It was one thing to face conditions of extreme cold and bitter exposure; it was quite another to do so while moving not laterally across a landscape but vertically to heights where the very air itself could not sustain life.

In the years before the war, Kellas made two other vital contributions to the Everest challenge. If Charles Bruce was the first to draw attention to the remarkable qualities of his Gurkha soldiers, Kellas was the one to elevate in the European mind the Sherpas, ethnic Tibetans who had settled in the Solu Khumbu region of Nepal, on the southern approaches to Everest, in the fifteenth century. With the commercial growth of the Raj, many had migrated to Darjeeling to work as porters or laborers; some had prospered as merchants. In a paper presented at the Royal Geographical Society on the afternoon of May 18, 1916, "A Consideration of the Possibility of Ascending the Loftier Himalaya," Kellas reflected on the unique character and disposition of these remarkable people:

Of the different types of coolies the writer has found the Bhutia Nepalese superior to all others he has employed. They are

strong, good-natured and as they are Buddhists there is no difficulty about special foodstuffs. The Lepcha and Kumaonoi are of
inferior physique . . . The Kashmiri of the plains were not found
reliable on mountains. The Gahrwali is inferior to the Bhutia
at high altitudes, because he is a Hindu, and there is far more
difficulty with food supply. The writer has had no opportunity
of traveling with the Gurkha and Balti, who are highly spoken
of by those competent to form an opinion. A solitary traveler
might find it worthwhile to take a few carefully selected Bhutia
Nepalese with him as personal servants to any mountain region.

Such passages, reading as if reviews of livestock, are disturbing to
the contemporary ear, but in the context of the times come across as
ringing endorsements. Kellas, more than any other British mountaineer of the era, placed his life in the hands of his native companions. For
months at a time, year in and year out, he disappeared from the chemical labs of London to the freedom of the Himalaya. In the Sherpas
he found friendship, camaraderie, and the trust that can come only to
those who risk their lives together on glacial slopes and among the jagged ridges of unknown lands. In elevating the Sherpas he transformed,
for better or for worse, their fate. Their capacity for endurance, their
strength and ability to carry loads at altitude, their perseverance, loyalty, and discipline, together with a cultural disposition that led them
to embrace with magnanimity and apparent calm all the vicissitudes
of life, would make them the foundation upon which all of modern
Himalayan climbing expeditions would be grounded.

Everest, for Kellas, was both a scientific challenge and a deeply personal mission. Like so many of his generation, he had been nursed on
a mystic patriotism, a reflexive sense of belonging to something far
greater than self, an empire destined to do justice in the world. This
conviction, which fired the spirits of so many of the men who would
be killed in the war, was in the first years of the century still alive, an
impulse so powerful that it would sustain four years of carnage. Kellas himself would miss the war, having failed to secure a commission
because of his age. For him, Everest took on a resonance of personal
redemption.

On February 22, 1916, he wrote to a close colleague, A. F. R. Wollaston, the naturalist and explorer destined to serve as medical officer
on the 1921 Everest reconnaissance:

I state my opinion of the problem as follows: We missed both
Poles after having control of the sea for 300 years, and we cer-

tainly ought not to miss the exploration of the Mt. Everest group after being the premier power in India for 160 . . . I have not heard from Major Rawling since the war started and therefore do not know if Tibet is disposed to grant leave for a small expedition . . . I for one would be glad to go in with 2 to 10 coolies, or even solo, so as to secure this little bit of exploration for Britain. I'm afraid I regard the Himalaya as a British preserve at present . . . We must win this war and of course above expedition is quite a secondary affair. At the same time we surely could spare one or two men over military age. I would consider myself free to go if hospital people gave me leave.

A journey to Tibet was out of the question for Kellas himself, but he found a way to send a surrogate. The full circumstances remain unclear, but undoubtedly involved his trusted Sherpa friends and companions. The jumping-off point for Everest, Kellas learned, was Kampa Dzong, which could be reached from Sikkim by traveling up the Teesta River and across the Serpo La, as Younghusband had done when he first entered Tibet, in 1903. From Kampa Dzong there was a route leading to the northwest where the Arun River, a key obstacle, could be crossed. From there a track ran south, along the Arun and past the settlement of Pharuk to reach the community of Kharta, located some twenty-five miles northeast of Everest. From Kharta, the nearest route to the mountain carried one up the Kharta Chu and across the Langma La, a high pass that led to the glaciers of the Kama Valley, flowing from the eastern flank of Everest.

Kellas, unable to make the journey, trained one or more of his Sherpa guides in the use of his format camera and dispatched them to Tibet. The results were two panoramic photographs, perfectly exposed, of what is now known as the Rabkar Glacier. Had the anonymous photographers continued just another mile downstream, past the terminal moraine, and had the weather continued to be fair, they would have seen the entire Kangshung Face of Everest, as well as Lhotse and the South Col from a distance of less than ten miles. As it was, they returned to Sikkim to reward Kellas with both detailed information about the route and dramatic evidence, as he put it, that "the scenery of the Mt. Everest group is of a very high order."

In London, meanwhile, John Noel had his own designs on Everest. Noel was a soldier by profession, an artist in spirit, a brilliant camera technician by necessity. Born in Devon in 1890, christened with the name Baptist Lucius, he was the third son of the second son of the Earl of Gainsborough. Schooled in Switzerland, he was educated by his father, a historian and army officer who allowed his youngest son to accompany him to postings throughout the empire, from Gibraltar to India and the Far East. His mother was a fine painter, mostly of alpine flowers, and she had encouraged her son to study art at an academy in Florence. His father, however, wanted him to be a soldier, and inevitably, though failing once to secure admission, he entered Sandhurst. Upon graduation, in 1908, he changed his name to John and joined the East Yorkshire Regiment, stationed at the time in Fyzabad, in northern India, a region as remote, ferociously hot, and undesirable as existed on the subcontinent. For Noel it was ideal, as he hoped that service in a distant outpost, where the heat alone would limit military activity, might make him somewhat forgotten and thus free to pursue his main passions, exploration and photography.

Noel's immediate goal in 1913 was to find a way to reach the approaches to Everest from the east. At the time unaware of the efforts of Kellas, he planned his journey from the writings of Chandra Das, the highly educated Bengali who, posing as a Buddhist scholar, had slipped as a spy into Tibet in 1879 and again in 1881. Like the pundit, Noel would travel in disguise, cloaked in native garb, his hair and face darkened with dye, his pose that of a wandering Muslim from India. As companions he took only three men: a Nepalese Sherpa, an ethnic Tibetan from Darjeeling, and an old native friend from his days rambling in the Garhwal Himalaya. For gear they took no more than could fit in two small tin trunks purchased from the local bazaar, a supply of blankets, and two native tents. Concealed in the trunks were two cameras, instruments for drawing and mapping, a boiling-point thermometer for measuring altitude, a disassembled rifle, a revolver, automatic pistols for the men, and a generous supply of ammunition.

Noel began by heading up the Teesta Valley along the main trail from Gangtok to Lachen, but then, rather than continuing north to the Serpo La and the main crossing into Tibet, he turned west at the village of Thango to follow a tributary of the Teesta to its headwaters and the flank of the Chorten Nyima La, a little-used and formidable pass fully two thousand feet higher than the Serpo La. Unfortunately, once they'd gotten across the pass, with the northern slope of the mountains falling away to the vast Tibetan plateau, "veritably the roof of the world," as Noel would recall, things became somewhat confused. The party, hoping to avoid settlements or nomadic encampments, headed west, maintaining elevation as they traversed the spurs, ridges, and glacier valleys of the mountainside, until finally being forced by a deep canyon to descend to the level plain. Traveling by night, giving wide berth to villages to avoid the vigilant and dangerous mastiffs, they made their way to the Langbu La, the pass that promised to open the way to the Tashirak Valley and thus to Everest.

When Noel reached the pass he was staggered, as he recalled, "by a magnificent view of towering snow mountains . . . fantastically corniced with overhanging ridges of ice." He consulted his map, the only one that existed. It showed the valley of the Tashirak running to the west and meeting the Arun River not far from the confluence of the Kama Chu, the river that drains the east face of Everest and the route that he had hoped to follow to the mountain. What, in fact, lay before him was an entire unknown range of mountains soaring to 23,000 feet barring the way to the west. Then, as he stared at the skyline, the clouds shifted to reveal higher mountains beyond, and among them a "sharp spire peak" with a thousand feet of its summit visible above the crest of the nearer range. From the compass bearing he knew that this was Everest. He remained at the pass for an hour, glassing the western horizon for any sign of an opening that might still lead him to the prize. Then, after his men had finished piling stones for a chorten and stringing prayer flags among the rocks, the party descended the steep grassy slopes to a small village, where they found shelter for the night among the sheep pens in huts plastered with mud and dung.

The following morning they continued down to the Tashirak River, which ran south and showed no signs of turning west to meet the Arun. A Nepalese trader encountered on the trail informed them that the confluence with the Arun was two full marches downstream at a crossing known as Hatia, which lay beyond the guarded frontier with Nepal. As Noel pondered his options, the fate of his expedition was decided by the unexpected arrival of a mounted party of six armed men, led by the *dzongpen* of Tinki, that had ridden 150 miles in three days to intercept the intruders. A heated exchange occurred, as the Tibetans insisted that Noel leave the country. In the end Noel had no choice but to yield. His party was low on food, and the men exhausted and weakened by the clandestine journey. The day before he had had to double their wages just to keep the expedition together. Violence in the moment was a real possibility. Noel feigned indignation, noted the power of the Raj, and demanded the respect due an officer of English birth. The *dzongpen* would not be moved. Noel feared not for himself but for his companions. He was well aware that the Tibetans who had aided the pundit Chandra Das had been sewn alive into leather bags and thrown into the Brahmaputra River to drown. The following morning, even after Noel had agreed to retire, there was a final altercation, and shots were exchanged from a distance. Reluctantly, a mere forty miles from Everest, Noel retreated to Sikkim.

Once back in London, on leave after five years in India, Noel compared notes with Kellas, who became a friend and mentor. As Noel recalled in his memoir, "In the long gap between my own journey of 1913 and the Everest Expedition of 1921, I talked with Kellas whenever I had a chance about Everest, and he told me many things that have never been made known about his plans and work concerning the mountain. He told me how he got his wonderful photographs of Everest's glacier from the Tibetan side. He had shown them to geographers, but would tell no one how he obtained the pictures."

The men often met at Kellas's chemistry laboratory at the Middlesex Hospital Medical School, and one afternoon in 1914, the older man shared his remarkable secret. There were many ways to the mountain, many means of crossing the Arun River and its gorge, the key impediment once a party had traversed the Himalayan divide to reach the slopes that fell away to the Tibetan Plateau. He had publicly outlined several of these approaches in informal discussions with colleagues at both the Alpine Club and the Royal Geographical Society. The route of choice, however, he confided in Noel, was a pass never traversed by Europeans but known to Tibetans; it offered a route through the very mountain range that had barred Noel's passage at Tashirak. Kharta could be readily reached. The Arun could be crossed on a bridge made of yak-hide rope. Once beyond the river, it was an easy march up the Kharta Chu to the Langma La, the pass that led to the Kama Valley and the eastern approaches to the Kangshung Face of Everest. It was a route used all the time by the herding people of Kharta, who had summer encampments in the high meadows in the very shadow of the summit.

Kellas had worked out an elaborate plan to place reserves of food and supplies at hidden depots in high, uninhabited valleys west of Kangchenjunga. His trusted Sherpas would do the work in secret. He would then enter Tibet unofficially, proceed to Kharta and the Kama Valley, and assault Everest from the east. It was a plan, Noel recalled, "thought out to the last ounce of food and water." Kellas asked Noel to join him on the adventure, as soon as the war was finished and both could get away. They would go either before the monsoon in June, or possibly later in the summer, after the worst of it had passed. Perhaps Rawling would come along, or Longstaff, Morshead, Wollaston, Bailey, or Bruce. With such a team, Kellas believed, nothing could keep them from having a serious go at the mountain. Noel, of course, immediately agreed to join. All that was needed was for the war to end; it surely could not go on forever.

CHAPTER 3

The Plan of Attack

O N THE EVENING of March 10, 1919, Sir Thomas Hungerford Holdich, then president of the Royal Geographical Society, arrived at Aeolian Hall on New Bond Street and hurried into the foyer, making his way past marbled columns and Venetian doorways, past the large oak-walled showroom crowded with the latest models of pianolas and other musical instruments made by the New York company that owned the building, and entered the concert hall at the rear of the main floor. He was late, and the room already was filled to capacity with fellows and guests of the society. It was the eighth evening meeting of the year, and it promised to be a momentous occasion. In the audience sat the patriarchs of British mountaineering, Douglas Freshfield of Kangchenjunga fame; Percy Farrar, then president of the Alpine Club; and Norman Collie, who had been with Albert Mummery and Charles Bruce on Nanga Parbat in 1895 and was destined to succeed Farrar as president of the club in 1920. Alexander Kellas, who had shared his plans for Everest with John Noel, was also there, as was Sir Francis Younghusband, who had, in fact, quite deliberately orchestrated the entire event with the hope of sparking new interest in an assault on the world's highest mountain.

Holdich took the stage to make some brief remarks before introducing the guest speaker. As he surveyed the hall, his mind slipped effortlessly to the years before the war. He was seventy-six years old, and the war was just a blur to him. Tibet and Everest he remembered vividly, however. In 1906 he had published *Tibet the Mysterious*, a book focused on the economic potential of the land, the almost limitless reserves, as he imagined, of wool, silver, musk, copper, lead, iron, and, above all, gold that might well be exploited in the wake of the Younghusband Mission to Lhasa. These resources, he maintained, dwarfed anything that had been found in the Yukon and the frenzy of the Klondike rush of 1898. He had also, in his book, celebrated the exploits of Cecil Rawling and Charles Ryder, and the explorations that had carried them to the source of the Brahmaputra and beyond. As a geographer, he knew that trade was the reason for engagement with Tibet. Still, he felt, as did many of his peers at the RGS, the lingering impulse that had always drawn the British to this highest of mountains. In 1912 an article in the *Badminton Magazine* had boldly asked why the summit of Everest had yet to be conquered. In the previous century alone, it noted, more than £25 million had been exhausted in the quest for the North Pole. Four hundred men had died and two hundred ships had been lost. And still no serious effort on Everest, hardly a farthing spent, and not a life lost.

On December 19, 1918, barely a month after the Armistice, Holdich had written to Edwin Montagu, Lloyd George's secretary of state for India, making inquiries about the possibility of launching an expedition toward the mountain. A draft of the letter had circulated the week before and had been edited by Freshfield and endorsed by Farrar. It raised several immediate concerns, problems to be faced and overcome. An oxygen helmet had to be designed that would somehow enrich the attenuated air, and a diet conceived that would mitigate and guard against the expected loss of appetite at extreme altitude. A preliminary expedition had to be launched to a significant yet manageable peak, perhaps a renewed attempt on Kamet, in the Garhwal Himalaya, at 25,643 feet still unclimbed yet known to Bruce and C. F. Meade, Kellas, Longstaff, and Mumm. There issues of oxygen deprivation could be addressed and solutions found. The approach to Everest would come from the north, through Tibet with the practical assistance of the Survey of India, which could be counted upon to produce men for whom the most remote and impossible reaches of the Himalaya were as a playing field. The letter ended with a note of urgency. Should action not be taken, and promptly, the challenge of Everest might well devolve to a foreign party of men who were not subjects of the king. This missive reached the government of India as Dispatch No. 1, received and dated January 17, 1919.

Weeks went by without a response. Clearly, as Younghusband conveyed to Holdich, some prodding was in order. Thus the decision to bring to the podium a relatively unknown man with a unique story to tell: John Noel, the photographer and veteran soldier who had in disguise in 1913 reached Tashirak and the closest approaches to the mountain.

To considerable applause, Noel moved toward the stage. A tall man of twenty-nine, with piercing eyes and delicate features, he placed his hands firmly on either side of the lectern, as if to steady himself before reading his paper. At his instructions the room went dark, leaving him in a small pool of light, silhouetted against a stunning image of a Himalayan landscape projected onto the stage screen from the back of the hall. The projector blinded him for a moment, until his eyes adjusted and he could see the shadowy outline of his audience. The beam of the projector was infused with the smoke of cigars and cigarettes.

"Attention during the last few years," he began, "has been focused more and more upon the Himalayas; and now that the poles have been reached it is generally felt that the next and equally important task is the exploration and mapping of Mount Everest. It cannot be long before the culminating summit of the world is visited, and its ridges, valleys and glaciers are mapped and photographed. This would perhaps have already been done, as we know, but for the war and the lamented death of General Rawling. This piece of exploration had been his life's ambition. May it yet be accomplished in his memory!"

With these words the hall erupted in applause as all those present rose in tribute to the fallen hero. Noel stepped back, slightly shaken by the noise, and then leaned forward and peered into the assembly of fellows. Most wore black, evening dress, formal and reserved. But his eyes were drawn to those in khaki, perhaps thirty or more scattered throughout the audience, soldiers like him who had endured the slaughter, the coughing of the guns, the bones and barbed wire, the white faces of the dead. Only they could possibly know what the vision of Everest had become, at least for him: a sentinel in the sky, a place and destination of hope and redemption, a symbol of continuity in a world gone mad.

CECIL RAWLING had fought throughout the war, at the front, in many of the most horrific engagements. He survived the fighting at Hellfire Corner, the most dangerous point in the Ypres Salient in the summer of 1915, and was present at Hooge, two miles down the Menin Road, on July 30, when the Germans attacked at 3:15 a.m. and sheets of liquid fire swept over the British line. It was the first time British troops were exposed to flamethrowers. Those soldiers not immediately incinerated fought hand to hand throughout the night before abandoning the trench with the dawn. A midmorning counterattack retook some of the lost ground, but at nightfall on the second day the British had to repulse yet another flamethrower attack. Such was the pattern of Rawling's life in those dark days, so far removed from his visions of Everest and the snow and ice. Even on a quiet day in the Salient, with the lines so close, the artillery so restless, some 300 British men would suffer wounding or death. And these were minor engagements. As Rawling rallied his troops late that summer, he knew that some short distance to the south another battle loomed, the first all-out British assault of the war. It was known among the officers as the Big Push, a desperate attempt to break the German line and return movement and even glory to the battlefield. Failure was inconceivable: with the Germans fighting the Russians in the east, the Allies in France outnumbered their enemy by thirty divisions, at least 300,000 men.

The British, as it happened, were not ready. There was a massive shortage of shells, too few guns, and an appalling dearth of machine guns. What was at hand in Artois was chlorine gas, and on September 25, 1915, the British used it for the first time, killing more of their own men than the enemy, as the generals sent the Territorials and what remained of the regular army over the top to attack German positions firmly entrenched among the slag heaps and pit heads of the coal mines of Loos. With officers on horseback, the infantry advanced, ten columns extended in a line, each of more than a thousand men. As the diary of the 15th German Reserve Regiment would record, "Never had the machine gunners such straightforward work to do nor done it so effectively. With barrels burning hot and swimming in oil, they traversed to and fro along the enemy's ranks unceasingly; one machine gun alone fired 12,500 rounds that afternoon. The men stood on the fire steps, some even on the parapets, and fired triumphantly into the mass of men advancing across the open grassland. As the entire field of fire was covered with the enemy infantry the effect was devastating and they could be seen falling literally in hundreds."

That night another twenty-two British battalions were raced to the front. Men who had not eaten in sixty hours, whose feet were raw and bloodied, were flung into the line and cast the following day into another storm of shell fire. The Germans could scarcely believe their eyes. Of the 10,000 who attacked in the first wave on the second day, the British lost—killed or wounded—385 officers and 7,861 men. "The massacre," reported a German battalion commander, "filled every one of us watching with a sense of disgust and nausea." Such was the carnage that the German soldiers, following the collapse of the fifth and final British assault, on September 26, held their fire in pity and simply watched as the wounded wreckage of the British force crawled or stumbled from the field. In a battle that lasted barely a fortnight, the British would suffer more than 60,000 casualties. Among the dead were the poet Charles Sorley, in whose bloodstained tunic was found the beginnings of a poem that spoke for the "millions of mouthless dead," and John Kipling, the only son of Rudyard, who after Loos would never again write fiction, or any work of the imagination.

Even to live through Loos was to suffer a thousand small deaths. In the wake of the battle Roland Leighton sent a letter to his fiancée, Vera Brittain, a nurse who had already lost her brother and her two best friends, and in time would lose Roland as well. "The dugouts have been nearly all blown in," he wrote,

> the wire entanglements are a wreck, and in among the chaos of twisted iron and splintered timber and shapeless earth are the fleshless, blackened bones of simple men . . . Let him who thinks war is a glorious, golden thing, who loves to roll forth stirring words of exhortation, invoking honour and praise and valour and love of country . . . Let him but look at a little pile of sodden grey rags that cover half a skull and a shin-bone and what might have been its ribs, or at this skeleton lying on its side, resting half crouching as it fell, perfect that it is headless, and with the tattered clothing still draped round it; and let him realize how grand and glorious a thing it is to have distilled all youth and joy and life into a fetid heap of hideous putrescence! Who is there who has known and seen who can say that victory is worth the death of even one of these?

This was an intimation of something that would haunt the nation for a generation, the impossible chasm between those who had been to war and those who remained at home to revel in its imagined glories, spouting idle rhetoric, struggling to retain a sense of normalcy, dreaming old dreams of a world the very memory of which had been obliterated in the trenches. In England the newspapers dutifully recorded the names of the dead—four full columns of print in the *Times* in the aftermath of September 25 alone—even as they lied about the soldiers' fate. "Two real victories at last," proclaimed the *Daily Mail* on September 29, five days into the battle. Within a week, with the consequences of the disastrous attack undeniable, the paper would temper its optimism with a new set of deceptions. The men in the trenches knew the truth and found such rhetoric hateful.

The enlisted soldiers coped with the insanity in their own way. They read in these same newspapers of work stoppages in the munitions factories, initiated for the most trivial of reasons, yet resulting in

literally millions of hours lost, time that might have been spent manu-
facturing shells. Soldiers who faced death for a mere shilling a day had
little sympathy with union rules that cloistered those left behind. Men
who knew their fate was a firing squad should they desert their posts
had little patience with workers who went on strike only to return to
the comfort of their families. Leave for the enlisted man was rare. The
average soldier got ten days for every fifteen months of field service,
but as late as 1916 many men in the trenches had not been home in
twenty months.

For the officers, it was different. Leave came more frequently, but
with it an ever-deepening realization of how absurd their existence had
become. The writer Paul Fussell later called it "the ridiculous proximity of the Front," the fact that just sixty miles from the trenches
awaited the comforts of England, a trivial distance that both belied and
deepened the psychological rift the war had created. London to Ypres
was a mere 130 miles. The guns could be heard in Kent. For those
safely ensconced in England, the only link to the front was the army
postal service, which by 1916 was processing over eleven million letters a week and sixty thousand parcels a day, all dispatched into a void
in which loved ones could be addressed only by name and regiment.
In dugouts rotten with putrescence, young officers received scented
letters from home, and by subscription the latest issues of *Country Life*
and *Tatler,* the *Spectator* and *Sphere*, along with gift parcels of ginger-
bread, pâté, chocolates, and cherry brandy specially packaged for the
troops by Harrods and Fortnum & Mason. Granted a fortnight's leave,
these same young officers would abandon the mud and degradation of
the trenches in the morning and by evening be dining with their wives
or parents at Claridge's in London, en route to the theater or a private
club.

Such encounters, as Robert Graves wrote, could be sheer agony,
for the families at home had no idea what youth had endured. The
temptation to scream was ever present, yet almost always muted. Conversations remained trivial, the truth concealed not only out of concern for loved ones but because words did not exist to describe the
reality, and thus any attempt to do so was pointless. Still, the relent-
lessly upbeat rhetoric, the patriotic banter, the illusion of normalcy
clung to so desperately by mothers and fathers and wives who saw the
stranger in a soldier's eye left the men hollow and often angry.

This chasm between those who knew and those who only imagined would be a defining reality of British life in the immediate years
after the war, a current of memory and distinction flowing beneath

the survivors, never spoken about and never forgotten. The war itself had ended in stunned disbelief. In the fall of 1918 the German home front had collapsed, the nation on the brink of starvation and revolution. But German armies still controlled the field, and there was not a single Allied soldier anywhere near the approaches to the Rhine. The carnage continued until the end. With the German Spring Offensive in March 1918, the fighting had reached new levels of violence. In the Allied counteroffensive that won the war, the British lost 300,000 men in less than three months. The guns fired literally until the eleventh hour. When, on November 11, word of the Armistice spread up and down the line, it was greeted with relief and jubilation leavened by numb exhaustion, like the slow fading of a long and violent hallucination. The British had been preparing for another two years of war; many simply thought it would go on forever.

The old men who had talked their nations into a war they could not escape had no idea what they had wrought. Nearly 1 million dead in Britain alone, some 2.5 million wounded, 40,000 amputees, 60,000 without sight, 2.4 million on disability a decade after the end, including 65,000 men who never recovered from the mental ravages of shell shock. For the moment it seemed a tremendous victory, despite the terrible losses. Germany and its allies lay prostrate, Russia convulsed in upheaval and revolution, France bled white and reeling from losses from which it might never recover as a nation. The British emerged from the conflict with the most powerful army in the world, its navy supreme, its empire enhanced by a surge of colonial acquisitions that would not end until 1935, when it would finally reach its greatest geographical extent.

That the war had destroyed the prosperity of a century of progress was not immediately evident to the average Englishman still marching to the rhythms of tradition. That it had birthed the nihilism and alienation of a new century was a thought impossible to anticipate. During the war there had been sacrifices, even for the wealthy. Cricket and racing were curtailed, and the wearing of evening dress to the theater was deemed poor form. Food was rationed for everyone and became so scarce that it was made illegal to throw rice at a wedding, unlawful to feed pigeons or stray dogs. The rationing of coal left people cold all the time, most especially in the dreadful winter of 1917, the most severe in a century. By a regulation that echoes to this day, pubs were closed during midday working hours to foment sobriety in the munitions plants. Irritations to be sure, but hardly deprivations of a sort to match what the men in the trenches endured.

The men who had fought in the trenches encountered peace on very different terms. While those at home had remained safe, and in many cases had profited from the crisis, the veterans had lost years of their lives and endured unspeakable hardships, only to return to a nation that wanted to forget everything about the war. They, too, wanted to forget. Robert Graves and T. E. Lawrence famously made a pact never to speak of it. What they wanted was quiet. But for Graves at least, as for many, it was impossible to escape the memories. There was always the night, waking to a pool of sweat, nightmare visions of bayonets and blood.

Graves, who was Mallory's student at Charterhouse, and for whom Mallory would serve as best man at his wedding, had enlisted at nineteen in the Royal Welsh Fusiliers at the outbreak of the war. On July 20, 1916, in a reserve trench awaiting an attack on High Wood at the Somme, his battalion was caught by German artillery fire that left a third of the men dead, and Graves seriously wounded. A metal splinter split his finger to the bone. Another metal shard went through his thigh, near the groin. Yet a third piece of shrapnel pierced his chest, slicing a hole through his body, and destroying his right lung. Unconscious, he was carried to a dressing station and left among the dead. Notice of his passing reached his mother four days later, on what would have been his twenty-first birthday, and his name appeared in the "Honour Roll" of the *Times*. But Graves, in fact, had survived the first night, and when the burial detail came by on the morning of July 21, he was found to be breathing. In agony he was carried to a casualty clearing station, where, because of the sheer numbers of wounded, he lay on a stretcher in the summer heat for five days before finally being evacuated to a hospital at Rouen, and then by ship and train to London. Two days later, he arrived at Victoria station, the Gate of Good-bye, where the living and the dying crossed paths, and crowds gathered throughout the war to herald the wounded home from the front.

Such an experience left him mentally unprepared for peace. Graves remained, as he wrote, nervously organized for war. Shells burst above his bed as he slept. Strangers in the street assumed the faces of friends lost at the front. He could not use a telephone. Train travel made him ill. To encounter more than two people in a day cost him his sleep. He could not walk in a field without reading the lay of the land as if on a raid. The sound of thunder made him shake. A sharp retort of any kind—the backfiring of a car, the slamming of a door—flung him face-first to the ground. The smell of cut lumber recalled the blasted pines and the corpses suspended from broken snags. His marriage dissolved, and he left England for Majorca, never to return to live in his native land.

Of the war he remained mute, as did so many of his generation, simply because language itself had failed them. Words did not exist to describe what they had endured. After the war, as John Masefield wrote, one needed a new term for mud, a new word for death. Only the wordless, said Virginia Woolf, "are the happy." And only those who had fought understood. "The man who really endured the War at its worst," wrote Siegfried Sassoon, "was everlastingly differentiated from everyone but his fellow soldiers."

With the peace, two million parents in Britain woke to the realization that their sons were dead, even as the first of some three million veterans returned to a land socially and politically dominated by those who had not served. "I simply could not speak to such people," recalled Captain Herbert Read, who lost a brother in the last month of the war and was himself awarded the Military Cross and the Distinguished Service Order for valor, "much less cooperate with them. It was not that I despised them, I even envied them. But between us was a dark screen of horror and violation; the knowledge of the reality of war. Across that screen I could not communicate. Nor could any of my friends who had the same experience. We could only stand on one side, like exiles in a strange country."

John Noel's audience that evening at Aeolian Hall embodied the divide that now marked a nation. Douglas Freshfield had been born in 1845, Farrar and Collie a decade or so later, Holdich in 1843. Dr. Kellas had been deemed too old for active service and had spent the war working with Professor John Scott Haldane at the Air Ministry, continuing his studies on high altitude and oxygen deprivation, research that had taken on a new urgency as pilots of the Royal Flying Corps pushed their planes to heights unimaginable at the outbreak of the conflict.

Sir Francis Younghusband had spent the war as a propagandist, rallying the British public to the cause. His mission began in the heady days of August 1914, when the war still seemed sublime and glorious. The spiritual impulse he had brought away from Lhasa, together with his mystic sense of patriotism, came together in a new calling, service in a national movement called Fight for Right. "For we will fight," stated the organization's manifesto, "not for the Highest but for a Higher than the Highest—for the sky beyond the mountain top! We mean to see to it that the code of the gentleman and not the custom of the barbarian shall be the rule among nations." The country was fighting "the battle of all humanity," and Younghusband took it upon himself to rouse all men and women for service in the sacred cause, and to sustain those already at arms and ready to die. The intention of the movement, announced a widely circulated pamphlet, was to stage on Sunday afternoons throughout the country a series of meetings "of a definitely spiritual character," at which time men and women inspired by the Fight for Right would through music, song, and speeches share their inspiration with others and thus buck up the national morale.

Such rallies, the first of which took place on November 7, 1915, in this same Aeolian Hall where the RGS was now gathered, were small comfort for the men returned from France, but they served the needs of a government increasingly concerned about unrest and discontent on the home front. As early as the end of August 1914, the foreign secretary, Edward Grey, and David Lloyd George had established the Secret War Propaganda Bureau, the goal of which was to promote British war aims, both at home and abroad. On September 2 of that year a meeting held at Wellington House, Buckingham Gate, brought together Britain's most prominent writers, Thomas Hardy, H. G. Wells, Arthur Conan Doyle, John Masefield, Rudyard Kipling, G. M. Trevelyan, G. K. Chesterton, and J. M. Barrie. The previous day Robert Bridges, the poet laureate, had described the conflict in the *Times* as a holy war, a conviction heralded in a manifesto that appeared in the newspaper two weeks later, signed by each of these well-known writers. Within months several of them, including Masefield and Conan Doyle, were on the government payroll. Within a year the Propaganda Bureau had produced and distributed 2.5 million copies of books, pamphlets, and speeches. Robert Bridges wrote only three poems during the war; his time went into editing an anthology of English verse, *The Spirit of Man*, which deliberately avoided the subject of war. Intended to inspire the public after the disasters of 1915, it was poetry as propaganda. Curiously, it was this book that Mallory carried with him to Everest, and from which he read aloud to his companions while camped in the ice and snow at 23,000 feet on the flank of the mountain.

In 1917 the Propaganda Bureau was taken over by the Department of Information. It was headed by John Buchan, who, as a friend of Cecil Rawling's, Tom Longstaff's, and Francis Younghusband's, had been recruited to help with the media and publicity for the proposed 1913–15 Everest expeditions that had been aborted by the outbreak of the war. By 1917, as Prime Minister Lloyd George wrote, the "terrible losses without appreciable results had spread a general sense of disillusionment and war weariness throughout the nation." John Buchan's mandate was to quell and counteract pacifist sentiment and maintain the fantasy that the war remained something honorable, even as serious statesmen in all nations began to call for a negotiated end to the slaughter. "If the people really knew," Lloyd George told C. P. Scott of the *Manchester Guardian* in December 1917, "the war would be stopped tomorrow."

Buchan's task was to ensure that they did not know. In this, his closest allies were the Harmsworth brothers, Lord Northcliffe, owner of the *Times* and the *Daily Mail*, and Lord Rothermere, who controlled the *Daily Mirror*, the *Sunday Pictorial*, and the *Glasgow Daily Record*. Together they set the tenor of the British media, controlling, as they did, the most important of London's thirty-seven daily newspapers. Censorship left journalists at the mercy of their imaginations. Anything might be written as long as it vilified the enemy and propped up morale. "So far as Britain is concerned," recalled Buchan, "the war could not have been fought for one month without its newspapers." The truth itself became a casualty. "While some patriots went to the battle front and died for their country," wrote A. R. Buchanan, "others stayed home and lied for it."

As John Noel read his address at the Aeolian that evening, slipping in and out of memory, recalling the view of Everest over the crest of the unknown range, the standoff with the Tibetan *dzongpen* and his troops, his frustration at being unable to secure an image of the mountain due to the ferocity of the winds, he could see John Buchan in the front row, seated between Younghusband and Farrar. Buchan had been recruited by Younghusband to handle the media for the new Everest effort. It was already anticipated that the sale of the expedition accounts and progress reports, in the end negotiated by Buchan as an exclusive arrangement with the *Times*, would provide a significant percentage of the expedition's budget. Buchan would later wax eloquent about the purpose of the Everest mission. "The war," he wrote, "had called forth the finest qualities of human nature, and with the advent of peace there seemed the risk of the world slipping back into a dull materialism. To embark on something which had no material value was a vindication of the essential idealism of the human spirit." These words, which could only have been written by someone who knew nothing of the reality of the war, nevertheless reveal the sentiments that led a desperate nation to embrace the assault on Everest as a gesture of imperial redemption.

Noel might parrot such phrases, but as he looked around the hall he also saw the faces of comrades who had known the war, and for whom survival had been reward enough. Of the fifteen men elected to the Royal Geographical Society that evening, ten were officers, seven with the rank of captain. Their duties at the front had included writing the letters that notified the families of the death of a son. These were gentle missives, quiet lies intended to soften the pain. They spoke of courage and valor, glorious charges and heroic stands. As the war went on they became ever more sadly abstract, the language as predictable as that of the precensored postcards issued to the troops, with boxes to be checked off: am well, am wounded but well, am sick but recovering. The truth was reserved for entries in private journals, such as that written by Captain Theodore Wilson on June 1, 1916: "We had to collect what had been a man the other day and put it into a sandbag and bury it, and less than two minutes before he had been laughing and talking and thinking."

These were the men who understood, as Noel did, what had really happened to Cecil Rawling. He had survived the long winter of 1915 in the Ypres Salient and the fighting at the Somme, the taking of Fricourt, Mametz Wood, and the capture of Gueudecourt. Promoted to brigadier general, he spent the spring and summer of 1917 engaged in the fighting on the Hindenburg Line, before moving north for the assault on Passchendaele, a battle that would be remembered by the historian A. J. P. Taylor as "the blindest slaughter of a blind war."

The goal was yet another fantasy of General Haig's, a plan to break out of the Ypres Salient and capture Antwerp and the channel ports of Belgium. For the British soldiers it was the worst battle of the war. The ground was flat, sodden, shattered by shell fire. On the first night of the assault, the last day in July, the rains began, and after a brief respite in September, they did not cease until November. Three thousand British guns fired more than four million explosive shells, nearly five tons of high explosive for every yard of German trench. The result was a muddy quagmire, a sea of black waste and shell holes, carcasses of horses and men, rats the size of cats, clouds of yellow and brown mist, an unbearable stench of rot and gangrene, and the sweet scent of violets, which was the smell of gas and thus also the odor of death. To slip wounded off a duckboard was to drown in the fathomless morass. Gunners worked thigh-deep in water. To advance over open ground, soldiers used the bodies of the dead as stepping-stones. On the day after the final assault, a senior British staff officer close to Haig, Lieutenant General Sir Launcelot Kiggell, made his first ever visit to the front. Reaching as far as his car could advance, appalled by the conditions, he began to weep. "Good God," he said, "did we really send men to fight in that?" The man beside him, who had been in action, replied flatly, "It's much worse farther up."

After three months, during which time the British suffered some 400,000 casualties, the village of Passchendaele, the objective of the first morning, had yet to fall. Once again, as at the Somme, it was noted in official documents that "the clerk power to investigate the exact losses was not available." The German high command compared Passchendaele to Verdun, a battle where more than a million French and German soldiers had been killed or severely wounded. "The horror of Verdun," wrote Erich Ludendorff, "was surpassed. It was no longer life at all. It was mere unspeakable suffering. And through this world of mud the attackers dragged themselves, slowly but steadily, and in dense masses. Caught in the advance zone of our hail of fire they often collapsed, and the lonely man in the shell hole breathed again."

The Germans simply fell back to a second and a third line of defense. British generals begged Haig to call off the attack, but he refused. When the onset of winter finally drowned out the guns, Haig famously asked Sidney Clive, his senior liaison to French headquarters, "Have we really lost half a million men?" He had, and all for an advance of five miles. Among the dead was Brigadier General Cecil Rawling, killed on October 28 when a shell landed outside his field headquarters at Hooge. Nothing of his body was found. The corpses of more than 90,000 British dead at Passchendaele were recovered too severely mutilated to be identified. Rawling was one of 42,000 who disappeared without a trace.

MORE THAN ANYONE in the hall, John Noel had reason to be haunted by Rawling's fate. At the outbreak of the war, with his own regiment still in India, he had been attached to the King's Own Yorkshire Light Infantry, which he'd joined in Dublin on August 13, 1914, the day before the battalion embarked for France. Within a week he was at Mons, in defensive positions on the south bank of the canal, as the Germans launched their all-out offensive. The fighting on August 23 was intense, and though the British line held, in the evening orders came to retreat. The Germans had broken through the French on the right, and reports of enemy cavalry sweeping in great numbers through the open country between the British and the seacoast left the entire British Expeditionary Force in danger of encirclement.

Noel's battalion retired, marching twenty miles through the night

to take up new positions at Le Cateau on the afternoon of August 25.
The following dawn they faced the overwhelming force of the German army. By noon the Suffolk Regiment, to their right, had been
destroyed, exposing their flank, and in the attacks that followed, Noel's
battalion lost 600 men and 20 officers. The official casualty list in the
Times reported Noel "Missing, believed killed." In fact, he'd been
taken prisoner, one of a handful of survivors. He somehow managed to
escape before reaching a prison camp, and for ten days made his way
back to the British forces. He had no map or compass, no knowledge
of the war-torn country, and his only source of food was what he could
scavenge from the pockets of dead men. He took his bearing from the
star Arcturus.

It is impossible to know what he saw and experienced in those
days. The British positions were still fluid; the front had yet to form.
The fields he crossed by night were a harvest of mutilated bodies. He
reached a British unit on September 5 and was evacuated as a casualty
to England, a fate reserved for those very seriously injured. His medical report shows that on September 14, at Queen Alexandra's Military
Hospital in London, it was decided to keep him away from active duty
for at least two months, when his health would be reviewed. Again this
was a drastic diagnosis, for the army at the time desperately needed
professional officers. His disability was described as "strain of active
service," a curious euphemism that suggested that the doctors had no
idea what they were seeing. "He is suffering," the report noted, "from
symptoms of marked nervous breakdown and is weak and debilitated."

At this early stage in the war, no one spoke of shell shock, a diagnosis that had yet to be distilled in medical language. Soldiers in past
wars had no doubt experienced the trauma, but it took the battles of
France, of unprecedented scale and horror, to bring both the military and medical professions to a point when the truth could not be
denied. The full realization took a year, for it was only after Loos that
a British medical officer, Captain W. Johnson, noticed the correlation
between what he witnessed after that disastrous engagement and what
he had seen during the retreat from Mons. Strong men, young and
old, reduced to hysteria, twisted and contorted, mute with fear, shaking with tremors, eyeballs protruding with the brightness of madness.
These were the refugees from a place that Siegfried Sassoon described
as "the looming twilight of hell." In quiet moments they sat in a daze,
a state of coma, as if deaf and dumb, incapable of speech. Incontinent,
they spewed apologies, cried aloud in their sleep, returning each night
in haunted memory to the sector of the front where they had first confronted the livid faces of the dead.

John Noel returned to active duty after two months and spent the first winter of the war in the Ypres Salient. He was there on April 22, 1915, when the Germans attacked, using poison gas for the first time. Entire British brigades were wiped out, and it was only the suicidal resistance of the 1st Canadian Division that prevented a massive enemy breakthrough. The gas corrupted the lungs, causing the victim to drown in his own toxic froth. "The men came tumbling from the front line," wrote W. A. Quinton of the 2nd Bedford Fusiliers. "I've never seen men so terror-stricken, they were tearing at their throats and their eyes were glaring out. Blood was streaming from those who were wounded and they were tumbling over one another. Those who fell couldn't get up because of the panic of the men following them, and eventually they were piled up two or three high in this trench."

Noel witnessed the attack, and on the same day was nearly killed by a high-explosive shell that dropped beside him. Severely concussed, he was evacuated from the field and once again to England. A medical board eleven days later, on May 3, 1915, at Caxton Hall noted of the patient, "He had been sent home last September for the same reason but returned to duty. He is in a very nervous condition and on one occasion threatened to take his own life." Noel's case of neurasthenia, or shell shock, was classified as "severe," and it was anticipated that he would be incapacitated for three months. In fact, he would never return to the front. On August 3 a medical board remarked that he was "improving slowly but cannot sleep well and still feels weak." Yet another review, at the military hospital at Grantham on November 6, found that "there are still marked symptoms of neurasthenia which will probably last for many months." It was not until March 9, 1917, nearly two years after the trauma, that a medical board finally concluded that he had "practically recovered." He spent the rest of 1917 on light duty as a revolver instructor in the Machine Gun Corps and writing army manuals, including a recipe book for soldiers cooking in the trenches and a veterinary first aid guide for treating horses. It was not until February 1918 that he returned to field command, in a small force of six thousand men dispatched to northern Persia to prevent the Russian Bolsheviks from taking the oil fields of Mesopotamia. Of his medical condition during the war, he would never speak a word.

AT THE CLOSE of Noel's lecture, as was the tradition at meetings of the Royal Geographical Society, distinguished members of the audience were invited to comment. The first to speak was Douglas Freshfield, who made some general remarks about climate and geography before endorsing an approach to the mountain from Kampa Dzong through Tibet, thus avoiding the problem of Nepal. Kellas agreed and outlined in considerable detail the various routes from the north and east, including the one that Noel had taken in 1913. Farrar then suggested the use of modern airships as a way of overcoming the problems of supply that had, as he put it, "baulked previous travelers." More important, as president of the Alpine Club, he promised financial support and the services of "two or three young mountaineers quite capable of dealing with any purely mountaineering difficulties as are likely to be met with on Mount Everest." The floor then yielded to Sir Francis Younghusband, who spoke on behalf of the RGS.

"It is now twenty-six years ago," he began, "since our old friend Captain Bruce—now General Bruce—made the proposition to me that we should go up Mount Everest. It did not come to anything then, but years afterwards, in 1903, when I was at Kampa Dzong in Tibet I had for three months a magnificent view of Mount Everest . . . The lecturer hoped that it would be an Englishman, or at any rate a Scotsman, who would first climb Mount Everest, I need only say I think we are all determined that it shall be a British expedition. Our own Society is interested in the project, and we have heard the president of the Alpine Club say he has magnificent young mountaineers ready to undertake it, and it must be done."

When the applause died down, Holdich, as president of the RGS, closed the evening, thanking the speaker for a splendid account of "his most adventurous and plucky journey." He then remarked that while he looked forward to hearing more about the proposed expedition, it was his conviction that any successful effort to reach the mountain must come through Nepal.

In truth, no one present that evening, with the possible exception of Kellas, had any idea what was in store for those destined for the mountain. Something of their naïveté was captured the following morning in a satirical report, "Himalayans at Play," published in *Punch*. "Sir Francis Oldmead said his preferred route to the summit was up the Yulmag valley to the Chikkim frontier at Lor-Lumi, crossing the Pildash at Gonglam and skirting the deep gorge of the Spudgyal . . . The chairman having expressed his regrets that Sir Marcon Tinway was not present to describe his experiments with manlifting kites and trained albatrosses, the assembly dispersed after singing the Tibetan national anthem."

Buoyed by the success of the evening, not to mention the attention of the press, however irreverent the coverage, on March 28, 1919,

Younghusband sent a letter seeking a meeting with the secretary of state for India, Edwin Montagu. His faith in the goodwill and reason of his government, expressed forcefully in his remarks following Noel's speech, was not rewarded. A wire received back from the government of India on April 19 reminded Whitehall that the Japanese were actively seeking control of all of China's internal telegraph and wireless infrastructure. To counter the aggression, the British had entered into secret negotiations with the Tibetans, seeking approval for the installation of wireless stations at Gyantse and Lhasa. The outcome was uncertain but, the wire noted, "the presence of a party of explorers on the borders of Tibet would not be likely to make the execution of this scheme any easier."

Younghusband was not about to be rebuffed and, despite the setback, proceeded with Farrar of the Alpine Club to devise plans for a two-year Everest effort, much along the lines of Rawling's original proposal: a reconnaissance mission that would chart the approach and identify the route of attack, and a second expedition the following season during which the summit would be attained. As Farrar considered personnel and logistics, Younghusband set his considerable will toward influencing the political process, a task made easier in June 1919 when he succeeded Holdrich as president of the Royal Geographical Society. The key, as he saw it, was to circumvent Whitehall and the India Office in London and seek influence directly with the viceroy and the government of India, where he believed the real power in regard to Tibet resided. He had just the man for the job, Lieutenant Colonel Charles Kenneth Howard-Bury, an officer and a fighting soldier whose experiences of death and survival lay far beyond those of ordinary men. Mentioned in despatches on seven occasions, the recipient of every medal of valor save the Victoria Cross, he was linked by blood and class to the highest levels of British society, and as ward of his cousin Lord Lansdowne, former viceroy of India, he had ready access to the halls of power in Simla and Calcutta.

HOWARD-BURY, for his part, knew nothing of Holdrich's approach to the India Office in the last weeks of 1918, and he was quite unaware at that time of any official plans for an Everest expedition. What he knew of the mountain lay in his own imaginings, nursed through four years at the front and several months in captivity. As late as December 1918, he remained a prisoner of war in a German camp at Clausthal, 2,000 feet up in the Harz Mountains, where he had been transferred after a daring escape from Fürstenberg, another POW camp south and west of Berlin. As his fellow officers created diversions, he had cut through three ranks of wire, tearing his clothes and skin to shreds in the process, only to be seen at the last moment as he scaled the final palisade. A hail of gunfire chased him to a nearby woods, and by the time he regained his breath he could hear the approaching dogs and the sentries beating the bush. He crawled into a ditch and submerged himself among the nettles and reeds. The water was cold, and he remained in it for two hours, motionless even as one of his pursuers parted the reeds not three feet from his head to drink from the stream. An hour after dark, he crawled out only to run immediately into a sentry, who fired a revolver at close range as he raced for the woods. There among the Scotch pines Howard-Bury hid out for another six hours until, with the dawn, he stripped off his khaki outer garments to reveal a peasant disguise, a farmer's corduroy trousers and waistcoat, which he augmented with a black coat and German felt hat. A green rucksack completed the feint, and with a stout walking stick cut on the spot, he began a long march north toward the Danish frontier.

In driving rain and darkness Howard-Bury covered some twenty to thirty miles each night. For food he had only what he could scavenge from damp fields—raw turnips, cabbage, and potatoes. By day he holed up in whatever shelter he could find, but with the sleet and cold, sleep was not an option. For nine days he did not rest. His luck ran out on the tenth night, when he drifted off to sleep just after midnight only to wake an hour or so later to a dog barking in his ear and the muzzle of a rifle in his face. Taken by train to the nearest prison camp, he was thrust into a punishment cell, where he remained in solitary confinement until released for escort back to Fürstenberg. In another war he might well have been shot. But the Germany of 1918 retained a sense of honor and deference, especially for those of aristocratic rank.

In Howard-Bury they had captured the great-grandson of the sixteenth Duke of Suffolk. His father, Captain Kenneth Howard of the Royal Light Horse, was a lover of plants, a world traveler, a big-game hunter, and a very fine painter who worked mostly with watercolors. His mother was an Irish heiress, Lady Emily Alfreda Julia Bury. They had met and fallen in love on a botanical expedition in Algeria and after marriage had settled at Charleville, a Gothic castle in Ireland that was the ancestral home of the Bury lineage. When Charles Howard-Bury was three, his father died, and Lord Lansdowne, confidant and counselor to King Edward VII, became his guardian. Charles remained, however, at his mother's side, moving between Charleville and a family chalet in the Dolomites, where he developed a love of mountains and mountaineering. Privately educated by a German governess, he entered Eton in 1897, where he excelled in history and languages, and though he could have matriculated to Oxford or Cambridge, he chose a career in the army and entered Sandhurst in 1902, graduating three years later with the rank of captain.

In India his travels began in earnest. In 1905 he slipped into Tibet in disguise, crossing the high passes that led to the flanks of Kailash, the sacred mountain. Severely reprimanded by Lord Curzon for the unsanctioned adventure, he turned his attention to Russia, and in 1906 he traveled south from St. Petersburg to the Pamirs and Russian Turkistan, again in disguise, his skin stained brown with walnut juice. A year later he spent his leave in Kashmir and the Karakorum. Drawn always to the sacred, he read the works of Krishnamurti and Kahlil Gibran, and visited in his many journeys the Buddhist monks of Angkor Wat, the high priests and shrine guardians of China, the mystics of Tibet. In India he embarked on pilgrimage along the waters of the Ganges, anointing his body with scented oils to receive the teachings of Sanskrit scholars at Badrinath. In the holy city of Amarkantak, his reputation was made when he shot and killed a tiger that had carried off and eaten twenty-one fakirs, or holy men. A brilliant writer, a fine photographer, and a keen and accomplished naturalist, he became fluent in no fewer than twenty-seven Asian and European languages. Not surprisingly, a military report dated December 17, 1908, recommended him as a "splendid candidate for diplomatic or intelligence work, or for any missive of secret service requiring a clever brain and active body."

His army career, however, came to an end in 1912, soon after he inherited Belvedere, a vast estate on the shore of Lough Ennell in the Irish county of Westmeath. With the land and the main house, built as a hunting lodge in 1740, came an astonishing collection of Italian art, including works by Titian and Raphael. At the age of thirty-one, Howard-Bury had become a very wealthy man, and he soon resigned his commission to devote his life to travel. In 1913, with his one constant companion, his beloved dog Nagu, he went overland from Siberia to spend six months exploring the Tien Shan, the Mountains of Heaven, a range far older than the Himalaya that traverses western China and forms the northern wall of the Tarim Basin where the Silk Road skirts the forbidding dunes of the Taklamakan Desert. Howard-Bury was drawn to the oases, and the spiritual resonance of an ancient trade route where Taoist thought had encountered the wisdom of the Buddha and the religious insights of Greece and Persia informed the faith of the Mongols. He spent his time collecting plants, taking notes, and living a life of freedom and whimsy.

At Omsk, in Russia, he filled his railway carriage with wild lilies of the valley, purchased for a penny a bunch from the ragged children on the platform. Later he would plant acres of the same flower at Belvedere in memory of the Russian children killed in the revolution. In a local market, he bought a baby bear, which he named Agu. He nursed and protected the cub throughout his expedition, carrying it with him on his horse, and eventually bringing it home to Ireland. Agu grew to seven feet and lived out its life in the arboretum at Belvedere. Wrestling with a mature bear from the Tien Shan would be, for Howard-Bury, a favorite form of exercise. He also brought back from central Asia a large number of mountain larks with the hope that their beautiful songs might always remind him of the lands that had so inspired his heart.

He was not a man ready for war, and yet when it came he returned immediately to his regiment. Like Rawling, he was at Hooge, in the Ypres Salient, in July 1915 when the Germans attacked for the first time with flamethrowers; he bore witness to the slaughter at Loos in September and spent the cruel winter of 1915 in the trenches at Arras. The summer of 1916 brought the Somme, which, like a vortex, drew nearly every unit of the British army to the battlefield. Howard-Bury was there by August 10, a day that broke to a drizzling rain and a visit from the king, as well as news of the slaughter of the entire 16th Battalion at Delville Wood, a place the British soldiers knew as Devil's Wood. Five days later was his birthday; it passed uneventfully until the evening, when he was ordered to lead a work party of three hundred men to dig a communication trench five hundred yards through Longeuval to the very sector where the battalion had perished, the bloodied remnants of Delville Wood. It was more than six miles to where the work was to begin, and in the darkness the men, each laden with a rifle and ammunition, a pick and a shovel and sandbags, struggled through the mud and mire, not reaching their destination until 10:30 p.m. They had until dawn to complete the work, a task that three other divisions had declared to be impossible, for the entire route of the trench to be dug lay exposed to a German artillery barrage. Howard-Bury wrote of the experience in the regimental diaries:

I have never seen any country to equal the sense of desolation: there was not a blade of grass to be seen anywhere, the ground had been so shelled and shelled that all the shell holes overlapped, some were enormous, some were quite small and through this we had to dig a trench. The latter part lay through orchard and ruined houses of which there was nothing left. The stench was too awful. We kept up digging corpses. They were lying everywhere, ours and Boche dead, heads, arms, limbs in the most advanced state of decay crawling with maggots were to be seen and smelt on all sides. The horror of the place is almost impossible to describe and the revolting sights were almost beyond belief. Barely had we started digging before six or seven large shells landed within a few yards of us and hit two men: never have I seen men dig so quickly after this, within half an hour they had buried themselves and then began to join up the holes to make a trench.

Howard-Bury remained at the front throughout the war, fighting at the Somme until the November rains, taking part in the attacks on the Hindenburg Line in the spring of 1917, and in the subsequent struggles at Arras. Every day brought a new indignity and horror, which he recorded in his diary: wounded men cowering in the mud and filth, a soldier with his feet blown off in a trench on a cold January morning, a young officer white with fear crying like a child and carried from a trench, his lower body burned beyond recognition. On April 11 he was ordered to lead his men on a charge that in the circumstances, with an adjacent hilltop German position untouched, was sure suicide. He protested to the divisional staff, safely secure ten miles behind the line. Not one of the staff officers responsible for the order had scouted the ground. They insisted that the attack proceed. British shells landed among his men. Those who managed to climb out of the trenches were immediately mown down by enfilade machine gun fire, just as Howard-Bury had predicted. In the snow and ice the wounded lay all day. Within forty-eight hours the Germans had abandoned the promontory and the British walked to what had been their objective. The entire attack had been a waste, caused by the stubborn idiocy of the staff officers, who, as Howard-Bury bitterly wrote, "remained in safety and comfort far behind; for this they will no doubt get many DSO's and foreign decorations."

As the war went on, battle after battle, the heroism of his men betrayed by the folly of the generals, a slow corrosion of spirit tempered his diary entries and letters. By 1917 the word "depression" had no relevance, no meaning. On May 15 Howard-Bury wrote, "Went round the trenches at 4 a.m. The smell is horrible. Many bodies lying out in front and also buried in the parapet." On August 18, writing from Ypres on the eve of Passchendaele: "The ground that I had been over in 1914 was absolutely unrecognizable. The country was ghastly, not a leaf or a blade of grass anywhere but shell holes full of water. Horrible smells and sights." Four days later British tanks came close to crushing his men, who trembled in trenches as the water rose to their waists. One sentry was blown to pieces before his eyes, another burned beyond recognition by phosphorous. Fragments of arms and other body parts lay scattered amid the corpses disinterred by the shells. "What an existence this is," he wrote in despair. "It is only the politician and staff that wish to prolong the war."

By 1918 the ranks of Howard-Bury's command, the 9th Battalion, King's Royal Rifle Corps, had been replenished so often that only memories and shadows remained of the original force of 1914. That he had survived was statistically a miracle. Mauled once again at Passchendaele, the battalion was finally taken out of the line in the spring of 1918 and sent south beyond Saint-Quentin to take over from the French what had been a quiet sector of the Western Front. But at 4:30 on the morning of March 21 he was aroused by a sudden and terrific bombardment up and down the line, north and south, a cacophony of guns louder than anything he had heard in the war. He went to inspect the wire only to encounter in the darkness a fog so thick it was quite impossible to see three feet in any direction. Communication with the rear was cut by the bombardment, and with the fog came the scent of poison gas.

As it happened, Howard-Bury and his men were about to endure the brunt of the most powerful German attack of the war, the Spring Offensive of 1918. Desperate to end the struggle on the Western Front before American forces in the millions might join the fray, the officers of the German high command elected to commit their entire strength in a final effort to defeat the Allies. With the collapse of Russia, they shifted their armies to the west, bringing their total strength to 192 divisions. The Allies had only 169, and these were spread out from Switzerland to the sea. The bombardment that awoke Howard-Bury was the most intense and concentrated of the war. The Germans had assembled 730 aircraft, 3,500 mortars, and 6,600 guns, which fired over a million shells that first night alone. On the initial day of the attack they captured more ground than the British had taken in the 140-day battle of the Somme. By the end of the third day, XIX Corps could muster only 50 men of the eight battalions that had held the line; 7,950 men had been killed, wounded, or captured, including all those who fought alongside Howard-Bury.

The fog had allowed the German storm troopers to infiltrate the British positions, and when it lifted, around 11:00 a.m., Howard-Bury realized that his battalion headquarters, with its small garrison of fifty men, was completely surrounded. He sent off a passenger pigeon to alert the rear that they were holding on. The Germans brought to bear trench mortars and a hail of machine gun fire. Flamethrowers swept the British line. The handful of survivors, including Howard-Bury, overwhelmed in a final assault that came from all sides, surrendered around 3:30 p.m. For him the war was over. Immediately he turned his attention to the wounded, and helped carry several men to a nearby dugout where the Germans had established an aid station. As he was escorted to the rear, he was astonished to see German staff officers, close to the front, orchestrating the attacks. He knew that the outcome of the war hung in the balance, even as he began the long march on foot and by train to the POW camp at Fürstenberg.

ONE OF THE PECULIAR and unexpected outcomes of peace was the desire of many veterans to go anywhere but home. For those who survived, as Paul Fussell writes, travel became a source of irrational happiness, a moving celebration of the sheer joy of being alive. For these men England offered only a memory of lost youth, betrayal and lies, the residue of "four years of repression, casualty lists and mass murder sanctioned by Bishops." The poet and composer Ivor Gurney, gassed and wounded, died in 1937 still believing that the war raged and he was part of it. Before his descent into madness, he had a moment of clarity. Returning from the front, and before he was institutionalized, he set out from Gloucester on foot to find a ship, any ship, that might take him away. H. M. Tomlinson, who nearly froze to death at Ypres, and whose memory was haunted by shell fire splintering the marble earth of winter, escaped as soon as he could to bask in the Caribbean sun and write exquisite elegies of the tropics. Maurice Wilson, who earned the Military Cross at Passchendaele and later had his arm and chest ripped open by machine gun fire, a wound that never healed, wandered the South Pacific for a decade before conceiving a wild scheme, long after Mallory's death, to climb Everest by fasting and mystic levitation. He bought a Gipsy Moth, learned to fly, and managed by air to reach Darjeeling, where he sold his biplane and, accompanied by two Sherpa guides, began the walk that would lead to his solitary death on the ice of the mountain approaches.

From his diaries there is no evidence that Howard-Bury shared such obsessions and afflictions. A month to the day after the Armistice, a train carried him and his fellow officers from the Clausthal prison camp to the coast, where a Danish vessel awaited to transport them to Copenhagen. There, in an atmosphere of joy and gratitude, they feasted on fine food and freedom for four days before shipping out on a British ship, which landed them at Leith a week before Christmas, "thankful," as he wrote, "to find ourselves once more on British soil."

Still, it is curious that a man who had been at war for four years, a captive prisoner for an additional nine months, who owned and was responsible for a beloved estate in Ireland, an island at the time convulsed in upheaval and revolution, with terror bombings and acts of arson threatening all the landed gentry, would volunteer within ninety days of his liberation to travel at his own expense to India with the goal of securing the connivance of the Raj for an approach to the Tibetan authorities, all with the dream of obtaining permission to have a go at Everest. But this is precisely what Howard-Bury proposed in an unsolicited letter to Arthur Hinks, the secretary of the Royal Geographical Society, on March 19, 1919, one week after Noel's tour de force at Aeolian Hall.

In the letter Howard-Bury outlined a plan to visit both Shigatse and Gyantse, with the goal of obtaining an audience with the Panchen Lama. If rebuffed by the Tibetans, he would proceed to Kathmandu to seek the cooperation of the maharaja for an expedition through Nepal. In either event he would meet with India's director general of flying and arrange for an aerial reconnaissance to photograph the mountain at close quarters. All of this he would endeavor to do with his own resources. It was this last offer that most certainly caught the attention of the notoriously parsimonious Arthur Hinks; he immediately contacted Younghusband, who enthusiastically welcomed Howard-Bury's participation. Unfortunately for all of them, the government of India remained completely opposed to any effort to insert a team of explorers into Tibet and quite unwilling even to raise the prospect of an Everest expedition with the Lhasa authorities. Younghusband, though infuriated by this bureaucratic recalcitrance, reluctantly concluded that a Howard-Bury mission to India would be premature.

NEARLY A YEAR LATER Younghusband wrote to Howard-Bury at the Grand Hôtel Nice, on the French Riviera, and enticed him to return to London from his meanderings in northern Italy and the Dolomites to attend, on April 26, 1920, a private meeting of key representatives of both the Alpine Club and the Royal Geographical Society. By this time Younghusband, ten months into his tenure as president of the RGS, had made Everest his mission in life. "I want to get the idea enshrined in the very heart of the society," newspapers throughout the country quoted him as saying. "We refuse to admit that the highest mountain in the world cannot be scaled. The man who first stands on the summit of Mount Everest will have raised the spirit of countless others for generations to come, and given men a firmer nerve for scaling every other mountain." The climbers would lead the way, he believed, and the soldiers, political officers, lowly geographers, and all the myriad functionaries of the Raj, not to mention the common workingmen and -women of Britain, would be inspired by their example. As media interest grew, and the mountain emerged as a powerful distraction from the reality of the times, one senses the hand of John Buchan at work, spinning the story, building interest and momentum, drawing the public in ever-increasing numbers toward the embrace of a climbing expedition that would become the ultimate gesture of imperial redemption.

In the short term, the April 26 meeting resulted in a number of specific resolutions that defined the parameters of the Everest effort. The approach to the mountain would indeed be through Tibet, not Nepal. The RGS would be responsible for the preliminary negotiations with the British, Indian, and Tibetan governments, and a formal deputation led by Younghusband would immediately seek the support of the secretary of state for India. A joint committee representing both the RGS and the Alpine Club would begin work on the organization and planning of an expedition to extend over two seasons. The climbers would be British. Cooperation with foreign elements would be neither sought nor tolerated. To make all of this possible, the committee formally solicited the assistance of Colonel Howard-Bury, and granted him the mandate to go out to India and set in motion the very initiatives that he had first proposed to Hinks in his unsolicited letter of March 19, 1919.

A month later, on May 31, 1920, Younghusband used the occasion of his inaugural address to the anniversary meeting of the RGS to herald a new era of geographical exploration, one in which mere material pursuits would be transcended by a new aesthetic of the spirit and the earth would no longer be seen as "a magnified billiard-ball but as a living being—as Mother Earth." In florid language that anticipated his later metaphysical writings, he boldly claimed that the characteristic of the world most worth knowing was its natural beauty, a universal force that grows in power and resonance "the more we see of it and the more of us see it." The RGS under his leadership, he continued, would demand a new standard of exploration, with every geographer expected to bring with him into the field the eye of a poet, the sensitivity of a painter.

On a night when the RGS recalled the heroics of Sir Ernest Shackleton in Antarctica and celebrated a presentation by General Sir Frederick Sykes on the "air routes of empire" in the wake of the war, "a topic of the highest Imperial interest," it is difficult to know how Younghusband's summoning of the spirits went over with the assembled fellows. But it did provide him with an opening to address those critics who had questioned the purpose of risking human life to reach the summit of Everest:

> If I am asked: What is the use of climbing this highest mountain? I reply, No use at all; no more than kicking a football about or dancing or playing on the piano or writing a poem, or painting a picture . . . But if there is no use, there is unquestionably good in climbing Mount Everest. The accomplishment of such a feat will elevate the human spirit. It will give men a feeling that we really are getting the upper hand on the Earth, that we are acquiring a true mastery of our surroundings . . . If Man stands on Earth's highest summit he will have an increased pride and confidence in himself in his struggle for ascendancy over matter. This is the incalculable good which the ascent of Mount Everest will confer.

The day after his inaugural address, which was widely reported in the papers, Younghusband once again wrote to the secretary of state for India, Edwin Montagu, urging him to support the Everest expedition. A month later a deputation that included Younghusband, Howard-Bury, Farrar, and Charles Bruce, on leave from India, gathered at 4:55 p.m. in the waiting room of the India Office in London. As the prime minister had summoned the secretary of state unexpectedly, they met with Lord Sinha, the undersecretary, and a number of his staff. With Howard-Bury scheduled to sail for India in two days, it was highly desirable, if not essential, that he embark with the tacit support of the India Office and Whitehall. After reviewing the history of their efforts, the outline of the various approaches, and the challenges of the mission, Younghusband dramatically unveiled a panoramic photograph that captured the entire northern flank of the Himalaya from Kangchenjunga, in the east, to Everest, in the west. A composite of images taken by the geologist J. Hayden during the Younghusband Mission and forwarded to the RGS by Lord Curzon, the image was stunning, though its scale was deceptive. It suggested, as Younghusband told Lord Sinha, that access would not be problematic. "There is a fairly even slope on this northern side," Younghusband noted, "so that it looks comparatively easy . . . Compared with other peaks of the Himalayas its form, at any rate, promises well. Another point in its favour is that it stands back from the monsoon influence. Certainly during the three months of July, August and September that I was up there I could see Mount Everest pretty nearly every day."

On both points Younghusband was dead wrong, but his confidence appeared to sway Lord Sinha, who, in the manner of all functionaries, enthusiastically offered a conditional endorsement, with the caveat being that the government of India had to independently back the effort, after fully taking into account the sensibilities of Tibet. It was not the major victory Younghusband had been seeking, but it was enough to encourage him to send a follow-up note to Howard-Bury the next day, instructing him to proceed directly upon arrival in India to Simla to seek a personal interview with the viceroy. The British knew so little of the mountain, its scale and its wrath, that Younghusband naively suggested that permission be sought for a party of only three, "an experienced mountaineer, a surveyor, and one other European," to scout the mountain and prepare the way for the three climbers who would establish a route to the top the following season.

AFTER A LONG, hot voyage through the Red Sea, a rough passage from Aden to Bombay, and a surprisingly cool, dust-free rail journey across the plains of India, Howard-Bury arrived at Simla, the summer capital of the Raj, on Monday, July 12, 1920. He did not waste a moment. Three days later, in a letter written from the Hotel Cecil, he informed Younghusband that he had already met with the acting surveyor general, a Colonel Coldstream, and secured his promise to provide the expedition with a team of surveyors, men with climbing experience whose expenses would be paid by the government of India. He then contacted Acting Foreign Secretary Cater, who assured him that relations with Tibet were favorable but nevertheless delicate, hinging as they did on the outcome of a vital decision currently under review by the secretary of state at the India Office at Whitehall. Though the details were vague, they clearly involved a shipment of arms and ammunition anticipated by the Tibetan authorities. Until this issue was resolved, there could be no guarantee, Cater said, of support from either the government of India or the Tibetan authorities.

Howard-Bury's next meeting, at the Royal Flying Corps headquarters, was disappointing. The costs of an aerial reconnaissance were prohibitive, and from the existing airfields at Allahabad and Calcutta there was no machine capable of reaching the flanks of Everest. The air force would lend cameras and offer advice, but the suggestion that a temporary base be established closer to the mountain, at Purnea, was dismissed out of hand. This curt rebuke from the flying corps did not please the viceroy, with whom Howard-Bury met on the morning of July 15. Lord Chelmsford was excessively sympathetic and vowed to provide the expedition with every possible support. But again, as he informed Howard-Bury, even his hands were tied. Everything would depend on the outcome of the negotiations currently under way with the Tibetans. The viceroy then made a remark that struck Howard-Bury as curious: he advised him to travel overland to Yatung, in Tibet, to confer there with Charles Bell, the political officer of Sikkim, and to do all that was possible to interest Bell and the Tibetan authorities in the project. Howard-Bury had been told something similar by Basil Gould, the assistant foreign secretary, who had been in Tibet, at Gyantse, in 1913. All roads to Everest appeared to run through Charles Bell, a solitary frontier administrator to whom even the viceroy evidently deferred.

Five days later, having secured formal permission to cross into Tibet to Yatung, the British trading mart established by the Younghusband Mission in the Chumbi Valley just beyond the frontier with Sikkim, Howard-Bury had a disappointing lunch with Acting Foreign Secretary Cater, who had just received a wire from none other than Charles Bell.

"Bell says some poet-saint is buried near Everest," Howard-Bury reported to Younghusband in a letter of July 20, "and that the Tibetans are likely to be very suspicious . . . I am afraid that Bell is another obstacle and that as long as he is in his present position, he will put every difficulty he can in the way."

The full content of Charles Bell's telegram of July 19 was cited by the viceroy in a wire marked "Secret Mount Everest" and dispatched to the India Office in London on July 24. "Regarding the expeditions to Mount Everest via Tibet in 1921 and 1922," Bell had written, "there are several sacred places in the vicinity of Mount Everest as Milarepa the Tibetan poet-saint who attained Buddhahood lived there. Tibetans would not like Europeans moving about in those places . . . The Tibetans do not believe that explorations are carried on only in the interests of geographical knowledge and science. They will suspect that there is something behind what we tell them . . . Until the Tibetan question is settled with China these expeditions to Mount Everest should not be allowed."

Lord Chelmsford appended his own concurrence as viceroy: "Until question of the supply of arms and ammunition and other outstanding political matters in regard to Tibet are settled we feel strongly that we cannot approach Tibetan Government on behalf of Society. Bury has arrived here and position has been explained to him."

A week later, on July 27, Howard-Bury again wrote to Younghusband: "The entire problem is the failure of either Montagu or Curzon to agree with the Government of India's request to sell arms to Lhasa." Then, after asking Younghusband to use his influence to have the matter settled in favor of the government of India's position, Howard-Bury added, "The more I hear of Bell, the less I fear he will help us. They all say he is a most tiresome man to deal with because he is very slow and cautious and does not make any mistakes."

This assessment, as Howard-Bury would himself discover in the ensuing days at Simla, and in his later inquiries in Calcutta, was uncharitable. Charles Bell indeed did not make mistakes; if he was cautious, it was because he knew that upon his watch, the future of Tibet might turn. While his loyalties remained with the British crown, his affection lay with His Holiness the Thirteenth Dalai Lama, who considered Bell his friend and a close and trusted confidant. Younghusband rejected as ludicrous Bell's concerns about mystic saints and the mountain approaches, arguing in a wire sent from Brussels to the India Office that the "sacred places that Bell talks of could very easily be avoided." Howard-Bury, for his part, was less dismissive of Tibetan sensitivities and increasingly disinclined to question Bell's motivations. From conversations with various officials subsequent to his July 27 letter to Younghusband, he had learned enough about Bell's remarkable background to withhold judgment.

Born in India and schooled at Winchester and Oxford, Bell had joined the Indian Civil Service in 1891. In 1900 he was posted to Darjeeling, where he became enamored of Tibet. He learned to speak the language fluently, and in time would compile the first Tibetan grammar and dictionary. Appointed acting political officer of Sikkim in 1906, he formally replaced Claude White in 1908 and served until 1918, when he retired to pursue his academic research. Unlike Younghusband, Bailey, O'Connor, and most of the frontier officers of the Indian Civil

Service, Bell was not a soldier but a scholar with a deep and sincere interest in the civilization of the Himalaya, an avocation that immediately set him apart from the vast majority of the British in India. His relationship with His Holiness had been forged during the years of the Dalai Lama's exile in Darjeeling, beginning in 1910. Largely because of Bell, the Tibetans had rallied to the British cause during the war. At the outbreak of war in 1914, the Dalai Lama had raised a thousand men to fight for the British, an offer that was diplomatically declined, though the military unit was kept on call throughout the war even as monasteries throughout Tibet held special religious ceremonies to pray for the success of the British cause. It was his friendship with Charles Bell that led the Dalai Lama to write, "Thus all the people of Tibet and myself have become of one mind, and the British and Tibetans have become one family." That such sentiments would be expressed less than a generation after the Younghusband invasion and the massacre of the Tibetan army at Guru was in itself remarkable.

On July 31 Younghusband received word in London from the India Office that the government of India had formally turned down the Everest Committee. He absorbed the news without bitterness and immediately wired Howard-Bury, encouraging him nevertheless to press on into Tibet to meet with Bell, who had at this point emerged as their final hope.

To GET TO YATUNG, where Bell at the moment was based, Howard-Bury followed the route taken by the Younghusband invasion, climbing in a day from the tropical forests of Sikkim to the snows of the Jelep La at 14,390 feet, and then beyond to the temperate beauty of the Chumbi Valley. After the leeches and monsoon rains of his long approach march, he found enchantment among the silver firs and rhododendron forests of Tibet, the meadows of clematis, purple iris, and wild strawberries. The precipitous rise in elevation, however, left him exhausted. Ascending the Jelep La, as Bell later wrote, "felt like climbing up a continuous ladder, each step higher than the one before. Up. Up. Up right onto the roof of the world. Your head felt light and your limbs like lead and all that could be heard was the strange laboured breathing of men and mules, with occasional fits of coughing."

By the time Howard-Bury reached Yatung, he felt weak and retired to bed immediately, without dinner. The following day, August 14, he awoke fully restored and spent an idle morning reading his mail and some newspapers that had just arrived. Though it appeared isolated on a map, Yatung was in fact a small but bustling depot through which flowed fully half of the entire trade between Tibet and India, a continuous traffic of yaks and mules bringing wool, salt, musk, and medicinal herbs down from the plateau and tea and manufactured goods up from the foothills and the cities of the Raj. The 175 miles from Gangtok, in Sikkim, to Gyantse, in Tibet, took eleven days at a steady pace, but could be covered by native runners in as little as seventy-two hours. Letters and newspapers from Calcutta could reach Lhasa in ten days. In many ways, communication in 1920 was far better than it would be fifty years later. Since the Younghusband invasion, the British had maintained not only a telegraph line to Gyantse but also a string of eleven *dak* bungalows, a day's walk apart, equipped with beds and small tea shops where officials could purchase food and basic supplies, services that were available for Howard-Bury and the later climbing expeditions. Bell's predecessor, Claude White, had decreed these facilities off-limits to natives for fear that they would be rendered unfit for Europeans, a contemptuous regulation that Bell immediately reversed on becoming political officer.

Late in the morning Howard-Bury conferred with the British trade agent, David Macdonald, a slight man, barely five feet tall, who had been appointed to the post by Bell in 1909. The son of a Scottish tea planter and a Lepcha mother from Sikkim, Macdonald had been born with the name Dorjee, but grew up fully in the shadow of the British, attending boarding school in Darjeeling and later becoming Christian under the influence of his wife, herself the product of a mixed marriage of English and Nepalese blood. A close friend and confidant of Bell's, fluent in many tongues, Macdonald had been with the British in Lhasa in 1904 and had briefly acted as Younghusband's translator during the invasion.

At noon, Macdonald and Howard-Bury joined Charles Bell for lunch, escorted to his quarters by a Tibetan military band of drums, bugles, and fife playing a rousing rendition of the British national anthem. Bell impressed Howard-Bury as being pleasant and hospitable, but adamant in his views. In a letter to Younghusband, he reported that Bell was particularly concerned that the home government had yet to reply about the question of sending arms to Lhasa: "He told me frankly that he did not care for the idea of an expedition until the whole question of the relations between China, India and Tibet had been settled . . . At the same time he said that he could ask the Tibetan government today and he was quite certain that they would allow the expedition, but that he did not think that it would be advisable at the present time."

Bell permitted Howard-Bury to proceed farther up the Chumbi Valley, on the condition that he not go past Phari, and that once there he say nothing of his proposed expedition to Everest to the local authorities. A request to return to Sikkim via Kampa Dzong was firmly denied as being diplomatically provocative. As Howard-Bury left Yatung on August 15, walking past the European cemetery on the edge of town and climbing the wild slopes of the Amo Chu Gorge, he remained puzzled by this extraordinary figure, a man whose knowledge of the language and culture of Tibet was clearly encyclopedic, who read the classics by night in the original Greek and by day had such fine intuitions concerning the ways of the Buddha, the spirit of the place, that he could decipher and anticipate the most subtle features of etiquette and ceremonial form. It was this sensitivity that so impressed Howard-Bury, who was himself deeply intrigued by all things spiritual and metaphysical. Bell, he had learned, deliberately rode a horse of a color deemed auspicious to Tibetans and arranged his diplomatic business according to the dictates of the Tibetan calendar. When monks remained indoors during the rainy season, for fear of harming the abundant insect life, he cast no judgment. He viewed sky burial not as something morbid, but as a proper and efficient means of diposing of the dead in a land where the ground lay frozen most of the year.

Out of respect for his formal position and the Tibetans he so admired, Bell retained his English dress and bearing, the proper behavior of an objective British officer. Only in this way could he exert authority and influence both in Lhasa and in the highest diplomatic circles of the Raj. Yet his knowledge, unequaled in the Indian Civil Service, gave his words precise and undeniable credence, allowing him, when appropriate, to slice through the most opaque of diplomatic niceties. Of the Chinese he spoke directly of their "tendency to treat the Tibetans as a people far inferior to themselves, and to apply to them methods of oppression at once brutal and stupid." And without apology or qualification, he accounted for the spiritual authority of His Holiness the Thirteenth Dalai Lama. "An unearthly light," he wrote, "is believed to issue from his brow when he blesses pilgrims; his back reveals the imprint of Chenrezi; he is known as Kundun, the Presence." Tibetans had their own explanation for Bell's cultural sensitivity and genius: they maintained that he had been a Tibetan in a previous lifetime, a high lama who had been reborn in a more powerful nation that he might return to help his people.

HOWARD-BURY SPENT TEN DAYS exploring the Chumbi Valley, slowly making his way to Phari and just beyond, to the southern edge of the Tibetan Plateau. It was rich land, at least in the lower reaches, with verdant fields of barley, wheat, and potatoes, pear and apple orchards heavy in fruit, wild azaleas and dwarf rhododendrons on the mountain slopes, and roses in such abundance that the entire valley was sweetly scented. The individual farmsteads were charming, the houses with their gently sloping roofs of pine shingles, split in six-foot lengths and held in place by heavy stones, each home draped in prayer flags, each flag a mantra blown to the wind. The men who greeted him, tongues darting out at the end of every phrase as a sign of deference and respect, were generous and welcoming, and the women less shy than those of Sikkim and India. He found that they stared at him quite unabashedly. Bell later showed Howard-Bury a Tibetan book, one of seventy-six in his library, written by Rin-chen Lha-mo; one passage in it summarized a woman's view of the Western man: "The average European is not good looking according to our ideas. We consider your noses too big, often they stick out like kettle spouts; your ears are too large, like pig's ears; your eyes blue like children's marbles; your eye sockets too deep and eyebrows too prominent, too simian."

Howard-Bury, like others before him, found Phari to be a miserable place, a windswept hovel built on its own waste with mud streets as open sewers and only the frozen air of morning to offer a respite from the all-pervading stench of human waste. But beyond Phari, the white summit of Chomolhari brightened the sky, and his track carried him up a marshy valley between grassy hills and then across the Kambu La, a 16,000-foot pass that led to a deep, narrow valley literally colored blue with wildflowers, gentians and bluebells, columbine, monkshood, and forget-me-nots. Farther up the valley he came upon a series of nine sacred springs, all sulfur, in one of which bathed a high lama, surrounded by his attendants. They welcomed him warmly, with butter tea and a plate of English biscuits. More food followed, minced mutton and diced vegetables, eggs and macaroni, which Howard-Bury, to the delight of all, attempted to eat with a pair of chopsticks. As they ate, any number of people of the valley, suffering from various afflictions, came before the lama, prostrating themselves three times on the ground, and then, having received his blessing, slowly walked away without turning their back to the master. The lama later accompanied Howard-Bury back to Phari to show him a shorter route. In his red robes and rosary, his oiled hair hanging on long plaits on either side of his brightly decorated saddle, wearing a hat of several tiers and shaped like a pagoda, yellow in color and decorated with Chinese characters and the portrait of a saint, the lama was, as Howard-Bury wrote, "the most picturesque individual I have yet seen."

In the last week of August Howard-Bury returned the twenty-eight miles from Phari to Yatung, where he was warmly welcomed by Macdonald, fed vast amounts of food, and even cajoled into playing a tennis match one quiet afternoon. Over two days at Yatung, beginning August 25, he met several times with Charles Bell, encounters that were both intense and revelatory. He noted in his diary, "Bell gave me the whole history of our relations with Tibet since 1904 and said that at the present moment they were in a worse condition than they had been for ten years, thanks to our not keeping our promises. He said that the Chinese are working hard and are gradually regaining their lost influence and that practically it is only the Dalai Lama now that prevents the Chinese from being complete masters again and that he may be poisoned at any time."

The story Bell recounted was indeed one of duplicity and betrayal. The Younghusband invasion had intended to keep the Russians out of Lhasa and secure Tibetan allegiance to the Raj, if only through commercial interests. The 1904 convention, forced on the Tibetan government in Lhasa by the British, included provisions for a punitive indemnity of £500,000 to be paid in seventy-five annual installments, terms that effectively guaranteed a British presence in Lhasa and indefinite control of the Chumbi Valley, the only conceivable invasion route between the two countries. The Chinese were deliberately excluded from the convention. In a letter to the secretary of state for India on January 8, 1903, Curzon stated the British position unequivocally: "We regard Chinese suzerainty over Tibet as a constitutional fiction." Tibet, according to the viceroy, was a free and independent country.

The repudiation of the Younghusband expedition by the Liberal government that came to power in 1905 sent a very different signal to Peking. Committed to abandoning Curzon's aggressive forward policies, yet anxious still to blunt Russian intrigue, the British elected to placate China, embargoing all arms sales to Tibet and reducing the Younghusband indemnity to £166,000, payable in five installments, a minor sum that China readily paid off, thus reaffirming, in effect, its control and political legitimacy in Lhasa. By the terms of the 1906 Anglo-Chinese Treaty, negotiated bilaterally in Peking without Tibetan involvement, the British government discarded everything the Younghusband invasion had achieved and formally returned Tibet to the Chinese orbit. A year later the Anglo-Russian Convention secured Russian recognition of Chinese suzerainty in Tibet in exchange for British acceptance of Russian domination of Mongolia. The Younghusband invasion had crushed the Tibetan army and left the nation defenseless even as it provoked the wrath of the Chinese and challenged them to exert their influence in a distant land they had long been content to ignore. The subsequent diplomatic betrayal of Tibet not only opened the door to Chinese aggression, it virtually obliged Peking to act.

The Chinese responded with an invasion force led by a notorious warlord, General Chao Erh-feng, who would become known throughout Tibet as Butcher Chao. A ruthless fighter who vowed to leave not a person or a dog alive, he marched his army through Batang and Derge, subduing all of eastern Tibet, leaving in his wake ravaged monasteries, devastated villages, and rivers stained with blood. Arriving at Bah in 1905, he murdered four monks. When word reached him that a neighboring monastery at Lithang was restive, he summoned two Tibetan officials, and when they confirmed the report, he promptly had them beheaded. When the people of the valley proved unruly, he dispatched his troops and slaughtered 1,210 monks and laymen. In June 1906 his forces surrounded the Gongkar Manling monastery, decapitated the four monks sent out to negotiate, and proceeded to kill and pillage, burning sacred texts, melting down for coinage the gold and copper icons, looting the temples, and reducing the sacred enclosures to ashes and dust. On the third day of the first Tibetan month of the Iron-Dog year, Butcher Chao and his army marched into Lhasa, blasted the Jokhang and Potala Palace with artillery fire, and looted the city, raping women and children and slaughtering any monk who resisted. By the end of February 1910 he had quelled resistance and taken control of the capital, leaving tens of thousands of Tibetans dead.

The Dalai Lama, having only returned from exile in China in December 1909, fled in advance of the Chinese armies to Phari, where the entire population of the Chumbi Valley rallied to his defense. He reached Yatung the following day, where he was sheltered by David Macdonald, who offered his own bedroom to His Holiness and fed him a proper English dinner of chicken soup and roast mutton, with baked custard apple for dessert. That night while the Dalai Lama rested, Macdonald placed a guard at his door, and when, the following morning, Chinese officials appeared, demanding that the British hand over the revered lama, Macdonald had them seized and searched for weapons. Learning that a larger Chinese force would soon be descending upon Yatung, the Dalai Lama, disguised as a common postal runner, escaped in the night and with his entourage braved the ice and snow of the Jelep La to reach Gnatong, the Sikkimese village nearest the frontier. There the Tibetan party found safety and rest in a telegraph hut, protected throughout the following night by two British soldiers. At daylight they continued to Kalimpong and beyond to Darjeeling, where a house was placed at the Dalai Lama's disposal by Charles Bell. It was a kindness that would not be forgotten.

The British under Younghusband had been firm, even brutal, in their 1904 conquest of Lhasa. But compared to the savagery of the Chinese, their transgressions had been trivial. They had paid for food, firewood, and fodder, provided medical care for the Tibetan wounded, protected noncombatants, honored the terms of surrender, respected sacred sites, and done nothing to threaten the religion of the land. When, on March 14, 1910, the Dalai Lama, accompanied by Charles Bell, was welcomed in Calcutta by the viceroy, Lord Minto, and heralded by a seventeen-gun salute, he had reason to look forward to the support of the Raj in his struggle against the Chinese. This was not to be, however. While the viceroy remained sympathetic, his hands were tied by Whitehall. Lord Morley, secretary of state for India and the architect of the Liberal policy, welcomed the Chinese invasion of Tibet as the legitimate assertion of China's claim to the land. He dismissed the Dalai Lama as a "pestilent animal who should be left to stew in his own juice." In May 1910 His Holiness was informed that despite the ongoing slaughter in Tibet, the government of India could not intervene.

What ultimately saved the Tibetans was the October 1911 revolution of Sun Yat-sen, which overthrew the Ch'ing dynasty and destroyed the power of the Manchu Empire. With Chinese forces in Lhasa now stranded, a general uprising led by the monks of the Sera and Ganden monasteries reclaimed the city. Butcher Chao retreated to Sichuan, where he was himself captured and beheaded. In June 1912 the Dalai Lama left India and slowly made his way back to Tibet, marking his time until word reached his entourage that the last Chinese official had vacated the city. At Yatung he stayed five days with David Macdonald. When he left, every object he had touched was deemed a holy relic, and Macdonald had some difficulty preventing the pilfering of door handles and chairs, brooms and washbasins. In January 1913 the Dalai Lama finally made his triumphant return to Lhasa. For twenty years, until his death in 1933, he refused to tolerate a single Chinese representative in his capital.

Charles Bell, appalled by the litany of British betrayals, decided that if Whitehall would not protect Tibet, he would do everything in his power to ensure that Tibet had the capacity to defend itself. With his encouragement, the Tibetan government created the symbols of an independent state: a national flag, a currency, postal stamps, and even a football team. He heralded the Dalai Lama's efforts to reorganize the economy and modernize the bureaucracy, with new policies that shifted the burden of taxation, redistributed land, and abolished the most draconian of punishments, the mutilations for criminal deeds. Bell worked tirelessly to increase commercial, diplomatic, and military ties to the Raj. With the active support of the Dalai Lama, he saw to it that the telegraph line from India to Gyantse was extended to Lhasa. A diesel generator carried overland in pieces provided electricity to the homes of the wealthy, many of whom had been educated in Darjeeling and spoke fluent English. The Dalai Lama himself owned a phone and two cars, including an American Dodge with the license plates reading TIBET 1; it also had been carried overland through the Chumbi Valley and reassembled in Lhasa. Perhaps most important of all, Bell had encouraged the Dalai Lama to modernize his military, increasing the size of the army from 5,000 to 15,000 and equipping it with proper arms.

In September 1913 Bell was ordered to Simla to enter into negotiations on behalf of the British government with China and Tibet. The ostensible purpose of the summit was to delineate the border between the countries, an 850-mile boundary from Bhutan to the Irrawaddy-Salween divide that became known as the McMahon Line. The true thrust of the conference, however, was an attempt by the British to formalize the political and territorial realignment that had taken place in the wake of the collapse of the Ch'ing dynasty. With China's hold on Lhasa broken, Britain once again reversed policy and acknowledged Tibet as an independent state. Whitehall continued to recognize the suzerain rights of China over Tibet, but denied China the right to intervene in the internal affairs of the smaller country. For its part, Tibet came to Simla to affirm its independence; meanwhile, the British desired, as always, to secure a protected buffer on the northern frontier of the Raj. China, by contrast, came to recover its former position in Tibet. When this proved impossible, the Chinese delegation refused to ratify the treaty. Tibet and Britain went ahead bilaterally, effectively reducing China to a bystander.

By the final terms of the Simla Convention, signed on April 27, 1914, the Tibetan authorities ceded to the Raj a small outcrop of territory bordering eastern Bhutan. More significantly, they agreed to divide their country into an inner and an outer Tibet, a decision that haunts Tibetans to this day. For diplomatic reasons there was no mention of arms in the agreement, but within weeks the government of

India shipped to Lhasa 5,000 rifles and 500,000 rounds of ammunition, a consignment later augmented by an additional 200,000 cartridges. Three months later, war broke out in Europe.

With the crisis in Europe, Tibet faded from the British mind, which inevitably provided another opening for China. Violence flared in Kham, and by the beginning of 1918 Tibet and China were engaged in open if sporadic warfare, with the Tibetans moving on Chamdo and occupying all the land west of the Yangtze. The government of India sent Tibet 500,000 rounds of ammunition for self-defense. But preoccupied in France, unwilling to antagonize the Chinese, and keen, if possible, to defuse the crisis, the British denied desperate Tibetan requests for the additional arms, machine guns in particular, that had been promised them, according to Charles Bell. The British did attempt to place a military officer in Lhasa, if only to send a message to the Chinese, but the Tibetan authorities would have nothing of it. By the summer of 1920, as Howard-Bury conferred with Bell, the situation had come to a head. The failure of the British to make good on arms shipments reinforced the suspicions of conservative elements in Lhasa who were already highly critical of the Dalai Lama's efforts to modernize the country along Western lines. This made it that much more difficult for him to take the steps necessary to protect his people from the Chinese, even as it opened the door to their influence.

As Howard-Bury informed Younghusband in a letter of September 2:

> Bell told me that politically the state of affairs between us and Tibet is worse now than it has been for 10 years . . . They are turning now to China again, as they say we only make promises and do not keep them. I fully agree with this point of view. We gave them rifles before and now when they have no ammunition, we make excuses. The Dalai Lama is still our friend, but his council is all going over to the Chinese, even the general in command of the forces supposed to be fighting them is pro-Chinese. Bell has just heard privately from the Dalai Lama all about this and he had wired to the Govt of India for leave to go see the Dalai Lama, before he gives up his job and this I think he will be allowed to do.

Bell, in fact, had come out of retirement in late 1919 with the specific goal of aiding the Dalai Lama. Throughout the summer and early fall of 1920, even as Howard-Bury continued his scouting journey with a monthlong trek up the Teesta Valley along the route taken by Noel in 1913, where he, too, was rewarded with a fleeting glimpse of Everest, Bell anxiously awaited word from Simla and Lhasa. Though eager to reach the Tibetan capital, he had no intention, as he had told Howard-Bury, of going empty-handed. He was not about to play a role in yet another betrayal of the Tibetans.

By mid-October Howard-Bury, having conferred with the maharaja of Sikkim, was back in Darjeeling, where he stayed with Lord Ronald-shay, governor of Bengal. His journey was nearing an end, and it was not at all clear what good had come of it. On October 13, he wrote to Younghusband, "I sail from Bombay on Nov 20th in the Kaesar-i-hind, which ought to reach Marseille on December 4. Lord Ronaldshay here will help us in every way and so will the local officials. The Maharajah of Sikkim will do his best and Macdonald the trade agent at Yatung and Gyantse can be most helpful." He added however: "As long as Bell is there we are badly handicapped, but I am trying to find out who his successor is to be."

It was not as if Howard-Bury disliked Bell. On the contrary, the more he knew of him, the more he admired the man. His frustration was with his own mission. Only the Dalai Lama could deliver the path to Everest. Bell held the key to the Dalai Lama and was not about to call in a favor unless the Tibetans were given the arms they so desperately needed. It was a position that Howard-Bury both agreed with and respected. It just did not help him with Everest.

On October 28, he wrote to Younghusband once again, this time with some startling news: Bell had been allowed to go to Lhasa to confer with the Dalai Lama. The Foreign Office had not yielded on Tibet's request for arms, as far as Howard-Bury knew, and it was not at all clear how Bell would be received, but it was nevertheless a highly significant diplomatic opening. "So now it all depends on how Bell puts it before the Dalai Lama and we shall have to wait for his answer, which will not be for a couple of months."

Bell had waited ten years for the orders that finally came through from Simla on October 15. His would be the first European party ever to be invited to Lhasa by the Tibetan government. He planned the journey with care, arranging transport such that they might enter the holy city on November 17, a day he knew to be highly auspicious on the Tibetan calendar.

On December 10, 1920, less than a month after his arrival in Lhasa, Bell sent a telegram to the foreign secretary of the government of India. The wire reached Delhi on December 13. Two days later the viceroy conveyed its contents to the India Office in London, and on December 20, Younghusband received a personal note from the political secretary, J. E. Shuckburgh.

"My dear Sir Francis," Schuckburgh wrote, "you will be interested to know that we have just received a telegram from the Viceroy in which the following passage occurs: 'Bell telegraphs that he has explained to Dalai Lama object of desired exploration and necessity of traveling through Tibetan territory and obtained Tibetan Government's consent.' We shall no doubt write to you officially about this; but meantime I wish to lose no time in letting you know personally what has happened. The human obstacles—of which you recently spoke—are beginning to drop off!"

On Christmas Eve 1920, Bell sat down in Lhasa to write a note of explanation directly to Younghusband in which he referred to Howard-Bury's visit. "At the time I was bound to oppose the exploration of Everest through Tibetan territory," he told Younghusband. "But by my coming to Lhasa and the personal intercourse with my Tibetan friends that results from this visit, circumstances have changed. It was therefore a great pleasure for me to gain the Dalai Lama's permission to [unreadable] this exploration, which is to be conducted under the auspices of the Royal Geographical Society, yours sincerely, C. A. Bell."

Precisely what circumstances had changed remains unclear. Bell would stay in Lhasa for nearly a year. It was a perilous period, and at times his life was in danger. His support of the army threatened the power of the monasteries, and during the Monlam Chenmo, the Great Prayer Festival, placards appeared throughout Lhasa calling for his assassination. He was protected by His Holiness the Thirteenth Dalai Lama, who personally urged him to remain in the Tibetan capital throughout the long winter of 1920. His initial orders from the government of India insisted that he make no offer of arms. Yet before he left Lhasa, in October 1921, he had apparently achieved the impossible: a complete reversal of British policy, an agreement whereby Tibet would receive arms, ammunition, military training, and technical assistance. The arsenal arrived in 1922: mountain artillery, Lewis machine guns, 10,000 Lee-Enfield rifles, and hundreds of thousands of rounds of ammunition, the very basis of a modern fighting force. There can be little doubt that permission for the British to assault Everest was but a small piece of a very large and complex diplomatic initiative, imagined and brought into being by Charles Bell, an arms deal upon which rested the very future of a free Tibet.

CHAPTER 4

Hinks's Watch

NEWS THAT TIBET had sanctioned an Everest expedition broke over London on the morning of January 11, 1921, following an official announcement the evening before by Sir Francis Younghusband at a meeting of the Royal Geographical Society. The press, orchestrated by John Buchan, did not disappoint. British dailies from Liverpool to Glasgow, Plymouth to Edinburgh headlined the story. Yet even as the papers heralded the imminent adventure, the enormity of the challenge was brought sharply into focus by some of the leading figures of British mountaineering.

Some weeks before, following a presentation by General Charles Bruce at Aeolian Hall, the highly regarded Himalayan climber Sir Martin Conway had offered a sobering assessment, reminding readers of the *Daily Chronicle* that for all the excitement, nothing whatsoever was known of the mountain. No European had ever reached its base; the immediate approaches remained uncharted. Little was understood of its structure, the character of its snow and ice, its silhouette and topography, the nature of the rock formations that made up its formidable bulk and narrowed to its imposing ridges. A week later Conway went further in an interview with the *Observer*. On the upper slopes of Everest no man could be expected to ascend more than 2,000 feet a day, he said. This implied that high camps would have to be established and equipped at 25,000 and 27,000 feet, elevations to which no one had yet climbed, let alone slept overnight. The greatest height achieved to date was a single ascent to just over 24,600 feet by the Duke of Abruzzi in the Karakoram, while the highest camp on record had been established at 23,420 feet by C. F. Meade on Kamet in 1913. What would happen beyond such heights was a total mystery. When, in a notorious nineteenth-century experiment, the French meteorologist Gaston Tissandier had ascended rapidly in a balloon, he'd passed out at 26,500 feet and upon regaining consciousness had found himself deaf and his two companions dead. In the war, pilots had typically donned oxygen masks above 18,000 feet, and reported severe problems above 20,000 feet if the gas was not available. Acclimatization promised to mitigate some of the effects of oxygen deprivation. Still, in climbing beyond 25,000 feet, men would be entering a zone virtually as hostile and mysterious as the surface of the moon. "The man who hopes to climb Mount Everest," predicted the *Daily Mail*, citing the well-known Keswick climber George Abraham, "must be able with no training to run at fair speed up the last 300 ft of Mount Blanc." And, it might have added, in air that had but a third of the oxygen encountered at sea level.

On January 12 Sir Francis Younghusband convened the first formal meeting of the Mount Everest Committee. Representing the Alpine Club were its president, Percy Farrar, and two of its most prominent members, Norman Collie and C. F. Meade. The Royal Geographical Society brought to the room Younghusband, a Colonel E. M. Jack, and a banker by the name of Edward Somers-Cock, who was appointed honorary treasurer. All agreed that the ultimate objective was the summit, a goal to which the preliminary reconnaissance would be directed. The primary task in the first year was to identify the best route of approach. Should time and conditions permit, the party would be allowed and encouraged to ascend as high as possible, but only once the mountain had been completely reconnoitered and the most viable line of attack determined.

Inevitably, this resolution would be interpreted somewhat differently by the two societies. For the Alpine Club, the climb was all that mattered. The RGS had a broader mandate, which included the exploration and mapping of the unknown lands along the flanks of the mountain. At Younghusband's insistence the party would include topographers and cartographers recruited from the Survey of India, a geologist from the Geological Survey of India, and a naturalist charged with the duty of compiling a botanical and zoological inventory. One of the first orders of business was the appointment of two honorary secretaries, Arthur Hinks of the RGS and J. E. C. Eaton of the Alpine Club. In short order Hinks, with Younghusband's tacit approval, would usurp virtually all administrative authority, reducing Eaton to irrelevance and eclipsing even Farrar, himself a dogmatic and formidable adversary; after numerous battles with Hinks, Farrar would ultimately resign from the committee in 1922.

Arthur Hinks was a complex and difficult man. A fellow of the Royal Society, he was a brilliant mathematician and academic cartographer, a world authority on map projections who, ironically, had little interest in exploration and no experience whatsoever of life on an expedition. Before coming to the Royal Geographical Society in 1913, he had spent much of his career sequestered at Cambridge on the staff of the University Observatory, calculating the mass of the Moon. Born in 1873, he had a codger's disdain for modernity. "The telephone is a great mistake," he cautioned General Bruce, "and you will do well to be rid of it. I would not have one in my house for anything." Disagreeable, intolerant, sarcastic, utterly lacking in tact or discretion, he was parsimonious and priggish, enamored of his own genius and convinced always of the infallible wisdom of his opinions. His letters suggest an individual imprisoned in a state of contempt and indignation.

At the same time, he was ferociously hardworking, meticulous, and exacting, with a bureaucrat's obsession with process and control. From the outset he would orchestrate virtually every aspect of the expeditions, from the raising of funds and the recruiting of personnel to the purchasing of supplies and the design of equipment. No detail escaped his attention, whether the comparative costs of a passage to India or the proper brand of chocolate, the engineering of high-altitude stoves or the appropriate modifications of cameras, fuel supplies, oxygen cylinders, alpine boots, sun goggles, or chemicals for developing film and printing photographs at high altitude. He choreographed all interactions with the press, oversaw all travel arrangements, and negotiated for the publication of expedition reports, the production of documentary films, the sale of photographs and botanical specimens, the drafting of maps, the bookings of the international lecture tours that would play an essential role in fueling public interest in the expeditions. Every decision, conflict, debate, and controversy passed over his desk, and though he never left his London office, he was without doubt the nexus for the entire enterprise, the glue that held everything together. His correspondence fills some forty boxes, scores of files, in the Royal Geographical Society archives. He was liked by virtually no one, and yet without his irascible and indomitable will the expeditions might never have happened.

Even before his formal ascendancy Hinks had begun working behind the scenes, recruiting and vetting men for the team. As early as December 30, 1920, he wrote to John Noel, who was stationed at the time at the Small Arms School at Hythe, in Kent. Noel accepted, with the caveat that the War Office might not be willing to grant him leave, which turned out to be the case. A year later Noel would resign his commission in order to join the second climbing expedition, in

1922. Tom Longstaff, who had spent an easy war in India attached to the Gilgit Scouts until invalided home in October 1917 as a result of a direct blow to the temple by a polo ball, offered to join the expedition as medical officer, with the understanding that he had no interest in actually serving as a doctor. He, too, would have to wait until 1922. In an awkward interlude, Norman Collie, a member of the Everest Committee, proposed himself for inclusion on the roster. He was sixty-two. That such a suggestion could even be tabled reveals how little was known of the horrendous conditions the men would face in Tibet. His offer was politely declined. John de Vars Hazard, a serious climber whom Alexander Kellas had invited to Kamet in 1920, was also denied, though he had been in touch with Hinks about Everest since 1919. Among his challenges were open wounds on his back and one thigh, excruciating injuries that would never heal, sustained at the Somme. John "Jack" Hazard's turn would come in 1924, when, despite constant pain, he would reach as high as the North Col.

Within days of the official announcement of the expedition, even as Hinks considered the list of established British climbers, scores of unsolicited applications poured into the RGS. From Texas a William Russell Bradford wrote of a sacred fire burning within him, an inner strength that had never failed. He also, it was noted, could ride and shoot well. From India came a letter from an ambitious policeman fluent in ordinary and honorific Tibetan, Nepali, and Bengali. An RGS fellow employed with Barclays Bank offered his considerable talents as a stenographer and typist, along with his skill at driving cars and handling "various native tribes." The majority of applicants were ex-servicemen. A plaintive appeal came from an F. Vankinsburgh, who had been severely wounded at Gallipoli and later nearly killed when his hospital ship was torpedoed. "I served all through the Egyptian, Palestine and Syrian campaigns [sic]," he wrote. "I'm 24 years old. Since being demobilized in March 1919 I have worked in a warehouse, and I feel stifled. I'm always thinking of the open spaces of the desert and I think I'd give anything to get out abroad somewhere." From Birmingham came a letter from a Lionel Mason, who flaunted but a single credential: the man had served at the front from November 1914 to April 1919, and in all that time had spent but a week in the hospital. He was evidently both tough and astonishingly lucky. That he had never been on a mountain was clearly, to his mind, irrelevant.

Perhaps the most unexpected appeals came from two veterans of ill-fated Antarctica expeditions. Ernest Joyce had served under both Scott and Shackleton, and his application to Hinks was supported by references from none other than Sir Clement Markham, former president of the RGS and a well-known patron of polar exploration. In 1915 Joyce had set out from the Ross Sea to establish a relay of supply drops for the Shackleton expedition, which was expected to be coming across the continent by way of the South Pole. Marooned from their ship, the *Aurora*, Joyce's party covered eighteen hundred miles in six months, struggling overland across the ice, sometimes making as little as two miles in a fifteen-hour march. Suffering from scurvy, tormented by delirium, three men would die. Joyce, surviving on raw seal meat, patiently awaited an expedition that never appeared. For two years he was totally stranded, with no contact with the outside world and no knowledge whatsoever of the fate of the expedition he had risked his life to provision.

Shackleton had sailed from London on August 1, 1914, the day Germany declared war on Russia. He offered to turn back, but was urged not to abandon his mission by Churchill himself, as First Lord of the Admiralty, who wired a single word: "Proceed." On January 18, 1915, within sight of land, Shackleton's ship, the *Endurance*, became stranded in the Weddell Sea, where it lay frozen for nine months before being crushed by the pack ice. The crew, camped on the floe, drifted for another five and a half months before reaching open water and Elephant Island, a rocky crag eight hundred miles from South Georgia, the nearest point of rescue. Shackleton, in one of the epic sea journeys of all time, set out in an open dory with five of his crew, washing ashore on South Georgia seventeen ferocious winter days later. When they finally reached a whaling station on May 20, 1916, they were to learn that war still raged in Europe. After recuperating for only three days, Shackleton returned to sea to rescue his men. Beaten back repeatedly by the weather, he would not make landfall on Elephant Island until his fourth attempt, fully eighteen weeks after he had departed. Not a man was lost. In January 1917, in a separate mission, Shackleton plucked Joyce off the shore of the Ross Sea.

Among the rescued at Elephant Island was Theodore Orde-Lees, who would repeatedly write Hinks seeking a place on the Everest expedition. He noted his record of "73 parachute descents from aeroplanes" and, in a letter dated January 26, 1921, enclosed a classified photograph of himself in free fall, just before his parachute opened. Convinced that the mountain would never be scaled without the aid of supplemental oxygen—a conviction certain to offend Hinks, a mountaineering purist—he outlined a plan to drop gas cylinders from the air. When this letter provoked no positive response, Orde-Lees wrote a final note on June 14, 1921: "My age is 42. I am a public school boy (Marlborough), 20 years military service, and was with Shackleton on his last expedition. Six months on an ice floe, 4½ under a boat on a dessert [*sic*] ice-covered island, very little food and never washed nor had my clothes off for 10½ months. I can stand anything and, though impious by instinct, I made up my mind never to use an expletive on that expedition, and never did, nor even lost my temper."

If such letters from Joyce and Orde-Lees failed to sway Hinks, one can only imagine his reaction to a request forwarded by the India Office from an Austrian, a military officer who had served the German cause throughout the war. On September 23, 1921, Hinks responded acidly to Leonard Wakely, whose office had passed along the application: "I thank you for your letter of September 17 asking that we shall undertake to reply to Herr Lechner, and I have today sent him a formal statement that in my opinion there is no possibility of employing him on the expedition. I have hitherto put straight in the waste paper basket all applications from ex-enemies to take part in this expedition."

Hinks was adamant that the expedition be exclusively British, a conviction that undercut Farrar's desire to recruit the very best of international climbers, such as the distinguished Swiss cartographer and surveyor Marcel Kurz. The exclusion of all foreigners, including those untainted by the war, a position endorsed by the committee, raised a fundamental challenge, which Tom Longstaff identified in an understated note to Sydney Spencer, editor of the *Alpine Journal*: "Owing to the War the supply of young climbers is less than formerly."

That the pool of fit and serious players was not large may account for the deeply flawed selection of an irascible Scot, Harold Raeburn, to lead the climbing party. On paper it seemed a reasonable choice. A keen birder who had grown up scaling the sea cliffs of Scotland, Raeburn was an acclaimed climber whose book *Mountaineering Art* had only just been published to exalted reviews. Climbing without guides and often solo, he had pioneered routes up Ben Nevis, established a strong record in the Alps and the Himalaya, and made no fewer than nine first ascents in the Caucasus. But at fifty-six he was, as Mallory would describe him, a "crabbed and crusty old man," well past his prime. A serious fall on a Scottish face had robbed him of courage and nerve. He suffered constant abdominal pain, most likely from an undiagnosed gastric or duodenal ulcer. His temperament was dictatorial and defensive, utterly bereft of humor, incapable of calm. In the end he would survive the first Everest expedition, but the effort would drive him mad. A broken man, certain in his delusions that he had been a murderer responsible for the fate of Kellas, Raeburn would himself fade into delirium and pass away at the age of sixty-one, in 1926.

The obvious candidate to lead the overall expedition, including the climbing party, was Charles Bruce, who had been thinking of Everest since 1893, when he and Younghusband first spoke of the mountain on the polo grounds at Chitral. The general's address to the RGS on November 8, 1920, at Aeolian Hall, in which he reviewed the history and challenges of Everest, had been widely reported in the London and national papers and later published in its entirety in the *Geographical Journal*, the official publication of the RGS, appearing in January 1921, just as the team was being assembled. As early as November 12, 1920, the newspaper the *Western Mall* reported that the general had already been formally selected to lead the assault.

Arthur Hinks, whose affection for Bruce was limited, clearly had other plans. Within days of the initial announcement, Hinks, acting on behalf of the Everest Committee, offered the leadership instead to Charles Howard-Bury. On January 21, 1921, Howard-Bury wrote from his estate in Ireland, accepting the position, even as he hinted at domestic political troubles that within months would leave one of his mother's homes in ashes, noting, "Everything is fairly quiet round here but we never know from day to day what may happen." A week later Howard-Bury wrote again and generously proposed that Bruce be given the leadership in 1922, pointing out, "It is only right and his due that he should have it when the really serious attempt is made to climb Mount Everest."

The official news of Howard-Bury's appointment went public on January 24. General Bruce, it was said, was unavailable, having recently taken up an appointment with the Glamorganshire Territorial Association. On the face of it, this seems dubious. In the summer of 1920 Bruce had formally retired from active duty with his regiment, and his new assignment was less a military transfer than a ceremonial posting typical of what awaited officers of the Indian Army upon their return to live out their last years in England. It is difficult to imagine that Bruce would not have been able to secure leave, as he indeed did in 1922, had the position been offered him. Clearly the Everest Committee believed that Howard-Bury was the better man for the job, as Hinks explained in a letter of January 22 to J. E. (John) Shuckburgh at the Foreign Office: "The Expedition will announce on Monday night that the Chief of the Expedition will be Colonel Howard-Bury who is already well known to the Govt. of India and the local Tibetans from his successful mission on our behalf last year. I think that the Secretary of State may feel confident that with him in general charge of the expedition everything will be done to make relations with the Govt. of India and the Dalai Lama as smooth and pleasant as they can possibly be."

Howard-Bury had earned the right to the job and, having established relationships with Charles Bell and other key figures in the Indian government, possessed the diplomatic skills required. Delicacy, tact, and discretion were not among General Bruce's prominent traits of character. There was also a lingering question as to whether the general was physically up to the task. In closing the November 8 meeting of the Royal Geographical Society at Aeolian Hall, Younghusband, while praising Bruce for his presentation, had also reminded the audience of Bruce's stellar record in the war: "It is known probably to most of you that in the Gallipoli campaign his presence alone was considered worth a whole Brigade." Indeed, this was the problem. After what Bruce had endured in combat, it was not clear that he would ever again walk, let alone climb the flank of Everest.

CHARLES BRUCE had been on an expedition in India, en route to Ladakh, when he first heard news of the outbreak of war in Europe. By November 1914, Bruce and his command, the 1st Battalion, 6th Gurkha Rifles, were in Egypt, detailed to protect the Suez Canal, the lifeline to India and the oil fields of Mesopotamia. Initially theirs would be a quiet war. In five months more of his men were hurt playing rugby, scaling the Pyramids, or wrestling their commander than were injured by their Turkish enemy. In the spring of 1915, however, this would change.

The specter of war without end had by then indeed begun to haunt the British. One who shuddered at the thought of generals, as he wrote, "content to fight machine gun bullets with the breasts of gallant men" was the First Lord of the Admiralty, Winston Churchill. As a member of Parliament Churchill refused to gloss over the reality of the trenches: "In the house I say to myself every day, what is going on while we sit here, while we go away to dinner or home to bed? Nearly 1,000 men—Englishmen, Britishers, men of our race—are knocked into bundles of bloody rags every twenty-four hours, and carried away to hasty graves or to field ambulances." Resisting the notion that the war had to be won in France, he conceived a strategic alternative, a naval assault on the weakest link in the enemy alliance, a bold move on the Dardanelles that would capture Constantinople, knock Turkey out of the war, and bring relief to the Russians by opening a supply line through the Bosporus, from the Mediterranean to the Black Sea.

It was a dangerous plan. To the west of the Dardanelles lay the arid slopes of the Gallipoli Peninsula. To the east shone the mountains of Anatolia. The strait, which separates Europe from Asia, runs forty-one miles from the Aegean to the Sea of Marmara and at one point narrows to a mere mile in width. Turkish batteries lined both shores, and the passage was sown with mines.

On March 18, 1915, an Allied force of ten battleships, accompanied by a flotilla of minesweepers and cruisers, sailed into a maelstrom. Within hours three British battleships had been destroyed and a fourth severely damaged, with a loss of 700 men. The French battleship *Bouvet* exploded and sank in three minutes. Rather than expose the fleet to further losses, the British elected to silence the Turkish guns by storming the Gallipoli Peninsula from the west, by sea, in the most ambitious amphibious assault yet attempted in the war.

From the start things went wrong. The organization of men and matériel in England was so ill conceived that the entire force had to disembark in Egypt just to reorganize equipment and supplies. Every dockworker in Alexandria and Port Said knew the timetable to the day, while Turkish and German agents in Cairo reported every activity to Berlin. The British commander, Sir Ian Hamilton, planned his campaign equipped with only two tourist guidebooks, an out-of-date map, and a 1905 textbook on the Turkish army. Professing disdain for the fighting abilities of the Turks, he anticipated light resistance and expected to capture the lower half of the peninsula in three days.

On April 25 the British 29th Division, supported by 30,000 troops of the Australian and New Zealand Army Corps, landed at Cape Helles, at the southern tip of the Gallipoli Peninsula. The Turks were ready. The ANZACs went ashore not on a gently ascending beach, as had been promised, but in an inlet dominated by steep cliffs and swept by Turkish machine gun fire. Assault boats filled with the dead would float in the cove for days. At a beach to the south of the ANZAC landing, 2,000 Irish troops packed onto the deck of a collier, the *River Clyde*, encountered such withering fire that men leapt in desperation into the sea, where they were slaughtered, as one Turkish officer wrote, like shoals of fish. The Irish dead lined the beach in such numbers that those British troops who followed had to walk astride the corpses to reach the shore.

Three days after the initial landings, Charles Bruce and the 1st

Battalion, 6th Gurkhas, came ashore just after midnight at Sedd el Bahr, in the lee of the wreckage of the *Clyde*, to reinforce the 29th Indian Brigade, the only reserve force in the Allied order of battle. As they made their way onto the beach, the night sky flared as the British fleet bombarded Turkish positions. A mile inland an intense artillery assault presaged a series of desperate frontal attacks by the Turks that continued day and night until May 6, when the British once again took the offensive in a futile attack that left both armies exhausted. Dominating the British left still was a bluff 300 feet high that had to be taken. Two assaults on May 8 and 9 by the Royal Munster and Royal Dublin Fusiliers ended in disaster. On the evening of May 9, Bruce and the 1st Battalion, 6th Gurkha Rifles moved into the line, with orders to renew the attack at dusk on May 12. Traversing a ravine swept by machine gun fire, they fought their way to the base of the bluff only to be repulsed with massive casualties by a Turkish counter-attack. For ten days the Gurkhas hunkered down in trenches separated from the enemy by mere yards. Then, on May 22, the Turks rushed the British line. Fierce hand-to-hand fighting left hundreds of dead, unburied and bloating in the sun. Soldiers on both sides of the line were killed upon capture. In gullies choked with dust and infused with the scent of thyme and cordite, the agonies of the wounded haunted the survivors.

On May 27 the men awoke to discover that the British fleet had abandoned Gallipoli for safer anchorages. That same morning the Gurkhas took over the extreme left of the British line. The futile, even suicidal, British attacks continued, climaxing on June 4, when an all-out assault collapsed within forty yards. On the left the Gurkhas reached the height of the bluff before being forced back by a Turk-ish counterattack, at a cost of 7 officers and 121 men. The following morning Bruce was ordered to renew the attack, this time with the 5th Gurkhas, one of his former commands, coming up in support. Bruce knew that he was leading the battalion to almost certain annihilation. "I don't think," he recalled, "I ever had a more unpleasant task given to me in the whole of my life, knowing full well the most hazardous nature of their task under these conditions and the practical certainty that I was saying goodbye to my best friends. Naturally the attack was a complete failure."

The survivors slunk back into trenches, where for the ensuing weeks they would be tormented by dysentery, plagues of flies that coated khaki twenty-five to the square inch, and a stench of death so foul that men stuffed their nostrils with flannelette and breathed through their mouths. General Hamilton ordered another attack for June 28. The objective given the Gurkhas demanded that they assault and overwhelm five lines of Turkish trenches. On July 1, safely aboard a destroyer at sea, Hamilton wrote in his diary, "Good news from the Helles continues . . . Headed by Bruce their Colonel, whom they adore, they [the Gurkhas] retook the trench and, for the first time, got into the enemy with their kukris and sliced off a number of their heads. At dawn half a battalion of Turks tried to make an attack along the top of the cliff and were entirely wiped out."

In fact, the Gurkha force itself was virtually destroyed. Every officer save the doctor was wounded or killed. Bruce lost all of his friends in the battalion. He himself was cut down with machine gun fire that nearly severed both his legs. As he later put it, "I got my little present which took me off the Peninsula and sent me to England to hospital for a year or nearly so." His medical records indicate that a bullet had entered his right leg with a three-quarter-inch hole in front of the tibia and emerged at the same level, an inch below the knee joint, while a bullet to his left leg had shattered the fibula. As he lay helpless in his bed on the hospital ship carrying him to the Isle of Wight and home, he watched through a porthole as a German submarine sank two ships in his convoy, both within a mile of his own. In England a medical board advised him to retire to a quiet life and to be especially careful never to walk strenuously uphill.

WITH BRUCE FOR THE MOMENT out and Howard-Bury and Raeburn in, Hinks turned to an old friend to fill the vital post of expedition doctor and naturalist. Alexander Frederick Richmond Wollaston, Sandy to his family, was a shy yet generous man with a wry sense of humor who could, as his friend John Maynard Keynes wrote, "unlock hearts with a word and a look, and break down everyone's reserves except his own." The war led to his service at age thirty-nine as a surgeon on an armed merchant cruiser, a converted P&O luxury liner patrolling the North Sea from Scapa Flow to Norway and beyond, to the Faroes and Iceland, through winter storms where, as he recalled, the sea surged not in "waves but moving mountains," where the word "wind" could not begin to describe the "force that lives in these latitudes." After nine months he transferred to HMS *Agincourt*, the largest dreadnought battleship in the British fleet.

His own experience of battle came early in 1916, when he was ordered to join a naval landing party in German East Africa. In five months of fighting, Wollaston and his marines advanced into the interior, one small contingent in a British force of 80,000 soldiers supported by 500,000 native porters, charged with the duty of finding and engaging the enemy in a roadless track of thorn scrub and forest twice the size of Germany. In a forgotten campaign of the war, a struggle of attrition and extermination, more men would die from disease than from battle. After two years in Africa, Wollaston returned to sea and blockade duty, which carried him into 1919, until finally in October, after several harrowing voyages to Murmansk, he was demobilized.

Life in London proved intolerable. "If you know a war profiteer who wants to support geographical exploration," he wrote to a friend in early 1920, "please introduce me. I do not find myself in tune with the people of this country." Thus his delight when he received from Hinks, in January 1921, a note making vague inquiries as to his interest and availability for an Everest expedition. On January 16, he replied on the letterhead of the Savile Club:

> If your question means that in your opinion I have any fitness for the work, you pay me an exceedingly high compliment, which I value at its proper worth. The answer is of course and most emphatically in the affirmative. I should not have dreamed of submitting my name to the Committee, supposing that there must be many others better fitted in every way for the Expedition but if there is any chance of joining it, of course, I should jump at it. Rawling wanted me to join his proposed M.E. Expedition of 1914 or 1915, which he thought might be possible, but like many other plans, that came to nothing. I shall not be disappointed if you don't ask me to join this venture, but if you do I should be more proud than I can tell you.

A week later Wollaston followed up with a note from his home in Sloane Square: "Nothing would please me more than an invitation to join the expedition." On February 6 Hinks replied, formally offering him a place on the team, even as he asked Wollaston if he might be prepared to bear the weight of his own expenses. They met the next night, and Wollaston, as Hinks put it, agreed to "find his own way to Darjeeling."

Wollaston, like Howard-Bury, could readily afford to pay his own passage to India, and there was no one in England better equipped to find his way anywhere. He came from an illustrious line of scholars, painters, and scientists, a family that had placed more members in the

Royal Society than any other in the history of Britain. His father, a housemaster at Clifton College, was austere and unforgiving, a dominating disciplinarian as happy to thrash his own son as any student in his form. His one brother having wisely bolted for Canada, Sandy grew up a solitary male in a home dominated by six sisters. He found his escape in nature, on the open moors of the West Country, and in the forested expanses of Lapland, where he wandered at the age of twenty-one while on holiday from his undergraduate studies at Cambridge. Though he loathed the thought of becoming a doctor, he pursued medicine as the one profession that would allow him to travel. While still in medical school he escaped London in the winter of 1901 to join Charles Rothschild on a zoological expedition to the Sudan. Elected to the Alpine Club in 1903, the year he completed his studies, he was saved from the dreaded life of a doctor by an invitation from Rothschild to return to the Sudan for a collecting foray that would yield over six hundred species of rare birds and mammals.

With Rothschild as both patron and friend—they would agree to burn the letters between them when they each married—Wollaston embarked on a series of journeys to Ceylon, Australia, New Zealand, and, later, New Britain and the Bismarck Archipelago, along the coast of New Guinea, and through the Dutch East Indies. These travels only whetted his desire for true exploration. Back in London in 1905, he made a vain attempt to settle down and took a job as house surgeon at Addenbrooke's Hospital in Cambridge. The experiment lasted two days. Word reached him of a British Museum expedition to the Ruwenzori Mountains on the border of Uganda and the Belgian Congo that had sailed for Africa still in need of a botanist, an entomologist, and a doctor. Wollaston was all three. To catch up with the party he embarked by ship within days for Mombasa, where he boarded a train that carried him along the escarpment of the Rift Valley and the flanks of Kilimanjaro to Lake Victoria; then a steamer brought him to the colonial outpost of Entebbe. A rickshaw carried him to Kampala, and from there it was a two-week march into the forest. Merely to rendezvous with the expedition implied a journey of some ninety days.

For the next eight months he lived in the forest, a place, he recalled, of sunbeams and mysterious shadows where the sheer wonder of the flora and fauna fired a desire always to see more, beckoning him from tree to tree, as he collected everything because virtually everything was new to him and thus to science. Enchanted by the wild but drawn always to the heights, he scaled one of the highest peaks of the Ruwenzori, a snowy crag of 15,286 feet. When later he learned that the Duke of Abruzzi, with an entourage of four hundred, was also engaged in exploration in this limitless expanse, he thought nothing of walking sixty miles through the jungle to pay his respects and offer scientific advice. Remembering this kindness, the Duke would later name the summit for him, a gesture that Wollaston, as a gentleman, acknowledged but deflected, for he preferred native names and such personal recognition was to him unsettling.

When the British expedition came to an end, Wollaston and the naturalist Douglas Carruthers headed west across Africa. Following the old Arab slave route through the Congo, they walked for a month through swamps and thickets of elephant grass until reaching a gray slick of water that turned out to be a tributary of a larger river. Traveling downstream by dugout canoe, past villages decorated with human skulls where children on the shore shouted, "Meat! Meat!," Wollaston and Carruthers encountered all of the madness and evil that was the Belgian Congo: a houseboy given twenty-five lashes for breaking a cup; a young soldier driven mad by fear that leopards or cannibals lurked behind every bush; a crazed trader who dressed for dinner and was joined each night by a well-mannered chimpanzee who took his soup with a silver spoon.

The key to travel in Africa, Wollaston later maintained, was to break camp before dawn, when the grass glitters with dew, and to walk some distance behind the porters. "I shall never come to tolerate," he wrote, "the peculiar bouquet of the African." Controlling the natives, he declared, required hard work, plenty of tobacco, and the liberal use of the stick, which was much preferred by them to a cut in pay. He thought nothing of slapping a man who demanded exorbitant fees for his labor, and he once broke an umbrella over the head of a porter. "Don't laugh at the natives," he advised, "but learn their greetings and submit to any ceremony of blood-brotherhood." As for maintaining morale and decorum in the wild, all that was required for an Englishman was "a hot bath or sponge down every night, regular bowels with porridge for breakfast and a night dose of 'Livingston Rouser' and a good book." With this remarkable creed guiding their way, Wollaston and Carruthers would travel the entire length of the Congo River, becoming the first party since Henry Stanley's to complete the journey across the African continent.

His book *From the Ruwenzori to the Congo* had barely been published when Wollaston decided to join a 1909 expedition of the British Ornithologists' Union to New Guinea. The lead surveyor was none other than Cecil Rawling. The goal was to find a way to the unexplored Nassau Mountains, the backbone of the island, and to map the approaches from the mangrove swamps of the coast to the summit of snow-covered Mount Carstensz, the highest point in Oceania and the tallest island peak in the world.

It was an unwieldy expedition, in many ways doomed from the start, consisting of six naturalists, three Dutch soldiers, forty Javanese troops, sixty convicts, ten Gurkhas, and scores of East Indian porters, who mutinied, collapsed, and died with terrible regularity. With the rivers and low-lying forests in flood, it took nearly a year simply to move supplies twenty miles from the coast to a forward base from where a thrust to the interior might begin. "Never," Wollaston wrote to a botanical colleague, "was there such vile country . . . There was nothing of beauty in it, nothing of romance, nothing to stir the soul. If I don't get a foot onto that snow I shall consider it a year of my life wasted."

One researcher died and two others became so tormented with fever that they had to be evacuated. Two convicts quarreled over food and killed each other with knives. A surveyor was found dead in the forest. Another man grew so paranoid that he had to be restrained with chains. In his journal Wollaston describes a lunatic scene as the river rises yet again and begins to inundate their camp. One of the three white men left is delirious with malaria, prostrate on a bed raised above the ground on tins. Wollaston and the other survivor are seated at a table eating their dinner as the water reaches the level of their knees. To wash their dishes between a main course of biscuits and sardines and a dessert of the same biscuits with marmalade, they merely dip their plates beneath their chairs into the flowing water of the river and continue their conversation.

Just as the expedition faced complete collapse, two natives appeared from the forest, naked save for penis sheaths, fifteen-inch gourds held at the waist by a string. Led by these strange men, Wollaston made one final effort, a forced march high into the cloud forest and beyond the tree line to open slopes where, for the first time in a year, they could see the horizon. The forest slipped away to the sea, which was only forty miles from where they stood. Above them beckoned the snow and ice of Mount Carstensz, but in their exhaustion after fifteen months in the jungle, they were incapable of reaching the summit spur.

Incredibly, within a year Wollaston would return to New Guinea to have another go at Carstensz. He would stop first in Borneo to recruit seventy Dyak headhunters, men of the forest he could trust. It made for an enormous party, 220 men altogether, with seventeen tons of rice, a ton of dried pork, half a ton of dried fish, along with tents, blankets, cots, rifles, trade goods, and equipment. In four months they managed to penetrate as far as a hundred miles, a distance that took Wollaston close to the snows, but once again death and disease and foul weather forced him back, though he did make it to within an hour of the summit ridge.

In a desperate retreat, Wollaston, in a malarial fever, glimpsed an apparition that would haunt him for the rest of his life. In the mist and rain, he saw another European moving ahead in the jungle, as if leading him to the sea. Though the pace was impossibly fast, the stranger was always there. When Wollaston reached the coast he made inquiries, only to learn that no other white man was in the region. Years later, while having a suit fitted in London, he would glance toward the mirror and see this same figure, a spirit of his imagination, a guardian angel in the form of an iconic explorer and guide. In 1912 Wollaston published *Pygmies and Papuans*, his second book. Two years later, as he was about to return to New Guinea for a third attempt on Carstensz, word reached him at his London club that Britain had declared war on Germany. He headed immediately to the Admiralty to volunteer as a medical surgeon.

EVEN AS HINKS engaged Wollaston, he was editing for publication in the *Geographical Journal* a note on the oxygen problem on Everest written by the one man whose inclusion in the party was taken by everyone as a given, a climber who in fact ought never to have been considered and who, because of this oversight, would be the first to die in Tibet. After some eight expeditions to the Himalaya, Dr. Alexander Kellas had more experience above 19,000 feet and knew more about the approaches to Everest than any living explorer. He had identified the Sherpas as the best native porters. He had considered and rejected as impractical the use of aerial support. His wartime experiments had left him with more knowledge about the physiological effects of altitude and oxygen deprivation than any other scientist, information he had shared frequently with Wollaston in an active correspondence that continued throughout the war, even as Wollaston served in Africa and the North Sea.

In June 1920 Kellas had gone to Darjeeling and with Henry Morshead of the Survey of India initiated a series of scientific experiments designed to test the structural integrity of oxygen cylinders and the practicality of carrying compressed gas to elevation. Reaching as high as 23,600 on Kamet, he concluded that the weight of the apparatus, an obvious detriment, more than offset any advantage provided by the supplemental oxygen. He also determined that the Primus stoves intended for use on Everest were woefully inadequate, difficult if not impossible to use above 20,000 feet. All of this vital information and more he conveyed to Hinks in a report, three weeks in the writing, which he dispatched on January 12, 1921, a day after the launch of the Everest expedition had made headlines in the London papers. A letter from Hinks to Kellas inviting him to join the climbing party must have crossed this document in the mail, for on January 26, from India, Kellas wrote to Norman Collie at the Alpine Club acknowledging that he had been selected for the mountain. On the same day, Kellas sent a cautionary note to Hinks advising him to recruit only British climbers, saying, "The expedition would be to some extent spoiled if any foreign guides were employed. Their use would be a reproach to all concerned, and would seem that we had not learned the technique of the game."

Such sentiments were bound to delight Hinks, who remained, like many others, blinded by Kellas's achievements in the laboratory and field, and oblivious to the fact that at fifty-three Kellas was simply too old for Everest. It was a myopia clearly shared by Kellas himself. In a letter written some weeks later, on April 9, after Howard-Bury, Mallory, and other members of the expedition had sailed from England for India, Kellas in all seriousness shared his hopes that another man long past his prime, Norman Collie, aged sixty-two, would indeed join the expedition.

Not all members of the Everest team were so incautious. On January 27 Howard-Bury wrote to Younghusband and promised to give Harold Raeburn, as climbing leader, a completely free hand on the mountain, a deferential gesture that belied the serious doubts he had about Raeburn's health and fitness. Wollaston was forty-six, Raeburn ten years older. At thirty-seven, Howard-Bury appeared young, though given the task at hand, he was not. For political and logistical reasons the climbing party was limited to four, which made it absolutely essential, Howard-Bury insisted, that the final two slots be filled by young, supremely fit, and seriously accomplished mountaineers.

In all of Britain two men stood out. One, of course, was George Mallory, the finest rock climber of his generation to have survived the war. The second climber proved more problematic and controversial. If George Mallory represented the British ideal, scion of the public schools, graduate of Cambridge, a perfect portrait of Uranian beauty and masculinity, George Finch was a child of the sun-burnt rocks of the Australian outback, the product of a family that defied orthodoxy and gave the lie to illusions of Victorian perfection, the kind of man the empire had been content to send to the slaughter, yet reluctant to acknowledge as one of its own. He was, to be sure, a complex personality. But on ice and snow he had no equal, and this is what counted for Percy Farrar, who had singled him out for Everest as early as March 1919.

George Ingle Finch was born in New South Wales in August 1888. As a boy he grew up in the open air, riding a pony ten miles each way to school, his closest companions being his brother, Max, and the poisonous viper he kept as a pet and fed with small saucers of milk. His father, Charles, forty-five when George was born, was the fourth son of a wealthy rancher. His mother, Laura, twenty-four years younger than her husband, had been married off to cover her own father's debts.

Life on an isolated and remote cattle station did not sit well with a young woman born to privilege who always carried with her a silver box containing a single piece of Melba toast, with which to instruct hotel waiters as to the proper preparation of her breakfast bread. When George was six, his mother attended a lecture in Sydney by the theosophist leader Annie Besant and was so inspired by the talk of latent powers and universal brotherhoods that she persuaded her husband to take the family to Paris, where in 1902 they settled into a mansion overlooking the Luxembourg Gardens. When, after a year, his father had to return to Australia, his mother refused to go. His heart broken, Charles Finch would continue to support the family for the rest of his life, though never again would he see his sons or utter the name of his wife. Not that it mattered to her. She had already fallen in love with a French painter, who gave her a new child, even as she flung herself into the bohemian life of Paris. Spiritualism, the occult, legends of the cosmic east, all distilled in the writings and ravings of Madame Blavatsky, became her obsessions. The further she slipped toward the mystic, the more estranged she became from her son, who never forgave her for what she had done to his father.

George despised the metaphysical nonsense, as he saw it, that had shattered his family, and with each academic opportunity he moved closer to the precision of the rational. He studied first at the École de Médecine, in Paris, and then attended the Swiss Federal Institute of Technology, in Zurich, before completing his studies of physical chemistry in Geneva. Awarded a gold medal as the top student in his school, he sold it immediately to finance a climbing expedition. He was first drawn to the mountains while living in Zurich in 1907, and from the start he brought to the sport the discipline and inventive curiosity that allowed him, throughout his career, to thrive as a scientist. At a time, for example, when most British climbers wore the same Norfolk tweed jackets they might don for a country walk, Finch designed and produced a light windproof anorak, unprecedented in its utility. For Everest he would invent the first down coat. In an article published in 1913 he celebrated the techniques of modern climbing, and provocatively reminded members of the Alpine Club that their average age was over fifty. Finch considered the traditional reliance on local guides, said to be the only "proper" way to climb for an English gentleman, an outdated and even dangerous practice that dulled the senses of the athlete.

As strong as any guide, and quite incapable of yielding control of his fate to anyone, Finch climbed alone or with his brother Max, sometimes with the sun, sometimes at night, always planning his routes with meticulous care, taking into account conditions of snow and ice, the play of light and shadow, the shifting temperatures over the course of a long alpine day. His reputation grew with each first ascent: the north face of Castor in 1909, the southwest ridge of the Aiguille du Midi in 1911, the west ridge of the Bifertenstock in 1913. In 1909, only two years after Finch began seriously to explore the heights, the highly regarded Italian mountaineer Count Aldo Bonacossa described the young Australian as the greatest climber and the most outstanding personality in the Alps. Tall and physically powerful, with eyes the color of glacial ice and hair long and untamed, Finch had, the count recalled, "an exotic look, quite unlike other men in Switzerland."

Finch's unorthodox background did not disturb Percy Farrar, who had himself been educated in Germany and Switzerland. But it deeply unnerved Arthur Hinks and challenged even Francis Younghusband, who, in dismissing Finch, did not deign to commit his name to paper. "As a mountaineer," Younghusband wrote, "this other was all that could be desired; but he had characteristics which several members of the committee who knew him [thought] would cause friction and irritation in the party and destroy the cohesion which is vitally necessary." In truth, the only mark against Finch was the land and culture of his origins. Though he thought of himself as British, and had responded to the outbreak of war in the true spirit of empire, he would never be able to dispel a certain cloud hovering over his character.

Nevertheless, on February 16 the Everest Committee, encouraged strongly by Geoffrey Young, who had maintained an active correspondence with Finch since 1911, voted to have both George Mallory and George Finch on the 1921 expedition. Finch, who had been first interviewed on February 9, received a formal letter of offer on February 17. In the interim Hinks, in a gratuitously provocative note, asked Mallory whether he would be prepared to share a tent at 27,000 feet with such a man as Finch. Mallory knew Finch well, having met him at Pen y Pass in 1912. As editor of the *Climbers' Club Journal*, Mallory had published Finch's dramatic account of his 1911 effort on the Aiguille du Dru. In the summer of 1920 they had climbed together in the Alps, reaching the summit of the Matterhorn and the Zinal Rothorn. Mallory responded to Hinks that he did not care who he slept with so long as they both got to the top of the mountain.

Thus, despite the concerns of Hinks, Younghusband, and especially Bruce, who profoundly disliked the rogue Australian, George Mallory and George Finch, the two finest climbers in Britain, one a master of rock, the other of ice, were scheduled to sail for India on SS *Sardinia* on April 8, 1921. They had barely seven weeks to equip themselves and plan their attack.

On March 7 every member of the team—indeed, every major player in the entire Everest saga—came together for a meeting of the Royal Geographical Society called to discuss the organization and logistics of the expedition. The first to speak was Younghusband, who uttered his familiar clarion call, invoking the names of Curzon and the late Cecil Rawling. Norman Collie focused on the scientific promise of the expedition: the expectation that fully 60 percent of the plant and animal species encountered in Tibet could be new to science. Howard-Bury spoke very simply, anticipating "a wonderful expedition, full of interest of all kinds. When we come back I hope we shall have a very interesting tale to tell." Harold Raeburn emphasized the need to find a route up a sheltered face, with sun in the morning to mitigate the perils of cold and altitude. Colonel Jack described the optical instruments to be taken, the pocket aneroids and the cameras, whereas C. F. Meade, who had reached 23,420 feet on Kamet, dwelt on the importance of sunproof flies for the Whymper tents, solid boots with coverings, and ample and desirable food for the high camps, where appetite fades. Wollaston stressed that the most interesting biological observations would be of the men themselves, their minds and bodies, but mostly their minds. "I have been told when you get above 16,000 feet the temper becomes very short," he remarked. "What it will be like when they have been to 29,000 feet remains to be seen." John Noel introduced the challenges and delights of mountain photography, the difficulty of shooting in the snow, the need for yellow filters to reduce the ultraviolet light, and a developing agent that would result chemically in a slow emergence of the image.

Of all the speakers only George Finch, the outsider, had concrete and truly important things to say. The climbers would face, he predicted, great difficulties and hazards. Comparisons to polar expeditions, drawn-out struggles of endurance lasting many months, were pointless. The approach march to Everest would be pedestrian; the ascent to 20,000 feet, assuming a route could be found, without serious dangers. It would be the last 9,000 feet, he noted, the last ten days, that would require a "concentrated effort and strain such as no other expedition has ever demanded . . . Every one of us will have to call up all he ever knew about snow conditions." Citing the experiments of Kellas, Finch reminded the audience that on the summit of Everest, temperatures of sixty degrees below zero Fahrenheit were quite likely, indeed highly probable. "That in itself may not at first be considered a serious matter but it must be borne in mind that at high altitudes the rate of evaporation of moisture and the loss of heat from the human body will be far greater than at sea level," he said. "At high altitudes there are large quantities of ultraviolet light not kept back from the atmosphere. At sea level we are protected. Ultraviolet light rays impinging on the skin literally burn it, and the burning is followed by a feverish condition which hardly seems to me to be conducive to health and well-being."

It is unclear whether any of these scientific insights registered on Younghusband, who in closing the evening once again invoked British pluck. Difficult as the challenges might be, he said, "You can depend upon these younger men to ascend as far as they can."

THERE REMAINED one unexpected hurdle. Less than a fortnight before Mallory and Finch were scheduled to depart England, a plan was floated by Hinks and Wollaston to have the climbers examined by two physicians chosen by the Everest Committee, Drs. Graeme Anderson and F. E. Larkins, who shared a practice at 75 Harley Street in London. Why it was decided to assess the climbers at such a late date was never revealed, but the results were dramatic in the extreme. Anderson's medical report indicated that at five foot eleven, 159 pounds, with a chest of thirty-five to thirty-seven inches, a pulse of 68, and a blood pressure of 115, Mallory was a "fit type," or, as Larkins would add, a "man in every respect fit." Finch apparently was a different story. Larkins's report, dated March 18, indicated that his nutrition was poor, his general appearance tired, his complexion sallow, his physique fair with evidence of recent exposure to malaria. Seventeen teeth were missing. "The man," Larkins concluded, "is not at the moment fit. He has been losing weight. He is slightly anemic and his mouth is very deficient in teeth. He may improve with training." Anderson, writing the day before, had come to a similar conclusion: "sallow, nutrition poor, spare, flabby, physical condition is poor." On March 18, the same day Finch wrote to Hinks indicating that he had selected berths 45 and 46 on the SS *Sardinia* for Mallory and himself, these damning medical reports were passed along to Wollaston, who, as expedition physician, had the final say. On March 22 Wollaston conveyed the news to Hinks: "Mallory—excellent in every way, Finch described as 'not fit at present.' I am strongly of the opinion that a substitute should be found if possible." The news was released on March 24. Only days before Finch was scheduled to sail for India, he was informed that he had been dropped from the expedition because of his health.

Both Percy Farrar, the only member of the Everest Committee who knew Finch well, and Finch himself were furious and immediately suspected the hand of Hinks or Bruce. To be fair, questions about Finch's condition had been floated earlier in the spring. Knowing that neither Kellas nor Raeburn would be able to go higher than 24,000 feet, if that, Mallory had written Geoffrey Young on February 21 and expressed concern about Finch's fitness. On April 3, after Finch had been rejected, Mallory wrote once again to Young, saying, "Finch always seemed to me rather a gamble. He didn't look fit and I had no confidence in his stamina. I feel sorry for Finch. The medical exam ought to have been arranged at a much earlier stage. But he forfeits sympathy by his behavior."

Mallory's reservations aside, there can be little doubt that George Finch was treated in a cavalier manner by a medical-review process that was at the very least highly subjective. Only a year later these same Harley Street physicians, once again acting on behalf of the Everest Committee, would pass as fit for Everest General Bruce, a man of fifty-six with a diagnosed heart condition requiring medication, who walked on legs weakened by severe battle wounds, and whose own physician had advised him to stay home, lead a quiet regular life, and not travel even to Darjeeling. "Taking the medical details alone," Larkins wrote of Bruce in his report of October 27, 1921, "one would conclude that this man is unfit; but I must say that looking at it from a wider view, I consider he is very suitable for the undertaking. Various scars due to accidents and wounds of no importance." If Larkins, perhaps encouraged by a third party, was willing to compromise his medical objectivity to yield a diagnosis in favor of Bruce, he presumably would have been prepared under similar circumstances to modify his ethics in order to disqualify Finch from consideration. Or so it would seem from the results of a subsequent and more thorough examination of Finch that occurred within days of his dismissal.

Four days before his position on the expedition was officially given to another climber, Finch, still loyal to the team, traveled to Oxford to work with Professor P. J. H. Unna to improve the performance at altitude of the Primus stoves. Percy Farrar had arranged for him to enter a low-pressure chamber designed during the war to prepare pilots for high-altitude flying. Professor Georges Dreyer, who had pioneered the use of bottled oxygen for the RAF, submitted Finch to a thorough medical examination, mandatory for anyone about to enter the decompression chamber. Dreyer's report of March 28, just ten days after those of the Harley Street physicians, found Finch to be slightly underweight, but with an excellent physique and such a high degree of physical fitness that he "should be able to stand great exertion at high altitudes better than most persons." In fact, Finch's "unusual powers of resistance to the effects of high altitude" were so remarkable that Dreyer described him as the most fit of the thousand young men examined to date by the facility, noting, "We have not come across a single case where the subject possessed the resisting power to such a high degree." His proportions were normal, chest measurement ideal, lung capacity 40 percent greater than the average, blood pressure slightly below average—all signs of superb physical fitness.

On March 29 Percy Farrar wrote to Hinks: "Finch's being thrown out at this late date upsets everything. I am the more surprised, as on Friday at Oxford I saw him for about 2 hours in the vacuum chamber with the Primus stoves at 30,000 ft. with oxygen supply. He was able to talk and take all his notes and act in the most natural manner. I left him there that night, and next day [at] Professor Georges Dreyer's suggestion he spent about the same time in the vacuum chamber without oxygen at 21,000 ft, and with a load of about 35 lbs. on his back went through all sorts of evolutions. I shall have the full report later. This is the weakling whom we have flung out!"

As if further vindication were required, Finch, having been denied by the Everest Committee, spent the summer of 1921 in the Alps engaged in some truly ambitious efforts, such as the opening of the Eccles route on Mont Blanc from the Freney Glacier. In a letter of September 9, Percy Farrar took delight in reminding Hinks that "our invalid Finch took part in the biggest climb done in the Alps this summer."

But there was more to the story. To be sure, Finch had his enemies, and as a climber he struggled with the values and biases of a British class society that was anything but inclusive. The RGS and the Alpine Club were hardly meritocracies. There was a well-known account of an aspiring applicant, Arnold Lunn, later Sir Arnold Lunn, who was excluded from the Alpine Club simply because his last name happened to be that of a popular tour company, even though he had nothing to do with the enterprise. In another notorious incident, Sydney Spencer, while speaking about the Finch case with Scott Russell, Finch's son-in-law and biographer, glanced out the window at a street sweeper and mentioned casually that his Alpine Club would never admit such an individual, even if he were the best climber in the world.

Such petty prejudices notwithstanding, it is difficult to believe that Finch's medical records would have been falsified simply to keep him from the team. Such a conspiracy would have had to involve Sandy Wollaston, who by all accounts was incapable of deceit. Mallory said as much in a letter to Young: "I can't imagine him a party to that sort of thing, however much the idea of an examination may have been the hope of the party opposed to Finch." In Wollaston's letter to Hinks of March 22 he specifically noted that the two physicians, Larkins and Anderson, "knew nothing more of these two young men than their names at the time of examination." If true, as almost certainly it was, then there could have been no deliberate attempt on anyone's part to manipulate the medical results to exclude the candidate from the field. So what was going on?

The phrasing of both medical reports on Finch leaves little doubt that the examinations were superficial, even impressionistic. The two doctors use the same language: complexion sallow, nutrition poor, general appearance tired. There is no suggestion or diagnosis of any form of pathology or specific infirmity. All Larkins and Anderson were really suggesting was that at the time of their examinations, Finch had been eating poorly and looked like hell, exhausted, anemic, and sickly. As it turns out, Finch had good reason for appearing so drained on the particular day in question. Events in his personal life had taken a tangled turn that would have unnerved the strongest of men.

It all began at an officers' dance in the late spring of 1915. Finch, a second lieutenant in the Royal Field Artillery, had served at the front since the outbreak of hostilities, surviving the retreat from Mons and all the terrible battles of the first months of the war, and was temporarily stationed at Portsmouth, awaiting orders. Alicia Gladys "Betty" Fisher was a twenty-two-year-old aspiring actress, coquettish and dangerously pretty. They had little in common, save the moment, which was enough. Without notifying either of his parents, they married on June 16, 1915, with Finch registering his home address as "No Man's Land." Their plan was for Betty to wait out the war at Southsea, a suburb of Portsmouth, while he returned to the fighting.

Finch's orders finally came through in the fall of 1915, and he shipped out not for France but for Egypt, where, soon after arriving, in January 1916, he suffered a nearly lethal attack of cerebral malaria that left him severely incapacitated for several months. After partial recovery, he was attached to the Royal Army Ordnance Corps and sent to the Salonika front in Macedonia, where he spent the rest of the war experimenting with ordnance, dismantling bombs, testing detonators, and inventing explosive devices. Among his innovations was an aerial bomb that could be sent aloft in a balloon and fired electronically from the ground; on its first trial Finch brought down a German plane. His most significant contribution came in July 1916, when it was discovered that virtually all of the artillery shells in the theater, the ammunition for every sixty-pound gun, 4.5-inch and 6-inch howitzer, and most of the bombs of the Royal Flying Corps, had been compromised by the heat, which had caused the amatol to ooze, rendering the fuses inoperative. With the supply lines back to Egypt precarious, it was essential that the shells be salvaged. Finch devised a method of doing so, using paraffin wax to fill the cavity after it had been cleaned out and the compromised fuses replaced. It was incredibly dangerous work—one explosion nearly cost Finch his life—but in the end some sixty thousand shells were defused and repaired. For his contribution Finch would be mentioned in despatches and highly decorated, ultimately receiving the MBE (Member of the Order of the British Empire) at an investiture at Buckingham Palace in December 1919.

In the last days of 1916 word reached Finch that his wife was seriously ill. Securing compassionate leave, Finch arrived in London toward the end of January 1917 and was at first delighted and then horrified to learn that Betty was both perfectly healthy and the mother of a young boy, Peter, who had been born on September 28, 1916, fully ten months after he had shipped out. Though Betty had vowed to remain faithful, her fidelity had lasted scarcely a month. When Finch had left for Egypt she had been joined at Woodleigh, their home on Palmerston Road in Southsea, by a Mrs. Powys Sketchley, whose own husband was away fighting in Gallipoli. In January 1916, as Finch lay struggling for his life with cerebral malaria, Powys Sketchley's brother, a Captain Wentworth Edward Dallas "Bertie" Campbell, of the Poona Horse, returned from France on ten days' leave and, while visiting his sister, seduced Finch's wife. To his credit, Finch took pity on the infant Peter and gave him his name, registering his birth on February 5, 1917. With the remainder of his leave, Finch went to France and tracked down his rival. He later recalled, "I found him, thrashed him into unconsciousness but unfortunately did not kill him."

Narrowly avoiding a court-martial, and having exacted new promises from his wife, Finch returned to his command, reaching the Salonika front by the end of February. Regular letters from home reassured him for some three months, but as the correspondence slackened, his suspicions were again aroused and he arranged to have Betty watched. His worst fears were confirmed.

In the meantime Finch himself had met and fallen for another woman, Gladys May, a nurse with the Voluntary Aid Detachment in Salonika. On October 10, 1918, he wrote to Gladys May to tell her of his first wife; in a letter of November 16 he promised her that his past would not haunt their future, saying, "In all fairness to you, and the dream boy we are going to have, you and yours must come first. Peter will not live with us, for my mother, who knows nothing of the truth about him, is going to bring him up in the company of my younger brother, Antoine, who is fourteen."

As soon as he was able to secure leave, Finch returned to London and sought to sever his legal ties to Betty. The petition of divorce noted that she had committed adultery with William [Wentworth Edward] Dallas Campbell on April 4–12, 1918, at the Moorlands Hotel in Hindhead, and on May 2–3, 1918, at the South Western Hotel, Southampton.

Finch's divorce came through on September 29, 1920. Five weeks later, on November 6, 1920, he married Gladys May. On April 10, 1921, she gave birth to a son, Bryan Robert, a child that had been conceived in the summer of 1920, when Finch was still legally wed to his Betty. Given subsequent events, it is clear that when Finch learned that Gladys May was pregnant, he elected to do the honorable thing and marry her as soon as his divorce from Betty was finalized. By then, however, his feelings for Gladys May had faded, leaving her five months pregnant and heartbroken. On December 5, 1920, Gladys May wrote to him from the Gables, Witney, Oxon:

My dearest Geoff: I am heartbroken at the way you have treated
me and the letter you wrote after you went away last week
has crushed me and means more to me than you can possibly
realize. I entreat you to return to me and live with me as your
wife, letting all that has passed be forgotten. Whatever you have
done I am only too willing to forget if you will only come back.
Ever your loving wife, G.

In a note postmarked the following day and written from 30 Sussex
Place in London, Finch responded coldly:

My dear Gladys, I have received your letter of the 5th inst.
When I left you I also wrote explaining my reasons for going.
I regret to say that nothing you may say or do would cause me
to deviate in any way whatsoever from the course I have taken.
I am sorry for having caused you pain. I shall continue your
allowance at the rate of 100 pounds a year. Geo I Finch.

The following spring, with Gladys May due to give birth within the
month, the situation came to a head. On March 2, 1921, a judge filed a
petition accusing Finch of desertion and ordering him to return home
to his wife within fourteen days and "render to her conjugal rights."
He was also obliged to pay the costs of the legal proceedings.
    Finch was not about to yield. Two weeks later he deliberately set
out to create a situation that would lead inevitably to the dissolution
of his second marriage. Further court documents reveal that on the
nights of March 15–17 Finch was guilty of committing adultery with
an unknown party in room 477 of the Strand Hotel. Such a flagrant
act of infidelity was a standard practice at the time employed by
gentlemen seeking a quick and easy divorce. As intended, it left Gladys
May with a choice between enduring public humiliation and granting Finch his freedom; his second divorce was finalized on December 12, 1921.
    Within two weeks Finch would marry yet again, this time to the
love of his life, Agnes Isobel "Bubbles" Johnston, a kindly woman who
would bear him three children and remain by his side for the rest of
his years. He would never tell anyone, not even his beloved Bubbles,
that Peter was not his biological son. Even after Peter Finch went on
to become a famous British actor, George Finch never mentioned his
name. As for his second wife, Gladys May, her existence was expunged
from memory. In Scott Russell's comprehensive biographical essay
written as the introduction to the reissue of Finch's classic book *The*

Making of a Mountaineer, there is no mention of a second marriage, and her name does not appear.

The extent to which members of the Everest Committee were cognizant of Finch's entanglements is uncertain. Clearly Younghusband had concerns, and when it came time to assemble the team for the 1922 climbing expedition he wrote to Professor Collie. In his response on November 26, 1921, Collie offered a grudging endorsement of Finch: "Of course I know that as a climber he is as good a man as we can get. I have never heard anything about Finch's matrimonial arrangements. If I hear anything I will let you know."

Collie may have been unaware of Finch's situation, but it is difficult to believe that in the rarefied realm of London society, the scent of scandal had not reached members of the RGS and the Alpine Club. What is certain is that on March 17, 1921, the day he was examined by the Harley Street doctors Larkins and Anderson, George Finch had a number of things on his mind. Two weeks previously he had been ordered by a judge to return to the bed of a wife he disdained who was in the ninth month of pregnancy and about to give birth to his child. Out of another disastrous relationship he had inherited responsibility for a four-year-old boy who bore his name but was not of his blood. In an attempt to rid himself of his second wife, he had taken on the obligation of providing her indefinitely with an annual indemnity of £100, a not inconsiderable sum in 1921, especially for a man whose only source of income was his work as a lecturer. All of his family money, invested in stock of the Trans-Siberian Railway, had evaporated with the Russian Revolution. And, on the very day of the medical examination, he was scheduled to commit adultery at the Strand Hotel, in a contrived situation intended to free him at last to marry the woman of his dreams. It is no wonder that he had lost his appetite and that his complexion was "sallow, his general appearance tired, his condition poor."

THE LOSS OF FINCH was a stunning setback for the expedition. His own humiliation was intense and public, as his name had already been published as a member of the expedition in the February issue of the *Geographical Journal.* Percy Farrar was not only livid but also deeply concerned about the implications for the climbing team. On March 4 he had cautioned Younghusband, "If for any reason either of the men, Finch or Mallory, were to fall out, I am bound to say that I know nobody who would be capable enough to take their place, and I speak with probably an unrivalled knowledge of the capacity of every English climber, and a good many foreign climbers of the day."

Mallory, too, was angry, especially after learning that Harold Raeburn had promoted as a replacement for Finch his old friend and climbing partner William Ling, president of the Scottish Mountaineering Club and a man of forty-eight. Ling, after some consideration, turned down the offer. Other names were floated, including Howard Somervell and Noel Odell, fine climbers who would make their marks on the 1922 and 1924 expeditions. Odell, recently married, declined; Somervell was inexplicably passed over entirely. Wakefield, also considered, proved impossible to reach. As Farrar wrote in a letter to Geoffrey Young on February 25, 1921, he was "away in Canada. I am informed his wife will not let him go." In truth, in the shadow of the war Wakefield had retreated to a remote region of Canada, in the dark forests of New Brunswick, with the hope of regenerating a life. "I regret Wakefield," wrote Mallory, "in a way more than Finch."

In a letter to Young on March 24, the day Finch was publicly dropped from the team, Farrar went so far as to suggest that the mountaineering component of the 1921 expedition be eliminated in favor of a purely geographical reconnaissance. Finch, he suggested, "had as wide a knowledge of the conditions of winter and summer snow as any man, not even excluding Raeburn himself, and, if there is an insufficient knowledge in the party of such conditions, there is going to be an accident. Moreover, he is the only skier [*sic*] in the party. I am half inclined to think that unless the mountaineering party this year is really strong, it would be better to let the RGS revert to their original plan of exploration only this year and then form a really strong party next year. But next year does not always come."

George Mallory already had his doubts about the strength and cohesion of the team. On March 9, a month before his scheduled departure for India, he wrote to Young complaining that Raeburn had yet to secure high-altitude tents or make provisions for the intense cold anticipated at the heights of Everest. Raeburn, he concluded, "is quite incompetent. He even advised us not to take pith helmets, an omission which is pronounced to be mere madness by such men as Meade and Longstaff."

Mallory was more impressed by other members of the Everest endeavor. "I very much like the look of Wollaston and Howard-Bury seems like a nice gay person though I don't accept him yet without reserves. Finch and I have been getting on well enough and I'm pleased by the feeling that he is competent; his scientific knowledge will be

useful and has already borne fruit in discussing equipment. Younghusband amuses and delights me more than anything—grim old apostle
of beauty and adventure! The Everest expedition has become a sort
of religious pilgrimage in his eyes. I expect I shall end by sitting at his
feet, hearing tales of Lhasa and Chitral."

Mallory wanted Finch with him on the mountain and was quite
prepared to forfeit the expedition were his concerns not addressed. On
March 27 he wrote to Hinks: "Since receiving your letter telling me
that Finch is not coming with the expedition to Mount Everest I have
been thinking very seriously of my own position. We ought to have
another man who should be chosen not so much for his expert skill but
simply for his power of endurance. I have all along regarded the party
as barely strong enough for a venture of this kind with the enormous
demand it is certain to make on both nerve and physique. I wanted to
have Finch because we shouldn't be strong enough without him. You
will understand that I must look after myself in this matter. I'm a married man, and I can't go into it bald-headed."

In response Hinks reminded Mallory that Henry Morshead, who
had been with Kellas on Kamet, had been seconded to the expedition
from the Survey of India. He went on:

> I don't think you need feel any anxiety about your own position,
> because you will be under the orders of very experienced
> mountaineers who will take care not to call upon you for jobs
> that can't be done. The fact that you have been in close touch
> with Farrar all along has no doubt made you imbibe his view
> which is hardly that of anyone else, that the first object of
> the expedition is to get to the top of Mount Everest this year.
> Raeburn has been given full liberty to get as high as possible
> consistent with the complete reconnaissance of the mountain,
> and it is left at that. As for Morshead after all, he has been more
> than half as high again as you have been, and he did this at
> rather short notice. I suspect you will find him a hard man to
> keep up with when he has been in the field for several months
> on his survey work, which is I should imagine the best possible
> training.

This patronizing response from a man who had never climbed
higher than a desk only further enraged Mallory. In his letter to Geoffrey Young of March 9 he had acknowledged Morshead's anticipated
involvement, which he welcomed: "I'm very glad Morshead is coming.

I know two of his brothers; they are a nice family and from what I have heard I feel sure he must be a good chap." But this recognition did not change the fundamental issue. Having joined the expedition somewhat reluctantly, Mallory—Hinks's opinion notwithstanding—now found himself alone, the only climber fit for the task in terms of age, experience, and physical and mental conditioning.

His solution was to go around Hinks and draft to the team an old friend from school, Guy Bullock. On March 31 he pitched the idea to Younghusband:

> The facts about G. H. Bullock are briefly these: I knew him
> at Winchester where he was a scholar and a very good runner,
> the best long distance runner that anyone remembered in my
> time, good at all games and stolid, a tough sort of fellow who
> never lost his head and would stand any amount of knocking
> about . . . He seemed to me then to have extraordinary stamina
> and looking back I can think of no one else about whom I have
> felt in the same way that he would probably last longer than
> myself . . . I feel that he would be a valuable man in the party,
> level headed and competent all round—a man in whom one
> would feel confidence in an emergency as one of the least likely
> of men to crack.

Guy Bullock was no George Finch, but if there had to be a substitute, he was an inspired choice. Like Mallory, he was a protégé of Graham Irving, their schoolmaster at Winchester, and they had climbed together as boys, reaching the 14,293-foot summit of the Dent Blanche, for example, in the Pennine Alps in the summer of 1905. Elected to the Alpine Club at the age of twenty-two, in 1909, a year before Mallory became a member at twenty-four, Bullock was a solid climber, as organized and efficient as Mallory was chaotic and forgetful, with a generous disposition and an even temperament that would prove to be a perfect foil to Mallory's volatility on the mountain. Impervious to the cold, willing and able to sleep anywhere in virtually any conditions, he was calm in a crisis and placid in the face of conflict. His father had been a diplomat, an authority on China, and later a professor of Chinese at Oxford, and Guy had followed him into the consular service in 1913. His first assignment had been New Orleans, where he dealt mostly with British refugees of the Mexican uprisings of Zapata and Pancho Villa. Leaving Louisiana in April 1914, he was assigned to Fernando Póo, where, with the coming of war, he orchestrated operations against the German colony in the Cameroons. A posting in Marseille brought him back to Europe in November 1916, and the following year he was dispatched to Lima.

With Mallory and the others scheduled to depart within a fortnight, Younghusband wrote immediately to the Foreign Office requesting that Bullock, still stationed at the time in Lima, be allowed to join the expedition. Turned down initially on the grounds that a man as experienced as Bullock could not be spared for eight months, Younghusband took his plea directly to the foreign secretary, who happened to be Lord Curzon. With Curzon's support and intervention, Bullock was freed from his duties in Peru and even kept on half pay for the duration of his absence. On April 1 he was formally invited to join the Everest expedition. Granted leave until December 31, 1921, with no chance of renewal, Bullock would have only one go at the mountain.

THERE REMAINED one minor challenge to overcome before the expedition could with confidence sail for India: money had to be found to fund it fully. In January, Younghusband with considerable fanfare had launched a formal appeal to fellows and friends of the Royal Geographical Society to contribute to the Mount Everest Fund. "In other days," he noted, "the Society would have been able to contribute largely from its general funds. But subscriptions to the Society have fallen. We have scarcely recovered the losses of the war." General revenue to the RGS had declined significantly simply because so many fellows and members had been killed in France. The Alpine Club faced the same dilemma; hence the general appeal. The goal was to secure £10,000, the estimated cost of a two-year effort. The Alpine Club did well, raising roughly £2,000 by March 4. The RGS attracted less than half that amount, though it had a far larger membership, leading Younghusband to issue a second appeal on February 25. The response improved somewhat, especially after March 16, when it became known that the Prince of Wales had pledged £50 and his father, King George V, twice that amount.

With the subscription drive less than fully successful, the Everest Committee turned to other means of financing the expedition. Arthur Hinks, to his credit, aggressively and quite remarkably took the lead, setting aside pride and any personal reservations he might have had to cobble together support from any source, through virtually any means. As a result the expeditions, though conceived in the gentlemanly traditions of Edwardian England, became surprisingly modern in execution, underwritten ultimately not by the government of India or the Foreign Office or private societies such as the RGS but, rather, through a combination of endorsements, discounts, and exclusive marketing arrangements for media, film, lecture, and book rights that would later become the norm in the mountaineering world. Hinks, despite his prudish sensibilities, cut deals and drove bargains with mercenary zeal, securing free passage on the Darjeeling railway, reduced fares on the shipping lines, and the suspension of import duties on the vast stores of equipment being sent to India. He made arrangements for the sale of botanical and zoological specimens to the Natural History Museum and obliged the Royal Horticultural Society and the Royal Botanic Garden Edinburgh, as well as wealthy private individuals, to bid for the rights to the first seeds, whether they arrived viable or not. Lionel de Rothschild offered £100 for rhododendrons and magnolias, while an A. K. Bulley of Birkenhead subscribed a similar sum for the rights to alpine wildflowers.

To equip the expedition, Hinks sourced goods and services from no fewer than thirty-three major suppliers. He sought discounts from each one: Benjamin Edgington, makers of camp equipment, sleeping bags, and the Meade and Whymper tents; the Army and Navy Stores, which packed and shipped all food supplies; the Hudson's Bay Company, provider of woolen blankets; and W. H. Smith, the source of the expedition's letterhead and stationery. Hinks's parsimony enveloped even the members of the expedition. Aside from leaning on Wollaston and Howard-Bury to pay their own costs, he shamelessly attempted to squeeze money out of virtually every other member of the expedition. When in 1922 Tom Longstaff, who had also agreed to finance his own way, sought £10 to pay for a scientific illustration for a publication celebrating achievements on the expedition, Hinks responded with miserly indignation, "It seems a sad state of affairs when no one but the Mount Everest Committee can pay for a colour plate of a species they have been responsible for collecting."

In addition to marketing virtually every aspect of the adventure—cablegrams reporting progress of the party, magazine articles by expedition members, articles about the effort by experts in the United Kingdom, photographs, special maps, cinematographic film—Hinks ruthlessly protected the back end, ensuring that the Mount Everest Committee would control and benefit exclusively from every commercial opportunity. Lectures promised to be particularly lucrative. When first Ashley Abraham, former president of the Fell and Rock Climbing Club, and later Sir Martin Conway, then director of the

Imperial War Museum, asked to borrow a few images for their public presentations, they were categorically turned down. The Bible Society and the Regimental Journal of the 17th Lancers fared no better. The same fate awaited a publisher of children's books. The National Geographic Society was told in no uncertain terms to bid high, if only to obtain the right to publish images after they had appeared in Britain. In four years, Hinks would give away only two items: a small packet of seeds to the king, and a single photographic image of Everest to the son of the maharaja of Nepal, who intended to use it for his Christmas card.

In Hinks's view, not a penny could be spared that might otherwise support the expeditions. In 1922 a letter reached him from a Miss Jessell of the Invalid Children's Aid Association, whose patron was Her Majesty the queen, seeking permission to set up a collection box for the children outside a Christmas Day screening at the Philharmonic Hall of the Everest film of 1922. On December 28, Hinks responded: "I venture to think that in general it is inconvenient and undesirable that such collections should be made at lectures of this kind . . . I am sorry therefore to have to refuse your request."

Hinks's ruthless pursuit of the commercial both pleased and horrified members of the Everest Committee. On February 26 Norman Collie wrote to Hinks with a modest proposal, suggesting a possible sponsor. "Go to Lord Leverhurlme [sic] and say give us 1000 pounds and we will take a large cake of Sunlight Soap and a flag also with Sunlight Soap emblazoned on it and we will plant them on top of Everest. Than he will be able to say 1) Sunlight Soap beat the record. 29002 tablets sold hourly 2) Sunlight Soap towers aloft, and dominates the Kingdoms of the Earth 3) Avoid worry use Sunlight soap and for Ever-rest."

The secretary of the RGS was not amused, and neither was Collie when he learned of Hinks's boldest scheme. In connivance with John Buchan, Hinks arranged to sell the exclusive rights to the Everest story to two newspapers, the *Times* and the *Philadelphia Public Ledger*, with the photographs going to the *Graphic*. According to the deal, any dispatches or news from Tibet would be released to the media twenty-four hours after having been reviewed by the *Times*. Predictably, the other papers went ballistic, both in Britain and in India, where a vibrant press would have to wait for Everest stories to be first wired to London and then telegraphed back to Calcutta. The viceroy intervened and put pressure on Colonel Ryder, the surveyor general of India, to have the members of the survey team, which was not funded by the Everest

Committee, supply reports directly to the Indian papers. The news blackout, it was maintained, would simply compel the other papers to print wild speculations that could do a disservice to the expeditions, not to mention relations with Tibet.

Hinks, in response, professed his lifelong disdain for the media, a "rotten lot . . . all sharks and pirates." In a letter to Howard-Bury, he wrote, "No one regrets more sincerely than I do that any dealings with the Press was ever instituted at all. I was, as you remember, always against it but I am not in a position to do more than make the best of the instructions from the Committee."

Hinks was indeed ambivalent about the press. Even once the deal had been signed, he gave the media no more than absolutely necessary, denying it basic biographical material on the climbers, refusing access to the men or their families, even going as far as to slip the men out of England without allowing any interviews or photographs to appear in the press. To Mallory in India he wrote, "We were very proud of our success of getting the whole party off without interviews and photographs and cinematograph films and we are anxious to repeat this success. Please use a little cunning in making your return. It would be a great pity if we let reporters in now when we have kept them out with so much success."

But whatever their reservations, Hinks and Younghusband were not about to give up the money: £1,000 secured from the *Times* in the initial deal, with the promise of an additional £2,000 should the summit of the mountain be achieved. On April 28 Hinks was able to report to Howard-Bury that, after paying all expenses in Britain and sending £2,000 to India, there remained a reserve in a London bank of some £1,000.

The expedition was on its way. Alexander Kellas was already in India, as were the survey officers Henry Morshead and E. O. (Oliver) Wheeler, as well as the geologist Alexander Heron. Harold Raeburn had left England from Birkenhead in mid-March on SS *City of Lahore*. By April 13, after a rough and cold journey across the Mediterranean, Howard-Bury was already off Port Said on the deck of the SS *Malwa*. Three days later, Sandy Wollaston and Guy Bullock sailed from Marseille on SS *Naldera* of the P&O line, destined for Bombay. Mallory went out on his own with much of the expedition gear and equipment on April 8, one of forty-three first-class passengers on SS *Sardinia*, bound for Calcutta.

In London Percy Farrar remained pessimistic, writing Geoffrey Young on April 12, "I do not expect they are going to do much this season. The party, to my mind, is not strong enough, nor has it any but scant experience of winter conditions." To the Everest Committee he had gone further, naming names: "Mr. Mallory and Mr. Bullock, whose mountaineering experience is limited and not of recent date, do not form a party sufficiently qualified to continue with safety the reconnaissance beyond the point at which Mr. Raeburn finds himself unable to lead." Young knew little of Bullock, but had no doubts about George Mallory, who most assuredly would not restrict his own ambitions to those of Raeburn. At the same time, Young remained haunted by an image of Mallory conveyed to him by Farrar and Younghusband. When first offered a place on the expedition at a luncheon on February 9, Mallory had accepted, as Younghusband noted, "without visible emotion," as if a weight of destiny had landed on his shoulders.

On April 26 a wire arrived in London from Charles Bell in Lhasa. It included a translation by Bell of a decree promulgated by the supreme Tibetan authority, His Holiness the Thirteenth Dalai Lama, and addressed the *dzongpens* of Phari, Tinki Dzong, Kampa Dzong, and Kharta, all forts and settlements on the route through Tibet to Everest. It was this document that would serve as their passport to Everest, once the expedition crossed the Tibetan frontier. The decree stated:

> The British Government has deputed a party of Sahibs to see the Chha-mo-lung-ma mountain [as the Tibetans referred to Everest]. They will evince great friendship towards the Tibetans. The Great Minister Bell has asked us to issue an order to the effect that these Sahibs may be supplied with riding ponies, pack animals and coolies. So on the arrival of these Sahibs and servants you should supply them with all the necessary transport, the rates for which should be fixed to the mutual satisfaction according to the prevailing rates in the country. Any other assistance that the Sahibs may require either by day or by night, on the march or during halts, should be faithfully given in the best possible way, in order to maintain friendly relations between the British and Tibetan governments. Issue the necessary orders to those in your jurisdiction. Dispatched during the Iron-Bird Year, Seal of the Sha-pes.

On April 28, 1921, Sir Francis Younghusband sent a wire to Howard-Bury in Darjeeling, saying, "We shall drink to the expedition at the Anniversary Dinner (May 31) and hope to have a telegram by that time to say you have reached Tibet." A fortnight earlier Younghusband had written the expedition leader a long letter with precise instructions as to the importance of the dispatches from the mountain, noting, "You will literally have the whole world for your audience." To Colonel Ryder, surveyor general of India, Younghusband sent a more cautious note: "To make the affair successful they will have to work together like a band of brothers."

CHAPTER 5

Enter Mallory

THE MORNING OF APRIL 12, 1921, found George Mallory alone, a shadowy figure peering through the blue half-light of dawn into the rising ocean mist from the upper bow deck as SS *Sardinia* slipped through the Strait of Gibraltar and into the Mediterranean Sea. A reluctant traveler, he had had a miserable time since embarking at Birkenhead, on the Mersey, four days before. The passage down the flank of Europe to Cape St. Vincent had been cold and wet, the *Sardinia* old, slow, dank, and claustrophobic. In England he had left behind a beloved wife, Ruth, and three young children, daughters Clare and Beridge, six and four, and his youngest, John, an infant only seven months old. In a letter home, he compared his quarters on the ship unfavorably to what he had known in France for sixteen months on the Western Front. With the groaning of the ship's hull, the clanging of its engine, the light shining into his room at all hours, there was no privacy, "no sense of remoteness or isolation." The dugouts and trenches had been a subterranean existence, but at least, rats and mice aside, "one was alone, alone as almost nowhere else with the silence of the dumb earth."

He found no comfort in his fellow passengers. "At the present," he wrote to his wife after but a day at sea, "I hate the sight of them—worse, Bon Dieu, I hate them." Meals were particularly trying, with dinner invariably a low point. "I found myself between one Colonel Frazer and a very undistinguished man called Holyoake, who has not originated a single remark to either of his neighbours at table since the voyage began—but his table manners are not in any way disgusting. The Colonel is a tall gaunt Anglo-Indian of rather forbidding appearance—but the mildest of human beings and also I should say the slowest. I feel he has a really nice character but absolutely not the faintest glimmer of an idea as to how to get any interest from conversation—he smashes a leading remark with dreadful truncheon blows or stamps them in the dust. I gasp."

The captain, a "gay raconteur," offered some relief, as did a returning veteran of the Indian Army, a soldier who had been captured by the Turks at Kut and somehow survived the death march through the deserts of Mesopotamia, where Arabs in every settlement stoned the prisoners and scavenged the clothing from the wounded, stuffing sand into their mouths to stifle their cries. Mallory recoiled from such images and, in describing the man in a letter to Ruth, retreated into condescension, a protective armor he had cultivated since his first years at Cambridge. "In an ill bred and too hearty way, he is good natured," Mallory conceded, but "the trouble with him is not that he is repulsively ugly or a cannibal, as one might suppose, but simply that he is a bore."

Mallory found relief only in the open wind, in his aerie on the ship's bow, or in the release of physical activity. He paced the deck, thirteen circuits to a mile, and worked out to a set of exercises designed to render the muscles, as he wrote to Ruth, "supple and ready and elastic." As he had periodically since first conceiving the project when an artillery subaltern at the Somme, he revisited the manuscript of his "Book of Geoffrey," a compendium of moral and patriotic lessons intended to inspire a new way of teaching the young, a text that would never be published. He read Dickens's *Martin Chuzzlewit*, dabbled in Santayana, and devoured *Queen Victoria*, written by his friend and former suitor Lytton Strachey. But mostly he thought of Ruth and home.

His depression finally began to lift as he beheld at last the gray shadow of Gibraltar slowly dissolving to reveal the full dimensions of the rock, silhouetted against a blue Mediterranean sky. "It grew in the growing day from the vague delineation to a defined shape," he wrote to Ruth, "very grand, as Browning said, majestic and impressive and also in the simplest way beautiful—the most splendid imaginable headland." Reflexively he sought a climber's line to the top. "It is a very fine face; its sheerness is no fable and one could almost leap clear into the sea from the summit, a vertical distance I suppose of 700 to 800 feet."

For Mallory, the Mediterranean was another world, a place of warmth and luminosity, far removed from the "wild ocean with its ceaseless swells." With the rise in temperature, a pleasant change came over him: "I felt we had now entered the world of pleasure, the cloudless sky above and everywhere else the placid shimmering sea." To the north, banks of pink clouds rose from land that had to be Spain, and from out of the pale horizon emerged a range of "clean and radiant mountains, snow covered to the waist . . . The loveliest imaginable sight, snow mountains over the sea."

With each day came splendid new sights. To starboard lay the coast of North Africa, so close that with field glasses Mallory could distinguish individual houses in small villages and identify crops of maize and wheat planted on slopes that rose to a horizon burnished in haze and dust. Beyond the sky, hovering in the sunset, were the white summits of the Atlas Mountains, crowning the crest of Africa. On April 15, on the eve of landing in Malta, he wrote to Ruth of "the beauty of the sunlit Mediterranean and the slow peace which comes as we steam gently and I sit up in the bows alone watching the wide sea and the passing land . . . We shall have six hours in Malta and I must go and see some flowers. Farewell sweet angel. Ever so much love to you and many kisses to the children."

After Malta it was on to Egypt. As the *Sardinia* entered the Suez Canal, both sides were strewn with the detritus of battle, wreckage of Turkish attacks in the early years of the war. The desolate scene, this "great ugly conglomeration of things meant for war," provoked in Mallory "disgust and contempt." The *Sardinia*, in his imaginings, appeared to glide over the sands, and the passage through the canal was uneventful, save for a growing mood of melancholy, which Mallory initially dismissed as a symptom of the dysentery that had run through the passengers and crew, laying low even the captain. But the despair deepened, and by the time the ship steamed out of the Red Sea and approached the fueling station of Aden, Mallory had been touched by a darker intuition, a foreboding sense, as he wrote to Ruth, "of the nearness of disaster or danger." By night it was too hot to sleep, and he lay naked on his bunk with the fans whirling the languid air. By day there was only the sea and the horizon, its monotony broken by schools of porpoises and flying fish scudding over the surface of waves. On the eve of reaching Colombo, having crossed the Indian Ocean, he had once again slipped into gloom. "All this appearance of a civilized life is a hollow sham," he wrote on May 2. "The Sea is as deeply evil as it is attractive . . . There's an unquiet spirit in the ocean—even at the dead calm times when the surface really appears frozen in stillness, the heart seems to go on beating with a long slow swell and we go perpetually rolling and pitching in a lazy gentle fashion as though we might so go on to the end of time . . . so that we seem to be pursued by the shadow of its brute nature, not allowed to forget the violence of which it is capable."

Nothing if not mercurial, Mallory was back to his ebullient self on May 9 when he woke in keen anticipation of Calcutta. Already he had been touched by the wonder of India. In Madras he had spent several hours ashore and, as he wrote to Ruth from the approaches to the

Bay of Bengal, his experience in the native quarter had been "thrilling beyond description—the mere presence of so much humanity in so small a space and at every turn some inconceivable sight revealing a manner of life and a manner of people as unlike the West as a Pyramid from Westminster Abbey."

Reality reconvened in Calcutta on the morning of May 10. There was no one to meet him. A letter received on board the *Sardinia* the night before from Howard-Bury, leader of the expedition, had instructed him to make his own way up the docks to the customs house, two miles in the hot sun, to clear the several thousand pounds of gear and supplies dispatched in his care by the Everest Committee. The letter concluded, with the casual assurance of one who knew the Raj and understood its ways, that Mallory, having secured transport to Darjeeling for the vital supplies, was to then proceed, at his leisure, to the rail station, where he might catch an overnight train for the mountains. "I start for Darjeeling this evening at 5 and get there midday," Mallory wrote to Ruth from Calcutta. "I am to stay with the Governor of Bengal—very splendid and comfortable but I don't look forward to official circles and would rather have been at the Hotel Mount Everest where I imagine Bullock is. The rest are now in Darjeeling. All except Kellas, who was last heard of as having climbed a mountain on April 5th. Raeburn was evidently a shade anxious about him. It's dripping hot here now, but I greatly enjoyed a good walk before breakfast. Farewell, George."

THE MAN WHOSE DEATH on Everest would cause an entire war-stained nation to weep was born in modest circumstances on June 18, 1886, the first son of the vicar of Mobberley, a large and prosperous Cheshire parish located sixteen miles outside of the industrial center of Manchester. His father, the Reverend Herbert Leigh Mallory, was devout, respectable, and staid, the scion of a lineage that had placed family members in the village pulpit as far back as 1621. His mother, Anne Beridge Jebb, herself the daughter and granddaughter of vicars, was, by contrast, emotionally chaotic, impetuous, indecisive, and unpredictable. Hopelessly disorganized, profligate in her spending, and yet much of the time great fun, she was a loving if unhappy person, reverent in her own way, and quietly tolerant of the unorthodox. Given to bouts of hypochondria, and a compulsive eater who insisted that her servants lay out each day a full complement of meals—breakfast, elevenses, lunch, midafternoon snack, high tea, dinner, and supper—

she was a conflicted woman and would, in the spring of 1904, suffer a nervous breakdown. Her husband's response to her quiet desperation was to feign deafness, even as he summoned the servants to every meal so that they might listen as he read aloud from the Bible.

Elements of his mother's character shadowed Mallory throughout his life. He flirted with the unorthodox and, like her, was emotionally volatile, constantly concerned about money, and so absentminded that he would drive his colleagues on Everest to distraction. But there is little to suggest that her unhappiness registered on him as a child. He was a beautiful if mischievous boy, doted on by his two sisters, Avie and Mary, lionized by his younger brother, Trafford, and already given to adventure by the time he could walk. Dispatched at the age of seven to his room for misbehaving at tea, he soon appeared, catlike, on the roof of the church, having scaled the downspouts of the house and scrambled up the sheer rock wall of the ancient bell tower. His younger sister, Avie, described him as an inspiration: "He had a knack of making things exciting and rather dangerous. He climbed everything that it was at all possible to climb. I learnt very early that it was fatal to tell him that a tree was impossible for him to get up. 'Impossible' was a word that acted as a challenge for him. When he once told me that it would be quite easy to lie between the railway lines and let the train go over him, I kept very quiet, as if I thought it would be quite an ordinary thing to do; otherwise, I was afraid he would do it."

At thirteen, George won a mathematics scholarship to Winchester. Arriving in September 1900, he was assigned, along with the brightest academic prospects, to College House, where he slept that first year high above the quadrangle in a fourth-floor dormitory shared with ten other boys, all children of the British elite. Mallory loved everything about Winchester: the games at which he excelled, the spirit of ardent patriotism, the value placed on honor, loyalty, sportsmanship, and duty, the prayers and hymns, and the rousing renditions of the national anthem that summoned the boys to ever higher imperial challenges.

His was a generation nursed on empire, born at a time when British suzerainty over the entire world was simply the way of things. A year before Mallory's birth, General Gordon had been martyred at Khartoum. At nine, he was able to read, in the *Boy's Own Paper*, of Kitchener's revenge, and see photographs in the newspapers of the Mahdi's bloodied head, skewered on a pike. He and his peers grew up to tales of imperial adventure, with dashing heroes who, through English pluck and courage alone, overwhelmed far superior forces of savagery and wickedness. From the Klondike to the Guianas, from Sarawak to the

Zambezi, from Hong Kong to Calcutta, the map of the world was red. To be British was to ride a wave of destiny, and to do so with moral rectitude. "We happen to be the best people in the world," Cecil Rhodes famously said, "and the more of the world we inhabit, the better it is for humanity."

The British public schools, some with ancient traditions, like Eton, Harrow, and Winchester, others born of the nineteenth century, reached their apogee in the decades before the war. The schools existed to create a cadre for the empire, civil servants to man the distant outposts, officers to lead the armies, politicians to determine the fate of millions of dark-faced subjects of the crown. Education was valued, with more than half of classroom work devoted to the classics, but for the most part the atmosphere in the schools was fiercely anti-intellectual. Their real purpose was to infuse students with a certain ethos, a blind obedience to those of higher rank, a reflexive inclination to dominate inferiors, and, above all, the cultivated air of superiority so essential to the stability of the empire.

Boys from the highest levels of wealth and society entered the lower forms of schools like Winchester and were immediately stripped of their identity. Dressed in uniforms, deprived of personal possessions, billeted in open dormitories, they lived a spartan existence of cold baths, miserable food, and intense physical activity. Exposed to the caprice of older students, who were empowered as prefects to discipline on a whim, and subject to the wrath of cloistered masters who enjoyed the proper use of the cane, young boys learned to conform in a thousand ways, suppressing emotions behind a thick skin of wit and repartee. What counted most was not academic excellence but character, which was measured in grit, toughness, loyalty, stoicism, uniformity, and, most important, success on the playing fields. One could be neither too smart nor too slow. Crying was not an option. What went on behind closed doors was never mentioned.

At Winchester, Mallory fell into the orbit of an unusual teacher, a college tutor, Graham Irving, who at twenty-seven was already a member of the Alpine Club and an accomplished if unorthodox climber. Irving was the first of many mentors to draw attention to Mallory's physical beauty. "Mallory was just an attractive, natural boy," he wrote, "not a hard worker and behind rather than in front of his contemporaries in intellectual attainments, a boy thoroughly at home and happy in his milieu . . . He was tallish with long limbs, supple and not over muscled as gymnasts are apt to be. He was extremely good looking, with a gentleness about his features, and a smoothness of skin that might suggest effeminacy to a stranger; it never did to a friend." Writing Mallory's obituary in the *Alpine Journal* in 1924, Irving in remembrance would be even more effusive: "He had a strikingly beautiful face. Its shape, its delicately cut features, especially the rather large, heavily lashed, thoughtful eyes, were extraordinarily suggestive of a Botticelli Madonna, even when he had ceased being a boy."

In the summer of 1904, Irving invited George and another schoolboy, Harry Gibson, to accompany him to the Alps. In a season so wild it would result in a formal letter to the Alpine Club from Geoffrey Young, Tom Longstaff, and Douglas Freshfield, renouncing the reckless tactics, Irving, Mallory, and Gibson climbed without guides, surviving rock falls, a nearly fatal slip into a crevasse, desperate winds, and storms so fierce they were battered off the flanks of mountains. Mallory loved every moment. On his very first alpine ascent, he vomited a dozen times but kept climbing, until finally forced to turn back just below the ice summit of Vélan, even as the sun rose over Mont Blanc. Irving was astonished by Mallory's athletic ability: "It was not till you saw him at work on steep rocks or ice, the perfect balance and the completely natural grace of upward movement, that you knew his body to be the perfect servant of his mind; and that mind was, above all, a climbing mind." After a particularly dangerous and exposed traverse of Mont Blanc, Irving recalled, "from that day it was certain that he had found in snow mountains the perfect medium for the expression of his physical and spiritual being."

Their response to the reprimand from the Alpine Club was to keep climbing, and upon their return to school in the fall they formed the Ice Club, recruiting to the effort, among others, Guy Bullock. Increasingly, as Mallory entered his final year, Winchester felt like home. In the summer of 1904, while he had been away climbing in France, his father had inexplicably traded parishes with the rector of a church in Birkenhead, in the grim industrial docklands of the Mersey. A scent of scandal hovered over the move; there was talk of debts, and perhaps emotional entanglements. Whatever the provocation, the family crisis propelled George Mallory forward. At seventeen, having failed the entrance exams to Woolwich and happily forgone a career in the army, he switched his academic interests from math to history and earned a scholarship to Magdalene College. Before moving to Cambridge, he returned to the Continent in the summer of 1905, where with Irving and Bullock he climbed the Dent Blanche, a 14,293-foot peak in the Swiss Alps. The dawn of August 21 found them on the exposed and hazardous south ridge, making their way toward the summit. "Peak after peak," Mallory later recalled, "was touched with the pink glow of the first sun, which slowly spread until the whole was a flaming fire—and that against a sky with varied tints of leaden blue." They reached the top just before noon, a singular achievement for a party of schoolboys, on a mountain that had claimed the lives of mountaineers.

AWAITING MALLORY at Cambridge was a cloistered world, monastic in its ideals, a place of "books, music and beautiful young men," as the essayist Arthur Benson recalled, and yet swirling with the intellectual, political, and emotional possibilities of a new century. Benson, who would become Mallory's tutor at Magdalene and guide his studies for three years, had come to Cambridge after leaving Eton in scandalous circumstances, having taught there for twenty years. He was a complex, tormented scholar, a poet and prolific author who recorded every twist and turn of his emotional life in a diary that stretched ultimately to four million words, all of which he ordered sealed until fifty years after his death. Now largely forgotten, in his day he was one of the most respected writers in Britain.

Benson's private melancholy was rooted in a brutal past. His father, headmaster of Wellington and later archbishop of Canterbury, endorsed the liberal use of the whip. His mother, broken and abused, suffered a mental collapse. Of their six children, two would die young, none would marry, and two, including Arthur Benson himself, would live with manic depression, inherited from the father. It is perhaps no wonder that Benson turned for solace to youth, the beauty of words, and a platonic ideal of friendship reaching across time, linking mentor and student as father and son, as brothers, and sometimes, in fleeting moments of yearning, as much more. At a time when Cambridge dons were obliged to resign should they elect to marry, Benson recalled the joys of university life in a popular collection of essays, *From a College Window:* "I love the youthful spirit that flashes and brightens every corner of the old courts, as the wallflower that rises spring by spring, with its rich orange tawny hue, its wild scent, on the tops of our moldering walls. It is a gracious and beautiful life for all who love peace and reflection, strength and youth."

No one brightened Benson's firmament as intensely as George Mallory. He first saw the young man in King's College Chapel during morning service on the Sunday before the first day of Michaelmas term in the fall of 1905. Mallory was only a few weeks removed from the mountains of Switzerland. "I noticed in King's in the morning a fine looking boy, evidently a freshman, just in front of me—lo and behold the same came to call on me, and turns out to be Mallory, from Winchester, one of our new exhibitioners at Magdalene. He sat some time; and a simpler, more ingenuous, more unaffected, more genuinely interested boy, I never saw. He is to be under me, and I rejoice in the thought. He seemed full of admiration for all good things, and yet no touch of priggishness."

Through the ensuing months, as Mallory adjusted to life at Cambridge, getting over his longing for Winchester, taking delight in rowing for his college, he and Benson met frequently, both formally as Mallory prepared for various academic hurdles and informally as Benson introduced him to the works of Boswell and Trevelyan, and a life of reading, scholarship, literature, and the arts. By December 1906, when Mallory agreed to join him at Hinton Hall, a country home Benson had rented for the holidays some ten miles outside of Cambridge, the older man was smitten.

For Mallory, just twenty, the sojourn at Hinton Hall was innocent, as, indeed, were all of his subsequent visits. "It is a jolly place to stay," he wrote. "One generally arrives back in time for a late tea after which A.C.B. produces gems of literature and we both read till dinner at 8:15 . . . The joy of the place is that one can do exactly as one likes, and everything is so peaceful and quiet and comfortable."

For Benson, by contrast, every encounter unleashed emotions and desires, which he struggled to sublimate. Mallory's departure, a fortnight before Christmas, plunged him into despair. He noted in his diary, "I came back, through melting snow and saw my dear companion off . . . We were photographed at the door, but the results were somewhat grotesque. He appears impish. I like an old bear . . . I then took a lonely walk."

Through the spring of 1907 Benson's diary reveals a growing infatuation. In May, after a day together, he asked, "Why should I pretend that I do not love this young friend, and take deep pleasure in his company?" Later in the summer, when Mallory fell ill with hepatitis, a bouquet of lilies of the valley arrived at his bedside, a gift, he was told, from a gentleman who'd given no name but had left a note signed "From a Fair Unknown." At the end of June there was another overnight visit to Hinton Hall. Mallory read his poetry, which Benson considered "rather conventional in expression, but full of the joyful melancholy of youth." Benson was tempted to profess love, yet tormented at the prospect and repercussions of doing so. "There was much romantic friendship in the air—and then dipped into a darker moral region, the shadow that lies behind such friendships. That is one of the few things about which I do not speak my real mind."

Whether these hidden sentiments, recorded in a private diary, were known or sensed by Mallory is uncertain. He clearly admired Benson as a scholar and writer and felt true affection for the older man. When, in the summer of 1907, Benson collapsed into suicidal despair, a depression that would ultimately force him to retire from the Cambridge scene for many months, Mallory literally rushed to his side, still dressed in costume and makeup from the stage of a university play. Throughout that dark fall, Mallory remained Benson's most loyal friend and frequent visitor. That the relationship stayed platonic, as most certainly it did, is beside the point. Their friendship, highly important to Mallory and pivotal to his intellectual and personal growth, can be understood only within the context of a culture that allowed a certain kind of love between men to exist, affections of a resonance and character so unique to the times that contemporary reference points and labels—heterosexual, homosexual, gay, or straight—lose all relevance.

Edwardian men and women knew little of each other until plunged into intimacy by marriage. Men married late, often after thirty, and four out of five brides were virgins. Celibacy for young men was no more appealing a prospect then than it is today. Before marriage, there were but two outlets: prostitutes who earned in an hour what housekeepers made in a month, and other men. "My experiences of friendship are with my own sex," Mallory confided in a letter to Cottie Sanders, the first woman he really knew aside from his sisters and family. "To confess the truth I don't much understand women and they make me feel like a mouse."

The handful of female students at Cambridge provoked confusion, if not misogynous contempt. After a two-hour class in which women were present, John Maynard Keynes shared his irritation in a letter to the painter Duncan Grant. Both were good friends of Mallory's. "I seem to hate every movement of their minds," wrote the man who would define and personify modern economics. "The minds of the men, even when they themselves are stupid and ugly, never appear to me so repellant." Keynes, who would invent the financial mechanisms that allowed the British to pay for the war, or at least pretend to do so, was drawn only to men. At Cambridge he was known for both his promiscuity and his sexual stamina. One contemporary described him as "the iron copulating machine."

The British, it was said, kept their dogs at home and sent their young boys away to kennels. Certainly the pattern of a young man's life in Edwardian England was established at boarding school. It is not known whether Mallory, while at Winchester, was sexually intimate with other students, but the possibility was in the air. The school, according to Oscar Wilde's biographer Neil McKenna, was "a den of intense sexual activity between boys." Lord Alfred "Bosie" Douglas, Wilde's lover, who attended Winchester only six years before Mallory, claimed that at least 90 percent of his classmates had experienced sex with other boys. Those who remained celibate were the exception. "The practice of Greek love is so general," he wrote, "that it is only those who are physically unattractive that are reduced to living without love."

Winchester was not alone. Oscar Wilde was famously imprisoned for homosexual acts, but his real crime was less what he did than his decision not to deny it. As W. T. Stead wrote in reviewing the Wilde case, "If all persons guilty of Oscar Wilde's offences were to be clapped in gaol, there would be a very surprising exodus from Eton and Harrow, Rugby and Winchester, to Pentonville and Holloway [prisons] . . . Public school boys are allowed to indulge with impunity in practices which, when they leave school, would consign them to hard labour."

The very culture of the public schools made such sexual ambiguity inevitable. Young boys of ten or thirteen, raised by nannies, with little casual contact with their parents and virtually no exposure to women outside of the home, were sent away for years to be educated by male teachers and headmasters, themselves products of the same schools. Nurtured on Greek myths that celebrated the love between men and boys as the natural ideal, they were sequestered in a world dominated by adolescent prefects, boys of eighteen infused with hormones. It was no wonder, as Robert Graves wrote, that the "air was always heavy with romance."

So, indeed, was the air at Cambridge. On November 30, 1906, Mallory and Arthur Benson attended the opening performance of the Greek play *Eumenides*, by Aeschylus, at the New Theatre. With Mallory was Charles Sayle, a university librarian, late of New College Oxford. A friend of Oscar Wilde's, to whom he had sent his anonymously published book of homoerotic poems, Sayle had been forced out of Oxford after a sexual fling with an undergraduate. At the age of forty-three, he had established himself in Cambridge, at 8 Trumpington Street, an address that became the locus of an expanding menagerie of young men and modern thinkers. Also in the audience was Edward Marsh, Winston Churchill's private secretary, who in time would become enamored of both Mallory and Rupert Brooke, who happened to be onstage that night playing the Herald. Brooke had no lines. All he had to do was look stunning and place a trumpet to his mouth while the actual instrument was played in the orchestra. This was more than sufficient for his admirers. W. B. Yeats described Brooke as a golden-haired Apollo, the most handsome man in England. Upon meeting him on a visit to Cambridge in the summer of 1909, Henry James eagerly asked John Maynard Keynes whether the young man was in fact a good poet. Keynes said no. "Thank goodness," replied James. "If he looked like that and was a good poet too, I do not know what I should do."

Through Charles Sayle, Mallory was introduced to a circle of friends that took him far beyond the modest constraints of Arthur Benson. His mind was already open. After but a year at Cambridge he had turned away from any thought of following his father to the pulpit. He became agnostic, embraced Fabian socialism, and represented his college in the Cambridge University Women's Suffrage Association. Fascinated by the arts, most especially the new wave of postimpressionists—Picasso, Cézanne, and van Gogh, painters little known at the time—he grew his hair long and began to dress flamboyantly in black flannel shirts and brightly colored ties. Drawn to the theater, he joined, along with his good friend Geoffrey Keynes, brother of Maynard, the University Amateur Dramatic Club, taking a role alongside Rupert Brooke in Marlowe's *Dr. Faustus*. Geoffrey played the Evil Angel, Mallory, the Pope. Both performances were deemed to be dreadful by Brooke, who shone as Mephistopheles.

This growing network of friends had its roots in family and school. Rupert Brooke and Geoffrey Keynes had known each other at Rugby. Through Brooke, Keynes and Mallory met James Strachey, who had been with Brooke as a boy at Hillbrow School. James's cousin was the painter Duncan Grant, his older brother the critic and biographer Lytton Strachey. Through Lytton and Charles Sayle, Mallory was introduced to the Apostles, a secret society whose members included the philosopher Bertrand Russell, Churchill's man Eddie Marsh, as well as the writer E. M. Forster, who would use Mallory as the model for George Emerson, a leading character in his 1908 novel *A Room with a View*. Maynard Keynes was the secretary of the club, and thus primarily responsible for trolling the campus for potential "embryos," the two or three young men who would be admitted each year.

The Apostles, founded in 1820, was a fraternal circle, exclusive and elite, where it counted to be clever and, better yet, beautiful. There were weekly lectures by such luminaries as Henry James, Hilaire Belloc, and H. G. Wells. Each member had to be prepared at any moment to debate the entire society, on any subject. Failure to rise in readiness was grounds for expulsion. Among the Apostles, love between men was not only tolerated, it was embraced as a creed. Rupert Brooke joined in January 1908. Mallory, while a frequent guest, was never offered membership, though this did not limit his social life, which soon expanded to include the historian George Trevelyan; the Huxley brothers, Aldous and Julian; and the entire Bloomsbury set: Virginia and Vanessa Stephen; their husbands, Leonard Woolf and Clive Bell, both Apostles; the Stracheys, also members; as well as the artist and critic Roger Fry; and, of course, Duncan Grant. Mallory, as Geoffrey Keynes recalled, "came naturally into our circle."

What drew these friends together was a tumult of ideas born of the possibilities of a new century. The inspiration was a book, *Principia Ethica*, published in 1903 by G. E. Moore, a Cambridge philosopher and, predictably, a member of the Apostles. Moore challenged the very notion of moral certitude. Social mores, he argued, rules of protocol, concepts of rectitude and honor had no objective basis. They were only reflections of public and private fears. What truly mattered was the state of the individual human mind, the truth and freedom of friendship, "the pleasures of human intercourse and the enjoyment of beautiful objects." The book called on young people to live transparent lives, deliberately and consciously, acknowledging the consequences of actions and speaking always the absolute truth, openly, without hesitation. For students but a generation removed from the stultifying conventions of Victorian England, Moore's book was an inspiration. Lytton Strachey ranked it on par with the writings of Aristotle and the teachings of Christ.

Bloomsbury was simply a neighborhood in London where a number of these friends lived: Duncan Grant and Maynard Keynes in Fitzroy Square, Clive and Vanessa Bell at 46 Gordon Square. "Neo-pagans" was just a term Virginia Stephen, later Virginia Woolf, used to describe the crowd that hung around Rupert Brooke, who always invited visitors to swim nude in a pool near his home at Grantchester, just outside Cambridge. These social and artistic movements, so celebrated today, were at the time mere clusters of individuals, artists and thinkers, poets and playwrights—and, in the case of Mallory, a climber—who sought new forms of expression, lives of new freedoms. As Mallory would try to explain some years later in a letter to his father written but five days after the end of the war, "My generation grew up with a disgust for the appearances of civilization so intense that it was an ever present spiritual discomfort, a sort of malaise that made us positively unhappy. It wasn't that we simply criticized evils as we saw them and supported movements of reform; we felt such an overwhelming sense of incalculable evil that we were helplessly unhappy."

Mallory landed in their midst as an experiment in aesthetics, a beautiful object to be appreciated, observed, and desired. Opinions as to his intelligence varied, but of his looks, there was no doubt. Duncan Grant wrote to Maynard Keynes, his lover at the time, "I had heard . . . of Mallory. He looks like, is called and apparently is an Arthurian hero." Lytton Strachey, who had coupled with both Grant and Brooke, could not restrain himself:

> Mon dieu—George Mallory—When that's been written, what more need be said? My hand trembles, my heart palpitates, my whole being swoons away at the words—oh heavens! Heavens! . . . he's six foot high, with the body of an athlete by Praxiteles, and a face—of incredible—the mystery of Botticelli, the refinement and delicacy of a Chinese print, the youth and piquancy of an unimaginable English boy. I rave, but when you see him, as you must you will admit all—all! . . . I'm a convert to the divinity of virginity and spend hours every day lost in a trance of adoration, innocence, and bliss. It was a complete revelation, as you may conceive. By God! The sheer beauty of it all is what transforms me . . . For the rest, he's going to be a schoolmaster, and his intelligence is not remarkable. What's the need?

Lytton's problem was one of timing. He was too late. Maynard Keynes had already introduced George to Lytton's younger brother, James. On February 8, 1909, Maynard wrote to Duncan Grant, "James and George Mallory fell into one another's arms." Three days later, a follow-up letter from Keynes to Grant reported that Mallory had confided in Rupert Brooke that he was "uncertain whether he liked James or loved him." On February 28, Keynes reported, "James and George now stroke one another's faces in public."

James Strachey, by nature cautious, elusive, and restrained, remained coy, expressing disinterest in a manner that astonished the ever-willing Maynard Keynes. "How does James manage it?" he asked in a letter to Grant. "How could one help having real affection for him [Mallory], if he made love to one; and even if he didn't. Finally he has offered to copulate; and even that doesn't melt James's stoniness."

On March 3 Lytton sent a teasing note to his younger brother: "Please tell George Mallory he's making a great mistake. It's James' brother who's the really fascinating person."

James, not amused, responded on March 8: "I've not even copulated with George. I don't much want to. In fact nowadays I see him so much that he bores me incredibly."

Fear of boredom did not stop James from inviting Mallory to accompany him to Paris at Easter. George demurred. He was already committed to join for the first time Geoffrey Young's climbing party at Pen y Pass, in Wales.

Mallory's passion for climbing, which remained his greatest joy throughout his university years, only strengthened his connection to a Cambridge scene that embraced mountaineering as part of its ethos. Arthur Benson had nearly died falling into a crevasse in the Swiss Alps. Leslie Stephen, father of Virginia and Vanessa, had been president of the Alpine Club and written a highly regarded book on European mountaineering. Charles Sayle was a founding member of the Climbers' Club, established in 1898 to promote the new sport of rock climbing. Mallory met Young, then Britain's most prominent climber, through Sayle and Maynard Keynes at the 1909 Charles Lamb dinner, an annual highlight of the Cambridge social calendar. Young, like Benson, had been dismissed after five years from the faculty of Eton, also for indiscretions. Maynard Keynes had been his student, and they had climbed together in the Alps. Young's younger brother Hilton lived with the Stephen family. Hugh Wilson, who often climbed with Mallory and Geoffrey Keynes, and who would be killed in the war, was the brother of Steuart, who was Rupert Brooke's lover. Duncan Grant climbed with Mallory and Young in Wales. As Mallory's biographer, David Robertson, himself a climber, noted, "It would have been difficult to move in any Cambridge intellectual circle without encountering someone who climbed or had a climber's blood in him."

Geoffrey Young, like so many others, was much taken by Mallory's appearance, which he described in his diary as "six feet of deer like power concordant with the perfect oval of his face, the classic profile and long, oval violet eyes . . . [and a] gravely beautiful tenor voice." They became, as Young wrote, "fast friends at once. I invited him to Wales." Maynard Keynes, who was present at their first encounter, later gloated, "I tried to get up an affair between him and George Mallory with the greatest possible success. They'd never met before, but George Mallory asked Geoffrey Young to breakfast next morning." Two days later, Mallory introduced Young to Rupert Brooke. Young proposed George for membership in the Climbers' Club, and then offered to cover all expenses if Mallory agreed to join him for a week in Venice and a season of climbing in the Alps. Mallory accepted both invitations, joining Young in Wales at Easter and then, in the summer of 1909, traveling with him to Europe. Young was thirty-three; Mallory was just twenty-three. Though Young would struggle with his sexuality all his life, slipping away from his marriage to indulge strange passions in the underworld of Berlin, there is no suggestion that he and Mallory became lovers.

Mallory remained smitten with James Strachey, whose indecision was driving him mad. On July 7, 1909, he sent James a note: "Will you, damn you, come to lunch tomorrow?" Finally, not long before Mallory left for the Continent, Strachey succumbed. They borrowed the Cambridge rooms of a friend, Goldsworthy Lowes Dickinson, another Apostle. James Strachey recalled the awkward encounter in a letter to Rupert Brooke written from Stockholm on September 13: "Poor George has returned, he tells me, from the Alps. By the way, I never had the courage to tell you that he insisted, before we parted, on copulating. No, I didn't in the least lead him on. In fact I was very chilling. But as he seemed so very anxious, and I couldn't pretend to have all that virgin horror, I submitted. So we went through with it—in poor old Dickinson's bed. Are you dreadfully shocked? I didn't enjoy it much—I was rather bored. Nor, oddly, did he. He, I think, was shocked. At any rate he showed no desire to repeat the business. Really, you know, it's only in the most special circumstances that copulation's tolerable . . . Yours James."

Mallory buried the experience in a series of extraordinary climbs, beginning on August 4 with the first ascent of the southeast ridge of the Nesthorn, a fearsome peak rising out of the ice of the Aletsch Glacier in the Bernese Alps. "We were out twenty-one hours," he wrote to his mother, "and were altogether pleased with ourselves." In fact, as we have seen, Mallory came close to death. Confronting a massive overhang, with sheer walls of rocks falling away on both sides, he took the lead, inching his way across the face, secured by his fingertips. Paying out the rope from below was Young, who could not discern a single toehold on the approach. Mallory fought his way up to the base of the overhang, and then, with an explosive move that astonished Young, propelled his body up and over the cornice, seeking a hold above the hazard. He failed, and in an instant plummeted off the face. Young, who had had the foresight to pass the rope behind a blade of rock as a precaution, was just able to hold the belay, even as the fall stretched the rope to the breaking point. Mallory, dangling in midair, used his ice ax to pull himself back to the face. Completely unfazed, he made his way back up to Young, who, stunned by his companion's nonchalance, found a safer line around the barrier. They reached the summit just in time to witness, as Mallory wrote, the most wonderful sunset he had ever seen.

"That young man will not be alive for long" was all the Austrian climber Karl Blodig could say after but a day on rock with Young and Mallory. Blodig, who had reached the summit of over fifty 12,000-foot peaks in the Alps, misunderstood Mallory's brash confidence as a climber. As a friend and fellow climber remarked, Mallory was actually "prudent, according to his own standards; but his standards were not those of an ordinary medium good rock-climber. The fact was that difficult rocks had become to him a perfectly normal element; his prodigious reach, his great strength, and his admirable technique joined to a sort of cat-like agility, made him feel completely secure on rocks so difficult as to fill less competent climbers with a sense of hazardous enterprise." Another Pen y Pass climber, H. V. Reade, said very simply that George Mallory "couldn't fall even if he wanted to."

Mallory brought to climbing an unprecedented level of athleticism, combining the grace and strength of a gymnast, another sport at which he excelled, with a mental focus utterly modern in its intensity. Though he could be absentminded in daily life, once he was on rock, seeking a line up a face, his concentration came together like a laser. "His memory," one climbing friend remarked, "bad for a good many things, was almost perfect for this." He could find a route up glass. The one photograph that survives from their summer in the Alps, taken by Geoffrey Young during their descent of the Moine Ridge of Mont Blanc, reveals Mallory perched by his nailed boots on a narrow ledge of rock and snow, his hawklike silhouette peering into a distant knot of mountains. With one hand on the rock face, the other confidently resting on his waist, he appears oblivious to the exposure, the void at his feet. He is not taking in the view. His eyes are charting a route, perhaps up the Dent du Géant, the Grand Flambeau, or the Aiguille Noire de Peuterey, all peaks within his vista. He is, as they say, "in the zone."

Such precision of intent dissipated the moment Mallory was off the mountain. At the end of August, Cottie Sanders, a young English traveler, noticed George sitting alone in a crowded café at the Hotel Monte Rosa in Zermatt. He was reading a novel, she later recalled, "in a sort of oblivion . . . only sometimes raising a hand to push back the shock of brown hair which fell constantly over his forehead. He was picturesque and untidy, in loose grey flannels with a bright handkerchief around his neck; but the things which chiefly aroused attention were his good looks and his complexion . . . his skin was clear and fair as a girl's."

Over the next week they met often, sometimes alone, sometimes joined by Geoffrey Young. They spoke mostly about mountains and the essence of their beauty. But Cottie picked up on something more: "He made one feel at once that here, in him, was the authentic thing, the real flame and passion. His talk, in his beautiful voice, with the careful choice of words, in its quality stood out extraordinarily from the ordinary run of conversation at the Monte Rosa." Of his own achievements in the mountains, he was very modest, recounting even "his more desperate escapades" with an endearing sense of whimsy that left her completely enchanted. Before they went their separate ways, Cottie had accepted an invitation to join the climbing party at Pen y Pass in the fall.

Cottie Sanders, in time the unhappy wife of a miserable Irish aristocrat named O'Malley, and later to be known as the novelist Ann Bridge, came to understand George Mallory as few others did. They met again in London in December, and later in the mountains of Wales. At Pen y Pass Mallory introduced her to his favored routes: the Girdle Traverse on Lliwedd, Parson's Nose on Clogwyn y Person, and Tryfan's Central Buttress. Cottie, in turn, introduced him to the possibility of friendship and platonic love with a woman. She was first and foremost a climber, but she had an interest in politics, literature, and the arts as passionate as his own. She shared his ideals, and understood how they intersected in a mystical love of mountains. "His great desire," she wrote very simply, "was for the spirit of man to exercise itself as freely and fearlessly and joyously as a climber on a hill."

Though, as a woman, excluded from much of Cambridge life, she sensed in an uncanny way the bonds that brought Mallory and his friends together. Gossip and whimsical promiscuity aside, these friendships were founded on powerful ideals. "They held personal relationships as so important," she wrote,

> that they held only a few other things as being of any
> importance whatever. Conventional inessentials simply had no
> meaning for them. They were extraordinarily attached to one
> another; they stuck closer than brothers; there was, literally,
> nothing they wouldn't do for one another. They enjoyed each
> other furiously; delightedly, they examined and explored every

means of knowing people better and liking them more, from
the simplest pleasures of food and exercise taken together to
the final closeness of the common acceptance of some sorrow
or some truth . . . They brought their whole intellectual energy
to bear on their relationships; they wanted to know not only
that they loved people but how and why they loved them,
to understand the mechanism of their likings, the springs
that prompted thought and emotion; to come to terms with
themselves and with one another; to know where they were
going and why. This passion for understanding was new; it
looked cold-blooded.

Mallory, by all accounts, had indeed been "shocked" by his tryst
with James Strachey, but he saw no reason why the clumsiness of that
encounter should ruin the friendship. He had written Strachey in
August from Switzerland, and received no reply. Back in England in
the fall, he visited his family at Birkenhead and then returned to Cambridge to finish work on his biography of Boswell, the only book the
aspiring author would ever complete and publish.

Finished with university and at loose ends, Mallory decided to
return to the Continent, stopping in Paris before continuing to the
south of France, where he stayed for several months just outside Monte
Carlo as a guest of the French painter Simon Bussy and his wife, Doro-
thy, the sister of James and Lytton Strachey. He spent his time reading
French novels, slipping down the hill to swim in the sea, staying up late
over wine to discuss the paintings of Matisse and Renoir, both good
friends of his hosts'. He explored on foot the hills above Roquebrune,
though his outings were limited by an injured ankle, still very sore
three months after a serious fall at, of all places, an abandoned quarry
near his parents' home in Birkenhead. Mostly he thought about his
future and his friends, especially James Strachey, who had remained
silent.

Finally, on December 20, 1909, Mallory swallowed his pride and
unleashed a letter of peevish recriminations: "Write to you I will at
last. What do you think of me? That I'm proud? That I'm injured?
That I'm angry? That I've forgotten? It is six weeks since yesterday
since I said goodbye to you at Hampstead and I haven't sent you a
word. I who love you! Probably you know the reason for my silence as
well as I do. There has never been anything to say since the day I told
you I loved you. Am I to repeat continually the wearisome news that
I want to kiss you? It is about all I am capable of . . . You had better

forget that I was ever your lover. If you could treat me as an ordinary friend I might manage to behave like one. How pleasant it was! For you I believe as well as for me, wasn't it?"

A month later, there was still no response. Mallory was almost out of money and wrote to Maynard Keynes, requesting a loan of £10. Keynes forwarded the money. Mallory responded with a gossipy letter of thanks. His financial situation did not improve until the early summer of 1910, when he received a letter from the headmaster of Charterhouse School, G. H. Rendall, inviting him to teach history, math, French, and Latin. His starting salary for the instruction and other duties would be £270 a year, a generous sum at a time when a country doctor might live well on an annual income of £400.

THOUGH MALLORY accepted the offer and would remain at Charterhouse for a decade, he was from the start ill suited to the task. As his friend David Pye remarked, Mallory, at twenty-six, was so youthful in appearance that parents mistook him for a student and students had difficulty accepting him as a master. After his years at Cambridge, he found little to admire in a rigid pedagogy that had not changed since his time as a student at Winchester. At a point in his life when he was rushing off with Cottie Sanders to admire the "exquisite economy of line and colour" in an exhibit of Chinese paintings, or staying an extra night in London to hear Debussy's *Pelléas et Mélisande* or to be painted in the nude by Duncan Grant, he could summon little enthusiasm for a regime of arbitrary discipline, in which boys could be caned on a whim and all that really mattered occurred on the playing fields. He did his best to infuse the school with another spirit. He gave subtly crafted lectures on Botticelli, Raphael, and Michelangelo and organized a debating society that brought into the school a world of politics, ethics, and philosophy. With three of the more imaginative students he published the *Green Chartreuse*, a parody of the official student magazine, the *Carthusian*. The cover of the first issue was illustrated by Duncan Grant and featured a green monk, suggestively inebriated, quaffing from a glass.

Mallory's rooms were always open for serious discussion, whether on the shifting tides of politics and culture, the Irish crisis and the looming threat of European war, the meaning of a painting or a phrase of poetry, or the new writings of George Bernard Shaw. But his classroom, by all accounts, was complete chaos, with noise levels that left no doubt as to the identity of the teacher in charge. After all he had experienced, all he had come to believe, Mallory was simply incapable of perpetuating the traditional roles of student and master. Many students saw this as weakness, and responded with contempt. Other, more sensitive souls saw Mallory as an inspiration. The poet Robert Graves, only sixteen when they met, remembered Mallory as the finest teacher he had ever known, writing, "From the first he treated me as an equal, and I used to spend my spare time reading books in his room or going for walks with him in the country. He told me of the existence of modern authors . . . I had never heard of people like Shaw, Rupert Brooke, Wells, Masefield." Mallory introduced Graves to Duncan Grant, Lytton and James Strachey, and, later, Eddie Marsh. With Duncan they went to Pen y Pass, where Geoffrey Young anointed young Graves, telling him he had the finest natural balance of any climber he had known. This was heady praise for a young student who had spent much of his time at Charterhouse the victim of bullies.

Graves and Mallory remained friends for life. Mallory, Graves recalled,

> was wasted at Charterhouse where, in my time at least, the boys generally despised him as neither a disciplinarian nor interested in cricket or football. He tried to treat his classes in a friendly way, which puzzled and offended them, because of the school tradition of concealed warfare between boys and masters. We considered it no shame to cheat, lie, or deceive where a master was concerned, though the same treatment of a schoolfellow would have been immoral. George also antagonized the Housemasters by refusing to accept this state of war and fraternizing with the boys whenever possible. When two housemasters, who had been unfriendly to him, happened to die within a short time of each other, he joked to me, "See Robert, how mine enemies flee before my face." I always called him by his Christian name and so did three or four more of his friends in the school. This lack of dignity put him beyond the pale with most boys and all masters. Eventually the falseness of his position told on his temper; yet he always managed to find four or five boys who were, like him, out of their element, befriending and making life tolerable for them.

Mallory's biggest challenge as a schoolteacher was coming to terms with the latent hypocrisy of his own position. G. H. Rendall, the headmaster of Charterhouse, famously told a conference of his peers that

the boys of his school were "amorous but seldom erotic." He intended
to keep it that way, and it fell to the junior masters to patrol the halls
and dormitories at night. Mallory was well aware of what was going
on. He knew his own young charge Robert Graves was involved with
a boy he called Dick Tiltwood—actually G. H. Johnstone, later Baron
Derwent. Mallory himself was deeply intrigued by Raymond Roda-
kowski, one of his many students later killed in the war. And he was
still coming to terms with his feelings for James Strachey, even as he
dodged the advances of James's older brother.

The fall of 1911 brought a new headmaster to Charterhouse: Frank
Fletcher, a mountaineer and member of the Alpine Club, but also a
strict and rigid disciplinarian whom Mallory came to detest. Increasingly disillusioned by his obligations at the school, George spent more
time in London. In February 1912 he met Eddie Marsh, who later
chastised Rupert Brooke for having failed to make the introduction
sooner. "Besides the great beauty of face," Marsh wrote, "I think he
has enormous charm of mind and character."

Marsh, still private secretary to Winston Churchill, who had been
elevated to First Lord of the Admiralty, moved in the highest circles of
British society and the arts. His friends and associates included Prime
Minister Herbert Asquith, writers as divergent as Rudyard Kipling,
Henry James, and D. H. Lawrence, and poets such as W. B. Yeats, John
Masefield, Walter de la Mare, Siegfried Sassoon, and Robert Bridges,
soon to be appointed poet laureate. Fourteen years older than Mallory, Marsh had traveled on foot to the source of the Nile and had
once stood down a charging rhinoceros by intrepidly opening a pink
umbrella in its face. But he was better known as a patron of poetry, and
his offer to help edit for publication the draft of Mallory's biography of
Boswell, which Mallory had completed at the end of 1911, was happily
accepted. Over the next many months, they met infrequently in London, sometimes joined by Rupert Brooke, or at Charterhouse, where
Marsh read aloud the latest poetry to catch his fancy. In the first days
of 1914, they went together to the opening of an exhibit of paintings
by Duncan Grant, Vanessa Bell, and Roger Fry at, of all places, the
Alpine Club.

In the summer of 1912 Mallory went back to the Alps for the
sixth time, climbing once again with Geoffrey Young. Mallory, Young
later reported, climbed as never before, with "a continuous undulating movement so rapid and so powerful that one felt the rock must
either yield or disintegrate." They reached the summit of the Pointe
de Genevois, a 12,000-foot spire, and later found a new route on the

Dent Blanche, which Mallory had first climbed as a schoolboy. But in Zermatt came word that two close friends, Humphrey and Muriel Jones, had fallen to their death in a terrible accident on Mont Rouge de Peuterey. A guide had lost grip on a hold and tumbled down the face, knocking the couple off the mountain. Geoffrey Young was the one to retrieve their bodies. Their death cast a pall over the season, Mallory's last in the Alps for seven long years.

In early 1914, when he was twenty-eight, Mallory's life shifted in an instant. He had taken a role in a local garden play. Among the other players was a young woman, Ruth Turner, an angelic girl of ethereal beauty. She was, he discovered, the middle daughter of a prominent architect, Thackeray Turner, a widower who lived with his three girls at Westbrook, a fine country home built on a hill across the Wey Valley from Charterhouse. Ruth was only twenty-two, somewhat shy but transparently decent and kind. It was more than love at first sight. For Mallory it was as if a dam had burst and the impounded emotions of a young lifetime had found immediate release. He was positively giddy. The loops in his handwriting, he told her in one of his first love letters, "are all kisses and the tall strokes and the tails are all arms to embrace you. Shall I go through my letter and make them longer?" At Easter, George was invited to join the Turner family in Venice, a city unlikely to dampen the passions of first love. "Life with you is going to be very perfect," Ruth told him. He replied that they would need to create a new vocabulary of love words. On May 1 they became engaged, with the marriage set for July 29. Ruth's father offered as dowry a guaranteed income of £750 a year, as well as the promise of a new house, the Holt, valued at £1,600, which he gifted in perpetuity to Ruth. In a material sense, Mallory was set for life.

Meanwhile, he planned his honeymoon. Ruth was a good walker and he wanted to bring her to the Alps, but he was uncertain whether after their marriage night she would be up to the challenge. His mother quite approved of the idea, insisting that newly wedded women ought to be exposed to rigorous exercise. The wives of several of his fellow schoolmasters at Charterhouse, however, were equivocal. He wrote to his best man, Geoffrey Young, who replied urging caution. By then Mallory had sought the advice of a Dr. Wills, who reassured him. He responded to Young as if discussing the well-being of an exotic and unknown creature: "At present I can't see that any purely physical considerations rule out the kind of things I had in mind—though your observations naturally make me all the more anxious to take care not to overdo it and to proceed experimentally."

The honeymoon in the Alps, as it turned out, would have to wait. On June 28, 1914, in distant Sarajevo, Archduke Francis Ferdinand fell to an assassin's bullet. A month later, the day before Mallory's wedding, the Austro-Hungarian Empire declared war on Serbia. In the shadow of a growing international crisis, the wedding ceremony was subdued yet pleasant, and the bride and groom, according to a witness, "were too good to be true." Six days after the ceremony, Britain declared war on Germany. In place of the Swiss Alps, George and Ruth went to the cliffs of North Devon and tramped along the coast, a brief idyll cut short when they were detained on the suspicion of being German spies. A blanket of fear and mistrust had already fallen over the British Isles.

THE WAR CHANGED everything. In the winter of 1910 Duncan Grant, Adrian and Virginia Stephen, and several other friends had disguised themselves as Abyssinian princes and, with Adrian playing the interpreter, managed to board a dreadnought battleship. They'd demanded and received full military honors, having deceived the officers in command into believing they were an official delegation, headed by a Prince Makalin. Adrian spoke to his cloaked and bejeweled friends in Latin, reciting long passages of Virgil's *Aeneid*, which he had memorized as a boy. His princes grunted in return. The flag commander, W. W. Fisher, who happened to be Adrian's cousin, was completely fooled. He apologized for not having an Abyssinian flag on board, ordered the ship's band to play the national anthem of Zanzibar, the only vaguely proximate score at hand, and then offered an eighteen-gun salute, which the delegation declined, citing a tight diplomatic schedule. In fact, the cast of characters was on the edge of panic. It had begun to rain, threatening their makeup, and Duncan Grant's mustache had begun to peel away. The caper was off. On their return to the train station by private carriage, the entourage, still in disguise, insisted that the waiters don white gloves before serving them food. When the hoax came to light, Duncan and Adrian were asked only to apologize as gentlemen to the First Lord of the Admiralty.

By the end of October 1914, with tens of thousands of young men dead and the nation mobilized for a war beyond all wars, such a stunt would have been inconceivable. The war obliterated sensibilities, laid waste the precious conceits of this small constellation of friends who had with such confidence graced the social scenes of London and Cambridge. Within days many of Mallory's friends had signed up, his younger brother, Trafford, his former student Robert Graves, Cottie Sanders's brother Jack, the climbers Siegfried Herford and Hugh Wilson. "We have," wrote Rupert Brooke, "come into our heritage." Within a fortnight Geoffrey Young was at the front, first as a journalist and later as a medical transport officer. Geoffrey Keynes, Mallory's closest friend, was soon performing surgeries in the shimmering light of kerosene lamps in the cellars of bomb-blasted ruins. As a schoolmaster Mallory was exempt, and, though fully committed to the defeat of Germany, he remained apart, reduced to giving lectures at Charterhouse on the causes of the conflict.

The heart of Bloomsbury wanted nothing to do with the war. "I work for a government I despise for ends I think criminal," confessed Maynard Keynes in a letter to Duncan Grant. But work he did, twenty hours a day throughout the war, bringing his financial wizardry to the highest levels of government. Others clung to principle or retreated into passivity. Bertrand Russell went to prison. E. M. Forster signed on with the Red Cross in Egypt. Duncan Grant was allowed to perform alternative service and spent the war on a farm growing turnips, as did Adrian Stephen. Clive Bell wrote that he was opposed to the war, not because of the tragic loss of life but because it promised to leave the world poorer in the pleasures of life. Asked why he was not fighting for civilization, Lytton Strachey, then thirty-four, replied, "I am the civilization for which you are fighting." Appearing before a military tribunal as a conscientious objector, Strachey was asked what he would do if he saw a German soldier violating his sister. "I would try," he responded with an air of virtue, "to get between them." As the casualties mounted, such wit fell flat.

Through the dark first autumn of the war, as the British regular army was destroyed as a fighting force, Mallory often slipped away from school to visit the wounded, convalescing in a nearby hospital in Godalming, where Ruth worked as a volunteer. His only contacts with the front were the jingoistic newspapers and his correspondence with Geoffrey Young, which always rang true. "It becomes increasingly impossible to remain a comfortable schoolmaster," he wrote to Young in late November. "I read this morning the dismal tale of wet and cold, which made my fireside an intolerable reproach . . . Naturally I want to avoid the army for Ruth's sake—but can't I do some job of your sort?"

With each passing day his dilemma deepened. He feared for his wife, who in December would be pregnant with their first child, but he was haunted by the wounded. Every week brought news of the death of another friend or a former student of the school; twenty-one Charterhouse graduates alone were killed in the first three months of the war. Every afternoon, he saw boys being prepped for war as cadets of the Officer Training Corps. Each month the army required 10,000 new officers of the lower ranks simply to replace the rosters of the dead. These recruits in the first years of the war came almost exclusively from the universities and public schools; entire graduating classes went directly to France as newly commissioned second lieutenants. In 1915 Winchester sent not a single student on to Oxford. That same year Charterhouse graduated 411 upperclassmen, all of whom proceeded directly to the trenches.

The chances of emerging unscathed were slim. Indeed, in 1914, the chances of any British boy aged thirteen through twenty-four surviving the war were one in three. Schools, on average, lost five years' worth of students. The student body of Eton numbered 1,100; in the war, 1,157 Old Etonians would perish. Wellington, a school of only 500, would sacrifice 699. Uppingham would lose 447, Winchester 500, Harrow 600, Marlborough 733, and Charterhouse 686. The Public Schools Club in London lost over 800 members, forcing it to close for lack of numbers. Of the thousands of public school boys who entered the war, one in five would perish. The lucky ones served on staff positions behind the line. Of those young officers who fought in the trenches, half would die.

In the early spring of 1915, with the help of Eddie Marsh, Mallory made inquiries at the Admiralty. Fletcher would have nothing of it. Mallory, he claimed, was too valuable an asset at the school, and government policy left the decision strictly in his hands as headmaster. Other Charterhouse masters, however, he allowed to enlist. Harold Thompson signed up in January 1915 and was killed at the Somme. Harry Kemble joined the London Regiment and rose to the rank of lieutenant colonel before being killed in action in 1917. William Gabain was attached to the Intelligence Corps, serving in France until invalided back to England in November 1916. Lancelot Allen served as a chaplain at the Somme. Bernard Willet was stationed in the artillery with a siege battery. Philip Fletcher entered the Signal Corps in the first weeks of the war.

With so many colleagues gone, often replaced by old men or crippled veterans, Mallory felt increasingly isolated on a campus where with each passing week more and more of the boys sported black armbands, indicating the loss of a father, an uncle, or a brother to the war. Then, in April, came word that his good friend Jack Sanders, Cottie's brother, had been killed by gas at Ypres on the very day Rupert Brooke had died of blood poisoning on a small island in the Mediterranean.

Brooke had joined the navy, witnessed the siege of Antwerp, and then upon his return to England, while staying at Walmer Castle with Violet Asquith, daughter of the prime minister, had written "The Soldier," a sonnet that became the most famous poem of the war:

> If I should die, think only this of me:
> That there's some corner of a foreign field
> That is forever England. There shall be
> In that rich earth a richer earth concealed;
> A dust whom England bore, shaped, made aware,
> Gave, once, her flowers to love, her ways to roam,
> A body of England's, breathing English air,
> Washed by the rivers, blest by suns of home.

"The Soldier," along with four of his other sonnets, was published in *1914 and Other Poems*, a slim volume that in five years would go through twenty-eight printings. Brooke did not live to see its success. En route to Gallipoli from Egypt, his ship stopped off at the island of Skyros on Saturday, April 17, where, feverish, he wandered for several hours through olive groves scented with thyme and sage. A letter reached him from Eddie Marsh, with a clipping from the *Times*, which had printed "The Soldier." On Easter Sunday the dean of St. Paul's Cathedral had read the poem from the pulpit before a congregation of several hundred widows, parents, and orphans. A solitary young man had leapt to his feet, disrupting the reading with a harangue against the war. By Thursday morning, April 22, Brooke was comatose, his temperature rising by late afternoon to 106 degrees. The following day he was dead of sepsis, brought on by an infected mosquito bite. He was buried in a "corner of a foreign field" on the isle of Skyros.

Mallory was stunned. "It is true, I'm afraid," he wrote to Arthur Benson on April 25, "that I've been too lucky; there's something indecent, when so many friends have been enduring such horrors, in just going on with one's job, quite happy and prosperous. I hear this morning that Rupert Brooke is dead of blood poisoning. I expect my friends to be killed in action, but not that way. It seems so wanton."

Rendering the loss even more painful was the exploitation of Rupert's death by those desperate to find a hero in a war that had made a mockery of the notion. Eddie Marsh wrote the obituary for the *Times*, which was signed by Winston Churchill. Tributes and proud eulogies appeared everywhere. Brooke, who never experienced the trenches, never wrote of the war as would Siegfried Sassoon and Wilfred Owen. But he had seen enough to know that it held no mythic glory. "It's a bloody thing," he wrote on November 5, three months into the carnage. "Half the youth of Europe blown through pain to nothingness, in the incessant mechanical slaughter of these modern battles. I can only marvel at human endurance."

In May came more bad news: Mallory's brother, Trafford, initially so keen on the war, wrote home of piles of dead bodies, the overwhelming stench of the trenches, a fellow officer's skull blasted by a bullet. Within a fortnight he had been badly wounded in the leg. Fortunately, he survived. Another good friend, Harry Garrett, died in Gallipoli, shot through the head by the Turks. Under the naive impression that the life of a pilot might be safer than that of a soldier, Mallory wrote to Eddie Marsh, seeking a connection that might land him a commission in the Royal Flying Corps, but nothing came of it. That spring at Charterhouse, Mallory had twenty students in his Under VI Modern History class. All but one graduated to war, and four were killed in action. Mallory sat out the summer of 1915 at Pen y Pass, while in France the British Army readied itself for the slaughter at Loos.

In September, Ruth gave birth to a girl, Clare, even as word arrived that Mallory's friend and climbing companion Hugh Wilson had been killed at Hébuterne. Robert Graves was at Loos with the Royal Welsh Fusiliers. In eight months, he wrote, his battalion had lost its full fighting strength five times over. The best way to survive the war was to get wounded. The best wounds, he advised, came on quiet nights in the open, when the chances of a bullet hitting an arm or a leg were highest and the calm on the line implied that the casualty clearing stations would not be too busy. Night patrols between the lines were the ticket, though that could mean crawling through corpses and watching rats tussle for the possession of a severed hand or head.

In the late fall of 1915, Charterhouse's headmaster finally relented and granted Mallory leave to join up. Mallory wisely sought a commission in the Royal Garrison Artillery and after a three-month training course he was posted to an artillery unit that, he assured Ruth, would be positioned safely behind the lines. On the eve of heading to the front, he had dinner with a young officer just out of the trenches, returning home on leave for the first time in eight months. "To think what those men endure," George wrote somberly to Ruth, "life seems to mean nothing if war has a place in it."

There was, in fact, nowhere at the front that was secure. On his first night near the line, a bullet passed between him and a soldier walking three feet ahead. "We settled long ago," he later reflected, "that there's no reckoning with death."

Mallory's orders directed him to a unit of four six-inch howitzers operating north of Armentières, eight miles south of the Ypres Salient. Commanding the battery was Captain J. Lithgow, a kindly and effusive Scotsman. Mallory, a second lieutenant, shared a billet with Lieutenant D. A. Bell, who was in charge of No. 4 gun. Mallory first came under fire on the night of May 14, 1916. Ten days later a German shell destroyed the back of their cottage but spared his room. "I'm not in the least bit nervy yet," he assured Ruth on May 27. "We haven't been badly shelled. One constantly hears the long crescendo whistle and bang or the quick whiz-bang; the ear becomes unconsciously trained in almost no time to note the changes of tone and observe the approximate distance of bursts."

Two days later, in the middle of a black rain, his unit was ordered south by night to occupy a new position in Picardy near Albert, the staging ground for the Somme. "Evidently we have come to a hot part of the line," George wrote to Ruth. "Be brave dearest. I came out here to fight."

"I shall never forget the night we left Armentières en route for Vimy," recalled G. Ramsay, Captain Lithgow's batman, who was with Mallory on the march south. Teams of horses strained in their harnesses, hauling guns and caissons of shells. Trucks and lorries inched forward. Troops bent into the rain, trudging facedown along the muddy tracks.

"After a few days bombardment at Vimy," wrote Ramsay, "we made our way to the Somme where we again joined up with the other half of the battery to take up our position at Pioneer Road, near Albert . . . This position was well remembered for hard work and no play, with continuous unloading and fusing shells, gun barrels almost red hot with excessive firing, shell dumps and artillery everywhere, with 8″ and 12″ howitzers on our left, 4.5s and 18 pounders behind us, French 75s in front, all raining shells on the German positions. While we were in this position our sister battery 41 lost all officers in one night while they were in their mess at dinner. Two of our junior officers were sent as replacements and the same thing occurred the following night."

Mallory made no specific mention of the loss of these men, but in a June 16 letter to Ruth he alluded to the danger of being strafed from the air. The more immediate horror, he wrote, was the prevalence of dead bodies and the difficulty of digging in soil certain to yield corpses. He lived now in a dugout, carved into the chalk terrain. Below ground was the scent of decay and the stink of rats, above the smell of cordite and sweat. His unit, the 40th Siege Battery, was attached to the 30th Heavy Artillery Group, which, in turn, was a part of 2nd Corps

Heavy Artillery. For the assault at the Somme, the British had in place a howitzer or mortar for every seventeen yards of the German line. In seven days, beginning on June 24, they blasted the German trenches with more shells than had been fired in the entire first year of the war. Mallory and Bell and their crews worked around the clock in four-hour shifts. Every morning broke with a withering barrage that lasted eighty minutes, with guns firing along the entire front. The remainder of the day saw a continuous bombardment, with perhaps a thousand shells fired by each gun. At night half the artillery rested, as the rear of the German lines was swept by heavy machine guns, with the intent of slicing down the enemy's efforts to replenish their lines.

The Germans returned the fire, and the ground around Mallory's emplacement trembled and groaned with the concussion of shells, field batteries, and giant sixty-pounders that blew out the lamps and shook the timbers in the deepest of dugouts. On the eve of the assault on July 1, Mallory wrote Ruth a long letter, "a spasm of thought," as he called it, on the nature of religion and his hopes for the spiritual education of their daughter, noting, "The conception of God must be formed very gradually out of the child's own spiritual experiences."

Three days later, a thunderstorm broke and the weather turned cold. The battery fired night and day, the barrels of the guns glowing red in the darkness. A field gunner visited with horrific tales from the trenches. Mallory sought solace in Shakespeare, poring over a pocket edition of four plays, *Romeo and Juliet*, *Hamlet*, *Othello*, and *King Lear*. To his father he wrote of the dead and the dying, of reports of entire regiments "being cut up by machine guns." On July 11, just before the second phase of the battle began, he was sent to the trenches, where for three days he occupied an advance observation post, a "bed of rabbit wire in a wet clay hole." His task was to register artillery fire on a distant redoubt, a windmill at 8,500 yards. The landscape was torn, the remnants of trees tattered and forlorn, the trenches awash in the "rotting bodies of the enemy and manifold horrors." He witnessed for the first time flamethrowers incinerating soldiers, "liquid fire exploding with great flashes."

On July 25, he finished Henry James's novel *The Wings of the Dove* and wrote to Ruth of purity and truth, qualities he cherished in their love. But his reality was gruesome. "My nerves are quite unaffected by the horrible—not so my nose; but oh the pity of it I very often exclaim when I see the dead lying about. And anger I feel too sometimes when I see corpses quite inexcusably not buried."

On July 29, Mallory came close to breaking. He had been leading a work detail away from the trenches when the party came under artillery attack. Lagging behind him were two of his men, young soldiers burdened by a heavy load, a spool of barbed wire. As shells burst on all sides, Mallory and those with him leapt into an adjacent communication trench, where they huddled for several minutes, waiting out the storm of fire. As the last of the 5.9s exploded, he climbed out and saw the spool of wire on the road, and the two lads, facedown in the mud, bundles of blood and bone. He had been with them all day. Both were Scots from Port Glasgow, on the Clyde. Alexander Craig was nineteen, John Forrest just twenty-two. Mallory insisted that they be carried to an aid station, though it was obvious they were dead; their heads were half severed from their bodies.

His letters through the long summer of the Somme record a descent toward despair. On August 2, from the mud hole crawling with rats where he slept, he wrote, "The surroundings are indescribably desolate and dotted with little crosses . . . The fighting here is very stiff . . . It's a slow business; I'm not such a hero as to refrain from putting often enough to myself the question: How much longer?" A fortnight later, on August 15, he confessed in a letter to Ruth, "I don't object to corpses so long as they are fresh. I soon found that I could reason thus with them. Between you and me is all the difference between life and death. But this is an accepted fact that men are killed and I have no more to learn about that from you, and the difference is no greater than that because your jaw hangs and your flesh changes colour and blood oozes from your wounds. With the wounded it is different. It always distresses me to see them."

Two days later he learned from Ruth that Robert Graves had been listed among the dead in the casualty rolls of the *Times*, only to reappear, as if by a miracle, among the living. Mallory responded to the news in a manner that suggests his senses had been completely dulled by the banality of death. "I missed Robert's name in the casualty lists," he wrote to Ruth on August 18. "I look at them in the Weekly Times. He must have had a lucky escape. He is a nice creature but I'm disappointed in his poems and wish he hadn't published them."

In mid-September, back in the trenches, Mallory drifted by a soldier and paused to examine his face, as if gazing into his own past. He was initially uncertain whether the man was alive or dead, an actual soldier or a ghost. He wrote to Ruth, "He had a rare dignity; for him clearly there were things beyond his surroundings. He had beautiful visionary eyes which looked at me thoughtfully before he answered my remarks and I felt that, if I had timidly asked him 'Do you hate it all very much,' he would probably have replied with infinite reserve."

By October Mallory's horizon was a flat, desolate plain, which the autumn rains had turned to mud. There was not a single square inch of ground, he wrote, unaffected by shell fire, not a blade of grass to be seen. In the mire men drowned unnoticed. "If hereafter I say to a friend 'Go to Hell,' " he mused in a letter home, "he'll probably reply 'Well I don't much mind if I do. Haven't I perhaps been there?' "

On October 4 came the welcome news that Robert Graves had been staying with Ruth. Graves wrote to Eddie Marsh on October 29, telling him that George had not had leave in six months. In a letter home on December 9, Mallory said that he had not seen the sun but once in twenty days. "Like the life?" he reflected after his most recent spell in the trenches. "I prefer to say that I like living."

CHRISTMAS 1916 marked a turning point for Mallory. Thanks to the intervention of Eddie Marsh, his leave came through and he spent ten glorious days at home with Ruth and Clare. Returning to duty on Boxing Day, he was reassigned as an orderly officer to one of the many colonels who flocked about the headquarters, safely decamped three miles behind the front. His task was to look after the colonel's needs, which were few, for the man, as far as Mallory could tell, didn't actually do anything. He resembled, Mallory wrote, a Chinese mandarin in a Gilbert and Sullivan opera. Mallory's own batman had been a barber in civilian life, so his mornings now began with a shave in bed. After the horror of the trenches he found life as an officer's valet, pampered in turn by his own servant, to be surreal. "I feel somewhat of a stranger in a strange land," he wrote to Ruth on February 4, 1917. Three days later he learned that he had been recommended for a staff position, to serve as a liaison officer with the French command. After two months of tedium, he applied to return to his battery. By April 7, he was again at the front, in an exposed observation post, directing artillery fire in the prelude to the Battle of Arras. In six days beginning on April 9, fourteen Allied divisions supported by 2,817 guns advanced three miles, with the Canadians capturing Vimy Ridge. Casualties were a mere 40,000 dead and 128,000 wounded. The British deemed it a great victory.

The day before the attack Mallory, by good fortune, was invalided out of the line. For some months his ankle had been bothering him, the same one he had hurt eight years before while scrambling in the quarry near his parents' home at Birkenhead. The injury, never diagnosed, had in fact been serious; the bone had fractured, healed improperly, and was now literally coming apart. The only solution was surgery.

By the beginning of May he was back in London, convalescing at the Officers' Hospital at Portland Place. Mallory felt no shame in having been spared death at the front. The injury was for him deliverance. "Trafford, My dear Trafford," he wrote to his only brother, not long after his return to England, "I have come back for good, the Lord be praised."

His respite was brief. Though the ankle remained problematic well into September, he was returned to active duty in the summer and stationed at Winchester to train with a new generation of heavy artillery, guns with a range of over six miles. Happily he was free every weekend to be with his young family, Clare and his beloved Ruth, who was pregnant with their second child. Geoffrey Young wrote joyfully from Italy agreeing to be godfather. Beridge was born in the third week of September, on the same day they received the terrible news that Geoffrey, wounded earlier in the month, had lost his leg. For Mallory it was the death of a dream, as if every mountain had instantly eroded into the sea. "It's the spoiling of some flawless, perfect thing," he wrote to Lady Alice Young, Geoffrey's elderly mother. "We had promised each other days on the mountains together, if we should meet again, and I can't separate my own loss in it from his."

In October, Mallory was promoted to full lieutenant and destined for France. In Belgium the battle of Passchendaele had raged since the end of July. After three months of steady bombardment, the entire universe of the British Army was a sodden wasteland of churned mud, poisoned by gas and fouled by the litter of war, dead horses and mules, headless corpses, bits and pieces of bodies, entire gun crews blasted into the air and staked headfirst in the mud when they fell back to earth. The only way to avoid being swallowed by the quagmire was to stick to the duckboards, wooden tracks laid upon the muck. Readily targeted by the enemy, these ran threadlike among the shell holes, vital supply lines that could be used only by night. As men walked blind, clinging to lifelines strung along the planks, they could hear from the darkness the groans and wails of the wounded, the despairing shrieks as men crawled into shell holes only to be swallowed by the fathomless mud. "The monstrous disgrace of Passchendaele," wrote the playwright R. C. Sherriff, himself wounded in the battle, "was proof, if proof was needed, that the Generals had lost touch with reality."

Having escaped the fight at Arras, saved by an old climbing injury, Mallory was spared the agony of Passchendaele by a freak accident. On October 8, as he rode his motorcycle into Winchester to post a letter, his back wheel locked just as he rounded a corner on St. Giles

Hill. The bike spun out and he crashed into a gatepost, crushing his right foot and injuring his thumb as well. Released from Magdalen Hospital on October 16, though still incapacitated, he returned to the Winchester camp, where all talk was of the battle.

On November 3 all leave in the British Army was canceled and those on leave were ordered immediately back to duty. There was a crisis at the front. Senior officers in the battle line called for an end to the slaughter in Flanders. General Haig insisted on pounding on, revising his strategic and tactical goals by the day to rationalize the pointless slaughter. Mallory was resigned to dying. "For my part," he wrote to Geoffrey Young on December 5, "I don't intend, for what ever little that might be worth, to be alive at the end." Fortunately, the injury to his foot was serious enough that it was not until after Christmas that he was deemed fit for service, by which time the onset of winter had finally silenced the battle.

The New Year brought a brief moment of joy. Robert Graves, at twenty-two, was to be married to Nancy Nicholson, a beautiful artist of eighteen, with Mallory standing as best man. He was, Graves wrote to Eddie Marsh on December 29, 1917, "my oldest surviving friend." The wedding was set for January 23, 1918. Among those invited was the poet Wilfred Owen. Graves knew Owen through Siegfried Sassoon, a fellow officer in the Royal Welsh Fusiliers. The wedding, Graves later recalled, "was both wild and subdued." He was outfitted in his dress uniform, field boots, spurs, and sword. Nancy wore blue, and balked at the formality of the service. With wartime rationing there was no sugar or butter, and when George Mallory "lifted off the plaster cast of imitation icing from the cake, a sigh of disappointment rose from the guests . . . champagne was another rare commodity and the guests made a rush for the dozen bottles on the table. Nancy decided to get something out of her wedding and made off with a bottle."

Through the spring of 1918 Mallory continued to be haunted by good fortune. On March 21 the Germans launched the Spring Offensive, which began with the most intense bombardment of the war. In five hours more than three million high-explosive and gas shells fell upon the British Fifth Army. Attacking out of the fog, German storm troopers retook in days what the British had struggled six months to capture at the Somme. Within twenty-four hours 21,000 British soldiers were taken prisoner; in nine days the number captured rose to 90,000. Thirteen hundred British gun emplacements were overrun. On April 9 the Germans attacked again at Ypres, prompting General Haig to issue his fateful proclamation to the troops: "With our backs to the wall and believing in the justice of our cause each one of us must fight to the end." By the beginning of June the Germans had reached the Marne and were within striking distance of Paris, just as they had been in the summer of 1914. Desperate to turn the tide, the British raced every able-bodied man to the front. From the hospitals alone they returned 60,000 a month, soldiers whose wounds had been deemed sufficiently healed to let them be cast again into the cauldron.

Assigned inexplicably—indeed, miraculously—to yet another training course, this time a battery commanders' session at the artillery school at Lydd, Mallory remained at home through the entire crisis. There is a gap in his correspondence from late 1917 through September 1918, during which time he lived happily with Ruth and his family at Littlestone, a seaside village near Lydd on the coast of Kent. From the channel ports one could hear the distant sounds of the battle in France. During the summer of 1918, as the French counterattacked at the Aisne and the Americans, in their baptism of fire, drove the Germans from Belleau Wood, as 15,000 tons of gas fell upon the Allied line in a single assault and German casualties rose to over a million dead and wounded, George Mallory and Ruth went on a climbing holiday to Scotland. How he avoided the front for sixteen months during the climax of the war is a mystery, though one senses the hand of Eddie Marsh. By the time he finally returned to France, in late September 1918, he had been reassigned to the 515th Siege Battery, positioned between Arras and the coast, a safe distance from the front. His commanding officer was Major Gwilym Lloyd George, son of the prime minister. The British had already lost one son of a prime minister, Raymond Asquith, shot fatally through the chest at the Somme in 1916; they were not about to lose another. Mallory had his ticket out of the war.

On November 3 Major Lloyd George was summoned to Paris to be with his father. "Lucky dog!" George wrote to Ruth. "I wish my father were P.M." Five days later, on "a lovely morning, frosty and sunny," he announced his intention to "go forth somewhere today—possibly to search for Geoffrey Keynes who is about 20 miles from here." Keynes was posted at a casualty clearing station near Cambrai. On the night of November 11, the two friends shared a tent and awoke to the noise of shouting and engines whistling. As they looked out into the dark they saw the entire front erupt in the flares of thousands of Very lights, ignited in celebration of the Armistice. Mallory's brother, Trafford, appeared on November 12, and they welcomed peace with a party at the officers' club in Cambrai.

"It was a good evening," George wrote to Ruth in the morning, "altogether of the kind one would expect from the public school type of British officer. The prevalent feeling I make out, in part my own, is simply the elation that comes after a hard game or race of supreme importance won after a struggle in which everyone has expended himself to the last ounce. What a freedom it is now! I seem to be inundated by waves of elation and to be capable now of untroubled joy such as one hasn't known during these four years since the war began. I doubt if I quite realized before what a load we were carrying about with us constantly . . . I want to lose all harshness of jagged nerves, to be above all gentle. I feel we have achieved victory for that almost more than anything—to be able to cultivate gentleness."

Robert Graves did not celebrate the end of the war. He felt only despair and sadness. As the guns fell quiet in Flanders, he went out that night, "walking alone along the dyke above the marshes of Rhuulan, cursing and sobbing and thinking of the dead."

Wilfred Owen's brother Harold, serving in the navy and stationed off the African coast on the cruiser *Astraea*, saw that same day an apparition of his brother, sitting peacefully in a chair in his cabin, smiling the most gentle of smiles. On the small table was a letter written to Harold the previous April in which Wilfred had anticipated his death, saying, "I know I shall be killed. But it's the only place I can make my protest from." Harold Owen wondered if he was dreaming. He glanced down, and when he looked up the chair was again empty. Harold fell asleep, only to wake to the perfect certainty that his brother was dead. Wilfred had, in fact, been killed on November 4. Word of his death would reach his parents at Shrewsbury on November 11, 1918, the same day as Harold's vision, even as the church bells in their village tolled the news of victory and the Armistice.

WITH THE END of the war came the challenge of peace, and the immediate need to demobilize six million men and find work for them in an economy that had geared two-thirds of its industrial capacity and workforce toward the production of weapons of war.

On paper the victory had been complete. Britain emerged supreme, her cities and fields unscathed, her navy unchallenged, her armies triumphant, her enemies vanquished. In reality, the war left the nation bitterly divided, spiritually exhausted, and financially ruined. The gold reserves had been drained, and the national debt surpassed the gross national product. Inflation and unemployment soon reached levels not

seen in a century. Taxes and death duties alone provoked such economic agonies that between 1918 and 1921 a quarter of all English
land would change hands, a shift in fortunes and ownership on a scale
not experienced in Britain since the Norman Conquest.

"In the autumn of 1919, in which I write," stated Mallory's old
friend John Maynard Keynes, "we are at the dead season of our fortunes. The reaction from the exertions, the fears, the sufferings of the
past five years is at its height. Our power of feeling or caring beyond
the immediate questions of our own material well-being is temporarily eclipsed. The greatest events outside our own direct experience
and the most dreadful anticipations cannot move us . . . We have been
moved already beyond endurance, and need rest. Never in the lifetime
of men now living has the universal element in the soul of man burnt
so dimly." By 1922 there would be two million unemployed and half
a million veterans living on the streets, going door-to-door, seeking
help, begging for clothes and food.

The long hallucination of the war induced a universal torpor and
melancholy, a sense of isolation, a loss of center, a restless desire to
move—what Christopher Isherwood called the "vast freak museum
of our generation." For some, like Robert Graves, the conflict had
marked their entire adult lives, with each moment of it, as he later
recalled, having provoked an inward scream, the duty to run mad.

"We left the war," wrote Herbert Read, "as we entered it: dazed,
indifferent, incapable of any creative action. We had acquired only one
quality: exhaustion." The entire futile exercise, wrote Vera Brittain, had
amounted to "nothing but a passionate gesture of negation—the negation of all that the centuries had taught us through long eons of pain."
Having lost her fiancé, her brother, and her two best male friends,
she had "no one left to dance with. The War was over; a new age was
beginning; but the dead were the dead and would never return."

As formal negotiations in Paris stretched into 1919, the British government formed the Peace Committee to determine how properly to
commemorate the victory. The initial meeting, chaired by the foreign
secretary, Lord Curzon, proposed a four-day celebration to be held in
August 1919. Under pressure from veterans and the million or more
soldiers still awaiting demobilization, who deemed it a waste of money,
the event was scaled back to a single parade, scheduled for July 19.
Thousands of citizens descended on London to watch fifteen thousand
servicemen parade past a temporary wood-and-plaster monument
erected in Whitehall, a cenotaph dedicated to "The Glorious Dead."
Had the actual dead walked abreast down Whitehall, the parade would

have lasted four days. Had each man who died in the war been granted a single page upon which to inscribe his life, it would have yielded a library of some twenty-six thousand volumes, every book six hundred pages long.

As a schoolmaster George Mallory was one of the first to be demobilized, and by the end of January 1919 he was back at Charterhouse, recalling all the reasons he had come to despise the headmaster (though, ironically, Frank Fletcher may well have saved his life, simply by keeping him out of the conflict for the first two years of the war). He returned to a school haunted with the spirits of vanquished youths, boys he had taught. The school's arcane rituals and rules, meanwhile, chafed; he found them more intolerable than ever. A compromising letter had come to light, and he faced sanctions because of his friendship with Robert Graves, who evidently as a schoolboy had been intimate with another schoolboy, who was now, at any rate, dead.

Mallory tried to reinvent himself as a schoolmaster. He wrote his old friends David Pye and Geoffrey Young, offering a vision of a new kind of school, one that would not separate boys from their families but rather bring them together, a pedagogy that would celebrate the imagination and reward experimentation, all with the goal of fostering personal growth, a school where sports would be an option and not the ultimate measurement of man.

It was a forlorn hope, a dream impossible to realize. Knowing that he had no future at Charterhouse, Mallory wrote to the League of Nations Union, a peace organization, seeking employment. On August 25, 1920, his third child was born, "a thumping great bruiser of a boy with fists and feet, a chin and very fat cheeks." In the fall he was hired by the league to go to Ireland and report on the troubles. Since the Easter Rebellion of 1916, the island had been convulsed with violence. The vast majority of the people supported Sinn Fein, the political party of independence. The British had responded by dispatching forty thousand troops, outlawing the Irish parliament, suppressing the press, and implementing a wave of repression known as the Terror. Mallory, clearly a sympathizer, was perfectly positioned. He had a friend, Conor O'Brien, a Pen y Pass climber, who ran guns for the Irish. Mallory sent word, and was invited deep into the movement. He learned of the sinister chambers at Dublin Castle, bore witness to raids by the notorious Black and Tans, watched as the Royal Irish Constabulary lined up the innocent to be searched. One night in Dublin he was himself awakened at night by a stranger with a gun in one hand, a flashlight in the other, demanding to know if he was Protestant. "There has been wrong on both sides," Mallory wrote, "but national aspirations, a passionate idealism, are to be found only on one side. It is to this fact that Irishmen appeal when they exclaim, 'If only the people of England knew! If only they would come and see!' "

Returning to London in the first days of 1921, Mallory was at a loss. He wanted to leave Charterhouse, and knew that his literary aspirations, such as they were, would not be realized as a schoolmaster. His friends—those who'd survived—had not deserted him, but circumstances had changed. Duncan Grant, who'd never known the front, was living after the war with both David Garnett and Vanessa Bell, who was still married to Clive. The first time Duncan made love to Vanessa, her husband passed through the room and without missing a beat said, "Oh don't stop. Please go on." Others had settled down to more conventional affairs. In 1917 Geoffrey Keynes had married Margaret Elizabeth Darwin, the granddaughter of the great naturalist. In the spring of 1918, Geoffrey Young, with Mallory as best man, went to the altar with Len Slingsby, a young climber and actress. That same year, against all expectations, Maynard Keynes, whose promiscuity at Cambridge had been so legendary, had also fallen for a woman, Lydia Lopokova, a Russian ballerina, whom he ultimately married. By 1920 even James Strachey had settled down, and with his wife, the psychoanalyst Alix Sargant-Florence, buried himself in his life's work, the English translation of the works of Sigmund Freud. Mallory, of course, was already the father of three children, a loyal and devoted husband, grateful to be home and alive.

The spasm of domesticity, though a fine antidote, could never mitigate the hangover of the war, which lingered even as talk of the conflict was banished from polite conversation—displaced, as Robert Graves scoffed, by the trivial, the marriage of London's reigning beauty, Lady Diana Manners, or the success of a favorite horse at the Derby. The final betrayal of hope came with the Treaty of Versailles, negotiated by the same coterie of old men responsible for setting fire to civilization in 1914. Siegfried Sassoon described it as "a peace to end all peace." Vera Brittain could not bear to read of its terms, so completely did it betray everything for which youth had fought and died. "They knew it was destined to cause another war," wrote Graves, and yet "nobody cared."

Such sentiments could not have been lost on Mallory, who, like so many of his generation, faced in the winter of 1921 an uncertain future. Charterhouse had become intolerable, a place of ghosts run by a headmaster who, knowing nothing of the front, expected life to continue as it always had, as if the war had been a mere interlude. The only anchor in Mallory's life was his family, and the only endeavor at which he truly excelled was climbing. "The war had knocked the ball-room floor from under middle-class English life," wrote Stephen Spender. "People resembled dancers suspended in mid-air yet miraculously able to pretend that they were still dancing."

George Mallory was still very much in midair on January 22, 1921, when he received a curt letter from Percy Farrar of the Alpine Club, noting, "It looks like Everest will really be tried this summer. Party would leave early April and get back in October. Any aspirations?" Initially Mallory hesitated, reluctant to leave his young family, especially his son, John, an infant of only five months. Geoffrey Young, who had proposed Mallory to the Everest Committee, saw the expedition as George's ticket out of Charterhouse and onto a larger stage. Ruth was against it, and Mallory almost refused. Young traveled to the Holt and made his case. He recalled, "I saw them both together, and in 20 minutes talk, Ruth saw what I meant: how much the label of Everest would mean for his career and educational plans. She told him to go."

On February 9 Mallory met in London with Farrar, Sir Francis Younghusband, and Harold Raeburn, the expedition's designated climbing leader. Mallory, Younghusband observed, accepted the offer "with no visible emotion." A day later he thanked Geoffrey Young for providing the contact, writing, "I am just fixed for Everest . . . It seems rather a momentous step altogether with a new job to find when I get back, but it will not be a bad thing to give up the settled ease of the present life. Frankly I want a more eminent platform than the one in my classroom—at least in the sense of appealing to minds more capable of response . . . I expect I shall have no cause to regret your persuasions in the cause of Everest; at present I am highly elated at the prospect and so is Ruth: thank you for that." The die was cast. In two months George Mallory would sail for India in what seemed at the time a good career move.

CHAPTER 6

The Doorway to the Mountain

FOR A FORTNIGHT the steamer *Hatarana*, carrying masses of equipment and stores destined for the expedition, lay at anchor in the languid waters of the Hooghly River, awaiting a berth at the Calcutta docks. A slot finally opened on May 10, the morning George Mallory disembarked from the *Sardinia*. Though the *Hatarana*'s cargo would be unloaded within a day, Mallory, ever impatient and encumbered with thirty-five pieces of luggage of his own, arranged for the bulk of the goods to follow and left that afternoon for Sealdah Station to catch the Darjeeling Mail, the evening train that ran north overnight to Siliguri. The terminus of the line, Siliguri, a small trading settlement scattered on a stony plain, lay seven miles from the slopes that rose out of the flatlands of India to form the foothills of the eastern Himalaya. From there he would transfer to the Darjeeling Himalayan Railway, a narrow-gauge ribbon of track that zigzagged and looped its way some 7,000 vertical feet up the flank of the mountains to the hill station of Darjeeling, the summer seat of the government of Bengal and the staging point for the assault on Everest.

His journey of some four hundred miles began in sweltering heat and dust as the Darjeeling Mail steamed and clattered through a monotonous landscape of paddy fields and bamboo, plantations of coconut and betel palms, bananas and plantains. Three hours from Calcutta came a deafening roar as the train pounded over the Sara Bridge across the Padma, and then, with the night, long shadows from the moon and the faint light of scores upon scores of silent villages, a concentration of humanity unlike anything Mallory had ever seen. At dawn, nearing Jalpaiguri, he had a first fleeting glimpse of ice summits on the horizon, a vista at once daunting and exhilarating. Reaching Siliguri just after six in the morning, he took tea in a pleasant refreshment room reserved, as were all such establishments on the line, exclusively for Europeans. Native porters, meanwhile, hustled to transfer his gear to the Darjeeling Himalayan line, which departed punctually each day thirty-five minutes after the arrival of the mail train from Calcutta.

Leaving Siliguri, the track ran seven miles through fever-haunted ground, past a vast, empty field where the Younghusband Mission had encamped before its 1904 invasion of Tibet to the station at Sukna, where finally it began to climb, first gradually, through a rich forest of semul and sal trees, and then up a steep gradient that carried the train cars, almost toylike in scale, higher and higher into the mists. At Kurseong, some thirty-two miles from Siliguri and nineteen shy of Darjeeling, Mallory got off the train and walked ahead, making better time on foot as he took in the stunning views of the green plains of Bengal, some 5,000 feet below, across which ran rivers he compared to ribbons of silver. Looking above and to the skyline, he saw for the first time the summits of Kabru and Kangchenjunga, soaring to heights that dwarfed any mountain he had known in the Alps. Fields of tea glowed with a deep uniform green, but what most impressed him, as he wrote to Ruth in his first letter home from Darjeeling, "was the forest itself, the incredibly touching and mysterious beauty of a tree clad hillside with all its wealth of growth and variety of greens and darkness and brightness. In one spot especially where I was walking ahead of the train I was irresistibly reminded of wooded hillsides in Chinese pictures where they are used to express some deep religious feeling."

Through a soft rain the train continued to climb, past fields of maize and dairy cattle, and forests of pine and fir that challenged all memory of the sultry lowlands abandoned but hours before. The air at Ghoom—at 7,400 feet, the highest station on the line—was actually cold and the wind penetrating as the train made the final descent over four miles to Darjeeling. Mallory strained for another view of Kangchenjunga, but the horizon was cloaked in clouds.

At Darjeeling Station a gaggle of female porters, tumplines in hand, waited to hoist his luggage up the hill to Government House, where he was scheduled to stay as the personal guest of Lord Ronaldshay, governor of Bengal. Mallory, for his part, reached the mansion in a rickshaw, pulled and pushed by a team of three men, all Lepchas, indigenous hill people of Sikkim. Mallory referred to them simply as coolies, a term applied casually by the British to any working native, be they Tibetan, Nepali, or Indian. He would have preferred to stay at the Mount Everest Hotel, on Auckland Road, where he understood Bullock and his young American wife to be waiting, or even at the Bellevue, on Commercial Row, where the officers assigned to the expedition from the

Survey of India, Oliver Wheeler and Henry Morshead, had been staying with their wives since arriving from their headquarters at Dehra Dun, the Wheelers on April 30 and the Morsheads three weeks earlier. But expedition leader Charles Howard-Bury had decided to billet both Mallory and the naturalist and physician Sandy Wollaston at Government House, where they would share the guesthouse, posh accommodations with a commanding view of the town. Mallory arrived just after three in the afternoon on May 11, only to learn that he was expected that evening at a formal dinner and reception, being hosted by Lord Ronaldshay himself.

It was, Mallory reported to Ruth, a "swagger" affair, complete with printed guest list and embossed invitations, servants dressed in red livery and gold and silver braid, a proper orchestra, and a table laid with a dazzling array of plates, flatware, bowls, and crystal. There were thirty guests, fifteen couples, who arrived two by two. Mallory escorted Evie Morshead. He had known her husband's brothers at Winchester. Henry gave his arm to Mrs. Graham, whose husband ran the mission and vocational schools at Kalimpong. The Wheelers, who had married only seven weeks before, in Bombay, arrived with the Bullocks and immediately made their way to Sandy Wollaston, who had sailed from Marseille with the Bullocks on the P&O ship *Naldera*, reaching Bombay on April 30. "A comfortable journey out," Wollaston reported in a letter to Arthur Hinks of the RGS, "but a villainous journey across India" had delayed his arrival until May 9. He had been in Darjeeling for only two days.

Harold Raeburn, the leader of the climbing party, had been staying at the Mount Everest Hotel since April 23. He had occupied his time profitably, engaging four cooks for the expedition and some forty porters, Sherpa Bhotias, as he described them, men of Tibetan ancestry whose homes lay in Solu Khumbu, the high alpine valleys of northeast Nepal that reach to the very southern flank of Everest. With the help of Howard-Bury, who had made his way to Darjeeling at the beginning of May after paying a social call on the viceroy, Lord Reading, in Simla, Raeburn had outfitted each hired man with boots, blankets, cap comforters, fur gloves, and warm clothing. Those destined for the high camps were given eiderdown sleeping bags. As only Henry Morshead spoke Tibetan, interpreters had to be found. Howard-Bury identified two ideal candidates. Gyalzen Kazi, raised in Sikkim, was fluent in the language, capable of reading and translating even the most obscure Buddhist scriptures. Chheten Wangdi was himself Tibetan, a former officer in the army of the Dalai Lama who had later served with the Indian Army in Egypt during the war.

Raeburn, a Scot not much given to British pomp, was in muted conversation with Alexander Heron, who had been appointed to the expedition by the Geological Survey of India, when Howard-Bury arrived, closely followed by Lord Ronaldshay, who was accompanied by two aides-de-camp in full dress uniform. The room fell silent as the governor made his circuit, shaking hands with each guest, engaging in the small patter of conversation that protocol demanded. From this point in the evening everything unfolded like clockwork. The servants stood by to usher each diner to a proper place at the table, and they hovered throughout the service, ready to top off each fluted glass with champagne. Music played and the conversation remained light until dessert, when Lord Ronaldshay rose to pay homage to the health of the king-emperor. Everyone stood in silence as the orchestra played "God Save the King."

The only unscripted moment occurred some ten minutes after everyone had been seated, when an odd rumpled figure burst into the hall. Alexander Kellas, whose absence from Darjeeling had been the cause of much anxiety for both Howard-Bury and Wollaston, arrived at Government House dressed for the field and soaking wet, having walked the four miles from his lodgings at Ghoom. In India since June 1920, he had been almost continuously on expedition for close to a year, exploring the mountainous ridges that formed the northeastern Nepalese frontier and testing the oxygen apparatus destined for Everest. He had returned to Darjeeling only on the evening of May 10. Exhausted and feeling ill, he'd taken to his bed and rested most of the next day, very nearly sleeping through the governor's dinner. At fifty-three, he was too old for such a pace. Though utterly spent, and suffering from obvious symptoms of enteritis and dysentery, he shared no word of his condition with Howard-Bury or even his old friends Morshead and Wollaston, who were all delighted that the veteran climber, deemed indispensable to the expedition, had finally appeared.

Mallory, who, like Raeburn, disdained formalities, took to Kellas immediately. "Kellas I love already," he wrote to Ruth on May 17. "He is beyond description Scotch and uncouth in his speech—altogether uncouth. He arrived at the great dinner party ten minutes after we had sat down, and very disheveled . . . His appearance would form an admirable model to the stage for a farcical representation of an alchemist. He is very slight in build, short, thin, stooping, and narrow-chested; his head . . . made grotesque by veritable gig-lamps of spectacles and a long pointed moustache."

Though by his own admission it was "early to be writing about the personnel," Mallory had within days of arriving in Darjeeling formed strong opinions about all his colleagues, judgments that for the most part he clung to for the remainder of the expedition. Bullock, of course, was an old friend from school. Wollaston he also knew and admired, "an absolutely devoted and disinterested person." Morshead seemed "a very nice man, quite unassuming and gentle, resembling his brothers a good deal in both face and manners, but considerably shorter than either of them."

His other companions fared less well. The geologist Heron he dismissed as dull. He described Harold Raeburn as "extremely irritating" and dictatorial, a man with no sense of humor, utterly lacking in calm, and consistently "wrong in his facts." As for expedition leader Howard-Bury, Mallory found him to be "too much the landlord, with not only Tory prejudices but a very highly developed sense of status and contempt for . . . sorts of people other than his own; he makes himself very pleasant with H.E. [Lord Ronaldshay]—too pleasant I sometimes think."

Mallory reserved his harshest comments for Oliver Wheeler, a man he had never met and whose stunning achievements on Everest he would never acknowledge. "Wheeler I have hardly spoken to, but you know my complex about Canadians. I shall have to swallow before I like him, I expect. God send me the saliva."

OVER THE FOLLOWING DAYS, even as the men and their wives enjoyed the popular amusements of Darjeeling—tennis, badminton, and golf at the Gymkhana Club, leisurely teas amid the potted plants and chintz and leather chairs and month-old copies of the *Times* and the *Illustrated London News*, the afternoon horse races at Lebong, dances and drinks in the evening at the Everest Hotel—the broad outline of the expedition came into focus. As Howard-Bury explained to Mallory, Bullock, and Wollaston—all newcomers to the Himalaya—at a meeting on the morning of May 12, there were two approaches to Tibet from Darjeeling, both well known to the British since the days of the Younghusband Mission. One, he indicated, ran directly north through Sikkim to Kampa Dzong via Gangtok, the Teesta Valley, and the Serpo La, the pass Younghusband had crossed in July 1903 on his first diplomatic foray into Tibet. This route would be taken by Henry Morshead, whose primary duty as an officer of the Survey of India was to fill in the map by completing a quarter-inch plane table survey of the crown of the Himalaya, a swath of unknown land 65 miles wide and 225 miles long that lay north of the Nepalese frontier and south of the drainage of the Tsangpo/Brahmaputra River, which had been mapped by Ryder during the Rawling expedition in 1904. Morshead's survey, if successful, would add some fifteen thousand square miles to the map of the Raj.

The second approach to Tibet followed the traditional trade route between India and Lhasa, taken by Younghusband's invasion force in 1904 and by Howard-Bury himself during his scout in 1920. It ran from Darjeeling to Kalimpong, across the Jelep La and the Tibetan frontier to Yatung, and then up the Chumbi Valley to Phari and thence north to Gyantse and Lhasa. Some thirty miles beyond Phari a track branched off the main road, crossed a pass called the Dug La, and then ran west, reaching Kampa Dzong in four to five days, according to Howard-Bury's sources.

The route to Kampa Dzong that Morshead would take, due north through Sikkim, was somewhat shorter but, as Younghusband had discovered in 1903, impractical for a large mounted force. It passed for several days along the feverish and sweltering Teesta Valley, where the rainfall was heavy and leeches abounded. For long stretches it was but a narrow trail, carved into rock overhangs above the Teesta and Lachen Rivers, quite unsuitable for mules and horses. With the season already late and monsoon clouds hovering over the plains of Bengal, both approaches to Tibet already promised to be very wet. In Darjeeling, the rains had begun, and not a day went by without torrential downpours. Time was of the essence, Howard-Bury insisted. It was vital to get the expedition across the divide into Tibet as quickly as possible, with the hope that the mountains would block the full force of the monsoon from reaching the Chumbi Valley and the northern approaches to Everest.

Howard-Bury's plan called for Morshead and his survey crew to depart Darjeeling on May 13. The main body of the expedition would go by way of the Jelep La, leaving in two parties, each with fifty mules and twenty porters, one group on May 18 and the other on May 19, so as not to overtax the accommodations, the *dak* bungalows conveniently spaced a day's march apart all the way through to Gyantse. Wollaston, Wheeler, Mallory, and Howard-Bury would head off first, followed by Raeburn, Kellas, Bullock, and Heron. Until branching off this major north-south artery and heading west to Kampa Dzong, the expedition would remain in ready communication with the outside world. Telephone and telegraph lines ran from Darjeeling to Gyantse, and letters mailed from Phari reached Darjeeling by postal runners in but three days. Morshead's survey team and both parties of climbers and support

staff would rendezvous at Kampa Dzong. From there they would literally walk off the map, following a route that in seven days promised to
reach Tingri Dzong, the Tibetan military garrison and trading depot
that had long been anticipated as the base for the initial explorations of
the northern approaches to the mountain.

IF THERE WAS one man Howard-Bury could with complete confidence send alone into the unknown, it was Henry Morshead. Born in
Cornwall in 1882, and ultimately murdered under mysterious circumstances in the jungles of Burma in 1931, he was a man of action and
deed, a true explorer, decisive and contained in temperament, ferociously strong and fit, at five foot nine a pocket Hercules, as one friend
described him, hard as nails, utterly indifferent to personal comfort,
blessed with an impregnable digestive tract, fully capable of eating
anything or nothing, of going without food or even water for days.
Trained as a military engineer, with a specialty in topography, mapping,
and the design and construction of fortifications, he'd joined the Survey of India in 1906. Thereafter he'd embarked on a decade of extraordinary expeditions, none more dramatic than a series of thrusts up the
Brahmaputra from the southern side of the Himalaya to the jungles of
northeast Assam and, ultimately, into the heart of the Tsangpo Gorge.
    Neither China nor Britain had been able to garrison the borderlands
of the North-East Frontier, which was the reason the six-hundred-mile
border, stretching from Bhutan to northern Burma, remained unde-
fined. Between 1858 and 1894 the Raj had made four failed attempts
to pacify the region. In every instance the British political officer had
been killed by the Abors, a fierce tribal people, notorious for their
use of arrows and buried stakes poisoned with aconite paste, deadly
venom derived from plants. When, in 1911, yet another political officer had been murdered, the Raj had had enough. With the pacification
of the Abors the immediate intent, and the penetration and mapping
of the high affluents of the Brahmaputra the strategic goal, the British
launched a massive punitive expedition, of which Morshead's survey
detachment was a key component. Two thousand soldiers, mostly Gurkhas, were each dosed with quinine and given in their kit an antidote
to aconite poison. They were supported on the march by thirty-five
hundred Nagas, sworn enemies of the Abors, each armed with a spear
and hoping to return with an enemy head as a trophy. It was an uneven
fight: British rifles and Maxim guns against rocks, spears, poisoned
stakes, and arrows.

Once the Abors were subdued, the exploration could begin. Survey teams went up the Dibang, Lohit, and Dihang, all major high tributaries of the Brahmaputra. The conditions were beyond terrible: mountainous slopes of forty degrees covered by dense jungle vegetation, river torrents that fell fifty feet in a mile, unbearable heat and leeches in the lower elevations, while at the heights such cold that men died of frost. "Personally I would give the frontier to the Chinese if they want it," one officer wrote to his mother. "I have never seen a more awful spot."

Morshead was in his element. In 1911, he spent four months ascending the Lohit, living on rice, dog meat, and beetles, hacking his way through tangles of creepers and toxic plants, threatened by tigers and elephants, in a pestilential climate as humid, he recalled, as a Turkish bath. All this simply to plant the Union Jack in disputed ground, claimed by the Chinese and marked with a single wooden post that identified the spot as the southern limit of the Empire of the Great Pure (Ch'ing) Dynasty.

By May 1913 he had successfully mapped the entire drainage of the Dibang, tracing the tributary to its source and thus proving that it did not pierce the Himalaya. While exploring its upper reaches, he met some Tibetans from Kham who offered to guide him up the Brahmaputra and into Tibet. Here was an opportunity to solve one of the great puzzles of Himalayan geography, the mystery of the Tsangpo Gorge. In 1884, as we have seen, the pundit Kinthup had proved that the Tsangpo River, flowing east from Kailas along the northern flank of the Himalaya, and the Brahmaputra, coming out of the mountains 12,000 feet lower, in the forests of Assam, were one and the same, but no one believed him. Now, with the Abors quelled and the other affluents of the lower Brahmaputra successfully surveyed, Morshead joined forces with F. M. Bailey to seek a final answer to the mystery.

Heading into the unknown on May 16, 1913, they crossed two high passes to reach a hamlet called Showa on the upper Dihang, where they were promptly arrested as Chinese spies by Tibetans who had never seen a European. After escaping with their lives, they made a wide circuit north, westward, and then to the south to reach the Tsangpo. They attempted to follow the river downstream to India but found their way blocked by a roaring chasm from which soared mountain walls to 23,000 feet. Returning upriver they reached Tsetang, not far from Lhasa, and, after extensive explorations, arrived back in India via Bhutan in the middle of November, with Morshead having mapped their entire journey. They had confirmed that the river did indeed fall through one of the deepest, longest, and most magnificent gorges on earth, and that, having sliced through the mountains, it turned back on itself in a great bend to run parallel in the opposite direction for sixty miles before heading south again into the forests of Assam. It was this curious and unexpected configuration that allowed for the dramatic drop in elevation, 7,000 feet in less than a hundred miles as the crow flies.

When, finally, Bailey and Morshead, having covered 1,680 miles on foot, reached India, they were penniless and bedraggled. Bailey recalled their attempts to mollify the Indian police and border guards: "I began to look at Morshead more closely. I had not paid any attention to how he dressed while we were in Tibet. The values there were spiritual not sartorial. But face to face with the police inspector I was forced to admit that sartorially Morshead did not look impressive."

F. M. Bailey was himself no slouch. A veteran of the Younghusband invasion, he had been with Ryder and Rawling on the 1904 exploration of the Tsangpo/Brahmaputra headwaters, reaching Kailash and beyond. In 1910 he'd come up with the plan to disguise the Thirteenth Dalai Lama as a postal runner during his escape to India—the only time, he later quipped, that a god incarnate had carried His Majesty's mails. In 1911 he'd walked 1,715 miles through southeast China, crossing the headwaters of the Mekong and the Salween to approach India from the northeast, through the very jungles of Assam. A brilliant naturalist, he discovered scores of new species, including the legendary Himalayan blue poppy that bears his name. He once saved his own life by using a butterfly net to self-arrest and thus escape a snow slide as it grew into an avalanche. Seriously wounded three times during the war, in France and Gallipoli, he became a British spy, a master of a dozen disguises, traveling as a Buddhist priest, an Austrian soldier, and an Armenian prisoner of war, and causing the Bolsheviks in Tashkent and Samarkand such grief that he would live with a Soviet bounty on his head for the rest of his days.

But in Henry Morshead, Bailey found his match. Four days into their Tsangpo expedition, he recorded in his diary, "I had noted another characteristic of Morshead which rather alarmed me. No one can avoid picking up leeches and one cannot stop to remove them while one is on the march. On one occasion I found at a halt that I had 150 leeches on me. Morshead appeared indifferent to them. I thought at the beginning that this indifference might be the residue of his fever; but later I found that this was not the case. When his temperature was indubitably normal, he would stand there covered in leeches and with blood oozing out of his boots, as oblivious as a small child whose face is smeared with jam." Eventually Bailey came to understand that Morshead simply did not notice impediments of any kind, certainly nothing so trivial as a parasitic leech. Not only was the man utterly fearless, Bailey discovered; he "thought so little about danger that he didn't realize that there was such a thing as risk."

Although Morshead was not a climber—indeed, his 1920 Kamet expedition with Kellas was the only time he had attempted a serious mountain—he had long had Everest on his mind. In May 1914, catching wind that Rawling was planning a reconnaissance in the summer of 1915, with an assault scheduled for 1916, Morshead had immediately offered his services as surveyor and had been accepted. Everest, however, would not be enough. With the enthusiasm of a schoolboy, he'd rushed a note to Bailey: "During the winter of 1915–16 while the rest of the Rawling's party return to vegetate in Darjeeling before the final attack, you and I could go off and explore the northern border of Bhutan and possibly revisit those Ammon on the Nyala La. Let me know as soon as possible what you think about it."

Before Bailey had a chance to reply, war clouds over Europe rendered the issue moot. Morshead, posted to a field company of Royal Engineers, had an active war, as would be expected, crossing the channel in time for the Battle of Loos. Mentioned twice in despatches, recipient of the Distinguished Service Order, he somehow survived the Somme, the Battle of Arras, and Passchendaele. A bout of trench fever sent him back in England, where, dressed in civilian clothes, he was approached on a tram by a member of the white feather brigade, self-appointed guardians who challenged the patriotism of any man found out of uniform. Morshead said nothing. His war ended on September 25, 1918, when, scouting canal crossings near Cambrai, he was severely wounded in the leg by a shell splinter. Carried to the 48th Casualty Clearing Station, he was operated on the following day and evacuated to a hospital at Rouen. By December 1919 he was back in India on active duty on the North-West Frontier with the Waziristan Field Force, an assignment that yielded yet further decorations, the Indian Service Medal with three clasps. No sooner did he return from the North-West Frontier than he was off to climb Kamet with Kellas.

"I wasn't long left in peace at Dehra Dun," he wrote to his old friend Jack Hazard, his second-in-command at the Somme. "Had to dump the wife in a hurry at Rurki and rush off." Dumping his wife meant that Evie arrived in India for the first time with no money, no friends, and no one waiting for her at the pier. Whatever these men were, sentimental they were not. As Morshead gathered his survey team in Darjeeling on the morning of May 13, they had already mapped twenty-five hundred square miles of Sikkim in the weeks before the rest of the Everest party had even reached the hill station. He saw the task ahead as a technical challenge, an opportunity to complete something that had been initiated years before by men he admired, Rawling, Bailey, and Ryder, and the pundits Hari Ram and Kinthup before them. Leaving his wife behind, along with a four-month-old child, their first, was simply what the job demanded.

WHEN GEORGE BERNARD SHAW saw a portrait of the 1921 Everest expedition—the men dressed in Norfolk jackets, knickerbockers, and puttees, the geologist Heron in a camel-hair greatcoat, Howard-Bury in Donegal tweed, with matching dark tie and waistcoat, Mallory wrapped in a woolen scarf—he famously quipped that the entire scene resembled a "Connemara picnic surprised by a snowstorm." There was, indeed, something less than heroic about the first few days as the expedition got under way.

On May 18 Mallory and Wollaston made their way to Wheeler's lodgings at the Bellevue around 11:00 a.m., only to find the porters, eighteen of whom had arrived with three mules three hours before, still sorting and arguing about loads. Joined finally by four cooks, an orderly, and an additional forty-seven mules, the party set off, with Mallory, Wheeler, and Wollaston traveling by car. The destination was Pashok, a *dak* bungalow located on a spur overlooking the confluence of the Ranjit and Teesta rivers, seventeen miles away and 5,000 feet below. A motor road reached six miles beyond Ghoom, and from there the men would walk.

Unfortunately, the car broke down almost immediately, obliging Mallory and Wollaston to ride ponies. Wheeler, an old Asia hand, flagged a rickshaw. Then came the rain. As Howard-Bury, who had stayed behind to see the second party off on May 19 with the intent of then doing a double march to catch up with the vanguard at Kalimpong, wrote to Younghusband, "the monsoon broke properly that night and we had a deluge which has continued ever since." Actually, it was not the monsoon but what the locals knew as the *chhoti barsat*, the rains that herald the arrival of the monsoon; it would only get worse. Mallory rode with a sun umbrella in hand, an oiled silk cover on his topee, and a rucksack on his back, humping out of his cycling cape. He looked, as he admitted in a letter to Ruth, ridiculous. But he was delighted to be leaving Darjeeling, "a devastating place—or rather it is a wonderful beautiful place almost incredibly bedeviled by fiends."

The track ran from Ghoom along a ridge forested with evergreen oaks and then dropped steeply through tea plantations and copses of tree ferns thirty feet high, with trunks covered in orchids and delicate polypodium and maidenhair ferns. The increasingly humid air left the men dripping with sweat, and the rains never let up, even as they finally approached the bungalow around 6:00 p.m. Perched 2,000 feet above the river, built of wood, with four rooms (one occupied with stores, two by other travelers, with one reserved for the three of them), it looked out over a valley across which could be seen the outline of Kalimpong, their next destination. Their arrival was late and, Wheeler recalled, somewhat chaotic. It poured all night, and "the rain sounded like a great windstorm."

Wollaston, nevertheless, was delighted. He had never in his wildest dreams anticipated such luxury, especially after what he had known in Africa and New Guinea. "You just walk in," he wrote in his amazement, "and find furniture, knives and plates, lamps and oil, even a library of old magazines and novels." This was not an expedition but a tour, in the inimitable style of the Raj. Each bungalow came staffed with a *chowkidar*, who provided firewood and milk, and was equipped with cooking utensils and cutlery, beds and even mattresses. A posted notice advised parties of two to travel with three servants: a cook, a bearer, and a sweeper, the latter charged with the duty of cleaning toilets and sweeping the bungalow after use. The addition of a *tiffin* coolie to prepare picnics and assist the cook was optional but highly recommended. No coolie was to be made to carry more than fifty pounds, and each should be paid, the notice continued, a third the daily cost of a mule. If proceeding to Tibet, the traveler was advised to carry several tins of biscuits, bottles of scented water, and boxes of toilet soap as gifts for high officials, lamas and *dzongpens*. These were to be presented on a tray by a servant, along with ceremonial *khatas*, or scarves.

The following morning was slow, the rain discouraging, and Wheeler elected to walk while Mallory and Wollaston rode. A steep track dropped 2,000 feet in three and a half miles to the Teesta River and then divided, the cart trail zigzagging its way ten miles up the mountain while the coolie track, which Wheeler took, rose five miles straight up more than 3,300 feet through dense forests to Kalimpong, a comparatively large settlement with shops, churches, tea gardens, a post office, and a telegraph line. The *dak* bungalow was large and elegant, six rooms and a veranda with beautiful gardens of roses and scarlet hibiscuses. Wheeler arrived around 3:00 p.m., wrote all afternoon, and then with Mallory, Wollaston, and Howard-Bury, who arrived by mule late in the day, joined a local missionary and his three daughters for dinner. The food was delicious, but not so the drink. "TT!" Wheeler scratched in his diary, his shorthand for "tea toddler." They were in their beds by ten, after some bad news from Howard-Bury.

The army mules, which had arrived in Darjeeling fat and sleek, had proved to be completely unfit for work in the heat and the mountains. Six had collapsed on the first day, and several more on the steep climb to Kalimpong. As it was, the expedition was severely underequipped in its transport. Of the 100 animals, 27 were loaded with the personal effects of the muleteers. Under the best of circumstances each could carry no more than 160 pounds, and with only 73 animals available to haul expedition supplies, Howard-Bury had been forced to leave much behind at Government House. Heading into the mountains, they had what was needed for three and a half months. To stay through September, as was their intent, they would have to bring up the remainder of the goods in July or August. If the army mules faltered completely, the expedition would be totally dependent on local transport, and the goodwill of Tibetans who less than a generation before had seen their fathers slaughtered by the British under Younghusband at Guru. The good news, however, was that Howard-Bury had run into David Macdonald, who was acting political agent in Sikkim until Morshead's old friend F. M. Bailey, recently appointed to the post, could get out from England. Macdonald had immediately telegraphed Yatung and the Tibetan authorities at Phari, instructing that supplies and transport be made available throughout the Chumbi Valley.

The following day, May 20, called for an easy march of fourteen miles. The route ran along the most wonderful datura hedges Howard-Bury had ever seen, dense thickets twenty feet in height, decorated with beautiful white trumpet-shaped blossoms eight inches long, phosphorescent in the dusk. But his thoughts were on the mules, which continued to cause trouble. The rain was also a curse, falling in such torrents that oiled waterproofs were rendered useless in minutes.

From Pedong to Rongli, the next stage, was only twelve miles, but the track dropped more than 3,000 feet to the Rishi Chu, where, crossing the Sikkim border, it rose 3,000 feet, along a steep path broken by paving stones and cobbles that made the walking difficult. They lunched at the modest bungalow at Ari and then continued down another 2,000 feet to reach Rongli Bridge, a hot and feverish crossing, where they paused for the night. Howard-Bury again arrived enchanted by the flora: sprays of orchids, a delicate pink-blossomed ground cover, rich plantings of mulberry and walnut, and everywhere in full flower a stunning forest tree with white blooms known locally as *chilauni*. Wheeler, for his part, nursed a blister the size of a shilling. His stomach was also giving him trouble. One of the mules had died en route of sheer exhaustion, and Wheeler feared that some of the men might follow. Things were so bad with the transport that Howard-Bury was forced to order a stop, instructing the first party to rest for a day at Rongli, while the second group advanced to stay three miles back at Ari.

May 23 dawned in hot sun, and Bullock was out chasing butterflies soon after first light. Down below at Rongli, Wheeler, Mallory, and Wollaston got an early start, and after following the right bank of the Rongli Chu for five miles, through forests of massive hardwoods some forty feet in diameter, they began the steep climb to Sedongchen, a dreary settlement of bamboo huts only nine miles away but perched at 7,000 feet. Of the fifty mules the advance party had led out of Darjeeling, only fourteen were fit to carry, and by the time even these reached Sedongchen, not one remained able to proceed. Howard-Bury had no choice but to send the entire lot back to Darjeeling and find new transport by negotiating on the spot with the wool traders, whose narrow traffic out of the Jelep La and Tibet was a constant flow. Their faces blackened with grease, their long dark hair bound up and tied in red, wearing exquisite earrings of coral and turquoise, they "were full of friendly smiles and greetings," Howard-Bury recalled, but they drove hard bargains, and the British had few options.

The following day was less a walk than a climb, 5,000 vertical feet up a stone causeway, more a series of steps than a road, that left the jungles and leeches behind and led the men into a fairyland of oaks, magnolias, and silver firs, delicate primroses and flowering rhododendrons of every hue and color, crimson, magenta, mauve, yellow, and white. The weather cleared and the hill ponies and mules hired locally proved more than up to the task. Sure-footed and strong, capable of carrying the heaviest of loads, they relieved Howard-Bury of his greatest immediate concern.

The climbers stayed the night at Gnatong, at 12,000 feet a scattering of stone huts in a hollow on a grassy spur, beyond which every tree had been cut for firewood, leaving the place, Wheeler noted in his diary, "filthy, dry and bleak." A cemetery of the dead from the 1904 Younghusband invasion did not elevate the spirits. Howard-Bury described the hamlet as "a most depressing place" that owed its existence only to the fact that it was the first British outpost this side of the Jelep La and the Tibetan frontier. With the constant mist and precipitation, two hundred inches a year, the mud was as wretched as anything Howard-Bury had known in France. Still, thanks to the presence of a post office and a telegraph line, he was able to place a call that one would be hard-pressed to make today, over the Jelep La to Yatung, to a "Mr. Isaacs, Mr. Macdonald's head clerk, to ask him to make arrangements for ponies and mules at Yatung and Phari."

Howard-Bury then proposed to Mallory and Wheeler that as a cost measure they be prepared to dispense with their Darjeeling saddle ponies immediately after crossing the Jelep La, a move that promised to save a few rupees but did not endear him to either man. Mallory held his tongue, though he vented his feelings in a letter to Ruth written that night: "I felt I should never be at ease with him, and indeed in a sense I never shall be. He is not a tolerant person. He is well informed and opinionated and doesn't at all like anyone else to know things he doesn't know. For the sake of peace, I am being very careful not to broach certain subjects of conversation; there are realms that are barred to our entrance altogether." Mallory further confessed that Raeburn, too, remained a problem. The climbing leader and Howard-Bury were as oil and water, and Raeburn's personality—critical, unappreciative, defensive, humorless—was already alienating Wheeler and Bullock, not to mention Mallory himself. Such tensions after but a week did not bode well. "Goodbye beautiful wooded Sikkim," Mallory wrote on May 24, "and welcome—God knows what! We shall see."

THE FOLLOWING MORNING Wheeler was up at 5:00, but thanks to the refusal of one of the Tibetan sirdars, or camp managers, to get out of bed, the party was delayed until 8:30, by which time mist had veiled every slope and rain was falling in freezing torrents. Wheeler walked to warm up and then rode to the top of the Tuku La (13,300 feet) before following an undulating track to a second summit that slipped away to a miserable place named Kupup, where a ford carried him across a stream flush with rain. He then continued up a steep path through dwarf willows and rhododendrons and over rock and scree to reach, in two and a half miles, the Jelep La—at 14,390 feet the gateway to Tibet. In the rain and clouds, with a biting wind, the pass was no place to linger. Taking little notice of the stone cairns and the prayer flags strung across the heights, he kicked his mule on and toward the green forests of Tibet. Within minutes, as he hurried down a steep and stony path, he emerged out of the mist and rain and saw for the first time in weeks a sky of lapis blue and, in the distance, the white snow summit of Chomolhari soaring to 24,000 feet.

Partly to spite Howard-Bury and partly to test his wind, Mallory had climbed to the Jelep La on foot, and found to his surprise that it was the descent of 5,000 feet from the top of the pass that caused him headache and distress. Bullock, a day behind, also felt ill from the altitude, and went to bed without eating the night before crossing the Jelep La. Both parties had climbed 12,000 feet in three days.

Wheeler, by contrast, was in good form, delighted to be over the divide and beyond the worst of the rain, walking down through forests of pine and silver fir that reminded him of the Canadian Rockies, where he had spent his youth. His father, a brilliant surveyor and cartographer, had founded the Alpine Club of Canada, and Wheeler had begun serious alpine ascents at the age of twelve. From the age of fifteen, he'd spent four months every summer humping loads and exploring the most remote reaches of the cordillera. His skill and prodigious strength came to the attention of Tom Longstaff, who traversed the summit of Mount Assiniboine, also in the Canadian Rockies, with him in 1910, a twenty-one-hour ordeal that Longstaff later described as the hardest climb he had ever done; Oliver Wheeler at twenty impressed him as the toughest and strongest climber he had known. In 1911 Wheeler became the youngest person ever elected to the Alpine Club, his nomination being endorsed by luminaries such as Collie, Mumm, and Longstaff, who had all seen him in action in Canada.

Despite this remarkable record, no one associated with the 1921 expedition thought of Wheeler as a climber. He was designated strictly as a surveyor, his primary duty to get in close to the mountain. While Morshead's task was to map several thousand square miles of unknown geography, Wheeler's mission was to map with precision the topography of the immediate environs of Everest itself, two hundred square miles of some of the roughest mountain country in the world. For two months he would be virtually on his own, staying higher and for longer, with more exposure to the wrath of the mountain, than anyone else on the expedition. "He had the hardest and most trying time of all of us," Howard-Bury later wrote, "and deserves the greatest credit for his work." Wheeler, not Mallory, he might have added, would be the one to find the doorway to the mountain.

The track dropped steeply to the Chumbi, and Wheeler kept up a strong pace, reaching the river bottom by 3:00, and making his way up the right bank of the Amo Chu to the hamlet of Chumbi, where he crossed the river once more and continued to Yatung, arriving at the *dak* bungalow around 5:30. Only Howard-Bury was ahead of him. They were greeted by a pot of tea with, Wheeler noted in a letter to his wife, "fresh milk and clean sugar—all on a tray!" sent over by Mrs. Macdonald, the wife of the British trade agent. Wheeler was delighted to learn that letters were waiting from his wife, Dolly, posted from Darjeeling as late as May 23; it had taken only two days for the mail to cover a hundred miles. The postal runners, Howard-Bury explained, traveled the route in five-mile relays, working night and day, each runner eventually trotting the entire way. By extending the system, he hoped to maintain regular postal deliveries to the very flank of Everest.

When the others arrived, Mrs. Macdonald outdid herself, as Wheeler recorded in his diary, by sending over a "topping dinner . . . white tablecloth and napkins, soup, chops, turkey and vegetables, cold meat and salad, strawberries and cream, biscuits and radishes and coffee, washed down by whiskey and soda and crème de menthe." The meal was most welcome, for as Mallory wrote to Ruth, "We've been living very badly. The substitutes for bread are abominable and our cooks produce nasty messes which are most unappetizing."

Howard-Bury wisely ordered a day of rest at Yatung, allowing them time to resupply, with purchases of sugar, barley flour, potatoes, and to secure a new set of porters and mules for the climb up the Chumbi and onto the Tibetan Plateau. The latter was "some job," Wheeler remarked in his diary, and the heated negotiations and arguments he overheard from Howard-Bury's billet made him glad to be free of the responsibility. Altogether seventeen replacement porters were recruited, along with forty-six mules and four ponies, and this just for the vanguard of the expedition.

The new men all mustered in good time on the morning of May 27 and the party was off, a rather imposing procession, Howard-Bury recalled, with Wollaston and himself on ponies, along with interpreters Gyalzen Kazi and Chheten Wangdi, both mounted, and a small escort from the military garrison, red-coated soldiers of the 73rd Carnatics. Before leaving Yatung, Howard-Bury dispatched a telegram to Younghusband, announcing the arrival of the expedition in Tibet. It reached London just in time to be read at the anniversary dinner of the Royal Geographical Society, where the news was received with an ovation from the assembled fellows.

Joining the expedition for the day was Mr. Isaacs, the head clerk at Yatung, who had kindly agreed to escort Howard-Bury on a visit to two Buddhist monasteries. The track followed the banks of the Amo Chu through a rich valley of wildflowers, yellow barberry, and dwarf rhododendrons, white clematis and delicate orchids, and with every breeze came the scent of wild roses, a fragrance Howard-Bury recalled fondly from his passage the previous year. Three miles from Yatung the valley narrowed, and just beyond the ruins of a defensive wall built by the Chinese, they saw high on the hillside and well away from the trail the Punagang Monastery, a refuge of the ancient Bonpo sect, Isaacs explained. At the prosperous hamlet of Galinka, they paused to visit another temple, newer and belonging to the Gelugpa, or Yellow Hat, sect, the monastic order of the Dalai Lamas. Here Howard-Bury paused before a massive prayer wheel, mounted so that it reached to twice his height and perhaps six feet in diameter. Inside the wheel were inscribed on paper over a million prayers, and with each rotation of the wheel, a bell sounded, indicating that the prayers had ascended into the sky. *Om mani padme hum.* Hail, the jewel in the lotus. Howard-Bury made a clumsy translation, but he spun the wheel several times and later wrote only partly in jest that he hoped "the many millions of prayers sent up may benefit us."

From Galinka, the river was broken by a series of dramatic falls, and as the trail climbed through a copse of wild cherry trees, the wind blowing off the water filled the air with white petals. Before long the trail crossed back over the river and rose through a massive boulder field, only to open onto a beautiful grassy plain, the Lingmathang Valley, the remnant of an ancient lake bed, perhaps two miles long and half a mile wide. At the height of a spur overlooking the valley stood the Donka Monastery, where Howard-Bury hoped to see his old friend the Geshe Lama, "a man of very great learning and held in high veneration." The rinpoche, as it turned out, was away in Lhasa, but the young monks warmly welcomed the British travelers. Howard-Bury marveled to see the 108 volumes of the Kangyur, the written repository of the dharma, and he compared the artistry of the calligraphy to that of the finest illuminated manuscripts of the Middle Ages. He was then shown the sanctuary of the oracle, who too was away, taking the medicinal waters at the hot springs at Kambu, which Howard-Bury remembered well. The sacred pools were said to be capable of curing each of the 440 diseases suffered by humanity.

The oracle's throne was golden, his robes crimson, and the ornate headdress he wore when in trance was adorned all around with silver skulls, symbols of the impermanence of life—a notion understood by every man on the expedition. Led out of the sanctuary, lit dimly with butter lamps, to an open veranda for tea, Howard-Bury hesitated as his eyes adjusted to the sunlight. They sat on low benches as a monk presented a tray of agate cups with silver covers. Howard-Bury winced; it was not his first taste of Tibetan tea. Made with butter and salt, it was to the English palate more soup than tea, but decorum dictated that they drink it with pleasure. Howard-Bury never became accustomed to the somewhat rancid flavor, though over the course of the expedition he would drink many hundreds of cups as a gesture of etiquette and protocol.

Departing the monastery, they dropped into a draw, then enjoyed a gallop across the open plain until the valley narrowed and the path again ran through forests of birch and larch, juniper, spruce, silver fir, and mountain ash. Crisscrossing the stream, climbing more steeply into a narrow gorge, after twelve miles the route reached Gausta; the name means, in Tibetan, "meadow of joy." It was not a hamlet, simply a post for the *dak* mail runners, with a small two-room bungalow, several mud hovels, and a single tea shop, all at 12,000 feet in the middle of an enormous gorge. For Wollaston and Wheeler there was little joy to be found, as both were ill. Wheeler took to his bed immediately and skipped dinner—which had, at any rate, little appeal. He did manage to write to his wife, beseeching her to send chocolate. What the expedition has, he noted, "will not compete with my appetite . . . [Mallory] says he eats ¼ pound of chocolate a day while climbing and I agree. One must have sweet stuff."

It rained throughout the night, but the morning dawned bright, with fresh snow within 1,500 feet of the bungalow. Howard-Bury ate wild goose eggs for breakfast and took delight all morning in the vegetation, plants that were new to him, a pale iris and a pink viburnum, a large yellow-belled honeysuckle, several unusual rhododendrons, and beautiful specimens of Bailey's blue poppy. Wheeler, for his part, ate nothing but was able to travel. His diary suggests that the day was damp and cold, with heavy rain as they trudged the sixteen miles to Phari, climbing from 12,000 to 14,300 feet. Wheeler rode Howard-Bury's mount for part of the way, then took Wollaston's, before walking the last easy miles with Mallory. Four miles out, in a gentle landscape of rolling downs soft underfoot, they saw for the first time the fortress at Phari and, beyond, the ice peak of Chomolhari, the Mountain of the Goddess, looming in a brilliant blue sky. They could see the impact of the wind on the summit, the fresh snow being blasted into the air, and felt no small sense of trepidation. As Mallory would later write to Ruth, "Chomolhari, rising abruptly out of the plain to more than

9000 ft above us, was certainly a very tremendous sight, astounding and magnificent; but in broad daylight, however much one may be interested by its prodigious cliffs, one is not charmed—one remains cold and rather horrified." They all knew that Everest reached another 5,000 feet into the heavens.

In the shadow of the mountain lay the village of Phari, its name Tibetan for "the hill made glorious." It was hard for the British to imagine a more inappropriate moniker for a settlement literally buried in its own filth. Situated at 14,300 feet on a broad, flat desert of stone, all barren rock and gray horizons, exposed to constant winds, with only sod houses for shelter and yak dung to fuel fires against the bitter cold, it was, Mallory wrote, "the most incredibly dirty warren that can be imagined." In streets fouled with waste, mangy dogs fought over dried carcasses, while open-air shops displayed hanging racks of rancid meat and cheese, and children with matted hair begged for food, their eyes bloodshot and their faces dark with grease.

The expedition had no choice but to linger, if only to allow time for the following party to catch up and have a day of rest. From Phari the real challenge of transport began, for there remained but one stage before they would turn west toward Kampa Dzong and away from the main route between Darjeeling and Lhasa. Howard-Bury needed a few days both to hire new men and animals and to renew his acquaintance with the *dzongpen*, the governor of the district, without whose cooperation they could not proceed. What's more, the expedition rather desperately needed to regroup. They were only eleven days and 122 miles removed from Darjeeling, but as Mallory wrote home:

> I suppose no one who could judge us fairly as a party would give much for our chances of getting up Mt Everest. The hardships such as they have been so far have not left us scathedless [*sic*]. Dr. Kellas arrived at Phari suffering from enteritis and though he is somewhat better now has been carried from there on some form of litter. Wheeler has constantly been suffering more or less from indigestion and has been sufficiently bad these past two days to make it a real difficulty to come on. Raeburn seems frail. All have been more or less upset inside at different times. However Heron, Howard-Bury and myself are all very fit and Bullock and Wollaston seem likely to survive.

The *dak* bungalow was a miserable affair, too small for the entire group and without firewood, but at least it was some distance removed from the village. Howard-Bury's decision to break into the expedition stores did wonders for morale. The men were sick of inadequate rations and local food prepared by the "same abominable cooks." Mail also lifted the spirits, and Wheeler was astonished to receive letters from his wife posted in Darjeeling only forty-eight hours earlier.

In the afternoon the *dzongpen* came by with several officials and a gift of a sheep. "It's customary," Wheeler later wrote, "to present a scarf, which is given back when it is time for him to leave. Laid on the table for superiors, handed to equals and put around the neck of inferiors." In lieu of a *khata*, Wollaston gave the *dzongpen* a large cigar, which "he apparently did not appreciate a bit. He looked very sick."

The following day Howard-Bury paid a call on the *dzongpen*, presenting a gift of several new electric torches, the first flashlights, which frightened and then delighted their host. After tea and various pleasantries, Howard-Bury and Heron rode to a monastery Howard-Bury had visited the previous year to give the monks photographs and other presents. He found them in the middle of ritual service, in a dark temple illuminated by hundreds of butter lamps, as they chanted their scriptures. Later, upon their return to Phari, they accepted an invitation from the *dzongpen* to dine with him the following evening, though few of the men could manage. Kellas, in particular, was very weak, and had not left his bed since arriving with the second group at half past one. Wheeler had spent the morning supervising the pitching of tents. A small troupe of dancers arrived in the late afternoon and put on a modest performance in the courtyard of the bungalow. Dressed in masks and red pantaloons, with crimson tunics hung with tufts of yak hair, they performed, Wheeler wrote, "various meaningless stunts and some ½ cartwheels. One man played the drum, the woman the cymbals. Bury gave them two rupees which pleased them no end."

The next morning Howard-Bury took a break and with only the *chowkidar* as a guide rode through the mist across the plain to reach some small hills, with the hope of finding a good spot from which to photograph Chomolhari. Soon they were above the clouds, looking out across a sea of white, with the sun overhead shining in a brilliant sky. After reaching 16,000 feet on horseback, they scrambled up another 1,500 feet on foot, until they could see directly across to the mountain. The winds were fierce, and after making several exposures, Howard-Bury hurried off the ridge.

Elated by the outing, he returned to a crisis in Phari. There was a mutiny of sorts among the porters, sparked by the sirdar as a way of diverting attention from himself and his own crimes. Since the start of the expedition he had been shaving the food rations and selling the surplus on the side. He would go, as would the least desirable of the cooks, those given to drink. With better food and rest, both Wheeler and Wollaston recovered somewhat, but not Kellas, who, Howard-Bury reported, "refused food and became very depressed about his condition."

Only Bullock, Mallory, Raeburn, and Howard-Bury were fit to join the *dzongpen* on the night of May 30. It was a fine dinner of small cakes and dried fruit, followed by minced mutton, pasta, and steamed vegetables, all washed down with brandy and strong ginger wine, deeply soothing to the digestion. With the help of interpreters, the *dzongpen*, who had been born in a small hamlet between Kampa Dzong and Shegar, directly upon their trajectory to Tingri, provided much useful information about the route, the names of settlements and village leaders, the availability of transport, and the quality of forage and water along the track. He also offered to write to his brother, who was acting as his agent in his village, to solicit his aid. Howard-Bury left the dinner deeply impressed by the authority of the Dalai Lama, and grateful to his old friend and colleague Charles Bell, whose combined efforts had so clearly and effectively opened the way to the mountain. A single order from Lhasa had spread like a wave before their path, ensuring that the cooperation upon which everything depended would be forthcoming.

Wheeler and Heron, meanwhile, busied themselves with the stores, breaking open twenty-one cases to rearrange the contents, which had been shipped sorted by food type, rather than by allotments for various camps. Wheeler, who had expedited dozens of survey parties as a youth in Canada, took charge, repacking the supplies in six lots of two- and three-week stores, "the way it should have been done," he noted in his diary. He went to bed early, worried about Wollaston, who remained unwell, and especially Kellas, who was "very sick, the usual complaint." The wind, which normally died down at night, had picked up to a howl, and the air was bitterly cold as he wrote the last lines in his diary and heard Howard-Bury and the others returning to the compound from dinner. Despite the frost, Mallory hesitated before slipping into his tent. It was only in the late evening that he found this new land of Tibet to be beautiful. At dusk, he wrote to Ruth, "this country becomes subdued; shadows soften the hillsides; there is a blending of lines and folds until the last light, so that one comes to bless the absolute bareness, feeling that here is a pure beauty of form, a kind of ultimate harmony."

With the help of the *dzongpen*, Howard-Bury was able to secure forty donkeys to accompany the expedition all the way to Kampa Dzong. Another forty-four animals—ponies, mules, donkeys, oxen, and yaks—would be changed at every stage. The men would ride mules, all save Kellas, who had to be carried. Wollaston, who had left Darjeeling on May 18 and not seen Kellas until the day before, spoke with him about staying behind in Phari. Kellas insisted that he was fully capable of continuing. He was stoic and, as Mallory later reflected, "very sly about being seen in the act of retiring." To mask his condition, Kellas had, since leaving Darjeeling, insisted on starting in the morning after the rest of his party. Departing Phari on May 31, however, Kellas reconsidered, his courage at the last moment faltering, and he offered to stay behind. But by then the entire expedition had set out, and all the cooks and porters and supplies were strung out across the wide plain. No one, including Wollaston, the expedition's physician, seems to have been aware of just how sick Kellas had become. Wheeler's diary entry for May 31, the day they left Phari, noted simply: "Bought a high Tibetan saddle, a rather swish affair made of silver and sharkskin . . . Eventually got away about nine. Kellas being carried in a chair by six coolies. It was a raw day." More attention was paid to Raeburn, who managed to get tossed from his mule twice before leaving Phari, and to two of their cooks, found drunk in the road, than to Alexander Kellas, who was slowly dying.

FROM PHARI the track rose gradually over eight miles to the Tang La, at 15,600 feet the actual Himalayan divide. Once beyond the pass they would enter the drainage of the Yaru Chu, a major headwater tributary of the Arun, the river that plunges through the Himalaya just to the east of Everest. Their route to Tingri would essentially follow the valley of the Yaru Chu to Kampa Dzong and west as far as the fortress town of Tinki. There they would spur north and west, flanking several mountain massifs and crossing one major pass before dropping back to the Yaru Chu at Shiling, an insignificant way station just above the point where the Yaru comes together with the Phung Chu to form the Arun proper. By following the Phung Chu upstream, again to the west, they would reach their immediate goal, the trading center and garrison of Tingri Dzong.

Leaving Phari they moved quickly, riding all day in the shadow of Chomolhari, with a bitter south wind blowing at their backs. They passed herds of kiangs, or wild asses, and any number of goas, Tibetan gazelles. Behind them billowed the dark clouds of the advancing monsoon, but to the north and over the Tang La the sky was brilliant and blue. After twenty miles, they stopped for the night at Tuna, where Younghusband had spent several months in the winter of 1903–4. It was nothing more than a cluster of stone huts on a barren, windswept gravel plain. The eight expedition members crammed into a bungalow, and the night was miserable.

The following morning Kellas appeared to be somewhat improved, and Howard-Bury felt confident leaving the main group and, accompanied by only a local villager, setting off across the Tang-pun-sum Plain in search of gazelles. He saw many, though always from a distance, and the elusive creatures never gave him a chance for a shot. But the entire day was blessed by glorious views of Chomolhari and, as always, he took great delight in the flora, cushion plants and a curious trumpet-shaped purple blossom that burst from the sands and carpeted the plain. In the early afternoon he rejoined the track, which ran for several miles along the shores of the Bam Tso, a shallow lake some sixteen miles long and ten miles wide, saturated with minerals and salts. He had never seen a body of water with so many colors, deep blues, purples, greens, and even bright red where certain algae grew. The bungalow at Dochen, thirteen miles from Tuna, stood right on the shore of the lake, which shimmered with the reflections of soaring snowcapped mountains and the slow movement of hundreds of waterfowl, bar-headed geese and Brahminy ducks, terns and wagtails.

But the news from the men was not good: Wollaston and Wheeler were still suffering, Raeburn was not well, and there was no chance that Kellas would be able to walk or ride on his own the next morning. He had lost fourteen pounds even before arriving in Darjeeling; now, after a fortnight with no appetite for food, he was withering away. The only moment of levity came with the news that one of the cooks, who had never seen canned food, had placed a tin of fish into boiling water to cook it. When he went to open the can, the contents had exploded all over the kitchen. Word spread through the camp that all of the British stores were explosive, a rumor Howard-Bury did nothing to quell. Henceforth pilfering from the supplies became less of a problem.

From Dochen the expedition at last departed from the Lhasa road and headed northwest across the 16,500-foot Dug La, a short march of only eleven miles that led to the small and dirty village of Khe. It was a bleak place, Howard-Bury would later recall, haunted by a more illustrious past, for there were several ruins and evidence of an ancient lakeshore long since reduced to dust. "The wind is the curse of the country," wrote Wheeler, "your face simply goes to bits." Mallory called it "our great enemy . . . the dry, dusty unceasing wind . . . The real problem for comfort now is to get a tent pitched so as to have some shelter when the day's destination is reached." They had seen the last of the comfortable government bungalows. The following morning, June 3, dawned bright. Wheeler felt poorly but noted that "a little lead opium improved matters considerably." Raeburn was still low, but Kellas, mercifully, seemed somewhat better. He was, as Wollaston later reflected, very difficult to read. Though obviously suffering and somewhat humiliated by his weakness, "he endured long marches with wonderful fortitude and was invariably cheerful."

The day was hot, and Howard-Bury elected to stop after but ten miles at Kheru, where new transport was to be secured. Some twenty families of nomads were encamped in a small side valley. Expecting the British, they had pitched a black yak-hair tent and welcomed the men with tea and sweets. Wheeler took comfort in the warmth and spent the afternoon curled by the brazier and the yak-dung fire. Howard-Bury went hunting for gazelles. Bullock shot a bar-headed goose. That evening Wheeler invited Heron, Wollaston, and Bury to his tent for cocktails, a fine brandy, and the men later dined on an excellent menu of soup, Bullock's goose with peas and potatoes, rice pudding, and cocoa. "I enjoyed it thoroughly," Wheeler wrote, though he would need more opium in the night.

Saturday, June 4, broke well, with Wheeler much improved and Wollaston fully recovered. It was an easy march of sixteen miles over two high passes to Tatsang, "the falcon's nest." Howard-Bury again abandoned the main track to follow the crests of the hills. Kellas, perhaps inspired by the sight of the great peaks of Chomiomo, Pauhunri, and Kanchenjhau, all of which he had climbed, began the day feeling better, and elected to ride a yak. Wheeler and Wollaston rode with him as far as the second pass; there, at 17,100 feet, they left him behind. Kellas was uncomfortable, Wheeler later confessed, but seemed to be fine.

By good fortune Mallory, Bullock, and Heron had remained behind, riding high onto the ridges to hunt bharal. They had just reached the pass and settled down to lunch when the translator Gyalzen Kazi arrived breathlessly to say that Kellas had collapsed just below the windward side of the pass. Leaving Heron and Mallory to tend to the older man, Bullock rode hard to overtake Wollaston and Wheeler. Wollaston went back and found Kellas utterly incapacitated, shivering in the wind, his lips blue. He gave him hot Bovril, brandy, and milk.

There was not much else to be done but to get him to camp. In his diary Wheeler later described the crisis rather casually: "When about 3 miles further on, we heard that Kellas was on top of the pass . . . so Wollaston went back. Bullock and I came on crossing a barren plain to the Ta-tsang, a tiny village and monastery on top of a rocky bluff. Camp was in a hollow by a nice little stream." Several porters were sent back with a stretcher. "Goodness knows," wrote Wheeler, "when they will get him in." Bullock, meanwhile, went fishing, managing to catch several trout with his butterfly net. Howard-Bury busied himself with the cooks, instructing them how to prepare the meat of a gazelle he had shot that day. The temperature dropped to seventeen degrees Fahrenheit and the streams were frozen by the time Kellas was finally carried into camp.

The following day, again reportedly in good spirits, Kellas started off on a litter at 7:00 a.m. The destination was Kampa Dzong, where Henry Morshead and his survey team awaited. To reach there Kellas had to travel twenty-one miles and cross a 17,200-foot pass. Wollaston and Howard-Bury had by this point decided to send him back to Darjeeling at the first opportunity, but for the moment there was no choice but to continue. Howard-Bury saw him off, then paid a visit to a nearby nunnery, where thirty women, their heads shaved and adorned with marvelous wool headdresses, sat quietly in meditation in a small, dark room before dozens of statues of the Buddha, all covered in gauze veils. Silently they spun prayer wheels, some small and others large enough to contain parchment inscribed with half a million prayers.

After begging leave of the elderly abbess, Howard-Bury, keen to catch up with his men, cantered along a dry and barren valley. He reached Kellas and his small party of porters well before the slow rise to the second pass leading to Kampa Dzong. The invalid seemed quite cheerful, so Howard-Bury continued on at a brisk pace until, reaching the pass, he sighted three Himalayan blue sheep, all large rams. He gave chase and after a mile managed to shoot the grandest of all. Triumphant, he rode down the pass toward Kampa Dzong, across fields of blue-and-white irises, until the valley narrowed to a limestone gorge and he saw, towering 400 feet above him, the silhouette of a great fortress crowning a massive cliff of upturned sedimentary rock. Camped at the base of the fortress, on an exposed grassy flat, were the Indian surveyor Gujjar Singh and Henry Morshead. Wheeler was already there, having pushed on ahead of the others, keen to retrieve his mail, and with much to discuss with Morshead. They found Morshead and Singh to be well, though nearly out of food and impatient, having arrived nine days earlier. They had passed the time checking Colonel Ryder's triangulation stations of 1904.

The *dzongpen* appeared around 4:00 to welcome Howard-Bury and offer gifts to the expedition: five live sheep, a hundred eggs, and a small carpet woven in a workshop within his own fortress. Their cordial formalities had scarcely begun when a man came rushing up to say that Kellas was dead. Wollaston, who had just arrived, could not believe it. Coming down out of the pass, he had received a note indicating that the doctor was well and, after a rest of an hour or two at the pass, would be arriving late in Kampa Dzong. Wollaston rode back immediately to verify the news. He found, to his horror, that his patient had suffered a massive heart attack, undoubtedly brought on by complete exhaustion. "Need I say," he wrote on June 11 to Younghusband, "that it was a very bitter shock to me and I feel myself very greatly to blame. Had I suspected earlier that he had so little reserve strength he would never have left Phari. But having left that place there was no turning back. I believe now that he should never have left Darjeeling."

Of all the men, Mallory was the most shaken by Kellas's death. "Can you imagine," he wrote to his good friend David Pye, "anything less like a mountaineering party? It was an arrangement which made me very unhappy and which appalls me now in the light of what has happened—he died without one of us anywhere near him." He went on, however, to explain, rather weakly, that Kellas had insisted on bringing up the rear. "Well, once one is in front, one doesn't linger much in dusty places on a windswept plain; and after our first anxieties none of us lingered much for Kellas. After all, there was nothing to be done for him if one did stay to see him, and he didn't want it."

Wheeler recorded the event with a nonchalance that seems shocking to the contemporary reader: "Shortly after arrival we heard that poor old Kellas had died at the pass. He has been getting weaker and weaker and the jolting and height did him in. It is very rough luck and everyone was very much upset. However, it can't be helped." The very next lines in his diary read, "It is not so cold here as at Tatsang. A fine evening with good views of Chumyomo [*sic*], Kanchenjunga and the Lhonak group to the west, a long way across rolling plain."

The following morning, June 6, the expedition gathered to bury Kellas on a slope just south of Kampa Dzong, in a place overlooking the broad plains of Tibet and beyond to the great wall of the Himalaya. On the horizon loomed Chomiomo, Pauhunri, and Kanchenjhau, peaks Kellas had known better than any person alive. Farther to the west, perhaps a hundred miles away, partially hidden in the clouds, soared Chomolungma—Everest—the mountain for which he had staked so much. The funeral was, Mallory wrote to Geoffrey Young, "an extraordinarily affecting little ceremony, burying Kellas on a stony hillside. I shan't easily forget the four boys, his own trained mountain men, children of nature, seated in wonder on a great stone near the grave while Bury read out the passage from I Corinthians." Stones were gathered for a cairn, and Kellas's initials were scratched into the memorial.

Not all of the members of the expedition felt so moved as Mallory. Or, to be fair, they may have lost the very capacity to be touched by something as commonplace as death. Wheeler's entire diary entry for the day of Kellas's burial reads: "Abdul Jalil and a local man go to Phari to send news of Kellas and to change rupees to tonkas—so everybody took the opportunity of sending in letters. Temperature in tent at 6:30 a.m. 36 (sun not on tent). I spent the day developing—and got some fair results. I seem to be underexposing my Kodak pictures—so must raise the normal factor from 200 to 100 for a trial. The Survey ones are more or less ok. Kellas was buried during the morning. I did not know—as it was originally timed for the afternoon and so missed it. I was sorry not to be there—but I do hate funerals."

"WHEELER CAN be a bore in the colonial fashion," Mallory confided to Ruth in a letter written from Phari seven days before Kellas's death, "but I don't dislike him." Oliver Wheeler was not an overly complicated man, and if Canada more than fifty years after its confederation remained in Mallory's view a British colony, perhaps some part of his comment to Ruth was true. But a bore, Wheeler most certainly was not, and of death he knew more than Mallory would want to imagine.

Keen since youth to be a soldier, Wheeler had entered the Royal Military College, Canada's equivalent of Sandhurst or West Point, in the summer of 1907, the top qualifying candidate in his class. For each of his three years at RMC he ranked first in every category, and upon graduation in June 1910 he won twelve of the thirteen prizes given to the matriculating class, including the coveted Sword of Honour. At five foot ten, with dark hair and deep brown eyes, he was, like Mallory, a superb athlete, excelling at tennis, hockey, boxing, football, riding, and gymnastics. A fine actor and a highly skilled mathematician and topographer, he would in time be appointed to lead the Survey of India. Promoted to brigadier general in 1941, he was knighted by King George VI in 1943. His work as surveyor general resulted in the publication, during the Second World War, of 20 million maps a year, a vital contribution to the Allied war effort. As much as any other single man, Wheeler was responsible for foiling Japanese plans to invade India after Japan's conquest of Burma in 1942.

But as a young officer, fresh out of RMC and stationed for two years at Chatham in England for training, Wheeler was known simply as a brilliant prospect with a pleasant and engaging disposition. Dispatched to India in 1912, he served for two years as garrison engineer, first at Dehra Dun and later at Meerut. Then came the war. A young subaltern of twenty-four, he was posted to the 3rd Field Company, 1st King George V's Own Bengal Sappers and Miners, and attached to the 7th Meerut Division. Ordered to mobilize on August 9 and directed to Karachi on August 23, Wheeler sailed with the first transport of Indian troops destined for France, embarking on September 16 on the *H.T. Pundua*. Their convoy entered Suez on October 4 and steamed into Marseille ten days later. In less than a week, 45,000 Indian troops, for the most part men from tropical climes ill equipped for European weather, entrained for northern France.

By the end of the month they were in the trenches at Richebourg, having relieved the devastated British II Corps on a line that reached from Givenchy past Neuve-Chapelle to Fauquissart. The day before Wheeler himself came into the line, four companies of Indian troops had attacked an enemy salient, covering seven hundred yards of open ground and driving out the Germans after fierce hand-to-hand fighting. The Germans had counterattacked with devastating force. By the end of the day the Indians had lost, killed or wounded, every officer and a third of their men. "It is not war," wrote a sepoy from France, "it is the ending of the world." In only two months at the front, the India Corps lost 9,579 men, and this at a time when Indian soldiers were not permitted to dine with other imperial troops or to be medically treated by white nurses.

As sappers and miners, Wheeler's command had two primary duties: protecting and reinforcing the Allied trenches—which included laying wire, defusing bombs, reinforcing dugouts and traverses—and doing whatever was necessary to destroy the trenches and defenses of the enemy. The work was done at night, and almost always under enemy fire. In November 1914, when Wheeler was stationed near Festubert, it became clear that the Germans were systematically digging saps, trenches extending at ninety degrees from their line and reaching dangerously close to the British defenses. The order went out to eliminate these saps and in a manner that would make the Germans reluctant to repeat the tactic. On November 16 sentries in Wheeler's sector noted that two such enemy saps had been pushed within thirty feet of the front held by the 107th Pioneers. The following night 125 sepoys under the command of a Major P. H. Dundas, supported by Wheeler and a Captain R. E. Kelly, conducted what was later reported as "a dashing little raid."

At 8:55 the men went over the top, with strict orders to maintain silence until they reached the enemy saps. But no sooner had they cleared their own wire than withering fire came down from two flanks. Dundas and his command headed diagonally for the right sap, while Wheeler and his section raced for the other. Both were full of Germans, by chance waiting to launch their own trench raid on the Indians. The result was a melee of terror as men fought hand to hand in the dark with knives and clubs and bayonets. The Indians lost thirty-four men but cleared out the enemy. Wheeler saw to the wounded and then, under constant fire, directed his men through the night, equipped only with shovels as they filled in the saps, burying the dead from both sides who lay at the bottom of the trench, bodies entwined as they had fought, bloody faces frozen in puzzled and startled stares, the bewildered death masks of boys far too young to die. The officer compiling the war diary noted, "I should like to bring to your notice the coolness and dash displayed by Lt. Wheeler in the handling of his section."

This was by no means Wheeler's first experience with combat and death; for two months since he arrived in France, these had been the only constants in his life. But it was quite possibly the first time he had killed with his own hands. And there remained the haunting possibility that some of the lads at the bottom of the sap, in the darkness, with his men under duress and exposed to shell fire, may have been buried alive. In the immediate aftermath of the raid his journal reports simply that "the next few days passed fairly quietly, in the sense that nothing occurred beyond the usual shelling, sniping and bombing. The weather was very cold and frosty rendering the roads slippery and difficult for horse transport."

Wheeler remained in France from October 1914 through the last days of 1915, one of a small army of military engineers who designed and built what became the Western Front. He drew maps of enemy trenches and tunnels, installed machine guns and sniper emplacements for maximum effect, and trained blindfolded men to build in the dark, in silence and stealth and under enemy fire. Men under his command, all Indians, took the lead in improvising new weapons for a new kind of war: trench mortars, grenades, periscopes, Bangalore torpedoes for blowing wire. At Loos in September, he and his men, working within fifty yards of the German line, erected fourteen hundred yards of wire in a single night, only to watch the following day as 4,000 of their comrades in the Indian Corps perished in a single attack. On December 24, 1915, the Canadian papers reported that Wheeler had been awarded the cross of the Légion d'honneur (Chevalier 5th Class). By then he and the Indian Corps had left France, en route to the fighting in Mesopotamia. In thirteen months on the Western Front the Indian Corps, two divisions of a total of 48,000 men, had lost 1,525 officers and 32,727 men of other ranks. More than 1,000 British officers of the Indian Army had fallen. Wheeler, who had fought at the front from the start, was lucky to be alive.

Wheeler and the Indian Corps arrived in Mesopotamia at a low point in Allied fortunes. At the outbreak of the war a British force had sailed from Bombay, with the mission of securing the oil fields. By November 1914 Basra was firmly in hand and the strategic problem solved. But as the war moved into the spring of 1915, a desire to curb Turkish ambitions and relieve pressure on Gallipoli, together with the allure of capturing Baghdad, led the British to launch an all-out invasion of the country, which ended in disaster. Wheeler fought through the entire campaign, earning the Military Cross; he was mentioned in despatches seven times, and these were only the moments when someone of authority was there to notice. After enduring and surviving so much, he collapsed with typhoid fever at the end of June 1916 and was invalided back to India. By the time he was deemed fit for duty, in the fall of 1917, the British had taken Baghdad and his tasks became more pedestrian: securing military camps, positioning searchlights and wire, building bridges, roads, and rail lines.

The end of the war left Mesopotamia a backwater, but a land in turmoil and revolution. War-weary as they were, the British, afflicted by the hangover of empire, struggling with the remnants of the Ottoman Turks, invented a country they named Iraq, and then sought men who might understand it. In June 1919 Wheeler, promoted to the rank of major, was instructed to conduct a reconnaissance from Aliaga to Süleymaniye, 136 miles across an unknown desert occupied by peoples thought to be hostile to the British. His orders delineated his responsibilities. He was to describe the topography, note the condition and direction of trails, and identify sources of water, food, transport, and fodder. He was to discover the names of the nomadic tribes, place on the map points of potential ambush, and anticipate escape routes from enemy enfilade fire. He pursued this mission just as he had done things as a young surveyor in Canada, just as he had killed his first German soldier, and just as he proposed to find a route up the flank of Everest: by getting close, closer than anyone else would dare to do.

IF ANY MEMBERS of the expedition were upset with Wheeler for missing Kellas's funeral, there is no mention of it in the documents. Mallory, whose letters to Ruth are full of small confidences, does not bring it up. Howard-Bury, quite prepared in his correspondence with Hinks and Younghusband to speak critically of colleagues (Mallory and Raeburn in particular), says nothing. Bullock's diary is mute. No reference is made in the letters of Wollaston, Heron, or Morshead, or in the biographies, expedition reports, or memoirs of any member of the expedition. Wheeler's own journal records not a hint of disapproval from the others. To a contemporary reader this seems rather strange. It would be almost inconceivable on a modern expedition for a team member present in camp at the time of the ceremony simply to miss the interment of a fellow climber. But for these men the war had changed the very gestalt of death. In the trenches, they lived it every moment—some, like Wheeler, for years. By the time he was twenty-eight he had witnessed the death of hundreds, encountered the shattered bodies of many thousands. Death's power lies in fear, which flourishes in the imagination and the unknown. For Wheeler there was nothing more that death could show him, short of his own.

In the months and years immediately after the war the essence of death became redefined, even as survivors sought new ways to deal with the inexorable separation it implied. In the 1890s the practice of cremation hardly existed, with fewer than a hundred bodies being so disposed in all of Britain in a year; by the 1920s cremation was the choice of tens of thousands. Daily exposure to the horror of rotting flesh and bodies gnawed by rats made it seem a clean, pure, and highly desirable alternative to burial. If faith and traditional religion were among the casualties of the war, the rivers of dead inversely caused a surge of interest in unconventional notions of the spirit, the more esoteric the better, for mystics and oracles, mediums and soothsayers all promised the possibility, however remote, that communication with the dead might be achievable.

Hundreds of thousands of parents in Britain had never found out what had happened to their boys. They'd simply received an official telegram that read, "Regret—no trace." More than 200,000 soldiers simply vanished, obliterated by shell fire. In 1918 there were still

500,000 unmarked graves in the war zones. The carefully manicured cemeteries built after the war by the Imperial War Graves Commission, maintained beautifully as memorials to this day, promoted the illusion that there were actual bodies buried beneath the neat rows of individual headstones. The inscriptions remember the dead, but the graves, for the most part, contain nothing but the hopes and dreams of the living.

Those who had experienced the worst of the war shared no such delusions. Death had been the backdrop of their lives. On any given day, most expected to die. The odds against a young subaltern like Wheeler surviving four years at the front were enormous. With death looming at all times, each man was granted license to deal with it as he saw fit. If there was decency to be found in the trenches, it was in the private sphere of dignity, respected by all, that each soldier cultivated within himself as he anticipated his own end and that of his friends and brothers. No one intruded into that space, just as no one on the expedition would have judged Wheeler for what he did or did not do on the morning of Kellas's burial.

HOWARD-BURY, at any rate, had little time to mourn the loss of Kellas. Harold Raeburn was fifty-six and had been suffering bouts of dysentery and acute abdominal pain since leaving Darjeeling. Twice he had fallen from his mule and twice been kicked in the head. Having lost Kellas, Howard-Bury and Wollaston were not about to risk another man. At Kampa Dzong it was decided to send Raeburn back to Sikkim, where he might convalesce at lower elevation in Lachen, at a Christian mission run by Swedish Moravian nuns. Wollaston and Gyalzen Kazi would escort the patient as far as the mission and then by double marches return to the Tibetan Plateau to rendezvous with the expedition in a fortnight at Tingri. Thus within twenty-four hours the expedition lost the only two climbers with Himalayan experience and, at least until Wollaston's return, its two medical doctors.

But out of disaster came the promise of new possibilities, especially the composition of the climbing party. Raeburn, as Mallory explained to Ruth, was already a write-off, quite unfit for high-altitude work, "a worn out factious old person, not at all suitable for the job." His departure promised, if anything, to improve morale. Kellas, on this expedition, had never been destined for higher than base camp, given his condition and age. Heron had turned out to be a "solid treasure," superb at handling porters, but he was no climber. Wollaston, Mallory's closest friend to date on the expedition, was a fine naturalist but, at forty-six, not one for the ice and snow. Bullock was fit and had a particular knack for reading topography, and Mallory saw great things in him. He was also much taken with Morshead, "who has been walking everywhere on the hills up to 18,000 [feet] all the way from Darjeeling and looks as fit and strong as possible." Howard-Bury was a strong walker and showed promise, a possible fourth for the climbing party. "Wheeler the other surveyor," he wrote to Young, "though he has considerable mountaineering experience in Canada, is a lame duck with a stomach out of order. He may pick up but I've very little hope he'll prove much use."

Already one senses the hand of fate. Though no one on the expedition knew it at the time, Everest was already turning out to be Mallory's mountain. Raeburn's medical complications and the devastating loss of Kellas had simply helped to clear the decks. On the day of the funeral, just after dawn and before any in the camp had stirred, Mallory and Bullock had scrambled up the barren slope leading to the fortress to experience "the strange elation" of seeing Everest for the first time.

"It was a perfect early morning," Mallory wrote. "We had mounted a thousand feet when we turned and saw what we came to see. There was no mistaking the two great peaks in the west; that to the left must be Makalu, grey, severe, and yet distinctly graceful, and the other away to the right—who could doubt its identity? It was a prodigious white fang excrescent from the jaw of the world. We saw Mount Everest not quite sharply defined on account of a slight haze in that direction; this circumstance added a touch of mystery and grandeur; we were satisfied that the highest of mountains would not disappoint us."

In truth, it was impossible to get a fully unobstructed view of Everest from Kampa Dzong. The mountain was still more than a hundred miles away, and its lower flanks were blocked by a nearer group of mountains, the Gyangkar Range, which rose to 22,000 feet and ran north–south, perpendicular to the Himalayan wall, roughly forty miles to the west of their camp. But from the roof of the fortress, where the *dzongpen* had entertained Howard-Bury, Morshead, and Wollaston on the afternoon of the funeral, it was possible to discern several important things. Seen from the north, the vertical gain climbers would have to achieve appeared far less daunting than what they had observed from Darjeeling. The northern slopes seemed less steep, and the snow line appeared to be several thousand feet higher. The great masses of cumulus clouds that rolled north with the monsoon appeared to collapse against the southern side, blanketing even the lower elevations with rain and snow. Sikkim received as much as two hundred inches of precipitation a year, the Tibetan settlements on the plateau about fourteen. Perhaps, Howard-Bury suggested, the northern side of the mountains would be quite unaffected by the monsoon, in which case their prospects would improve considerably. As they would discover soon enough, he could not have been more wrong.

The challenge of assembling new transport, dispatching official letters and a telegram to Younghusband with news of Kellas's fate, as well as preparing Raeburn and Wollaston for their retreat south to Sikkim, held the expedition in Kampa Dzong until the morning of June 8, when, after much haggling and arguments over loads, they set off to the west, into country through which no European had traveled. The first day took them sixteen miles across the Yaru Chu, still a small stream, through beautiful groves of willows, onto a rocky spur that led to what Wheeler described as "the most beautiful valley yet seen on the trip," a great verdant plain that stretched all the way to Tingri. Bullock and Mallory, riding together, as always, ascended a small hill that rose out of the valley and spent an hour and a half at midday "basking in the sun and surveying the country around," Mallory wrote, noting that "it was very beautiful in its Tibetan way; there is more water over here and a very dark green broad undulating strip made a great contrast to the base gravelly sand or yellow dried grass. But the beauty is really one of form—gentle slopes rising from the plain as tongues of hill land projecting into it . . . surrounding hills and on all sides an almost infinite number of graduated ridges."

The expedition halted for the night at Lingga, a small village surrounded by marshes and ponds, with wild grasses growing alongside tender plantings of new barley. To the south extended the entire flank of the Himalaya, and throughout the day there were periodic sightings of Everest, which, like a lodestone, drew them on. Morshead was off on his own, camped a few miles to the north at a monastery, intent on following the crest of a ridge that paralleled the main valley. From the heights he could scan to both the north and the south, surveying the unknown country before rejoining the party the following night. The journey from Lingga to Tinki Dzong continued thirteen miles across the flat plain, through grasslands and marshes and small ponds crowded with teals, mallards, and bar-headed geese. Vast herds of yaks and sheep reached to the horizons. It was rich land with abundant water, and the day was bucolic, save for the torment of thousands of midges and sand flies, which hovered in clouds over every animal, including each rider.

The trail to Tinki Dzong led them through a curious belt of sand dunes, some twenty feet high, moving inexorably with the wind the length of the verdant valley. Beyond the dunes, great sheets of water spread to the horizon, shimmering in the afternoon light. Out of the sun, Howard-Bury saw riders approaching. It was the *dzongpen* of Tinki, mounted on a beautiful white pony, accompanied by several other men. He was a man, Howard-Bury later recalled, of impeccable grace and manners, Chinese in appearance, wearing embroidered silk robes, with a long pigtail and a most curious hat.

After brief salutations, the *dzongpen* escorted the British to a glen beside a pond where several tents had been pitched and women waited with refreshments, tea and great vats of frothy barley beer. Beyond the water stood the dilapidated walls of the fort. Above the camp was a small village and a monastery enveloped in a sacred grove of ancient willows. In his more formal welcome, the *dzongpen* presented Howard-Bury with four sheep and some two hundred eggs, even as he gently admonished the British not to shoot or molest any of the waterfowl, the ducks, terns, and geese that in their thousands dipped and dove in the marshes and ponds of the valley. Some years before, he explained, the Dalai Lama had sent a monk from Lhasa with specific instructions to tame the creatures of Tinki. Since that time all birds had been deemed sacred. That night Howard-Bury was astonished to find bar-headed geese and wild ducks, normally the most skittish of animals, waddling about his tent, squabbling and squawking and scavenging for food, even as he tried to settle down to his correspondence.

Delays in securing transport obliged Howard-Bury to halt for a day at Tinki. The expedition required ninety animals, but this meant recruiting yaks, ponies, and mules from as many as forty-five families, each convinced that its beasts were being asked to carry the heaviest loads. The solution was to place in a sack an embroidered garter taken from the boot of someone in each family. These were shuffled and then dropped randomly, one by one, as the sirdar moved from load to load. The weight of one's load became a matter of destiny, and no one could fight karma. Still, it made for slow departures, and it was remarkable that the expedition, after a day of rest and letter writing, managed to get off by 8:00 on the morning of June 11.

The track took them up the valley behind Tinki, in a slow, gentle rise to a 17,100-foot pass that fell away to the west to the valley of the Yaru. Howard-Bury paused at the summit and, with the weather fair, decided to scramble another 600 feet up the slope. From the rise he saw to the east Tinki and Kampa Dzong and the entire northern flank of the Himalaya reaching more than a hundred miles to Chomolhari. To the south and west unknown ridges still blocked the view to Everest, but he could see that in two days, once they had passed through and around the flank of the Gyangkar Range, the mountain would be unveiled. He plucked a blossom from the ground, a curious white-and-pink flower reminiscent of a daphne, slipped it into the buttonhole of his jacket, and made his way back to his mule and the men waiting for him at the summit of the pass. Only when they had ridden down to the Yaru Chu and found their camp pitched on a grassy flat just below the village of Chushar Nango, with its ruined stone tower and great gatherings of black ravens, did the men tell him that the flower was deadly poisonous and certain at the very least to give him a severe headache.

With every day, and every mile gained, the mountain took on a more powerful resonance. For Mallory it was something visceral. Unlike some of the others, who still suffered from the diet or the lingering effects of dysentery, he only became stronger, his mind more active, as he plotted and anticipated his moves. At Tinki he and Bullock had paraded the porters, selecting the twelve best to begin training for the snows. By night he hammered nails into their boots, cobbles to grip the ice. "My job begins to show like a flower bud soon to open," he wrote to Ruth from Tinki. "This begins to look like business." And to Geoffrey Young that same day: "We're just about to walk off the map—the survey made for the Lhasa expedition. We've had one good distant view of Everest from above Kampa Dzong and I'm no believer in the easy north face. I hope we shall see from some 30–40 miles off from some slopes this side of the Arun Valley in the next week or so. Geoffrey, it's beginning to be exciting."

THERE WAS rain in the night, but the morning dawned clear. With another change of transport, their departure was not until 10:00, and then, within a mile and a half of camp, there were further delays as they forded the Yaru Chu, a considerable stream some eighty yards wide and three feet deep. The new yaks, in particular, were very wild, and the plain was soon strewn with equipment and supplies as the stubborn creatures stomped and bolted, shedding their loads.

The track ran wide and clear for eight miles along the foot of hills rising on the west side of the valley, but then entered a broad wetland, where it disappeared into a score of narrow trails running off in every direction. Waiting at the junction was the headman of Gyangkar Nangpa, their next destination, who turned out to be the brother of the *dzongpen* of Phari. He guided the expedition to his village, where a feast of dumplings awaited. The women had never seen Europeans but had been told they were monstrously large, and so had prepared fifteen dumplings for every man, to be washed down with soup, chili sauce, and *chang*, barley beer. "Quite nice but not suitable for the state of stomach," Wheeler recalled. "The tea is distinctly nasty." They camped that night in one of the headman's green fields, protected from the wind by a stone wall. "Crossed the Yaru River today," he wrote to his wife, Dolly. "We are off the map now and have only an enlargement of the map of Tibet to go on, mostly computed from old explorer's reports and distinctly sketchy. But it makes it all the more interesting."

The following morning Mallory and Bullock were off by seven, riding alone, charged, too, with the excitement of entering uncharted land. They followed the Yaru and soon entered a dramatic gorge where the water cascaded along a deep riverbed, falling perhaps 200 feet in a mile. The dirt track rose for three hours, until a shallow ford led out of a confined draw and onto a wide plain where the Yaru took a turn to the south. Mallory knew that they had reached beyond the Gyangkar Range, the mountains that had blocked his view of Everest from Kampa Dzong. To the south the Yaru ran away to its confluence with the Phung Chu to form the Arun, which flowed south and west, eventually picking up three successive tributaries, the Dzakar, Kharta, and Kama Chu, all flowing off the eastern flanks of Everest before plunging through the Himalaya to Nepal. Two days later Mallory shared his sense of exhilaration in a letter to Ruth:

> As we rode out into this sandy plain to take stock of our surroundings and make out the map, such as it is, I felt somehow a traveler. It was not only that no European had ever been here before us, but we were penetrating a secret: we were looking behind the great barrier running north and south which had been a screen in front of us ever since we turned our eyes westwards from Kampa Dzong. From the most distant viewpoint, it is true, Makalu and Everest had peeped over the top; but for some days now, since the morning of our first day's march from Kampa Dzong, even the ultimate tops of these great mountains had been invisible. What were we to see now? Were they really to be revealed to us in their grandeur? We knew them to be somewhere at the end of the Arun Valley as we looked down it. There was nothing to be seen there at present but a bank of cloud.

Mallory and Bullock decided to tether their horses and scramble up a small peak, hoping for a better view. After an hour of hard climbing, they paused to glass the horizon, as if "some miracle might pierce the veil." The miracle happened. "Suddenly our eyes caught glint of snow through the clouds," he wrote to Ruth.

"A whole group of mountains," Mallory later recalled,

> began to appear in gigantic fragments. Mountain shapes are often fantastic seen through a mist. These were like the wildest creation of a dream. A preposterous triangular lump rose out of the depths; its edge came leaping up at an angle of about 70 degrees and ended nowhere. To its left a black serrated crest was hanging in the sky incredibly. Gradually, very gradually, we saw the great mountainsides and glaciers and arêtes, now one fragment now another through the floating rifts, until far higher in the sky than imagination had dared to suggest the white summit of Everest appeared. And in this series of partial glimpses we had seen a whole; we were able to piece together the fragments, interpret the dream. However much might remain to be understood, the centre had a clear meaning as one mountain's shape, the shape of Everest.

"We saw not only the summit," he told Ruth, "but the whole of the east face, no less than four groups of peaks which form its northward continuations, immense and quite unknown peaks, perhaps 1,500 feet lower than Everest itself and very nearly connected to it to the southeast, and finally two most notable cols to the left and right, dividing the great mountain from its neighbours.

"It was a gradually clearing view. The dark clouds were brightly lit, but still a great band lay across the face of Everest when we turned at last to go down and catch up [with] our train of coolies and donkeys, which we had observed crossing the plain to the west."

The main body of the expedition did not have quite so inspiring a day. In the morning Wheeler, still sick, shifted to a diet of porridge, soup, eggs, and milk pudding. There had been yet another change of transport, with the usual arguments and shouting, the headman collecting the boot garters and tossing them down, the loads flung over the wooden saddles and bound with yak-hair rope. The *dzongpen*'s brother guided the procession through the Yaru Gorge as far as the small village of Rongkong. Three miles beyond, the track divided, with the left fork following the Yaru south toward its confluence with the Phung

Chu. Bidding farewell to its escort, the expedition took the right fork, which rose through sandy, gorse-covered hills to a wide plain of shifting dunes and quicksand. The wind came up, as it always did in the afternoon, only it grew to galelike intensity. Violent sandstorms swept the valley, reducing the visibility to nil.

Howard-Bury contemplated a halt, but the guides insisted that the wind would make the crossing easier by blowing dry sand over the wet. So they started off, Howard-Bury recalled, "dressed as though for a gas attack, with goggles over the eyes and with mouth and nose covered with handkerchiefs and mufflers." Gusts off the dunes rendered everyone mute, making it impossible to hear the shouts of the porters, scattered by the storm and completely disoriented. Howard-Bury rode back and managed to rally them with a strict order to stay within sight of the man ahead and behind. The passage took on an almost hallucinogenic quality. The wind muffled the senses. There was no horizon, and no sense of sky save a brown haze filtering the sun. Spindrifts of dust and sand blew over the ground, making it impossible even to see the hooves of one's mule, let alone another rider. In places the ground quivered and shook and the mules lunged in panic for solid footing. The men clung to their saddles, facedown and bent into the wind. Eventually it became impossible to continue. Howard-Bury ordered a halt, and the men made camp in a howling gale among the sand dunes.

Mallory and Bullock did not fully escape the storm, but by the time they reached camp, the worst of it had passed, and in the falling light, Mallory recalled, a remarkable scene was unveiled: "The wind was blowing the sand as we followed up the party, and all the landscape to leeward was like a wriggling nightmare of watered silk. We found them on a little green bank rising from the dry plain, where by some miracle is a spring of water. Our friends were shuddering in their tents; but the wind dropped towards sunset, and they came out. We walked 200 yards or so to a little eminence, and there to the south was Everest absolutely clear and glorious."

Mallory was up early the next morning, unable to sleep, obsessed by what he had seen of the mountain. Wheeler spied him walking over the dunes, just after dawn, still clad in pajamas and bedroom slippers.

As THE EXPEDITION moved west, leaving the crescent sands and heading up the valley of the Phung Chu, only Wheeler, who was better but still weak for lack of food, stayed with the pack animals. Howard-Bury left the main party and climbed 3,000 feet up a spur dominating the valley from the north and was rewarded with an astonishing panorama of some 250 miles from beyond Chomolhari, in the east, to the summit of Gosainthan, in the west. Everest, at dead center, seemed to tower over the world. He sat down and remained there for five hours, enjoying the hot sun, simply staring at the mountain. At one point he noticed Morshead and several men far below, making their way quickly up the slope. Howard-Bury smiled to recall the night at Chushar when Bullock and Mallory had returned to camp exhausted, having spent but a day trying to keep up with the veteran surveyor. The three of them had climbed 1,000 feet up a ridge until, played out, the other two paused to rest. They had stared in amazement, they'd later reported to Howard-Bury, as Morshead stormed another 1,500 vertical feet up the mountain without stopping. There was no one stronger or fitter on the expedition. Howard-Bury had known from that moment that if and when an assault on Everest could be launched this year, Morshead would be among the climbers.

After exchanging pleasantries with Morshead and his companions, for they had not seen each other in several days, Howard-Bury left the survey team to its work and made his way off the mountain and headed west to catch up with the transport. There was an infestation of rinderpest in the valley, and only donkeys had been available. He wondered about the loads and how the diminutive animals had fared.

While Howard-Bury had climbed high to gaze upon Everest from the northern spur, Mallory and Bullock had set off in quite another direction, hoping to gain a different perspective on the mountain approaches. Abandoning camp early, they backtracked toward the Arun, fording the Phung Chu just above the confluence. Although Bullock crossed without incident, Mallory led his horse into a deep channel and was nearly swept away. The skittish ponies refused the steep sand that rose directly away from the river, but after some searching the men found a cleft in the cliffs that led onto the plain. From there they rode up the most prominent mountain on the west side of the river. Tethering their ponies on a broad spur a thousand feet above the valley, they scrambled up scree for another 2,000 feet to the north summit, an elevation of 17,650 as measured by their aneroid altimeter. Clouds obscured the peaks to the west, but Everest itself was visible, as was the dramatic summit of Makalu, just to the east. Both Mallory and Bullock felt again a peculiar sense of elation and foreboding. They simply had no reference points in their experience for mountains of such a scale. No one did. Heading for the summit of Everest in 1921 was as exotic as heading for the surface of the Moon.

Sir Charles Bell and His Holiness the Thirteenth Dalai Lama (seated, right) with Maharaj Kumar Sidkeong Trul-ku (standing)

General Charles G. Bruce drinking *chang*, fermented from barley, during the 1924 expedition. Photographed by Bentley Beetham.

The ice pinnacles of the East Rongbuk Glacier, photographed by Bentley Beetham in 1924

Right: Geoffrey Bruce and George Finch returning to Camp IV at 23,000 feet after their record climb in 1922. Photographed by John Noel.

An expedition party heading up the North Col to Camp IV, photographed by Bentley Beetham, 1924

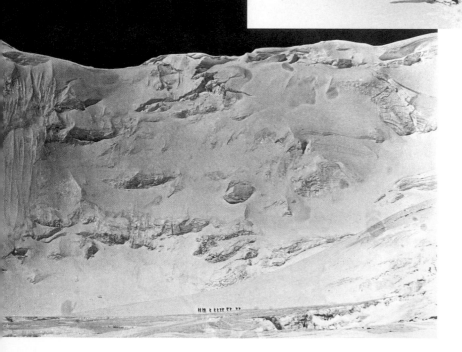

Everest, the Northeast Ridge, photographed
by Sandy Wollaston, 1921

Left: George
Mallory and
Teddy Norton
approaching their
highest point,
26,985 feet, on
May 21, 1922.
Photographed
by Howard
Somervell.

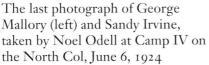

The last photograph of George
Mallory (left) and Sandy Irvine,
taken by Noel Odell at Camp IV on
the North Col, June 6, 1924

A self-portrait of John Noel filming the ascent of Everest from the Chang La, the North Col, 1922

Below: Another self-portrait: Noel Odell camped in the Zemu Forest, Sikkim, en route to Everest, 1924

The 1922 expedition at base camp, photographed with tripod and timer by John Noel. Back row (left to right): Henry Morshead, Geoffrey Bruce, John Noel, Arthur Wakefield, Howard Somervell, John Morris, and Teddy Norton.
Front row (left to right): George Mallory, George Finch, Tom Longstaff, General Bruce, Edward Strutt, and Colin Crawford.

Oliver Wheeler with his photographic survey team, photographed by Sandy Wollaston, 1921

Howard Somervell, photographed by Bentley Beetham, 1924

The camp at Windy Gap, on the Lhakpa La (22,500 feet), photographed by Charles Howard-Bury, 1921

Members of the 1921 expedition with Lord Ronaldshay, governor of Bengal, photographed by Guy Bullock's wife, Alice, outside Government House, Darjeeling. Left to right: Sandy Wollaston, George Mallory, Bullock, Ronaldshay, Charles Howard-Bury, and Harold Raeburn.

Summit of Everest and the North Col from the Lhakpa La, photographed by Charles Howard-Bury, 1921

The dedication of the
Fell and Rock Climbing
Club war memorial on
the summit of Great
Gable, June 8, 1924

George Mallory on the
Moine Ridge of the Aiguille
Verte, photographed by Geoffrey
Young, 1909

George Mallory (right)
and Siegfried Herford at
Pen y Pass, photographed
by Geoffrey Young, 1913

George Mallory and Sandy Irvine, photographed by Noel Odell, at the Pang La, looking southeast toward Everest, 1924. On the skyline to the right are Gyachung Kang and Cho Oyu.

The 1922 expedition heading overland, through Sikkim, to Everest, photographed by Howard Somervell

John Morris, photographed by his tent mate, George Mallory, 1922

John Noel captured the last climb in 1922. Within an hour this party would be swept off the face of the North Col, and seven Sherpas, seen here bringing up the rear, would be killed.

Shegar Dzong, with the tents of the 1924 expedition in the foreground, photographed by Noel Odell

The Himalayas from Darjeeling, circa 1890

Henry Morshead, Teddy Norton, Howard Somervell, and George Mallory after their 1922 summit attempt, photographed by John Noel. Only Somervell escaped frostbite.

The 1924 expedition, photographed by John Noel. Back row (left to right): Sandy Irvine, George Mallory, Teddy Norton, Noel Odell, and John Macdonald (translator). Front row (left to right): Edward Shebbeare, Geoffrey Bruce, Howard Somervell, and Bentley Beetham.

The fortress of Kampa Dzong, photographed by John Noel

The burial site at Kampa Dzong of Dr. Alexander Kellas, who died en route to Everest in 1921. Photographed by John Noel in 1922.

The 1921 expedition, photographed by Sandy Wollaston. Back row (left to right): Guy Bullock, Henry Morshead, Oliver Wheeler, and George Mallory. Front row (left to right): A. M. Heron, Sandy Wollaston, Charles Howard-Bury, and Harold Raeburn.

Geoffrey Bruce (left) and George Finch, photographed by John Noel, after their record climb to 27,300 feet in 1922

Teddy Norton in 1924, photographed by Howard Somervell, just before Norton turned his back on Everest at 28,126 feet. In the history of photography, no image has ever been exposed at a higher elevation.

The Rongbuk Monastery with the North Face of Everest in the background, photographed by John Noel in 1922

Members of the 1922 expedition enjoying an English breakfast in Tibet, photographed by John Noel. On the left of the image sit Arthur Wakefield, John Morris, and General Bruce. On the right, Geoffrey Bruce, an unnamed Gurkha, and Teddy Norton. Standing at the rear is the interpreter, Karma Paul.

Camp IV on the North Col, at 23,000 feet, photographed by John Noel, 1922

Seated left to right are Geoffrey Bruce, George Mallory, and Teddy Norton at the Rongbuk Monastery, awaiting the blessings of the high lama, Dzatrul Rinpoche, photographed by Noel Odell, 1924.

George Mallory's and Guy Bullock's camp at Pethang Ringmo with Chomo Lonzo soaring behind, photographed by Sandy Wollaston, 1921

Sherpas in 1924 climbing the North Col with the help of Sandy Irvine's rope ladder. Photographed by Howard Somervell.

Dzatrul Rinpoche, the abbot of Rongbuk Monastery, photographed by Noel Odell in 1924

George Mallory (upper left) and his team of Sherpas, photographed by John Noel on June 7, 1922, as they rested en route to Camp IV. None would make it to the North Col. Within the hour an avalanche would sweep seven of these men to their deaths.

Sandy Irvine with oxygen apparatus, photographed by his mentor, Noel Odell, at Shegar, 1924

They took photographs but did not linger. They had climbed 3,650 feet, and had not started until 4:00 p.m. Partly because the hour was late, and partly to test their wind, Mallory and Bullock ran down the mountain, reaching their ponies in thirty minutes. Darkness was coming on by the time they once again crossed the Phung Chu and caught up with the expedition at an old Chinese rest house at Trangso Chumbab, just across the river from the village of Chukor. For Bullock it was a cold ride, as he was wet to the knees from the river.

Morning found them in a rich valley, with the prospect of an easy march along the right bank of the Phung Chu seventeen miles northwest to the village of Kyishong. Howard-Bury did not keep to the road, but crossed a broad plain to explore a side valley, as always taking delight in the flora: a new black clematis, several species of broom, a meadow carpeted with wild yellow roses. He shot a gazelle, and later bagged a partridge and several hares. For a time he rested by a spring, taking notes for Wollaston of the birds that came to drink: blackbirds, rock doves, and Brahminy ducks, all surprisingly tame.

In the early afternoon the weather, hot and sultry that morning, suddenly changed as dark thunderclouds rolled over the mountains. Great sheets of hail pounded the ground, laying flat the barley and wild grasses, and blanketing the valley in white. The monsoon had broken, and by morning there would be snow on the hills. As he hurried on, dropping back into the main valley, he came upon a sacred monument, four large white chortens built as the corners of a square, at the center of which stood a stupa, a larger structure. To Tibetans, chortens and stupas are symbolic mountains, ritual daggers used to suppress darkness and plant the Buddhist mandala upon the earth. Howard-Bury would later learn that a demon lay beneath the largest of the structures, and that the four others helped hold the demon down, crushed by the weight of the millions of prayers buried in their stone.

The next day's march followed the main valley of the muddy Phung Chu through fertile marshlands of stunted willows, valerian, and clematis and then entered a series of conglomerate gorges and open flats thick with buckthorn. Six miles on, the track turned north, away from the river and up a side valley that in time opened onto the most astonishing sight Howard-Bury had yet seen in Tibet. In the distance, isolated amid rich fields of barley that shimmered in the morning light, a castlelike massif rose perhaps 3,000 feet to a sharp pinnacle of a summit. It seemed less a mountain than a feature of fantasy. Nestled on its sheer walls, halfway up the cliffs, a warren of white structures clung like swallows' nests to the precipice. These buildings, scores of them,

were connected by walls and turrets to an imposing fortress much farther up the mountain, from which massive defensive walls rose to the
very summit, crowned by a round Gothic-like tower out of which billowed white plumes of smoke. A lacework of prayer flags, strings of
banners in red, blue, green, and yellow, hundreds of feet long, decorated every flank of the mountain, as if to animate every rock and link
every gesture to the wind and the sky.

As Howard-Bury and the expedition came nearer, they could see at
the base of the mountain the whitewashed walls of the town of Shegar,
the district capital, gleaming in the sun. Most of the town turned out
to greet them. None of the residents had seen a European before. A
small tent had been pitched, but the pressing crowds were so bother-
some that Howard-Bury retreated behind a wall of stones. There were
two *dzongpens* stationed at Shegar, one secular and the other a monk,
but neither appeared. Howard-Bury dispatched Chheten Wangdi to
see what was going on. Before long he returned with one of the officials, bearing a basket of eggs as a gift. There had been some kind
of mixup, and no formal word had reached Shegar from Lhasa. Initially somewhat suspicious but soon deeply apologetic, the *dzongpen*
led them to a grassy enclosure in the shade of a willow grove, where a
festive Chinese tent had been erected for their kitchen. Howard-Bury
asked him rather emphatically that drink not be passed to any of the
expedition porters. The *dzongpen* demurred, then stiffened as he saw
several of the British strip down to wash. Like all Tibetans, he bathed
but once a year, late in the fall, and he was shocked to see men washing
themselves in June.

The expedition rested at Shegar for a day. Bullock chased butterflies for two hours and considered climbing a striking limestone
mountain to the northwest with the hope of seeing Everest, but instead
scrambled up a ridge on the south side of the Phung Chu. Mallory busied himself making preparations for an overnight bivouac. His sights
were on Everest, and a mountain between Shegar and Tingri promised
excellent views. In his diary Bullock makes little mention of their halt
at Shegar, save for the fact that on the night of June 16 "the camp was
attacked by a madman . . . I chased him out of camp with an ice axe
and captured his gun rest." As they later discovered, the culprit was a
deranged young man, normally kept by his parents under lock and key
on the night of a full moon. By chance he had escaped on the very day
the British had arrived.

Howard-Bury, for one, was astonished by what he saw of the monastery and the fortress perched above their camp, silhouetted against

the moon. Mallory often condemned him for being closed-minded and narrow in his convictions, but in realms of the spirit Howard-Bury was in fact completely open to the world, and in ways Mallory could never be. Howard-Bury had studied with Sanskrit scholars at Badrinath, sought the wisdom of Theravada teachings among the monks of Indochina, and anointed his body with scented oils and embarked on pilgrimages down the Ganges. Spiritual seeking had inspired the journeys of his youth, and though the war had stolen nearly everything, it had not quelled his fundamental curiosity; if anything, it had enhanced his yearning.

In the morning he went with Morshead to pay a perfunctory call on the *dzongpen*, who lived modestly in a small house at the base of the track that rose to the fortress and temples. His official residence was in the fort, but he was elderly and the climb was too much for him. Invited to eat the usual fare, sweetmeats and tea, minced meat and noodles spiced with chili, Howard-Bury and Morshead made inquiries about the road to Tingri and asked that word be sent ahead outlining their needs for accommodations, transport, and supplies. But in the moment Howard-Bury's real interest lay far above them, along the small paths that climbed through the archways leading to the inner sanctum and courtyard of the temple complex.

He reached there around three, accompanied by Wheeler and Morshead. Entering the dark recesses of the sanctuary he was astonished to see a dozen statues all decorated with turquoise and precious jewels, and behind them an enormous Buddha, fifty feet high and completely covered in gold. Strange figures with demonic grimaces circled the shrine as protector deities. Butter lamps cast shadows and brought a sparkle to the jewels, and provided enough light to the many mirrors to create the illusion that the chamber reached back to infinity, with the limitless potential of the Buddha mind.

The open air of the temple rooftop, where they paused for tea, offered astonishing views of the fields 1,000 feet below and the distant Phung Chu running away to the west. Howard-Bury asked permission to photograph a group of novices, and discovered that none of them had ever seen a camera. Before leaving they had an audience with the head lama, Lingkhor Rinpoche, who had lived at the monastery for sixty-six years. The incarnation of the previous abbot, he was a living Buddha, a bodhisattva who had achieved enlightenment and yet chosen to remain in this earthly realm to help all sentient beings escape the illusions of samsara. At Howard-Bury's behest, he agreed to have his photograph taken and was escorted outside to the courtyard, where he posed, Howard-Bury later wrote, "dressed in robes of beautiful golden brocades, with priceless silk Chinese hangings arranged behind him while he sat on a raised dais with his dorjee and his bell in front of him, placed upon a finely carved Chinese table." The fame of this photograph spread, and for the rest of the expedition, Howard-Bury would be besieged by requests for copies, for the man was a living saint and worshipped as a god incarnate.

There was, of course, a complex story to Shegar, only a small part of which Howard-Bury came to understand that day. Situated astride the crossroads of two major trade routes, one running to the north and south, the more prominent arching east to west from central Tibet to Nepal, Shegar Dzong had long been of strategic importance. The fortress had been forged in blood, in conflicts between rival Tibetan kingdoms in the fourteenth century and as recently as the devastating wars with Nepal; a Gurkha army of eight thousand had laid siege to the rock in 1788.

The monastery, by contrast, was said to have been born in prophecy. The story, as told to Howard-Bury, went like this: To the north of Bodhgaya, in India, where the Buddha Shakyamuni attained enlightenment, there was a land of high mountains rising like pillars to the sky. Below the mountains were beautiful lakes, mandalas of turquoise. The snow and ice were stupas of white crystals. The ocher slopes were of gold. In a kingdom, it was said, where autumn was colored with golden flowers and summer meadows had the scent of incense and the hue of turquoise, there would be found the true spiritual paradise, the home of the protector of the Land of the Snows. Among these mountains, the domain of the Chenrezig (or Avalokitesvara), the Bodhisattva of Compassion, there stood a rock in the shape of the Tara, the female essence. The prophecy maintained that one day, kings, monks, and lamas would reside on this pinnacle, and that it would become a great center for learning and the transmission of the dharma.

In the eighth century, when Padma Sambhava brought Buddhism to Tibet, he came upon such a place, inhabited by demonic mountain goddesses. Padma Sambhava tamed their wild natures, converting them to dharma protectors, with the darkest of all becoming transformed into a transcendent figure whose white body was a shimmering crystal. The mountain itself took her form, becoming the seat of the goddess, queen of the *dakinis*, or sky dancers. Her body became literally the foundation of the monastery, the first temple of which was constructed over her left breast. A white conch shell was buried beneath her vulva, in a secret place out of which flowed all wisdom and doctrine.

In time the Shining Crystal Monastery at Shegar became a major center of Buddhist scholarship and teachings, attracting learned lamas from throughout Tibet. Though a mythical being and divinity, Padma Sambhava was also an actual person, and his transmission of the Buddhist teachings to Tibet was one of the seminal acts of history. He supervised the construction of the first monastery at Samye, and translated the canon of Buddhist scripture from Sanskrit. He invited Indian scholars to Tibet, and dispatched hundreds of young Tibetans to India to study. After the Islamic invasion of India at the end of the twelfth century, when Muslim persecution over a century led to the slaughter of monks and the destruction of monasteries and libraries, Tibet became the repository of Buddhist dharma. Shegar, located close to the Nepali frontier, was, in part, a sanctuary. The temple, the main hall, and the first Sakya college were completed in the Wood-Ox year of 1385. In 1643, the Water-Sheep year, the Fifth Dalai Lama transformed Shegar into a Gelugpa monastery. For centuries the reputation of the sacred center grew. At Shegar, it was said, the color saffron filled the space between earth and sky with vermilion light, and everywhere holy precepts and wise learning resounded.

At the time of the arrival of the British expedition, there were twenty-one colleges at Shegar dedicated to the study of tantra, debating, and metaphysics, with hundreds of monks sitting in spiritual examinations for *geshe*, the highest of scholastic degrees. The rituals and debates the members of the British expedition witnessed, and the timing of the tea breaks they sat through, had not changed in essence or in practice for nearly four hundred years.

Curiously, only Howard-Bury seems to have recognized the power, meaning, and significance of the place. Bullock and Mallory scarcely noticed. Wheeler wrote to his wife, acknowledging that Shegar was "quite the most picturesque spot we've been in." He found the people to be "infernally curious" and later confessed, "I'm not much good at descriptions I'm afraid, but will send a photo later."

To be fair, none of them had any context for understanding what they were seeing. Images of Tibetan cruelty and barbarism invoked in the writings of Henry Savage Landor and Perceval Landon near the turn of the century, during Younghusband's invasion, had for the most part been discredited. Yet Tibet the mystical, as we know it today, had yet to be invented. Walter Evans-Wentz was in Darjeeling in 1919, but his translation of *The Tibetan Book of the Dead* did not appear until 1927. The theosophist and artist Nicholas Roerich did not begin his four-year sojourn in Tibet and India until December 1923, and *Heart of Asia*, his account of his travels, was published only in 1930. Alexandra David-Neel first visited Sikkim in 1912, but the journey to Lhasa that would gain her international fame did not occur until 1924. Her accounts of flying yogis and lamas with tantric powers did much to influence later publications, such as *Lost Horizon*, James Hilton's 1933 fictional account of Shangri-La, the world's first mass-market paperback best seller. But her books *My Journey to Lhasa* (1927) and *Magic and Mystery in Tibet* (1929) came after the early British efforts on Everest. Like the outpouring of war memoirs that ultimately defined our notions of the Lost Generation, the wave of travel accounts celebrating the mystic wonders of Tibet, including the possibility of reincarnation and rebirth, appeared in the late 1920s and early '30s. The two trends were not unrelated, but both came too late to influence Howard-Bury as he stood before the wonder of Shegar Dzong.

In this void created by the absence of expectation, Howard-Bury simply reported what he saw, and he did so with an open mind and remarkable tolerance. Asked to report on the life and customs of Tibetans in one of his dispatches to the *Times*, he mentioned that they wore clothes made at home from sheep wool and that their crops of barley and peas thrived at the highest elevations. They did indeed bathe only once a year, simply because of the cold. The women smeared their faces with grease and soot to protect their skin from the weather. The people practiced polyandry, with the wife of the eldest brother also belonging to other brothers, an arrangement that, as Howard-Bury noted, rephrasing the issue with some delicacy, also allowed a woman to be free to have relations with and receive support from more than one man.

The oddest custom, he confessed, concerned the disposal of the dead. A special class of men cut up the bodies and fed each fragment to vultures. "The practice is perfectly clean," he hastened to add, "for all the scraps disappear very quickly, as after all everything is frozen for six months of the year." Life on the Tibetan Plateau was not easy, he indicated. Winter cold came with every night, and the heat on summer days was so intense that it "drew all life out of one the moment the sun was up." But, he added, the people had shown the British the "very greatest kindness. It must be remembered that these Tibetans had never before seen a European, but they were wonderfully hospitable to us." Such sentiments stood in marked contrast to those of Mallory, who in a petulant moment would famously describe Tibet as "a hateful country inhabited by hateful people."

Mallory and Bullock left Shegar with half a dozen porters at 7:00 on the morning of June 18, equipped with only a pair of Mummery tents, blankets, and modest supplies for the men. Their plan was to establish a fly camp for two nights, south of the Phung Chu, with the goal of climbing as high as possible to obtain a closer view of the Everest massif. "Everest had become something more than a fantastic vision," Mallory explained to Ruth. "One began to know it as a peak with its individual form; the problem of its great ridges and glaciers began to take shape, and to haunt the mind presenting itself at odd moments and leading to definite planes. Where can one go for another view, to unveil a little more of the great mystery? From this day that question has always been present."

With Bullock distracted by his spirited pony, they reached the Phung Chu, but they mistook it for a side stream. Still seeking the main river, they followed an insignificant affluent into a side valley and then doubled back, fording deep streams, their porters waist-deep in water, only to find themselves, after seven hours, back on the south side of the Phung Chu just five miles from Shegar on the road they ought to have followed in the first place. Mallory, in particular, was a wet mess. He had lost his mackintosh cape, soaked his field glasses, and reduced his hat to a pulp. The two men were not an impressive sight when first seen by Howard-Bury and the rest of the party, which, because of various delays, had not left Shegar until noon. Wheeler reported the incident with a single line in his diary. "Mallory and Bullock had started around 7 am and at 2:30 Howard-Bury met them. They had forded the river pretty well up to their necks after completely losing themselves!"

Bullock and Mallory swallowed their embarrassment and continued south, up a valley that led to the town of Pang La, where they made their camp at 14,300 feet. The next day they were up before light. Setting off at 4:30, they walked steadily for nearly two hours, reaching a high pass that offered an astonishing view of the entire Everest group, from Makalu all the way west to a series of unknown summits, all towering, it seemed, to heights of 26,000 feet or more. Everything they could see lay unexplored. To the west some twelve miles beyond Everest, the Nangpa La led to Nepal and the Solu Khumbu, the homeland of the Sherpas. Soaring above the pass was Cho Oyu, at 26,906 feet the world's sixth-highest summit. Moving along the horizon toward Everest, Gyachung Kang stood at 25,990, itself taller by 3,000 feet than any mountain in the Americas. Everest (29,035 feet) loomed over all, but was shadowed by Lhotse (27,890 feet) and, to the east, Chomo Lonzo (25,604 feet) and its sister summit, Makalu (27,765 feet). These appeared less as separate mountains than elements of a whole, a massive wall of ice and rock that stretched in a curve some forty miles before the ridge fell away into the great gorge of the Arun, which cut through the range to the east. Although Mallory and Bullock did not know it at the time, in the fifteen minutes they had at the summit of the Pang La before the clouds rolled in and blanketed the horizon, they were looking at four of the six tallest mountains on earth. Even the cols that separated the summits—and from where the real climbing would begin—stood 10,000 feet higher than Mont Blanc, the tallest mountain in Europe and the highest point Mallory had ever achieved as a climber.

Humbled and inspired, quivering with the daunting task ahead, they headed down the Pang La, returning to camp at 8:00 a.m., and were on their way again within the hour, riding through hot sun and then a small hailstorm, passing the village of Tsakor to reach the meadows of Memong in early afternoon. The following day they were off at 6 a.m. and, leaving the porters behind, pressed ahead across the great plains of the Phung Chu to reach Tingri by midmorning.

The main party, meanwhile, had pushed along the direct road from Shegar, camping the first night at Tsakor. The pack train did not appear until long after dark, and the entire team slept in a large kitchen tent kindly provided by the local yak herders. The following day they got an early start and moved at an easy pace across the expanding valley of the Phung Chu, which ran wide between shallow banks. In another month the rains would obliterate any sense of a river and water would flood the entire breadth of the valley. The marshes and fields were already sodden, and there were scores of wading birds, egrets and black-necked cranes. The flies and midges were dreadful. Howard-Bury had just covered his mouth with a kerchief when he saw the most arresting of sights: a solitary man, well in the distance, who seemed to be stumbling repeatedly, only to regain his feet with the predictability of a metronome. He would then stand erect for a moment, only to stumble once more. As they came closer Howard-Bury recognized the man as Mongolian. He wore layers of sodden wool and both his hands and his knees were wrapped in filthy rags. His hair was matted, his face black with grease, and his forehead shone where the grease seemed to have been rubbed away.

The man was a pilgrim eleven months out of Lhasa, moving 650 miles toward Kathmandu, one body length at a time in ritual prostration. From a standing position, he would look ahead, lift his hands touched in prayer over his shoulders as high as he could reach, and then, bringing them back to his forehead, throat, and chest, he would bend forward to the ground. Touching the earth on all fours, with hands flat and squarely on his knees, he placed his forehead on the ground, making five points of contact. Thus he would purify from his being the five poisons of hatred, desire, ignorance, pride, and jealousy, that they might be replaced with the five corresponding aspects of wisdom. Standing once more, he drew his hands again in prayer to his chest, a symbolic gesture indicating his willingness as an aspiring bodhisattva to take on the suffering of all sentient beings. With each silent prostration he moved that much closer to his goal, which was not a place but a state of mind, not a destination but a path of salvation and liberation that is the ultimate quest of the pilgrim.

For Howard-Bury, less than three years removed from the blood and horror of Flanders, it was a stunning affirmation of religious purpose. He moved slowly past the man and listened. As his pony clip-clopped along the track, he could hear over his shoulder the rustle of woolen cloth and the sound of hands passing over the dirt. To the south all of the peaks came clear and the snows of Everest could be seen looming against a lapis sky. The expedition reached Tingri just after noon on June 19, exactly one month and 362 miles after leaving Darjeeling.

CHAPTER 7

The Blindness of Birds

IN THE EIGHTH CENTURY the Tibetan armies of King Trisong
Detsän sacked the Chinese capital, crushing the Tang dynasty
before turning west to threaten the Arab caliph and the lands of the
Middle East. Then, at the height of his power, with Tibet in control
of much of central Asia, the king decided to free his countrymen from
their violence and barbarism. He called on a great Indian sage, Padma
Sambhava, to introduce the Buddhist dharma, the teachings that might
tame the demonic heart of the nation, silence the jealous mountain
gods, and bring peace, wisdom, and transcendence to the people.

Uncertain where and how to begin, Padma Sambhava sought
help from the Buddha himself, who had long since passed into the
realm of nirvana. Buddha Shakyamuni, returning in resplendent form,
picked up a stone from the ground, a sphere as light as a dove, spun it
between his fingers, and then threw it high across the Himalaya. When
it landed, a single perfect note resounded through the universe. The
Buddha called the place T'ing Ri, and dispatched Padma Sambhava to
find the stone and begin his teachings.

Padma Sambhava went first to the mountains north of the Phung
Chu, the river the British under Howard-Bury had followed on their
march from Shegar. There, in a place of power and pilgrimage known
today as Tsibri, Padmasambhava met a *dakini*, a sky dancer, a female
protector and mountain goddess who led him back across the valley to
the hills of Langkor, where he actually found the sacred stone cast by
the Buddha.

For the rest of his life, until finally ascending to the Copper Mountain Paradise, Padma Sambhava remained in the T'ing Ri Valley,
meditating and teaching, inspiring the construction of monasteries,
infusing the very land with the essence of the dharma, which the Buddha had distilled in the Four Noble Truths. First, all life is suffering.
By this the Buddha did not mean that all life is negation, but only
that terrible things happen. Evil was not exceptional but part of the

existing order of things, a consequence of human actions, or karma. Second, the cause of suffering is ignorance. By ignorance the Buddha did not mean stupidity. He meant the tendency of human beings to cling to the cruel illusion of their own permanence and centrality, their isolation and separation from the stream of universal existence. The third of the noble truths was the revelation that ignorance could be overcome, and the fourth and most essential was the delineation of a contemplative practice that, if followed, promised an end to suffering and a true liberation and transformation of the human heart. The goal was not to escape the world but to escape being enslaved by it. The purpose of practice was not the elimination of self but the annihilation of ignorance and the unmasking of the true Buddha nature, which, like a buried jewel, shines bright within every human being, waiting to be revealed. Padma Sambhava's transmission, in short, offered nothing less than a road map to enlightenment.

Revered as Guru Rinpoche, Teacher of Teachers, Padma Sambhava, "Lotus Born," was in time deified by the Tibetan people. His wanderings were as prayers, his very presence a sign of the sacred, imprinted on the landscape for all time. The wonder of his memory and the miracles of his deeds drew an endless stream of pilgrims and mystic saints to T'ing Ri and beyond, to the wild reaches of the mountain streams that drained the glaciers and ice fields of the highest and most rugged knot of mountains in the world. He was the hero of heroes, a true bodhisattva, the wisdom hero, the realized being who had found enlightenment and yet remained in the earthly realm of samsara, of suffering and ignorance, to help all sentient beings achieve their own liberation.

To guide the people in their quest, and to ensure the eternal resonance of the wisdom doctrine, Guru Rinpoche planted along his path spiritual treasures, sacred texts and tantric teachings that might survive times of persecution, remaining magically hidden in the landscape until ready to be unveiled. Some were actual manuscripts sealed away in chortens or cached in caves. Others were instructions passed down in mystic script and concealed within the five elements, earth, water, fire, air, and ether. Some were sequestered in meditative space alone. To facilitate the endless flowering of the dharma, Guru Rinpoche through prophecy reached into the future, empowering a tradition of treasure seekers, tertöns, spiritual adepts destined to discover over time these dharma treasures, advanced and esoteric techniques that, like flashes of the spirit, allowed the seeker to bypass the mundane liturgies, yogas, and visualizations of orthodox practice and cut through to the very essence of Buddhahood.

In addition to these treasures, deposited as a ring of bone along the body of the Himalaya, Guru Rinpoche scattered throughout the mountains sacred valleys, or *beyuls*, hidden lands of fertility and blessings, secret places where simply to be born and to live was to be liberated from the endless cycle of life, death, and rebirth. These hidden valleys, like the mythical kingdom of Shambhala, said to be found in the north of Tibet beyond the limitless horizons of the Chang Tang steppe, inspired the Western notion of Shangri-La. But for Tibetans, the Himalayan *beyuls* were actual places, landscapes that existed simultaneously in both physical and metaphysical space. They were true geographical refugia, verdant valleys dominated by protective mountain deities where people could seek solace as lonely pilgrims, or flee violence as a community in time of war.

Beyond the material plane, the *beyuls* also existed in mystic dimensions visible and accessible only to the most advanced practitioners of the Buddhist way. Ancient texts known as lamyig (neyig), guidebooks said to have been written by Guru Rinpoche himself in the eighth century, described their locations and landscapes, noted the ritual activities to be performed before crossing their thresholds, and identified the days and months of the year when a journey through the portals of the divine might prove to be auspicious. These conditions were delineated with great specificity, as were the consequences of violating the sanctity of the hidden lands. Those who entered the sacred space did so with both care and intense anticipation. Merely to walk through a landscape sanctified by Guru Rinpoche was to gain merit and obtain realization and great power, provided one's intentions were pure and the timing propitious. To enter a *beyul* without preparation, or before it had been spiritually opened by an enlightened being, was to risk catastrophe. Guru Rinpoche left a clear warning to guide pilgrims on the perilous path:

"You blessed ones who will discover my treasures in the future, keep this testament in your minds. If you cannot sustain the teaching, misadventure will certainly befall you . . . If you reveal the secret teaching before it is time, you will be struck. Make your vision as high as the sky . . . your activity heroic and confident . . . If you act according to my advice, blessings will spontaneously accrue. You will find Buddha within yourself . . . Failing to do as I advise, you will disgrace the Buddha . . . and, setting yourself on the road to hell, you will waste your precious human body."

HOWARD-BURY HAD no idea that the mystic tracks of pilgrims radiated in every direction and dimension from the town of Tingri. It seemed to him on arrival to be a modest place, a warren of stone, and very much of this world. He noticed the absence of wood. The smoke of dung fires hovered in the early afternoon light. The street stalls and shop fronts were stacked with wool and salt, piles of red chilies and great mounds of white butter, barley flour, and chips of dried meat. His soldier's eye took in its strategic position: two hundred houses packed closely along the flank of a high, solitary hill, remarkable in its isolation, that rose some 300 feet above the valley floor, a wide and windswept plain beyond which mountains towered on three sides. The local people, he was told, the nomads in particular, knew the town as Gang-gar, or "high encampment."

Located at the crossroads of ancient routes that led east to Shegar and Lhasa, west in sixty miles to Nyenyam and beyond to Kathmandu, and south directly across the Himalaya to the Sherpa homeland of Solu Khumbu, Tingri had long anchored the border trade with Nepal. Like most frontier outposts, it was no stranger to vice. A way station of gambling, drinking, and brawling, it was a sleepless settlement of dark, smoky inns where brigands and thieves mingled with artisans and monks, and runaway debtors hid out among scores of harmless serfs fleeing the monastic estates. For the British climbers, who would make it their base for nearly a month as they probed the approaches to Everest, it was, Wollaston later wrote, a place of "unimaginable filth inhabited by people vile in their habits." English sensibilities were readily inflamed, but even within Tibet, Tingri had a certain reputation. The town had one of the highest rates of illegitimate birth in all of the country, and also the lowest birth rate, for so many of its residents were sterile due to the high prevalence of venereal disease.

On top of Tingri Hill was an old Chinese fort, falling into ruin but only recently abandoned. Howard-Bury found the ground still littered with papers and books with Mandarin script, the inner walls adorned with bright frescoes, winged dragons and warriors riding stags into battle. When Hari Ram, the explorer and Indian pundit, had gone through Tingri in 1885, the garrison had numbered close to six hundred, Chinese and Tibetan troops positioned to defend the country against Gurkha invaders from Nepal. By 1921 this had been reduced to a shadow force of just four soldiers, plus a sergeant and *depon*, or military governor, whose main task was the transfer, each year, of 5,000 rupees as tribute to the Nepalese, a people the Tibetans still feared, even as they loathed the Chinese, expelled at last only a decade before.

At the base of the hill was a large rest house, built by the Chinese, and used to accommodate visiting government officials and dignitaries. Few Tibetans, however, were prepared to stay in the complex, haunted as it was by the ghosts of the many Chinese who had been killed within its walls. For the British it made for ideal lodgings. The rooms were small with mud floors; the roofs, as they discovered the first night, were in desperate need of repair; but the buildings, quaint and picturesque, with fantastic murals of flying dogs and demons, were fundamentally sound. There were three concentric courtyards, allowing Howard-Bury to billet the entire expedition: the porters in the outer ring; the survey parties, Morshead, Wheeler, and Heron in the middle; and the core expedition members in the inner sanctum. Water initially presented a problem, as the local supply was brown with mud. But a clear spring was soon found, not half a mile away. Once they had sorted through the supplies and equipment, determining what, if anything, had been lost or damaged on the journey from Darjeeling, the first priority was the construction of a darkroom, for they had to process film and make prints in the field, in a space free of dust and sheltered from the wind. Within hours of arrival they had plastered the floor, ceiling, and walls of a small chamber with mud, and by the end of the day, the first wet prints hung from a line of cord strung between posts carved in the shape of dragons.

The following morning, June 20, Howard-Bury and the entire party, save Mallory and Bullock, who had yet to arrive in Tingri, clambered up the hill, reaching the summit just after 6:00 a.m. with the hope of obtaining a view of the mountains to the south. Clouds, unfortunately, obscured much of the horizon, though Everest could be plainly seen and, to the west, some twenty or thirty miles away, the great summit of Cho Oyu, rising to 26,906 feet. It was a daunting sight, one that only reinforced their sense of the unknown. Their first task, as Mallory would later reflect, was to find a way to the mountain, and in the face of a dark and gathering monsoon. Each of Everest's lateral valleys, radiating to all sides, would have to be penetrated and explored. These, no doubt, would be separated one from the other by formidable ridges, across which routes would need to be charted, passes identified and traversed. Once they were at close quarters, the real work would begin. Every face and ridge would need to be studied, the approaches to every saddle, or col, scrutinized. The very form and structure of the mountain—the character of its sedimentary rocks, the nature of its ice and snow—held mysteries waiting to be unveiled. "We must distinguish," Mallory wrote, "the vulnerable places in its armour and finally pit our skill against the obstacles wherever an opportunity of ascent should appear until all such opportunities were exhausted."

The British knew something of the basic geography. From Kampa

Dzong, where Kellas had been buried, they had marched west to the confluence of the Phung Chu and the Arun, and then, following the Phung Chu upstream, had proceeded northwest to Shegar and then west again to reach Tingri. At Tingri the Phung Chu takes a dramatic turn to the north. Its headwaters, uncharted and unexplored, lay somewhere along the mountainous heights that formed the divide between the drainage of the Arun and that of the Tsangpo, Tibet's greatest river, which flows across the plateau west to east before plunging through the Himalaya to become, as Morshead with Bailey had confirmed on their 1913 expedition, the mighty Brahmaputra.

Joining the Phung Chu at Tingri and flowing directly from the south was another river, which the Tibetans identified as the Ra Chu. By following this modest tributary upstream and due south, Howard-Bury understood, they would reach in a day, or perhaps two, a vast ice field descending from the flank of Cho Oyu, the Kyetrak Glacier, at the head of which rose the 19,050-foot Nangpa La, a treacherous pass open only half the year that led to Solu Khumbu and the southern side of the Himalaya in Nepal. East of the Nangpa La and beyond Cho Oyu, in a tangle of ice and rock the scale of the sky, stood the other great summits of the Everest massif: Gyachung Kang, Lhotse, Everest itself, Chomo Lonzo, and Makalu, as well as several lesser peaks, Pumori, Lingtren, Changtse, and Pethangtse. These mountains, piled one upon the other, stretched from the Nangpa La for forty miles before collapsing just beyond Makalu in the great gorge of the Arun, which delineated Everest from the east.

Clearly, the traditional trade route up the Ra Chu to the Nangpa La offered an opening to Everest from the west. To learn more, Howard-Bury paid a call on the acting governor, whom he found that afternoon at home, in a quarter of town favored by wealthy merchants, surrounded by his family. He was a cheerful man, surprisingly young, and dressed in elegant embroidered robes. An earring of pearls and turquoise dangled six inches from his left ear. His wife and mother-in-law wore their hair up in great halos of string pearls and coral. Long chains of turquoise and coral beads and lumps of amber hung from their necks, along with small golden amulets, boxes of prayers, inlaid with precious stones. They were exceedingly shy, having never seen a European, and in their nervousness their fingers ran stiffly over the beads of their rosaries. Howard-Bury's offer to photograph the family provoked tears and protestations that took the husband some effort to quell.

The *depon* was not from Tingri, and his knowledge of the country to the south was inspired as much by rumor as by geography. Like all Tibetans, he measured distance not in miles but in increments of time. He spoke less of places than of personalities and events, the great yogis and their mythic deeds that had brought the landscape alive. All this left Howard-Bury rather baffled, though he did distill from the conversation some important information. The trade route up the Ra Chu to the Nangpa La in summer months had modest traffic, though it remained dangerous at all times of the year. In spring and fall it was impassable, in winter suicidal. But from the Ra Chu Valley itself other tracks provided access west and south across a pass known as the Phuse La to the drainage of the Rongshar Chu and to Lapche, a valley made sacred by Milarepa, the beloved bodhisattva who had lived and died there, and beyond to the Nepalese border town of Nyenyam. Howard-Bury recognized the name Milarepa, for it had been Tibetan reverence for this legendary mystic saint and poet that had led Charles Bell initially to oppose any suggestion of an Everest reconnaissance.

There was a second route, the *depon* continued; this one ran east from the Ra Chu Valley, crossing a high pass, the Lamna La, to reach the Dzakar Chu, another tributary of the Arun, which flowed east and northeast, parallel to the Phung Chu and about fifteen miles to the south of it. The Dzakar Chu was itself formed by two smaller streams, one of which, the Rong Chu, was said to be born in the very glaciers that enveloped the northern base of Everest. Located at the edge of the ice was a monastery, and in caves farther up the flanks of the valley lived hermits, pilgrims who had settled into a lifetime of retreat, isolation, and prayer. At night, it was said, they danced alone, untouched by the wind and cold, chanting to the rhythms of two-headed drums while playing trumpets carved from human thighbones, all the time invoking the spirits and deities of the universe. By following the track that led to Rongbuk, the highest of all monasteries in Tibet, the British would reach, the *depon* cautioned, the very heart of the mountain.

Howard-Bury incorporated the *depon*'s advice, obscure though it was, into his plan of attack. With the monsoon threatening, and now certain to cross the Himalaya, he elected to scatter his men in search of an approach to Everest to maximize the reach and efficiency of the reconnaissance. Henry Morshead's first priority would be the exploration and mapping of the upper Phung Chu, with the goal of linking the survey work he and his team had done since leaving Darjeeling into the map of the Tsangpo drainage completed by the Rawling expedition of 1904. Major Wheeler, accompanied by the geologist Dr. Heron, would explore the Ra Chu, surveying and photographing the western approaches to Everest from the Nangpa La and Cho Oyu. One of their primary tasks would be to determine whether the Kyetrak Glacier, at the base of Cho Oyu, might be continuous with some as yet unknown ice field coming off Everest to the west. If so, this might open another avenue to the mountain. The climbing party of Mallory and Bullock, meanwhile, would head south directly for the Rongbuk Chu and the lower flanks and glaciers of Everest itself. Howard-Bury would act as a liaison between all parties, doing double marches whenever necessary, even as he anticipated the second major phase of the expedition, the approach to the mountain from the east. He had gathered from his conversation with the *depon* that Everest, or Chomolungma, was revered as a place of particular power. He mistook this to mean that the mountain was deemed to be sacred. Everest, in fact, was no more holy than the other mountains, and far less than some. What was sanctified was the land itself, for everywhere they intended to go—west toward Lapche and Rongshar, east toward Rongbuk, eventually around the far side of the mountain to Kharta and the rivers draining its Kangshung Face into the Arun—they would follow the paths of Guru Rinpoche, enter the hidden valleys, and thus tread in the footsteps of the divine.

MALLORY AND BULLOCK arrived in Tingri at midmorning on June 20, conferred with Howard-Bury, and made immediate plans to leave. Already on the long approach march from Kampa Dzong, Mallory had identified a select group of sixteen Sherpas, equipping each man with climbing boots, an ice ax, and a suit of underwear. He recruited Dukpa, the best of the cooks, and selected a sirdar who was trustworthy and energetic. To communicate with the sirdar, who would be in charge of the men, he had memorized 150 words of Tibetan, which he kept at hand in a small notebook. They would have fifteen yaks as transport, and food and supplies for two weeks—a fortnight that, as Mallory later wrote, would spin out into a month. Their departure was set for June 23.

With clouds thick over the mountains, Bullock rested on June 21, taking to his tent to read *The Three Black Pennys* and Oscar Wilde's *The Happy Prince and Other Tales*, a book of fairy tales. The following day he rearranged his gear, leaving his pink umbrella and large kit bag behind, along with some souvenirs picked up in the Tingri market that morning: a dagger and two bracelets, purchased for two rupees apiece.

That afternoon, to the astonishment of all, Sandy Wollaston, the expedition doctor, after an absence of only thirteen days, rejoined the expedition, having safely escorted the invalid Harold Raeburn from

Kampa Dzong south across the Himalaya to the mission at Lachen, in Sikkim. It had been a hazardous passage. Crossing the Serpo La in a biting wind, they had been forced to bivouac in the open and had very nearly died of exposure. Leaving Raeburn in the care of the nuns, with instructions to an assistant surgeon that he be evacuated to Gangtok, Wollaston had after but a day of rest set out to regain the Tibetan Plateau, accompanied only by Gyalzen Kazi, the expedition interpreter. To reach Tingri by June 22 they had ridden hard, overnight from Shegar, arriving not a moment too soon. Howard-Bury's orderly was gravely ill with typhoid fever, as was Wheeler's man, Asghar Khan.

With Wollaston in Tingri to care for the sick, Howard-Bury set the plan in motion. Morshead, accompanied by his Indian colleague, Gujjar Singh, went north to explore the headwaters of the Phung Chu. On June 24 Wheeler and Heron would set off for the Kyetrak Glacier and the Nangpa La. Their team would consist of three porters equipped for high altitude, ten others assigned from Morshead's survey party, and, as Wheeler wrote, in place of Asghar, one "drunken mess cook." Several of the men hailed from the Khumbu Valley of Nepal, just beyond the pass. They warned Wheeler that the trail would be desperate, and that their eight yaks would have difficulty reaching the divide. Few traders hazarded the climb. Their party would most likely be completely alone, a prospect that secretly delighted Wheeler, who had every intention of crossing the forbidden frontier. "I hope there will be no one in the neighbourhood," he confided in his diary the day of his departure. "I shall be able to nip into Nepal a bit and see the southern ridges of Everest."

MALLORY AND BULLOCK, having recruited the translator Gyalzen Kazi to their party, left Tingri at 7:00 a.m. on Thursday, June 23. Almost right away they ran into difficulties. Their immediate goal was Chöbuk, a small hamlet and monastery on the banks of the Dzakar Chu, close to its confluence with the Rongbuk, the stream they hoped to follow to its source on Everest. Not three miles from Tingri, it became apparent that the local transport was leading them astray, heading south by southwest up the wrong side of the open plain, all with the apparent goal of extending the journey. After an "interminable three-cornered argument," Mallory and Bullock left Gyalzen to deal with the porters and stormed on, heading east for the base of a great moraine that spread across the entire valley. They paused around two in the afternoon and, with rain threatening, pitched a Mummery tent. For two hours they waited anxiously for a sign of the yaks. Joined finally by Gyalzen and the rest of their party, they climbed 1,000 feet up a steep rise that led across the moraine and down to the banks of a narrow stream, where, in sight of wild gazelles, they camped in a meadow behind a stone shelter, a mile below a bridge that crossed the river at Nazurga. Bullock, cursed all day by a "rotten pony," took solace in the mail, which had arrived that morning: letters from his wife, along with a box of chocolate and fudge. Mallory found comfort in the fact that he "had foiled the natives, whose aim was to retard our progress."

The following day they crossed at Nazurga and made their way back up and over the moraine, moving south and east across a number of massive spurs until they reached the head of a valley that led to the Lamna La, a 16,200-foot pass that brought them by late afternoon to the village of Zambu, in the valley of the Dzakar Chu. From the heights they had another glimpse of Everest, and could just make out the junction of the northwest and northeast buttresses. The North Face, Bullock noted in his diary that evening, was "very steep, also the West Ridge." Some of the porters, he added ominously, were already "rather tired."

Saturday dawned in intense anticipation as the party turned upstream, toward the confluence with the Rongbuk Chu and a much-anticipated route to the mountain. In little more than an hour they reached Chöbuk, where they paused to unload the pack train. Men and supplies crossed the river by way of a rickety cantilevered bridge. The yaks plunged into the torrent, driven by a barrage of stones and shouts. Once on the right bank of the Rongbuk Chu, it was simply a matter of following the stream to its source. By noon they had entered a narrow gorge, dominated by red limestone cliffs where the rainwater gathered on the rocks and pooled below in lush meadows of yellow asters and primulas, dwarf rhododendrons, and wild roses. It reminded Mallory of the Alps: the hot summer sun, the still air, the fragrance of juniper crushed underfoot. He was sorely tempted to lie down and drift into sleep, for he had seen nothing this green since reaching Tibet. Instead he pushed on, climbing the length of a long valley, once again surrounded on all sides by barren hillsides, monotonous and dreary in the harsh light. On either side of the path were small piles of stones, heaped up by pilgrims.

The trail rose to a height of land and passed between two white stupas, or shrines, draped in a lacework of red and yellow prayer flags. Each of the porters paused and shouted a salutation to the mountain.

Several tossed packets of white papers to the wind, each imprinted with the mantra of Guru Rinpoche, *Om mani padme hum*, six syllables representing the six realms that must be passed before the whole of samsara is emptied and complete purity embraced through the heart essence of the Buddha. They reached out and touched a rock cairn, as did Mallory and Bullock, who hesitated at the pass to stare south in "sheer astonishment." They had half expected, Mallory later recalled, to see Everest from the divide, and in the back of their minds had a "host of questions clamoring for an answer. But the sight of it banished every thought. We forgot the stony wastes and regrets for other beauties. We asked no questions and made no comment, but simply looked."

Ahead of them stretched one of the most remarkable mountain vistas on earth. The Rongbuk Valley spreading south toward Everest rises in twenty miles but 4,000 feet, and it runs remarkably straight. From even a slight elevation, it appears to be flat, with its massive ice fields seeming to lie prostrate along the valley floor, as if detached from the mountain from which they flow. High ridges on both flanks draw the eye irresistibly to the head of the valley, where the sheer scale of the North Face, towering 10,000 feet, collapses perspective, creating an illusion of both proximity and depth, as if the mountain could be reached in a moment, or never reached at all. "At the end of the valley," Mallory wrote, "and above the glacier Everest rises not so much a peak as a prodigious mountain mass."

In bright sunlight, with not a cloud in view, Mallory wasted not a moment. He was a ridge walker, and with the North Face clearly out of the question, his eyes went immediately to the skyline. He had no idea what lay on the southern side of Everest, but from his vantage on the north, two prominent ridges splayed the mountain. One ran to the west, falling precipitously several thousand feet, first through rock and then continuing for perhaps three miles along an impossible knife edge of ice and snow. The second, by contrast, left the summit pyramid at a more reasonable pitch, dropping perhaps 1,000 feet over half a mile, before continuing at a much steeper angle of descent north and east, again for perhaps three miles.

This Northeast Arête, or Ridge, was at its lower elevations no less imposing than the West Ridge. But Mallory could see that at just the point higher on the mountain where the slope became manageable, even gentle, a clearly defined shoulder fell away from the ridge to the north. He could not make out its base, which was hidden behind by "a northern wing of mountains" that formed the eastern flank of the

Rongbuk Valley to his left. But he surmised correctly that these mountains formed a continuous ridge, perpendicular to the Northeast Ridge, which implied that the shoulder in question dropped to a col, a saddle separating the heights. Reach the col and a route up the shoulder could land a climber beyond the hazards of the Northeast Ridge, with what appeared to be a possible route up the skyline to the summit. It would not be easy. He wrote to Ruth later in the day, "Suffice to say it has the most stupendous ridges and appalling precipices that I have ever seen and all the talk of an easy snow slope is a myth." Nevertheless, with a single glance, and from a distance of nearly twenty miles, Mallory had identified what would turn out to be the key to the mountain, the North Col, what he later called the "col of our desires." Now the challenge was to find a way to get to it.

HOWARD-BURY INTENDED to leave Tingri with Wheeler and Heron on the morning of June 24, but chemicals in the darkroom, fumes given off by the acid hypo, left him "gassed" and incapable of speaking. For two days he remained mute as Wollaston, to the horror of the local people, kept his men busy killing rats, birds, lizards, beetles, and fish for the British Museum. Finally, on the morning of June 26, Howard-Bury headed south to join Wheeler and Heron. Crossing the Tingri Plain, he reached in nine miles the small village of Sharto. Along the way he picked up a new servant, a Tibetan named Poo, a "sensible fellow, very seldom drunk." Poo turned out to be a splendid cook and would remain at Howard-Bury's side for the rest of the expedition. That first night, with the wind blowing fiercely and the heavens illuminated by curious rays of light cast upon a purple sky, Howard-Bury dined elegantly on wild greens, garlic, and turnip leaves, and watched as a herd of kiang, wild asses, grazed freely in the barley fields that surrounded his camp.

The following morning he was off early, intent on climbing a small hill of some 17,700 feet as he made his way south. The route proved longer than anticipated, the mountain more distant, the glacial stream of the Ra Chu difficult to ford, and it was not until nearly 9:00 a.m. that he reached the summit. From the heights, he could see north a hundred miles to the watershed of the Tsangpo and beyond, a "charming picture," he recalled, of light, shade, color, and clouds. To the east the top of Everest emerged from a sea of icy peaks, and ahead in the direction he was traveling, Cho Oyu dominated the sky. Howard-Bury had never seen such rock, immense granite precipices descending

sheer for several thousand feet until reaching "great winding glaciers."
At first the Nangpa La was clear, but as he glassed its slopes, long
wisps of clouds whipped across the ice, within minutes obscuring the
pass and all the surrounding mountains. Even in summer, he had been
told, entire yak trains had simply disappeared, snuffed out by sudden
blizzards that spun fine, powdery snow into such whirlwinds that men
and animals suffocated in the open air. In these mountains, he mused,
exposure was the danger, with every change of weather bringing the
possibility of peril.

WHEELER AND HERON were camped at 16,500 feet near the small
hamlet of Kyetrak, a bleak and grassless cluster of stone houses located
about a mile below the snout of the glacier, altogether some twenty
miles south of Tingri. Howard-Bury caught up with them late in
the day, just after they had returned to base camp and were resting
against the walls of the crumbling chorten that dominated the village.
Howard-Bury mentioned Wheeler's orderly Asghar, who had fallen
into delirium from typhoid. Wheeler shared what he had learned of
the land. By good fortune a Gurkha salt trader from Nepal had come
down out of the Nangpa La, and they had conversed for a time in
Hindustani, which Wheeler spoke fluently. Wheeler himself had completed two brilliant days of survey work, under mostly clear skies, with
little wind. Just that morning in bitter cold he had left camp before
dawn and climbed high up the eastern flank of the valley. From that
station he had photographed Cho Oyu, Gauri Sankar (23,405 feet),
and Gyachung Kang (25,990 feet), as well as the entire length of the
Kyetrak Glacier, including the approaches to both the Nangpa La, in
the south and west, to the Phuse La, a second and lower pass that led
to the Rongshar Valley and the sacred homeland of Milarepa.
    Wheeler had reason to be pleased. With his camera he was not
simply photographing scenery but, rather, beginning one of the more
remarkable experiments in the recent history of the Survey of India.
Since the seventeenth century surveyors had relied essentially on the
same basic field techniques. A plane table, a flat wooden surface, supported generally by a tripod, was set over a known point, oriented by
compass, and brought to the horizontal by adjusting the legs of the tripod and verifying the inclination with a bubble level. A sheet of drawing paper was attached to the table, and surmounting the paper was
positioned a telescopic sight connected to a flat, straight-edge ruler.
Distances, angles, bearings, and elevations along a line of sight were
measured and then inscribed directly onto the paper. The drafting

work was done in the field, as the map sheet literally came into being point by point.

This traditional methodology, suitable for the soft downs of Suffolk and the leisurely pace of the Ordnance Survey of the home islands, had proved impossibly cumbersome in the high mountains of the empire, be they the Ruwenzori, Himalaya, or Pamirs, where the weather alone demanded that men work quickly and with far greater efficiency. Wheeler's father, Arthur Oliver, had pioneered what came to be known as the Canadian photo-topographical method, a clever innovation that substituted a theodolite and a fixed-focus F45 camera for the sight rule and plane table. Stations were established, as always, by rigorous triangulation, and notes on angles and exposure carefully recorded in the field. The photographs, composed as true perspectives, captured the country precisely as it would be seen through the eye of a surveyor working with telescopic sight and plane table. The image, secured on a glass plate negative, could be developed later, the print studied at leisure back at base. No drafting was done in the field, which freed up time, allowing for more stations to be established and much more ground to be covered. Accuracy was also enhanced, since the surveyor as cartographer had not only his memory but also an actual image of the landscape as a visual reference to complement the raw data.

The Canadian photographic technique naturally had its limitations. As in all cartography, it depended on the precision of the triangulation that was the foundation of the survey. Fixed points had to be true. High stations had to be established, the more the better, and not necessarily mountain summits, for it was essential to secure multiple images of the same topography from distinct points of reference, the greater the overlap and coverage the better. Above all, the weather had to be clear, the winds moderate, the camera position steady and secure to allow for sharp three-to-five-second exposures. And, although the new method required less cumbersome equipment, the essential gear was not insubstantial.

On behalf of the Survey of India, Wheeler had purchased and assembled the basic kit in Canada while on leave in 1920. He carried the camera, a supply of eleven glass plates, as well as notebooks and pencils in a stout leather case in a knapsack that weighed some thirty pounds. The theodolite broke down into two parts, each stored in a protective wooden box. Together with the tripod, this added another twenty-seven pounds. The leveling base for the camera, spare plate holders, measuring tapes, three-cornered canvas bags to fill with dirt or stones to steady the tripod, and other miscellaneous items brought the total field kit to nearly 100 pounds. In addition, there was the supply of glass negatives, which Wheeler had packed himself, wrapping each plate in dry botanical paper, then placing them individually in one-inch protective sleeves in tin-lined boxes, which he personally sealed with solder. Each of these boxes weighed thirty-two pounds.

Wheeler had conducted some initial trials at Dehra Dun before leaving for Darjeeling. But time had been limited, and the real work, as had always been anticipated, would begin in the field, on the unknown slopes of Everest. "This area seemed suitable for the experiment," he later wrote. "It contained some 1200 square miles of country—about a season's work, given fine weather—and gave opportunities for photographing all types of country from rolling hills with villages and cultivation, through steep gorges, to glaciers and tremendous snow and ice clad peaks. With Major Morshead's approval I therefore decided to tackle this area with a view to fair-mapping both on 1 inch and ¼ inch scale."

Wheeler was embarking, as Howard-Bury well appreciated, on the most challenging of all assignments. Over the five-and-a-half-month length of the Everest reconnaissance, he would be isolated with his native men for nearly three months, far longer than any other British member of the expedition. Altogether he would spend forty-one days camped on moraines and glaciers between 18,000 and 22,000 feet. He would secure and develop 240 images. Each of these photographs implied a dawn departure and a grinding ascent, fully laden with gear. For each good day, there were a half dozen when the wind blew ice and snow on the heights, and stations were attained at enormous effort only to have the camera enveloped in cloud and the entire exercise rendered pointless. It challenged morale, but it also obliged Wheeler to remain constantly vigilant. He saw the landscape through the precision of a lens, with the discipline of one who could not squander an instant. The literal burden of his load slowed him down. But with his measured pace, there was little on the horizon that escaped his notice.

On the night of Monday, June 27, there was a sharp frost, and the following morning, while Wheeler readied his kit and crew, Howard-Bury and Heron started early for the Nangpa La. For the first seven miles they rode together up the moraine on the east side of the glacier. Heron moved slowly, trying to make sense of the landscape. As a geologist, he struggled to understand the presence of marine fossils and great bands of sedimentary rock at heights previously unimagined by science. Howard-Bury grew impatient, eager to reach the pass before it might be obscured by cloud. Abandoning his pony and his colleague, he pressed ahead on foot, with one porter, climbing in four miles up a steep and slippery moraine, setting an impossible pace, as each new side valley revealed yet another magnificent river of ice. By the time he reached the end of the moraine, his porter's boots had literally fallen to pieces. Shouldering the heavy camera, Howard-Bury headed on alone, across firm ice that soon turned soft. Floundering in wet snow and water to his knees, he made his way to the edge of a crevasse, which he followed for half a mile to a rock wall that led, after much effort, to the heights of the Nangpa La.

Exhausted, he glanced into Nepal, saw little, and then lay down in the hot sun and fell asleep. Some minutes later he awoke to a storm, and found himself, to his astonishment, beneath an inch of snow. By the time he made his way back down off the pass, having lugged the camera for some six hours, he could barely walk. Heron and his porter awaited at the edge of the moraine to lead him back to Kyetrak, where, somewhat to his surprise, he discovered that Wheeler had himself headed up the Nangpa La, intent on spending a fortnight on the ice.

That evening Wheeler, camping at 18,180 feet just four miles shy of the pass, rested alone in a Meade tent, "comfortable enough inside but horrible to get in and out," he reported. It measured seven feet by six, and stood about five feet high, thin canvas with pegs and poles weighing perhaps fifteen pounds. His three high-altitude assistants, Ugyen, Dawa, and Rinjia Namgya, shared a larger Whymper tent. Unable in the cold to kindle a yak-dung fire with flint, they took advantage of the double-barreled Primus stove Wheeler had picked up in Calcutta. Though difficult to ignite at high altitude, it burned decently once it got going. Together they fed well on oxtail soup, mutton, fried potatoes, sweet biscuits, and prunes. Wheeler retired to his tent with a cup of cocoa and a copy of Douglas Freshfield's *Round Kachenjunga*, lent to him by Heron. He was having trouble sleeping. "I find that I am on the point of dropping to sleep," he confided in his diary, "when I seem to hold my breath and wake up gasping. Am ready enough to go to sleep but can't quite bring it off." The dark, restless hours of the night brought quiet concerns. "The going is bad," he wrote on June 28, a Tuesday. "Huge moraines, side glaciers shooting rocks down. The natives say that a good many people lose their lives . . . Everywhere the rocks are frightfully loose—falls go on all the time on all sides. The peaks are all so steep, particularly the screes. I have never seen such consistently steep faces and ridges."

THE DAY AFTER cresting the Nangpa La, Howard-Bury and Heron set out to scout the Rongshar Valley, fording the Ra Chu at Kyetrak at dawn and climbing the moraine on the western side of the glacier to reach the grassy hills that rose gently to the 17,700-foot Phuse La, the second of the major passes. Clouds hid much of the horizon, though one magnificent peak showed through from the south. Howard-Bury came upon a herd of female bharal so docile he passed on his pony within fifty yards. The long descent west beyond the pass toward the Rongshar Valley was a well-traveled track, a proper trail engineered into the rocks above the Shung Chu, a wild torrent that became quite impassable as it picked up other glacial streams coming off the divide. Alpine meadows of barberry and honeysuckle, white and pink spireas narrowed into a great gorge that after some distance opened upon the green barley fields of Tasang, a small settlement where on a terrace above the hamlet the party camped for the night. They had dropped more than 4,000 feet from the pass, and were delighted to be once again in a land of forests and fields. They cooked that evening on a fire made of juniper, a pleasant change from the acrid scent of yak dung, a fuel that ruined the taste of every meal.

In the morning, Howard-Bury awoke in a holy valley, a place sanctified in part because of the abundance of juniper, a wood sacred to Tibetans. The scent of the tree always reminded him of his home in Ireland. On all sides of Tasang, he was told, hermits and nuns lived in caves. They used juniper branches as incense, and each morning and evening lit fires at the mouth of their dwellings to purify the space. The villagers supplied them with food each day. Just above the British camp, high in the rocks, lived one man who had gone into life-long retreat. Howard-Bury could see the blue smoke of his fire. It was said by the locals that after meditating for ten years, he would be able to live on only ten grains of barley a day. "There was another anchorite female," Howard-Bury wrote, who was said to have lived in the valley for 138 years and "was greatly revered. She had forbidden any of the animals in the valley to be killed, and that was the reason why the flocks of burhel [bharal] we had passed were so extremely tame."

Resting the transport for a day, he and Heron walked alone farther down the trail, covering perhaps eight miles, descending much of the time through narrow ravines and low forests of birch, willow, and wild rose. At every spring grew great masses of anemones and yellow primulas, while on drier ground were thickets of gooseberries so plump with fruit that the two men gathered in an hour a supply sufficient to last for several days. According to the aneroid, they'd reached as low as 12,000 feet, where they learned from a local herder that the trail continued down for three more days before entering the chasms that marked the boundary between Tibet and Nepal.

The exploration of these borderlands would have to wait. Howard-Bury's more immediate concern was the situation of Mallory and Bullock in the Rongbuk Valley on Everest, the most promising of all approaches to the mountain. On the last day of June Howard-Bury and Heron turned their backs on the Rongshar Valley and retraced their path to Tasang, arriving in a cold rain after a long and exhausting slog. The following morning, in thick mist, they recrossed the Phuse La and dropped once more into the valley of the Ra Chu. At Kyetrak they learned that Wheeler remained at his high camp, isolated on the flank of the glacier just below the Nangpa La. As they turned north, seeking a ford across the river and the track that would lead them to the Lamna La pass and the Rongbuk approaches to Everest, Howard-Bury looked back to see thick sheets of sleet and freezing rain darkening the moraine. He would not set eyes on Wheeler again for nearly three weeks.

THE MONKS of the Rongbuk Monastery did not look favorably on the strange guests who arrived uninvited in the sixth month of the Iron-Bird year at their high mountain retreat in the shadow of Chomolungma. When Howard-Bury attempted to present his credentials, a passport bearing the seal of the Thirteenth Dalai Lama, he learned that the head lama was in retreat and unavailable for an audience. Only twenty monks lived permanently among the low stone chambers of Rongbuk, but several hundred came and went through the summer months, and in cells and caves the length of the valley lived between three and four hundred other recluses and hermits, men and women who had taken lifelong vows of isolation and retreat. The presence of the British was certain to disturb their meditations, not to mention upsetting the wild creatures, as well as the demons and deities of the mountains.

Howard-Bury begged pardon, and through his interpreter promised to be respectful and refrain from all further hunting. On the approach march, he had again marveled at the docility of the wildlife. "They seemed to have no fear whatever of human beings," he wrote. "On the way up the valley we passed within forty yards of a fine flock of rams, and on the way back we passed some females that were so inquisitive that they actually came up to within ten yards of us in order to have a look. The rock pigeons came and fed out of one's hand, and the ravens and all other birds were equally tame." It was most interesting, he remarked, "to watch all their habits and to see them at such quarters." These were the words of an English naturalist. But what was going on at Rongbuk was something altogether different and new to him. "With my own eyes I watched the wild sheep coming down in the early morning to the hermits' cells and being fed not 100 yards from our camp," he noted. As he walked away from his first inconclusive interview with the attendants of the lama of Rongbuk, he passed a large white chorten, propped up by long wooden poles. A narrow crack ran down its side, and it appeared ready to topple at any moment. Like the entire monastery, it had the feel of something very old and very new, as ancient as the land and as timeless as the sky.

Rongbuk had, in fact, attracted Buddhist seekers since the time of Guru Rinpoche, Padma Sambhava, who was said to have spent seven months in dark retreat in the valley while sowing the land with sacred treasures. In the eleventh century the tantric wizard and mystic yogini Machig Labdrön, heroine of all Tibet, came to the frozen reaches of Rongbuk to shatter orthodoxy through a spiritual practice that became known as *chöd*, literally the "cutting through" of attachment. A Buddhist scholar of renown as a young woman, she later sought to free her mind of all intellect, believing that only by severing attachment to the conceptual realm could true liberation be achieved. The catalyst of transformation was the wild, the most fearful places, cemeteries and charnel ground, sky burial sites and the most ragged and exposed of landscapes. "Unless all reality is made worse," she wrote, "one cannot attain liberation . . . So wander in grisly places and mountain retreats . . . do not get distracted by doctrines and books . . . just get real experiences . . . in the horrid and desolate." Face your demons was her message; annihilate pride and vanity, and make a gift of one's body to the wilderness.

Illumination in sacred madness was the essence of the *chöd* practice. Men and women went to the most desperate reaches of the mountains, not simply to live in caves but to retreat into an inner cavern, the universe of one's being. In time they took on the appearance of the very demons they sought to vanquish, faces black with soot, fingernails never cut, hair matted in tangled locks hanging to the ground. Exposed to the coldest winters, they possessed nothing more than a trident and a scrap of cloth for shelter, a human skull for a bowl, a ritual bell, a two-headed drum, and a trumpet made of human bone. When they slept they remained in an upright posture. In the morning, before drinking hot water, they swallowed dried barley powder to feed

the worms in their stomach. At night, drum and trumpet in hand, they danced before all the deities and *dakinis*, trampling underfoot the fetters and attachments of samsara. When they died, it was said, rainbows crossed the sky, a sign that their minds had dissolved back into clear light.

AMONG THOSE who sought refuge in Rongbuk in the late nineteenth century was a young monk by the name of Ngawang Tenzin Norbu. Born in Kharta, close to Everest, in the Fire-Rabbit year, 1866, he had grown up to a hard life of poverty and loss. A brother had died at fourteen, a sister in childbirth at twenty. His father was a dharma practitioner but also a drunkard. The lad studied at the Mindroling Monastery but without money or support had been obliged to beg to stay alive. Undaunted, he went on retreat for the first time at fourteen, and so great was his compassion that the sound of birdsong only reminded him of the depth of human suffering. When he emerged, his lama, Trulshik Rinpoche, instructed him to go to Rongbuk. At first he protested, dismissing it as an uninhabitable land, a country of bears and yeti. "Who says we need grass and trees to study dharma?" his teacher famously replied. So Ngawang Tenzin Norbu went, and for more than three years meditated in a cave without a door, certain that at any moment a yeti would arrive and devour him. Abandoned by his attendant, who found the conditions impossibly arduous, he persevered despite privations—no clothes, no shelter, and little if any food. Finally at twenty-five, he returned to Shegar to formally take monastic vows.

At the time the only permanent structures at Rongbuk were a cluster of meditation huts, inhabited by ascetic nuns. But in 1901, at the age of thirty-five, Ngawang Tenzin Norbu returned to the valley, determined to build a monastery at this highest of sanctuaries. With immense personal energy, he expanded a small lodge into a temple, and built housing for a growing circle of students, both young monks and nuns. He secured the patronage of merchants in Tingri and of the Sherpas of Solu Khumbu, beyond the Nangpa La pass in Nepal. His profound spiritual charisma in time inspired the loyalty of the entire rural population living in the environs of Everest, in both Tibet and Nepal.

Children startled by his uncanny physical resemblance to Shakyamuni called him Sangye Buddha, the Buddha of Rongbuk. To their parents he was Dzatrul Rinpoche, revealer of hidden treasures, a living embodiment of Guru Rinpoche. A spiritual master of *chöd*, he dispatched over the course of his life more than a thousand seekers into the mountains to confront their demons. Asked in later years by a novice ascetic the proper course of action should a yeti appear at the mouth of a cave and disrupt one's meditation, the master responded, "Why, of course, invite him in to tea!"

Like many great Tibetan lamas, Dzatrul Rinpoche dictated a *namthar*, a spiritual autobiography—less a personal account of a life than a celebration of the ritual practices that gave a life meaning and transcendence. The text documents in numbing detail his mastery of well over a hundred esoteric rites, vows, transmissions, blessings, and purifications, as well as all the baroque happenings of an existence dedicated to devotional ceremony. But it also returns time and again to actual events, though not always in linear chronology. The great stupa at Rongbuk, the *namthar* reveals, was built only in 1919, two years before it appeared so decrepit to Howard-Bury. The rinpoche himself had mixed the mortar, combining earth, water, and sacred relics: the flesh of realized beings, salt from the mummified remains of treasure seekers, bits of hair said to be that of Milarepa. With the construction finished, he traveled to Nepal to consecrate a new monastery, Tengboche, a *gompa* he had first envisioned in a dream. To reach Khumbu, he crossed the Nangpa La, carried over the 19,050-foot pass on an eight-man palanquin, an honor reserved for only the highest lamas. The day was beautiful, he remembered, "no snowstorms, only a spring like rain." When the party reached Tengboche, a five-colored rainbow arose over the new monastery, and the following day, as Dzatrul Rinpoche sang the juniper offering, the sun, moon, and stars appeared in the sky at the same time.

Travels and pilgrimage consumed much of 1920, including a journey to Kharta, on the east side of Everest, to perform a sky-cleaning *puja* and make offerings to the protector of the hidden valleys of Guru Rinpoche, a white-haired woman enveloped in jewels who came to him in a vision. But in 1921, he remained at Rongbuk, taking care of the business of the monastery, the mundane demands of an abbot: construction projects, paperwork, bureaucratic challenges, taxes to pay to the government at Shegar. In the fifth month, according to his *namthar*, Dzatrul Rinpoche had a powerful dream. "From the east a roaring sound with light appeared . . . After this," he wrote, "six English Sahibs, 30 servants and 70 animals carrying loads arrived here. They camped close to the eastern spring and stayed there. The leaders went to the snow mountain. They stayed for 20 days and couldn't climb the mountain. They returned without making any trouble or harm to the local animals or the humans in the region. They left through Kharta."

The presence of the Everest expedition, the first Europeans the monks of Rongbuk had ever seen, warranted but a cursory mention in the *namthar*—these few lines and nothing more. For Dzatrul Rinpoche, it was a busy summer. There were more than 450 monks in residence. There were tantric initiations to perform, the entire Kangyur (the essential canon of the Buddhist religion) to recite, great feasts to be prepared. At the end of the retreat, the entire community performed a long-life ritual for him, creating a mandala so radiant that "the sky filled with rainbows and flowers in five colors rained down." Beyond the monastery, the *chöd* practitioners emerged from their caves to dance, utterly grounded in purpose, for there was no place in Tibet more desolate than Everest, and for them, desolation was good.

IN THE EARLY predawn hours of June 27, from their camp just beyond the monastery, Mallory and Bullock set off by moonlight with five porters to explore for the first time the Rongbuk Glacier. They reached the terminal moraine after ninety minutes, and then, crossing in the darkness the torrent that poured out of the ice, made their way across a basin of massive boulders and hummocks to a dry stream-bed that ran up the western side of the glacier. The sun found them around 7:00, as they paused for breakfast in the lee of a great dark stone. Another hour of hard walking left the porters exhausted. They had climbed barely 2,000 feet, Mallory noted, and already their spirits were gone, their laughter displaced by grunts of fatigue. Bullock, too, was suffering. In this altitude, they were all like infants in a new world, learning to breathe for the first time. They had set out from a camp at 16,000 feet, a modest height by Himalayan standards but still higher, as Mallory noted, than the summit of Mont Blanc. He decided to test his own endurance, informally, walking steadily faster as one of the porters remained at his heels. The man was slightly built, Mallory would write, "strong and active, compact of muscle; but he had not yet learnt the art of walking rhythmically and balancing easily from stone to stone."

Mallory raced ahead, still following the lateral edge of the glacier, which gradually seemed to be trending to the west. He waited for the others, and then, leaving the porters to rest, he and Bullock scrambled up the mountainside to have a look. As suspected, they were coming to the mouth of a lateral valley where a second glacier came in to fuse with the Rongbuk from the west. They were now at 18,500 feet. Clouds obscured the source, but this new sheet of ice, named by Mallory the West Rongbuk, seemed to rise higher and higher, reaching toward a broad basin that, if anything, challenged the scale of the main glacier at the foot of Everest. Clearly, this would all in due time have to be explored.

But it was 11:00 a.m. and the sun was getting hot. They had been walking for well on eight hours. Rather than retracing their route, Mallory and Bullock elected to return to camp by crossing the main glacier to explore its opposite bank. This was something of a miscalculation. In the Alps, glaciers, unless severely crevassed, offer the easiest route of approach to or egress from a mountain. In the Himalaya, they are a climber's slow route to purgatory, difficult to traverse, generally impossible to descend, a maze of meltwater ponds and giant seracs of unworldly scale and constant danger. For three hours Mallory cut steps in the ice as they struggled through a "jumble of surprising pinnacles, many of them over 50 feet high." It was good training for the men, none of whom were familiar with a climbing rope. But it was exhausting for Mallory, who twice fell through the ice, soaking his clothes. The direct sun reflected off the white surface, leaving them weary with a lassitude that hinted at heatstroke. When finally they reached the far side, having in all that time crossed little more than a mile of ice, they halted for an hour to rest. Then, following a shelf that ran above the lateral moraine, they trudged back toward their camp, arriving utterly spent at 8:15 p.m., seventeen hours after setting out.

The following morning, somewhat humbled, they rested. Bullock fitted the men with crampons for the ice. Mallory spent much of the morning glassing the upper reaches of the mountain. The long, gentle snow slopes suggested by early photographs taken from afar most assuredly did not exist. "We'll want climbers and not half dazed ones," he later reflected, "it's a tougher job than I bargained for ... The mountain appears not to be intended for climbing." Bullock dismissed the West Ridge as simply impossible. Mallory was less pessimistic. But clearly the preferable route ran up the Northeast Ridge. The key would be to get closer to the mountain, first to scout the North Col, and second to get around to the west and south, with the hope of encountering a side of Everest less intimidating than the North Face. The decision was made to leave one man behind at base and advance the rest of the party four hours farther upvalley to establish an alpine camp about a mile below the mouth of the West Rongbuk. From there they would explore the upper reaches of both glaciers, all with an eye to the summit. Mallory, his mind in motion, was elated. "My darling this is a thrilling business altogether," he wrote to Ruth later that day. "I can't tell you how it possesses me and what prospect it is. And the beauty of it all!"

That afternoon around 5:00, in part to secure their supply lines, Mallory and Bullock paid a visit to the Rongbuk monastery. They saw the central shrine and an ornate, newly constructed prayer hall, but the place did not impress. "Not particularly interesting, after Shegar Dzong," Bullock noted in his diary. "No prominent monk appeared to show us around. In the morning the lama, who is seeing no one for one year, sent us presents of flour, salt and milk."

BULLOCK AWOKE on June 29, a Wednesday, to cloud and low mist coming off the glacier. He had not slept well, and he had a slight headache that would linger through the day. Mallory was irritable. A task that ought to have been completed the night before—the filling of small tins of kerosene and alcohol for the Primus stoves—had been neglected. Gyalzen Kazi, the translator, felt his ire and, being Tibetan, responded with passivity. "Loads must be arranged better if anything is to be done efficiently," Mallory wrote. "Gyalzen's response to being hustled is to tie knots or collect tent pegs—with no idea of superintending operations." They finally broke camp at 8:00 a.m., an hour later than planned, and with thirteen heavily laden porters, along with Dukpa the cook, began a slow, ponderous walk to an uncertain destination. They carried two Whymper and two Mummery tents, with rations and fuel for four days for only six porters. Mallory's plan was to establish the higher camp, dispatch most of the men back to base, and then in the coming days divide them into three parties, rotating each group through the advanced alpine camp, where they might be trained as mountaineers, while those at base camp maintained the flow of food and fuel.

He again underestimated the difficulty of the terrain. The men reached the glacier in good order, but climbing up its face left several deeply fatigued. By the time they reached the spot where Mallory and Bullock had paused for breakfast on the morning of June 27, four hours from base camp, several of the older porters in particular, including one named Nyima, were coughing badly. The loads, Mallory noted, would need to be lightened. He ordered a halt, permitting the men to eat while he and Gyalzen went ahead, climbing a steep moraine to a high shelf, which he followed for forty minutes, looking for water and a good place to establish the camp.

He had given up, and already turned back, when he spotted a beautiful pond and a spring, an ideal spot sheltered from the wind, with good ground for the tents. The elevation was 17,400 feet, much higher than Rongbuk and, more important, six hours closer to Everest. "It should now be possible to carry reconnaissance well up the main glacier and to the basin Westwards without moving further," he wrote, "once we get accustomed to this elevation." The porters, who stumbled into camp as late as 4:30 p.m., long after the sun had been lost to shadow, were less sanguine. Bullock's diary entry for the day concluded with a single phrase: "All coolies remained the night contrary to plan."

During the night it snowed, and the morning dawned cold, with no sun. No one felt fit. Mallory and Bullock took an easy day, leaving the new camp as the weather cleared around 9:30 a.m. and making their way along the shelf that led, in little over a mile, to the junction of the Rongbuk Glacier and its western branch. They could see that where the two rivers of ice collided, a bank of stones had piled up against the pinnacles and seracs of the main glacier, forming a causeway leading across the entire width of the West Rongbuk. This path they followed, crossing in little more than an hour, and returning at a leisurely pace late in the day, having found, to their satisfaction, a route to the upper reaches of the Rongbuk Glacier and the North Face of the mountain. They returned exhilarated but exhausted in a cold rain that left bits of ice on the stubble of their beards.

Bullock, who had felt poorly all day, decided to rest and took to his bed for a dinner of tinned chicken and peas. "Pretty fair especially the peas," he scribbled in his diary. "Probably better cold in jelly." Mallory, who preferred his food hot, nearly burned down the mess tent attempting to light the Primus stove; the following morning he did it again.

While Bullock remained in camp chasing butterflies, catching three species as well as some flies and bees, Mallory took five porters back to the ice, with the goal of reaching the head of the main glacier at the foot of the North Face. After traversing the West Rongbuk with ease, they soon became bogged down in soft snow, which they fought for three hours, even as the weather closed in. "In a race against clouds," he later wrote, "we were beaten and failed to find out what happened to the glacier at its Western head under the North-west arête."

Despite this setback, the day was a considerable success. They reached 19,100 feet and were within a mile of the one feature that had obsessed them since first setting eyes on the Rongbuk Valley. Though the visibility was limited, Mallory was able to look up to the shoulder coming down off the Northeast Ridge and make out the outline of what he now called the North Col, the Chang La in Tibetan—the saddle between Everest and the ridge that ran away to the north, the highest point of which was Changtse, the North Peak. Mallory had already seen enough of the Northwest Ridge to dismiss it as an option of last resort. The broken ice and steep slopes leading up to the North Col from the west seemed equally uninviting. As Mallory led his exhausted party back to camp, he knew without doubt that if the North Col were to be the opening to the mountain, the chink in its armor, as he had come to believe, he would have to find a way to approach it from the east, a task of exploration easier said than done.

Thirteen hours in the snow left the men spent, and with Bullock still feeling low, Mallory had little choice but to rest on July 2, despite the fair weather. While his companion pursued more butterflies, four new varieties caught by noon, and Gyalzen brought up supplies—the high climbing box, two tins of biscuits, and, by error, Bullock's leather bag—Mallory took advantage of the respite to write a long report to Captain Farrar at the Alpine Club.

"You will be wanting to know," the letter began, "something of the mountain and in one respect it is very easily told. It's a colossal rock peak plastered with snow, with faces as steep as any I have ever seen."

Their camp, he continued, was positioned above the left bank of "a surprisingly narrow glacier, whose right bank is the North Ridge of the mountain. This glacier runs itself up into a cwm like the charge of the Light Brigade, up under a 10,000 ft precipice and, as I saw it yesterday, round to the left towards something like the Col du Lion on the Tiefenmatten side. The slopes of the first peak on the north ridge (Changtse it is) beyond the col are impossibly steep except perhaps near the col. I could not make that out through the mist."

Turning his attention to the other rim of the great basin of ice that formed the head of the Rongbuk Glacier, Mallory noted, "the west side of the cwm is formed by a huge buttress (the northwest arête) coming steeply down from a snowy shoulder to a low broad col where the glacier presumably sweeps around into the WNW bay into which we have not penetrated."

This second col, the Lho La, Mallory had not reached on July 1, and for most of the day it had been obscured in cloud. Yet he anticipated correctly that beyond the saddle would be found another basin of ice, running along the opposite side of the Northwest Ridge of Everest. This was, in fact, the Western Cwm, the route that Edmund Hillary and Tenzing Norgay would ultimately follow in 1953 when they successfully climbed the mountain from the south. In 1921 it was formally off-limits to the British, as Nepal remained closed. Political considerations alone would not stop Mallory from seeking every avenue to the summit. Even as he wrote Farrar, he was making plans to reach the Western Cwm, either by means of the Rongbuk and the Lho La, or via the West Rongbuk, the head of which, he believed, might be contiguous with the ice fields of the Western Cwm. If this meant crossing the Nepalese frontier, so be it.

Still, the immediate prospects for Everest were not good. The entire arc of the North Face was, he wrote,

> completely unassailable. The WNW face is impossible near the top; and the same, roughly speaking, though with less certainty, must apply to the northeast and southeast faces—all this from a number of distant views. There remain the arêtes. The west ends in very steep rocks—we have seen no more. The northwest could be ascended to the snowy shoulder I mentioned if we met it in the Alps—a crampon job, I should say. Above this a long stretch of snow ridge leads to a steep pitch of rocks; and there is a further but shorter steep pitch where one of the vertical bands meets the ridge; but in both places the rocks appear broken by gullies, and I don't think them impossible. The actual summit is rock at a moderately easy angle. The North arête does not come down from the summit but from the E arête, which is comparatively flat and snowy above the point. I think it might go if one could reach the col between it and the 1st peak to the North.
>
> Well, that is about all we know of the mountain from the point of view of attack . . . All the faces on the north are frightfully steep, so I doubt there being an accessible col on this side near Everest, even should the west arête be a line of attack . . . You'll understand from this that we have a formidable job. I've hardly the dimmest hope of reaching the top, but of course we shall proceed as though we meant to get there.

Mallory closed his report with a quick review of the men. The porters received high praise, as did Morshead, who, regrettably, had yet to join the climbing party. Mallory added, "Bullock is feeling the height at present. Wheeler continually suffers from indigestion and I've no hope of him being any use to us. Personally I'm as fit as can be."

ON JULY 3 Mallory decided to test the porters on ice. Leaving camp just after 5:00 a.m., they made their way up the shelf to the

West Rongbuk, and once having traversed the glacier, continued up its southern side. Their training goal was a snow saddle between two high, unnamed peaks, both of which were, according to Bullock, "continually dropping stones." The col itself was protected by "steep ice and shabby shales" and a crevasse, or bergschrund, that ran across the entire slope at 21,000 feet. Mallory tied two ropes together and, while Bullock waited below the bergschrund with the men, proceeded to cut steps in the ice, a steep traverse that brought him in a hundred feet to a rock island in the snow.

The men followed, inching their way up the staircase, with Bullock in the fourth position. None of the Tibetans had ever been on hard ice. One slipped, the man behind Bullock, and would have plunged to his death had Bullock not arrested his fall. Mallory agreed to forgo the exercise and retire. The descent, he wrote, was a "better performance." Bullock made no further mention of the incident in his diary, save to say that they were both pleased by their overall fitness at high altitude. But it may well have been the beginning of tension between the two climbers. Writing some forty years later, in 1960, Guy Bullock's widow, Alice, recalled, "My husband considered Mallory ready to take unwarranted risks with still untrained porters in traversing dangerous ice. At least on one occasion he refused to take his rope of porters over the route proposed by Mallory. Mallory was not over pleased. He did not support a critical difference of opinion readily."

Mallory's singular goal was the summit, and the next step, as he saw it, was to get high, away from the valleys with their impossible glaciers to elevations where he might make further sense of the land. He had in mind an isolated peak rising above the confluence of the glaciers, just west of their camp. They were about to set off on the morning of July 4 when word reached them that other Englishmen were in the valley and climbing toward their camp.

Howard-Bury and Heron, having departed Rongbuk at dawn, had enjoyed a most pleasant scramble up and over the snout of the glacier, a seven-mile walk in bright sunshine, which landed them at the alpine camp around 9:30 a.m. for what turned out to be a short but, as Mallory recalled, "very pleasant visit." Howard-Bury commented on the curious lodgings they had passed, small monasteries perhaps, as well as the numerous cells where "hermits and recluses were living in retirement and meditation." Bullock was more interested in what Heron could tell him of the rocks. "Black rock here is a hornblende schist. Lower is granite," Bullock noted that night in his journal. They compared their aneroid altimeters, remarking that Bullock's seemed to be reading a bit low. Howard-Bury was delighted to see the camp well established, the exploration under way, and the porters being properly trained for ice. He had no word of Wheeler, still alone high on the Nangpa La, though he did report that the weather on that side had been horrific. To the delight of Mallory, he and Heron had brought some wild meat, gazelle: "a fine leg of goa—very much better than the skin and bone which passes for mutton in these parts."

The main purpose of Howard-Bury's visit was to inform Mallory and Bullock of his plans to proceed east in search of Kharta, where they would establish a base for the second phase of the reconnaissance, the exploration of the Kangshung Face and the eastern approaches to Everest. Should all go well, Howard-Bury expected to return to Tingri around midmonth in order to shut down the compound there and begin the transfer of the entire expedition to Kharta. He instructed Mallory and Bullock to be ready to move by July 20, though the date might change. He and Heron took their leave late in the afternoon, just as the light became beautiful. The summit of Everest, Howard-Bury recalled, soared high above the clouds, silhouetted against a perfectly clear night sky. They reached Rongbuk just after dark, met by a number of monks seeking medical attention; the same monks appeared the following morning with a large bowl of fresh eggs as a parting gift.

MALLORY AND BULLOCK left the following morning, July 5, at 4:15, climbing up the steep scree that rose immediately behind their camp. They halted briefly at dawn to photograph a glorious sunrise, but otherwise kept up a steady pace, climbing 2,500 feet to reach a high shoulder by 7:00 a.m. After roping up, they traversed a broad and exposed south-facing slope of rock and ice, taking fully three hours to attain the security of a snow saddle beyond which rose the ascending ridge of the peak. Two of the men, including one who had been carrying the quarter-plate camera, were played out and, despite a forty-minute rest, could not proceed. Bullock instructed them to remain at the col. Mallory, meanwhile, looked ahead to the route, a long curving snow ridge, slightly corniced, leading to a rocky shoulder that rose to a snow-covered peak, beyond which stood the true summit, slightly higher and perhaps fifty yards farther along the ridge. They set off up the snow. Within an hour each of the four remaining porters, one by one, succumbed to exhaustion and had to be escorted back to a point where they could retrace their steps down to the saddle to join the others.

The angle grew steeper. With Bullock fading, Mallory took the lead. "We moved very slowly," he later reported, "keeping up muscular energy and overcoming lassitude by breathing fast and deep. It was a colossal labour." They reached the rock ridge, and from that point Mallory's memory faded, as the summit itself seemed to recede with each step, even as the slopes on either side of the ridge became more exposed. His pace faltered as his body defied his mind, forcing an endless series of halts simply to breathe.

At last they reached the base of an ice wall. It took all of Mallory's remaining strength to cut a way back up to the crest of the ridge. With a few more steps, they found themselves on the summit. It was already 2:45 p.m. Weather threatened from the southwest and north, and at his feet a thunderstorm hung over the Rongbuk Valley, darkening the glacier with clouds. Bullock's aneroid, though it had been reading low, recorded an elevation of 23,450 feet, which implied a vertical ascent from their camp of over 5,500 feet, a remarkable achievement at such altitude. "We puffed out our chests as we examined it," wrote Mallory a day later in a letter to Ruth. "Longstaff climbed one 23,600. After a week at our camp I consider this a good performance." If the figure was accurate, they had just knocked off the second-highest peak ever climbed. Mallory wanted to call it Mount Kellas, but the Tibetan name, Ri-Ring, would prevail. As it turned out, its true elevation was only 22,520 feet.

But height records in the moment were of little concern. They had had no water all day and little food, and Mallory felt "distinctly mountain-sick." Below them six porters had been huddling in the snow for over three hours. Mallory allowed just fifteen minutes on top, and he made the most of it. As a crow flies, he was only ten miles from the summit of Everest. Looking to the west, he saw the great peaks of Gyachung Kang and Cho Oyu and for the first time grasped the geographical alignment of the Ra Chu and the Kyetrak Glacier, where Wheeler was working, and the valley of the Rongbuk, which lay at his feet to the east. To the south he could see that beyond the Northwest Ridge of Everest there was indeed a second, equally massive ridge running parallel to it. This arête, he estimated, soared above 25,000 feet for much of its length, with individual peaks, including one he named Nuptse, rising higher. What's more, it buttressed not Everest but, rather, a second enormous summit, "a fierce rock arête," which he dubbed South Peak. In Tibetan this was Lhotse. Between the two ridges lay the Western Cwm, a valley of ice, and between the rocky black crest of Lhotse and Everest was a dramatic saddle, the South Col, which offered a line to the summit, "the easiest we have seen."

This indeed would be the route followed by Hillary and Tenzing in 1953. But from Mallory's perspective on Ri-Ring in 1921, it was not at all clear how one could reach the South Col itself. It was "almost certainly inapproachable from the east side," he would write to Ruth. "We have yet to find out whether it can be approached from the west." He would not know for certain without a closer examination of the Western Cwm, the base of which could not be seen from Ri-Ring.

His attention turned east. It was at this point, with a storm gathering, that he made a fateful miscalculation. He was by now familiar with the basic structure of Everest, certainly the architecture of the Northeast Ridge. His eyes quickly scanned from the summit pyramid down to the shoulder that fell away steeply to the North Col. Beyond the saddle rose Changtse, or North Peak, the highest point on a ridge running away to the north and forming the eastern flank of the Rongbuk Valley. This wall, he could see, was broken at a single point, perhaps a mile or two from their camp, across the glacier and up the valley, where a stream pierced the mountains from the east. Mallory knew the spot. Returning to base camp late on June 27, their first day on the glacier, they had come upon the draw, dangerously swollen with snowmelt, impossible to cross. In their exhaustion they had been obliged to follow the stream down to its confluence with the glacier, where it disappeared under the ice. Mallory intended in due course to explore the headwaters, but it was not a priority. The valley seemed too small and narrow to be of serious consequence, an impression now only reinforced in his mind by what he could see from the summit of Ri-Ring. As it turned out, he was deeply mistaken.

One other observation compounded the error. His obsession remained the North Col, the only viable route that he could see to the summit, which he had determined could not be climbed from the Rongbuk side. But from Ri-Ring he saw that from the top of Changtse, on the northern flank of the col, there was a second ridge, heading to the east and forming, he assumed, "the side of whatever valley connected with the Arun River in this direction." In this unknown valley, logic suggested, would be another river of ice flowing to the east but also leading at its head to the desirable side of the North Col. Changtse and its ridge appeared to bar any access from the west or north. Unable to anticipate the serpentine flow of glaciers in the Himalaya, Mallory concluded that to have a chance at Everest, they would have to abandon Rongbuk and approach the problem from the east. Half blinded by certainty, he retreated from the summit of Ri-Ring, exhilarated at the prospects. Howard-Bury had been right to press on for

Kharta. "Fortune favoured us," Mallory later wrote. "The wind was no more than a breeze; the temperature was mild, the storm's malice was somehow dissipated with no harm done. We rejoined the coolies before five o'clock and were back in our camp at 7:15 pm, happy to have avoided a descent in the dark." Bullock did not get in until 7:30, the last to arrive. At 21,000 feet, he had seen "a handsome black butterfly with red markings."

ON THE night of July 6, the monsoon broke in earnest. Snow blanketed the camp, leaving the climbers tent-bound for two days. Mallory's spirit dampened. His letter that day to Ruth began, as always, with a description of the mountain. These short passages had become like mantras, each a perfect reflection of his mood. "As to the general shape of the mountain," he began, as if for the first time, "in the first place it is a great rock peak plastered with snow and having prodigious precipices . . . a rock peak a little blunted at top, but white from the fresh snow which seems never to melt—immeasurably bigger and higher than any mountain I have seen in the Alps, not a slender spike but built up on its great arête with the limbs of a giant, simple, severe and superb. From the mountaineer's point of view so far as we have seen it no more appalling sight could be imagined."

Toward the end of the letter, which for the most part reads as a mountaineer's account, he apologized for the formal tone and wrote more personally:

> And what of my thoughts about it all? Well, in the first place
> all the driving power comes from me and it makes me a little
> dispirited sometimes to be giving out so much . . . I could do
> without the coolies and the problems with rations and supplies
> from base camp. I weary of the discomforts, the cramped style
> in this tent and the sand which blows in and the little problems
> every night of arranging one's bedding comfortably and the
> cold of evenings. I began this letter in the sun among the rocks;
> now I am sitting on my rolled up bedding with my sheepskin
> boots on. Two months or more of such a life let alone the
> discomforts at higher camps seem a long stretch in front of me
> and I look forward to the time when we shall be trekking back
> to Darjeeling and I shall be drawing nearer to you. However
> you mustn't think I am depressed. It is an exhilarating life on the
> whole and I am wonderfully fit—never a moment's trouble with

my digestion . . . There'll be something to be told even if we don't climb Everest, as I can hardly think we shall . . . Well, now I must write a report to Howard-Bury to send along with this letter tomorrow. Good night and great love to you. We see the same stars.

MALLORY WAS NOT the only man sitting out the weather with thoughts of home. On the Nangpa La moraine, things could not have gone worse for Wheeler, who had been camped alone with his porters for twelve days. June 30 had brought such rain that there had been nothing to do, he'd noted in his journal, "but stay in bed and make the most of it." The following morning, July 1, Canada's Dominion Day, he and two porters had climbed for several hours to reach the shoulder of Chorat-Sung, lugging the theodolite and all the gear past "rock hopelessly rotten, blocks weighing several tons ready to slip at the slightest touch." At noon, just as they finally reached a spot suitable as a surveying station, it began to snow, "a beastly wet storm until 3:30." He had just cached all of the instruments when the weather "cleared in a miraculous fashion." Then, just as he was measuring the angles, another blizzard struck. He headed home defeated in the dark, having wasted the entire day, "tired and just about ready to drop."

The next day he had to rest the men, "so naturally it was a most beautiful morning." Leaving camp alone, he scouted several possible stations and made the decision to move even farther up the moraine. A foot of snow fell that night. He woke on the morning of July 3 "simply loathing the idea of breaking camp and doing a day's work." All the cooking had to be done outside, and in the wind the Primus stove failed to ignite. He breakfasted without tea, and then, leaving camp by 7:45, spent the morning at a station south of what he called "Dirty Glacier." He secured some useful photographs, but was still unable, because of the weather, to get a decent read on a defined survey point. "I must get something fixed!" he wrote in some desperation. Returning around 10:30, he revived his spirits with a bit of food and then, around noon, led the porters up the ice to establish the higher camp. They set up beside a small meltwater pool on a moss-covered moraine only two miles from the Nangpa La. The aneroid indicated an elevation of 18,500 feet, his highest and coldest camp yet.

A blizzard blew in the following day, confining him to camp. Fortunately, the mail had arrived the evening before, and he busied himself with correspondence. "My tent looked exactly like Xmas morning," he noted; his wife, Dolly, had sent a box of ginger nuts, which disappeared "exceedingly rapidly." Wollaston, ever loyal, had dispatched a box of food, special treats, along with the sad message that Wheeler's orderly, Asghar Khan, had finally succumbed on June 27 from typhoid. "Poor devil," Wheeler wrote. "He was very bad. Delirium for three days before he died. I shall have to do something for the family. Perhaps I can get a government pension for them."

Wheeler expected to remain at the higher camp for four days. He stayed for eight, even as the monsoon storms poured over the Nangpa La from Nepal. On July 5 they climbed at dawn, only to spend all day on top of a shoulder doing nothing. On the way back they became disoriented in a whiteout, and wandered blind among the seracs and crevasses of the glacier. When the clouds did clear, the porters suffered from the sun, for they had neglected to wear their goggles and several became snowblind. "I rather lost patience with them," Wheeler wrote, "for they will not do as they are told!" He threatened to dock their pay, to no avail. The bigger problem was food. His supply line stretched back to Tingri, twenty miles of flat, open ground followed by eight miles "of poisonous going" to reach his high camp on the Nangpa La. Out of goodwill, he had taken as his servant and cook a man Howard-Bury had exiled from headquarters: "one of the expedition's scallywags," Wheeler called him, a hopeless sort incapable of making a meal.

Wheeler's luck changed the next day. It dawned bright and he was able to return to the high shoulder and a "glorious panorama at last for 2–3 hours." He spent the afternoon plotting his work and establishing the height and precise geographical positions of two key peaks that became benchmarks of his survey. "Everything now fits around them ok," he wrote that night. "Another two stations ought to do me here to get the pass and watershed and amphitheatre fixed. The watershed is a bit doubtful I think but tomorrow might settle it."

The morning resolved nothing. He woke to a snowstorm, pushed off from camp in bright sun, and climbed to 21,000 feet to a spur that promised vistas to the east, south, and west, only to be enveloped in cloud, where he sat until 4:45 p.m. The next two days sleet and snow encased his tents. Things began to fall apart. "One can't camp half clad men," he wrote, "on a glacier 19,000 ft up with weather as it is now. I'll need half a dozen primus stoves and gallons of fuel to feed them and Mallory and Bullock are using about all there are. The expedition is equipped to climb Everest, not to map it."

Wheeler gave it one last go on July 10, climbing alone in light mist and terrible cold to another station. "The coolies as usual I had to leave behind . . . The weather is awful," he recorded. "It snowed all afternoon and my station was in the clouds all day. It is the monsoon good and proper and with a vengeance . . . It's still snowing this evening and seems likely to go on. I think the best thing to do is clear out . . . A beastly day . . . bitterly cold, a blinding snowstorm, damp snow all night, coat, breeches, puttees and boots simply soaked . . . 10 degrees of frost."

After another day tent-bound by the snow, with four men sick and his own health failing, Wheeler finally headed down on July 12 to his lower camp, where a relay of porters awaited with mail and supplies. Howard-Bury and Heron, he learned, in anticipation of the major move scheduled for later in the month, were off scouting Kharta, leaving Morshead and Wollaston, "much to their disgust," in Tingri. In the upper Phung Chu, Morshead and Gujjar Singh had "mapped some 3000 square miles of new country ¼"," a singular achievement that only highlighted his own frustrations. "It is simply disgusting," he wrote, "going up these infernal grinds to do nothing, but what can I do? Back home in Canada it would be nothing—a 2 hour grind, nothing at all; but here at these beastly altitudes it literally takes the life out of you."

He felt rotten, the weather remained bad, and the porters were on the verge of breakdown. He was also out of money, down to his last fifty *tankas* of silver and copper, with one gold *srang* and a five-rupee note, nothing to pay the men or purchase firewood and yak dung. "Time is moving on," he noted. "Distances are so huge in this country. Of course, this is the real monsoon."

He still had several stations to attempt on his way north, and it would be six days before he finally arrived back in Tingri, where his reward was a hot bath, a cup of whiskey, and the first decent food in nearly a month. Howard-Bury had returned with good news from Kharta, and the two of them stayed up late into the night of July 18 "swapping lies." The next day Wheeler slept. "It is ripping," he wrote, "to have nothing strenuous to do."

WHILE WHEELER was still toiling on the Nangpa La, Mallory and Bullock fought the weather in the upper Rongbuk Valley. On July 8, with a fresh party of seven porters, taking the minimum of gear and food for just three nights, they set out into the face of the monsoon, hoping in a quick two-day thrust to solve the mystery of the Western Cwm. They followed the shelf to its confluence with the West

Rongbuk and, rather than crossing the glacier, continued along its northern moraine, reaching a rare patch of grass and moss, exposed to the south and the sun, perhaps five miles from their alpine camp. They realized almost immediately, Mallory noted, the "error of our ways." The Mummery tents, with their thin canvas and low profile, decent enough in fair weather, were hopeless in the snows of Everest. Mallory's congenital incompetence with anything technical made a mess of the Primus stoves, leaving both him and Bullock nauseated by kerosene fumes. No one slept. In the morning, they found snow piled high around and over the camp. The weather forced them to rethink their scheme. Were they to reach the Western Cwm, and explore in a meaningful way what lay beyond the Northwest Ridge and the upper reaches of the West Rongbuk, they would need proper support.

Despite the heavy snow, on the morning of July 9 Mallory returned all the way down to their base near the Rongbuk Monastery. His plan was to move the base, including the men and adequate supplies, up to a point just below the snout of the Rongbuk Glacier, within a single march of their highest bivouac, or what he now called the Second Advanced Camp. Bullock, meanwhile, was charged with returning to the alpine camp, to shift the bulk of its equipment, most notably the Whymper tents, up to the higher camp. The alpine camp, stripped of much of its equipment and supplies and now dubbed by Mallory the First Advanced Camp, would serve, according to Mallory, as "a half-way house with our big 80-foot tent standing in solemn grandeur to protect all that remained there." It was no simple task, as the notes in Bullock's diary attest: "Beastly weather, cold sleet and snow, wind in our faces. Changed tents in driving snow. Coat and trousers wet. Water in pockets of waterproof. Cold night, snowing at four am."

Within forty-eight hours the move was done, and by the evening of Sunday, July 10, they were established as a proper team, ready to advance, or so they believed. But that night the snowfall was the heaviest they had yet experienced, and in the morning they were unable to move. The porters could not kindle a fire, and men had to be sent down to the lower camp to fetch a sack of dried yak dung. Finally, late in the day the clouds broke and Mallory beheld for the first time the range of mountains on the Nepali frontier that anchored the head of the West Rongbuk, the highest of which was Pumori, which soared to nearly 24,000 feet. "The clinging curtains," he wrote, "were rent and swirled aside and closed again, lifted and lowered and flung wide at last; sunlight broke through with sharp shadows and clean edges revealed—and we were there to witness the amazing spectacle." Directly across the ice from their camp was Lingtren, a mountain massif rising to 22,025 feet. The head of the glacier stretched away to the west, but an arm branched south, wrapping around the flank of Lingtren and separating it from Pumori. The geography suggested that this southern reach of the West Rongbuk had to be continuous with the Western Cwm or at least separated from it only by a high saddle. Either way, for the moment, it held the key.

On July 12, they set out at 5:45 a.m. with great hopes. Exhilarated at last to be walking, as Mallory wrote, "under a clear sky," they crossed much of the glacier with ease, "delighted to think that a large part of the task was accomplished when the sun rose full of warmth and cheerfulness." Then they ran literally into a wall, "a stream of white ice, so narrow" they expected to get through in thirty minutes. They entered by way of a bay with "high white towers and ridges" all around. A side passage led to another, and another. To escape the maze Mallory finally cut steps up an ice wall, which landed them on the crest of a sheer precipice that dropped 100 feet to the moraine. Having wasted nearly three hours, they were forced to backtrack; weather set in, and the only option was an early return to camp in anticipation of better luck the following day.

It was a crushing blow to their morale. They had taken four and a half hours to cover little more than a mile. That evening the mail came up, and Mallory wrote to his old friend Rupert Thompson:

> I think of you as especially a civilized man with somehow the capacity of sympathizing with the barbarous life and habits of a poor devil like myself, you may even be able to tell me why I embarked on an adventure such as this. Here in this outlandish spot we two—Bullock is the other—sit in a tent listening to the fine grains of sand beating against its sides, content, in so far as we can be content simply in the fact that we are writing letters to our wives and friends and that a coolie will bear them away on the first stage of their journey tomorrow . . . I sometimes think of this expedition as a fraud from beginning to end, invented by the wild enthusiasm of one man; Younghusband—puffed up by the would-be wisdom of certain pundits in the A.C.; and imposed upon the youthful ardour of your humble servant. Certainly the reality must be strangely different from their dream. The long imagined snow slopes of this Northern Face of Everest with their gently and inviting angle turn out to be the most appalling precipice nearly 10,000 ft high. It is

a great rock peak plastered with snow, built of gigantic arêtes, which enclose impossible faces. The prospect of ascent in any direction is about nil and our present job is to rub our noses against the impossible in such a way as to persuade mankind that some noble heroism has failed once again. And the heroism at present consists in enduring the discomforts of a camp at 19,000 ft in company of a band of whose native tongue I can scarcely understand a syllable, in urging these good folk to rise before daylight, and by the same token urging oneself, in the most usually vain hope that by the time we have got somewhere something may still remain unhidden by the clouds.

Mallory had inadvertently anticipated precisely the outcome of their next foray. Leaving camp at 4:20 on July 13, again a fine morning, they traversed the glacier in just ninety minutes, successfully avoiding the worst of its hazards. Clinging to the edge of the moraine, they moved steadily around the shoulder of Lingtren, west and then south, coming back onto the ice just as the clouds rolled in from Nepal, obliterating everything. They continued on a bearing, walking blind. Mallory could sense the unknown peaks even as he felt the presence of "yawning crevasses as dim labyrinths on every side." At 9:30 they reached a crest of snow, what they assumed to be the col, but they could scarcely see each other, let alone the mountains of Nepal and the valley of the Western Cwm. Yet again they were forced to retreat.

For three days they regrouped at their high camp. After resting on July 14, Bullock with two porters made another stab at reaching the mysterious col, only to be again stymied by clouds. Mallory climbed alone the next day, July 16, setting out in the middle of the night to scramble up a spur of the Lingtren massif, directly across from their camp, reaching the top at sunrise. He struggled with his Kodak, though what he saw was illuminating. He confirmed that, as suspected, there were two approaches to the Western Cwm: one at the head of the main Rongbuk Glacier, which he had already identified as the Lho La, and the second, known to Tibetans as the Nup La, which had been their elusive goal for the past week. He remained on the summit until 7:00 a.m., exposing altogether a dozen photographic plates, before returning to camp in time for breakfast, astonished by what a clear sky could yield. With Bullock resting after his own photographic excursion, Mallory spent a pleasant morning collecting flowers, "not a great variety but some delicious honey scents and an occasional cheerful blue poppy."

If they had learned one thing for their troubles, it was the predict-ability with which the weather rolled in every day as the sun approached the zenith. To have any chance of reaching the Nup La and the West-ern Cwm before the clouds, they would have to begin from a higher point on the ice. Mallory instructed the sirdar to assemble rations for two days for ten men. On Monday, July 18, the same day that Wheeler returned to Tingri, Mallory and Bullock, equipped with snowshoes and carrying their own gear, accompanied by eight porters, moved up to establish a spike camp at 18,600 feet. In a flimsy Mummery tent that evening they waited for the moon. At 3:00 a.m., with black shadows on the snow, they set out for the col, keenly anticipating the dawn. As they came near, Mallory recalled, "the whole scene opened up. The North Ridge of Everest was clear and bright even before sunrise. We reached the col at 5 a.m., a fantastically beautiful scene; and we looked across into the Western Cwm at last, terribly cold and forbidding under the shadow of Everest."

After all their long struggles to lift the veil, what they saw provoked only disappointment. On the skyline the great white peaks stood out, radiant in the morning sky. At their feet, however, was a 1,500-foot drop, a "hopeless precipice" of ice. Mallory scouted the length of the crest, seeking in vain a traverse that might lead safely down to the val-ley. "That, too, quite hopeless," he lamented.

But as he and Bullock studied from on high the contours of the glacier of the Western Cwm, their disappointment quickly turned to relief. "We have seen this Western glacier," Mallory later wrote, "and are not sorry we have not to go up it."

From their vantage they could look directly into the basin of ice that swept to the South Col and the summits of Lhotse and Everest. The Lhotse Face has a pitch of seventy to eighty degrees; even today, with fixed ropes and modern equipment, it is a grueling three-hour climb. The front-pointed crampon was not invented until 1929, so for Mallory the only way up would have been an ice stairway, cut step by step with his own power, an impossibility. Even more intimidating was the fierce tangle of ice at the entrance to the Western Cwm, the Khumbu Icefall. The glacier, moving at an astonishing speed of four feet per day, literally tumbles 2,000 feet off the mountain, creating an unstable maze of crevasses and ice towers the size of small buildings. Mallory had never seen a glacier so "terribly steep and broken." Even had they been able to reach the floor of the valley, the route to the mountain, as Bullock concluded, was "out of the question."

·   ·   ·

"WITH THIS EXPEDITION of July 19," Mallory wrote, "our recon-naissance of these parts had ended." By nightfall of the following day they had broken camp and retreated, bringing all stores and gear back to their base at the snout of the main Rongbuk Glacier. They had both succeeded and failed. If Everest were to be climbed, Mallory con-cluded, "the route would not lie along the whole length of any of its colossal ridges." Their sharp crests and towers would bar the way. Nor would it be found on any of the approaches from the south, west, or north, all of which had now been explored, or so he believed. Only one side of the mountain remained. "The great question before us now was one of access. Could the North Col be reached from the East and how could we attain this point?"

At base camp near the Rongbuk Monastery word awaited Mallory that Howard-Bury would soon be making the move to Kharta, leav-ing Tingri on July 23 and, two days later, passing through Chöbuk, where he proposed they rendezvous. This gave Mallory five short days to pull his men out of Rongbuk, even as events, in a fateful way, spun out of his control. Weather shrouded the camp for two days, rain and sleet; the snow lay a foot deep and down to 16,000 feet on the morn-ing of July 23. The porters were exhausted. There was a small crisis of organization and logistics. In the official expedition account, Mallory famously blamed the sirdar, "a whey-faced treacherous knave whose sly and calculated villainy too often, before it was discovered, deprived our coolies of their food, and whose acquiescence in his own illimitable incompetence was only less disgusting than his infamous duplicity." These were strong words indeed to describe a man Mallory had per-sonally vetted and who by definition had kept the expedition running in the most difficult of circumstances for a month. Had he been so truly incompetent, why had action not been taken sooner? In truth, Mallory was spinning a moment of intense humiliation.

On the night of July 22 a note had arrived from headquarters at Tingri, indicating that every photograph taken by Mallory with the quarter-plate camera had been ruined. In a monumental gesture of technical incompetence, he had inserted the plates back to front. It was a crushing blow. "I knew nothing of plates," he lamented in a let-ter that night to Ruth, "and followed instructions given me by Heron. I have taken enormous trouble over these photos; many of them were taken at sunrise from places where neither I nor anyone else may go again . . . However I'm determined to replace them as far as possi-ble . . . It will mean two days spent in the most tiresome fashion, when I thought all our work in those parts was done."

It was, of course, impossible to reproduce in two days what had been accomplished in thirty, though Mallory, to his immense credit, did his best. Bullock, meanwhile, was not idle. On Sunday, July 24, he pounded his way back up the entire length of the main Rongbuk Glacier, both to examine once more the North Col and to scout at last the Lho La, the saddle at the head of the basin that looked down into Nepal. He reached 19,500 feet and stared into mist, just able to make out the outline of the Khumbu Icefall at the foot of the Western Cwm. It did not look appealing. He returned to base camp, three hours in the sleet, arriving just before dark.

A heavy snow fell in the night, dispelling a vague notion Mallory had of crossing the mountains directly to reach Kharta. It would have been a horrendous passage, especially in such weather. But had it been attempted, there would have been only one possible route. Along the entire flank of the Rongbuk Valley, from Everest down to the North Col and from Changste along the full length of the jagged mountain skyline running to the north, there is but a single cleft that opens to the east. Mallory and Bullock had walked right by the narrow mouth of the valley on their first day on the ice. Its outlet stream, a torrent of meltwater, had forced them to detour onto the glacier. From the summit of Ri-Ring they had seen the drainage again and remarked upon it. Their achievements on the mountain had been considerable, even noble, but given that their primary task was reconnaissance, their failure to explore this opening, given the ease of access, was a remarkable oversight, if not a dereliction of duty, and ultimately far more embarrassing to Mallory that his struggles with the camera.

Instead, on the morning of July 25, exhausted from their efforts and keen to get a fresh start at Kharta, they hurried the porters down the Rongbuk, past the monastery, and along the track to Chöbuk. As they descended from the rock and ice, Mallory experienced an odd sensation: "The valley was somehow changed and more agreeable to the eye. Presently I discovered the reason. The grass had grown on the hillside since we went up. We were coming down to summer green."

In his haste to leave the valley, Mallory had missed the key to the North Col and thus to the mountain.

CHAPTER 8

Eastern Approaches

As Mallory and Bullock struggled in the snows of Rongbuk, and Wheeler, high on the ice of the Nangpa La, waited in vain for the sun, Charles Howard-Bury was making plans for the final phase of the 1921 reconnaissance: the exploration of the eastern approaches to Everest through Kharta and the unknown rivers that fell away from the glaciers of the Kangshung Face, a vertical wall of ice two miles high. On July 5, accompanied still by Alexander Heron, he had left Mallory and Bullock after the brief visit with them and began the long slow descent of the Rongbuk Chu, leaving behind what he later described as a "wild and gloomy but strangely holy valley." From the monks at Rongbuk he had learned that Kharta lay but an easy two-day march from the monastery. Rather than returning to his headquarters at Tingri, he decided to scout the route directly, with the goal of identifying a site from which to base the expedition during what he knew would be the critical months of August and September. With the expedition stymied in the north and west, and with the government of Nepal precluding an assault from the south, all their hopes now lay to the east.

Howard-Bury and Heron started out on a cold morning after a night of sharp frost that left the summit of Everest radiant under a fresh cover of snow. With yaks for transport, the pace was slow and it was midday before they reached the first signs of cultivation at Chöbuk, rich fields of barley eighteen inches high and coming into ear. The crop had barely sprouted when they had first set out from Tingri; the season, Howard-Bury noted with some concern, was moving along far too quickly. He decided to increase the use of baksheesh, cash incentives that would entice the Tibetan herdsmen to break tradition and cover longer distances rather than changing animals in every village, which caused impossible delays. Still, it was not until well after 3:00 p.m. that they began the steep 1,200-foot climb over a high pass that rose above Chöbuk and marked the route to Halung, a prosperous hamlet of well-irrigated fields of barley and mustard where they would halt for the night. In a grassy meadow by a mountain stream, the villagers had pitched three tents, and gathered fuel, cushions, and food for the comfort of the men. At 14,800 feet, the air was temperate and warm, and they slept well for the first time in days.

Morning broke bright and clear and, having moved their loads by hand across a rickety bridge, they drove the yaks and ponies across the ford and began a slow passage through a number of small villages laced together with irrigation ditches lined with an astonishing array of wildflowers, black and yellow clematis, monkshood, buttercups and primulas of a dozen hues. A change of transport delayed them at Rebu, a picturesque village that straddled a perfectly crystal river—a welcome relief, Howard-Bury later recalled, after the muddy glacial torrents of Rongbuk. When they paused for lunch, scores of small birds, all fearless and wonderfully tame, hopped about their legs, carrying off crumbs and small bits of food. It reminded Howard-Bury of the swifts and songbirds of France, which had always returned to alight on the torn and tangled branches of woodlands blasted apart by battle.

So much had been changed by the war, and yet so little had been won. Peace had given way to chaos, and everywhere the world of his youth was crumbling. Germany and Russia were engulfed in revolution. His beloved Ireland was a cauldron of violence and sectarian strife. A national uprising in Egypt in the spring of 1919 had been followed a year later by an Arab revolt in Mesopotamia that engaged thousands of British troops and left hundreds dead. In India, all the news was bad. On the North-West Frontier no fewer than 340,000 British and Indian soldiers, fully two-thirds of the entire military might of the Raj, were engaged in open war with Afghanistan and the Wazirs, Mahsuds, and Afridis. The air force bombed and strafed the tribesmen and there was talk of using poison gas, a proposal that horrified veterans of the Western Front.

More than 2.5 million Indians who had served with the British in the trenches had returned home expecting to be rewarded for their loyalty to the Crown. Instead, the Raj extended the laws that had suspended civil liberties during the war. Mohandas Gandhi called for a one-day strike, a boycott of British manufactured goods, and a national campaign of peaceful noncooperation. Invariably these protests, like all those initiated by the Mahatma, sparked the very violence and conflict he so earnestly condemned.

In April 1919 in the Punjab city of Amritsar an English missionary, a white woman, was brutally attacked and severely injured. In retribution the British military commander General Reginald Dyer ordered all Indians passing the spot where she had been assaulted to crawl on their hands and knees. This humiliation unleashed waves of demonstrations, which Dyer promptly banned. On the evening of April 13, in defiance of martial law, a crowd of several thousand unarmed men, women, and children gathered in the Jallianwala Bagh, an enclosed courtyard adjacent to a holy shrine, the Golden Temple, the most sacred site of the Sikhs. Furious at this affront, Dyer marched a detachment of ninety Baluchis and Gurkhas into the square, arrayed them in battle formation, and ordered them to open fire. There was no warning, no mercy, and for the victims no escape. For ten minutes Dyer obliged his men to maintain a constant fire. Howard-Bury knew well what this implied. A British soldier armed with a .303 Lee-Enfield rifle was trained to hit a target three hundred yards away fifteen times a minute; many could double this rate. Dyer had commanded his troops to fire at point-blank range into a dense crowd with a weapon that could kill at two thousand yards. Single bullets passed through three and four bodies. The dead lined the walls of the enclosure in bloody piles ten feet deep. In the end, 379 were killed and four times as many severely wounded. Dyer ordered that no succor be given to the injured or dying. Leaving children to wail for their slaughtered mothers, husbands to untangle the corpses in search of their wives, he simply marched his troops out of the enclosure. Had his vehicles with their mounted machine guns been able to fit through the narrow entrance to the Jallianwala Bagh, it was later noted, he would not have hesitated to use those weapons on the mob.

The Amritsar Massacre left a scar across India that would never heal. Dyer's only punishment was early retirement from the army. In many quarters of the Raj he was celebrated as a hero. English ladies took up collections to buy him a sword of honor. From supporters like Rudyard Kipling he received a gift of £26,000, a small fortune, to ease his way into his golden years. The agony and outrage united Indians in fury. In February 1921, even as the Everest Committee made plans for the mountain, the Duke of Connaught, the younger brother of Edward VII, declared that "the shadow of Amritsar has lengthened over the fair face of India." It was the beginning of the end of the Raj, even if few recognized it at the time.

For Howard-Bury, who socialized with royalty and knew the Duke of Connaught personally, India in 1921 remained the Raj of his youth, a land of old Sikh soldiers bedecked in medals, glittering assemblies of princes and elephants, and dashing young English officers posing beside racks of dead Bengal tigers. He had seen too much carnage in France to condone Dyer's actions at Amritsar, but he remained a dedicated imperialist with high Tory principles, convinced that British rule, firm and fair, was the best form of government for the subcontinent. In the House of Commons in 1923 he would speak out against Gandhi and insist that the Raj make no concessions to nationalist agitation. India, he maintained, was not ready for independence. The people did not understand democracy.

Like so many of his class, Howard-Bury loved the idea of India, the proud martial tradition of the Indian Army, the exotic features of its culture and traditions, the righteous sense of pride that came to all Englishmen with the spread of British civilization. But he had little time for those Indians who had actually achieved what the English aspired to offer, who had attended Harrow and Eton, Oxford and Cambridge, and returned home quite prepared to lead a free nation. Sir Francis Younghusband spoke for many when he wrote, "The best Indians . . . and those who have the highest and best qualities, are the soldiers and servants who can perhaps neither read nor write, but who have lived their lives within the honest atmosphere of Englishmen and Englishwomen. The worst are the so-called highly educated Indians who get a smattering of algebra and John Stuart Mill." This attitude, as much as the atrocity at Amritsar, drove Indian politicians and intellectuals and British social reformers to distraction.

Mallory had disliked Howard-Bury from the start, describing him in a letter to Ruth as a "queer customer . . . too much the landlord with not only Tory prejudices but a very highly developed sense of hate and contempt for other people other than his own." This last statement seems unfair, but in photographs the contrast between the two men is evident: Howard-Bury erect in his houndstooth jacket and tweed breeches, with his tie and gold watch chain, his felt hat perched at a rakish angle; Mallory impish, hands in mittens, a scarf casually dangling from his neck, legs pulled up to his chest almost like a child.

It could not have helped that Mallory had traveled to Ireland and was clearly sympathetic to the Republican cause; as far as Howard-Bury was concerned, the Sinn Fein had unleashed a terrorist war. For him the issue was intensely personal. Only ten months before, in September 1920, his mother's gamekeeper's cottage had been destroyed by arson, as had the bridge and the gates at her estate at Charleville. Within a year her own house at Brookfield would be torched. The crisis had caused Howard-Bury to accept the Everest post with some reluctance and trepidation. The fate of Ireland and his mother's well-being haunted Howard-Bury his entire sojourn in Tibet, and it was one reason he was so concerned about the timely delivery of the mail. He opened each letter from home less than certain that there would be a home to return to.

THE TRACK OUT of Rebu led for several miles through a valley flanked on both sides by great limestone and sandstone cliffs, and then gradually rose to the summit of the Doya La, a 17,000-foot pass that marked the boundary between two very different worlds. Just a quarter mile below the pass Howard-Bury picked up a first sign, a stretch of granite soil that supported an extraordinary growth of alpine flowers: blue poppies in great abundance, pink, yellow, and white saxifrages, purple gentians, and a dozen species that were completely new to him. North of the Doya La the land was dry, harsh, and barren save for the irrigated fields of mustard and barley. Beyond the pass the air was moist, and the entire landscape was swathed by the blanket of the monsoon, the damp clouds driven up the Arun River and its tributaries from beyond the Himalaya to the south. As Howard-Bury and Heron dropped away from the heights, they passed through junipers and willows, and entire forests of pink and white rhododendrons, meadows of dozens of wildflowers, clematis and currants, monkshood and blue anemones, wild roses and spiraeas.

If the landscape was welcoming, the people were not. None had ever seen a European. Having ridden twenty-six miles with no sign of Kharta, Howard-Bury and Heron needed information about the route, yet in every village the Tibetans scattered in fear as they approached. In the end the travelers gave chase and captured a man, who under some duress guided the party to Chulungphu, where they halted for the night. Only with reluctance did the locals emerge out of hiding to erect tents and provide fuel, as per the standing orders of the *dzongpen*. Howard-Bury and Heron slept that night in a field of scented yellow primulas and awoke to mist and a pattering of rain. It was the first precipitation of the year and the villagers, delighted by this auspicious turn of events, now begged the Europeans, for the sake of the crops, not to leave.

In the soft and mild air of morning, they pushed on down the valley, with each passing mile bringing richer fields and more fertile land, hillsides covered with junipers and willows, ancient terraces ablaze with yellow mustard, villages and country estates surrounded by groves of giant poplars. In due course they came to a large river, which Howard-Bury knew to be the upper reaches of the Arun, known in Tibet as the Phung Chu, which they had followed a month before on their exploratory approach to Shegar Dzong and Tingri. Only once it dropped into Nepal, passing through a deep, thunderous gorge flanked by great cliffs and towering peaks, was the river formally known as the Arun.

It was even here a formidable barrier. There was a rope bridge eighteen miles upstream, Howard-Bury learned, but it would be useless in high water. So the party continued south, following the main track of the river for three miles, until coming upon a wild glacial stream also quite impossible to ford. It flowed out of a valley that reached away to the west, the direction of Everest, though the mountain could not be seen. The local people professed to know nothing of the stream's source or of the lands that rose so dramatically to snow summits that fused with the clouds and sky. Heading up this valley, the travelers presently came to Kharta Shika, the hamlet that was home to the local governor.

Kharta, they discovered, was not a place but a district, a series of villages and religious retreats and monasteries clustered around the confluence of the Kharta Chu and the Phung Chu, in a temperate valley heavily influenced by the weather systems that swept up the Arun from Nepal. The governor welcomed them cordially with gifts of sweetmeats and ceremonial scarves, and invited them to camp in his garden, a beautiful copse of willows and wild rosebushes set off from the courtyard of his home, sheltered from the wind and dominated by an ancient poplar larger than any specimen Howard-Bury had ever encountered. A stream crossed the garden and in the shadow of the poplar was a painted prayer wheel eight feet high, which, driven by the water, turned in constant motion. To one side was a fine Chinese tent, their shelter for the night. It turned out, however, to be more beautiful than functional. The rains that heralded the full coming of the monsoon broke that evening, and they spent the night huddled in their mackintoshes as a fine mist sprayed through the roof and the sloping walls, soaking everything. But again the coincidence of their arrival on the eve of the first really heavy rains of the season did not go unnoticed by the *dzongpen* and the villagers, and it made for a very promising start.

In the morning Howard-Bury, leaving Heron to rest, set out with Chheten Wangdi, his Tibetan translator, the *dzongpen*, and a wealthy landowner named Hopaphema to search for an appropriate encampment for the expedition. They rode down toward the main valley, pausing to examine several houses before settling on one that stood alone on an old river terrace with fine views, a good supply of readily accessible water, and a lovely garden of poplars and willows where they could pitch their tents. The landlord agreed to let it for thirty *trangka* a month, a princely sum of three and a half pence a day. It was the first time anyone had attempted to rent a property in the valley and, as Howard-Bury mused, there were no real estate agents present to drive up the price.

After a lunch of macaroni and minced meat, tea, milk, and beer, the men headed back to Kharta, where the rains that day had never stopped. In the clearing light of evening Howard-Bury took a walk through the ruins of an old fort close to their camp, and came upon a dell of willows and scarlet roses where the ground was carpeted by primulas and giant poplars grew thirty feet in circumference. He felt renewed by the beauty of the place. It was fine country and would serve as an excellent base even as their explorations took them back up onto the ice and rock. He still did not know what lay at the head of the Kharta Chu, but he had learned that there was a parallel valley to the south, the Kama, accessible by three distinct routes, high passes crossed only infrequently by herdsmen, pilgrims, and the odd trader heading south across the Himalaya into Nepal. At the head of one of these valleys, Howard-Bury surmised, would be found the opening to Everest, the eastern flank of the North Col, and the route to the summit.

WHAT HOWARD-BURY did not know was that in crossing into the Kama Valley, the British would be entering one of the most beautiful and sacred places in Tibet, Khenbalung, the Hidden Valley of Arteme-sia, one of the *beyuls*, or spiritual refugia, created in mystic time by Padma Sambhava, Guru Rinpoche. Tibetans saw the valley as one vast cosmic mandala, the points of which were defined by sacred peaks, the homes of mountain deities, with the centrifugal heartland itself being a single Buddha energy field of such beneficence that merely to be there on the land was to know and embrace ever deeper levels of compassion, wisdom, and loving-kindness. The waters of Khenbalung were said to cure all maladies, be they of the mind, body, or spirit. Women who drank from the Kama Chu or any of the hundreds of snowmelt streams of the valley became instantly more beautiful, certain to give birth to an unbroken line of descendants. Men became as strong as the mythical warriors of the ancient Tibetan kings, as swift and skillful as the most brilliant of birds. To meditate for one year in Khenbalung brought greater merit than what might be secured by a thousand years of prayer in any other land.

The appropriate time to take refuge in Khenbalung, the location of its four sacred portals, and the rituals to be performed before crossing these thresholds of the divine were set out with precision in the *terma*, the concealed treasure document, the original guidebook deposited in both physical and mystical space by Guru Rinpoche. These heavenly lands were only for the faithful to find in times of danger and crisis. For sincere seekers they were places of peace and fertility, an ocean of positive energy, eternal youth, religious virtue, insight, and wisdom. For the advanced practitioner, Khenbalung was itself ultimate reality, a valley where spiritually awakened beings could slip silently and effortlessly into an aura of intense mystical ecstasy.

The beauty and benevolence of the *beyuls* was in a sense the perfect coefficient for the depravity, despair, and horror certain to have been suffered by all those who reached the mystical doorways. For it was written in the treasures that only when all civilization lay as shattered stones, when monks renounced their vows and wandered about like feral dogs, when people ate human flesh without shame, when wars drove men mad with depravity and blood ran like rivers throughout the world, would it be time for the virtuous to seek refuge in the hidden lands.

Once inside the sensory space of the hidden valley, in the full radiance of the Buddha field, the pilgrim, according to the guidebook, was certain to encounter endless magical possibilities, plants that knew no seasons and cured all diseases, fruits and flowers scented with the essence of the Buddha, sweat from his skin, and more animals than can be imagined, snow lions and foxes, bears, leopards, apes, jackals, black birds with red-and-yellow beaks floating in space. Clouds and mist darkened the dawn and from the sky resounded the roar of dragons. There was a poisonous burning lake and in the midst of white mountains a crystal palace, home of the secret protector of all hidden treasures, Chekyong Sura, a radiant deity with three bloodshot eyes.

For Tibetans it was inconceivable to enter Khenbalung without taking appropriate ritual precautions. Each traveler wore around the neck a small silver amulet containing written religious texts to be held close to the heart to ward off demons and empower the spirit. Each walked with a prayer wheel spinning in constant motion, a silver or copper vessel inscribed with the six-syllable mantra *Om mane padme hum*. Inside the wheel were rolls of paper printed with sutras and spiritual invocations designed to absorb and radiate Buddha energy. With every rotation both the supplicant and the land itself became charged with religious potential. In climbing to any pass, pilgrims carried small stones as offerings to the guardians of the mountains, and at the major divides they paused to string prayer flags printed with mantras, images of the Windhorse, in the colors of the five elements, yellow representing the earth, green for water, red for fire, white for the air, and blue for space, or ether. With each flutter of breeze, the prayers carried to the universe. As pilgrims crossed the heights, they shouted *Kiki so so lha so lha*, "May the gods be victorious," for each mountain pass recalls the triumph of Guru Rinpoche, when he tamed the resident deities and quelled the malignant forces of the land.

Still demons remain, and among the most terrible are those that dwell within mountain peaks. These are gods of fire and fury, pitiless in their wrath, merciless in their violence. They are the source of the poisonous mists that blind travelers. They launch thunderbolts, loose avalanches; they find gratification in tormenting human beings with hail, rocks, and freezing rain. These terrible and monstrous demons are only among the spiritual hazards awaiting the insincere. Every feature of the landscape is the abode of vital life forces, powerful spiritual entities that dwell everywhere, in caves, lakes, a glacial flow, a juniper leaf, a songbird, or a blade of grass. As pilgrims move through the sacred landscape, they engage in a constant reciprocal flow of spiritual energy, giving fully of themselves, sensing, hearing, seeing with both eyes and mind, speaking through prayers, taking from the land small symbolic gifts even as they leave in exchange something of themselves. When they circle a sacred site, circumambulating a chorten or shrine, perhaps in ritual prostration, it is with the purpose of focusing this energy, building a spiritual charge of empowerment about themselves and the place, like a coil of latent potential.

From the Tibetan perspective, to go into the mountains blind, knowing nothing of proper ritual protocols, living in complete ignorance of anything but what lies on the surface of perception, was an act of total folly. To enter the hidden lands of Khenbelung without adequate spiritual protection, as the British were destined to do, would seem a sign of madness.

Howard-Bury, naturally, knew nothing of this. He had with some sympathy and interest watched his porters make these curious gestures, particularly when crossing high passes. He had been touched by the sincerity of their spiritual intent. He had allowed them to pause at will on the trail to make offerings, to purify a space with juniper fire and smoke. But ultimately these rituals remained for him quaint and mysterious customs, without obvious meaning or significance. All he knew was that the Kama Chu lay beyond the height of land that flanked the Kharta Valley to the south and that somewhere near its source might be found the opening to Everest they had been seeking for these many long weeks. The spiritual potency of the valley, its capacity for grace or for harm, was the last thing on his mind.

ON THE MORNING of July 9 Howard-Bury and Heron, after a final breakfast of milk, turnip greens, and minced meat hosted by their new friend Hopaphema, began the long trek back to Tingri. They rode down the Kharta Chu and then, rather than returning west and over the Doya La, they followed the true right bank of the Phung Chu upstream for some ten miles, passing rich fields of barley, peas, and mustard that gradually gave way to an increasingly barren landscape. The river swept close to the mountains and the trail rose up the face of steep cliffs, dangerous with falling rocks, before crossing a series of broad stony terraces to reach the small hamlet of Dak, where they paused to change transport. Beyond Dak the Phung Chu took a dramatic turn to the east, disappearing into a formidable gorge. Abandoning the main river, the party climbed high into a lateral valley coming in from the west. This proved to be the lower reaches of the Dzakar Chu, a river ultimately born in the rock and ice of Rongbuk, where for much of its initial flow it is known as the Rongbuk Chu. Howard-Bury's plan was to follow the Dzakar Chu upstream for some forty miles, completing a great circle of exploration, and then strike out to the northwest for Tingri, thus adding several hundred square miles of new terrain to the reconnaissance.

They camped that first night at Lumeh, in the garden of a fine country home dominated by enormous poplars, which the villagers claimed had been planted some five hundred years before; one measured an astonishing forty feet in circumference at the base. Beyond the garden wheat grew alongside barley, though the elevation was 12,800 feet, and the fields were alive with hares and magpies. The rain that evening fell again in torrents, as it now did every night, and by morning fresh snow lay thick on the ridges down to an elevation of 16,000 feet, an ominous development that did little to assuage Howard-Bury's concerns about time and the changing of the seasons. The following day's march carried them up the Dzakar Chu, with much of the route requiring them to follow the actual bed of the river, which was hemmed in by cliffs, in flood, and dangerous. Occasionally the valley opened up and gravel bars and beaches thick with tamarisks and buckthorns allowed a brief respite from the wet and cold. But mostly they slogged upstream, fighting the current. Heron wanted to stop after fifteen miles, as the porters from Kharta were played out, but Howard-Bury insisted on pushing on another seven miles to Pulme, where in the rain and darkness they were delighted to find tents pitched and villagers waiting their arrival with hot food and frothy vats of *chang*, the local beer made from barley.

Eager to get back to Tingri, Howard-Bury woke before dawn on July 11 and, leaving Chheten Wangdi to guide Heron and the rest of the party at a more leisurely pace, set out in the darkness to ford the Dzakar Chu. The river was deep and running fast. His pony was swept off its feet, leaving him clinging to the saddle, his entire body flailing about in the current and freezing water. It made for a miserable start to what would be a very long day. Four miles on, at Tashi Dzong, he changed horses and found a guide to lead him away from the river, toward the distant passes that led to Tingri. A cold rain fell all morning, and the dark valley through which they rode was bleak, as if haunted by some ancient calamity. There were dozens of abandoned ruins, villages destroyed, Howard-Bury surmised, during the Gurkha wars of the eighteenth century, when Nepal had ravaged the Tibetan borderlands. It was with relief that they finally climbed away from the fields and found themselves again on a narrow track, slowly clip-clopping over the rocks toward a high saddle that fell away to the west and the vast Tingri Plain. With miles still to go, they leaned into the wind and rain, abandoning themselves to the journey. Not until early evening, having ridden some forty miles since dawn, did Howard-Bury, drenched to the bone, finally arrive at his headquarters at Tingri. With his personal kit still back on the trail with Heron, he slept that night wrapped in a spare tent, without blanket or sleeping bag, and without complaint.

The following morning Wollaston and Morshead gave him a full debriefing. During his time away, the survey party under Morshead had ranged north and west of Tingri, struggling all the time with the impending monsoon, which broke in full force on July 7, driving the men back to headquarters. Working from their base at Tingri, Wollaston, frustrated still by the refusal of Tibetans to kill, had nevertheless amassed a considerable collection of insects, rats, butterflies, birds, and plants. His opinion of the land and the people had not improved, and his mood was grim. Tingri remained, he wrote, "a place of unimaginable filth, with people vile in their habits. They are indescribably dirty and beyond words ignorant and superstitious. I see a large number of fat pink tongues daily." If the traditional Tibetan greeting did not impress, the stark landscape failed to inspire. "The air in Tibet is fine and exhilarating," he granted, "but it is not my country and I don't want much of it. There is nothing beautiful in huge snow mountains rising out of bare plain and I am not even sure there is any real beauty in a snow mountain pure and simple."

Wollaston's aversion to Tibet did not grow out of physical discomfort or dissatisfaction with his colleagues. The Everest expedition, he would write to Hinks, was a picnic compared to what he had endured in New Guinea. He liked Howard-Bury very much, admired him as a leader, and gave him full credit for the lack of friction among the men. Wollaston's fundamental problem, as his own son would later reflect on, was his hatred of all religion, a sentiment born of science but forged in certainty by what he had experienced in the war. Unlike Howard-Bury, whose empathy and curiosity about the Buddhist path increased with each exotic encounter, Wollaston felt only a growing rage at a theocracy that, as he saw it, allowed monks and nuns to live idle and parasitic lives, exploiting the hardworking peasants and extorting the wealth of the nation.

What ultimately interested him was not the culture or even the conquest of Everest but, rather, "the indescribable beauty of the flowers and the sight of these mountains, the glaciers descending among tall fir trees." Thus when Wollaston and Morshead informed Howard-Bury of an invitation that had come from the *dzongpen* to visit Nyenyam, a village and trading emporium on the Nepalese border well to the southwest of Everest, it was the opportunity to botanize in new country, see the great summits of Gosainthan and Gauri Sankar, mountains long confused with Everest, and add several hundred square miles of land to the map that galvanized their attention. To Wollaston, in particular, it was only of passing interest that their route would carry them by Lapche, home of Milarepa, the mystic saint of Tibet, and among the most sacred pilgrimage sites in Tibet. That their journey would begin with a visit to Langkor, a thousand-year-old temple that housed what was said to be the actual stone that the Buddha Shakyamuni had flung across the Himalaya to inspire Guru Rinpoche, was of considerably less significance to him than the possibility of encountering along the way plants, insects, and perhaps even animals unknown to science.

Morshead and Wollaston, accompanied by their Tibetan translator Gyalzen Kazi and the surveyor Gujjar Singh, set off on the morning of July 13 for a trip that would last three weeks. Howard-Bury, meanwhile, though keen to make the move to Kharta, had little choice but to remain at Tingri until Mallory and Bullock completed their explorations at Rongbuk, and Wheeler his photographic survey of the upper reaches of the Kyetrak and the Nangpa La. There was plenty of work to do: film from the various parties to be processed and printed, correspondence and reports to be written and dispatched, supply lines to maintain. Heron came and went, extending his geological surveys. Howard-Bury himself got away on a number of short excursions. He went north to the flank of the holy mountain of Tsibri, where scores of pilgrims from all corners of Tibet acquired, he wrote, "much merit" as they made the "circuit of the mountain," five days of prayer and ritual prostration. On another outing he crossed the marshes to the hot springs at Tsamda, where, just as he was about to slip into the steamy pools for his first proper wash in weeks, villagers appeared to urge him most ardently not to proceed; autumn, after the harvest, was the proper time for one's annual bath.

Wherever he rode on the plains of Tingri, Howard-Bury encountered herds of wild kiangs and antelope, and with each passing day the water rose higher, transforming the entire expanse of the valley into one vast wetland, alive with waterfowl, mergansers, bar-headed geese, and black-necked cranes. Thunderstorms rolled in every evening, and the nights flashed with lightning. The weather came mostly from the north, from beyond Tsibri and the mountain ridge that separated the Phung Chu from the Tsangpo, the valley of the upper Brahmaputra River. Rarely did rain come from the south, with the monsoon. Indeed, when a south wind blew, the rain stopped altogether, which both surprised and relieved Howard-Bury. Perhaps, he mused, they might still have time for a final go at the mountain. On the afternoon of July 22 a halo of yellow, green, and white light circled the sun. That evening, for the first time in days, there were lovely views of Everest and all the great summits stretching west as far as Cho Oyu.

But the pressure was on. Wheeler, who returned to Tingri on the night of July 18, painted a grim picture of conditions on the high flanks of the Everest massif. On the evening of Thursday, July 21, a message arrived from Mallory suggesting that the reconnaissance of the north and west sides was complete; they were ready to move to the east. "A chit in from M tonight," Wheeler recorded in his journal. "He does not say so in so many words but I gather the N and W are pretty much out of the question." The following day, Wheeler added: "A coolie in from Mallory to say that he is moving east, if possible over a pass between the 23,000[-foot] group of Everest which he hopes will lead to the Kharta Valley."

Unfortunately, even as Wheeler wrote these notes in his journal, on the afternoon of July 22, a courier was delivering to Mallory the letter from Howard-Bury indicating that all the photographs taken with the quarter-plate camera were useless. Mallory, as we have seen, had inserted the plates back to front. Thus ended any thought of heading directly to Kharta, east across the mountains, a route that would no doubt have led to their discovery of the way to the eastern side of the North Col, the key to the mountain. Instead, while Bullock made a final thrust toward the North Face, Mallory would have to exhaust two precious days scrambling to reshoot what he could of the lost images. Broken in spirit, at least for the moment, he sent word that the climbing party would retreat via the Rongbuk Chu and rendezvous as instructed with Howard-Bury and Wheeler on July 25 at Chöbuk, the small hamlet some five miles downstream where the river first takes the name the Dzakar Chu.

ON SUNDAY, JULY 24, leaving Heron to continue his geological work north of Tingri, Howard-Bury and Wheeler set off for Kharta, by way of Chöbuk, where they expected to meet up with Mallory and Bullock the following day. Their first march carried them south over familiar ground, some twenty miles across the Tingri Plain to Nezogu, where a bridge crossed the Kyetrak Chu. There, Wheeler had left his camp, and they were delighted to find tents pitched and food ready upon their arrival. Howard-Bury had shot a goa, and that evening they ate well. Snow fell overnight and well into the dawn, which made for a slow start to a day that brought them fifteen miles over the Lamna La to Chöbuk. Howard-Bury, despite a detour high along a ridge south of the pass, arrived early, well ahead of the rest of the party, which was still drifting in at 4:00 p.m. when Mallory and Bullock turned up, spent and exhausted from their time at Rongbuk.

Wheeler, by contrast, had never felt stronger. Quitting his horse, he walked all the way from Kyetrak that day, "feeling fit as could be, for the first time since I've been in Tibet." At the grassy saddle of the Lamna La, he abandoned the main track, which dropped down to the valley and Chöbuk, and set off on his own, reading the land. Staying high, he traversed several spurs until he reached the main ridge overlooking both the hamlet, now far below to the north, and the corridor of the Rongbuk Valley, which opened, he recalled, onto "a glorious view of Everest."

It was one month to the day since this same distant vista had left both Mallory and Bullock silent in awe. As had they, Wheeler first saw the looming North Face from a distance of fifteen miles on a perfectly clear afternoon. Little did he know that rarely again would he see the sun or, indeed, the mountain. His task was to map its every contour and outcrop. The weather that month would prove so dreadful that to establish a single station, he would have to trudge his crew and equipment three and sometimes four times thousands of feet up the same slope, racing the clouds just to secure a single photographic image. But for the moment the summit loomed clear, and having charted in his mind all the points of perspective that would reveal the whole, he recalled, "[I] dropped down the spur to Chöbuk, which I reached about 5:30. . . . We spent the evening gassing hard and swapping lies."

Mallory, for reasons difficult to ascertain, had an abiding dislike of Canadians, and since the beginning of the expedition he had treated Wheeler with some disdain. Now, in a quiet way, he had the beginnings of a change of heart. He and Bullock were off to Kharta and what promised to be more temperate climes. Wheeler, he knew, was heading back up to Rongbuk to attempt the impossible in conditions that were deteriorating by the day. In a letter to Ruth, begun on July 22, when he had first learned about the photographic calamity, and finished six days later at Kharta, he wrote, "Wheeler turned up late the same evening. He has been making his photographic survey to the west—doing much of what I did on that last day, but doing it alone! A dreary job in this broken weather. However he had had some rest at Tingri and seemed fit and cheerful. And now he was going up the valley we had just come down. It seems rather a silly business that he couldn't have joined forces with us up there. But we were able to tell him a good deal to help him."

Wheeler had the toughest assignment, and everyone knew it. That he was a highly accomplished mountaineer, stoic and focused, who never wavered from his duty and never complained was now evident to all, including Mallory. Morshead, in particular, had enormous respect for his fellow officer from the Survey of India. "It is difficult for those who have not actually had the experience," he would write to Hinks, "to conceive the degree of mental and physical discomfort which results from prolonged camping during the monsoon at heights of 19,000 ft or more, waiting for the fine day, which never comes. Such had been Wheeler's fate ever since leaving Tingri, three months previously."

ON THE MORNING of July 26, leaving Wheeler at Chöbuk with his porters, Howard-Bury, Mallory, and Bullock pushed on for Kharta. They had a slow start, not breaking camp until 9:00 a.m. During the night Howard-Bury and Chheten Wangdi, as well as several of the porters, had suffered severe inflammation of the eyes, the onset of snow blindness. The previous day had been overcast. But such was the power of the Himalayan sun that with even the slightest snowfall, Howard-Bury realized, it was imperative to wear goggles. He would not make the same mistake again, though others would and with dire consequences.

With good horses, they soon made up the time, cantering down the valley and up and over a low pass to reach Halung, where they paused to picnic in the grass. From a spur en route they had caught a dramatic glimpse of Everest, encircled by formidable black bands of perpendicular cliffs. It looked, Howard-Bury wrote, "as impossible as ever." Mallory, for the moment, wanted nothing to do with the mountain. He was still luxuriating in seeing the world green again. "To see things grow again as though they liked growing, enjoying rain and sun—that has been a real joy."

One would have thought that they had come down from the moon, and in a sense they had. "I have been half the time in ecstasy," wrote Mallory, referring to their short passage from Chöbuk and Rebu across the Doya La to Kharta. "We came up to a remarkable pass between two ranges of snow mountains—not a high pass, only about 17,000 ft. There the ground was a wilderness of flowers, rock plants nestling under the big flat stones; most beautiful of all the blue poppy and a little pink saxifrage growing almost like a cushion flower and there was a fine gentian . . . And here we are in the Arun Valley perched a little above its wide flat basin before it goes down in a narrow and fearsome gorge to Nepal and India, the valley of the monsoon."

That evening after dinner, Mallory returned from a stroll with a bouquet of wildflowers, including fringed grass of Parnassus, white and yellow anemones, larkspur, and potentilla. "My dearest Ruth," he wrote, "you can imagine how lovely all this has been after the stern world of glaciers and moraines! This is a good spot; Bury has chosen well." Bullock, if less effusive, was equally glad to be down at last in a land of forests and fields, though his eyes were still on the heights. "Makalu was visible through clouds due south," he wrote in his diary. "Rather a stony road and a long ride. Had rhubarb for dinner and juniper wood for fuel!"

The party awoke in Kharta late on the morning of Friday, July 29, delighted at the prospect of doing nothing for a day. Bullock wrote to his wife, Alice, while Mallory took in the lay of the land, walking to a high point above their base. Across the valley to the south the monsoon clouds came up the gorge in thin wisps, only to dissipate as rainbows in the sunlight. A dark band of fir and birch marked the boundary where the mist stopped and the valley opened onto rich fields and meadowlands. To the east sheets of distant rain veiled the horizon. To the north, beyond the mountain ridge that rose above their base, the sky was dark with heavy clouds. Kharta, by contrast, nestled in the rain shadow, enjoyed clear skies and a "delicious climate." By the time Mallory returned to camp, the air was actually hot. That afternoon, Howard-Bury recorded a temperature of seventy-five degrees inside his tent, a pleasant change after Tingri, let alone Rongbuk.

While Mallory and Bullock rested and regrouped, Howard-Bury, having seen to the construction of a new darkroom, elected to scout the Samchung La, the closest and most eastern of the three openings to the Kama Valley. Traveling light, he left Kharta early on July 30 and rode hard, crossing the Kharta Chu at the first possible ford, then climbing 3,000 feet up a steep and stony track to reach the pass. Unfortunately, clouds covered the heights, and it was only upon descending 500 feet on the other side that he suddenly beheld a beautiful lost glen and, beyond it, a string of fourteen lakes, each a different shape and color—turquoise, blue, green, and black—all flung like jewels the length of a hanging alpine valley that disappeared into the mist. Along a track of loose stones, he slowly made his way south, hoping to catch a glimpse into the Kama Valley. Instead he found himself climbing steeply once more, on a track carved through deep snow, to reach another pass, the Chog La, at 16,100 feet considerably higher than the Samchung La. At the summit fierce winds and blinding snow precluded any chance of seeing into the Kama, let alone tracking its course toward the eastern face of Everest. Taking shelter behind the ruins of a stone wall, he waited for an hour, hoping for a break in the weather, before reluctantly retracing his path through an alpine valley as beautiful as any he had ever encountered.

Crossing back over the Samchung La, with all the Kharta Valley now at his feet, Howard-Bury rested for a time, as was his habit when alone. The air here was clear and there was no sign of rain, let alone snow. He noticed a red-breasted rose finch perched on a dwarf rhododendron. From a willow thicket came the call of a laughing thrush and the squawk of blackbirds. Over the valley ravens and black-eared kites flew at extraordinary heights, and at the very zenith of the sky, he saw the dark silhouette of a lammergeier, soaring toward the east. From the pass the Kharta Chu appeared a sliver of silver, flanked by fields and villages that seemed toylike in the immensity of the landscape.

If geography defined the next challenge, circumstances, Howard-Bury knew, would determine the players. Kellas, the one Britisher who had probed the Kama—securing with the help of his native colleagues photographs, albeit from a distance, of the major glaciers and mountain approaches—was dead. Harold Raeburn, the titular head of the climbing party, the man expected to orchestrate the alpine assault on the summit, was lost to the expedition, evacuated by Wollaston to Sikkim, and not expected to return. With Wheeler preoccupied at Rongbuk, and Morshead and Wollaston not scheduled to reach Kharta from their explorations of the Nepali borderlands for some time, it would fall to Mallory and Bullock to follow the Kharta Chu to its source, cross into the Kama, and ascertain which valley, if either, offered an opening to the mountain.

At Kharta, Mallory, idle for the day, was having similar thoughts. Inactivity for him invariably provoked reflection, which slipped readily into melancholy. "It has been rather disappointing to see so little of Wollaston and Morshead," he wrote to Ruth on July 31. "Poor Wollaston has had a bad time of it altogether. He reached Tingri the day before we left after seeing Raeburn safely into Sikkim and almost at once had two cases of typhoid to attend at Tingri, a place he disliked as much as I did . . . Of Raeburn we have no further news . . . Bullock though a very nice fellow is not a lively companion."

On the same day, Bullock and Howard-Bury rode three miles up the valley to visit the *dzongpen*, who appeared with his wife, a young woman adorned in jewels, amethysts, turquoises, pearls, and uncut rubies. "She had a most elaborate head-dress of coral and pearls, with masses of false hair on either side of her head," Howard-Bury recalled. "It was not becoming."

Mallory, alone at base camp, remained focused on the challenge at hand. The locals knew Everest by name, Chomolungma, but aside from this it had been difficult to obtain any useful information, save that the mountain was to be approached only by crossing over the Langma La, a pass farther up the Kharta Chu leading to the south. On this they were quite specific. There the men would find another valley—clearly the Kama—that would lead right up to the base of the mountain. Beyond this, the local people appeared to know little. Where the Kharta Chu originated, they could not say. Whether it had its origins in the snows of Everest, they did not know. As to distances, they were hopeless. A journey could be measured in days or in cups of tea; it was only after some trial and error that the British determined that three cups of tea were roughly the equivalent of five miles. But again nothing was precise.

Even the Tibetan name of the mountain had any number of translations and meanings. Howard-Bury quoted yak herders who called it Chomo Uri, which he translated as Goddess of the Turquoise Peak. Back in London Douglas Freshfield, a veteran of Kangchenjunga and a former president of both the Alpine Club and the Royal Geographical Society, translated the name Chomolungma as Mother Goddess of the Country, which soon morphed into the even more fanciful Goddess Mother of the World. Charles Bell, the scholarly authority, claimed that the proper Tibetan name was, in fact, Kang Chamolung, meaning the Snow of Bird Land. David Macdonald, Bell's protégé as British trade agent at Yatung and Gyantse, offered yet another, more descriptive name, which, translated, was: "the mountain you can see from nine directions, the summit you cannot see from near, the mountain so high that birds flying over the peak become blind."

MALLORY'S PLAN was to set out up the Kharta Valley with Bullock on Tuesday, August 2. But first he faced a minor crisis with the porters, "who made a good deal of fuss enquiring what their rations were to be." He spent Monday and, in growing frustration, the first morning hours of Tuesday packing loads and securing additional supplies of salt, flour, and chilies for the men. The sirdar, Gyalzen, the man responsible for the job, had lost the confidence of all. Suspecting embezzlement, Howard-Bury had stripped him of his authority only the night before, and now he skulked about, sowing discontent. Mallory did not respond well. He drove the men hard, later commenting, "In a valley where there are many individual farms and little villages, the coolie's path is well beset with pitfalls and with gin. Without discipline the Sahib might easily find himself at the end of a day's march with perhaps half his loads." Such an approach, as Howard-Bury fully understood, only caused the men to accomplish less. On their first day out of Kharta, after a slow march of just eight miles, the porters simply stopped, all thirty, and pitched camp despite Mallory's protests. His response was to demand a double march for the following day.

Despite the setback, Mallory remained sanguine. Howard-Bury had assured him that Everest lay but two days to the west, and logic alone suggested that the glacial stream of the Kharta Chu originated on the mountain; its upper left branch, Mallory surmised, must surely come from the North Col. In his mind's eye, he wrote to Ruth, he envisioned a trek straight up the Kharta Valley to the "pass of our desire." Within four days he hoped at last to be on the North Col, staring down into the great cwm of the Rongbuk Glacier, making plans for the Northeast Ridge, what he believed to be the only viable route to the summit.

But something was amiss. The men had camped at a valley junction, as expected, but the route to Chomolungma, as described by a local leader who said the journey would take five days, climbed away from the Kharta Chu, rising beyond a track that crisscrossed a trickle of a stream, nothing like the glacial torrent one would expect to issue from the frozen heart of the mountain. Mallory, uncertain of their position, stubbornly insisted that Chomolungma could be reached within two days, as Howard-Bury had anticipated. The village headman shrugged, the sirdar said nothing, and the matter rested until the morning of August 3, which dawned in drizzle and fog. They broke camp, according to Bullock's journal, just after 7:00. The visibility only decreased as they climbed high through dense thickets of rhododendrons and junipers, reaching by midday a small blue lake on a flat shelf of rock. Mallory was completely mystified. With each step they had moved south and west, away from both the Kharta Valley and the known direction of Everest. That afternoon they continued to climb, a slow, ponderous slog in the rain and mist, to a pass that registered on the aneroid fully 4,000 feet above their camp of the previous night. They crossed the threshold of the Langma La, the most formidable of the passes leading to the Kama Chu, the northern doorway to the hidden valley of Khenbalung, in cloud cover so thick it muted the joyous shouts of the men.

Beyond the pass the track fell away due south, and Mallory, still perplexed by their direction of travel, noticed a shift in mood among the men. "Grumblings had subsided in friendliness," he wrote and, though burdened by sodden tents and heavy wet loads, the porters "all marched splendidly." When finally, two hours and some 2,500 feet below the pass, they halted for the day, making camp on a grassy bench where yaks grazed and stone huts offered shelter from the wind, he found the men "quite undepressed with the gloomy circumstance of again encamping in the rain." That night in a fragmentary conversation with the headman, with the sirdar acting as translator, Mallory solved a small part of the puzzle: there were two mountains known to the hill men of Kharta as Chomolungma. "It was not difficult to guess," he later recalled, that "if Everest were one, the other must be Makalu, which is twelve miles southwest of Everest. We explained that we wanted to go to the one to the right."

The morning of August 4 brought further confusion. Breaking camp again at 7:00, and again in cloud and drizzle, they followed the track down a steep moraine, dropping some 700 feet to the valley floor, where thickets of giant rhododendrons concealed a rickety bridge over a stream. They crossed and continued through wet meadows, eventually reaching the snout of a glacier that evidently crossed the valley from the south, at ninety degrees to the flow of the Kama Chu, the muffled roar of which they could hear. The trail carried them up and over the ice, and along the base of high cliffs obscured in mist. Toward midday the sky suddenly opened, just for a fleeting moment, to reveal "gigantic precipices looming through the clouds." This glimpse of Makalu, towering so high above them, unsettled their senses, and they almost welcomed the gray clouds that closed around them, darkening the Kama Valley with rain. They pushed on for another two, perhaps three, miles, following the lateral moraine of yet a second glacier flowing as a river along the valley floor, until coming upon Pethang Ringmo, a nomadic encampment where they stopped for the night. "There was no point in going further," Mallory wrote. "We had no desire to run our heads against the East Face of Everest; we must now wait for a view."

They woke to the sound of yak bells and the spacious silence of a broad expanse of meadows flanked by glacial moraine and ice. The elevation was 16,400 feet, and there was a dusting of snow. The "weather signs," Mallory recalled, "were decidedly more hopeful as I looked out of our tent, and we decided at once to spend the day in some sort of reconnaissance up the valley."

Finally they could see something. They were camped on the northern side of the valley. At their backs, running east to west, was a formidable ridge of uncertain height, with great spurs of rock, each separated from the next by basins of ice. This was the range they had crossed, the one broken by the Langma La. The glacier they had mounted and traversed the previous day was the Kangdoshung, which does indeed flow into the Kama from the south, from the lower face of Chomo Lonzo, at 25,604 feet the sister mountain of Makalu (27,765 feet). Acting as a dam, the Kangdoshung blocks the passage of a much larger glacier, the Kangshung, a mile-wide river of ice that flows from the base of Everest itself and dominates the upper valley floor, concealing the Kama Chu, which runs beneath it. From Pethang Ringmo, peering back down the valley to the east, Mallory could just make out the massive tangle of ice that marked the meeting of the glaciers. Of the mountains they knew to dominate the valley to the south, they could see little, save a glimpse of the white summit ice of Pethangtse (22,014 feet), which appeared out of clouds so close to the zenith of the sky that they questioned their vision.

Having dispatched the porters down valley to cut juniper for fuel, Mallory and Bullock lingered briefly in camp, waiting for the weather to lift, before setting out to explore the upper reaches of the Kang-shung Glacier. High winds spun the clouds, and though the weather remained gray, by late morning the sky over the mountains partially cleared to reveal a landscape of stunning scale. First the snow and ice faces of Makalu and Chomo Lonzo, soaring 11,000 feet above the valley floor, and then, as Bullock recalled, the "terrific" cliffs below Lhotse, the south peak of Everest. By noon they had reached high into the basin and climbed the shoulder of a ridge that formed a corner of the valley wall. For the first time Mallory, somewhat above Bullock on the slope, beheld the East Face of Everest and the formidable Northeast Ridge, "cutting across the sky to the right." All that he had previously experienced as a mountaineer receded in memory as his eyes beheld "a scene of magnificence and splendour" that provoked, he later recalled, a completely "new sensation . . . fresh surprise and vivid delight."

Everest and Lhotse, separated by a prominent saddle, the South Col, formed a single mountain wall, which fell away in a tumble of buttresses and ice fully two vertical miles in height. At the base of this imposing face, the head of the Kangshung Glacier widened into a massive cirque, with great tongues of snowbound rock and ice reaching from the valley to the skyline. Viewed from the east, Everest and Lhotse appeared not as individual mountains but as a single massif of impossible dimensions. From Lhotse a "prodigious" shoulder fell away to the southeast, merging into a ridgeline of wild precipices that swept the length of the Kama Valley only to be swallowed after about twelve miles by the equally formidable bastion of Makalu and the multiple summits of Chomo Lonzo. As Mallory's eye traced the lines of ascent to every spur, the broken edges of every hanging glacier, he stood in the shadow of three of the five tallest mountains in the world, Lhotse, Makalu, and Everest.·

Exhilarating as this was, his concern remained focused on the task at hand. The height of land dominated by the great summits on the southern side of the Kama Valley marked the frontier with Nepal. Had they presented an avenue of approach, Mallory might well have been prepared to violate the border, but they most assuredly did not. As Mallory looked west to Everest, it was the unknown ridge of mountains on his right that presented the immediate challenge. These extended in an easterly direction from the very foot of the Everest's Northeast Ridge. Mallory's goal on leaving Kharta had been to reach the North Col. Instead, "after three days traveling in the clouds," he wrote to Ruth, they had found themselves "in a different part of the world and cut off from our North Col by an impassable barrier." Bullock was certain that the Kama Valley would not lead them directly to the col, and he wrote as much in his journal on the night of August 5, upon their return to camp. But there remained a chance, which Bullock acknowledged, that closer to the base of Everest, or just beyond the height of land that formed this frustrating barrier and divide to their north, they might find a way.

At the same time, they had an obligation to complete a thorough visual reconnaissance of the East Face and the Northeast Ridge. This remained their mission. Mallory's solution was to climb. Even in the uncertainty of clouds, he had noticed a "conspicuous snowy summit," the second prominent peak along the divide on this wild side of Everest. His porters knew the mountain as Kartse. From its summit, they would be able to scan at close quarters the entire Kangshung Face of Everest, even as they determined what lay beyond to the north and west in the uppermost reaches of the Kharta watershed, ice fields that would surely flow, he anticipated, as far as the base of the elusive North Col.

On the morning of Saturday, August 6, they struck the Whymper tents and moved farther up the Kama Valley, following the edge of the glacier for some two hours before rounding a shoulder to pitch camp on a high shelf at 17,700 feet. Bullock spent the afternoon hunting butterflies in the snow. Mallory found shelter by a stream in the lee of a moraine, and did his best to study his proposed line of ascent. Though dwarfed by Everest, Kartse, at 21,348 feet, was nevertheless an unclimbed peak, some 5,000 feet higher than any mountain in Europe, located in unknown country, and exposed to monsoon winds and weather. Mallory and Bullock would scramble up its slopes merely to have a good look around. "Our object tomorrow is to discover what is behind the wall of this coombe [*sic*]," Bullock noted that night in his journal. "It is now snowing."

Morning came early for them: they woke at 2:00 a.m. and set off in the dark, with four porters, using lanterns and candles to light their way along a stony ridge that ran north of their camp. The new snow, icy and granular, crunched beneath their boots. The air was frigid but clear. "It was a night," Mallory recalled, "of early moons." They walked in keen anticipation, for the stars were bright and there was not a cloud in the sky. "Even before the first glimmer of dawn," he wrote, "the white mountains were somehow touched to life by a faint blue light—a light that changed as the day grew." The sun reached first the summit of Makalu, and as the glowing red light, "a flush of pink and purple shadows," fell upon the massive ice cliffs of Chomo Lonzo, Mallory turned to see Everest itself unveiled. "We were not kept waiting for the supreme effects; the curtain was withdrawn. Rising from the bright mists Everest above us was immanent, vast, incalculable—no fleeting apparition of elusive dream-form; nothing could have been more set and permanent, steadfast like Keats's star, 'in long splendour hung aloft the night,' a watcher of all the nights, diffusing, it seemed universally, an exalted radiance."

Such eloquence, summoned long after the event, belied the reality of the moment. The cold that morning was intense. The cook was sick. The porters, wrapped in wool blankets, had refused to stir until threatened. Boots, outer clothing, and gear were frozen stiff. It was only after considerable cajoling that Mallory had gotten his small expedition under way. The first goal was a conspicuous saddle, the Karpo La, lying to the east of Kartse. The most direct approach carried them up and over a steep outcrop of rock. Mallory took delight in the feel of firm granite, and the porters, though totally inexperienced as climbers, proved, if anything, too cavalier in their exertions; he had to throw down the odd stone to remind them of the perils of failure. As they scaled and traversed the bluff, Mallory cast his eye toward Everest and the daunting Kangshung Face. The most threatening feature, as he saw it, was a series of massive hanging glaciers that dominated the lower cliffs and buttresses. "It required," he recalled, "but little further gazing to be convinced—to know that almost everywhere the rocks below must be exposed to ice falling from this glacier; that if, elsewhere, it might be possible to climb up, the performance would be too arduous, would take too much time and would lead to no convenient platform; that in short, other men, less wise, might attempt this way if they would, but, emphatically it was not for us."

By the time Mallory and his small party crested the Karpo La, just before 9:00 a.m., both he and Bullock had dismissed any notion of a direct attack on Everest from the Kama Valley. (The Kangshung Face would prove to be the most difficult route up the mountain; it would not be successfully climbed until 1983.) There remained, however, the possibility of the Northeast Ridge, which Bullock referred to in his journals as the East Ridge. He and Mallory, it will be recalled, were obsessed with finding a way to the eastern base of the North Col precisely because they had seen from Rongbuk that from the col a manageable route rose up a steep shoulder to meet the upper limits of the Northeast Ridge, which led to the summit pyramid of Everest. Might the Northeast Ridge be followed all the way from its base? From the

Karpo La, it was impossible to know, for the view of Everest and the lower Northeast Ridge was blocked by the snow summit of Kartse.

After a quick breakfast, Mallory led the party along the snow ridge that reached west toward Kartse. At close to 20,000 feet, with storms threatening from the south, it was by no means a trivial ascent. The exposures were severe, the threat of avalanche a constant menace. To traverse a gully of deep, powdery snow, Mallory established a rope anchor on an island of rock and, using hand signals, patiently guided men who had never before faced such danger. Once all were safely across, he entrusted his own life to Nyima, a sturdy youth of eighteen who had been his most faithful and dependable companion since the beginning of the expedition. The only viable route led up an extremely steep slope, the head of which was blocked by overhanging ice and hard snow. Belayed by Nyima, Mallory "hewed at the cornice above his head, fixed a fist-and-axe hold in the crest and struggled over." Inspired by Mallory's example, the men followed, and with "explosive grunts" overcame in turn an obstacle unlike anything they had ever confronted. Exhausted, they huddled on the edge of the ice as Mallory worked on, cutting steps in the hard snow for some 400 feet, until finally a stretch of level ground was achieved. It was after midday by the time the men crossed the flat shoulder of snow and collapsed in a heap at the base of the final slope, some 500 feet below the Kartse summit.

Mallory had only begun. From this vantage he could finally look directly up Everest's Northeast Ridge, only some three miles distant. Its viability as an avenue to the summit was made moot by a single glance at the mountain. The ridge, as Bullock later noted, was "enormously long," in places formidably steep, with several imposing pinnacles, impossible to scale, impeding the route well below the junction with the north buttress, the shoulder that fell away to the North Col.

To the north the vista was more complicated. From the Karpo La they had stared down to a broad glacier running east. This sea of ice, they correctly surmised, was the head of the Kharta Valley. To the west the tangle of mountains and ridges included Changtse, the North Peak, the summit of which Mallory, with intense excitement, could just make out in the clouds. The elusive North Col was the saddle separating Changtse from Everest. For thirty minutes he strained his eyes to see more. But the col and all of its approaches remained hidden. He decided to go higher. Leaving Bullock with two of the men, he recruited Nyima and another strong climber, Dasno, and after a thirty-minute rest, they set off for the summit.

Almost immediately clouds billowed up from below, enveloping them completely. At the foot of the steepest slope, they removed their snowshoes and, struggling hip-deep in fresh snow, made their way across a dangerous crevasse. Dasno gave up and retreated to wait with the other men. Mallory and Nyima trudged on, up the steepest of slopes, pausing every few moments to listen to the sound of distant avalanches. Glancing over his left shoulder, Mallory suddenly saw the horizon to the west begin to clear and, through a hole in the clouds, once again spotted Changtse, the North Peak. His eye eagerly followed its ridge as it descended toward Everest. Then, for but a fleeting moment, the actual rim of the North Col came into view. He could see nothing of the slopes below it, nothing of the glaciers at its base.

Mallory and Nyima struggled on to the summit of Kartse, another hour of intense exertion. Again the mountain teased him with a glimpse of the glaciers to the north. But then came more weather, a thick veil of clouds that foreshadowed the night. His confusion was now confounded by frustration. "To be bewildered was all in the game," he later wrote. "But our sensation was something beyond bewilderment. We felt ourselves to be foiled. We were unpleasantly stung by this slap in the face. We had indeed solved all doubts as to the East Face and the Northeast arête, and had solved them quickly. But the way to Chang La [North Col], which had seemed almost within our grasp, had suddenly eluded us, and had escaped, how far we could not tell. Though its actual distance from our summit might be short, as indeed it must be, the glacier of our quest appeared now at the end of a receding vista; and this was all our prospect."

Disappointment spun Mallory into a whirlwind of thought and action. Moving off the Kartse summit in such haste that Nyima slipped and was nearly lost, he formulated a new plan even before reaching the deep snows of the couloir that in short order disgorged the party onto the glacier below and a rendezvous with Bullock and the rest of the porters. Bullock led the way from that point, freeing an exhausted Mallory to plan. Without delay, they would retreat across the Langma La. There had to be a glacier reaching to the face of the North Col, and that elusive river of ice had to flow east, "in which case its waters *must* flow into the Kharta stream," Mallory speculated. Their time in the Kama Valley, while useful, was ultimately a diversion, and with the season advancing by the day, they had not an hour to spare. The earliest they could get back to the Kharta Valley, crossing the Langma La, would be August 9, two days hence. By Mallory's reckoning, the initial reconnaissance would have to be completed by August 20, if they were to have sufficient time afterward to rest and regroup at Kharta before launching an actual attempt at the summit of Everest. This left little more than a week to complete the exploration of the unknown ice fields of the upper Kharta Valley, where the mystery of the North Col would surely be solved.

Unfortunately, Mallory's resolve did not take into account his own physical condition. He had sensed weariness earlier in the day, a fatigue that was less exhaustion than lassitude. By the time they trudged through the deep snow covering the glacier, sinking to their knees even with snowshoes, his head was pounding. Reaching camp in the early evening, he went right to his tent and spent a feverish night, shivering with sweat in the cold. It was all he could do to drag himself down valley the following day to their base at Pethang Ringmo. News that Howard-Bury had arrived unexpectedly and was exploring in the vicinity did not elevate his spirits. He took immediately to bed, and slept the entire afternoon of Monday, August 8, while Bullock collected flowers and butterflies in the sun.

CHAPTER 9

The North Col

CHARLES HOWARD-BURY had reason to be content on the afternoon of Tuesday, August 2. After some confusion, and no small amount of conflict with the sirdar, Mallory and Bullock, along with thirty men, had finally set off late that morning for their exploration of the Kama Valley. Just after lunch, which Howard-Bury took alone, eleven muleloads of rations had arrived, flour, potatoes, rice, and sugar, supplies that had been dispatched from the British trading mission at Yatung on June 15. The rivers apparently were all in flood and many of the routes severely compromised, but at least he now knew that the essential supply line from Darjeeling remained open. Then, to his surprise, not three hours after Mallory and Bullock had left Kharta, Wollaston and Morshead turned up, utterly bedraggled after a 250-mile slog from the Nepalese frontier at Nyenyam. As they plunged into a feast of fresh peas, potatoes and wild mushroom stew, minced meat and chilies, washed down with steaming bowls of hot milk, they had quite a story to tell.

Their goal had been to explore the country west of Everest; Wollaston, in particular, saw reconnaissance and exploration, not alpinism, as the expedition's essential mandate, as determined by Younghusband and the Royal Geographical Society. They had set out from Tingri on July 13, crossing the plain to reach the village of Langkor, where they camped beside the thousand-year-old temple. The following morning, in blinding sleet, they crossed the 17,981-foot Thong La to the desolate headwaters of the Bhote Kosi, which they followed south through massive granite gorges to reach, in four difficult marches, the border town at Nyenyam. The reception there was decidedly hostile. The *dzongpen* who had issued the original invitation, a dubious character in silk robes whose long fingernails celebrated his idleness, claimed to have no knowledge of it. In the market the traders, mostly Hindus, Newars from Kathmandu, refused the travelers' money. Information about routes and geography was impossible to obtain, or patently false.

Despite the difficulties, they stayed for three days. Wollaston expanded his collections, adding a number of curious plants and defiantly killing insects, birds, and small mammals to take back as specimens. Morshead, as a diversion, descended into the narrow chasm of the Bhote Kosi as he searched for traces of the pundit Hari Ram's 1871 expedition. The river, all waterfalls and cataracts, dropped 1,000 feet every two miles, and in one exhausting afternoon Morshead crisscrossed the torrent four times before turning back some ten miles this side of the Nepalese frontier.

Their return journey from Nyenyam began with a traverse of the Lapche Kang, an unknown range that led to the sacred valley of Lapche, birthplace of the mystic saint Milarepa, which no European had ever visited. When the terrain became too difficult for yaks, they hired as porters every able youth in the village of Tashishong and headed east, climbing a steep side valley to a massive moraine at the foot of a glacier. Suddenly overhead a lammergeier, or bearded vulture, the most majestic of all Himalayan birds, came sailing down in a wide circle to settle on the ice not a hundred feet away. Wollaston could see its black beak, the small circle of red around the eye. The enormous birds live by scavenging bones, which they drop onto rocks from great heights to free the marrow, the basis of their diet. Some swallow entire bones the size of a lamb's femur.

The men continued up the glacier, struggling through soft snow, crossing crevasses with rotten planks pilgrims had left on the ice, reaching the pass in a fog so thick that the stone cairns, bristling with prayer flags, seemed to move, as if a congregation of supplicants. Their porters stopped to make offerings, and by the time the party crested the divide and began the long descent, evening was upon them. They spent a miserable night camped on boulders at 14,600 feet, without proper shelter from a drenching rain and no fuel save twigs of dwarf rhododendron. The Tibetans huddled together in caves, laughing and drinking through the dawn.

The track that dropped to the valley led through meadows of yellow barberry and mountain ash before entering dense forests of juniper draped in wet lichen and prayer flags. Every rock, it seemed, had been carved with a prayer, every overhang transformed into a shrine, illuminated by butter lamps and festooned with blossoms. Great boulders had been engraved in letters several feet high proclaiming the universal mantra *Om mani padme hum.* In small caves solitary monks silently accepted offerings from a scattering of pilgrims who trudged by the British on the trail.

Lapche itself was a tiny warren of perhaps a dozen households, half

Tibetan and half Nepalese, families that came and went in service to the shrine. The famous temple was a simple but imposing structure, a square of stone perhaps two hundred feet to the side, each with a hundred prayer wheels set into the wall. It enclosed a courtyard paved in cobbles, with sheds along the perimeter to shelter the pilgrims; at the center sat a plain stone sanctuary, with a pagoda roof burnished in copper. Wollaston found it hard to believe that seekers came from all over Tibet to worship the footprint of a saint who'd once lived in a hermit cell beneath a rock, or that such a squalid building, reeking with butter lamps, could be one of the holiest sites of Buddhism. To make his stay even more unpleasant, he was forced to shield his eyes from the scores of new plants, animals, insects, and butterflies he was unable to collect for fear of antagonizing, as he put it, the "plodding dead faced pilgrims."

The old smugglers' route Morshead had chosen to reach their next goal, the Rongshar Valley, obliged them to cross two 17,000-foot passes and traverse "sundry glaciers . . . stumbling over moraines, and nearly always in an impenetrable fog." For the entire march the weather was so foul they could see nothing save the ground at their feet, but for Wollaston this was enough. He discovered several novelties, including two new species of primulas, one of which today bears his name. A delicate plant with a bell-shaped corolla the size of a "lady's thimble, of a deep blue colour and lined inside with frosted silver," it is found today in specialty gardens throughout the temperate world.

As they finally crested the Kangchen La, the second of the passes, and began the long descent into the Rongshar Valley, the clouds opened to reveal for a moment a quite unexpected sight: the stunning summit of Gauri Sankar, "blazing in the afternoon sun." Long mistaken for Everest, and never seen closely by a European from the Tibetan side of the Nepalese frontier, it was, at 23,440 feet, a much smaller mountain, but more beautiful. The following morning the weather cleared and Wollaston was able to photograph its entire form, soaring 10,000 feet above the pine and birch forests of the Rongshar, "a knife-edged ridge of ice" rising to a "glistening summit." Wollaston was among the most accomplished of all photographers on the 1921 reconnaissance, and of all the images he took, it was this single shot of Gauri Sankar, "pure and simple," that hung on the wall of his family home for the rest of his life.

Morshead and Wollaston were now in country familiar to the British expedition. In the last days of June, Howard-Bury and Heron had trekked into the Rongshar from its head, crossing the Phuse La from

Kyetrak, descending eight miles beyond the village of Tasang, reaching roughly the point where Morshead and Wollaston, coming out of the heights to the west, encountered the main trail. Yet another great circle of exploration had been completed. They turned upvalley, passing in time through the same beautiful thickets of red roses, the scent of which had so enchanted Howard-Bury. They, too, found that the entire valley was given over to the sacred. Everywhere they encountered prayer wheels, driven by wind or water. No animal could be harmed. As they pitched camp in a willow grove, a herd of gazelles, utterly fearless, grazed in the grass by their tents. The scene reminded Wollaston of a moment, half a lifetime away, long before the war, when on a sacred island in Japan he had fed wild deer from his hand. Now in need of food, Morshead and Wollaston purchased a goat. Out of respect for the people of Rongshar, they brought the animal alive up and over the Phuse La, before slaughtering it in the bright sun of Tibet. The meat lasted for four days, just the time it took them to reach the British base at Kharta.

WITH SUPPLIES IN HAND, and Wollaston and Morshead in camp, Howard-Bury was free to pursue Mallory and Bullock over the Langma La. Accompanied by Chheten Wangdi and a dozen porters, he headed up the Kharta Valley on August 5. The progress was slow, six miles in six hours. At every village, as he fully understood, tradition demanded that the men stop and drink. They finally halted for the night at 16,100 feet, the limit of firewood on the approaches to the pass. In the morning the men were fed and off by 5:30. Howard-Bury, as was his habit, brought up the rear, accompanied by two trusted porters, Ang Tenze and Nyima Tendu, who carried his rifle, shotgun, and three cameras.

They crossed the Langma La in mixed weather, with clouds hanging at 22,000 feet, obscuring the summits. Just beyond the divide, Howard-Bury caught a marmot with bluish-gray hair, a curious specimen, which he sent back with one of the porters to Kharta for Wollaston. The rest of the party continued down several thousand feet, passing through grassy meadows and alongside a beautiful blue lake before making camp in early afternoon on a long terrace perched perhaps a thousand feet above the floor of the Kama Valley. Howard-Bury spent the rest of the day lying among the rhododendrons, watching as the wind blew the clouds across the white cliffs of Makalu and Chomo Lonzo.

The following morning, in a burst of energy, he scrambled 1,000 feet up the ridge behind their camp, then made his way down into the valley, passing through copses of juniper and ash and meadows festooned with wildflowers, including a blue primula, which he recognized as a new species only just discovered a fortnight earlier by Wollaston at Lapche. He reached Pethang Ringmo by midafternoon and learned, to his satisfaction, that Mallory and Bullock had chosen it as their base. He enjoyed the rest of the day there, basking in bright sun, as he listened to the thunder of avalanches breaking on all sides of the valley.

Mist enveloped the camp the following morning, but there were glimpses of blue sky, and he made haste to march up the valley to reach a ridge directly across from Everest that he had noted the evening before. In the fog he walked almost directly by Mallory and Bullock's advanced camp, as they woke after their long day on Kartse. He saw no signs of them, but he did find the ridge he was seeking, which he climbed, some 3,000 feet in a long morning, to emerge from the clouds at 19,500 feet, no more than three miles from Everest. He remained on the summit spur for several hours, admiring the vegetation, chasing without luck a new kind of rat, listening to the sounds of great masses of ice exploding off the hanging glaciers of the Kangshung Face, and photographing the extraordinary panorama, from Everest and Lhotse, through Pethangtse to Makalu and Chomo Lonzo, and beyond a hundred miles to the east, where the summit of Kangchenjunga emerged from an ocean of clouds over Nepal.

Howard-Bury was in high spirits when he returned, in early afternoon, to the camp at Pethang Ringmo. Mallory was not. "Bury came in about two, full of talk and genial," he wrote to Ruth. "He bothered me a great deal about rations." In truth, as Bullock recorded, Howard-Bury simply confirmed that the unrest among the porters at Kharta had indeed been instigated by the sirdar, Gyalzen, who was now placed on probation, under threat of being reported to the authorities in Darjeeling. In a gesture that ought to have pleased Mallory, Howard-Bury had decided to distribute food, barley flour and rice, as well as salaries directly to the men, thus bypassing the embezzling hands of any intermediary. Mallory, sick with fever, was not in the mood to discuss it. He took to his bed and slept the rest of the day.

Briefed by Bullock about the Kartse climb and their plans to explore the glaciers of the upper Kharta, Howard-Bury agreed that, should Mallory be fit, they would return together in the morning to the base of the Langma La. While Bullock and Mallory made their way the following day over the pass, he would continue his explorations of the upper Kama Valley. Ten days earlier he had ridden out from Kharta, up and over the Samchung La, crossing the valley of the fourteen lakes to crest, in the clouds, the Chog La. This was the most eastern route into the Kama Valley, the one farthest from Everest. The Langma La they were coming to know well. There was evidently a third pass, the Shao La, halfway down the Kama, which also led back to Kharta. As long as he was on this side of the divide, why not have a look?

Mallory awoke feeling peevish but able to travel. It had rained most of the night, and he had slept poorly. He suffered from swollen glands, a raw throat, and a pounding headache. He ate little before they set off, in the damp and cold, just after 7:00. The pace of the yaks irritated him, as did the exuberance of Howard-Bury, who abandoned the party along the main trail to scramble 1,000 feet up the rocks in an attempt to photograph Makalu and the Kangdoshung Glacier, falling away from Chomo Lonzo. "Bury went ahead on some stunt," he later complained in a letter to Ruth. "Very unsociable I thought." Howard-Bury turned up late in the day, after they had set up camp, and then, having chatted briefly with Bullock, decided to pitch his own tents at a yak encampment some distance farther along the shelf. A storm of rain swept across the face of Makalu.

Writing some months later from the comfort of England, Mallory would wax eloquent about his time in the Kama Valley: "When all is said about Chomolungma, the Goddess Mother of the World . . . I come back to the valley, the valley bed itself, the broad pastures, where our tents lay, where cattle grazed and where butter was made, the little stream we followed up to the valley head, wandering along its well-turfed banks under the high moraine, the few rare plants, saxifrages, gentians and primulas, so well watered there, and a soft, familiar blueness in the air which even here may charm us. Though I bow to the goddesses I cannot forget at their feet a gentler spirit than theirs, a little shy perhaps, but constant in the changing winds and variable moods of mountains and always friendly."

In the moment, his thoughts were less gently crafted. He was both physically sick and increasingly bothered by his companions. Days had been lost and, after nearly seven weeks at close quarters with the mountain, he was no closer to solving the challenge of the North Col. Coming down valley this very afternoon, he had foolishly lost his waistcoat along the way, and would be forced to dispatch Nyima to search for it. He was famously absentminded, but not proud of the fact. It was a dark cloud indeed that carried him over the Langma La the next morning, Wednesday, August 10.

Howard-Bury, for his part, remained focused on his larger mission, which was not to climb Everest himself but to explore and chart the geography and natural history of the entire region. It was he, more than Mallory, whose thoughts always came back to the valley floor and the gentler spirits at the base of the mountains. The moisture that every night enveloped even the upper reaches of the Kama Valley in mist made possible the most luxuriant of forests. The Kama Chu, the river that bursts from beneath the ice of the Kangdoshung Glacier, falls over 14,000 feet in twenty-three miles, dropping over a spectacular series of waterfalls into the deepest ravine on earth, the canyon of the Arun, a river older than the Himalaya. Beneath the black cliffs and ice fields of Makalu, a mere fifteen miles from the base of Everest, thrive immense forests of junipers and silver firs, trees the size of redwoods, and farther downstream great thickets of bamboo grow, as well as mountain ashes, birches, and rhododendrons the size of a woodsman's cottage.

As Howard-Bury made his way down the valley, staying, for the most part, high above the river, he passed through acres of blue irises and lush hillsides of wild rhubarb with columns of pale leaves sheathing great spikes of flowers five feet or more in height. Every opening in the forest was carpeted in rare novelties, unknown flowers that he pressed between the pages of his Bible and the Book of Common Prayer, which he always carried with him. By midday the sun had burned away the clouds, and he saw silhouetted against the ice face of Makalu a ridgeline of silver firs. That night he made camp at the base of the Shao La in a dell known in Tibetan as the "field of marigolds." The following day he "crawled up to the top," crossing the 16,500-foot pass in driving rain, and was back in Kharta in time for tea.

THAT SAME EVENING found Mallory and Bullock well up the Kharta Chu, camped on a grassy shelf at 16,500 feet. Ahead of them they could see that the valley forked. Both arms would need to be explored. But after three exhausting marches, and with Mallory still ill with what he now feared to be tonsillitis, August 12 would be a day of rest. Bullock dispatched the men to gather firewood, while Mallory turned his thoughts toward home. He wrote to Ruth, proposing that she meet him upon his return in Marseille for a walking tour of Provence, or in Gibraltar, or in Italy, which he could reach by train. If Marseille, she was to stay at the Hôtel Louvre et Paix. If he did not find her at the hotel, he would leave a note at the post office and, as an added precaution, he would go there "every three hours beginning at 9 am and wait five minutes outside the main entrance."

Mallory's other proposal was perhaps more unsettling: he intended to bring back one of the expedition porters as a servant. His choice, he wrote, was Nyima:

> I don't know what his age may be, about 18 . . . He has the perfect temperament for what I propose he should do. He would naturally be turned on to all scullery work and floor scrubbing, carrying coals, cutting firewood, lighting the kitchen fire at as early an hour as you like, washing clothes . . . He could learn to bring in meals and wait at table . . . The boots, knives, swill pails, cinders and greenhouse stove would all be his province . . . And he would fetch and carry—he is a coolie whose job is to carry; and if you want a box weighing 70 pounds brought from the station, you would simply send him . . . He would save many a taxi drive by carrying luggage to the station . . . His present diet is chiefly flour and water, rice, occasionally meat and as luxuries a little tea and butter . . . He might inhabit part of the cellar or the outside coal shed might be freed by storing coal in the cellar . . . Would the other servants like him? Well, he is a clean animal and though he would look a bit queer to them at first they couldn't help liking him. He is not very dark skinned like a plainsman.

Fever and lassitude carried Mallory through the night and into the morning. Bullock could not remain idle for a second day. Though Mallory professed to harbor no thoughts of competition with his companion, the prospect of being left out at the moment of discovery depressed him. Still, as he put it, the hunt had to go on, and thus from the "ungrateful comfort" of his sleeping bag, he waved Bullock off on the morning of August 13, wishing him well.

From the summit of Kartse they had seen the southern branch of the Kharta Glacier and had not been convinced that it reached as far as the North Col. Bullock, accompanied by Sanglu, who spoke some English, therefore elected to explore the northern arm of the valley. They followed the glacier stream to the foot of the ice, and then, staying on the northern side, proceeded up and along the lateral moraine, climbing in a morning roughly 2,000 feet to reach the end of the rocks and a broad bay covered by a powder of fresh snow, where Bullock decided to establish a base. Word reached him that one of the porters, Ang Pasang, was played out on the trail. Bullock sent one of the men down for his load, and with him a note to go back to Mallory. The content of this note and the timing of its dispatch, as we shall see, were of considerable significance.

After a quick lunch, they set out onto the glacier, only to find it covered in deep snow. Bullock pressed ahead with Sanglu, leaving the porters with their heavy loads to plod at their own pace. It was late afternoon before Bullock himself completed the traverse, and well after 7:00 p.m. before the first of the exhausted porters arrived. They spread rocks to level a patch of ground and in the faint moonlight pitched a single Mummery tent. Bullock dined on tinned beef, biscuits, and jam. The following morning, August 14, dawned cold and clear, and with firm snow they reached, in two hours, the col at the head of the valley. Its elevation, Bullock recorded, was 19,770 feet. After crossing the saddle, they descended into the next valley just far enough to see that it ended close to a prominent mountain named Kharta Changri (23,149 feet). They most assuredly, as Bullock recognized, were not looking down upon the elusive North Col. Retracing their steps, they returned to the saddle by 10:00 a.m. and hastened down the glacier before the sun had a chance to soften the snow. They reached their base by midday. Leaving Sanglu and the rest of the men to break camp the following morning, Bullock and Dorji Gompa, after a brief halt for lunch, continued down the valley to rejoin Mallory.

TORMENTED STILL by the thought that he might miss "the joy of wresting from the mountain its final secret," Mallory had left his tent on the morning of August 13 and was sitting in the sun sharing his "dismal tale" in a letter to Ruth when he was interrupted by the unexpected but welcome arrival of a party from Kharta. It was Morshead, whom he had not seen in more than seven weeks. A favorite on the long approach march from Darjeeling, Morshead brought not only his stout character but also supplies and, from Wollaston, the expedition physician, "medical dope" to treat Mallory's fever. His presence was medicine enough, and Mallory immediately "began to entertain a hope for the morrow."

Just before dark that day, the porter turned up with the note for Mallory that Bullock had written earlier in the afternoon. The actual wording of this chit, which has not been preserved, is unknown. Bullock's journal entry of the day states only that he sent a "message to M. saying that this valley was not the one we were looking for." In the official expedition account, written months after the fact, Mallory quotes Bullock's note as having said, "I can see up the glacier ahead of me and it ends in another high pass. I shall get to the pass tomorrow morning if I can, and ought to see our glacier over it. But it looks, after all, as though the most unlikely solution is the right one and the glacier goes out into the Rongbuk Valley." Mallory goes on in the published account to suggest that he and Bullock had previously discussed the possibility that the glacier at the base of the North Col flowed not east but somehow north and back into the Rongbuk Valley. If so, there is no mention of it in either Bullock's journal or in any letters written during the expedition by Mallory. During their monthlong reconnaissance of the Rongbuk Valley they had in fact walked past the mouth of the East Rongbuk twice, failing to explore it. The size of the outflowing stream did not suggest a glacial watershed of any significance.

Bullock's note of August 13 was written before he had crested the saddle of the valley he was exploring. It's not clear how he might have anticipated what lay beyond and with the confidence that Mallory attributed to him. And had Bullock that day had some revelation concerning the East Rongbuk Glacier, as Mallory's recollection suggests, it is curious, given the significance, that he made no mention of it in his journal. Writing in the field on the night of August 13, Mallory himself makes no reference to Rongbuk or to any particular breakthrough in their understanding of the mountain. To the contrary, he simply writes, "Bullock's chit in the evening was very depressing—foreshadowing as it did fresh efforts of reconnaissance."

On the morning of August 14, Mallory and Morshead left to scout the southern arm of the Kharta Glacier, the branch that Bullock had not explored. With Mallory still recovering, they set a leisurely pace. Fortunately, the sky remained clear until noon, and they were able to reach high enough up the valley to see the ice of the Kharta Glacier rising to a shallow col on the skyline. Beyond this broad saddle, known to Tibetans as the Lhakpa La, they could just see, to their astonishment and delight, the tip of the summit of Changtse, the North Peak, which with Everest cradled the North Col. They could not tell what lay beyond the Lhakpa La, between it and the base of Changtse. But if the ground could be covered, it might offer at last an avenue of attack. Encouraged, they returned to base camp, keen to set out on a more thorough reconnaissance in the morning.

When they got back, however, eager to share the plan with Bullock, "a fresh bone," as Mallory later wrote, "was thrown into our stew." A letter had arrived from Howard-Bury, with an enclosure from Wheeler, a hand-sketched map that revealed the solution to the puzzle that had tormented them for all these many weeks. In the official expedition account, Mallory implies that this letter reached them after he and Bullock had effectively solved the mystery of the North Col.

Wheeler's map, which Mallory went to some length to disparage, may in fact have been the very first indication that he or Bullock had of the existence of the East Rongbuk Glacier, an embarrassing oversight that Mallory went out of his way in the official expedition account to obscure. One thing is certain: it was not Mallory or any of his English compatriots who first discovered the key to the mountain. It was the Canadian Oliver Wheeler, working alone in the solitude of the Rongbuk Valley.

ON THE EVENING of July 26, the day Howard-Bury, Mallory, and Bullock had pushed on to the new British base at Kharta, Wheeler, camped amid the buckthorn thickets at Chöbuk, had reasons to be optimistic. From what he had seen from the trail, the peaks of Rongbuk appeared more accessible, the side valleys shorter, than what he had confronted on the western approaches to Everest. Unlike the climbing party, his focus was less on the summit than on the satellite features of the massif, the lower peaks and ridges that might provide stations for his photographic survey. He required a certain number, and within limits, the more he could establish, the more proficient would be his map, but he had no desire to haul his hundred-pound kit up one more slope than was necessary. The unknown factor remained, as always, the weather.

From Chöbuk it was a ten-mile march to the Rongbuk Monastery, a climb of some 1,500 feet along a well-trodden track, fairly crowded on the morning of July 27 with the narrow traffic of yaks and porters carrying bundles of firewood and hand-hewn timbers destined for the *gompa* and the hermit cells of the valley. Making his first camp close to the monastery, Wheeler assessed his situation. The monks were unfriendly, resentful of his presence, and no one was willing to sell him supplies. "It is a bleak cold spot," he confided in his journal, "hemmed in by high shale peaks, changing to granite a bit further up." The following morning he left camp at 8:00 to climb to 19,900 feet, "a tremendous grind" to reach a summit spur, where he waited all day in the rain to secure a single image. It was a bitter taste of what was to come.

Over the next two days he had his camp moved, in stages, farther up the valley, eventually occupying a site a mile below the snout of the main Rongbuk Glacier, where Mallory and Bullock had their base. His focus for the moment was the "23,000 ft group to the east." His deliberate goal was to look "over into the Kharta side." On Saturday, July 30, he set out to establish a second station, climbing in three and a half hours to 19,400 feet, where again he was obliged to wait until early evening to "get a round of angles and some indifferent photos." Though stymied again by the weather, he was able to study the entire Rongbuk Valley, from a mile or two below the monastery to the massive cirque at the head of the glacier beneath the North Face of Everest itself. His surveyor's eye did not fail to notice that the mountain wall of the eastern side of the Rongbuk Valley was cleft at only a single point. He could not see beyond the ridgeline, but this opening became his goal.

The following morning, with a light camp, he moved four miles up the "main valley and a mile up the next side valley from the east, coming I think from the 23,000 ft group." To cross the outlet, he had stayed high on the ice. The glacial stream itself, roaring out of the mountains, proved too treacherous to ford. Wheeler made camp early, knowing that the water levels would drop with the dawn. One clue as to the size of the unknown drainage, he noted, was the surge of meltwater late in the day, an indication of a large surface of glacial ice exposed to the sun. "Anyhow," he confided in his journal that night, "it is a very big valley, and where it goes remains to be seen."

The next day, Monday, August 1, was a disappointment. The water had indeed dropped, but it remained a torrent, and with the rocks glazed in ice, "it was the devil crossing the stream" to reposition the camp, though they managed to do so. Wheeler then set off on another horrendous climb, only to wait in the rain and clouds until 5:00 p.m., failing to fix a single point due to the "cursed weather." Feeling ill, he nevertheless moved camp yet again the following morning, pushing a further four miles up what he now recognized as the East Rongbuk Valley, establishing a bivouac on a miserable patch of debris-covered ice. His four porters failed to arrive until dark. They slept without blankets. He rewarded each with a Tibetan coin, "which seemed to satisfy them perfectly."

Feeling fit by morning, August 3, a Wednesday, he traversed the slush and ice for half a mile to reach a prominent shoulder, which carried him over frozen scree to a high ridge, where he established a station at 20,000 feet. For once the clouds cleared, and he realized the significance of his discovery: "The valley tends a bit to the south and reaches right past Everest to a pass at the end of its E ridge—vastly bigger than I had imagined." From its confluence with the main Rongbuk Valley, he estimated, the East Rongbuk reached for some fifteen miles to the very foot of Everest; a single branch of its glacier directly opposite his station stretched to the northeast for five to six miles,

reaching toward a tangle of mountains anchored in the far distance by
Kharta Changri. To the southeast, he had a sighting of Makalu, which
implies that his vista on this clear afternoon took in as well the Lhakpa
La, the high saddle at the head of the Kharta Glacier, which Mallory
and Morshead would not see until the morning of August 14. Wheeler
returned to camp by 3:30 p.m. after a "glorious glissade down perfect
snow, the first I've had in this country, about 1000 feet of it." The porters, he reported in his journal, "funked" at the opportunity. They had
never seen someone ski down a mountain on his boots.

The snow began to fall that night and did not let up for thirty-six
hours. At noon the next day, August 4, a party of porters appeared
out of the storm with supplies and a precious delivery of mail, including delicacies from his wife, Dolly, and some real cigarettes, which he
smoked with such fervor that he nearly made himself ill. By the next
morning, after a sleepless night, he really was sick, and with three feet
of fresh snow on the ground, there was nothing to do but lie in the tent
and busy himself with his correspondence. "So long as I can get the lie
of the land this side in my head," he wrote to his wife, "September's
work will be pretty easy. And I think I'm well on the way to it now."
He went on to describe the difficulty of the terrain on the surface of
the glacier. Between the lateral moraines the ice formed pinnacles a
hundred feet tall, impossible to climb, stacked one upon another for
miles. To cross the glacier implied tackling each in turn, struggling
up vertical walls only to tumble down on the other side into hollows
and ponds of ice water. To cover a mile of ground took him on one
occasion four hours, and he and the men were "cooked before we ever
started the days work." The valley, he wrote in a subsequent letter to
Dolly that went out on August 6, "runs along the whole north face of
Everest, from the north to the east, which I think can be done. The
existing map is of course totally wrong."

After a week in the East Rongbuk, Wheeler had a sketch of the
actual geography in hand. To establish new stations would require
crossing the full length of the upper glacier, an impossibility given the
condition of the men. His own clothes and boots were riddled with
holes. One of the porters, a Pashtun, was dangerously ill. Wheeler had
little choice but to return to the main Rongbuk Valley, where, at any
rate, much work remained to be done. After a long slog, he arrived
back at his base at the snout of the Rongbuk Glacier late on the afternoon of August 7, some hours ahead of the porters. Two of them finally
arrived just after 8:00 p.m. with his bedding, just as, he noted, he had
"settled down to make the best of it with my spare underwear, socks

under me and myself wrapped in the waterproof cover of the sleeping bag Mallory had given me." The following day, or possibly as late as August 9, he sent a letter by *dak* courier to Howard-Bury, with the map that revealed the most direct and efficient route to the eastern base of the North Col. It was not through Kharta, but via the main Rongbuk Valley, and the ice-studded moraines of the East Rongbuk Glacier.

Wheeler remained in the Rongbuk Valley for another sixteen days, cursed on every one by inclement conditions. He awoke each morning hopeful, only to pound up some ridge and be frustrated by clouds. On Thursday, August 11, he ran out of food. By Saturday, though resupplied, he was despondent; on August 18, from his highest camp on the glacier, he nearly broke down. "Weather, weather, weather!" he lamented. "It is this infernal Nepal frontier again; the monsoon clouds simply pour over—but this time the passes are in the main Everest ridge and I've got to stay till I map them. I must admit I'm fed up with this uncomfortable camp and this small tent (9 days in it now) and short rations. I'm smokeless! It was bad smoking mildewed stuff but infinitely better than nothing. I used the last this morning when I broke up three remaining stubs and rolled them into a fresh cigarette. Somewhat rank but smokeable." Two days later, in the middle of the night, a blizzard blew through, crushing his tent under three feet of snow. The following morning he retreated down the ice in a blinding storm, three hours to his main camp, where he arrived drenched, hungry, tired, "but fit thank the Lord." There was a message waiting from Howard-Bury, telling him to come down and around to Kharta, where much work was to be done and the climate was temperate. There were fruit trees and meadows, glaciers flowing down to 12,000 feet, and wonderful views of Makalu and Everest. On the morning of August 22, a Monday, he sent back by courier a note to Howard-Bury: "It is cold and cheerless now the clouds down. I've never seen such weather. Hopeless for survey work." With that Wheeler finally abandoned the Rongbuk Valley, making his way down to Chöbuk, where he, like Mallory before him, took immense delight and pleasure from green fields and creeks running through glens, with no ice in sight.

MALLORY'S FIRST REACTION to Wheeler's map was to question its accuracy. While it clearly showed, he wrote, a "glacier of enormous dimensions running north from Everest and draining into the Rongbuk Valley . . . its obvious inaccuracies in some respects had made us discount his conclusion perhaps too much . . . In my case I had little hope it would be of service to us." The map was indeed just a sketch, intended only to brief Howard-Bury as to the significance of the East Rongbuk Glacier. But Wheeler was a skilled professional surveyor, an engineer who would one day become the surveyor general of India and later be knighted for cartographic work during the Second World War. His abilities as a topographer and mapmaker were exceptional, as Morshead and other members of the Survey of India acknowledged. Mallory's real concern, beyond his lingering disregard for Wheeler and the possibility that he had been trumped, was his sense that the expedition, firmly entrenched in Kharta, could not possibly pull back and reposition for an assault on the mountain from the Rongbuk side. Time and the advancing seasons would not permit it. Nor would the morale of the men tolerate such a move. Everyone was exhausted and nerves were frayed. If they were to have a chance at Everest this season, it would have to come from Kharta, where supplies could be had and comfort found as the men prepared for the ultimate test.

On the morning of August 15, having seen Wheeler's map, Mallory, Morshead, and Bullock set out to reach the high saddle at the head of the southern arm of the Kharta Glacier, the wide col beyond which they had seen the summit of Changtse, the North Peak. They expected to get there in a day. It took four, and from the start things went poorly.

Bullock's porters, slow withdrawing his equipment and supplies from the northern arm of the glacier, delayed the advance, and the climbing party was obliged on the first evening to make camp on an awkward slope of rock, in whirling snow. Thick mist obscured the terrain the following morning, and they elected to leave the ice and scale the stony ridge immediately behind their camp, with the hope of finding a way to traverse to the col at elevation. Instead, having climbed 1,700 feet by 6:30 a.m., they discovered that only by dropping 1,000 feet might they regain the glacier, which they did, taking another two hours to do so. Exhausted, blinded by clouds, they trudged on snowshoes until late morning when, confronted by an ice wall impossible to turn or, in their weakened condition, to scale, they reluctantly gave up the day. Efforts to resupply and move their camp farther up the glacier, thwarted and compromised by the muddling incompetence of the sirdar, lost them another twenty-four hours, during which time snow fell constantly. Not until late in the afternoon of August 17 had they established a high camp at close to 20,000 feet.

That night—actually, 3:00 a.m. on August 18—the three Englishmen, accompanied by a single porter, the strong and dependable

Nyima, departed for what Mallory would later describe as the most critical foray of the whole reconnaissance. He had long determined August 20 to be the cutoff, the date by which a final route would have to be known, or all the expedition's efforts to climb Everest abandoned. In his mind, they had but a day, possibly two. A lingering hope that the cold might have hardened the surface of the snow slipped away the moment they moved onto the glacier. The snow was deep, and even with snowshoes they sank to their knees. Every step registered. Their greatest enemy, however, was not the fresh powder but the impossible heat that rose from the ice once the sun broke the horizon. In all their time in Tibet they had never experienced anything like it. Mallory tried to describe it in a letter to Ruth: "We were enveloped in a thin mist which obscured the view and made one world of snow and sky—a scorching mist, if you can imagine such a thing, more burning than bright sunshine and indescribably breathless. One seemed literally at times to be walking in a white furnace."

Morshead compared it to the unbearable heat of the Indian plains, only far worse, mist that became steam, enveloping and exhausting the body. To halt for even a moment was to be overcome with inertia. One could only plod on. "Never before had our lungs been tested so severely," Mallory later recalled. Even with Mallory taking the lead, breaking trail in the snow, Morshead could not keep up and was forced to fall out just below their goal. Mallory went on, in what he would later describe as the toughest push he had ever done on a mountain. With Bullock and Nyima behind, he finally crested the saddle at half past noon, after a steady climb of more than nine hours. To their delight, the indomitable Morshead joined them after fifteen minutes.

Clouds obscured the view, and the wind was fierce. The entire ridge from Everest to Changtse and beyond, all the peaks above the Rongbuk Valley, were hidden in white. But they could look down upon the head of the East Rongbuk Glacier and across at last to the face of the Chang La, the North Col, a sight that after so many weeks of effort, discipline, and longing must have left Mallory shaking with relief. He guessed that the drop from where they were to the glacier was 800 feet; it turned out to be closer to 1,200 feet and more difficult than his initial assessment. Still, it could be done, and crossing the head of the glacier to the base of the North Col would be a walk. The actual face of the col, which he guessed to be 500 feet—again an underestimate—presented at least from afar no insurmountable challenges. What lay beyond the col, on the shoulder rising to the Northeast Ridge, remained to be seen. All of Everest was veiled in cloud.

Still, success seemed potentially at hand. "We saw what we came to see," he later wrote to Ruth. "We have found our way to the great mountain." The Lhakpa La, a pass soon to be dubbed Windy Gap by the British, offered without doubt an avenue to the foot of the North Col, to Mallory the only viable route to the summit of Everest.

Their return to base was a long, anticlimactic trudge, with Morshead utterly played out. They were not off the glacier until after dark. They lost the route, and only the "faint misty moonlight" allowed them to retrace their steps, a long, arduous ascent up a steep slope, stepping from boulder to boulder, until finally, just after 2:00 in the morning, fully twenty-three hours after setting out, they reached the safety of their lower camp. It had been an extraordinary triumph, marred perhaps only by Mallory's stubborn, even unseemly, refusal to acknowledge Wheeler's contribution. "The expedition was a success," he wrote to Ruth on August 22. "There, sure enough, was the suspected glacier running north from a cwm under the northeast face of Everest. How we wished it had been possible to follow it down and find out the secret of its exit. There we were baffled." In truth, even as he spun the story to his wife, making a second reference in the letter to the "glacier whose exit we have yet to find," Mallory knew where the East Rongbuk flowed. Wheeler's map had told him, more than a week before.

EVERYTHING NOW DEPENDED on the conditions, and the hope that the monsoon would break, as anticipated, at the end of the month and bring on a stretch of fine weather in the first days of September. Mallory, Bullock, and Morshead returned to Kharta on August 20. The geologist Heron had reached Kharta the previous day, having walked all the ranges north of Tingri and Shegar as far as the Brahmaputra drainage. Howard-Bury and Wollaston were already at base, and Wheeler was expected any day. Of the original party that had set out from Darjeeling three months before, almost to the day, only Harold Raeburn, invalided to Nepal, and Arthur Kellas, resting in his grave at Kampa Dzong, were missing.

Any question of returning to Rongbuk to reach the North Col via the newly discovered East Rongbuk Glacier had been rendered moot by the advancing season. There was no time. It would be the Kharta Valley or nothing. Mallory's plan, endorsed by Howard-Bury, was to establish a supply stronghold in relative comfort at 17,300 feet. From there they would reoccupy their advanced base at 20,000 feet and place

two, possibly three, additional tent camps on the mountain, one sheltered to the extent possible at Windy Gap, the Lhakpa La, at 22,200
feet, a second at the foot of the North Col, what they hazarded to be
an elevation of some 21,500 feet, and finally a third beyond the North
Col itself, "somewhere under the shoulder," as Mallory anticipated,
"at around 26,500 feet." From there they would go as high as possible,
hoping at the very least to reach the junction of the Northeast Shoulder rising from the col and the Northeast Ridge, which leads to the
summit pyramid of the mountain. "We saw no reason," Mallory wrote,
"to exclude the supreme object itself."

In retrospect, these were wildly ambitious, quixotic goals, revealing
how little the climbers actually knew about the mountain, the scale
of the endeavor, the danger of the undertaking, the power of Everest's wrath. They were like knights who had endured impossible hardships to reach the mouth of the dragon's cave, still to discover what it
really means to enter and confront the creature. The quest nevertheless preoccupied Mallory, who spent hours at Kharta calculating loads,
anticipating rotations of porters, constructing in his mind a ladder of
logistical support that would rise from a broad base to the ultimate
rung, a single step upon the summit of the world.

With the expedition now focused on the climb, Mallory's voice
within the group grew, and leadership shifted his way. The day after
returning to Kharta, he wrote to Arthur Hinks at the Royal Geographical Society. The letter's tone was both brash and defiant, as if to remind
the secretary at his desk in London that the climbers on the mountain
now controlled the narrative. He began with the practical, cutting a
lecture deal for money, and closed with the essential:

> As things have turned out it seems to me I am rather the obvious
> person to enlighten the public about the mountaineering part
> of the expedition; it is a good story, I think, so far, and I have
> every reason to expect the climax to be no less interesting . . . I
> suppose, before you receive this you will have heard our news
> in some other way and will know whether we have got to the
> top or how far we have reached "Height record beaten by two
> daring Englishmen," or some balderdash of the sort. Meanwhile,
> "as flies to wanton dogs are we to the gods." It's a very big
> game; we've been foiled ever so often merely in finding out the
> shape of the mountain, the nature of the approaches . . . We've
> a chance of getting up; one can't say more. Farewell. I hope we
> may meet sometime in December.

Among the men at Kharta, there were numerous tensions. Bullock and Mallory shared a small tent, and despite the soft weather, as wet and temperate as an English summer, they had been companions for too long. "We had rather drifted into that common superficial attitude between two people who live alone together," Mallory wrote to Ruth, "competitive and slightly quarrelsome, each looking out to see that he doesn't get done down in some small way by the other. I have been thinking B too lazy about many small things that have to be done, as a result of which I have sometimes tried to arrange that he shall be left to do them; and he has developed the idea that I habitually try and shift the dirty work onto him; and so we have both been forgetting Christian decency and even eyeing the food to see that the other doesn't take too much—horrible confession!"

Mallory and Howard-Bury remained at odds, in conflict now about food and compensation for the porters. From their own pockets Mallory and Bullock had been buying meat and tea for their men in the high camps. "Bury will allow nothing outside their base rations. He has economy on the brain and I can't bear his meanness," Mallory reported. For his part, Howard-Bury had had enough. On Tuesday, August 23, three days after the climbers had returned to Kharta, he and Wollaston took off for the Kama Valley to explore its lower reaches. Mallory was relieved. "Frankly I was quite glad Bury was away," he wrote. "I can't get over my dislike of him."

In six days Howard-Bury and Wollaston did wonderful things. They crossed the heights and descended into the Kama Valley, passing through the abandoned trading depot of Sakeding, ghost-riddled and haunted by demons, and then went down the gorge. They dropped more than 4,000 feet from the valley floor, following the Kama Chu for three days to its confluence with the Arun, where they stayed in a grove of blue pines and broad-leafed alders in a camp thick with leeches. They got away early the next morning and climbed high through black mud to reach the summit of the Popti La, at 14,000 feet a seasonal pass overlooking Nepal. There they found an ancient border stone, inscribed in Chinese characters. They remained at the pass for an hour, as Nepalese women trudged by silently in the rain, each burdened by eighty-pound loads of salt. That night they camped again in the wet forest, with a roaring fire of rhododendron and juniper wood to keep the leeches at bay. The following morning, they encountered langur monkeys in a valley scarlet with mountain ash and barberry. For both Howard-Bury and Wollaston, it was an inspired week away from the daily challenges of responsibility and leadership. As naturalists, they took delight in the fauna and flora, ignored all inconveniences, and found any number of new species. But by the time they retraced their steps, regained all the elevation lost, and crossed back over the divide to Kharta on August 29, the expedition and the story of Everest belonged to Mallory.

WHEELER HAD ARRIVED at Kharta two days earlier, on August 27, just before noon, looking "quite fit," Bullock noted that night in his journal. In ninety-three days, he had rested nine. When not moving camp, he had climbed every day, on one occasion going up to a 20,500-foot station three days in a row only to secure an indifferent photograph on the third attempt. Delighted at last to be back with the main party, he naturally offered to help. Mallory was uncertain. "Wheeler is intending to give us his service on the mountain," he wrote to Ruth, "while using our camps to some extent for his surveying; but he'll find it difficult to work the two objects together and I can't believe he'll be much use to us. He is continually complaining of a disordered inside and he doesn't look fit. Besides he won't be trained to the extent that B and I will be. Though he's done a good deal of walking and plenty of living at high altitude he's never been up more than 2000 ft in a day and hasn't gone on enough I should imagine when it requires a real effort to go on—which is the essence of training. However, we shall see."

Wheeler, having been alone for so long, was simply glad, he wrote, to "feed off a table again and to sit and swap lies after meals!" He missed Heron, who had set off again for another ten days on August 26, but shared what he had learned with the other men. "Wheeler was able to confirm," Morshead later wrote, "the important fact that the glacier on to which we had looked down from the Lhakpa La, drained into the Rongbuk valley, through a narrow gorge which had been overlooked by the mountaineers in the mists and clouds during their first reconnaissance of the Rongbuk glaciers." The sketched map had been correct, as Mallory now recognized. "But this certain knowledge," he wrote, "could have no bearing on our plans; we remained content with the way we had found and troubled our heads no more for the present about the East Rongbuk Glacier."

With the return to Kharta of Howard-Bury and Wollaston on the evening of August 29, Mallory and Bullock took advantage of what appeared to be a slight break in the weather to make immediate plans to move up the valley to establish the base camp at 17,300 feet. Bullock sent his mattress and spare clothes on August 30, keeping only his suitcase. He and Mallory set off the following day on ponies, with three porters to carry the rest of their kit. After two hours, they had to walk, and it was midafternoon before they reached the site for the new advanced base. Mallory felt ill. Leaving Kharta so soon was a mistake, as Howard-Bury had anticipated in a letter to Arthur Hinks on the first day of September: "Bullock and Mallory left yesterday for the upper camp, foolishly I think for they can do nothing in this weather, but I am afraid they are getting impatient and anxious to get back to their wives."

The locals had predicted one last blizzard before the turn of the season. For several days the weather stabilized, but there was little for Mallory and Bullock to do save wait as the porters, one load at a time, thirty altogether, supplied the upper camps with wood. The two climbers at the advanced base camp remained essentially idle for five days, in the damp and discomfort, when they could have been resting and conserving their strength down below at Kharta. Bullock passed the time by playing with two young buntings he had captured, letting them run about on a string, and taking great delight whenever the mother came to feed them. He made a cage from a basket, and they began to take seeds from his hand. But then on the night of Monday, September 5, wet snow fell and by morning the birds were dead.

At Kharta, meanwhile, Wheeler had been working intently on his photographic collection, processing the glass plates and printing the best of the images to be dispatched by *dak* courier to Darjeeling and ultimately to Arthur Hinks at the RGS. Wheeler was disappointed in several of the exposures. Clearly he had underestimated the brightness of Tibetan light even when filtered by clouds. On the afternoon of September 1, he'd left the darkroom and gone outside to get away from the chemical fumes and have a cigarette when suddenly he saw a short, ghostlike figure stumble toward their camp. To the utter surprise of all, it was the irascible Scot, Harold Raeburn, whom they had not seen or heard from since Wollaston had left him in the care of the Moravian nuns at Lachen in Sikkim on June 12. At the age of fifty-six, he had walked across Tibet to rejoin the expedition.

Stunned, they gathered in the mess tent to hear the tale. At the missionary post Raeburn had indeed come close to death. But, mercifully, his fever had broken on the evening of June 18. The maharaja of Sikkim had been kind enough to dispatch his personal bearers, who carried the invalid in a dandy three days across the mountains to Gangtok, where he convalesced at the British Residency. Regaining his strength by the end of July, he purchased four ponies and headed for Tibet. Accompanied by a single interpreter, he crossed the Serpo

La and reached Kampa Dzong on August 15. He rested for a day, paying his respects to Kellas's grave. He then set out for Kharta, though neither he nor the *dzongpen* of Tinki had any idea where to find it. But he recalled from the account of the pundit Sarat Chandra Das, published in 1885, mention of a bridge, said to be just a few strands of twisted hide, that crossed the Phung Chu some thirty miles east of Everest. He walked for five days, only to find the river swollen by the monsoon, a sea of water and quicksand. There was no sign of a bridge, save the trunk of an old tree poking out of the water. Backtracking, he found all the rivers swollen in flood, and it was only after several arduous days that he reached a possible ford. The men stripped naked and joined hands. Raeburn recalled, "The crossing was most painful and hard from the cold and the water and wind and the heavy quick sands. It took me up to the shoulders and in a small man up to the chin. On getting over I shivered for two hours." Only by good fortune did he then meet a native to the area, one of Morshead's porters from Kharta, who directed him to the valley.

In the official expedition account, the return of Harold Raeburn, the titular leader of the climbing party, was cause for celebration. "We rejoiced," Mallory wrote, "to see [him] again." Private thoughts were less charitable. "To our great surprise Raeburn turned up yesterday after a three month absence," Howard-Bury reported in a note to Sir Francis Younghusband. But his sin was unforgivable: "He passed five bags of our mails near Tinki . . . Can you imagine anyone being such a fool!"

Mallory spoke the harshest words, in a letter some days later to Geoffrey Young: "Raeburn turned up . . . looking extraordinarily old and grizzled and being no less old than he looks. When he is not being a bore I feel moved to pity. But that's not often. He takes no part luckily . . . Was he always such a very stupid man? It's impossible to understand how ever he can have got a party up a mountain."

Wollaston, the expedition doctor who had personally escorted Raeburn to safety in Sikkim, was appalled that he had returned. He felt that Raeburn was a serious liability to all, noting, "His internal trouble is at an end . . . But he is definitely an old man, in mind as well as in body, and I very much wish he had not come, as there is nothing whatever for him to do . . . He is become quite senile since his illness."

IN CLOUDS and drifting snow Wheeler and Morshead left Kharta on Saturday, September 3, keen to map the approaches to the Lhakpa La. It was their first opportunity to work together, and Morshead was eager to learn the Canadian photographic survey technique that had allowed Wheeler to accomplish so much, so close to the mountain. They walked seven miles up the valley, making camp at the last bridge. That afternoon they climbed 4,000 feet to scout a survey station, an exertion they repeated the following day, with Morshead setting the pace. On September 5 they moved eight miles farther up the Kharta Valley, past the last village, establishing a camp roughly five miles this side of Mallory and Bullock's advanced base. This same day, Howard-Bury, Wollaston, and Raeburn moved up from Kharta, making their camp two miles below that of Wheeler and Morshead. There were now three parties on the advance, all ultimately heading to the ice and wind of the Lhakpa La.

Howard-Bury, Wollaston, and Raeburn pushed through in the morning, joining Mallory and Bullock at their 17,300-foot camp by midday. On September 7 Morshead walked up to visit them, returning to Wheeler in the afternoon with word of Mallory's plan: Mallory and Bullock would wait at the advanced base until the first clear day and then immediately ascend to the 20,000-foot camp, where they would remain for four days, bringing up wood and supplies, before heading to Windy Gap at 22,200 feet. Mallory expected Wheeler and Morshead to follow on command. Wheeler was delighted, for the schedule gave him time to complete his work and still get up the mountain to join the assault, with twenty-four hours to spare for acclimatization.

Morshead also brought gossip from the upper camp. "Apparently Bury and Wollaston and Raeburn live in one mess alone," Wheeler confided in his journal, "and Mallory and Bullock in another! Rather funny. Bury and Mallory don't hit it off—nor do Raeburn and Wollaston, so if the weather lasts there may be some squabbles." Morshead also brought more important news, which Wheeler shared in a letter to his wife. Mallory intended for certain to cross the head of the East Rongbuk Glacier to establish a camp at "25,000 to 26,000 on the col joining the north to the main peak and so up the north ridge. Whether we shall be able to do all that is another matter. Anyhow Morshead and I are going to get in on that climb which is something!"

News that Mallory had included him and Morshead in the final climbing party inspired Wheeler, but what most lifted his morale that particular day had been his sighting of three heavily laden porters slowly making their way up the valley. "We examined them carefully through glasses," he noted, "and eventually decided that they must be the mail!"

Dispatched from Darjeeling as early as July 1, the post had taken six to ten weeks to cross the flooded uplands of Tibet. At the advanced base camp Howard-Bury alone received two hundred letters, along with various packages and papers. For Mallory, waiting out the weather in the damp and cold with not a candle to heat the night, the news from Ruth and home was nothing less than six "weeks of love" in envelopes. "It's always a wonderful moment," he later wrote, "when the mail comes and love flies in among us and nestles in every tent."

In an age of letters, it was not only the receipt of correspondence that maintained a lifeline, it was the grace and comfort that came in the moment of reply, when each man could share private thoughts, vent frustrations, and express fears, knowing that convention demanded discretion, and that a private letter between gentlemen or an intimate note between man and wife implied an inviolable trust.

Among the many letters to arrive that day for Mallory was one dated July 20 from his old friend and mentor Geoffrey Young. It urged caution: "The result is nothing compared to the rightness of the attempt. Keep it right then; and let no desire for result spoil the effort by overstretching the safe limits within which it must move . . . The summit may, in any particular case, lie outside the course . . . Good Fortune! And the 'resolution to return' even against ambition!"

Mallory responded immediately, even before writing to his wife:

Long before you get this you will know the result, which may make my speculations look foolish; but I must make them, I can think of nothing else. The excitement of the reconnaissance is over—it was exciting—and we have found a good way to the mountain . . .

The whole thing is on my shoulders. Bullock follows well and is safe; but you know what it means on a long, exhausting effort to lead all the time . . . Morshead and Wheeler are both joining us for the assault. M is wonderfully stouthearted, but hasn't the lungs for this job I fear. Wheeler hasn't been out with us as yet, but . . . I don't expect much of him. If they don't come on from the final camp I shall take coolies; one or two of them are wonderful good goers . . . It's all a question of lungs.

Lord, how I wish you were here to talk it all over. It has been rather a strain Geoffrey altogether . . . Relations with Bury have not been easy—they're reestablished pretty happily now I believe after a day's scrambling yesterday along an amusing little rock ridge; he's a queer customer as I'll tell you one day, and I don't support friction easily. Altogether it's a trying time . . .

Geoffrey at what point am I going to stop? It's going to be a fearfully difficult decision and there's an incalculable element

about other men's physical condition, and all the more so under
these strange conditions. I almost hope I shall be the first to
give out!

I shan't be sorry to get back to civilization and know
again what's going on in the world; it's a poor world perhaps
but it remains interesting even here—if only as a contrast
to Tibet, which is a hateful country inhabited by hateful
people. The great mountains give their flashes of beauty;
Makalu is indescribably impressive; but on the whole they are
disappointing and infinitely less beautiful than the Alps.

Mallory, of course, shared none of these private doubts and misgivings with the men. But he did feel the burden of the expedition
upon him, and he watched everyone for signs of weakness. His opinion
of Howard-Bury had indeed softened. The post had brought word of
a truce in Ireland, for which they both rejoiced. Their "most agreeable little scramble" the day before was actually the first time they had
climbed together, and they had confronted a number of sharp pinnacles with some exposure. "I found these gymnastics at a height of
over 19,000 feet to be very exhausting," recalled Howard-Bury, "but
Mallory did not seem to mind them in the least." Of Howard-Bury,
Mallory later wrote, "He went quite well, walked strongly and was by
no means so clumsy on rocks as one might expect of a novice of 40."

Still, despite Howard-Bury's evident strength and fitness, Mallory
did not trust him for the actual assault, any more than he did Heron
and Wollaston, both of whom he genuinely liked. He promised the
ever "cheerful and good natured" Heron "a bit of rock from the summit of Everest." Wollaston amused him, but he was no climber: "Wollaston, I find, a rather solitary bird, posing over his collections—a most
varied assortment they must be ranging from dead rats of which he
has an incredible number to poppy seeds and butterflies. He is always
jolly and friendly to talk with, but I've an impression that he is more
tired of the expedition than the rest of us. Of course, just now we are
all drifting as the clouds drift, forgetting to number the days so as to
avoid painful thoughts of the hurrying month."

Time was the challenge—and, of course, the weather. On September 10, Mallory rather impetuously decided to advance the schedule,
sending a chit to Wheeler and Morshead, summoning them to the
advanced base for a move to the 20,000-foot camp the following day.
"2 days instead of 4!" Wheeler scribbled in his journal. "He [Mallory]
changes his plans pretty frequently. There is nothing for it but to chuck

this and come up to the base camp tomorrow. How I shall finish work in this valley I don't know."

The next morning, a Sunday, they headed up, a 2,000-foot rise over five miles. They arrived at noon only to find that Mallory and Bullock had pushed on to the 20,000-foot camp. "It is distinctly colder here," Wheeler noted, "raw and beastly. Temperature 39 at lunchtime."

Mallory's haste was for naught. Within twenty-four hours he and Bullock were forced back from the higher camp. Four feet of fresh powder had fallen, and nothing could be done until they had sun by day and frost by night to harden the surface. On the descent in the sleet and snow, Bullock put up his pink umbrella. Mallory wore his shepherd's overalls, airplane wing fabric oiled to a dirty yellow sheen. He took two hours to get down to the advanced base, Bullock slightly longer. In that time an additional six inches fell. "Having only brought one coat which was wet," Bullock wrote in his journal that night, "Spent the evening in a sweater. Luckily I had two."

Inactivity now became a curse. "I've done precisely nothing since I left Kharta," complained Wheeler, "9 whole days gone to pot. It is disgusting. Mallory of course is bored to tears. He is such an excitable person."

The following morning, Tuesday, September 13, the snow and cold grew worse, with a morning sun blackened by cloud by breakfast. "It's distinctly raw in camp," wrote Wheeler. "There really is nothing to do but stay in bed. My feet are nearly frozen in spite of 2 pr of socks, wooly bedroom slippers and the whole ensconced in the wooly legs of my long boots. It froze in my tent during the night. A glass of water was frozen solid—also my boots."

That afternoon, with the temperature dropping to thirteen degrees, Howard-Bury, Mallory, Bullock, and Wheeler gathered in one of the tents to play bridge. "First time since March," Wheeler recalled. "I enjoyed it thoroughly. Pretty even cards. We had one of two quite exciting hands too—5 hearts doubled which we just made and 4 diamonds doubled our opponents just made." Outside, three feet of fresh snow had fallen. There was no fuel in camp, as every stick of firewood had to be carried up five miles from the valley below. The "raw cold cuts one to the marrow," Wheeler acknowledged in a letter to Dolly, his mind drifting to a case of fine Madeira wine that had been promised to the expedition, something to celebrate the king's birthday. Perhaps it was already in Kharta. "It would be nice—by Jove, it would! It just makes the mouth water."

Heron arrived the following day, without wine but with another cache of mail, including recent letters, some of which had been posted in Darjeeling only a fortnight before. But with the cold came a growing lassitude. Even at their advanced base camp they were sleeping at an elevation nearly 2,000 feet higher than the summit of Mont Blanc, the highest mountain in the Alps. Climbers had never before spent so much time at such altitude, and they had no idea that with every hour they grew weaker. "Mallory has now switched," Wheeler noted on September 14, "from violent hurry to waiting at least a week after the fine weather comes for the final ascent." The notion of waiting out the weather may have made sense in Europe, but it would prove disastrous on the slopes of Everest. By day Mallory dreamed of returning to Ruth, meeting her quayside at some sun-drenched Mediterranean port. By night Bullock was forced to shake him awake, for Mallory often ceased to breathe for what seemed like minutes at a time.

Morshead's clothes were stiff with sweat and frost, and his face blackened from the wind and cold. Raeburn suffered the most. In a letter to Ruth, Mallory dismissed him as "a senile, babbling, insignificant, almost broken and heart breaking figure." That night, in a curious gesture, Raeburn gave Wheeler a copy of his book *Mountaineering Art*, which had been published to strong reviews only a year before. It was a climbing manual as much as a book, and it summed up everything Raeburn knew and had experienced as a mountaineer. Wheeler enjoyed it, but was astonished that Raeburn had carried it all the way from Darjeeling.

Mallory sensed the gloom in the "strange bearded faces and teeth" of his companions. "The month is too late already for the great venture," he wrote to Ruth. "We shall have to face great cold, I've no doubt; and the longer the delay the colder it will be. But the fine weather will come at last. My chance, the chance of a lifetime, I suppose, will be sadly shrunk by then and all my hopes and plans . . . will be blown to wherever the monsoon blows."

Then, as if by a miracle, the weather broke and the morning of September 16 dawned with promise. "Wonder of wonders!" Mallory exclaimed in a note to Ruth. "We just woke and found it different—the sky clear and remaining clear—no dense grey clouds drifting up the valley, but a chill wind driving high clouds from the north." Wheeler got away early and established, on a high hill across from their base, his best station yet, composing his first full circle of images, eight photographs in all, with every feature of the land illuminated by a cloudless sky. Mallory, Morshead, and Bullock scrambled up the same side of the valley, became separated for a time but returned together, swept into the camp by an afternoon snowstorm.

By evening it had again cleared, and the eight men posed for a group portrait, the only one taken of the entire expedition party high on the mountain. Mallory, pipe in hand, sits stiffly in a camp chair beside Wheeler, and hovering over both is Howard-Bury, dapper in tie, waistcoat, and checkered coat. Every face is grim. "The party has been gathered for the great assault," Mallory wrote to his old friend Herbert Read. "Mountaineers and surveyors, the chief himself, the men of medicine, the geologist who demands a piece of the top, even old Raeburn who has rushed up again at the last moment—we're all here waiting for the indispensible friend who never will show himself, the Sun, to melt the snow for us. And every day we wait, the poorer our chances become, the later the season, the colder the nights, the more uncomfortable the coolies . . . The puffs of smoke from the fire give the faintest of blue cheer to our desolation."

Before renewing their quest, they had to wait for the sun and the cold to form a crust on the fresh snow of the glacier. But rather than rest, they made immediate plans to take advantage of the decent weather. On Saturday, September 17, Wheeler and Heron established two new stations at close to 20,000 feet. That same day Mallory, Morshead, and Howard-Bury set out just after 2:00 a.m. to climb Kama Changri, a dominant peak to the south, overlooking the Kama Valley. They began by the light of a full moon. There was, Howard-Bury later wrote, everywhere an intense stillness. To the south, lightning flashed constantly through the night and the mountains—Kangchenjunga in the east, Makalu and Everest closer at hand—emerged as islands above the clouds. "All of a sudden a ray of sunshine touched the summit of Everest, and soon flooded the higher snows and ridges with golden light, while behind, the deep purple of the sky changed to orange. Makalu was the next to catch the first rays of the sun and glowed as though alive; then the white sea of clouds was struck by the gleaming rays of the sun, and all aglow with colour rose slowly and seemed to break against the island peaks in great billows of fleecy white. Such a sunrise has seldom been the privilege of man to see, and once seen can never be forgotten."

With the dawn, however, "the climbing became more unpleasant," Howard-Bury noted. It took them more than six hours, much of the time in soft snow under a bright sun, to traverse the glacier and reach the summit at 21,300 feet. The heat was intense, and there seemed not to be a breath of air. Mallory and Morshead both felt the altitude, and that did not bode well for what was to come. They rested on the summit for three hours, then returned by an easier route down the glacier, reaching camp in time for dinner and, as had become their habit, a pleasant game of bridge. They had climbed more than 4,000 vertical feet, taking sixteen hours to do so, on the eve of the day they hoped to begin their final assault on Everest.

The next morning, Sunday, September 18, as it turned out, was a write-off, with snow and sleet rendering any movement pointless. Wheeler and the others played cards all day, setting, as Howard-Bury quipped, an altitude record. Mallory was in no mood for levity. "I am clearly far from being as fit as I ought to be," he confided in a letter to Ruth. "It's very distressing my dear but at this moment and altogether my hopes are at zero."

His latest plan, as outlined in a letter to Geoffrey Young, was straightforward, though in hindsight still impossibly optimistic. From their current position they would push up to their 20,000-foot camp, already established on a stone terrace and well supplied with wood, light tents, and food. From there they would advance as soon as possible over the heights of Windy Gap, the Lhakpa La, cross the head of the East Rongbuk Glacier, and establish a third camp, he wrote,

> at about 24,000 feet, I hope somewhere near what we call the "north col" between Everest and the first part of its north ridge—an easy stage. It's an easy slope up from there to a great shoulder of the N.E. arête which must be 27,000 ft or thereabouts, and from there to the summit there should be no obstacle unless on the steep final up, which looks all too formidable. Naturally much depends upon how high we can get the coolies up from the "north col" on the 3rd day from our first camp. And we still have to find a place where a tent can be pitched. If we can get them 2,000 ft [above the col on the Northeast Shoulder] we shall have a chance I believe, a bare outside chance perhaps of crawling to the top.

Precisely who would make this supreme effort, and how it might be logistically supported, preoccupied Mallory for much of the day. Both Morshead and Wheeler were now pledged to mountaineering, as was Bullock. In a divided camp, they had forged a unit and were getting along well. Morshead, Bullock, and Mallory shared a Whymper tent, and Wheeler joined them for meals with "plenty of talk and good cheer," while the "rest," as Mallory noted, referring to Wollaston, Howard-Bury, and Raeburn, "have lordly meals round a table in a pukka mess tent." Yet despite this new camaraderie among the climbers, Mallory retained doubts about Wheeler. "Wheeler still strikes me as not a fit man," he wrote to Ruth. "Unless he shows more stamina than I expect I can't take him with us on the final day."

How the porters would perform at severe altitude also remained a great unknown. If the British were to have a chance at the summit, they would have to establish a final camp at an elevation higher than any human had ever reached, let alone slept. From the North Col, Mallory estimated, it would take ten fifteen-pound packs, half the normal load, merely to position tents, sleeping bags, and food for a four-man climbing party. This implied fourteen porters reaching the highest camp, with four to remain with the climbers and ten returning to a lower camp at or below the North Col. Unescorted, these porters would nevertheless need shelter, which meant that six tents at least, along with food and fuel for eighteen men, would have to be carried over the Lhakpa La, across the head of East Rongbuk Glacier, and then up the unclimbed face of the North Col. The expedition had nineteen porters experienced on ice. Sixteen had been with Mallory and Bullock; Wheeler had trained another three. But not all were well, and the expedition did not have enough high-altitude boots to equip even those still sufficiently fit to attempt the ascent. The math did not compute. The plan had no chance of success, but at this point in the expedition, the mountain and the weather dictated events.

AFTER A FRIGID NIGHT, sixteen degrees of frost, Mallory, Bullock, Morshead, and Wheeler left advanced base at 8:30 a.m. on Monday, September 19, to make their way in four hours to the 20,000-foot camp. That evening the sky cleared, and Wheeler described in his journal a glorious sight, Makalu and the whole of the ridge leading to Everest, and to the east a "false sunset, great pink beams of light across a purple sky." There was later a beautiful halo around the moon, and in its light Mallory and Morshead, along with sixteen porters, set out at 2:30 a.m. for the Lhakpa La, carrying with them fourteen loads to provision an upper camp there. Bullock remained with Wheeler, traversing the ice that morning to establish a survey station at 20,000 feet on a saddle overlooking the Kama Valley.

For Mallory and Morshead, initially all went well. The night was colder than the last, twenty degrees Fahrenheit according to Wheeler's journal, and the surface of the snow "crisp and solid." Mallory and Morshead walked ahead, along with Sanglu, acting now as sirdar, and one spare porter, Dorji Gompa, who carried no load. The fourteen laden porters came in their wake. There was no need for snowshoes—

which, at any rate, had been left behind; there were not enough pairs to go around.

In less than an hour they reached the icefall that had blocked Mallory and Morshead on their first attempt at the Lhakpa La precisely a month before. Mallory had avoided it in August by scaling the rocks above the lateral moraine. Now, with men weighted down with loads, he was determined to find a way through. He pressed ahead, following a smooth and promising corridor in the ice that ended abruptly in a series of crevasses, dangerous to negotiate in the dim light. "We plunged into the maze and struggled for a little time," he later recalled, "crossing frail bridges over fantastic depths and making steps up steep little walls, until it seemed we were in serious trouble." The men, weighted down with loads, grew fearful, and Mallory's decision to leap across an especially formidable crevasse did not inspire confidence. The party halted on a "sharp little crest between two monstrous chasms" as Morshead and Mallory "discussed the situation." They decided to scout the ground to their left, whereupon they found another corridor leading up and through the final hazards of the icefall.

Dawn broke, and Mallory called a halt, giving the men a chance to rest and "knock a little warmth into chilled toes." The sun revealed a vast expanse of snow reaching toward the skyline of the Lhakpa La, but the conditions above the icefall were very different, and worse than anything Mallory had deemed possible. There was no crust, only deep powder so fine that every step they took was almost immediately obliterated by the wind. Dorji Gompa, the strongest of them all, led the way, plowing into the drifts—exhausting work that did little to relieve the porters coming up behind, each of whom, burdened by a thirty-pound pack, had to find his own way through the snow. The party, as Mallory recalled, "straggled badly." One porter, Kitar, and then two others, Nim Dorji and Angdanel, fell out and refused to go on. Mallory sent Dorji Gompa back to get one of the loads, while he, Morshead, and Sanglu pressed on, taking turns in the lead. Step by step the men made their way toward the saddle, with each porter setting his own pace. At one of the frequent halts Mallory and Morshead looked back and saw at some distance the last porter coming on, and beside his moving figure a dark hump in the snow. This was the dazed and nearly spent body of Dorji Gompa, who had retrieved not one but two of the abandoned loads.

Mallory, with Morshead and Sanglu just behind, finally reached the Lhakpa La at 11:20 a.m. The porters followed, dropping altogether eleven loads in a hollow between great flanks of snow, as sheltered a place as any on the windswept saddle. For the first time Mallory had a completely clear view of the Chang La, the North Col, less than three miles away across the head of the East Rongbuk. All his imagined plans, detailed in letters and discussed in huddled meetings, blew away in an instant. The North Col was itself a far more formidable barrier than he had anticipated, a steep and imposing wall of ice and snow at least 1,000 feet high, broken across its face by enormous bergschrunds, great crevasses formed as the glacial ice falls away from the underlying rock of the mountain. Climbing the slopes of Everest to the south was out of the question. The North Col was the only chance, and as he glassed its every approach, he decided that it could be done, but not as he had envisioned. "It would not be work for untrained men," he later recalled, "and to have on the rope a number of laden coolies, more or less mountain sick, conducted by so small a nucleus as three Sahibs, who would also presumably be feeling the effects of altitude, was a proposition not to be contemplated for a moment."

There would be no further talk of establishing camps high on the Northeast Shoulder—or anywhere else, for that matter, beyond the base of the North Col. The first challenge would be simply to find a route up its daunting face, and for this, Mallory concluded, he would have to assemble "as strong a party as possible." Only later, should their efforts prove successful, could they consider bringing up a camp, and only as a quite separate operation. As Mallory led his tired porters away from the Lhakpa La, back down over the Kharta Glacier and through the treacherous icefall to their highest camp, he knew exactly who should be in the final party. Howard-Bury and Morshead might still be of use on subsequent efforts, and certainly Wollaston, as expedition medical officer, would need to reach at least as high as the Lhakpa La. But "only Wheeler," Mallory wrote, "had sufficient mountaineering experience, and it was decided that he alone should accompany Bullock and myself on our first attempt to reach the col."

Even as Mallory and Morshead retreated from the Lhakpa La, the rest of the expedition moved up the mountain. Bullock and Wheeler, of course, were already at the 20,000-foot camp, and they would return from their survey work just after noon. That same morning, September 20, a Tuesday, Howard-Bury, Raeburn, and Wollaston, leaving Gyalzen Kazi, the Tibetan interpreter, in charge of the supply line back to Kharta, set out from the advanced base shortly after 8:30 a.m. Howard-Bury pushed too hard, reaching the upper camp in four hours; Wollaston and Raeburn struggled in just after 3:00 p.m. All three men were exhausted. "I had a thorough feeling of lassitude all the way," recalled Howard-Bury. "It required, indeed, some effort to walk at all, and a strong effort, both of mind and body, to reach camp." The challenges were the elevation and the heat, the scorching sun on the ice and, with it, the constant danger of dehydration. Frigid nights gave way to blistering days. "The sun at these great heights," he wrote, "is one of the great foes that we contend with. The whole climate is trying and the extremes are so great that your feet can be suffering from frost-bite while you are getting sunstroke at the same time."

Mallory and Morshead returned just after 4:00, with the last of their porters shuffling into camp just before dark. It was a beautiful, clear evening. As the sun fell behind Everest, a ring of clouds surrounding the summit glowed in amber light. The mountain itself was in shadow, save for great streamers of snow that blew off every face "the whole length of its crests," Howard-Bury recalled. The men stood silently "and watched this extraordinary sight for some time, devoutly hoping that the wind would die down. Unfortunately we were soon to experience what a strong wind meant at these heights."

Wheeler woke the following day determined to continue his work, and while the others rested in anticipation of the move to the Lhakpa La and the North Col, he established a station at 20,500 feet on a rounded hill just north of their camp. Howard-Bury spent the morning botanizing and was astonished to discover a dwarf delphinium and a delicate white saxifrage in full flower at such an elevation. That evening Wollaston monitored the physical condition of each man. Raeburn clearly was out and would remain behind at the 20,000-foot camp when the others pressed on. Wheeler's pulse was also worrisome. It had been fluctuating between 86 and 98; now it registered 93, higher than the other climbers' heart rates. "I seem to be pretty high," Wheeler admitted in his journal, "most of the others being about 90 . . . Snow falling at 2:30 p.m."

The following morning, September 22, a Thursday, Wheeler and his three porters were the first away, setting out in twenty degrees of frost at 3:30 a.m. It was his intention to work his way to the Lhakpa La, while establishing photographic survey stations en route. The rest of the expedition—Bullock, Wollaston, Mallory, Morshead, and Howard-Bury—left an hour before dawn, with twenty-six porters, divided into four parties, each properly roped. The snow was stiff, and they moved steadily, with each man breathing as Mallory had instructed: one breath as hard and deep as possible, in and out, for each step taken, with a short pause every few paces. Sunrise found them on the broad flat of the glacier, with the light falling on the summit of Everest, which lay directly ahead of them. Bullock and Morshead led the way, retracing the route Mallory had pioneered through the icefall and continuing up the soft, powdery snow toward the high pass.

Howard-Bury was astonished to see a red-billed chough, a blackbird flying overhead, and, in the snow, the tracks of foxes and hares.

Among the tracks was one that appeared uncannily like that of a bare human foot. The porters knew precisely what it was: the mark of a yeti, Metohkangmi, the "wild man of the snows," a monstrous creature known to descend upon villages to kill men, steal women, and drink the blood of yaks and children. Howard-Bury recognized the track as that of an animal, perhaps a wolf, and considered the yeti story folklore, similar to English beliefs in bogeymen or ghosts. But the mere mention of this quaint encounter in his report to the *Times* would spark wild speculation in London, adding fuel to the legend of the abominable snowman and reports of the reputed existence of a strange tribe of wild mountain men, "tall, muscular and very hairy," descendants of a vanquished race that found sanctuary in the ice caves of the high Himalaya. Howard-Bury would be astonished in time to learn that of all the achievements of the 1921 expedition, this would be, according to the popular press, the discovery that "evoked considerable discussion in scientific circles."

It was most assuredly not the topic of conversation as the men slogged toward the heights of the Lhakpa La. Howard-Bury was the first to reach the saddle at 10:30 a.m., just over six hours after setting out. The sky was clear, but the northwest wind was impossibly fierce. Fine, powdery snow blasted the side of his face as he peered for the first time across the wide expanse of the East Rongbuk toward the North Col. The descent to the head of the glacier alone, he estimated, was a drop of at least 1,200 feet. Then they'd need to traverse perhaps two, maybe three, miles to the base of what seemed to him a "steep and unpromising" wall of ice. He tried to photograph the approach, but his hands froze to the metal of his camera. He wondered where to establish a camp, and whether to push the entire party beyond the Lhakpa La and down onto the glacier before doing so. Looking toward the heights of Everest, he saw great banners of snow spinning from every ridge and spur. The winds and the conditions would only get worse, he realized.

As Howard-Bury turned his back on the mountain, Bullock and Morshead and several of the porters crested the rise. They had to shout to be heard. They had just passed Wheeler, but Mallory and Wollaston were well behind. "I found it hard work and went pretty slowly," confessed Wheeler that night in his journal, though he did reach the top by 11:30 a.m. Mallory, too, had a miserable morning, feeling "excessively and unaccountably tired coming up the col." He arrived to find the rest of his comrades, save Wollaston, who still struggled behind him, "sitting under the rim, the best shelter that could be found, and shuddering in the dry smother of snow blown up by every gust." Mallory resisted the "suggestion of going down to encamp on the other side," concerned about the condition of the men and the challenges of the return. He reported, "I observed no great sparkle of energy or enthusiasm among my companions; Sanglu was practically hors de combat, the coolies more or less exhausted."

It was all they could do to pitch seven alpine tents in a shallow basin in the snow that afforded only slight protection from the battering winds. Each man crawled into his hole. Bullock and Wheeler shared a Meade, as did Howard-Bury and Wollaston. Mallory and Morshead had a Mummery; the porters packed into the four other tents. Howard-Bury later compared it to climbing into a valise, but it was the only way to survive the cold. The very effort of crawling into the funnel of the tents, as if "entering a dog kennel," left the men breathless and exhausted. Though they were bivouacked at close quarters, not a word passed among them. Cooking was out of the question. Within mere minutes, Mallory wrote, "all was still . . . no hand stirred for a thought of comfort; only rest, not sweet but death-like, as though the spirit of the party had died within it. And so it had; we buried it next morning."

Through a long and cheerless afternoon the wind howled and the flaps of the tents, as Morshead recalled, rattled and beat like machine gun fire. Wollaston could not stand being confined. "We are all very stupid and muddle-headed," he wrote. "It's a wonder that we don't bite each other's heads off." Howard-Bury had no physical complaints, but "owned to feeling rather lazy" and had difficulty concentrating. He retained his appetite, but it was not until after sunset, when the temperature plummeted and the wind temporarily lulled, that Wheeler was able to light a spirit stove and heat some consommé, which they all shared, along with biscuits and tins of cold ham. Of all the men, only Mallory slept through the night, having wisely cut two slits in the roof of his tent. The others dozed fitfully or lay awake on the hard snow, unable to breathe freely in the suffocating enclosures and the impossibly thin air of 22,350 feet. By morning, Howard-Bury recalled, their "faces and hands were all a curious blue colour," which Wollaston diagnosed as cyanosis of the blood, caused by oxygen deprivation.

Everything was frozen, but the sky was clear and the winds, which had blown hard all night, once again moderated with the dawn. Wheeler managed to brew a little tea, which remained in a liquid state as long as drunk immediately. Mallory melted sardines. As the sun rose higher, the camp gradually thawed out and, Mallory wrote, "we all became more alive." The porters, however, did not. Of the twenty-nine who had set out from the lower camp the previous day, only eight remained capable. All felt the effects of altitude; several were severely ill. Just to assemble a team of ten, it was necessary to draw lots, with two of the debilitated men being forcibly recruited to carry.

It was clearly both impossible and dangerous for the entire expedition to continue to push on. At what Wheeler described as a "bit of a conference," it was decided that Wollaston, Morshead, and Howard-Bury would retreat. Only Mallory, Bullock, and Wheeler would go on. The decision made, Wheeler set off. The day before, even in the madness of the wind, he had deciphered the topography from the crest of the Lhakpa La. "As soon as I got to the top," he recalled in a letter to Dolly a week later, "I was able to recognize many old friends in that valley and got the geography completely straightened out which I had been very hazy about before."

Now, with Morshead's help, he set up a photographic station at the height of the Lhakpa La that allowed him to connect everything he had done on the East Rongbuk with the survey points of Kharta. It was not easy. The wind by this late hour of the morning had returned. He positioned his camera, and found that even with the snow so soft that one sank in "half way to the knee . . . both theodolite and camera would remain steady with the tripod resting either on ice axes or bags of grain." In this way Wheeler recorded the highest point ever achieved by the Survey of India.

Once the decision had been made to divide the expedition, Howard-Bury, Morshead, and Wollaston struck their tents and made haste to abandon the Lhakpa La, taking with them most of the porters and all of the gear that could be carried. Among the ten porters who remained were all three of Wheeler's men, Ang Pasang, Lagay, and Gorang, who stood silently, stiffly in the snow, watching their friends depart, before turning to the task of packing away the survey instruments, which were to be left behind on the pass. Mallory encouraged a slow start for the climbing party. Everything in the wind and cold took time: sorting out loads, deicing the ropes, caching emergency supplies for their return. They eventually got off around noon (half past eleven by Wheeler's notes), encumbered with light packs holding just the essentials: tents, sleeping bags, blankets, and a minimum of food. Water was a serious problem. Even Wheeler, acknowledged by Howard-Bury as their one expert with the Primus stoves, could not manage to ignite them at such altitude. Melting ice by spirit lamp was adequate for tea, but hardly sufficient for their needs. They set out suffering from thirst, Mallory and Bullock on one rope, Wheeler tied in on another. Mercifully, at the base of a bit of scree, Wheeler found water and was able to fill all of the bottles, "a great help provided it can be kept from freezing."

The drop from the Lhakpa La to the head of the East Rongbuk was longer and the distance across the glacier farther than anticipated. After an excruciatingly slow march, they made camp around 4:00 p.m., a mile from the base of the North Col, which now loomed above them. Their elevation was 21,500 feet. The spot was bleak, isolated, and bitterly cold. The snow stretched endlessly, and the scale of the relief intimidated even Mallory. "It was so flat," he wrote, "and the world was so big . . . the great cliffs on three sides of us were a felt presence." They had hoped at least to find in the shadow of the mountains, the depths of the basin, "tranquil air and the soothing, though chilly calm of undisturbed frost." But this was not to be: "The wind found us out and there was never a more determined and bitter enemy."

They struggled to pitch five tents. Mallory and Bullock shared a Meade. Wheeler was alone in another that also served as their kitchen. The porters huddled in two Mummerys and a Whymper. Wheeler was "chief cook," but all he managed to heat was tea, cocoa, and broth. Ham, biscuits, chocolate, figs, dates, and raisins they had cold. None of them had much appetite. "One does not eat very much," Wheeler noted, "at these heights and in that discomfort."

Night came. Fierce squalls battered their camp, threatening to tear the tents from their moorings. Wheeler lay awake, certain that his tent would collapse. Bullock spent "a rotten night," his feet cold, his body stiff, and his mind incapable of rest. "The atmosphere," noted Mallory, "discouraged sleep," but, in fact, he rested surprisingly well, as he had the night before at the Lhakpa La. The porters, however, did not, and as the sun broke over the glacier at 6:00 a.m. only three were fit for duty: Gorang, Lagay, and Ang Pasang, Wheeler's team.

The cold precluded an early start, and Mallory chose to wait for the sun. Wheeler heated water for tea and thawed several tins of sardines. Bullock wrapped himself in clothes for the climb, "3 prs of drawers and 3 shetland sweaters." Just after 7:00 a.m., the three ethnic Tibetans and three British set out on a single rope. Within thirty minutes they reached the rising slopes at the base of the North Col. In order to conserve the strength of the climbing party, Mallory instructed Ang Pasang and Lagay to take the lead and break trail. They moved across a broad debris field at a rising angle, climbing steadily over firm snow up to the right, or northwest, side of the face, and then turned left for a long traverse toward the crest of the col.

For Mallory, in particular, it was not technically a difficult route. "Nothing very remarkable remains in my mind about the ascent to the North Col," he later wrote, "except perhaps Wheeler's black beard coming up behind me." Aside from a few steps hacked into the ice to overcome the corner of a deep crevasse, it was a "matter of straightforward plugging." Naturally his eyes strayed to the bare face of Everest, over the immense rounded shoulder that rose from the col to the final rocks below the Northeast Ridge. From the first days of the reconnaissance he had recognized this as the only possible line of attack. Now that it was within his sight, he saw that not only was it viable, it looked easy—at least as far as the Northeast Ridge. The sheer scale of the mountain distorted perspective; the summit seemed near, within striking distance, and in truth it was close, little more than two miles away and 6,000 feet above. "If ever we had doubted whether the arête [Northeast Ridge] was accessible," he later wrote, "it was impossible to doubt any longer. For a long way up those easy rock and snow slopes was [*sic*] neither dangerous nor difficult."

Exhilarated by the prospect, and feeling supremely fit, Mallory moved into the lead to attack the only serious hazard they would face on the route up to the col, a passage of steep and soft snow just below the rim, "deep enough to be disagreeable." It was, as Wheeler recalled, "very hard work indeed," five hundred exhausting steps that lifted them at last to heights they had sought for so long. Their elevation was just over 23,000 feet. Mallory estimated the time to be shortly before 11:30 a.m., implying a climb of just over four hours. Wheeler wrote that they arrived at 10:00, "only 2½ hours from camp." Both could be forgiven for a lapse in judgment and precision, for what greeted them on the col shattered their senses.

A first sign appeared even below the rim: each man began to glow with a frigid halo, an "aureole of spindrift" and whirling snow. Then, as soon as they crested the height, a wind like nothing they had ever known plunged them into a maelstrom as mad and disorienting as anything Wheeler had experienced in France in all the noise, chaos, and shell blast of battle. At first, he confessed to his wife, he was "scared stiff," certain that they would all die, suffocated by swirling eddies of snow. Scarcely able to stand, he focused on his breathing, drew his hands around his face, and, with a discipline long ago honed in terror, slowed down the world until a new rhythm could be found, inhaling during the lulls between the blasts of the gale.

Bullock and Mallory fared no better. As they approached the crest, Mallory became aware of the presence of the devil, "dancing in a sudden tourbillon of snow which took away my breath." He turned his head away, reflexively, inclining it at an angle to the wind that allowed him to regain his center and discipline. He looked to the men—Gorang still strong, Ang Pasang and Lagay exhausted, huddled in the snow— waiting for orders. At once they disappeared behind a veil of spindrift. "A sudden gust of violent wind," Mallory later wrote, "made a minia- ture cyclone of blown snow which caught us in its vortex just below the crest." What saved them was the physical structure of the col, a double shelf with a higher band of ice and snow traversing its length and offer- ing at least some protection from the wind, which pounded from the west. They had yet to feel the complete force of the storm. Mallory drew the party together and, in a sheer act of will, moved them into the lee, where, he recalled, "we halted before exposing ourselves to the full blast, under the shelter of an ice wall."

The men took the measure of each other. Mallory was sound and felt good for another 2,000 feet of elevation, far higher than anyone had ever climbed. His reserves of strength astonished Wheeler. "Mal- lory was in the best shape of all of us," he wrote that night, "apparently perfectly fit. Bullock about cooked. I was fairly fit except for my feet. No bleeding from the nose or heart doing funny things." Wheeler had, in fact, lost all feeling in both legs and could not possibly con- tinue. Willpower and grit could propel Bullock higher, but as Mallory recognized, his old schoolmate, "though admirably game, had clearly no reserve of strength." Bullock himself confessed in his journal, "I was prepared to follow Mallory if he wished to try and make some height, but was glad when he decided not to."

In the end the issue was decided by the wind. As the men rested, Wheeler gnawing on a frozen fig, drinking the last of his water, Mal- lory focused on the mountain soaring above them. He strained his eyes to find a single impediment on the great shoulder that rose from the col to the Northeast Ridge. "We looked up at the flat edge ascending at no very steep angle," he later wrote to Sir Francis Younghusband, the old explorer who'd first sparked the British dream of Everest, "easy rocks and snow all the way to the north-east crest. All we had seen before to build hopes on was confirmed now by the nearer view. No obstacle appeared, none so formidable that a competent party would not easily surmount or go around it."

Transfixed by the mountain, Mallory appeared to Wheeler oblivi- ous to the fierce gusts that still swept over them, despite the modest protection of the wall. Ice formed in his hair and frosted his eyelashes. His eyes seemed as if settled in another realm. In truth, Mallory was tempted to go on, even alone. But as he studied the slope, his hopes sank. "It was impossible," he reported to Younghusband, "to look long without a shudder. From top to bottom this ridge was exposed to the full fury of a gale from the northwest." Violent blasts of wind-whipped snow shot across every slope. "The powdery fresh snow on the great face of Everest was being swept along in unbroken spindrift," he wrote, "and the very ridge where our route lay was marked out to receive its unmitigated fury. We could see the blown snow deflected upwards for a moment where the wind met the ridge, only to rush violently down in a frightful blizzard on the leeward side."

Their lines of communication back to base were also tenuous in the extreme, reaching from this desperate position on the col at 23,000 feet back down across the East Rongbuk Glacier and then over the 22,200-foot Lhakpa La to the camps of the Kharta Valley. The men were too weak for heroics. What good could come from achieving another 2,000 feet, even were it possible? A height record for Hinks and the Everest Committee, imperial glory for Younghusband and the British press; nothing could motivate Mallory less. It was folly to continue. Still he hesitated, and gathered Wheeler and Bullock to his side. By all accounts not a word passed between them. Then Mallory decided to challenge the wind. Leaving the porters, the three British sahibs went on, stumbling more than walking, making their way up the col to the upper ledge "to put the matter to a test." They continued for perhaps two hundred yards, and "for a few moments exposed ourselves on the col to the full blast, and then straggled back to shelter. Nothing more was said about pushing our assault any further." No man, Mallory ventured, could have survived such exposure for more than an hour. "No one," Wheeler wrote very simply, "could have existed on that ridge."

With disappointment and relief, but not a shadow of doubt in their mind, the first climbers ever to set foot on Mount Everest turned their back on the wind and began a long and agonized retreat. As they dropped over the lip of the col, they struggled to make their way down the steepest pitch. The steps cut into the snow with such effort were gone, obliterated by an avalanche. In the wind they had not even heard the ice break off from the mountain. Mallory took note of the instability of the snow and recognized that the face of the North Col would be ever changing. As the route to the summit, it would present different challenges every year, every season, and always would be dangerous. That it would within months sweep away seven of his men to their death, and leave even the British wondering about the true power and mystic endowment of the mountain, remained beyond the moment.

He had five men to get back to camp. Wheeler had no circulation below his knees, and stumbled as if walking on stumps. When they finally reached the base of the col, Bullock told the others to go ahead. They did, reaching their flimsy tents just after 1:00 p.m. It was nearly two hours before Bullock turned up. Disoriented by fatigue, dehydrated by the sun, he had only with great difficulty found his way to the camp. Mallory's attention was on Wheeler, whose feet were raw, "very nearly gone with frostbite." For more than an hour, Mallory stayed by Wheeler's side, rubbing his legs with whale oil, bringing them back around. In his journal Wheeler credits Mallory with saving his feet and, indeed, his life. Through a long, cold night, Mallory stayed by the invalid, while Bullock, unable to sleep, sat to one side, at last able to "smoke a pipe with pleasure."

HOWARD-BURY, WOLLASTON, and Morshead had without incident returned from the Lhakpa La to the 20,000-foot camp on the afternoon of Friday, September 23. The drop of just over 2,000 feet of elevation made for a different world, as did the luxuries of expedition life: proper mess tents and camp beds, decent food and plenty of it. All had slept soundly, save Howard-Bury, who was awakened by one of the Tibetan porters chanting prayers in the middle of the night. In the morning, there was some tension in camp as they waited the outcome of the climb. Wollaston, as expedition doctor, had from the start had great misgivings about the drive to the North Col. Raeburn, who had remained behind and not accompanied the others to the Lhakpa La, still indulged delusions that he had a role to play. The normally unflappable Morshead had been grieved by a number of frantic and petulant letters from Hinks at the RGS, suggesting that he focus less on climbing and more on his survey work: the Everest Committee was desperate for a map. Howard-Bury simply worried about the men. He glassed the mountain throughout the day, and could see how the wind mounted, growing much stronger by the hour, blowing huge clouds of snow off the slopes and all the adjacent ridges. The Lhakpa La disappeared in great wisps of white, and he could only speculate about the conditions on the North Col.

The following day was warm and bright, and the men ate all their meals outside at a table in front of their tents. Howard-Bury set off for a rise west of their camp, where he had "superb views of Everest and Makalu with their appalling cliffs and beautifully fluted snow slopes." But the wind clearly remained desperate on the upper slopes, and "every ridge of Everest was smothered with clouds of blown snow."

Only later would he realize that they were experiencing weather typical of the season. As the monsoon fades, gale-force winds pound the Himalaya from the northwest, striking especially violently at elevations above 23,000 feet, obliterating every major summit in a whirlwind of ice and spindrift snow. In climbing the North Col in the last week of September, the British, in effect, had walked directly into the face of a hurricane.

After a pleasant glissade back to camp, Howard-Bury basked in the sun, enjoying a cup of tea, still glassing the upper slopes of the Lhakpa La. Suddenly black specks appeared on the skyline and began to make their way steadily down the glacier. Wollaston counted and was relieved to discern thirteen figures spread out in the snow. He and Howard-Bury tracked their progress throughout the early afternoon, eager to learn of their fate.

The return trek for Mallory, Bullock, and Wheeler had not been easy. After a second bitter night of wind and cold camped on the glacier, with Wheeler in considerable pain, Mallory buried any lingering thought of returning for another go at the North Col. No one, save perhaps he, was fit. Several of the porters struggled to walk. Wheeler's condition was uncertain. That Mallory waited until dawn on September 25 to make the final decision was perhaps a measure of a growing obsession that in time would dominate his life and mark his death. In the moment, it was all he could do simply to assemble the men and strike the camp. They got away, according to Wheeler, at 8:15 a.m., with Mallory in the lead. With high winds evident on all the heights, he headed for a rock ridge just south of the Lhakpa La, where the porters might find better footing. Slowly they climbed toward the pass, step by step, each man buffeted by violent gusts that only grew in intensity the higher they reached. Dorji Gompa fell behind, forcing Bullock and Gorang, in their exhaustion, to retrace their steps to rescue the man. Wheeler and Mallory went ahead, leading the porters on two ropes.

When finally they reached the summit, nearly five hours after setting out, they encountered a whirlwind of snow so intense it caused them to stop in their tracks and gasp for air, uncertain whether to go forward or back, stiff with fear. Several of the men were on the verge of collapse. Mallory urged them into the shelter of the basin on the site of their old camp. As they shivered with their backs to the wind, he pointed to a cache of supplies, loads left behind by the other party. "Suddenly," he later wrote, "with one will we dragged them to the edge, hurled them down the slope, and stood there laughing like children as we watched them roll and roll, 600 or 700 feet down." It was an inspired gesture that gave courage to the men, even as it signaled the end of the expedition.

All tracks down the slopes from the Lhakpa La had been buried in drifts. The snow was deep, the descent from the saddle long, and a final rise of 300 feet from the glacier to the British camp excruciating. Wheeler got in "about 4 p.m. very tired but very pleased with life." Bullock turned up just before sunset. Mallory arrived shortly after. "I enjoyed the jaunt," Wheeler wrote to Dolly later in the evening, "but were I going again I would make proper provision for my feet." Bullock reflected in his journal on the warm camaraderie in the camp. "We spent a pleasant evening, being the last before the expedition finally broke up." And Mallory to Ruth: "I doubt if any big mountain venture has ever been made with a smaller margin of strength. I carried the whole party on my shoulders to the end."

AFTER SUCH EXERTIONS one might have expected the party to rest and regroup at the 20,000-foot camp before returning to Kharta and making plans for the long march back across Tibet to India. Instead, the men simply dispersed like players at the end of a long match. The following day, Monday, September 26, Wheeler, Wollaston, and Howard-Bury slipped away, crossing the divide to the south by way of the Karpo La to descend into the Kama Valley. Wheeler had yet to go there; damaged feet and all, he nevertheless persevered in his duty, establishing survey stations at the height of the Karpo La and on the Shao La and at points in between. For Howard-Bury something radiant and powerful drew him back to the valley, and though Mallory had doubted it could be done, he climbed to the summit ridge between Makalu and Everest, reaching 22,000 feet, helping to establish firmly his own credentials as a mountaineer in the process. Wollaston went for the plants, of course. He, in particular, had been delighted to abandon the heights. "The air in Tibet is fine and exhilarating," he later wrote, "but it is not my country and I don't want much of it."

Bullock remained at the high camp for a day, even as the last of the porters straggled down from the Lhakpa La and twenty-one additional men required to evacuate equipment and supplies arrived exhausted from Kharta, having slept under a rock ledge in the wind and sleet the night before. On the morning of September 26 Mallory and Morshead bolted for Kharta, where Bullock and Raeburn caught up with them, arriving just in time for lunch on September 28.

Bullock had long planned to travel back across Tibet with Mallory, taking the shortest and quickest route, south from Kampa Dzong across the Serpo La to the Teesta Valley and down to Gangtok and Darjeeling. But even he was surprised by Mallory's plan to leave on the morning of September 30. Bullock had but a day to bid farewell to the *dzongpen*, pick up a few souvenirs (a silver prayer wheel, an old sword, and a Buddhist painting), and pack his kit for the three-week journey. It was, as Mallory scribbled in a hasty note to Ruth on September 29, "now homeward with all speed."

Howard-Bury returned from the Kama Valley late in the afternoon of September 30 and was appalled to learn that Mallory and Bullock had left only hours before, after an early lunch, without so much as a proper farewell. He had charged them with the duty of evacuating all stores from the high camps of the Kharta Valley, a task they had evidently abandoned to Gyalzen Kazi and Chheten Wangdi. As expedition leader, he was in a less than charitable mood when he wrote to Arthur Hinks at the RGS on October 2, "Mallory and Bullock have been perfectly useless to me. They have never attempted to help in anything and now they are in such a great hurry to get back to civilization that they have rushed on ahead. They both dislike Tibet and the little discomforts incidental to travel." In a second letter that same day, he shared these sentiments with Francis Younghusband as well.

Mallory could not have cared less. He had been away from his family for five months. His daughters, Clare and Beridge, were six and four, both born during the war, when he had been at the front for many months. While in Tibet he had missed his son John's first birthday, as well as those of both girls, just three days apart in September. He had indeed carried the climbing party on his shoulders, and had done everything in his power to achieve success. In a manner that only time and history would reveal, he had attached his destiny to the mountain. But as he left Kharta on the last day of September, his only thought was of home.

THE REMAINING MEMBERS of the expedition went their separate ways as they wrapped up their work or satisfied a last-minute urge to see new country. To Wollaston's horror, the less than robust Raeburn set off on October 1 for a four-day jaunt in the Kama Valley. Morshead left Kharta on the following day, heading up the Phung Chu with Gujjar Singh to complete survey work north of Tingri on the southern flanks of the Brahmaputra. Heron, too, had gaps to fill in his geological survey. Both he and Morshead would catch up with the returning expedition at Shiling, on the Tibetan Plateau, four days short of Kampa Dzong.

On October 5, the day after the return of Raeburn, the main party, under Howard-Bury's command, left Kharta, altogether four sahibs and 150 porters. At Kampa Dzong, Wheeler, Heron, and Raeburn would head south, following Mallory and Bullock over the Serpo La to Sikkim. Howard-Bury and Wollaston, with the bulk of the stores, would continue east to Phari, returning to Darjeeling by way of the Chumbi Valley and Yatung, the British trading depot where, little more than a year before, on August 14, 1920, Howard-Bury had met with Charles Bell and sought initial support for an exploratory reconnaissance of Everest. As he passed through Yatung on the return journey, the entire detachment of the 90th Punjabis turned out in full dress to present arms and salute his achievement.

One by one the members of the 1921 reconnaissance found their way out of Tibet and home via India. Bullock met his wife, Alice, on October 8 at Lachen, the mission post in the upper Teesta Valley where the nuns had nursed Raeburn back from near death. Morshead arrived in Darjeeling on October 16 to find a young son with no memory of his father and a wife, Evie, pregnant with a second child. Wheeler was reunited with his wife, Dolly, on October 19 and spent a night with her at Pashok, in a *dak* bungalow eighteen miles outside Darjeeling, before heading into town the next morning. Raeburn and Heron drifted in that same day. Howard-Bury and Wollaston were the last to arrive, not reaching Darjeeling until October 25, twenty days after having set out from Kharta.

By then Mallory was long gone. He wrote to Ruth on October 20 from Benares, the midpoint of the rail journey from Darjeeling to Bombay, confirming that his ship, SS *Malwa*, would sail on October 29, expected to dock at Marseille on November 12. He spoke of small things—sightseeing along the Ganges, shopping for silks, the petty ailments he suffered: chills and swollen glands, a sore throat, rheumatic legs, stiff and painful. He said nothing of Everest, though he knew there was already talk of another expedition to the mountain. In the four days he had lingered at Darjeeling, "a very gay time," as he recalled, he had been feted at garden parties and singled out at a formal dress ball. Howard-Bury's reports to the *Times*, fifteen altogether, orchestrated in London by John Buchan, had been brilliantly effective. Sent from exotic Tibet by courier and telegraph, arriving intermittently, which only increased the suspense, they fired the British imagination as surely as a serial novel by Dickens. The fact that the *Times* had a window of exclusivity on each story only drove the rest of the press, in both Britain and India, to embellish and invent, which merely elevated the adventure in the public mind.

Arthur Hinks, secretary of the Royal Geographical Society, the Svengali of Everest, privately railed against the survey team, pestering Wheeler and Morshead to deliver maps. "We have nothing to go upon," he fumed to Morshead on October 12, "but rather vague accounts in telegrams and equally unsystematic titles penciled on the backs of photographs, and at present we cannot unravel the confused geography of the east Rongbuk Glacier and the head of the Kharta Valley and the several cols of the north ridge and its extension and the north east arête."

Morshead responded, "I fear you have perhaps scarcely grasped the difficulties under which we were all labouring at the time, owing to the appalling weather conditions . . . In August last we ourselves on the spot had by no means completely unraveled the geography of the East Rongbuk and Kharta Valleys, and we could scarcely send you information which we did not ourselves possess."

This did not stop Hinks, who replied five days later: "We are beginning to despair about the map from you."

Publicly the story was very different. The expedition and the surveyors, in particular, were hailed for what was in fact a remarkable achievement. Twelve thousand square miles of unexplored territory had been mapped on a quarter-inch scale, and an additional four thousand square miles of land previously surveyed had been revised with far greater accuracy. Wheeler and his photographic technique had documented the six hundred square miles of the immediate vicinity of Everest, the heart of the mountain, on a one-inch scale. This alone represented a considerable technical breakthrough. The cost to the Survey of India was measured with bureaucratic precision: 3.9 rupees a square mile—a bargain for the Raj that even Hinks, notoriously parsimonious, appreciated.

Even before the expedition sailed from Bombay, a preliminary six-color map was sent to the Everest Committee. By the end of November, Wheeler, still in Darjeeling, completed a rough half-inch-scale map of the Everest core. Over the winter months, stationed at Dehra Dun, he worked furiously to prepare a final map at a one-inch scale. When the three map sheets arrived in London, along with all numerical results, coordinates, and azimuths, it was noted that his intersected points were accurate within one to two seconds of latitude and longitude and within 50 feet of height. Given the conditions on the mountain, Wheeler's acuity was astonishing. His map would be the basis for all future endeavors. Wollaston, thinking of Hinks and other armchair members of the Everest Committee, deliberately wrote in his public report to the RGS, "Only you who have been at those great altitudes can realize the immense labour involved in this effort."

Of all the many achievements of the expedition—the discovery of new species of plants and insects, the far-reaching implications of Heron's geological survey, the extension of the British presence along the entire northern flank of the Himalaya—there was one revelation that Mallory could not get out of his mind as he made his way home across the great Gangetic plains of India. Rather naively, with perhaps the European climbing season in mind, the expedition had set off for Everest in May, reaching the mountain in mid-June, the height of the monsoon. This was the worst possible season in which to attack the mountain, with the possible exception of late September, when the hurricane winds blow. They had confronted both, and it was remarkable that they had all, save Kellas, come back alive. As Morshead wrote to Jack Hazard, his second-in-command at the Somme and a fine climber who had been kept from the 1921 expedition because of war wounds that would never completely heal, "It looks like May and June are the months for a successful climb and I doubt there'll be time to organize an expedition for May '22."

As Mallory half feared, this was precisely what the Everest Committee had in mind. Younghusband was keen to ride the wave of public interest, which he thought might wane should the next expedition be put off until 1923. Hinks was concerned that the opening to Tibet made possible by Charles Bell might close. Bell was still in Lhasa in the midst of secret negotiations, as he had been for the entire duration of the expedition. Though supported by His Holiness the Thirteenth Dalai Lama, he was bitterly opposed by a conservative faction of monks. Posters in the Tibetan capital called for his assassination.

Bell had been willing to help once, but he was not about to compromise British interests or his own position and security for a mountaineering expedition. Complaints about the behavior of the climbers infuriated him. On October 13, rather late in the game, he ordered Howard-Bury, then a fortnight out of Kharta, to stop the killing of wildlife. Morshead's general survey work presented enormous diplomatic challenges. Long before the Everest expedition set out from Darjeeling, Bell had issued specific instructions through the Foreign Office to the Survey of India that Morshead, in particular, do no survey work "off the beaten track and away from the vicinity of Everest to avoid arousing Tibetan suspicions." On March 29, 1921, the head of the Survey of India, Colonel Charles Ryder, cognizant of Bell's demands, wrote Younghusband, urging him to keep any reference to geographical exploration out of the press. Hinks and the RGS did quite the opposite, prompting a wry note from F. M. Bailey, which reached Younghusband a fortnight after the climbers returned to England: "Bell not exactly sympathetic. He thought it was pretty cool to get permission to climb a mountain and then go make a map."

The geologist Heron had also seriously offended Tibetan sensibilities. On September 28, four days after the assault on the North Col, Charles Bell received a telegram from the Tibetan prime minister relaying a complaint from the authorities at Shegar. The constant movements of the British, it was claimed, had disturbed the monks and hermits at Rongbuk. There was evidence as well, the telegram suggested, that the climbers had dug from the ground and carried away precious stones, turquoises from the sacred valley of Rongshar and rubies from Shegar Dzong. "It was agreed that Mount Everest might be explored," the prime minister wrote, "but if this is used as an excuse for digging earth and stones from the most sacred hills of Tibet, inhabited by fierce demons, the very guardians of the soil, fatal epidemics may break out amongst men and cattle. Kindly prevent officials wandering about and effect their early return."

Bell knew that no precious stones or metals had been found, let alone stolen, by the British, but given his knowledge of Tibetan culture and his awareness of diplomatic sensitivities, he could not have been pleased by Heron's explanation, especially in the wake of a scarlet fever epidemic that did indeed sweep Tibet in the last months of 1921. "I have to plead," Heron wrote, " 'Not Guilty' to the charge of being a Disturber of Demons. I did no mining and the gentle hammer tapping which I indulged in was, I am sure, insufficient to alarm the most timid of the fraternity. Perhaps it was Wheeler through his cairn-building propensity! However this time I shall exorcise them by the pious refrain of 'kiki so so lha so lha' to a hammer accompaniment."

It was precisely such an attitude that enraged Bell, and ensured that no geologist, most especially Heron, would ever accompany a future Everest expedition. Nor, given Tibetan concerns, would any subsequent expedition include officers of the Survey of India. A naturalist might go, but only on the condition that not an animal, bird, or butterfly would be harmed.

Hinks and the Everest Committee, acutely aware of Bell's influence both in Lhasa and in Calcutta, and within the Foreign Office in London, pressed ahead. On November 3, even as Mallory's ship was crossing the Indian Ocean, Hinks wrote to Wollaston of the "urgent need to carry on in case situation in Tibet changes." That same day he sent a letter to Mallory, sharing the news that there would indeed be a second expedition in 1922. Dates had been determined. In order to leave Darjeeling for the mountain on March 21, the climbing party would sail from England on March 1, in little more than three months' time. Passages had already been secured. It would be a strictly mountaineering affair, all climbers, making a direct line for the East Rongbuk and the North Col, everything geared to reaching the summit. Hinks hoped not only that Mallory would return as a member of the climbing party but also that he would spend much of January and February of the coming year touring the country, lecturing and raising funds for the expedition. "We could not wait until 1923," added Younghusband in a letter on November 9. "The public interest in the Expedition is now so extraordinarily keen we could not allow it to cool. So we are very much hoping you will be able to go out again next year."

Mallory's formal response was noncommittal. "I shall pay you a visit so soon as I get home," he wrote Hinks on November 10. "But when will that be? My wife is to be amused first for a little time, as she so richly deserves, in the South of France. Entre nous, I'm tired of seeing sights, sick to death of traveling and travelers, of remote places, of trains and ships, of garish sun and foreign ports, and of dark skinned faces. The sights I want to see are my own little home, and after that, the solemn in Pall Mall, the stately beauty of St. James's Square or perhaps Bloomsbury in a fog."

Privately, he was appalled. As SS *Malva* approached Marseille, where he knew Ruth to be waiting, he wrote a desperate note to his sister Avie. "They can't possibly organize another show so soon, particularly as I've also said that it's barely worth trying again, and anyway not without eight first rate climbers. They can't get eight, certainly not soon, perhaps not even the year after. Hinks already wants to know whether I'll go again. When they press for an answer, I shall tell them they can get the other seven first. How they'll pore over the AC list and write round for opinions about the various candidates. I wouldn't go again next year, as the saying is, for all the gold in Arabia."

The following day, November 11, was the third anniversary of the Armistice, which had ended the war. Throughout the British Empire men and women stood still in silence at the eleventh hour. The simple ritual of remembrance, honored by captain, crew, and passengers on board the *Malva*, provoked in Mallory an even stronger longing for home, family, and friends. "Never mind Everest and its unfriendly glories," he wrote to his old Cambridge mate David Pye, stealing some of his own lines from an earlier letter to Hinks. "I'm tired of traveling and travelers, far countries and uncouth people, trains and ships and shimmering mausoleums, foreign ports, dark-skinned faces, and a garish sun. What I want to see is faces I know, and perhaps Bloomsbury in a fog; and then an English river, cattle grazing in western meadows."

He felt grateful simply to be alive. The regrets that had haunted him after the retreat from Everest had been swept aside by time and reflection. In a letter to his friend and mentor Geoffrey Young, Mallory surrendered to God, thankful that the conditions on the North Col had been so severe as to present no possible "temptation to go on. We came back without accident; it seems now a question not as to what might have happened higher but what would have happened with unfailing certainty; it was a pitiful party at the last, not fit to be on a mountainside anywhere."

But as he recalled, that day, how close they had come to death, Mallory could not help but wonder who his companions might be should he accept Hinks's offer and return to Everest in 1922. Bullock was obliged to resume his diplomatic post at Le Havre. Wheeler, with eighteen months of accrued leave, was going home to Canada for the first time since the outbreak of the war. Raeburn, for obvious reasons, would not be back, or Heron. Wollaston had no love for Tibet and was not a climber. Morshead was game, certainly a possibility, provided he abandon all survey work and pass muster with Bell and the indecipherable Tibetan authorities.

Howard-Bury had been away from Ireland and his family lands for nearly two years and, as Mallory knew, yearned to return. He had written to Hinks from Kharta on October 2, at the end of the 1921 effort, indicating that he would not be back for a second year, what for him would have been a third season in the Himalaya. Howard-Bury reiterated his position in a letter of November 6, dispatched from Delhi: "Next year I am anxious to stop at home, as I want to see the Irish question settled and there will be developments of all kinds."

Mallory knew that Hinks, under pressure from Younghusband, had as early as February 1921 already promised the leadership of any future expedition to Charles Bruce. At the time, Howard-Bury had graciously supported the decision, saying, "I hope Bruce will be given the leadership of the expedition in 1922; it's only right and his due that he should have it when the really serious attempt is made to climb

Everest." But this endorsement came long before their experiences on the mountain, before the death of Kellas and the collapse of Raeburn. Both Howard-Bury and Mallory had great respect for the general, but his selection did not inspire confidence or suggest that the members of the Everest Committee had learned anything from the 1921 expedition. In a veiled reference to Bruce, who would be fifty-six in 1922, Howard-Bury argued that "a medical examination of anyone taking part in the next expedition should be insisted upon and anyone over fifty should be ruled out." Hinks informed Howard-Bury on November 3 that the general had indeed been seen by the Harley Street physicians Larkins and Anderson, who had passed him as fit, scars and bullet wounds being of no importance, nor apparently a blood pressure of 210/110. As if to add deliberate insult, Hinks publicly announced the appointment of General Bruce before Howard-Bury sailed from India, leaving the press to speculate that he had been relieved of duty for some perceived failure.

In truth, Hinks, who harbored his own doubts about the general's health, had urged Howard-Bury, in a letter of July 14, 1921, to accompany Bruce as his chief of staff. It was with some bitterness that Howard-Bury, who had done so much to make these expeditions possible and who, more than any other member of the expedition, had sensed and been moved by the mystic endowment of Tibet, wrote Hinks a final letter on the subject of Everest, noting, "I am glad the ordeal is over and that I can now sink back once more into quiet and obscurity." His contribution, in fact, would never be forgotten. More than thirty years later, when Edmund Hillary and Tenzing Norgay reached the summit for the first time, safely to return, the news was withheld from the British press for twenty-four hours so as not to compete with the coronation of Queen Elizabeth II. Only two people in all Britain were told in advance, the Queen Mother and Lieutenant Colonel Charles Kenneth Howard-Bury.

As Howard-Bury exited the scene in the winter of 1921, Mallory moved to center stage. He knew that the same physicians who had approved General Bruce had only months before rejected as unfit George Finch, who had gone on to set climbing records that summer in the Alps while they had been on Everest. Finch would have to be included. Mallory would insist. He was the best ice climber in Britain. Other names came to mind, men who had also been considered for 1921. John Noel, if he could secure leave from his regiment. It would be a fitting tribute to old Kellas, Noel's close friend and mentor. Geoffrey Young always spoke highly of Arthur Wakefield, who had declined an invitation in 1921. His age was a concern, but he could double as both physician and a climber. Perhaps he might be induced to come over from the backwoods of Canada, where he had fled after the war. Tom Longstaff would have been with them had he not already been committed to an expedition in Spitsbergen. At forty-seven, he was too old, but he might serve in 1922 as medical officer. Howard Somervell was a better candidate: another doctor, immensely strong by reputation, just thirty-two. To this list other names would be added as possible candidates: Teddy Norton, taught as a child to climb in the Alps by his grandfather Sir Alfred Wills, one of the founding members of the Alpine Club; Bill Strutt, a veteran guide and much decorated soldier; Noel Odell, another strong climber and, like Strutt and John Noel, fully recovered from wounds suffered in the war.

On November 12, the day his ship docked at Marseille, Mallory wrote Hinks a noncommittal letter, deferring his decision about whether to join the 1922 expedition until they had a chance to meet in London. But in this same correspondence—written, presumably, with his beloved wife, Ruth, at his side, the couple reunited after his absence of five months—he took the time to critique at some length the equipment of the expedition. He preferred the Meade tents to the Mummerys, easier to get in and out of. The sleeping sacks were fine, the sun goggles excellent, the Gletscher Crème face grease and whale oil very useful. The rucksacks were terrible, much too small, "artless square bags made of unsuitable material." The Primus stoves failed above 20,000 feet. Crampons too long, snowshoes invaluable, skis never used. Having sent off his report, he and Ruth went walking in the warm Mediterranean sun. Four days later, he would write Hinks again, from the Pont du Gard. "I don't know precisely what I may have said in my haste from Marseilles; but please don't tell the committee if the question arises that I don't intend to go . . . That's not my thought. I shall have to feel that with so many chances against us, we have some in our favour."

As he committed himself to return to Everest, he added a note of caution that proved prophetic. "We must remember," he wrote, "that the highest of mountains is capable of severity, a severity so awful and so fatal that the wiser sort of men do well to think and tremble even on the threshold of their high endeavor."

CHAPTER 10

The Summit of Their Desires

THE FIRST YEARS OF PEACE found John Morris in remote India, living a hundred miles north of Lucknow, close to the Nepali frontier, trying, as he wrote, "without much success, to mould my disorganized life into some sort of pattern." As a British officer in a Gurkha regiment, he could well have lived as a sahib, in imperial comfort and luxury. He chose instead to dwell in a tent, near the ruins of a British compound that smelled like a tomb, the gardens overgrown, the billiard table sickly with yellow mold, the plaster on the walls etched in cracks and decrepitude. His Indian servant, humiliated by the living conditions, resigned, unwilling to wait on an Englishman unprepared to accept his inherent superiority. Morris then took on a Gurkha lad, quite untrained but very beautiful, with an "easy almost animal way of moving. Subconsciously I suppose," he admitted, "I wanted to sleep with him."

This simple life, with its gentle conflicts, so far removed from the war, left Morris suspended between the past and a forgotten future. He remained the most unlikely of soldiers. Of strategy he knew little, of close combat a great deal. He was almost blind, utterly dependent on his eyeglasses, but in the trenches he had never failed to kill. Though a career officer, he had no military ambitions of any kind, noting, "The years of war had bred in me a distaste for the close company of my fellow men. I felt an urgent need to get away."

His obsession was Tibet; he had studied the language, read every available book and military report, and sought through his contacts information about the many routes to its interior. As closely as possible, given his isolation, he had followed the exploits of the 1921 reconnaissance, and for some months had been in correspondence with General Bruce. The general wanted Morris as part of the team, but leave for an officer on active duty was problematic. Bruce went to the highest military authorities in the Raj. When, finally, a telegram arrived from

Delhi requesting his release so that he could join the 1922 expedition, his commanding officer relented only on the condition that the months away on Everest count as home leave. Though this implied that Morris might have to wait another three to four years before returning to England and seeing his parents, he seized the opportunity. He had not been home since the end of 1915, and he had no overwhelming interest in going.

Unlike so many of his peers, Morris had not succumbed to the war fever that swept London in the summer of 1914. The dour and wooden face of Lord Kitchener, peering down and pointing from every recruiting poster, reminded him of a fanatical Old Testament prophet who had "grown a moustache and put on fancy dress." Morris felt no urge to answer the summons to serve his country. He worked at the time as a bank clerk. It was boredom that led him to enlist, and a class structure impossible to defy that elevated him—against all military reason, as he saw it—to an officer's rank in the 5th Leicestershire Regiment. Just before going out to France, he tried to lose his virginity to a Nottingham prostitute but froze at the last moment and bolted, fully dressed, from her room. The following morning he went to a doctor, certain that he had contracted some horrible disease, despite having not shed his trousers. He was only nineteen. He loved to paint, and his passion was music, the "delicate tapestry of sounds" of Debussy and the genius of Rachmaninoff, whom he saw perform at the pianist's London debut.

Morris arrived at the front in the terrible spring of 1915. His first recollection was of getting lost in the trench system and approaching a signaler standing alone in a side bay. The man wore headphones. He was dead, though there was not a wound on his body. Morris recoiled in terror, but then, to his shame, began to laugh, a reaction he would soon consider to be normal.

Months later he was ordered to lead a night raid on a German position. For several days he scouted the ground, crawling out of the trench after dark and inching his way through mud and tall grass soiled with the dead of 1914, the French and Belgians in tatters of red and blue cloth, the Germans in field gray, the British in decaying uniforms of khaki. On the night of the attack, twenty of his men would die and twenty others be wounded, though the raid accomplished nothing. The survivors returned with no useful information and not a single prisoner. The platoon to his right "managed to bring back a German helmet which had presumably belonged to a soldier who had been blown to pieces. It was half filled with glutinous blood and brains."

The very next day Morris was offered leave to return home for a week. As he headed for Calais, a freight train farther up the line broke its couplings and came crashing down on his troop transport, derailing the engine, which exploded in flames that swept over carriages crammed with soldiers. His car, by chance, was in the rear, and he suffered only minor injuries. For those up front, escape was impossible. He later recalled, "The screams of those trapped in the burning wreckage horrified me in a way that trench warfare never did. There was something obscene about this drawn out agony, so unlike the quick death of battle."

He reached London that night, just in time to join his mother at the theater, the Alhambra, for a performance by George Robey in the popular musical *The Bing Boys*. But his thoughts remained concentrated on the burning train, and "half way through . . . I could stand it no longer and we left." Like so many soldiers home from the front, Morris found it exceedingly difficult to be with his parents. "There seemed to be nothing to talk about," he explained. "I had entered into a world where they could not follow. I longed for my leave to end." On his last day in London he was accosted on Regent Street by a major of the provost marshal's department, a man who would never see the war, and severely reprimanded for wearing turned-up cuffs on his pant legs, a breach of regulations that had been invented in the months he had been at the front.

He rejoined his battalion in Marseille, destined for Egypt—an unexpected reprieve, he wrote, from the "sinister life in the trenches." But at the last moment, with half the men having embarked, those still marshaling in the docks were ordered back to the trains to return to northern France and the lines at Gommecourt Wood. It was the spring of the Somme. For weeks they would sleep by day and haul ammunition by night. In a shell blast Morris was wounded, a minor incident that took him to a field hospital, where a chaplain pleaded to minister to his soul. Morris refused. Recovered, he was sent directly back to the front on the very eve of the battle. At the last moment he was ordered out of the front line on the evening of June 30 to take up a position in support trenches a few hundred yards to the rear. While he waited through the night to learn the fate of his command, shells fell all around. A soldier crouching at Morris's side was struck by a large splinter that all but severed his leg. Morris was impressed by the absence of blood. The boy died stoically, without complaint.

The battle-wounded began to trickle back, among them Morris's platoon sergeant, who seemed to have aged twenty years in the minutes of the failed morning attack. His ashen face stained with blood, his uniform drenched by it, he screamed hysterically. Every lad had been mown down climbing out of the forward trenches. Not an inch of ground had been won. In all Morris's sector the story was the same. Bodies and parts of bodies trampled in the mud, limbs protruding from the timbers of shattered dugouts, and everywhere "the tattered remnants of annihilated battalions lay strewn over No Man's Land like a picnic that had gone terribly wrong."

In the night Morris and men like him retrieved for burial what remained of the dead. In the dawn an acrid pall of smoke hung over the battlefield. Men walked about without fear of the enemy, as if in a trance, like sleepwalkers. Morris wrote, "All noise has ceased; a stunned hush had fallen over the blasted moon-like landscape."

On the eve of Morris's twenty-first birthday he carried a mutilated soldier to an aid station behind the front. In the hospital tent, the sickening smell of gangrene and ether fascinated him. A voice came out of the haze, that of the surgeon about to go to work, warning him that what he would see if he stayed would not be pleasant. He returned to the line, which over the next days began to smell like a cesspool from the decaying dead. In the heat the bodies bloated and the faces took on a peculiar greenish pallor. "They haunt me still," Morris later wrote, "especially if I am alone at night in a forest."

In time everyone he had known in the army was dead. Morris only waited his turn. His salvation came quite unexpectedly, when a curious pamphlet reached the trenches, offering junior officers of British regiments the opportunity to apply for regular commissions in the Indian Army. Designed like a tourist brochure, the flyer gave the distinct impression that life in India was one long holiday. Morris knew nothing of the East, save that it was not France.

On March 30, 1917, even as the British launched attacks near Arras and made plans for the summer offensive at Passchendaele, Morris, in London, sat before a panel of beribboned officers and gave his reasons for joining the Indian Army. A general wanted to know why he was not wearing the customary gold stripe on his sleeve, indicating that he had been wounded in battle. Fighting soldiers, Morris replied, disdained such ribbons. The general nodded sympathetically. Morris had his ticket out of the war and away from the almost certain death that awaited him on the Western Front.

A soldier's life in India inevitably led to the North-West Frontier, then as now a cauldron of tribal violence. During the war Afghanistan remained neutral, but in 1919 the ruler of Kabul, Emir Habibullah Khan, sensing weakness, ordered his army to descend upon India. He was stopped, but a fire was ignited that would take years and the entire Indian Army to extinguish. In late 1921 Morris was again at war, serving on the frontier with the Waziristan Field Force.

On December 11 he led a convoy of supply transports and troops, Punjabis and Gurkhas, through the Spinchilla Narai, a strategic mountain pass. Morris rode with the vanguard. The Mahsud tribesmen attacked from the rear, an ambush that took the British completely by surprise. More than a hundred fell, including the senior officer, Major Paget, who was killed. The command passed to Morris. When the enemy closed from three sides, he had no choice but to fight through them, even at the risk of abandoning the wounded. A Mahsud warrior came out of nowhere. Morris drew his revolver but could not shoot. He defecated in his pants. Only thirty of his original command got away, falling back at a run to the protection of the nearby fort. Morris tried to rally the men and rescue the wounded, but the colonel in command, fearing more casualties, refused to allow the sortie.

Morris climbed to a sentry post overlooking the plain. There was no sign of anyone. But in the distance a cloud of vultures hovered in the sky, waiting for the dead. Morris stood there for a long time, "watching the shadows lengthen; thinking and yet not thinking, physically numbed and unable to move away. As dusk was falling I noticed a solitary figure, moving very slowly and apparently with great difficulty. As he came near I recognized one of my own men. He was stark naked. He had been knifed in the belly and his testicles slashed. They now hung by bleeding threads of sinew. He was unable to speak and collapsed as soon as we carried him into the camp."

At dawn Morris led a relief company back to the wounded. All were dead and each had been ravaged, their flesh flayed and their genitals "roughly severed and stuffed into the victim's mouths." There was little more to say, and nothing to do but seek revenge.

Within two months of this terrible moment, John Morris would be at the Mount Everest Hotel in Darjeeling, seconded to the 1922 Mount Everest expedition as transport officer, waiting to meet men he did not know. He had left Calcutta on the mail train and traveled across the Bengali plains, rising into the mountains at dusk. He had noticed the young boys perched on the front of the engine, ladling out handfuls of grit to give the wheels better purchase.

When, in his exhaustion, he had finally settled into his hotel room in Darjeeling, there came a sudden pounding at his door. Before he could respond, a great bear of a man lumbered into the room and unleashed a stream of fluent Nepali, "much of it abusive and obscene, after which he broke into roars of school boyish laughter." This was General Bruce, the leader of the expedition. They had never actually met. Bruce later confessed to having been horrified by Morris's bespectacled and unmilitary face. That the young soldier spoke excellent Nepali saved the day.

AS THE 1922 EXPEDITION came together in Darjeeling, with several of the men meeting for the first time, there was little sign of the camaraderie that in time would develop on the mountain. Conversations were formal and restrained as each took the measure of the other. "In that peculiarly British way," Morris recalled, "we attempted to elucidate the details of one another's upbringing and background without asking direct questions." The atmosphere was awkward in part because there were initially two distinct factions, the climbers and those in support, soldiers chosen by General Bruce because of their experience in India and facility with local languages. "At first the climbers tended to regard those few of us who were not climbers as slightly superior servants," Morris observed, "but this attitude faded as the climbers realized that they were dependent on the transport for every need."

Among those straddling both camps and, in a sense, belonging to neither was Colin Crawford of the Indian Civil Service. Known as "Ferdie" because of his uncanny resemblance to Czar Ferdinand I of Bulgaria, he had served with the Gurkhas during the war but was no longer a soldier. His climbing experience included seven seasons in the Alps and a number of excursions in Kashmir. In 1920 he had accompanied Harold Raeburn to Kangchenjunga. Brought on now, like Morris, as a transport officer, the thirty-two-year-old Crawford would prove to be "very cheerful but entirely useless," in Bruce's assessment, a decent rock climber but hopeless at altitude. Others on the expedition were less harsh, including Bruce's second-in-command, Lieutenant Colonel Edward Lisle "Bill" Strutt, who later acknowledged that "Crawford's great powers were neglected sadly almost to the end of the expedition—a crime for which I was chiefly responsible." Crawford would indeed be undervalued but he was a comforting presence, always personable and often laughing. He would die in his seventieth year with a smile on his face, having just hit a ball for six out of the local cricket ground at Rosemarkie, his hometown in Scotland.

The third transport officer was the general's nephew Geoffrey Bruce, a soldier since the age of seventeen and now, at twenty-five, one of the finest athletes in the Indian Army. He had never climbed a mountain, save to hunt, but he excelled at pig sticking, a sport long considered to be "of inestimable value in developing the manly qualities of the British soldier." The competition pitted an individual with a nine-foot lance on a galloping horse against a species of wild boar unique to India, a creature known to attack and kill elephants and tigers. The goal was to strike the pig immediately behind the shoulder, driving the spear through the lungs and out at the breast. Only the very best competed for the Kadir Cup, the most coveted trophy in India, and in 1920 young Bruce reached the semifinals.

Like Morris, Bruce had fought with a Gurkha regiment on the North-West Frontier since the outbreak of the Third Afghan War. Only weeks before arriving in Darjeeling with his uncle, at the beginning of March, he had been awarded the Military Cross for gallantry in action. The deadly skirmish had occurred on June 13, 1921, by chance the very day that Mallory and Bullock had, from the heights above the Yaru Chu, seen clearly for the first time the summit of Everest. The official report noted that Bruce and his men, "fresh from the rigours of the Great War," had been in "no mood to adopt kid-glove methods with the Mahsud tribesmen." Their tactics, in truth, had been so merciless that the high command had been obliged to move young Bruce's battalion to a quieter area, one less likely to provoke such politically problematic "incidents" of retaliation and vengeance.

The medical officer in 1922 was Tom Longstaff, at forty-seven a veteran mountaineer, too old for Everest but certain to be a steady and calm influence. He was the father of seven daughters. No proponent of large expeditions, he preferred simplicity: living off the land, moving fast, the climbers unencumbered by anything beyond the essentials. He had sought the position as physician and naturalist simply to return to Tibet and experience the approach march to Everest. His first love was ornithology, and with his slight build and curious face—a patrician nose, darting eyes, and a bright orange beard—there was indeed something birdlike in his appearance.

The night of his arrival in Darjeeling, March 13, an earthquake shook the walls of the Mount Everest Hotel. Longstaff blamed General Bruce for the tremor, encouraging him to shed some weight. He then clarified for his old friend the terms of his engagement, for he was independently wealthy and had paid his own passage to India: "I want to make one thing clear. I am the expedition's official medical officer. I am, as a matter of fact, a qualified doctor, but I feel it my duty now to remind you that I have never practiced in my life. I beg you in no circumstances to seek my professional advice, since it would almost certainly turn out to be wrong. I am however willing if necessary to sign a certificate of death." Longstaff, of course, would throughout the expedition remain deeply concerned about the well-being of the men, even as his own health failed. He was a good man, honest and direct. "His hatred of anything mean or shabby," one of the climbers wrote, "gave a spice of nobility to his personal charm and keen intellect. He used to rag Mallory for being a high brow, while his brow was anything but low."

IF THE CLIMBING PARTY appeared somewhat standoffish to Morris and the others upon its arrival in Darjeeling on March 20, it was in part because the men had already established a strong connection with one another on the voyage out from England and the subsequent rail journey across India from Bombay. In 1921, most of the members of the reconnaissance had traveled alone to Darjeeling. General Bruce had encouraged Hinks to have this year's party head out together, which they did, crossing from Folkestone to Boulogne on March 2, then continuing south across France by train to reach Marseille in time for the departure of SS *Caledonia*, which sailed with the rising tide on the afternoon of the following day.

Their titular climbing leader was Bruce's deputy, Colonel Strutt, a highly decorated soldier and diplomat. Aristocratic, wealthy, fluent in German and French, Strutt had been a fine alpine climber, but at forty-eight he too was old for Everest. His medical examination on November 20, 1921, passed him as fit, with a notation indicating that "the slight wound on the left side of the lower jaw which he sustained in 1914 has left no disability, except that he wears a denture which appears to be quite satisfactory." He was actually lucky to be alive. Commanding the 2nd Battalion of the Royal Scots during the retreat from Mons in the first autumn of the war, he had been caught in the open by multiple shell blasts, which left him severely concussed, partially paralyzed, and unable to walk for nine months. The debilitating effects lingered for nearly two years, and it was not until the summer of 1916 that he was deemed capable of taking up staff duties in Salonika, well away from the fighting.

Strutt emerged from the war a complex and difficult man, certain of his own opinions, and by all accounts pompous and arrogant. Morris described him as "the greatest snob I have ever known . . . kind and generous, but a survival of an age that had passed," a vestige of a world of privilege and honor that had died in the trenches. When, in the first months of peace, revolution convulsed Vienna, Strutt personally rescued the Austrian royal family, whose members he had known since childhood, escorting the last emperor, Charles I, and his empress to safety in Switzerland. It was a bold and courageous move that prevented, as Winston Churchill wrote, another Romanov massacre. It also earned Strutt the enmity of Lord Curzon, the foreign secretary, who accused him of being a traitor to his country and threatened a court-martial. When Mallory heard this story on board the *Caledonia*, he came away convinced that there had to be some good in a man who had stood up to the former viceroy.

Mallory clearly enjoyed his second voyage to India, a welcome respite from the whirlwind that had been his life over the preceding weeks. In addition to writing long sections of *Mount Everest: The Reconnaissance, 1921*, a book being rushed into print by Edward Arnold, and working through equipment reports and preparations for the new expedition with Hinks and the Everest Committee, he had traveled the length of the country, delivering thirty lectures in ten weeks to a public increasingly inspired by the story of Everest. At the Free Trade Hall in Manchester, three thousand people had filled the seats and hundreds more had been turned away. There had been hardly a moment for his family, and now he was away yet again, and for several months. On board he still sought solitude, moments of "seasoned silence," as he called it, when he could think and read. He had with him Virginia Woolf's *Night and Day* and *The Economic Consequences of the Peace*, a devastating critique of the Versailles Treaty written by John Maynard Keynes, brother of his good friend Geoffrey. But Mallory also enjoyed his companions, and felt little of the alienation that had soured his journey out in 1921. "We go smoothly along in the smiling sunshine day after day," he wrote to Ruth on March 7 as they neared Port Said, "and the members of the expedition are a happy smiling company with plenty of easy conversation."

His new companions were indeed a remarkable lot. Howard Somervell had registered more than 350 climbs in Great Britain alone before heading for the Alps, where, during one six-week holiday, he reached the summits of more than thirty mountains. Immensely strong, with a stout body and a head so large the men teased him about his hat size, Somervell was in fact the gentlest of souls, decent and compassionate, a devout Christian of unfailing good humor. At thirty-one, he was a brilliant surgeon, a painter of exquisite watercolors, and a highly accomplished classical musician who over the course of the expedition intended to conduct the first serious study of Tibetan ethnomusicology. As a climber he had infinite reserves of energy and, like Mallory, could not resist a pitch of rock. When the *Caledonia* docked at Gibraltar for but two hours, Somervell, one of the party reported in a letter to Hinks, "proceeded to scale the rocks making the ascent in 10 minutes, but was stopped by a policeman near the top who ordered him down again as he was on secret military ground."

Arthur Wakefield had been recommended to the Everest Committee by Mallory's friend and mentor Geoffrey Young, who had never forgotten the record Wakefield set in the Lake District in 1905: fifty-nine miles of mountain summits with a total vertical ascent of 23,500 feet in less than twenty-four hours. Young had wanted him on the reconnaissance in 1921, but Wakefield had been unable to get away from the medical practice he had established in a small town in the forests of eastern Canada. He was recruited to the 1922 expedition as a climber, not a physician, but his age, forty-six, was against him. General Bruce would later dismiss him as "a noble and worthy gentleman . . . [but] a complete passenger . . . does not stand heights well." Another of the climbers, George Finch, would have harsher words, suggesting that Wakefield "squandered his energy in a nervousness that amounted to hysteria."

It was true, Wakefield's family acknowledged, that the man suffered depression and nervous anxiety after the war. He had been, it will be recalled, a surgeon at a casualty clearing station behind the Somme front. On July 1, 1916, he witnessed the annihilation of the entire Newfoundland Regiment at Beaumont-Hamel, hundreds of young men whom he had, as a frontier doctor in Labrador, literally brought into the world. From this he would never recover, and the man who went to Everest in 1922 was certainly not the person Geoffrey Young had known before the war. But the actual record of the expedition, as we shall see, suggests that these judgments by Bruce and Finch were excessive and unfair. With Longstaff severely debilitated, Wakefield would step to the fore as physician, earning the lasting gratitude of the climbers whose lives he would save.

A war that came out of nowhere to consume a generation left in its wake a wasteland of isolation. Every man had to come to terms with the experience on his own. Somervell, too, had been a surgeon at the Somme. On that horrible first morning he walked alone through six acres of stretchers bearing the wounded and the dying. It was the most terrible experience of his life, but it led him only deeper into Christian devotion and compassion, which in the end freed him from trauma. Although he did not know it as he chatted up Strutt, played deck tennis on the *Caledonia* with Wakefield, or chess in the evenings with Mallory, Somervell would never return from this, his first journey to Asia. Forgoing a lucrative career as a Harley Street surgeon, with only £60 in his pocket he would travel through India, eventually settling in the south in Travancore, where he joined the staff of a mission hospital. For more than forty years he would sweep away all memories of the dead by saving the living, treating, with a small cadre of volunteers, more than 200,000 cases a year, performing as many as 15,000 surgeries, pioneering the treatment of leprosy. For the rest of his professional life Somervell alone would see 150 indigent patients a day, including Sundays if necessary. In his faith he was never dogmatic. On the *Caledonia*, it amused him when one night a fellow passenger, a narrow-minded Christian, chastised him for tolerating drinking and dancing.

The photographer John Noel was to Mallory's mind the wonderful surprise of the expedition. Formally engaged to document the climb on film, both through stills and moving pictures, Noel, it will be recalled, was a veteran of the Himalaya and the dream of Everest. With Alexander Kellas, his good friend and mentor (now buried at Kampa Dzong), he had long before the war hatched schemes to reach the mountain, even in defiance of Charles Bell and the Tibetan authorities. In 1913, disguised as a native, he'd gotten as far as Tashirak, a mere forty miles from Everest, before being forced back into Sikkim by armed Tibetan soldiers. And it had been Noel's Aeolian Hall lecture on March 10, 1919, for the Royal Geographical Society, that had inspired Younghusband and Percy Farrar of the Alpine Club to take action, setting in motion the chain of events that culminated in the reconnaissance of 1921.

Noel was an extraordinary character, an entrepreneur in a very modern sense and a born promoter given to wild schemes of the very sort that mountain climbing expeditions to this day cobble together to fund their efforts. Talk of using supplemental oxygen, the great debate of 1922, led him to propose the laying of a pipeline to carry gas to the top of the mountain. If steel cylinders were to be used, he suggested that they be dropped from airplanes. To maintain the supply line across Tibet to Everest, Noel suggested that a Citroën tractor car be carried over the Jelep La and up the Chumbi Valley. Cars, after all, had been delivered to the Dalai Lama in Lhasa—why not one for the Everest climbers? To raise money Noel was a fountain of ideas, which was one of the reasons Hinks thought so highly of him.

By all accounts a great raconteur, Noel, throughout the long voyage out to Bombay, regularly regaled Mallory and the others with stories of his travels in Labrador, his time in Persia as a spy, his early efforts to reach Everest, and his experiences in the war when, as a small arms instructor, he became one of the best pistol shots in the British Army. Naturally he said nothing about the months he had spent in hospitals suffering from shell shock, or of the nervous afflictions that tormented him for so many months of the war. But he did enthusiastically share his fascination with the new art of photography, and on this subject he was on very solid ground. As a still photographer he had been deeply influenced by the work of Vittorio Sella, the Italian pioneer who had virtually established the art of mountain photography, even as he invented the equipment that made it possible. Noel's inspiration in cinematography was Herbert Ponting, who documented Scott's Antarctic expedition of 1910–11, a film Noel had watched sixteen times before going to Everest.

Like Ponting and Sella, Noel would design or modify all of his kit for the mountain. In addition to cameras, tripods, and thousands of feet of raw stock, he brought along a lightproof tent for processing film; developing tanks and chemical fixers; and, for drying the negatives, a specialized stove designed to burn yak dung. His camera was modeled after the 35mm Newton-Sinclair model Ponting had used in Antarctica. Made of duralumin for lightness, it was eighteen inches long and a foot high, with special bearings that required no oil and a protective rubber cover that allowed him to press his face against the eyepiece without fear of his skin sticking to the metal. The magazine held four hundred feet of film, which could be advanced by battery or a hand crank. The lens was a twenty-inch Taylor Hobson telephoto, with optics honed during the war. Attached to the top of the camera was a customized six-power directional telescope to be used to locate and identify distant subjects on the mountain. Fully loaded, the camera weighed less than twenty pounds.

Noel brought to the 1922 expedition not only state-of-the-art equipment but also a sophisticated and thoroughly contemporary aesthetic, informed by a rare understanding of what film implied as a new medium. The technology, and the commercial industry it spawned, was not yet twenty years old. The British public, in particular, did not yet have a preference for features over documentaries, which competed head-to-head in theaters, each format having in common this new and astonishing capacity to conjure out of the darkness flickering images of wild and unimagined worlds. The most popular film produced during the war was the officially sanctioned account *The Battle of the Somme,* released in August 1916, even as the battle raged. Though highly sanitized, its live footage and the graphic display of life at the front stunned a nation largely unaware of the reality of the war.

With the peace, documentary films unveiled the promise of distant lands, the exotic allure of escape. While Noel and the others sailed for India, Frank Hurley was making his plans for New Guinea, a journey that would yield *Pearls and Savages*, and the most popular ethnographic documentary of all time, Robert Flaherty's *Nanook of the North*, was playing in sold-out theaters across Britain.

Noel's plans for Everest were very much part of a creative wave of adventure that throughout the 1920s propelled filmmakers to every corner of the world. It all fed into a greater quest, embraced readily by a tired and exhausted people, to show that the life and death of an individual could still have meaning, that the war had not expunged everything heroic and inspired. The image of the noble mountaineer scaling the heights, climbing literally through a zone of death to reach the heavens, high above the sordid reality of the modern world, would emerge first from the imagination and through the lens of John Noel. On the mountain, Mallory would famously complain to Noel that he had not come to Tibet to become a film star. But he would become one, whether he realized it or not. "St. Noel of the Cameras," as General Bruce affectionately called the filmmaker, who happened to be Catholic, would see to it. The two films Noel made, *Climbing Mount Everest* (1922) and *The Epic of Everest* (1924), transformed the challenge of the mountain into a national mission, a symbol of imperial redemption, even as they elevated Mallory, still a relatively unknown mountaineer, into the realm of the Titans. "If you had lived as they had lived," Noel would ask at the end of *The Epic of Everest*, "and died in the heart of nature would you, yourself, wish for any better grave?"

THE OTHER RADICAL innovation of the 1922 expedition was oxygen. Thanks in good measure to the research of Alexander Kellas both during and before the war, it was known that at the summit of Everest a climber breathing normally would absorb only a third of the oxygen available at sea level. Oxygen deprivation severely weakens the body and, more seriously, can lead to mountain sickness, a misleadingly gentle term for life-threatening cerebral edema. In compression chambers at Oxford, experiments had shown that the debilitating effects of high altitude could be readily mitigated with supplemental oxygen, and by the end of the war virtually every plane in the Royal Air Force was suitably equipped with an apparatus. The potential application on the mountain was obvious. All that would be required was a portable source: steel bottles of compressed gas, together with a secure regulator and a mask.

The challenge was less technical than ethical and aesthetic. Traditionalists such as Arthur Hinks and General Bruce questioned whether the use of supplemental oxygen was sporting. Wakefield remained highly distrustful. Mallory referred to it as "a damnable heresy." Hinks, who knew nothing of mountaineering, was the most vocal critic. "Only rotters would use oxygen," he insisted in a letter to Bruce. Those more scientifically inclined—Howard Somervell and George Finch, in particular—followed the evidence and considered the use of oxygen to be no more artificial than the selection of a good custom-made pair of boots.

The argument was actually more complex and substantial than either side acknowledged. On the one hand, there were dangerous uncertainties. Professor Georges Dreyer at Oxford, who had worked with Kellas, could guarantee nothing. "I do not think you will get up without oxygen," he cautioned, "but if you do succeed you may not get down again." No one knew what would happen at such heights, or what might occur should the apparatus fail and the flow of air suddenly cease. The very notion of using a gas mask was haunting. John Noel was the first to refer to the "dead world of Everest," the death zone rising above the "region of life" where a climber could be "suffocated as if by some subtle, invisible, odourless gas." To climb the mountain with one's face covered in anonymity by an apparatus so powerfully evocative of the trenches seemed less than heroic.

On the other hand, getting to the top was ultimately all that mattered. Professor J. B. S. Haldane, the world's leading physiologist whose opinion swayed Somervell, believed that while the summit could conceivably be reached without oxygen, only the use of supplemental gas would ensure success. Longstaff, initially strongly opposed, in time came around to the same position. On February 10, three weeks before the expedition sailed on the *Caledonia*, Percy Farrar of the Alpine Club, Hinks's rival for control of the Everest Committee, wrote to Younghusband: "I should like to state very explicitly that I would very willingly dispense with this oxygen. At the same time I am sure that Longstaff is right when he states we can only get to the top with oxygen."

The challenge was to invent an apparatus light enough to be carried to the summit, and then to identify a climber to take charge of the effort, someone technically capable of maintaining and repairing the equipment and training the other climbers in its use. The obvious candidate was George Finch, the finest ice climber in Britain and a scientist in his own right who had already worked closely on the oxygen problem at Oxford with Kellas and Haldane. Finch's participation in the 1921 reconnaissance had been denied at the last moment by the Harley Street physicians, and a cloud of controversy still hung over his name, but his credentials could no longer be denied. Mallory certainly wanted him along, if only for the challenge of the North Col. Farrar had never lost confidence in the man. "Finch was, so Strutt says, a gas expert in Salonika," Farrar wrote to Younghusband. "He is entirely qualified." When Younghusband made further inquiries, Strutt responded, "I personally, although my acquaintance with Finch is slight, have no objection to his inclusion. He served at the same time as I with the British Salonika Force, did good work and was popular with his unit. I think that Charles Bruce and I should be able to handle him. At the same time if the other members dislike him, which I fear is the case, it rather alters the situation. However in reply to your question I should like Finch to go. He is the one man I would back to reach the summit and we should always remember that!"

On December 3, 1921, Younghusband sent Finch a letter inquiring as to his availability in 1922. Hinks again ordered a medical examination, but went out of his way to inform Finch that passing the physical would not imply a place on the expedition. The radioactive Finch had to wait until December 15 for a formal invitation, and only after he'd signed a confidentiality agreement and endured a rebuke from Hinks concerning photographs that had appeared, without authorization of the RGS, in the press in 1921, was his place on the climbing party secured.

Finch, who had never been to the Himalaya, attacked the challenge of Everest with methodical rigor. Anticipating the cold, he contacted S. W. Silver & Co., a firm specializing in military uniforms and expedition gear, and ordered custom-made garments of his own invention: a knee-length coat, trousers, and gauntlets lined with eiderdown. These arrived for Younghusband's inspection on February 13, 1922. Compared to the cut of a Norfolk tweed jacket, the world's first down coat appeared inelegant in the extreme. But on the mountain, its worth would be proved.

Meanwhile, Finch worked on the oxygen apparatus with another innovative English company, Siebe Gorman, which had pioneered deepwater diving technologies based on pressurized helmets, sophisticated regulators, rubber tubes, and suits that insulated the diver from the dangers of the depths. The result was a relatively simple invention, a Bergen backpack holding four bottles of Swedish steel, each weighing 5.75 pounds fully charged, for a total weight of 32 pounds. The regulator was designed to deliver air as if at an elevation of 15,000 feet, at a rate of flow that provided a total of seven hours of supplemental oxygen. Anticipating that some might find a breathing mask claustrophobic, Finch designed a second delivery system, a simple mouthpiece of piped glass. He tested the prototype in the laboratory at Oxford and, having made a number of modifications, ordered eleven complete sets to be manufactured for the expedition. Ten of these were dispatched to India on SS *Chilka*. One set Finch kept aside to take with him on the *Caledonia*, where the entire climbing party, all the men, would be expected to participate in oxygen drills in order to familiarize themselves with the equipment.

Even this remarkable scientific and technical contribution did not earn Finch any respect. Indeed, if anything, it only further antagonized Hinks, who famously mocked the oxygen effort in a letter to General Bruce: "This afternoon we go to see a gas drill. They have contrived a most wonderful apparatus, which will make you die laughing. Pray see that a picture of Finch in his patent climbing outfit with the gas apparatus is taken by the official photographer. I would gladly put a little money on Mallory to go to 25,000 ft without assistance of four cylinders and a mask."

Bruce was no more charitable. In the same report in which he acknowledged Finch as being without doubt the best man on snow and ice on the expedition, as well as "extraordinarily handy in all kinds of ways outside his scientific accomplishments," the general added a personal note: "Cleans his teeth on February 1st and has a bath on the same day if the water is very hot, otherwise puts it off until the next year. Six months course as a Lama novice in a monastery would enable me to occupy a Whymper tent with him." It is difficult to know or imagine what provoked such contempt. By the time Bruce wrote these scathing remarks, Finch, at thirty-four a relatively young climber, had performed heroically on the mountain, establishing against all odds a new height record, even as he gave up a chance for the summit to save the life of the general's own nephew, his climbing partner, Geoffrey Bruce.

John Morris recalled an incident soon after the arrival of the climbing party in Darjeeling. A weekly parcel of English papers had arrived by post, among them an edition of the *Illustrated London News* with two middle pages devoted to photographs of Finch. One image showed him intently repairing his own boots. That Finch had not attended the proper schools was one thing for General Bruce and Colonel Strutt to endure; that he had chosen a career in the sciences, a profession unworthy of a gentleman, was quite another; but that he would cobble his own boots was beneath contempt. Strutt, in particular, was outraged. "I can still see his rigid expression as he looked at the picture," Morris wrote. " 'I always knew that fellow was a shit,' he said, and the sneer remained on his face while the rest of us sat in frozen silence."

As it turned out, Hinks had included the copy of the *Illustrated London News* in the postal dispatch as a deliberate taunt and provocation. The story was weeks old. The photographs in question had been taken long before Finch had been formally invited to join the 1922 expedition. The suggestion that Finch had violated his confidentiality agreement with the Everest Committee was absurd. The *Illustrated London News* printed the photographs only because of Younghusband's official announcement, which ran through all the papers, that the two-man climbing team chosen for the ultimate assault on the mountain would be George Mallory and George Finch. Bruce's slurs aside, Finch, a man in fact fastidious in his personal hygiene, would have his moment on the mountain.

ON BOARD the *Caledonia* the oxygen debate played out with its own small drama. Wakefield was on one side, highly doubtful, and Finch on the other, dogmatic and irritatingly competent. "I must say that in this company I'm amused by Finch and rather enjoy him," Mallory wrote to Ruth. "I'm much intrigued by the size of his head which seems to go out on the sides where it might go up. He's a fanatical character and doesn't laugh easily. He greatly enjoys his oxygen classes." Somervell lightened the mood with a series of sketches of climbers descending the mountain, sucking oxygen straight from the bottle. Finch was not amused. He was certain that only with supplemental gas would they reach the summit. It was an experiment that had never been tried, however, and there were considerable risks. The side of the mountain in a gale at 28,000 feet was not the place to learn how to use the apparatus. He believed it essential that each man practice until the tanks seemed but an extension of his own lungs. Few of the others shared his conviction that the benefit of supplemental oxygen would offset the burden of climbing with more than thirty pounds of steel on one's back.

Mallory, however, came away from Finch's lectures quite hopeful, convinced that the oxygen "will serve us well enough without physi-ological dangers from a camp at 25,000 feet." He was open to anything that would get them to the summit. But the idea of holding a rubber tube in his mouth he found disgusting. "I sicken with the thought of the saliva dribbling down," he wrote. And like the others, he thought he had mastered the contraption after a single try, and privately shared everyone's relief when Colonel Strutt called off the drills on the morn-ing the *Caledonia* steamed out of the Red Sea and into the Indian Ocean.

They arrived in Bombay on Friday, March 17, and had but five hours before their train departed for Calcutta. Word of the arrest of Gandhi had reached them in Aden, as had news of the general strike and the shutdown of the railways. Longstaff, heading for Darjeeling on March 12, had been caught in the chaos. But within days the interven-tion of the army had cleared the lines, and the men from the *Caledonia* experienced no delays. With Wakefield sharing a berth with Mal-lory, they crossed India in less than two days, pulling into Calcutta's Howrah Station just before noon on Sunday. After a lunch at Spence's Hotel and a quick visit to the native market and the infamous Black Hole, they made their way to North Station to board the 4:50 p.m. Darjeeling Express for the overnight run to Siliguri. The following morning General Bruce came out by car and rode with them the last few miles into Darjeeling, where they arrived not long after noon on Monday, March 20.

Mallory immediately slipped away to stay at Chevremont with the Morsheads, Henry and his wife, Evie, who had spent the winter in Darjeeling after the birth of their second son. After some diplomatic haggling, Morshead had finally secured permission to join the new effort, not as a surveyor but as a member of the climbing party. The Tibetan authorities wanted nothing more of maps, and Charles Bell saw to it that the Survey of India had no formal role on the second expedition. Mallory cared nothing for cartography, but he was deeply relieved to know that Morshead, the old workhorse of 1921, would be with him on the mountain. They walked into town that night to a din-ner hosted by General Bruce at the Mount Everest Hotel, where the rest of the party was billeted, along with Morris, Longstaff, Geoffrey Bruce, and the general. It was the first time the expedition had been together in the same place; hence the formality and awkwardness that drew Morris's notice.

To be sure, the men watched their words, even as they watched one another. No one fell under greater scrutiny than Finch, and no one was more judgmental than Finch himself, as his diary entries attest. In his journal, he began with a brutal assessment of India and its people, a place to which he had never previously traveled and of which he knew nothing. His only experience was the train trip, and the few moments in Bombay and Calcutta. "The country is wonderfully rich and very magnificent," he wrote. "The dweller in the plains is bodily poor and mentally most abased, little better than animals. I can see no hope for them except in the most autocratic government. These hills men up here are totally different. They are fine, well set-up self-reliant men. They despise the plainsmen, and I must confess I believe they have every right to."

Not an impressive or charitable judgment for one so new to India, but indicative of conventional British opinion, which was precisely why the Raj was falling apart. Mahatma Gandhi had indeed been arrested during the fortnight the Everest expedition had been at sea, accused of fomenting sedition and disaffection in the Indian Army, a charge to which he enthusiastically pleaded guilty. On trial he defended himself, reviewing his history with discrimination in South Africa, his service in the Boer War, the false promises from the Crown that the millions of Indians who had served in Gallipoli and on the Western Front would be rewarded for their loyalty, a dream betrayed by the Rowlatt Acts and crushed in blood at Amritsar. Britain, Gandhi said, had broken its word even as it shattered India's pride. "In my humble opinion," he had told the court, "non-cooperation with evil is as much a duty as is co-operation with good." He then asked the judge to impose the harshest penalty the law would permit. Two days after Finch and the men reached Darjeeling, Gandhi was sentenced to serve six years in the Yerawada jail. In Darjeeling the British enclave rejoiced.

As Finch cast a harsh eye over India and everything in his experience, his fellow climbers did not escape notice. In his journal entry of March 21, having known some of the men less than a day, he displayed the analytical rectitude—many would say arrogance—that drove his colleagues to distraction: "With a view to seeing later how far future events will confirm, or otherwise, my present opinion of each individual in this group I am putting against each individual's name the opinion I now hold of his chances of going far." General Bruce, Tom Longstaff, and John Noel he listed as nonstarters. Captain Bruce: "good for 23,000 ft. too young (lack of stamina) lung capacity not very pronounced (he is slightly narrow in chest from back to front) Not a climber." Captain Morris: "good for 23,000 ft. wears glasses. Not a climber. Rather clumsy. Body long, legs short." Captain Crawford: "good for 22,000. Nervous disposition, tending faintly to hysteria . . . To judge from appearances is now even suffering from mild insomnia."

One by one Finch worked through the list. Colonel Strutt might go as high as 24,000 feet were it not for his fundamental lack of confidence, certain to stop him at 23,000. Wakefield, like Crawford, appeared nervous, "distinctly hysterical and thus not likely to conserve his powers. Age very much against him." Major Morshead had possibilities but "is no born mountaineer." Howard Somervell would be good for 24,000 feet, though he was "rather heavy and likely therefore to become muscle bound. 23,000 ft in tank at Oxford finished him." Mallory alone was solid, a sure thing: "Good for from 24,000 to 25,000, perhaps a little more but not over 25,500 ft. I am inclined to look upon him as the strongest of all if he learns to go slow and not fluster himself." As for his own prospects: "Capt Finch would, I hope, hold his own with Mallory. But I also hope that I shall not be called upon to make an attempt without oxygen . . . Mt Everest will not, I am convinced be climbed without oxygen." Referring to the existing height record, set by the Duke of Abruzzi in the Karakoram, he added that anyone who tried to go higher than 24,600 feet without supplemental air would surely be incapable of another attempt, even should oxygen be available. There would be no second chances on Everest.

ONE FINAL MEMBER of the climbing party impressed even Finch: a new man for 1922, Major Edward Felix "Teddy" Norton, who had come up from Bengal only that day. For a week he had been convalescing in a Calcutta hospital, having suffered a severe case of piles after reaching the finals of the Kadir Cup. An operation had not been necessary, but his condition was serious. The pain of thrombotic hemorrhoids, a common affliction in the Himalaya, is intense and debilitating in the extreme. Mallory questioned whether Norton would be fit in time to join them. Finch saw only great promise: "Good for 23,000, trunk long, legs short in relation. Stamina good. He may do 24,000."

Teddy Norton, thirty-eight, was in fact the great discovery of the 1922 expedition, a man of extraordinary qualities of leadership, integrity, and grit. Commissioned as a graduate of the Royal Military Academy Woolwich in 1902, he had been a soldier since boyhood. Posted to the Royal Horse Artillery at Meerut at twenty-three, he had served throughout India, eventually becoming aide-de-camp to the viceroy before sailing with his regiment to France in the late summer of 1914. That he survived the war was a statistical miracle, for he fought in virtually every campaign, from the very first British attacks at Aisne and the Marne, through Ypres, Loos, and the Somme, and Arras and the German Spring Offensive of 1918. Mentioned in despatches three times, he was awarded the Military Cross, appointed DSO, and honored with every medal for gallantry and combat, save the Victoria Cross.

Norton was present at Bapaume on March 21, 1918, when the Germans unleashed the greatest bombardment of the war. Nine battalions were annihilated as a blanket of poison gas and shell fire ripped open the entire front of the Fourth and Fifth Armies, allowing forty-five German divisions to pour through. Norton's brother, also an artillery officer, was killed in action and Norton's own battery was overrun, his men torn apart by machine gun fire. Norton retired his guns in order, only to return to the fight. Six months later he was at Cambrai when the tide turned for good. Allied artillery, thousands of guns massed wheel to wheel in two enfilades that seemed to stretch the length of the world, flashed as a perfect sheet of flame, with unprecedented accuracy that allowed tanks and troops to roll forward in the massive final offensive that would end the war. It was the antidote to the Somme, though still a bitter fight. One German soldier singlehandedly knocked out five British tanks. Norton saw the man captured and bayoneted in cold blood. It was not a memory he would carry with him, any more than he would dwell on the certain knowledge that his brother had been killed by errant French fire. He had seen too much of death not to embrace the good fortune of his deliverance.

Major Norton emerged from the war with a certain quality of being, a serenity, confidence, and uncanny presence that caused men almost reflexively to follow his lead. "Norton is one of the best," Mallory exclaimed to Ruth in his first reference to the new man, "extraordinarily keen and active and full of interest and gentle and charming withal. He is to be my stable companion I understand and I don't doubt that I shall like him in that capacity as well as anyone." Two years later, when leadership on Everest in 1924 devolved to Norton, as fate inevitably would have it, one of the climbers marveled at how Norton, as commander, would make up his mind about a decision, then call in the entire expedition to confer, and "invariably they would after discussion come to his view."

In retrospect it was remarkable that Norton was even available to join the Everest effort. He had just passed through Staff College and was destined for great things in the army. Arthur Hinks had gone to the very top, Sir Henry Wilson, chief of the Imperial General Staff, to secure for Norton eight months of leave, which Wilson granted in a letter of January 23, 1922. One senses the hand of Younghusband, who perfectly distilled Norton's character and charisma in a brief biographical sketch written long after the expedition:

> Major E. F. Norton, D.S.O., was well known in the Alpine Club and well versed in the lore of mountaineering. He had the additional advantage of having served in India and been on shooting expeditions in the Himalaya. He could speak Hindustani and knew how to handle Indian peoples. Compact and collected, erect and direct, and with a habit of command, he inspired confidence at once. And there was a kindliness and suavity about him, which increased the trust placed in him. He was indeed a combination of many qualities. As an officer of the Royal Horse Artillery he was noted for the smartness of his battery; he had served with distinction in the War; for seven years he had run the Kadir Cup Meeting—the great pig-sticking event in India; he was a keen observer of birds; and he was an amateur painter of more than average ability. In everything he was methodical . . . In his punctuality he took great pride: he would be neither too early nor too late. It was not much more than a minute before the train left Victoria that he arrived at the station on his way to India and he was leisurely saying good-bye to his friends and the train was well on the move as he quietly stepped into it continuing his conversation. With him there would be no flurry in emergency.

THE RECONNAISSANCE of 1921 had left Darjeeling in mid-May and crossed Tibet in the early days of summer only to run up against the full force of the monsoon, which broke over the Himalaya in the second week of July. The challenge in the spring of 1922 was to advance into the mountains as late as possible, with the hope of avoiding the worst of the winter, but still in time to reach Everest and complete the assault *before* the arrival of the rains. This narrow window demanded all haste.

General Bruce, arriving with his nephew Geoffrey in Darjeeling on March 1, had sprung into action, immediately seeing to the stores and supplies, even as he vetted 150 porters, selecting fifty of the best, including thirteen who had served on Mallory's climbing party the previous year. The general elected to give Gyalzen, the sirdar who had caused such trouble for Howard-Bury, a second chance, and he took on as interpreter Karma Paul, a brilliant scholar and schoolmaster, a Tibetan born in Lhasa but living in Darjeeling. For cooks, Bruce insisted on the very best, and tested a number of men in the field before finally selecting four. Food, both quantity and quality, most especially for the porters, had been a major point of contention in 1921. General Bruce, a man of prodigious appetites himself, would not make such a mistake. The supplies for 1922, packed and shipped from the Army and Navy Stores in London, filled some nine hundred light plywood boxes. In addition to the standard rations—cheeses and ham, bully beef, biscuits, oatmeal, and dried soups—the expedition larder included such delicacies as gingered lemons and tinned quail in aspic, not to mention a case of the finest French champagne and several bottles of 120-year-old rum, with which the general intended to toast his own birthday on April 7. "Our messing and transport are lavish," Morshead remarked with delight in a letter to his wife, especially when "compared with Bury's frugal methods of last year's trip."

So, too, were the expenses. Within a fortnight of arriving in Darjeeling, General Bruce wrote the Royal Geographical Society demanding an additional £2,000, a wild request that sent the miserly Hinks into spasms of indignation. The general could not have cared less. His favorite party trick was to tear a pack of cards in half. For casual exercise he carried his adjutant on his back up and down whatever mountain was at hand. His body was a canvas of bullet wounds. In a struggle of wills, Hinks at his desk in London was but a flea on the body of a bear. If the Everest Committee expected Sherpa and Tibetan porters under Bruce's command to transport the deadweight of Noel's photographic gear and supplies, all the cameras, lenses, chemicals, developing tanks, specialized tents, tripods, and thousands of feet of film stock, as well as eleven ridiculous sets, as the general saw it, of oxygen racks and steel cylinders, weighing altogether some nine hundred pounds, his men would be well fed, whatever the costs.

It made for a dramatic convoy, ultimately more than three hundred yaks, fifty mules, riding ponies for the thirteen sahibs, Karma Paul, and the four Gurkha NCOs, along with cows, donkeys, oxen, and, at any moment, between fifty and a hundred Tibetan and Nepali porters. The initial route was that of the reconnaissance: down to Kalimpong and up the Teesta Valley, across the Jelep La to Yatung and then the long ascent of the Chumbi Valley to the Tibetan Plateau at Phari. As in 1921, the departure from Darjeeling was deliberately staggered. Longstaff and Morris left by rail for Kalimpong on March 22. General Bruce and Geoffrey, John Noel, Morshead, Mallory, and Wakefield joined them four days later. Strutt, Norton, and Somervell arrived on the evening of March 27. The geologist Heron, singled out by Tibetans for alleged transgressions in 1921, met up with the party in Kalimpong, still with the vague hope of being able to accompany the expedition. At dinner on March 27 General Bruce discreetly passed along the regrettable news that in deference to Charles Bell and the Tibetan authorities, permission had been denied at the last moment by the Foreign Office. Heron gracefully retreated to Darjeeling, where he and his wife were based. Morshead came close to suffering the same fate. Before setting out for Pedong on the morning of March 28, Bruce scratched a note to Hinks: "I must say I congratulate myself on having been able to smuggle Morshead in as not only can he talk Thibetan [*sic*] but he will be able to amplify his map." Enlarging the survey, of course, was precisely what the Tibetans did not want to occur, but such diplomatic nuances did not register with the general.

Finch and Crawford, meanwhile, remained behind in Darjeeling, awaiting the oxygen equipment. SS *Chilka*, having docked in Colombo and several Indian cities, was not expected in Calcutta until the end of the month. The delay did not bother General Bruce, whose disdain for the oxygen experiment was well known. But it provoked in Finch considerable anxiety. Every evening he scanned the *Statesman*, Calcutta's newspaper of record, for an announcement of the ship's arrival. The port list included vessels not due until April 5, but as late as March 29 there was still no word of the *Chilka*. He would need a day to discharge the cylinders, and three more to get the equipment to Kalimpong. He and Crawford, assuming they could find transport, would then be obliged to do a forced march with no medical support to catch up with the expedition in Kampa Dzong. The climbers, to make matters worse, would have no opportunity for further training with the apparatus. English pluck, Finch was certain, would not get anyone to the summit. Oxygen would, and now he would have neither tools nor the time to make essential modifications to the ten sets still stuck in the hold of the *Chilka*.

With little to do but wait in Darjeeling, Finch tinkered for four days, testing his Kodak Vest Pocket camera, making alterations to his high-altitude boots, assembling a "corking good catapult with rubber tubing" for hunting birds, and waterproofing his maps with a Duraprene concoction of his own invention. Finally, on March 31, a wire arrived reporting that the ship was at anchor in Calcutta, with its cargo scheduled to reach Kalimpong in four days. Finch and Crawford got off on April 2, a full week behind the expedition vanguard. At the railhead they hired ten mules just to transport the gas cylinders, another ten to carry their kit and supplies, and, finally, nine porters to lug the oxygen apparatus—backpacks, regulators, and breathing tubes—some 350 miles across Tibet to the lower flanks of Everest.

The rest of the expedition had crossed the Jelep La on the third day in April and slowly made its way up the Chumbi Valley to the planned rendezvous at Phari. They were on the whole a "cheerful and happy" mob. Morshead and Wakefield celebrated their escape from civilization by having their heads shaved at Pedong by Morshead's servant, Munir Khan, already a great favorite of the men. A few days later Norton and Longstaff were similarly scalped, as was Mallory, who reported in a note to Ruth, "I look rather like a Hun with my close crop and unshaven chin." Morris and Somervell discovered that they had both served at the Somme in the 46th Division, but they spoke little of the war. Somervell wanted to learn Nepali, and with Morris's help he did. Meanwhile General Bruce made "heroic exertions to get rid of his tummy," refusing his mount as he stormed ahead on foot, climbing as much as 5,500 feet in a day. "You know his figure," Mallory exclaimed in undaunted admiration, "and you may imagine how he watered the path, but what energy!" George, by contrast, lacking a ready change of shirt, chose to ride. He had fine sensibilities and a strong and perhaps unexpected aversion to the clammy sensation of perspiration next to his skin.

Norton and Longstaff, riding on their own, took great delight in the beauty of the Chumbi Valley, the primulas and blue poppies at the edge of winter snows on the flanks of the Jelep La, the "lovely glades and alpine forests," the unknown birds. Norton the soldier would collect more than four hundred botanical specimens during his time in Tibet, along with 120 varieties of butterflies and moths. Longstaff was enchanted by the "dream crag of Shegar, hung with forts and monasteries like martins' nests on a cliff" and the massive monastery walls of Tinki Dzong, "reflected in the mirror of the lake, the haunt of bar-headed geese, never hunted in this sacred spot." To experience these wonders on the approaches to Everest, he wrote, made up for the "penalty of being condemned to try to climb the monster; for monster it is, this relic of primordial chaos, murderous and threatening, the home of devils, not of gods."

Somervell embraced the new country through sound. At Sedong-chen, at the end of a hot and dusty trek, he and Morshead came upon four Buddhist monks chanting prayers to avert a hailstorm, accompanied by drums, cymbals, rattles, and a trumpet made from a human thighbone. Morshead was astonished to see Somervell decipher the cacophony into precise musical notations. Somervell marveled that the very first tune he heard in Tibet, "whistled by a lad at work in the fields," differed by only one note from the "little air played at the beginning" of Stravinksy's *Rite of Spring*. He later wrote, "Men working in the fields sing pentatonic tunes and this must be considered as the national mode. I have heard Tibetans whistling arpeggios of common chords and strangely enough of diminished sevenths; but never a semitone, which they do not seem to appreciate as an interval. They may strike E and E flat in this way, but never in succession."

Not all the men displayed such sensitivity or scholarly discipline. Mallory was frankly bored by the return journey. "The repetition of aesthetic experiences is not very stimulating," he wrote to Ruth from Tinki Dzong. "The march in the sun and the wind in camp have a somnolent effect; and one is apt to feel too much of an animal." Mallory's mind and spirit, his entire being, focused exclusively on the mountain. His personal deportment remained fastidious in the extreme, but his kit was always a shambles. Mallory moved with effortless grace, Morris recalled fondly, his body perfectly proportioned, "leaving trails of untidiness wherever he went." After a few days the other men decided to take turns cleaning up Mallory's scattered gear to ensure that nothing essential get left behind or pinched by the scores of young Tibetans who crowded around their every camp.

Privacy was never an option. The men were constantly on display, as Morris wrote, "like animals in an exhibition." Morris, always insightful, took note of how they coped with their basic needs, such as defecating in the morning. "The attitude of different members of the party was very revealing; the extraverts squatted down behind the nearest rock and paid no heed to the audience, while the others would saunter on until their pursuers lost interest." Among the priggish was most certainly Colonel Strutt, whose dislike of Tibetans grew with each passing day. "A usual and by now welcome sound in each new place," Mallory wrote, "is Strutt's voice, cursing Tibet—this march for being more dreary and repulsive even than the last one before, and this village for being more filthy than any other. Not that Strutt is particularly a grouser; but he likes to ease his feelings with maledictions and I hope feels better for it."

In Phari, where the expedition gathered on April 6, even Strutt had good reason to complain. Morris described it as the "most dreary place in the world." Rather than pitching tents, they crowded into a smoky *dak* bungalow vile with soot, its courtyard heaped with garbage and frozen filth, the narrow alleys infested with pigs and vermin. The air was viciously cold, the winter winds swirling with grit, dust, and powdered yak dung. "They huddled at the dining table," Morris recalled, "coughing in the ever thickening murk." On the second night it was the general's fifty-sixth birthday, but even a taste of 120-year-old rum did not elevate the mood.

No one the year before, and none of the men of 1922, had experienced the full wrath of a Tibetan winter. Their clothing was hopelessly inadequate. As in 1921, each climber had been responsible for his own kit, and the result was a motley assemblage, with each man layered in unique combinations of woolen underwear, flannel shirts, cotton outer garments padded with eiderdown, waistcoats and lambskin jackets, plus fours and cashmere puttees, stockings, knickerbocker suits, and Shetland pullovers. The only standard issue was a pair of thigh-length sheepskin RAF flying boots, which reduced all movement to "a clumsy waddle." Morris wore a suit of shoddy cashmere tweed. "It looked all right," he wrote, "but afforded little protection from the howling Tibetan gales."

In clothing suitable for a modest winter outing in the Welsh mountains, the expedition made plans for a three-week march across the frozen uplands of the highest plateau on earth. No one, Morris recalled, felt like talking. They were headed for Kampa Dzong, where Kellas was buried, and would travel in two groups. The climbers, with porters and fifty mules, would make haste over the shorter route, crossing the Tang La and the Donkar La, thus saving two days, though it implied desperate marches. The yaks and the bulk of the supplies, General Bruce indicated, would follow the road to Lhasa and head west to Kampa Dzong, crossing the Dug La some distance northwest of Bam Tso lake. At Kampa Dzong they would await the arrival of Finch and Crawford and the oxygen detail. As the men contemplated the journey, it could not have helped morale that Morshead, only a week before, had received word from London that old Harold Raeburn, the climbing leader in 1921, had gone "off his head" and been diagnosed as clinically mad, obsessed and tormented by the delusion that he had somehow murdered Kellas in cold blood in the wastelands of Tibet.

The three-day direct march to Kampa Dzong lived up to expectations: a bleak and arid landscape, blinding blizzards, and "poisonous" winds from the south driving snow and sand into the eyes and obliterating all signs of a track. The first day, with men and animals strung out across several miles, each leaning into the storm, five porters strayed from the rest and for several anxious hours were presumed lost and quite possibly dead. They had yet to be issued clothing for the heights, and that night they slept in the open without bedding or shelter. The temperature dropped to eight degrees Fahrenheit and the wind blew into the dawn. There was no water save what could be melted from ice, and with a crust of snow covering the ground they were unable to kindle a yak-dung fire. Geoffrey Bruce found them barely alive the following morning at a nunnery at Tatsang, where they had sought warmth at first light. As General Bruce remarked, "It made for a disheartening start."

By the time the expedition reached Kampa Dzong, on April 11, Somervell and Morris were both done in by the "diabolical" cold, and the general had also suffered severely. Within days Longstaff, too, would succumb, overtaken by a violent attack of vomiting and diarrhea, the first sign of the chronic health problems that would continue to afflict him for the rest of the expedition. Beginning on April 18, Wakefield, by now known to the men as the Archdeacon, would effectively take over the position of medical officer.

They made camp in a stone enclosure in the lee of the great fort, beneath the buttress ridge where swallows swept and spun across the rock face. The tireless Norton went birding. Enchanted by the falling light in the west, Somervell did a sketch of the fort, silhouetted by amber waves of color, the brown earth beneath a cerulean sky. Longstaff and Bruce paid a call on the *dzongpen*, and on the morning of April 13 they all visited Kellas's grave, adding stones to the memorial. John Noel captured the moment on film, but several of the men urged him not to allow the footage to be shown. Dignity and discretion, Longstaff insisted, most especially for the dead.

At 2:30 that afternoon, Finch and Crawford turned up, having reached Kampa Dzong in just ten days. Finch, his face blackened by the sun, was uncharacteristically cheerful. He was wearing a flying helmet, quilted trousers, flying boots, lambskin gloves, and his notorious knee-length down coat. Not once on the journey had he been bothered by the cold. "Everybody now envies me my eiderdown coat," he gloated in his diary, "and it is no longer laughed at." Finch was not one to wear success well. He was a skilled photographer, second in talent only to Noel, but no one in camp wanted to hear about all the images he had taken, the first of more than two thousand photographs he would expose in Tibet. His arrival implied a return to the dreaded oxygen drills, which most of the men loathed. "I'm bound to say I find Finch rather tiresome," wrote Mallory. "He is perpetually talking about science as practiced in his laboratory or about photography. In fact it is becoming a little difficult not to acquire a Finch complex. I hope we shall manage to get on."

Not everyone crossed swords with Finch. Around camp he was exceedingly helpful, fiddling with cameras and lenses, adjusting the stoves, even on one occasion shoeing Noel's horse. Finch joined Norton for bird-watching and often compared notes with Noel on photography. He was a keen observer with a trenchant sense of humor. "If one ever wishes to talk with a Tibetan," he wrote acidly,

> it is advisable to stand on his windward side. A noble Tibetan informed me with great pride that he had had two baths, one on the day of his birth and the other on the day of his wedding . . . In this matter of physical cleanliness the Tibetan priests are even worse offenders than the laity; doubtless because they do not marry. As two-fifths of the able bodied population of the country follow a religious calling, it will be readily understood that the odour of sanctity is all pervading. Only once did I see a Tibetan having a bath. It was at Shegar Dzong . . . Disporting himself in the waters of a pool, quite close to the village, was a Tibetan boy, stark naked. On closer examination it transpired that the boy was the village idiot.

Henry Morshead in particular quite admired Finch. "He is a good fellow," he wrote his wife, "and I don't know where all these yarns about him originated last year. We all like him and I personally consider him far more of a Sahib than our local representative of the ICS [Indian Civil Service] . . . We are a very happy party, absolutely no jarring elements, and my only complaint is the extreme cold compared with last year."

Small tensions did, in fact, erupt just four days before the expedition reached Shegar. In order to test the fitness of the men and their acclimatization, General Bruce authorized a short diversion, allowing two teams—Mallory and Somervell, Finch and Wakefield—to have a go at Sangkar Ri, an elegant peak that rose 7,000 feet above their camp at Gyangkar Nangpa. They would travel light, one Whymper and two Mummery tents, with six porters to carry provisions and gear. Before setting out, as Finch later wrote, he and Mallory "had a battle royal on the right way of approach to the mountain—settled by the General's casting vote in favor of my plan." Having assured General Bruce that they would be back down in the valley by 1:00 p.m. the following day, ready to rejoin the march to Shegar, the four climbers set out at

4:15 p.m. on April 20, a Thursday. "Mallory, of course, started to race," Finch recalled, "so, just to show there was no ill feeling, I acted as his runner-up and beat him by just over ¾ hr in the 3¼ hours it took to get to the site of our projected camp."

With both Finch and Somervell sick that night, the men did not get off the next morning until just after 4:00, having first dispatched the porters with tents and equipment back to the expedition. The climbers, now on their own, faced a four-hour slog simply to reach the base of a steep col on the northern side of the peak. "I was going strong being fit in wind," Finch scratched in his journal, "but was very sore in my tummy and vomited several times." Lagging behind Mallory and Somervell and only halfway up the col by 9:00 a.m., Finch and Wakefield decided to turn back to keep their promise to the general.

Mallory naturally went on, encouraging Somervell to join him. They struggled to within 500 feet of the summit. "We were neither of us well acclimatized at the time," Somervell later wrote, "moreover I had had a severe attack of dysentery, and frequent halts and slow progress were necessary for me. Mallory could, I think, have got to the top without me, but instead he chose the safety of a party of two. In his place I should continually have said to my companion 'Come along now, don't be slow,' and so on, but Mallory was absolutely patient and while one could see his eagerness to get on, one could see far more clearly his infinite considerations for his slower companion." This casual comment offers an important insight into Mallory's character as a mountaineer, particularly in regard to the fateful events of June 8, 1924, the day he and Sandy Irvine were last seen alive on Everest. However powerful the allure of a summit, nothing, according to Howard Somervell, would induce Mallory to abandon a weaker climber on a mountain.

The general was not pleased when Mallory and Somervell turned up at Shiling several hours after dark, but he did admire their stamina. In a day they had walked from their high camp for four hours to reach the base of Sangkar Ri, climbed several thousand feet to within reach of its 20,490-foot summit, and then returned in five hours to Gyangkar, only to face a ten-mile ride through "quick sands of evil repute" to rejoin the expedition. By morning all was forgiven. At breakfast the general lightened the mood with an off-color joke. Finch that same morning disarmed everyone by making a fool of himself riding the back of a yak, thus acquiring the nickname Buffalo Bill. Morris, who wore flamboyant native dress to dinner and, "after the manner of a Hindu" had shaved all but a lock of his hair, soon answered to the name Babu

Chatterjee. Mallory became, appropriately, Peter Pan. General Bruce naturally remained the general. "We could not have a better and more able leader than him," Finch confessed. "His immense power over the coolies is worth the presence of a dozen good men."

Morale soared later that morning when, not fifteen minutes out of Shiling, they rounded a rocky promontory and suddenly caught a clear view of Everest, some fifty-five miles away to the southwest. Reflected in the smooth water of the Yaru Chu, the summit seemed much closer. "It was a great and stirring sight," Finch recalled, "one which renewed the enthusiasm of all." Two days later, just before noon, the party reached the Shining Crystal Monastery of Shegar, where it remained for three days, as General Bruce met with the *dzongpens*, secured new transport and additional porters, and made all final arrangements for the mountain. Longstaff bought a rosary for his wife and several trinkets for his children, and with Strutt climbed to the very top of the fort, where juniper and incense offerings burned ceaselessly on a sacred platform surrounded by prayer flags. John Noel labored throughout the stay, securing extraordinary footage of ceremonial processions, monks in prayer, and the wildly theatrical rituals described by the British as devil dances.

Finch, too, set immediately to work, developing not only his own film but also that of Mallory and several of the men. Mallory's images were dreadful, frantically composed and impulsively shot. Finch's work was remarkably good, and his skill in the darkroom allowed him, in short order, to take portraits and deliver prints to the leading local authorities, something of a diplomatic coup for Bruce. "On the whole my photos have improved ever so much," Finch noted in his diary on April 25. "Noel's photos are to my mind not as good and they are far less numerous." In style immodest, but in reasoning quite true; Finch arguably secured the best still images in 1922.

GENERAL BRUCE'S aim was to reach Everest, the sooner the better. Rather than continue west as far as Tingri, as the 1921 reconnaissance expedition had done, he intended to strike south from Shegar, crossing the Pang La, a high pass that offered a direct route to the Dzakar Chu, the river that drained the Rongbuk Glacier. It was country largely unknown to the British, but well trodden by local traders, pilgrims, and monks. Within four days, the general had been assured, they would reach the monastery, poised to move straight up the East Rongbuk to the North Col, a goal that in 1921 had taken Mallory and Wheeler more than four months to attain. The plan after that was simple. Establish a base as near as possible to the mouth of the East Rongbuk, and then fix two or, if necessary, three camps between it and the foot of the North Col. A fourth camp would perch on top of the col, sheltered in the lee of the ice cliff that Mallory had described in his report. From there, a light camp would be carried high onto the Northeast Shoulder to provide the jumping-off point for the thrust to the summit. They would have five weeks, the general anticipated, to reach the top before the onset of the monsoon obliterated all approaches to the mountain.

The expedition left Shegar on Thursday, April 27, and crested the Pang La at midmorning the following day. The light lifted on a quilt of brown mountain ridges running up against a stunning panorama of ice peaks clawing at the skyline, Makalu, Everest, and Cho Oyu. With the exception of Mallory and Bullock, and possibly Heron, they were the first Europeans to reach the heights of a pass traversed today by every climber who comes at Everest from the north. Finch was astonished to see through scattered clouds that the "great northern flank east of the north ridge and the North Peak were almost bare rock. The N ridge also showed up almost wholly as rock." With Noel and Longstaff, he climbed a hillock rising 500 feet above the Pang La. In the few minutes it took them to reach the highest promontory, he noted, "Everest shook off its fleecy mantle [*sic*]."

Longstaff sat down to steady his breathing and the scope in his hands. It was quite wrong, he could see with the glass, to consider any part of the ascent of Everest to be easy, as many had inferred. The strata on the upper slopes of the North Face slanted down like tiles on a roof, the Northeast Ridge was far more serrated than he had anticipated, with great buttresses at several points, and even against the dark rock he could see spindrift sweeping across the face at tremendous velocity, evidence of the ferocity of the winds. The exposures would be formidable.

John Noel, the nonclimber, dwelt only on the aesthetic as he steadied his camera on its tripod. "For weeks," he later reflected, "we had toiled through the desolation of mountain and plateau. At last we sighted our goal and gazed spell bound at the sheer cliffs of rock draped in ice which seemed to form part of the very heavens above us."

Noel and others on the expedition, certainly Mallory and, in their own way, Somervell and Norton, like so many European climbers, projected onto mountains a sense of the spiritual, as if the alpine heights and icy crags were animate, responsive, infused with redemptive power. "I try to compose my pictures," Noel wrote, "as if to interpret, if pos-

sible, the soul meaning of these mountains. For me, they really lived."
Perhaps not surprisingly, Noel did not extend the possibility of such
inspiration or connection to the people of Tibet, who in his mind lived
both literally and metaphorically in the bottomlands, in the squalor
and filth of their hamlets and towns, "sunk in the most fantastic superstitions," their religion but a "solemn fantasy." Quaint and photogenic
as their customs and manners might be, their rituals fundamentally
provoked in him only "disgust." Morris thought otherwise. He found
the constant complaints about hygiene and sanitation a tedious refrain.
But Morris was exceptional, a refugee from his own culture living by
choice in remotest India, his sensibilities already informed by scholarly intuitions that in time would make him a fine ethnographer and a
world authority on the Lepcha people of Nepal.

The expedition reached the Rongbuk Monastery on April 30. Plans
to move immediately farther up the valley, closer to the confluence
of the East Rongbuk, were stymied by the cold and the late arrival of
the stragglers. Longstaff, weak with gastritis, did not stumble in until
well after 4:00 p.m., accompanied by Geoffrey Bruce. The general
decided to camp at the monastery and dispatched Finch to retrieve the
vanguard. The following morning General Bruce, Karma Paul, and a
number of the men went to pay a call on the lama of Rongbuk, Dzatrul Rinpoche, who the previous year had been in spiritual retreat and
unavailable to meet with Howard-Bury.

The lama had never seen an Englishman. The British had never
been in the presence of a living Buddha. Dzatrul Rinpoche was the
incarnation of Padma Sambhava, Guru Rinpoche. Bruce acknowledged
his host as the embodiment of a god, one "depicted with 9 heads." The
general had no idea what this actually meant, but he did take notice
of the cleanliness of the monastery and the reverence shown to the
rinpoche by all Tibetans. Karma Paul, Western educated and clothed,
precisely the sort of native Bruce most admired, positively "groveled"
at the lama's feet. They were clearly, Bruce later wrote, in the presence of a remarkable individual. "He was a large, well-made man of
about sixty, full of dignity, with a most intelligent and wise face and an
extraordinarily attractive smile. We were received with full ceremony,
and after compliments had been exchanged, the Lama began to ask
questions with regard to the object of the expedition."

Bruce's response has become part of the folklore of Everest. According to Finch, who was there, the lama, "an impressive bit of humbug,
with a huge face, almost twice as large as yours or mine," asked why we
would "spend so much money, endure hardships, and face the dangers

he was sure had to be faced, merely for the sake of standing on top of this loftiest of great peaks . . . General Bruce, as usual, rose to the occasion," explaining with irrefutable logic that as the summit was the highest point on earth, it was the location closest to heaven, a worthy goal for any man. According to Finch, this explanation, "which contains more than a germ of the truth, satisfied the revered old gentleman completely."

Given that Buddhists have no notion of heaven, Bruce's own explanation seems on the face of it more authentic: "I was fortunately inspired to say that we regarded the whole expedition, and especially our attempt to reach the summit of Everest, as a pilgrimage. I am afraid . . . I rather enlarged on the importance of the vows taken by all members of the Expedition. At any rate these gentle white lies were very well received, and even my own less excusable one, which I uttered to save myself from the dreadful imposition of having to drink Tibetan tea was also sufficiently well received. I told the Lama that I had sworn never to touch butter until [we] arrived at the summit of Everest."

Neither recollection, however, is consistent with what Dzatrul Rinpoche recalled in his spiritual autobiography. According to the *namthar*, the beginning of 1922 found the lama in his fifty-sixth year, gravely ill. After a slow recovery, the rinpoche, though still weak, returned to his labors as abbot of Rongbuk in the second month of the year, for the monastery was in a frenzy of construction and expansion. The monks had only just begun the murals of the sanctuary, and the painters had yet to color the pillars of the prayer hall, when the district authorities from Shegar arrived along with the thirteen sahibs and several hundred beasts and porters. They insisted that he give an audience to the leader of the English. Initially the rinpoche refused, citing his poor health. Relenting under pressure, he agreed to make himself available the following morning. He received three sahibs and their leader, to whom he gave "a picture of the 13th Dalai Lama and a piece of silk. I gave them tea, yoghurt and rice, and then asked them where they were going. They said, 'if we can climb the world's highest mountain, the English government will give money and high position.' "

With no mention of pilgrimage or heaven, the lama told them that the heights were extremely cold, with nothing useful to be done save the practice of the dharma. He then warned them of dangerous forces, wrathful protectors of the land. The British asked for his protection, sought permission to gather firewood, and vowed not to kill any creatures. "After they had gone," he recalled, "I sent a trunk of meat, four bricks of tea and one bowl of flour according to our local tradition of hospitality. They camped at the bottom of the mountain, then, I heard they camped for seven times for each level they reach, with great effort they use magical skills with iron nails, iron chains and iron claws, with great agony, hands and feet frozen . . . [Some] left early to have limbs cut off, the others stubbornly continue to climb . . . I felt great compassion for them to suffer so much for such meaningless work."

Of all the British, Morris was most affected by the encounter with the rinpoche. "I suppose the world would have called him illiterate," he wrote,

> but he was a man who radiated a sort of positive goodness, a true man of God, and it was impossible to conceive of his having an evil thought. He told us that great harm would come if we killed any of the animals or birds, which wandered tamely in the lower reaches of the Rongbuk. Everest, itself, the lama said, was the home of demons, but he did not fear that our activities would disturb them; they were sufficiently powerful to look after themselves. For his part he would intercede with them not to harm us. He smiled benevolently as he said this and asked us to approach him one by one. To each of us he gave a ceremonial scarf and then blessed us by lightly touching our heads with what looked like an ornate silver pepper pot . . . For our porters it was one of the great occasions of their lives. As they entered the presence each man prostrated himself and wormed his way forward to receive the blessing. None raised his head.

It is not good, one of the men later told Morris, "for mortal man to look upon God."

As the expedition moved up the Rongbuk on the morning of May 1, with the wind in their faces and twenty-three degrees of frost, the thoughts of both General Bruce and Morris turned to the hermit cells along the flanks of the valley. "How it is possible for human beings to stand what they stand, even for a year," Bruce pondered, "without either dying or going mad, passes comprehension." Even Morris was bewildered and offended by the austerity of the practice. "Tibetans regard these ascetic monks with the utmost veneration, but their vacuous faces, looking as though they had lost the power of thought, gave me nothing but a feeling of disgust. It seemed horrible thus deliberately to deny the purpose of life." The lama's talk of wrathful deities and wild creatures, yetis inhabiting the upper glaciers of the mountain, inspired confidence in no one.

The first away that morning were Somervell, Wakefield, Crawford, and Finch, detailed by the general to find a route through the massive moraines that dominated the valley, a track suitable for laden yaks and porters. The goal was to establish the expedition base camp well up the eastern side of the glacier, close to the mouth of the East Rongbuk. The burden fell largely on Finch. "I had to lose the others before anything good in this line could be accomplished," he wrote. "None of them have the slightest idea of route finding. It all involved three wearisome double journeys for me, but I had the satisfaction of getting the whole transport through onto the level plain stretching towards the foot of the Rongbuk glacier." Then a curious thing happened: the Tibetans simply stopped and refused to continue. "No argument or inducements by way of backsheesh," a bewildered Finch recalled, "was of the slightest avail. Fear of devils and lack of grazing for the animals were insuperable obstacles."

Finch had no choice but to order a retreat to Mallory and Bullock's old camp from 1921, a mile below the snout of the Rongbuk Glacier, where he furiously instructed the Tibetans to dump their loads. The result was chaos, scores of restless and hungry yaks snorting across the barren flat, ponies on the loose, hundreds of small heaps of saddles, boxes, tents, and equipment scattered in all directions. Aside from sixty porters brought on from Darjeeling, the expedition had picked up a hundred or more local "transport workers," men, women, and no few children. Shaken at the prospect of disturbing the demons of the ice, fearful of the wrath of the mountain, the Tibetans demanded to be paid immediately that they might abandon the valley in all haste. Tempers flared. Longstaff only just managed to "stave off a stoning match between Tibetans and our people." A few choice words from the general quelled the unrest. After several hours, all the yak herders had been dutifully compensated and dismissed, and the expedition, thirteen British and a small corps of Sherpa porters, was "left alone in its glory."

The site was not ideal. There was little forage, and with the ground still frozen, the only source of drinking water was the glacial surge of the Rongbuk Chu, fast and hazardous. The cold was intense, as was the wind, and there was little fuel to be had. The men struggled to erect mess and sleeping tents in the lee of great stacks of stores. John Noel pitched his developing facility close to the stream, using boulders and rope to secure the stays. That evening, "on a night cold beyond imaginings," Morris recalled, he broke open the champagne and each man had a mouthful as they toasted the general for safely leading them through Tibet. As night fell, the clouds cleared to reveal a magnificent view of the North Face of Everest. Though dwarfed by the mountain, their base at 16,500 feet was still nearly a thousand feet higher than the summit of Mont Blanc.

HAUNTED BY the specter of the monsoon, General Bruce did not waste a day. Wheeler's map of 1921 left little doubt that with the base established well below the mouth of the East Rongbuk, they would require three advanced camps running up to the flank of the North Col, not the two initially planned. Porters burdened by heavy loads could not be expected to carry for more than three hours. On that first morning, Tuesday, May 2, the general dispatched Strutt, Norton, and Finch up the East Rongbuk to select a site for Camp I. Wakefield and Longstaff took sick parade and then saw to the medical support, breaking open the boxes to assemble individual kits with all the necessary supplies, one for each of the upper camps. John Noel, meanwhile, worked alone, taking some satisfaction as he set up the world's highest photographic laboratory. Inside the darkened tent, he put together the lined plywood boxes in which he would process several thousand stills along with some seventeen thousand feet of film stock, and he positioned the stove, which, fueled with yak dung, would allow him to dry the negatives. He would work exclusively at night, in temperatures well below freezing. All the processing had to be finished by dawn, when the winds returned to whip up clouds of sand and dust, certain to ruin the emulsion.

The general spent the early afternoon filing one of the periodic reports for Hinks and the *Times*, an obligation he loathed. He paced in the mess while Morris did the typing. "It is a weakness of Bruce's," Mallory noted, "that he hates writing; if only he could realize how deplorable is the result of his dictating he would perhaps bring himself to the effort." General Bruce had more pressing concerns. He desperately needed men. Local supplies of barley flour, dried meat and grain for the porters, and dung to fuel the cooking fires had to be sourced some forty miles away. These loads could be brought up to the heights by yak, provided herdsmen could be found. But the upper camps on the East Rongbuk would need to be resupplied by relays of porters. The bulk of the stores and equipment, including oxygen tanks and apparatus, ropes, snow stakes, crampons, climbing gear, tents, and high-altitude boots and clothing, would have to be moved up the mountain to the foot of the North Col. That depot, Camp III, would anchor a supply line leading to the crest of the col. Camp IV, pitched on the col at an elevation higher than any human had ever slept, would in turn support a light camp somewhere high on the Northeast Shoulder, the jumping-off point for the summit.

Recruiting porters had been much more difficult than anticipated. It was the plowing season, and Tibetan men were needed in the fields. Unbeknownst to the British, the traditional rituals performed at the Rongbuk Monastery in the first days of May were believed by Buddhists to be especially irritating to the demons of the mountain, making it a highly inauspicious time to go anywhere near Chomolungma. As a result the expedition never knew, as the general complained, if "three or four or thirty" contracted coolies would report for duty. Bruce had hoped to reserve the Darjeeling Sherpas for the high camps, but in the circumstances he was obliged to put all officers and men to work. This labor shortage, ultimately resolved as word reached Nepal and enterprising Sherpa men and women from Solu Khumbu crossed the 19,050-foot Nangpa La, had two immediate and serious consequences: it placed added physical strain on the climbers even as it delayed, by several critical days, the arrival of the oxygen apparatus at Camp III. Both factors would prove highly significant to the outcome of the expedition.

Shortly after 4:00 p.m. the scouting party returned, having found, as Finch recalled, a "splendid" site for Camp I, near a stream about a quarter mile west of the snout of the East Rongbuk Glacier on the north bank. At an elevation of 17,800 feet, it was roughly three and a half hours, or three miles, from their base. The going was "poisonously monotonous" but without serious challenge, though at one point Finch had to cut a few steps. To his surprise, the first blow with his new and "beautiful Schenk ice-axe" bent the blade almost parallel to the shaft. It was his first experience of Himalayan ice.

The following morning, Wednesday, May 3, with Finch detailed to put in order the high-altitude kits, General Bruce sent Somervell, Crawford, and his nephew Geoffrey back to Camp I, along with forty-three porters laden with some twelve hundred pounds of yak dung for fuel. The day was cold but clear, with stunning views of Everest. They lingered long enough to build four roofless stone huts, which would later be covered with tarps and canvas, tents being in somewhat short supply. At noon the weather turned, as it did each day, with clouds covering the sun and the usual "pestilential wind" arising from the west. Meanwhile, at base camp, Mallory was restless. He had received no letters from home in nearly two months. Word that Finch intended to deliver a lecture to the entire expedition sent him literally running for the hills. He and Somervell persuaded the general that further acclimatization demanded an excursion.

On Thursday morning, even as Finch assembled his props—Primus stoves and various fuels: kerosene, petrol, and absolute alcohol—Somervell and Mallory set off early to climb a 21,850-foot peak high above the west bank of the Rongbuk. The scramble almost ended in disaster. On the ascent the nails of Mallory's boots slipped on a granite slab; in falling, he badly skinned the back of his right hand. Then, higher on the mountain, as he worked his way along a broken ridge, he dislodged a large stone, which fell heavily on his foot, badly bruising his big toe. He had just the strength to heave the boulder down the slope. Fortunately no bones were broken, but the pain was severe and Mallory was grateful to have a little whiskey in his tea when finally they returned to camp.

Finch, too, had a bad day. His cooking and stove demonstration went well enough. The Tibetans and "high-going coolies" had been impressed by the pyrotechnics, though the British climbers perhaps less so. But a second experiment ended poorly. In addition to cylinders of gas, regulators, and masks, Finch had devised a backup method for oxygen resuscitation. This involved a chemical reaction of sodium peroxide in what was known as an oxylithe bag. The idea was simple: at rest, the exhausted climber would lean face-first into a sack, add cold water, and absorb a blast of oxygen released by the reaction. For just this purpose Finch had brought across Tibet solid blocks of sodium peroxide weighing altogether no less than 125 pounds. Noel, working the previous night in his sealed and darkened tent, had found that the air quickly became deoxygenated, making it difficult to breathe. He complained to Finch, who gave him a tin of oxylithe just after the morning lecture. The filmmaker did as directed, but less than ten minutes after he added water the entire works exploded with a great flash of flame, leaving the interior of the tent thick with a caustic mist of soda.

"It strikes me that oxygen from oxylithe will want some watching," Finch conceded in his diary. "Tomorrow I am going to give one of Leonard Hill's bags a try-out, but I'm not going to take any chances!" Breathing the oxygen-enriched soda spray, he soon discovered, caused "violent coughing and produces . . . a vile slimy taste in the mouth which must be relieved by frequent expectoration." This dramatic and very public failure could not have inspired confidence in those skeptics already resistant to the entire oxygen scheme, especially when Finch, despite the fiasco, nevertheless insisted on sending bags of sodium peroxide up to the highest camps. It was perhaps no wonder that he became ever more isolated in what the others viewed as an oxygen obsession.

Friday, May 5, was, according to Wakefield, the "finest day to date," clear and sunny through the late afternoon, with only a slight breeze by evening. Strutt, Longstaff, Morshead, and Norton set off early on an extended reconnaissance, charged with the task of finding locations for Camps II and III and assessing the conditions of the ice and snow on the flank of the North Col. The year before, Wheeler had explored and mapped much of the East Rongbuk, and with Mallory and Bullock had traversed, from the Lhakpa La, the great cirque at the head of the glacier to climb the col. But to date no one had walked the entire length of the valley. Strutt, Morshead, and Norton would be the first to do so. Along with sixteen porters, they reached Camp I at 12:45 p.m. Longstaff arrived thirty minutes later, noticeably weak. While he rested, with Strutt staying at his side, Norton and Morshead pushed on.

General Bruce, meanwhile, secure as always at base camp, dispatched to Camp I a second party, a supply column of some fifty heavily laden porters escorted by Morris and Wakefield. It fell to Wakefield, bringing up the rear, to keep the small army moving. "It really was the funniest thing in creation," he recalled, "to follow from behind, keeping the flock together, preventing straggling and seeing that everything went ok. We patiently shepherded them from behind, cheering up the stragglers. I felt like an old Westmoreland farmer, driving a flock of sheep to market. We had with us several Gurkha non-coms, helping us like sheep dogs doing the barking (and biting) when necessary." The Tibetans, each carrying eighty-pound loads, were not amused. Just as they reached the head of the trough leading to Camp I, they struck for a second time, refusing to continue. Only Morris's skillful diplomacy, together with a promise from Longstaff to reduce the weight of the loads, defused a potentially disastrous situation. The expedition, already shorthanded, needed at least ninety porters; it could hardly afford to lose fifty that it had.

With Morris and Wakefield heading back to base camp, Strutt and his men pushed ahead on May 6, reaching Wheeler's old 19,360-foot camp just before noon. Finding it inadequate for a large party, they continued, eventually placing Camp II at 19,800 feet on the west side of the valley just below the spur that terminates Everest's North Ridge, some four hours beyond Camp I.

At this point, as if on cue, the strain of weeks of exposure and exhaustion caught up with several members of the expedition. Long-staff, severely depleted, could not continue and sent a note saying as much to General Bruce. At base camp Crawford was also down, as was Finch, who took ill on Saturday and remained, on medical orders, in bed through Tuesday, setting back the oxygen preparations by three days.

On Monday, May 8, leaving Longstaff to rest at Camp II, Strutt, Norton, and Morshead, with five porters, continued up the East Rong-buk. At first the ground was open, the way clear, but two miles out they ran into a maze of jagged ice pinnacles, which forced them onto the true left bank, the western side of the valley. Eventually they found a deep trough running through the seracs to the smooth surface of the glacier, ice so polished and hard they needed crampons, despite the easy angle of ascent. The distance from Camp II to Camp III, ulti-mately established at 21,000 feet on a broad snow plateau just below the steep slopes leading to the North Col, was only three and a half miles, but the route was not trivial. Broken by crevasses, swept by wind and snow, with towering ice distorting the senses, it demanded real mountaineering skills, something the porters would have to acquire.

At base camp, Wakefield and the general continued to worry about the health of the expedition. The advance reconnaissance party, returning just after lunch on Tuesday, May 9, brought word that Long-staff had managed to walk down as far as Camp I but was unable to go farther. That very morning Geoffrey Bruce, Morris, and a dozen porters had headed up with supplies, including flags, wooden stakes, and rope to mark the upper route through the ice pinnacles. Strutt reported to the general that Morris, too, was down, last seen vomiting, and severely depleted from "mountain lassitude."

On the morning of May 10 General Bruce ordered Wakefield to lead a stretcher party to Camp I to evacuate Longstaff. It was a bright morning, with five degrees of frost. The porters rushed ahead. Wake-field moved deliberately to the rescue, and after two and a half hours he met the Tibetan porters coming down the trail with the invalid. At base camp, Somervell gave up his place in Wakefield's tent so that Longstaff might have constant attention. It was a peculiar outcome: Somervell, the brilliant military surgeon, avoiding sick parade duties at all cost; Longstaff, the expedition's medical officer, now the patient; and Wakefield, the forgotten physician, moving reflexively into the breach.

Longstaff spent the next three days in bed, emerging only on the afternoon of May 13, voiceless and still very weak. Though the most experienced mountaineer, he never fully recovered and was essentially lost to the expedition. "A great heart in a frail body," a shaken Mallory wrote. "It is very distressing." Morshead feared "another Kellas case, unless the General insists on his staying down at base. It's a pity that people cannot learn that Himalayan mountaineering is a young man's game." In truth, Longstaff ought never to have been allowed to go to Tibet. His Harley Street medical exam, conducted by Dr. Anderson on December 20, 1921, had concluded that he "was not robust enough to stand severe strains." That Longstaff had been permitted to join the expedition, and appointed to the critical role of medical officer, suggests how much the British still had to learn about the challenges and perils of Everest.

Even before learning of Longstaff's collapse, General Bruce had been concerned about morale. An "epidemic" of influenza and diarrhea had swept through the porters. Many had simply "cleared off," as Finch recorded in his diary, "scared of the devils that haunt the snows." The news from home was bleak. Three bags of mail had arrived on May 6, with the last letters posted from England on March 29. One of them brought word to Wakefield that his wife, Madge, had suffered a severe infection in the mastoid cavity of her skull, a potentially lethal condition in the era before antibiotics. In their absence Mallory's wife, Ruth, had also been gravely ill. Morris, alone at Camp I, summed up the frustrations of idleness and isolation. There was little to occupy the long evenings. In bed by 5:00 p.m. after a dinner of lukewarm stew, the air so cold it was impossible to read a book for more than a few minutes, sleeping in fits and starts. "I should like to be able to say," he later recalled, "that on these occasions my thoughts were concerned with the nature of the universe, but they were not; the only thing I thought about was food."

When in doubt, the general always chose action. Even as Wakefield moved to the rescue of Longstaff on the morning of May 10, Bruce impulsively set in motion a new plan, ordering Mallory and Somervell, with all available porters, to head up that very afternoon, with the goal of establishing Camp IV on the crest of the North Col within two days. From there, as Mallory wrote Ruth, they would get "as high up the mountain as we can." It would be a "tremendous undertaking at this stage," Mallory noted, even as he hastily tore pages from his diary to send to her in lieu of a proper letter, which he had no time to write.

In retrospect, this was a critical moment, a hinge of fate that ultimately determined the outcome of the expedition. The general had always intended that Mallory and Somervell, climbing without oxygen, would have the first go at the mountain; Hinks and the Everest Committee back in London had virtually demanded as much. But even as Mallory and Somervell scrambled to organize their gear and grab a bit of lunch before their departure, George Finch was still under the impression that he and Norton would climb together with oxygen. "Mallory and Somervell start this afternoon upwards," he wrote in his diary on the morning of May 10. "In a few days time Norton and I start for the same thing with oxygen." Finch's main concern was how to get the apparatus and supplies up to Camp III with the "35 odd coolies we have of our own." As far as getting up the mountain, he wrote, "Personally I am quite optimistic (that is as far as the oxygen party is concerned), though I don't give Mallory and Somervell a foot above 25,000 feet."

For all of Finch's quirks of character, the petty antagonisms, the ridicule that greeted his drills and experiments, there was still, as of May 10, the full intention of giving the oxygen party a fair and equal shot at the mountain. For precisely this reason General Bruce, despite his reservations about Finch and the entire gas initiative, had assigned Norton, a climber of considerable experience and strength, to Finch's team. Then, disastrously, on the evening of May 10, Finch suffered a relapse of dysentery so severe that for five days he could barely move from his tent, incapable of even writing a note in his diary. When finally his stomach trouble passed, the entire momentum of the expedition had shifted. Norton and Morshead had gone up the mountain to join Mallory and Somervell. Finch had been relegated, if not to a secondary role, at least to a place of such handicap that success would demand almost miraculous exertions. "Hitherto I had been sanguine in the extreme about getting to the top," he later recalled, "but when I saw the last mountaineers of the expedition leave the Base Camp, my hopes fell low. Any attempt I could now make upon Mount Everest would have to be carried out with untrained climbers."

MALLORY AND SOMERVELL had set off from base camp with forty porters just after 1:00 p.m., crossing paths with Wakefield and the rescue party just below Camp I as they brought Longstaff down off the mountain. Without incident they reached Camp III on May 12, a Friday, whereupon they immediately sent all but two porters and a cook back to Camp I to fetch more loads. The following morning, accompanied by a single porter, Mallory and Somervell, with one Mummery tent, 400 feet of rope, and a bundle of wooden ice pegs, set out to establish a route up the North Col. Their challenge was not simply to reach the height of the col, as had been the case in 1921, but to lay down a line that could be repeatedly climbed by porters laden with supplies for the higher camps. Not unexpectedly, as Mallory soon recognized, the conditions and alignment of the snow had changed dramatically. The lower part of the previous year's approach now glittered in blue ice. Even had it been possible or practical to cut steps, the exposure would have been too severe and the footing too precarious for Tibetans with no mountaineering experience.

Mallory instead chose a route that led to the left and rose over firm snow to a steep slope, unchanged since 1921, that ultimately reached the shelf just below the summit crest. It was hard work, and they arrived exhausted at midday. The wind was moderate compared to the previous year's gale, but still strong. Fearful of the gusts, Mallory and Somervell roped up as they moved across the broad ledge of snow toward the lowest point of the col. They soon found their way blocked by a crevasse too wide to be jumped, and beyond it another obstacle insurmountable without a ladder. For a moment Mallory despaired that these single impediments might be, as he later recalled, the broken links in the chain that had carried them so far and brought them so close to the mountain.

Regrouping, he and Somervell backtracked along the shelf to where they had left their Tibetan companion Dasno resting out of the wind. They paused for a bit of food, mint cake and sweet biscuits. The snow cliffs above them were impassable, but Mallory discerned a gap marked by a great pinnacle of ice where a steep slope came down from Changtse, the North Peak. This carried them up to the ridge and onto the col. As they made their way over the snow, heading toward the Northeast Shoulder, each step opened wider the stunning view to the west: the North Face of Everest and the valley of Rongbuk at its base. At one point, having leapt across two serious crevasses, they simply stopped and stared in wonder. "For a time," Mallory recalled, "we completely forgot our quest."

But then, even as the wind grew, they could see the spindrift high on the Northeast Ridge. Everest seemed both near and impossibly distant. Dropping back to the shelf, they set up the Mummery tent, almost as an afterthought, though in doing so they established the highest camp in mountaineering history. Too exhausted for reflection, they returned silently to Camp III, pausing on their descent only long enough to fix ropes on two of the steepest pitches. They were in their sleeping bags by 5:30 p.m., each tormented by a headache and incapable of eating. But they slept with the satisfaction that a route had been found.

For three days they waited in the cold for the rest of the expedition. To pass the time they played cards or read aloud. Mallory had two books with him, a volume of Shakespeare's plays and a copy of Robert Bridges's wartime anthology, *The Spirit of Man*, a collection of poetry and short prose pieces compiled by the poet laureate in 1915 to buck up the morale of the nation and the soldiers at the front. Mallory considered Somervell his closest confidant on the expedition. He did not share Somervell's religious convictions, but he admired his friend's lack of dogma and open mind, his true and evident desire to serve God and love men. "The trouble with Christianity," Somervell told Mallory between readings of *King Lear* and *Hamlet*, "is that it has never been tried." Somervell later recalled these short days and long nights at Camp III: "I forget the details of George Mallory's views on most of the many subjects we discussed but in general he took always the big and liberal view . . . He hated anything that savoured of hypocrisy or humbug, but cherished all that is really good and sound."

While Mallory and Somervell waited in the snow at 21,000 feet, the rest of the expedition marshaled for the first assault on the mountain. On May 12 Crawford, recovered from influenza but still weak, headed up to Camp I. The following day Wakefield escorted nineteen porters to join him, returning to base camp the same day. On May 14 Strutt, Morshead, Norton, and Crawford, with a large convoy of porters, went up to Camp II, and then continued for the higher camp. Mallory and Somervell had that same day crossed the wide snow basin at the head of the East Rongbuk to take the measure of the approaching monsoon from the Rapiu La, a pass two miles due south of the Lhakpa La that looked down into the Kama Valley and beyond to Makalu. So far, so good, they reported to Strutt when the colonel arrived to take command of Camp III just after midday on May 16.

Over lunch, as the climbers huddled together, each with a spoon eating from a common saucepan of spaghetti, a habit that horrified Strutt, they made plans for the attack. Mallory, naturally, wanted as strong a party as possible. Crawford, the transport officer, knew that men were needed below. In a compromise they agreed that eight of Crawford's porters would remain at Camp III, giving the climbing party a total of ten, along with the cook. Crawford, himself weak with mountain sickness, would escort the remainder down the mountain to continue the work of provisioning the higher camps and moving up the oxygen equipment. Given the exertions of the morning and the demands of the North Col, it was also decided to rest the ten porters destined for the mountain for the remainder of the day, allowing time for loads to be broken down and reassembled in lots of no more than thirty pounds, each to be weighed with a spring balance.

Strutt, to whom General Bruce had delegated final authority at Camp III, would determine not only the timing of the attack but also the final configuration of the climbing party. Once again the fate of the expedition hovered in the balance. Strutt shared the general's concerns about the monsoon. Mallory's assurances aside, he could see signs of ominous weather to the south. While the porters rested that afternoon, he and a number of the climbers, including Mallory, crossed the head of the East Rongbuk to have a second look into the Kama Valley from the heights of the Rapiu La. What they saw did not inspire confidence. "The clouds," Mallory later recalled, "boiling up from that vast and terrible cauldron were not gleaming white, but sadly grey. A glimpse down the valley showed under them the somber blue light that forebodes mischief, and Makalu, seen through the rift, looked cold and grim. The evidence of trouble in store for us was not confined to the Kama Valley." As they moved off the divide, he noted, "The bitterest even of Tibetan winds poured violently over the pass at our backs. We wondered as we turned to meet it how long a respite was to be allowed us."

Strutt returned to Camp III convinced that it was now or perhaps never. Norton and Morshead, keen to have a go at the mountain, welcomed his sense of urgency. Mallory maintained that a party of four would have a greater chance of success than a team of two. He admired Norton, had confidence in Somervell, and had limitless respect for Morshead. In the pressure of the moment Strutt, who had no personal illusions of reaching any higher than the crest of the North Col, authorized Norton and Morshead to join forces with Mallory and Somervell. That this decision would leave Finch alone, stripping his oxygen party of any experienced climbing support, did not register as a serious concern.

On the morning of May 17, they set out to provision Camp IV, with ten porters carrying among them some three hundred pounds of gear and supplies, and the five British without loads but quite prepared to pitch in should any of the Tibetans falter. The wind, which had blown at gale force during the night, had quieted with the dawn, and the bright cerulean sky promised heat and glare on the ice. Mallory wore two felt hats. Strutt and Somervell both had their solar topees. Norton and Morshead foolishly went without protection from the sun, and would regret it. The porters trudged up the long slopes without complaint, but "more silent than usual." Mallory marveled that a destination that had been the climax of the entire effort in 1921 was now just another link in a logistical chain as they moved toward their higher goal.

Both he and Somervell were surprised by the relative ease with which they made this second ascent of the col. The strength and fitness of the porters, who readily carried their loads to 23,000 feet, higher than any laden man had ever reached, boded well for the coming trial on the mountain. When Colonel Strutt, gasping for wind, finally crested the height of the North Col, his first impulse was to curse photographer Noel for his absence. "I wish that cinema were here," he exclaimed in a rare spark of humor. "If I look anything like what I feel, I ought to be immortalized for the British public." As the porters dropped their loads and headed back down to Camp III, soon to be followed by the climbers, a bemused Mallory, taking in Strutt's "grease smeared, yellow ashen face," noted that they all looked like hell, wind-whipped and blackened by the sun. "And what do we do it for, anyway?" he asked.

JOHN NOEL was in fact on his way up the mountain, having spent the night of May 15 at Camp I with Morris. The next day, a Tuesday, Wakefield, Geoffrey Bruce, and Finch, with the last of the oxygen equipment, made their move, leaving only Longstaff and General Bruce at base camp. Chongay, among the most respected of the Tibetans, had assured the general that the weather would moderate after May 17, when the ritual at Rongbuk ended. And indeed it did. Wakefield in his diary recalled the beauty of the next day, the stillness in the air, the warmth of the sun by midmorning. The general proclaimed rather optimistically that the change might well be the beginning of the three weeks of fine conditions that typically precede the onset of the monsoon. Longstaff had his doubts.

Finch, by now fully recovered, rested his porters on May 17, even as he and Geoffrey Bruce busied themselves with the oxygen cylinders. All had kept their pressure; none showed less than 110 atmospheres, an excellent sign. On Thursday, May 18, while Mallory and his team took a slack day at Camp III in anticipation of their push up the mountain on May 19, Finch, Wakefield, and Geoffrey Bruce moved up to Camp II. En route Finch gave "G. Bruce, one goorka [sic] and two picked coolies a stiff lesson in the use of climbing irons so that no time need be lost when we arrive at Camp III."

Finch was not about to give up. Leaving Camp II just after 8:00 a.m. on May 19, he led his convoy of porters in four and a half hours to Camp III, arriving at 12:30 p.m. Only Strutt and the cook were there. Mallory, Norton, Morshead, and Somervell, along with nine porters, had left at 8:45 that morning with the last of the supplies for Camp IV. Their plan was to sleep that night on the col and strike out the following day for the higher flanks of Everest. They would establish a small camp at 26,000 feet, spend one night, and then have a go for the summit. At the very least they expected to climb higher than humans had ever been.

For Finch, these new plans—both the allocation of men and support and the configuration of the climbing party—must have come as a terrible blow. After months of prodigious effort, he had delivered the last of the oxygen equipment to 21,000 feet on the very flank of Everest. The apparatus had flaws, and after an overland journey across Tibet there was some damage. But the cylinders of gas were sound, and Finch had all the tools required to make the necessary repairs. His every instinct as a scientist told him that only with supplemental gas would climbers have a chance at the summit. He was equally certain that each man would be capable of just one attempt; the rigors of exposure and altitude would preclude a second effort. Not four hours before his arrival at Camp III, Strutt had effectively placed all of the expedition's eggs in one basket by sending every experienced and fit mountaineer, aside from Finch himself, up to the North Col to attempt Everest *without* oxygen. Why had not even one of the climbers been held back, as per the original plan? Why deplete four of the best men before giving gas a chance?

Finch, to his credit, did not view Strutt's decision as anything more than what it was: a lapse in judgment and leadership that squandered an opportunity and severely compromised their chances of achieving the ultimate goal. Finch saw it not as conspiracy so much as idiocy, but it left him angry and even more determined. The suggestion that Wakefield might qualify to join him as a climber was the final insult. His scratched notes that evening reflected his mood: "Wakefield has come up with us. I don't know what good he expects to do. He can barely crawl along, is always fussing and making a nuisance of himself. Generally speaking he is a busy old woman and good for nothing." Finch's focus instead was on young Geoffrey Bruce. He had forty-eight hours to transform the general's nephew into a mountaineer, a climber both physically and mentally prepared to take on the challenge of Everest.

BY UNCANNY COINCIDENCE, Mallory, Somervell, Norton, and Morshead, along with nine Tibetan porters, reached Camp IV, on the shelf just below the North Col, within minutes of Finch's arrival at

Camp III. Their thoughts turned immediately to shelter, and with the sun still warm they pitched five light tents, three for the porters and two set slightly apart for the British, all in a row along the terrace. Mallory noted the colors against the snow, the green canvas and the blue ice, and somehow it reminded him of ocean waves breaking over "swelling seas." "For the safety of sleep-walkers," he insisted that the openings to the tents be oriented inward, toward the ice wall, away from the exposed drop, an alignment that in any case provided better protection from the west wind.

While Somervell and Morshead set off to fix rope to secure the route from the shelf to the height of the col, Mallory and Norton saw to the food and water. They had two sources of fuel: absolute alcohol and, for emergency purposes, cylinders of white metaldehyde, or meta, a solid that burned readily at the strike of a match. The meta, smoke-less and highly efficient, was in short supply. To melt snow for water, they were obliged to use alcohol in a spirit burner, a laborious process that consumed much of the afternoon merely to yield six large thermos flasks of tea and water for the following day. For food they had cocoa, pea soup, biscuits, ham, and cheese. Well fed, they turned in for the night just after 4:30, as the sun left the mountain and the temperature plummeted. Norton and Mallory shared one tent, Somervell and Morshead the other. They lay with their heads to the door for air. Peering from his eiderdown bag, Mallory could see the crest of Everest sharply defined. All of the signs were favorable. "We had," he wrote, "the best omen a mountaineer can look for, the palpitating fire, to use Mr. Santayana's words, of many stars against a black sky . . . It remained but to ask, would the Fates be kind?"

The plan was to head up the mountain with as light a camp as possible, four loads in all, none exceeding twenty pounds, to be shared by nine porters: two small tents each weighing fifteen pounds, two double sleeping sacks, two thermos flasks, the minimum of cooking gear, and food for one and a half days. The intention was to gain 1,500 feet in elevation before the heat of the sun fully consumed the day, and then in fits and starts to move even higher, making an upper camp at 26,000 feet. Mallory had no illusions that they would reach the summit. "We shan't get to the top," he wrote on May 18 in his last letter to Ruth, but "if we reach the shoulder at 27,400, it will be better than anyone here expects."

Like so many Everest plans, this one did not survive the dawn. Mallory was the first up, and when he attempted to rouse the porters just after 5:00 a.m., he found them half dead, sickened with mountain lassitude, in part because they had sealed the flaps of their tent. Only five were fit to climb. Yet another delay was caused by a trivial oversight. The tins of spaghetti meant for breakfast had been left in the cold. Frozen solid, they had to be thawed, which took time. The climbers were finally off just after 7:00 a.m., with a cheerful Morshead setting the pace as they made their way up the steep slope of snow that fell away to the col from the Northeast Shoulder. Mallory followed with two porters. Norton and Somervell led the rest on a separate rope. They made good progress, following an edge of stones, a virtual staircase that gave firm footing and carried them readily 1,200 feet up the mountain.

The challenge was less the terrain than the cold and wind. Mallory found himself kicking the ground whenever they paused, simply to keep circulation in his toes. He had had the sense to add layers of warmth, a Shetland sweater and a silk shirt; Morshead had merely wrapped a woolen scarf about his neck. Their ability to cope with the cold was not helped by Mallory's rather clumsy blunder when they first stopped to rest. Norton was sitting slightly apart from the others, his knapsack resting on his knees. Gathering up the slack in one of the ropes, Mallory accidentally knocked the pack over. Norton made a desperate lunge, but it tumbled out of reach. Gaining momentum with every bound, it soon disappeared from sight, destined for the Rongbuk Glacier, several thousand feet below. Norton lost all of his warm gear, save what he was wearing, including Mallory's pajama legs, which he had borrowed. Fortunately, the other three had sufficient clothing in reserve, and they could all continue.

But by now the sun had slipped behind the clouds, and the wind grew like a tempest. They plodded up the slope, leaning forward into the gusts, each struggling to breathe. No climber had ever before faced such conditions. Windchill added the equivalent of forty degrees of frost to air already bitterly cold. Mallory took the measure of his senses and found that his extremities were numb. Frostbite threatened them all, and the danger grew with every passing moment. Morshead at last had the sense to put on his sledding suit—scant warmth but at least some protection from the wind. They desperately needed to get into the lee of the ridge, but to move toward the east meant cutting steps in hard snow, 300 feet of grueling labor at such altitude.

It was noon before Mallory, Somervell, and Norton finally attained shelter, behind a wall of rocks. The aneroid measured 25,000 feet. There was no question of going any farther. Morshead lingered well below, accompanied by three of the porters. They had two tents, sufficient only for the climbers. With the weather worsening by the minute, they needed to make camp to allow time for the porters to get down the mountain to the shelter of Camp IV. The challenge was finding anything resembling level ground. Somervell, eventually joined by Morshead, after fully two hours of searching finally located a spot out of the wind where stones could be piled into a low wall, and a small platform built the size of a single Mummery tent. Norton and Mallory searched for similar ground, and some fifty yards beyond came upon a sloping slab of rock, half the dimension of their tent. It would have to do.

The porters headed down at 3:00 p.m., by which time Somervell had set up a kitchen of sorts, just outside the flaps of his tent. They had a quick meal, tins of ham and hot Bovril to drink. None of them had much appetite. The day had been brutal. Norton's ear, severely frostbitten, was swollen to three times its normal size. Three of Mallory's fingers had also been touched by frost. Much more serious was Morshead's condition; he suffered not only from frostbite on the extremities but also a deep and disturbing chill, impossible to shake, and a weary lassitude marked by nausea.

No one slept well. Norton and Mallory crushed together at the bottom of their tent, the former in considerable pain and capable of lying on only one side, Mallory restless for the dawn, his pillow a pair of climbing boots in a wet rucksack. In an exhausting day they had managed to climb 2,000 feet in three and a half hours, albeit with modest loads. This left them lower than he had hoped, but another 1,000 feet would have taken three additional hours, never a possibility. Though still 4,000 feet below the summit, they were camped higher than anyone had ever slept, and in this achievement Mallory found some small comfort. The wind dropped in the night, and there were moments when stars could be seen. But with the dawn came snow, followed by hail, and to the east thick clouds, darkening with the growing light of day.

Mallory was the first to stir, prompting a stifled yawn from his tent mate. "I suppose," Norton said, as if awakening in a luxury cottage by the sea, "it's about time we were getting up." They both groaned at the prospect of leaving the warmth of the sleeping bag they had shared through a bitter night. Both had headaches, and Norton's ear did not look good. As always in the morning cold, it took time to accomplish anything, and finding but a single thermos (the porters having foolishly taken the others), they had to melt snow for tea. There was no flat ground, and as they stumbled about, one of them brushed against the rucksack that contained all their provisions. It fell from its perch and immediately tumbled a hundred feet, only by chance coming to rest on a narrow ledge.

Morshead offered to retrieve it, and suffered considerably for his efforts. When they finally pushed up the mountain at 8:00 a.m., he paused after only a few steps. "I think I won't come with you," he said. "I am quite sure I shall only keep you back." Morshead's withdrawal came as a complete surprise, for he had made light of his troubles of the previous day, and showed no outward signs of serious discomfort or injury. After a brief consultation with Somervell, all four men agreed that Morshead was capable of remaining alone for the day in the shelter of his tent. With not another word Somervell tied into Norton's rope and they set off as three.

Mallory privately wondered whether any of them ought to continue. Starting out, he later confessed, he lacked the power to lift his own weight, and he only hoped that if he did so, step by step, the machinery would somehow kick in. The summit remained their goal, but it took heroic efforts merely to work their way back up to the crest of the North Ridge, some 800 feet above their position. They advanced in spells of twenty minutes, resting for five and then plodding on, moving from ledge to ledge, all of which were tilted to their disadvantage. The angle of attack was severe, yet not steep enough to allow the use of their arms, an exhausting prospect. They were climbing, yet not climbing, and with several inches of fresh snow covering the ground, it made for slow progress.

When finally they reached the ridge, they took a long halt. Mallory's foot was painfully cold. Fearing frostbite, he removed his boot. Norton rubbed his foot warm and suggested that he shed one of the four pairs of socks he was wearing; the boot was too tight. Problem solved, they continued directly up the ridge, heading for a great tower of rock that marked the junction of the Northeast Shoulder and the Northeast Ridge of Everest. Their pace, as Mallory recalled, was no better than a "miserable crawl" and their rate of climb—400 feet per hour by his estimate—diminished with every step.

They had agreed in the lucidity of morning to turn back at 2:30 p.m., whatever their position. At 2:15 they reached the height of a steep pitch, beyond which was somewhat easier ground. They rested and snacked on a bit of food, sweets mostly—chocolate, mint cake, acid drops, raisins, and prunes. None felt truly spent, and the stunning view of the summit of Everest, seen from a vantage where no human had ever been, tempted them to continue. They were, Mallory estimated in his first report from the mountain, perhaps 600 to 700 feet below the Northeast Ridge, a figure he later revised to 400 feet in the official expedition account. Whatever the distance, given their rate of ascent, it would require at least four more hours to the ridge, a destination of no particular significance.

The summit was out of the question. Retreat was the only option. As Mallory later remarked, "We were prepared to leave it to braver men to climb Mount Everest by night." Their aneroid registered 26,800 feet. Certain that they were above the summit of Cho Oyu, which they saw to the west, Mallory later estimated their true height to have been 26,985 feet. Either way, they had clearly set a new record. None of them relished the thought of a second night in bivouac on the side of the mountain. And, of course, there was Morshead to consider. The decision made, they paused just long enough for a nip of brandy, "medical comfort," before starting down the shoulder.

Mallory led, followed by Norton and then Somervell. Dropping some 2,000 feet, they reached Morshead just after 4:00 p.m., and found him well and keen to head down to the relative comfort of Camp IV. Leaving the tents and sleeping bags in place, they gathered their few belongings and began a slow traverse back along the ledge they had followed the previous day. Camp IV was another 2,000 feet below, but with three hours of daylight, they anticipated no difficulties. Uncertain of Morshead's fitness, they tied into a single rope, with Mallory again in the lead; Norton and Somervell flanked Morshead, ready to assist him if necessary.

Fresh snow had obliterated their tracks, and Mallory inadvertently took a lower line, ending up in broken ground, difficult to negotiate: ice and old snow, dark rocks hidden beneath powder. As they crossed the head of a steep gully of snow, Morshead slipped at the precise moment that Somervell, bringing up the rear as anchor, was taking a step. Caught unawares, he, too, lost his balance. The force of their fall swept Norton off his feet. In an instant all three men were cascading down the couloir toward the glacier 3,500 feet below. Mallory, already alert to the hazards of the traverse, was cutting a step when he sensed as much as heard the accident. Before sound had time to form or take on meaning, he instinctively thrust his ax into the snow and spun a coil of rope around it as a belay. Somervell plunged his ax into the slope as a brake, as did Norton. But it was Mallory's reflexive response that saved all of their lives. No one was hurt, but all were deeply shaken, and whatever reserves of strength Morshead might have had were utterly spent.

Though Camp IV was not distant and there remained still an hour of light, they were now dealing with an invalid who could walk only a few paces at a time and whose critical judgment had slipped into the irrational. In his confused and weakened state, Morshead insisted on glissading down slopes that demanded the caution of steps. Only by propping him up and offering constant reassurances could they persuade him to move at all. He had entered that zone of lethargy brought on by hypothermia and provoked by altitude sickness that leaves a person perfectly content to lie down in the snow and die. Norton stayed at his side, lending the support of his shoulder and an arm around his waist, as Mallory sought the easiest line of descent and Somervell maintained the rear. The light faded, and in the gathering darkness they crawled down the mountain. There was no moon, only dark clouds and the occasional flash of lightning. Mallory could hardly see his companions, vague shadows against the snow. At last they reached the staircase of stones that had led them up the shoulder from the North Col. They had only to follow it down, through the long hours of the night.

When finally they reached the snows of the col, they still had to make their way, through the darkness, across a broad ice field fissured with dangerous crevasses. Somervell had a lantern in his pack, and mercifully the air was calm; after a dozen attempts he was able to strike a match and light a candle. In the flickering light, they made their way, eventually coming to the edge of a little cliff, a 15-foot drop. They lowered Morshead by rope and then had no choice but to jump. Groping in the snow, they found at last the fixed rope that guided them down to the terrace where their five tents still stood, pitched in a neat row. It was nearly midnight, the end of a day that had begun eighteen hours before. Not one of them had drunk a drop of water since noon. It had taken seven and a half hours to descend a mere 2,000 feet; nearly four hours merely to crawl the last 300 yards across the treacherous crevasses just above their camp. Now, to their horror, they discovered that the porters, heading down from the col to Camp III, had taken with them every cooking pot. They had no means to slake their thirst, save a mixture of canned milk, strawberry jam, and snow, devised by Norton on the spot. Not surprisingly, the concoction induced an agony of stomach cramps all around.

Their trials were not over. Snow fell heavily in the night, obscuring the old tracks and forcing Mallory and Norton to cut new steps in the snow the next morning. What should have been an hour's descent became four hours of "unbearable" labor, all beneath a strong sun, by men who still had yet to quench their thirst. When they finally reached the base of the col, their discipline collapsed. In the rush for water, the men in the lead inadvertently pulled those still coming down behind them off their feet. Mallory tumbled some 80 feet down the ice until the pick of his ax arrested him at the base of the slope. Photographing his fall was none other than George Finch, who, with Geoffrey Bruce, was heading up the mountain with a relief party of twelve porters. "I could have borne the ignominy of my involuntary glissade," Mallory later wrote, "had I not found Finch at the foot of the slope taking advantage of my situation with a Kodak."

Both Finch and Bruce had oxygen cylinders and a breathing apparatus strapped to their back. They also had two thermoses of hot tea, which they gave to the exhausted and parched climbers. "Most of them," Finch later recalled, "were hardly able to speak coherently. Norton, weather beaten and with obvious signs of strain, gave us a brief account of their climb." Finch had nothing but admiration for what Mallory and the others had achieved, a "magnificent record," not to mention a safe return. Little more was said. The climbers just wanted to drink. Wakefield now came up to escort them back to Camp III, where Noel waited to film the return, along with Strutt and Morris. Somervell alone drank seventeen mugs of tea. Morshead did not wait for camp. He drank his fill at a snowmelt stream. When he finally reached camp, he seemed a new man. "It was thirst that did me in and nothing else," he said, even as Wakefield bound up his black and swollen hands.

CHAPTER 11

Finch's Triumph

GEORGE FINCH AND GEOFFREY BRUCE, along with Arthur Wakefield, had arrived at Camp III on May 19 just in time to see the dark and distant figures of George Mallory and his party making their way up the final ice cliffs of the North Col. Swallowing his pride, Finch got immediately to work. There were, as it turned out, a number of repairs and adjustments to be made to the oxygen apparatus. Equipped with soldering iron, hacksaw, pliers, and other tools, he and Bruce created what was surely the world's highest open-air tinkerer's workshop. It was no small achievement. Working in temperatures well below zero, with steel tools often too cold to handle, he fixed various leaks and inefficiencies, even as he devised a completely new breathing mechanism. The valves of the face mask, as it turned out, stiffened so badly with the cold as to be rendered useless. Finch, anticipating potential difficulties, had brought from Darjeeling T-shaped glass tubes and toy football bladders, with which he managed to assemble a highly effective substitute. Within a day, with the help of young Bruce, he had four sets ready to go. On the afternoon of May 20, even as Mallory and the others struggled toward their high camp, Finch for the first time tested his invention in actual field conditions at high altitude. Just after lunch they set out across the head of the East Rongbuk for the Rapiu La. Wakefield and Strutt walked under their own power, while Finch and Bruce used gas. "The effect of the O_2 was remarkable," Finch later noted in his diary. Though the apparatus weighed some thirty pounds, "we two went ahead like a house on fire."

A heavy snowstorm overnight confined them to camp the following day. But their performance had been so remarkable that Strutt, concerned about the fate of Mallory and his team, dispatched Finch and Bruce with oxygen on a rescue mission the morning of May 22. When the climbers were at last seen coming down the col, Finch and

Bruce decided to head up anyway, both to resupply Camp IV and to conduct a second test of the apparatus. With them was Lance Corporal Tejbir Bura, in Finch's opinion "the most promising of the Ghurkas," whom Finch had recruited to the oxygen team. They met Mallory at the foot of the col around 11:00 a.m., and then moved up. Finch deviated from the established route, and with the new snow was obliged to do a "considerable amount of step-cutting," which he did almost effortlessly. The effect of oxygen, he reported, was to transform a horrendous slog into a "brief Alpine ascent." They readily outpaced the porters, who carried less weight, and reached Camp IV in but three hours. The descent was almost leisurely, fifty minutes altogether. En route they paused like tourists to take some thirty-six photographs, and arrived back at Camp III feeling "fit and fresh."

They had each consumed three bottles of oxygen; the apparatus had performed flawlessly. The Tibetans finally understood why they had been asked to carry steel cylinders all the way from Darjeeling. It was the "English air" that made the British so powerful. Bruce agreed, and to make the point Finch released a stream of pure oxygen over the glow of his cigarette, which flared in brilliant white light, dazzling the porters. As Finch later wrote, "All possible doubts as to the great advantages of oxygen were now at an end."

The following day the entire camp rested, save Finch, who continued to tinker with the oxygen equipment. There were metal joints to be soldered, gauges out of order, washers that had dried out and needed to be replaced. Wakefield dressed Morshead's wounds and saw to Mallory's frostbitten fingers before dispatching the two men, along with Norton, Somervell, and Strutt, down the mountain to base camp. Strutt was especially keen to convey news of the climb to General Bruce, who would in turn pass it on by *dak* runners to the telegraph at Phari to be wired to Hinks and the Everest Committee in London. All were delighted that the previous record, set by the Duke of Abruzzi in 1909 on Chogolisa in the Karakoram, had been broken without the use of supplemental gas. "Nothing pleased us more," Hinks would write Somervell, "than the exciting news which arrived on June 8 and was published the following day than the two words 'without oxygen,' reached 26,800." Hinks's triumph would be short-lived.

On May 24, Empire Day, George Finch and Geoffrey Bruce, along with Noel and Tejbir Bura, all using oxygen, headed back up the North Col. Tejbir and Bruce knew each other well, having served in the same regiment, 2nd Battalion, 6th Gurkha Rifles, on the North-West Fron-

tier. They had survived many a bloody skirmish, but this was an altogether new adventure for both of them. Neither man had any climbing
experience whatsoever, and both were about to attempt the highest
mountain in the world. Bruce stood five foot ten and a half inches and
weighed 165 pounds, shorter and slightly heavier than Finch, who, at
half an inch over six feet and 159 pounds, was rail thin. Tejbir, short
and squat, ferociously strong, appeared almost as wide at the shoulder
as he was tall. Finch had selected him for a simple reason: "The man
who grins the most is usually the one who goes farthest in the mountains." Noel, who planned to go no farther than the North Col, was
along to document their departure and stand watch for their return.
He had become, as Finch later wrote, "a new convert to the true faith,"
which was oxygen.

They passed an uncomfortable but uneventful night at Camp IV
and woke to strong winds and a clear morning. Such was Finch's confidence in the effectiveness of oxygen that he sent his twelve porters
on ahead, certain that he, Bruce, and Tejbir would readily catch up.
At 8:00 a.m. the Tibetans, carrying gas cylinders, tents, sleeping bags,
cooking gear, and provisions for one day, began the long traverse of
the snowfields leading to the Northeast Shoulder of Everest. Finch
and his party left fully ninety minutes later, and though each carried
a thirty-pound apparatus, more than the average load of the porters,
they readily overtook them at 24,500 feet, some 1,500 feet above the
North Col. "They greeted our arrival with their usual cheery, broad
grins," Finch later recalled, "but no longer did they regard oxygen as a
foolish man's whim." As Finch and the gas party pushed up the mountain, leaving the porters in their wake, more than one of the Tibetans
called out for a small sample of the "English air."

The climbers had hoped to camp at close to 26,000 feet, but soon
after 1:00 p.m., some 500 feet in elevation shy of that goal, the weather
turned and it began to snow heavily. Finch sensed the danger of the
coming storm, and for the sake of the porters, who had to get back
down to Camp IV, on the North Col, he ordered an immediate halt.
With the wind growing stronger, they struggled to find anything
resembling level ground for their one Mummery tent. They were on
the spine of the Northeast Shoulder. The windward side, exposed to
the full force of the storm, was out of the question. Yet to the east,
in the lee of the height of land, there was nothing but steep, exposed
slopes and jumbles of rock. They had no choice but to level off a small
platform on the very backbone of the shoulder, pitching the tent at
the edge of precipices that fell away 4,000 feet to the main Rongbuk

Glacier on one side, and on the other to the head of the East Rongbuk and their advanced base at Camp III.

When the last of the porters had scurried down the slope, Finch checked the ropes holding down the tent and then crawled in to join Bruce and Tejbir as they waited out the storm. The air was bitterly cold, and the tent filled with small crystals of snow, which alighted on every surface. Wrapped in every bit of clothing they had, they huddled together for warmth. Using blocks of solid fuel, they managed to warm some stew. Hot drinks were out of the question. At such heights water boils at too low a temperature to make proper tea. Finch consoled himself with a cigarette, even as he assured his companions that the summit was theirs for the taking.

But as the sun went down, the storm raged, growing to hurricane force. Gusts tore at their tent with such ferocity, Finch later recalled, that the ground sheet with all three men on it lifted off the packed snow. They had to force their weight fully against the canvas, leaning with all their strength into the wind, lest the entire tent be blown off the mountain. And even as they struggled to hold it down, they feared that at any moment its fabric would be torn to ribbons. No one slept. It was too dangerous even to attempt to do so. "We fought for our lives," Finch wrote, "realizing that once the wind got our little shelter into its ruthless grip, it must inevitably be hurled, with us inside it, down on to the East Rongbuk Glacier, thousands of feet below."

By midnight every surface was coated in frost, and frozen spindrift had entered every bit of clothing, including the insides of their sleeping bags, which were soon dangerously damp. An hour later, the storm reached its peak. "The wild flapping of the canvas," Finch noted, "made a noise like that of machine-gun fire. So deafening was it that we could scarcely hear each other speak." At 2:00 a.m. there was a lull in the wind. Finch summoned the strength to go outside and managed to tie down the tent by passing an alpine rope over the ridge and poles and fastening both ends firmly to boulders. He returned to the tent utterly spent and chilled to the bone. With the rope in place, they managed a few moments of rest, though sleep eluded them all.

"Dawn broke bleak and chill," Finch later wrote. "The snow had ceased to fall, but the wind continued with unabated violence." Throughout a long morning, they took turns venturing outside, never for more than a few minutes at a time, to tighten the ropes and build a small wall of stones on the windward side, which gave some protection. Until the storm abated, they were completely trapped and at the mercy of the mountain. Even had they wanted to abandon the climb, retreat was not an option. Outwardly Bruce and Tejbir stood up well, without complaint. Still, Finch wondered, "How much longer could human beings stand the strain?" They prepared another meal, and the flames from the spirit stove caused in Finch "an anxiety bordering on anguish lest the tent, a frail shelter between life and death, should catch fire." At noon the storm "regained its strength and rose to unsurpassed fury." A stone struck the side of the tent, leaving a great gash in the canvas. The situation was desperate, yet they had no choice but to endure. "No human being could survive more than a few minutes' exposure to a gale of such fury coupled with so intense a cold," Finch speculated.

Finally, close to 1:00 p.m., the wind broke and the worst of the storm passed. Sensible men would have returned to the North Col and continued down to the safety of Camp III. Finch wanted to stay another night and have a go at the summit the next day. He tentatively raised the question with Bruce, quite prepared to follow his lead. Bruce wanted nothing of retreat. Speaking Punjabi, he shared their thoughts with Tejbir, whose only response was to "broaden his already expansive grin."

The moment's elation was soon quelled by their circumstances. With the last of their fuel they had a meager meal, eating the last of their food, as well. If they were to climb Everest, it would be on empty stomachs. They were huddling in what remained of their tent when unexpectedly, around 6:00 p.m., they heard voices outside. Six Sherpas, led by the "indomitable Tergio," had on their own accord left the North Col that afternoon as soon as the storm passed. John Noel, in his concern, had sent thermos flasks of hot Bovril and tea. Finch thanked them for their efforts, but with the hour so late he sent them immediately back down the mountain, with instructions to return the following day at noon. He watched them scamper away, wondering how far they would get before darkness fell. They had left the North Col at 4:00 p.m., clearly risking their lives to bring comfort to the climbers. On the way down they would become lost, and not reach the shelter of Camp IV for five hours. Only a miracle kept them from death.

Unaware of the plight of Tergio and his men, the climbers settled in for another miserable night. Exhausted, on starvation rations, deadened by the cold, they wore the strain on their faces. In the moment Everest was forgotten. The challenge was to survive the night. They were all, Finch observed, "ravenously hungry, even, I think, to the point of cannibalism." The one thing they did have was tobacco. Finch loved to smoke, and he seriously believed that it had a "most beneficial effect on respiration at high altitudes." He was fully capable of sometimes glossing in technical language the most ridiculous of ideas. "Something in the smoke took the place of the carbon dioxide in which the blood is deficient, and acted as a nerve stimulant," he maintained. "The beneficial effect of a cigarette lasted as much as three hours. As luck would have it, we had with us a fair supply." A tent thick with cigarette smoke surely was not the best space for men already weak, hungry, and queasy from the altitude.

At their lowest ebb, Finch had an inspired idea. He hauled one of the oxygen sets into the tent and insisted that all take a shot of the gas. Tejbir resisted, but as soon as he relented, his face brightened. The effect on Bruce was also immediate and profound. Finch, after one inhalation, felt the "tingling sensation of returning life and warmth to my limbs." Here was the key to sleeping at extreme elevation. Finch was positively joyous as he rigged the tanks to allow each of them to breathe a small amount of oxygen throughout the night. The effect was miraculous. Not only could they rest, they slept well and remained warm. Finch later wrote that oxygen alone saved their lives.

They woke before dawn, feeling much stronger than they had the previous morning. Finch had slept with his boots on. The others had not, and it took a full hour with burning candles to thaw the leather. With nothing for breakfast, they set out at 6:30 a.m. as the first sunlight fell on their camp. Bruce and Finch, with water bottles, cameras, warm gear, and the apparatus itself, each carried forty pounds. Tejbir, with two extra cylinders of gas, shouldered nearly fifty. The plan was to have Tejbir accompany the climbers only as far as the junction of the Northeast Shoulder and the Northeast Ridge. Taking on fresh cylinders, Finch and Bruce would then continue, while Tejbir would head back down to await their return at the high camp.

They had not gone more than a few hundred feet from camp when it became clear that the tough old Gurkha soldier simply did not have it in him. Bruce exhorted him for the sake of the honor of the regiment to keep going. Shame lifted him to 26,000 feet, but then Tejbir completely collapsed, falling face-first into the rocks, and smashing the delicate glass instruments of his oxygen apparatus. Finch, more concerned about the equipment than the man, was furious. Bruce again challenged Tejbir's pride, but the Gurkha was beyond the end of his tether. After reviving him with oxygen, they directed him down the mountain, with orders to remain in the high camp, which could be readily seen some distance below.

Finch and Bruce lightened their loads by abandoning all but one of their ropes, even as they took on extra cylinders of gas from Tejbir's pack. Moving over easy rocks, they continued up the shoulder, making good time to 26,500 feet. But now the wind returned, blowing with such force that Finch had no choice but to abandon the shoulder and seek protection in its lee. They began to work their way across the North Face of the mountain and soon found themselves on the great sandstone slabs of the Yellow Band, a sedimentary formation that sweeps across Everest. Though technically not difficult, the rocks slope out and steeply downward and can be slippery with snow, with treacherous exposures that transform the simplest of falls into fatal disasters. To save time Finch did not rope up, leaving Bruce to traverse the "steeply sloping, evilly smooth slabs" without protection, a daring achievement for a man who had never before been on a mountain.

As they moved across the North Face they came ever closer to their goal, though they gained little in height. It was all exhausting work, rendered possible by the oxygen on their backs. When a cylinder emptied, they took great delight in flinging it down the slope, lightening their load by five pounds, even as they listened to the sound of metal tumbling over rocks, "the good steel clanging like a church bell at each impact." Finch paid close attention to his aneroid, measuring his advance, his challenge of Mallory. At 27,000 feet he had won, and all his thoughts turned to the summit. He abandoned the traverse and led Bruce upward, moving in a diagonal direction toward a point on the Northeast Ridge halfway between its junction with the Northeast Shoulder and the base of the summit pyramid of the mountain.

They had climbed perhaps 300 feet when suddenly Finch heard a cry from young Bruce: "I'm getting no oxygen!" Finch, perhaps 20 feet above, immediately raced down, reaching a desperate Bruce just in time to grab him by the shoulder as he was about to fall backward off the mountain. Finch dragged him forward, saving his life, even as he inserted his own breathing tube into Bruce's mouth. At an elevation where most men can hardly think, Finch worked the problem. "Systematically I traced the connections from the cylinder in use down to the pressure gauge and flow-meter and found both in action, the latter recording a flow of 2.4 litres per minute." The culprit was a broken glass T in the mask.

While Bruce regained his steadiness, Finch first modified his own apparatus that both men might breathe from the same cylinder. He then set about repairing Bruce's set, replacing the glass part with a spare he had carried from Darjeeling precisely for this purpose. With both sets functioning properly, the crisis resolved, he consulted his aneroid. Their elevation was 27,300 feet—the highest that man had ever climbed. Finch, pilloried from the start as an Australian, dismissed as a scientific eccentric, marginalized as a colonial irritant, had done the impossible, and in doing so had changed mountaineering history. The Duke of Abruzzi's record had stood for thirteen years until shattered by Mallory, who'd climbed 2,200 feet above the previous mark. Mallory's record had endured for less than a week until broken by George Finch and Geoffrey Bruce, climbing with oxygen.

Finch naturally wanted to go higher, but he knew there was no point. The summit, still 1,700 feet above, could not possibly be reached with any chance of a safe return. To attempt even another 500 feet, he recognized, would be suicidal. Geoffrey Bruce, badly shaken by the incident, which had almost led to his death, was in no psychological state to continue. The young soldier had set a world height record on his very first mountain climb. What more could Finch possibly ask of him? They were within half a mile of the summit. Finch could clearly distinguish individual stones scattered across the snow just beneath the slope rising to the peak. He was so close and yet so far, with no ethical choice but to retreat. "The realization came like a blow," he later reflected.

> My emotions are eternally my own, and I will not put on paper a cold blooded, psychological analysis of the cataclysmic change they underwent, but will merely indicate the initial and final mental positions. Reasoned determination, confidence, faith in the possibility of achievement, hope—all had acquired cumulative force as we made our way higher and higher; the two nights' struggle at our high camp had not dimmed our enthusiasm, nor had the collapse of Tejbir, rude shock and source of grave anxiety though it undoubtedly was. Never for a moment did I think we would fail; progress was steady, the summit was there before us; a little longer, and we should be on top. And then—suddenly, unexpectedly, the vision was gone.

They turned back at midday, roping up as a precaution. Finch, though concerned about the possibility of another failure in the apparatus, took comfort in knowing that men on oxygen at extreme altitude could in fact survive a sudden, if brief, stoppage. The worst fears of the physiologists—that such a cessation would result in instant death—were unfounded. Still, the experienced mountaineer moved across the North Face with extreme caution, never more than a step or two in front of Bruce. A simple stumble could prove fatal, and both men were exhausted.

They reached the spine of the Northeast Shoulder at 2:00 p.m. and dropped four cylinders to lighten their loads. The clear weather was gone, and Finch thanked the fates that he had not been tempted to go higher on Everest. They trudged down the broken rocks of the stairway, even as violent winds whipped small clouds across their path. Mercifully, there was no snow, and in only thirty minutes they reached their high camp, where they found the good Tejbir sound asleep, wrapped in all three of their sleeping bags. They were much relieved to hear voices from the mist just below: the porters coming up to retrieve their gear. They shook Tejbir awake and instructed him to await the relief. Bruce and Finch then continued down, grateful to see, after but a few moments, the warmth of welcoming Tibetan faces.

But now the sheer weight of their trials fell upon them. Their bodies had reached the limits of the possible. Knees buckled as they staggered down the slope. Bruce's feet were completely numb. He walked on stumps, with no feel for the ground. Finch said nothing but feared that his young companion might lose one or both feet to frostbite. When they finally reached the broken snows of the North Col, John Noel was there to greet them. General Bruce would famously describe the filmmaker as "the ever present Noel," adding, "There is no more thorough member of the expedition than he." This reputation came from moments such as this one. For four days and three nights Noel had maintained his vigil at Camp IV, scouring the upper slopes of the mountain with his distant lens as he tracked the movements of the men. He knew that climbers without food or support had never spent two nights essentially in bivouac at such heights. That Finch and Bruce had elected to go on, despite this ordeal, had astonished him, even as it had filled him with dread. He'd feared the worst when they were hours overdue. As clouds had swept over the Northeast Shoulder, he had burned, at intervals, piles of unexposed film as signal flares. When finally they stumbled onto the flat of the col, he had hot spaghetti and flasks of steaming tea ready for them.

Wakefield and Crawford had come up to the North Col on May 25, arriving just hours after Finch and Bruce had departed for their summit attempt. Despite his age and essential role as medical officer, Wakefield still saw himself as a climber. He and Crawford intended to have their own go at Everest, a plan that collapsed when Wakefield inadvertently overdosed his companion with morphine. As Wakefield later explained in a letter to his wife:

I have overdosed Crawford with morphia and am writing this
while he is sleeping it off, hours after we should have started had
we been able to go. We had not slept at all for 4 nights owing
to the altitude, and we both thought that a good night's sleep
before our attack would do him good. I happened to have some
morphia with me that I had been given for this very purpose.
So I gave him 0.1 gm by mouth and told him to take another
in an hour's time [if] the first had no effect. He took the 2nd,
had a magnificent night's sleep, but is now far too sleepy to
think of climbing even had the drink difficulty allowed us to go!
I remember now hearing somewhere that high altitudes may
reduce the doses of all medicines necessary. He'll be alright in
an hour or two, but it is dicky up with the attack.

Wakefield's medical error may well have saved both their lives, for
neither he nor Crawford was remotely prepared for the rigors of the
mountain. Their aborted effort did have one serious consequence:
with Wakefield and Crawford encamped at the North Col on May 27,
there was no tent available for Finch and Bruce, who were obliged to
continue down to Camp III. The indefatigable Noel escorted them,
"nursing them safely," as Finch recalled, in forty minutes to the base
of the North Col. They reached the relative comfort of Camp III at
5:30 p.m. After two horrendous nights fighting to survive the storm,
with no sleep or food for warmth and strength, they had from an elevation of 25,500 feet climbed 1,800 feet, only to descend more than
6,000 feet, all in less than eight hours. They were "dead, dead beat,"
but even more famished. Noel served up a feast, four whole quails followed by nine great sausages, and still they asked for more. That night
Finch took a tin of toffee to bed, tucking it away in the crook of his
elbow, and slept without stirring for fourteen hours.
    Finch had escaped serious harm, though the cold had penetrated
the half-inch soles of his boots and three layers of socks to burn four
small patches of frostbite on the skin, enough to make walking painful. Bruce's feet were bad, the left one useless. Neither man had the
strength to get off the mountain on his own. On the morning of
May 28, a Sunday, they piled onto a sled and were dragged down the
glacier by four of the porters. Once the ground became too rough,
about halfway to Camp II, Finch hobbled, supported by one of the
Tibetans, while the other three competed for the privilege, as they saw
it, of carrying the indomitable Bruce on their backs. Courage, strength,
equanimity, and perseverance were traits Tibetans both embodied and

admired. As they all left the shadow of the mountain, young Bruce glanced back over his shoulder. "Just you wait, old thing," he said, "you'll be for it soon."

Cadging food at every opportunity, with another great meal at Camp II, Finch and Bruce trudged back down to base camp, arriving just in time for lunch on Monday, May 29. News of their record climb had reached General Bruce the previous day, brought down the mountain by Noel and Somervell. No one could challenge the achievement. Finch and Bruce, as Percy Farrar of the Alpine Club would later write, had "added a page to the history of Everest that need fear no competition." Douglas Freshfield, another iconic figure of British mountaineering, described the climb as "one of the bravest feats of mountaineering on record."

On May 24, just days before the historic climb, Arthur Hinks had sent a petulant letter to General Bruce complaining that London had heard nothing of the expedition in four weeks; editors at the *Times* awaited three overdue cables. The first word to reach Hinks in response would be a copy of Finch's account, written at the request of the general, which detailed with some precision the success of the oxygen party. In six hours, starting from their high camp, Mallory and his team had climbed a vertical distance of 1,985 feet to reach 26,800 feet, a rate of ascent of 330 feet per hour. At their highest point, they were one and an eighth miles from the summit and roughly 2,000 feet below it.

Finch and Bruce had ascended to their high camp at a rate of 1,000 feet per hour. During their summit attempt, they climbed at 900 feet per hour, nearly three times the pace of Mallory, in spite of carrying loads weighing more than forty pounds. Their final point was 1,700 feet below and half a mile distant from the summit. They had gone higher and much closer. Mallory's party had had food, less severe weather, and spent but a night on the mountain. After two nights in bivouac, Finch and Bruce had set out on their climb half starved and half dead. Yet still they had achieved far better results. The difference could hardly be the experience of the men. Mallory, Norton, and Somervell were veteran mountaineers at the peak of their powers. Geoffrey Bruce was a novice, the untrained Tejbir most likely somewhat of an impediment to a climbing party. There was only one possible explanation. Knowing that his report would end up in the *Times*, Finch must have taken particular delight in writing his assessment: "The superior results obtained can only be ascribed to the fact that the weaker party made use of an artificial supply of oxygen."

· · ·

THE FATE of the expedition now hung on the opinion of the medical officer. Effectively there were two, Longstaff and Wakefield. At base camp Tom Longstaff, though still suffering from indigestion and insomnia, had recovered sufficiently to reassert his authority. He had been the first to greet Mallory, Norton, Morshead, and Somervell on their return in the late afternoon of May 23. As he saw to their injuries he had tried to lift their spirits, reminding them that they had performed heroically, breaking the long-standing height record by a stunning 2,000 feet.

Longstaff, a veteran climber, knew the dangers of the heights, what it meant to fail, the fine line between success and disaster. At thirty, climbing in Tibet, he had survived an avalanche that swept him 3,000 feet off a mountain by spending two nights in a snow cave at 23,000 feet. He had experienced directly how the brain suffers, how reason becomes impaired, how a body starved of oxygen becomes more susceptible to frostbite, how a climber's strength and resistance weaken with every day spent at extreme altitude. The condition of the men returning from the higher camps disturbed him profoundly. Norton's ear was bad; the top of it no doubt would have to be removed. The cold had entered his boots, damaging both feet. His heart had also been strained. Morshead was destined to lose three fingers, amputated at the final joint. When Geoffrey Bruce was carried into base camp on Monday, May 29, unable to walk, his feet severely injured, Longstaff decided to act. He resolved to give each man a thorough examination. "Must put my foot down," he wrote in his diary. "There is too little margin of safety. Strutt agrees."

That very day he submitted a full medical report to the general. Of all the men, only Somervell was fit. Morshead, suffering constant and severe pain, had to be evacuated immediately, accompanied by one of the medical staff. Norton and Geoffrey Bruce could barely walk. Neither could be expected to render further service. Strutt, too, was worn out, quite lost to the expedition. Finch was also weak, suffering from an enlarged heart. Mallory, with frostbitten fingers and a readily detectable heart murmur, was also deemed to be unfit. Longstaff put these opinions in writing, both to protect himself and to ensure that no man on the expedition be accused of cowardice. "Please impress on all," he wrote to his old friend Younghusband, "that this adventure is the very deuce. The cold at high altitude and the lack of desire for food is hard to stand. The climbers are heroes and saints. They are facing the utmost limits of endurance. It's harder than Polar work. And the climbing is none too easy; it's not an easy peak." Longstaff was clearly of the opinion that the expedition had shot its bolt. It was time to go home. What was the point of launching another assault on the North Col, he argued, when both the fitness of the men and the conditions on the mountain, with the monsoon imminent, precluded any possibility of reaching the summit?

Mallory was not about to give up. For nearly a week he had waited at base camp for word from the mountain and the fate of the oxygen attempt. "I think they will certainly break our record," he wrote to Ruth on May 26, three days after his return. "They have had very good weather. But I don't expect them to have reached the top at the first attempt . . . I shan't feel in the least jealous of any success they may have. The whole venture of getting up with oxygen is so different from ours that the two hardly enter into competition."

This was surely an instance of a man protesting too much, and it was not the first time Mallory had glossed over the truth in letters to his wife. Finch and Bruce had hardly benefited from finer weather. Even as Mallory wrote this note, they were trapped in bivouac for a second day in conditions unlike any ever endured by a climber. The men at base camp were not blind. If the efforts to climb without supplemental gas had been such a distinct endeavor, why did Mallory, upon learning of Finch's success, make immediate plans for a third attempt with every intention of using the apparatus? Mallory, in truth, simply wanted to be the first to summit Everest. He did not really care whether it was with or without oxygen. As for medical concerns, Mallory dismissed the messenger. "Longstaff is in one of his moods of bustling activity," he told Ruth in a letter on June 1, "when he becomes tiresome, inter-fering and self-important."

The medical challenge resolved itself. On May 30, the very day that Wakefield returned to base camp from the higher camps, Long-staff contracted severe conjunctivitis and for several days was unable to perform any duties. Finch, according to his diary, "heard a pretty little plot concocted in the tent next to me." Mallory was arranging for Wakefield to reexamine Finch, Somervell, and himself, all with the goal of foiling Longstaff and securing a clean bill of health. When Mallory's heart was checked the following day, Wakefield declared a satisfactory recovery, having found no evidence of any abnormality. Wakefield had his own motivations, as he wrote his wife, Madge, on May 31: "I am deeply chagrined to say that I am too old for the final summit attack . . . But no man of my age has been higher than me, in fact I am the only one who has stuck it up to 23,000 feet, and the others of my age who have been so high, are now on the sick list and returning home *quam celerrime* [as fast as possible] along with others who have not been so high." Wakefield no doubt sensed and resented the disdain with which others, as we know from their diary notes, viewed his capabilities and contributions. He had hoped to make a mark with Crawford, which was why he was at the North Col on May 27, when prudence would have had him at Camp III, awaiting the return of Finch and Bruce at a place far better situated and equipped to deal with a medical emergency. It was a quixotic notion in every way, but for Wakefield, broken in the war, the mountain offered redemption. Only Mallory had the influence to sway General Bruce, and counter the weight of Longstaff and Strutt, who were both opposed to a third assault.

Wakefield spent the afternoon of May 31 in the general's tent, writing and reading reports, and debriefing Bruce on the results of the medical examinations of that morning. The general, with one eye on London and the expectations of the Everest Committee, agreed to a third attempt. It was not an ill-considered decision. On May 27 John Macdonald, the son of David Macdonald, the British trade agent at Yatung, had arrived at base camp with mail and money for the expedition. He brought word of the political situation in Lhasa. British arms, rifles and ammunition, were finally arriving, but there was no stability. Charles Bell, the reluctant advocate of the Everest efforts, had left the Tibetan capital in October of the previous year. It was by no means certain that the Tibetan authorities would grant permission for another expedition. If the British team backed off now, there might not be another opportunity.

John Noel, present when Bruce made his decision, later cast it in the language of war: "In a struggle between man and mountain, such as this, as in any other battle . . . the moral effect of turning away from the enemy, after having once challenged and opened the fight, is fatal." General Bruce did not see it in this way. Writing to Hinks on June 1, he expressed concern about the weakness of the men and questioned whether any climber could endure more than one full exposure to the mountain. "I shall be very much relieved indeed," he confessed, "when this last attempt is finished because to tell you frankly I am afraid of Everest under the present conditions with the monsoon only within days of us."

To placate Longstaff, who was furious that his advice as both physician and mountaineer was being ignored, the general authorized his old friend to leave immediately for India, accompanied by the sirdar Gyalzen, in order to escort Morshead and Strutt to proper medical care. Traveling light by way of the Serpo La to Lachen, they might well reach Darjeeling in twenty days. Morshead would have to ride with his mutilated hands strapped to his shoulders, and his damaged feet stretched out before him in improvised stirrups. He would need opium for pain but was otherwise fit for the journey. The walking wounded, Norton and Geoffrey Bruce, would go with Tejbir to Kharta, where General Bruce intended to rest the main body of the expedition before undertaking the long journey home across Tibet. Once the general's decision was announced, a certain calm came over a previously anxious and restive camp. It was now a simple matter of each man to his duty.

Outwardly Mallory was sanguine, his only concern being the coming monsoon, which the lama of Rongbuk had predicted to break on June 10. But privately he was torn between caution and a growing obsession. On June 1 he wrote to his good friend David Pye, sharing doubts he would never express to Ruth: "David, it's an infernal mountain, cold and treacherous. Frankly the game is not good enough: the risks of getting caught are too great; the margin of strength when men are at great heights is too small. Perhaps it's mere folly to go up again. But how can I be out of the hunt . . . It sounds more like war than sport—and perhaps it is."

On Saturday, June 3, having bade farewell to their injured comrades, Mallory, Finch, and Somervell started for Camp I, preceded that morning by Wakefield and Crawford, who had gone up in support. Finch, weaker than imagined, could hardly walk and broke down completely when they arrived, just after 3:30 p.m. He was out, and would return to base camp the following day. Keen to be reunited with his wife, he gladly accepted the general's offer that he leave with Longstaff's medical party, scheduled to begin the long trek back to Darjeeling on June 5. It was an odd reversal of fortunes. One day heading for the summit of Everest, the very next joining a party of invalids, clip-clopping their way home.

The snow began to fall late on Saturday, the day of their arrival at Camp I, and continued all through the night and the following day. The climbing party, reduced now to four men, huddled in a small stone hut with walls half the height of a man and roofed with the outer fly of a Whymper tent. It was a miserable shelter in which to wait out the opening squalls of the monsoon. The one thought on everyone's mind was whether it made sense to be making an attempt in such weather. As no one wanted to give voice to the obvious, they spoke little. John Noel's arrival in late afternoon did little to break the monotony.

The morning of June 5 dawned with some promise, and though

the snow was wet and heavy, in six hours they pushed through all the way to Camp III. Morale did not soar when they arrived in the mist to find every tent flat on the ground and all the stores buried beneath eighteen inches of new snow. Fortunately, the next day was clear and bright, the warmest any of them had experienced at the high camp, and though there was little wind they managed, with the help of Morris, who had been ordered up by the general, to dry out most of the gear. The sun did its work on the snow, and with the intense heat by day and the cold by night, the surface hardened. Their plan was to move up to the North Col on Wednesday, June 7. Wakefield, for the moment, would remain in reserve at Camp III, awaiting Mallory's prearranged signals from the col indicating what supplies needed to be brought up by him on June 8. Crawford and Noel would accompany Somervell and Mallory as far as Camp IV, along with fourteen porters carrying food, fuel, and ten cylinders of gas and two sets of the oxygen apparatus. Somervell and Mallory would climb without oxygen as far as their high camp, and use the gas only once above 25,000 feet. This arbitrary decision suggests that while Mallory had no compunction about using oxygen, he had yet to absorb the lessons of Finch's record climb.

Amid great confusion, as Wakefield recalled, Mallory, Crawford, Somervell, and Noel, along with the porters, set out just after 8:00 a.m. They soon discovered that the sun had failed them. With each step they broke through the crust, sinking to the waist. Strung out on three ropes, trading off the lead at frequent intervals, they essentially plowed a track to the base of the North Col, taking two full hours simply to cross the snowfield to its base. Leaving the other men to rest, Somervell, Mallory, one of the Tibetans, and Crawford, roped in that order, began slowly to find a way up the ice slopes buried in wet snow. Any sign of their previous route had been obliterated. But to Mallory's surprise, even on the steepest pitches, the snow remained firm on the ice below, adhering to the surface so well that he did not need to cut steps. He carefully tested several slopes, trenching the snow to provoke slippage, as would occur in the case of an avalanche. If the steepest of gradients held firm, they would surely have nothing to fear on the gentler slopes higher on the face. "The thought of avalanche was dismissed from our minds," he reported.

The going was nevertheless brutal and excruciatingly slow. Somervell led on a long rope, replaced by Crawford, and finally by Mallory—a tedious rotation so exhausting that the men had to pause to gasp for air after every step. At 22,500 feet Noel turned back. The softness of the snow made it impossible with his heavy cameras. He would instead film the party from the base of the col with his long lens. The decision saved his life.

At about 1:30 p.m. the party halted. After nearly six hours they were still 600 feet beneath the col. The Tibetan porters, strung out on three ropes, clustered to the fore, bringing fifteen bodies close together in the snow. They were on a gentle flank, and had the hour not been late, they would have rested. Instead Somervell plunged ahead, advancing perhaps 100 feet up the slope. The air was still, with no wind, and there was no idle chatter among the exhausted men. The bright sun glared off the snow, and the only sound was that of human breath. Suddenly the quiet was broken by a noise that Mallory later compared to "an explosion of untamped gunpowder." In an instant the entire slope gave way. At first Mallory was able to ride the surge, but then the rope around his waist tightened and a massive wave of snow buried him alive. He thrust out his arms, as if swimming, struggling in the chaos of the tumbling snow in the dark, until mercifully, within seconds, it was over. His arms were free, his legs near the surface. The pressure of the snow grew in intensity. A brief struggle brought him to the surface, the rope at his waist still taut. Miraculously, the porter tied into his rope clawed out of the snow, unhurt, as did Somervell and Crawford, who had endured experiences similar to Mallory's.

Searching frantically about, they saw one group of four porters perhaps 150 feet farther down the slope. Of the other two ropes, one with four men and the other five, there was not a sign. The British began desperately to dig. When the Tibetans down below failed to join them, Mallory realized that their comrades had been carried even farther down the mountain. He rushed down the slope, only to find the Tibetans standing at the edge of an ice cliff 40 to 60 feet high, a formidable drop. The avalanche had filled the crevasse at its base with snow, even as it had cast the nine men into the void. Crawford and the four surviving Tibetans began to dig. Mallory and Somervell dropped over the edge of the crevasse. One man was quickly recovered, still breathing. The one beside him had been killed by the fall. Mallory traced a rope to a second corpse, but then found a man alive, barely breathing, trapped upside down with snow packed hard around his limbs. He had been carrying four oxygen cylinders on a steel frame, which had to be cut from his body before he could be dragged to the surface. Of the others on his rope, they found only one, who was dead.

At Camp III Noel and Wakefield had been watching—the filmmaker through his camera, the doctor through the same binoculars he had used on July 1, 1916, when his Newfoundland boys had gone over the top at Beaumont-Hamel. Wakefield saw everything, as he later wrote his wife: "I had been watching them through glasses winding their way up the steep wall. Then I glanced away for a moment. When I looked back the whole wall was white and there was no string of ascending climbers. At first I thought all had been wiped off by the avalanche. But as I kept looking, the fuzz of snow settled down, and I gradually made out most of the figures still on the slope. I hastily made up a relief party with first aid and hurried up." Wakefield ordered Noel to heat water for tea and then, with four Tibetan porters, headed up with shovels, ropes, dressings, and brandy. At 3:30 p.m. he met Crawford, coming off the mountain to fetch help. "All whites are safe" were Crawford's first words. Wakefield soon saw that he was not needed. Men had lived or they had died.

Of the nine Tibetans who had been swept into the crevasse, the two found still breathing by Mallory would live. Unhurt, they would walk down to Camp III, and within a day be fully recovered, by all appearances utterly free of the emotional fervor that had only begun to torment the British. When Mallory asked them whether an attempt should be made to retrieve the bodies for burial, the survivors replied that the men, their friends and brothers, ought to be left where they lay. The British saw this response as a sign of the universal spirit of mountaineers. For the Tibetans it was simply over. There was no need for explanations, and certainly no purpose to be found in imagining what might have been.

Mallory by contrast was haunted with regret, Somervell tormented by a sense of unfairness. "I well remember," Somervell later wrote, "the thought gnawing at my brain. Only Sherpa and Bhotias killed— why, oh why could not one of us, Britishers, shared their fate? I would gladly at that moment have been lying there, dead in the snow. If only to give those fine chaps who had survived the feeling that we had shared their loss, as we had indeed shared the risk." The bitterness, Mallory wrote, was "in the irony of fate." He and Somervell had been critical of what they viewed as Finch's cavalier treatment of the porters, allowing them, for example, to head up the mountain without escort and unprotected by ropes. They had been appalled to learn that the relief party of May 26 had returned from Finch's high camp at night, obliged to cross the dangerous crevasses of the North Col in the dark, arriving back at Camp IV at 11:00 p.m. They openly condemned such practices, and felt "consciously virtuous" for doing so.

Morris recalled the return of the survivors to Camp III: "I had thought they looked tired when they passed through on their way up, but now they were not only shaken and completely exhausted, but seemed to have aged considerably. It was obvious that we could make no further attempts that year." The question that haunted them all, most especially Mallory, was whether this third assault ought ever to have been contemplated, given the conditions.

General Bruce learned of the disaster within hours. A Sherpa runner dispatched by Morris raced the length of the East Rongbuk, arriving at base camp at 9:00 p.m. The general, who took particular pride in understanding what he saw as the Asian mind, presumed that the Sherpas would react fatalistically: "If it was written that they should die on Everest, they should die on Everest. If it was written they would not die on Everest, they would not, and that was all there was to be said in the matter."

Bruce sent word to Morris to begin the evacuation of the high camps immediately, and then set out to notify the lama of Rongbuk by runner and to offer, in writing, compensation to the families of the deceased, as he would in the case of soldiers killed in battle. Each family, he determined, would receive 250 rupees, roughly £13, in quarterly installments beginning on August 15. The names of the dead were duly recorded: Thankay, Sangay, Temba, Lhakpa, Pasang Namgyn, Norbu, and Pema. Norbu and Pasang, who were fathers, were allotted an additional payment of 50 rupees per child. In the case of the death of an heir, the general specified that the recruiting officer for the Gurkhas in Ghoom would disperse the funds, in consultation with the deputy commissioner and the superintendent of police. In Bruce's official account of the 1922 expedition, there would be no mention of the names of the Sherpa dead.

Among the victims were several of the men who had risked their lives to bring hot drinks and support to Finch and Bruce in their moment of crisis, and two, Sangay and Temba, who had worked closely with Wakefield throughout the expedition. Norbu had been Somervell's servant. The day after the accident, a devastated Mallory headed immediately to base camp to brief the general, while Wakefield remained at Camp III to build a memorial cairn for the fallen, stones that Somervell inscribed with verse and the names of the dead. In the afternoon they headed down to Camp I with Crawford, leaving Morris alone to close down the higher camp. It was a hot and clear day, not a cloud in the sky. The monsoon winds brought warmer air. By the time Morris abandoned Camp III, bringing with him what few supplies he could salvage, the valley had been transformed. The trough of black ice running up the center of the glacier was a raging torrent. The great pinnacles crumbled and toppled, with ice disintegrating until the entire landscape, he recalled, resembled "a vast ice cream that had been left out in the sun." It was no longer safe to walk the valley, let alone climb mountain slopes cascading with avalanches.

The mood at base camp over the next days was grim. The medical evacuees were long gone; Longstaff, Finch, and Strutt would not even learn of the accident until they docked in Dover in mid-July. Norton and Geoffrey Bruce had accompanied them for two days and then, on the morning of the fateful climb, headed south over the Doya La to recuperate at Kharta. They would learn of the disaster ten days after the fact. Mallory, sharing the camp on the night of June 8 with the general, blamed himself for the loss. He was haunted by the thought that children the same age as his own had been left without fathers. "The consequences of my mistake," he wrote to Ruth, "are so terrible; it seems almost impossible to believe that this has happened and that I can do nothing to make it good. There is no obligation I have so much wanted to honour as that of taking care of those men." Writing to Francis Younghusband, he took full responsibility, acknowledging that if he had known more about the snow conditions, the accident would not have occurred. To his old friend and mentor Geoffrey Young, he confided, in a tone both sincere and paternalistic, "I'm quite knocked out by this accident. Seven of these brave men killed, and they were ignorant of mountain dangers, like children in our care. And I'm to blame."

On Saturday, June 10, three days after the tragedy, Mallory, Wakefield, Somervell, and Noel visited the Rongbuk Monastery. They had all initially been uncertain about how the monks would respond. After their second attempt, Dzatrul Rinpoche had sent word congratulating the porters for their selfless devotion to Finch and Bruce, but he had also specifically warned the expedition to leave the mountain. He had foreseen an accident in a vision. When told that men had died, he had responded with sympathy and kindness. He asked only that the climbers attend a prayer service, as Morris recalled, to "honour the spirits of those we left behind."

As the climbers approached the monastery that day, they were astonished to see scores of pilgrims gathering for what turned out to be a most extraordinary pageant. Mallory likened it to Shakespeare, theater in the round. Noel called it a "devil dance." It was in fact the Mani Rimdu, a ritual of intense devotion that over the course of nearly three weeks recalls and celebrates the original dissemination of Buddhism to Tibet. The climbers happened to arrive on the climactic day, when masked dancers in great dramatic flourishes give form to all the forces of light and darkness, every demon and deity. The British stayed only until early afternoon, but before they left each was given a small red pill, a sacred offering that, if swallowed, literally allows one to eat the power of the Buddhist dharma.

FOUR DAYS LATER, the 1922 Everest expedition set out for home. They stopped at the monastery for a final audience with the lama, whom they now described in their journals as "the holiest man in Tibet." Butter tea was served. Noel astonished all by actually drinking some, the first of the English to do so. Dzatrul Rinpoche gave the general an image of the Green Tara for protection, and then blessed the dead, their families, and all who had survived. The Gurkhas were overwhelmed to be in the presence of the lama; they scarcely dared approach to receive his blessings. Several wept as the rinpoche draped ceremonial scarves around their necks.

The warmth and beauty of Kharta and the lower Kama Valley held General Bruce and the remnants of his force for nearly three weeks. They celebrated Mallory's thirty-sixth birthday in the shadow of a monastery at Teng, and the following day they all lunched at the mouth of the Arun Gorge, where Norton had found an enchanting glen. Noel and Morris took off on an exploration of the lower reaches of the Kama Chu, while the others botanized or loafed in the alpine meadows, where the flowers were at a peak. It was a welcome respite from the agonies of the ice. They gathered together at last on July 1. Mallory, still under a cloud, set off alone two days later.

The others started the following morning, and with various diversions and delays would reach Darjeeling in the first days of August. It was for the most part an uneventful journey, though Morris, as transport officer, had to struggle at times to maintain discipline among the porters, especially when it came to drink. "We decided that a man was not drunk," he reported, "so long as he could lie on the ground without actually holding on. It was, we felt, a generous interpretation, but there was one porter who was consistently unable to comply even with this simple test." As a lesson they loaded the man with a one-hundred-pound sack and made him carry it to Phari, across three 18,000-foot passes. With great enthusiasm, the Tibetan stormed up the first pass, sweating out his drunkenness.

On this, one of their last marches before dropping into the Chumbi Valley, they came upon an arresting sight, a pilgrim traveling from

Lhasa to Kathmandu in ritual prostration. It recalled Howard-Bury's similar encounter during his approach to Tingri in 1921. The young man, though dressed in rags, appeared strong and well fed. He hailed from Urga, in northern Mongolia. His journey had already consumed a year of his life. "It seemed to me not only a futile waste of time," Morris later wrote, "but a terrible denial of life, but when I came to consider it later I could not think it any more repugnant than the austerities practiced by some Christian orders."

JOHN MORRIS came back from Everest no longer able to endure the boredom of military life. In the end he managed to secure a long overdue leave, and returned to London for the first time in years. "There was nobody I particularly wanted to see," he wrote. "In any case mine was the generation that had suffered most in the war, and the few friends I had acquired during the course of it were dead. There were times when I wished that I, too, had been killed, for there seemed in those days to be an unbridgeable gulf between those who had been actively involved in the war and those who had not. I envied the ones who could take the easy way, but I disliked the taste and still more the effects of alcohol; and no love affair came my way." After eight months, he would pull himself out of a severe depression and once again turn his thoughts to Asia. Eventually he moved to Japan and became fluent in the language; he taught literature in Tokyo until, in the wake of Pearl Harbor in 1941, he had to escape.

Teddy Norton, who brought back from Tibet a collection of some 400 botanical specimens and 120 butterflies and moths, could not wait to get back to soldiering. Invited by Hinks to lecture on behalf of the Everest Committee, he scoffed at the thought. In September he rejoined his regiment and was immediately posted to Turkey, where he spent the winter in Constantinople and Chanak, as Britain and the Soviets edged ever closer to war.

Morshead endured several operations and was finally able to continue his survey duties in Dehra Dun. Finch reached England something of a hero; even Hinks had to acknowledge his record achievement, which he did grudgingly in a letter of June 22. Wakefield did not even bother to stop in London; he made a beeline for his wife and medical practice in Kendal, in the Lake District. Tom Longstaff, broken in health, wanted nothing more to do with Everest. "For Heaven's sake," he wrote, "climb the wretched thing and let's get back to real mountaineering."

Somervell remained in India after the expedition and, with £60 in his pocket, set off for several months to wander about the country. In time he would join the staff of the Neyyoor mission hospital in Travancore, in southern India, forgoing a prestigious post he had been offered at University College Hospital in London. But for the moment he was just a pilgrim, a spiritual traveler.

While still in India, Somervell began work on the score for Noel's first film, *Climbing Mount Everest*. The film initially was a disappointment, but gradually word of mouth carried the day. By the end of its ten-week run at the Philharmonic Hall, every performance was sold out.

Mallory, having resigned his teaching post at Charterhouse, found himself back in Britain without work and with a young family to support. His only income came from lecturing, fees he managed to squeeze out of Hinks and the Everest Committee. In a very practical sense, his fate was tied to the mountain. Noel ended his film with a melodramatic flourish certain to please the British press: "Though defeated this time, still our climbers will not accept defeat. They will make another expedition soon to complete the conquest of the mountain. They will return to this terrific battle with Nature and, despite the dangers, the storms and the cold, they will win through. They will conquer and they will stand on the summit of Everest—the very topmost pinnacle of the world."

Mallory was not so sure, but as the summer turned to the fall, there was never really any doubt that if another effort were to be made, he would be leading the charge. The mountain had become him, and he the mountain, not only in the minds of the British public but within his own.

CHAPTER 12

The Thread of Life

Tom Longstaff felt considerable relief on the morning of July 15 as SS *Macedonia* approached the harbor of Marseille shortly after dawn. Since taking leave of General Bruce and the expedition at Rongbuk, he had brought Henry Morshead home safely to Darjeeling, a grueling journey of some four hundred miles completed without rest in a mere nineteen days. Morshead had remained stoic throughout the ordeal, and without complaint had walked across 18,000-foot passes inaccessible to mounted ponies, on feet raw and blistered from frostbite. But, as Longstaff later recalled, the man "suffered abominably" and might well have died; blood poisoning was a constant worry. Opium did little to quell the pain and, as Howard Somervell had noticed at base camp, there were moments at night when in agony the tough explorer would "get away by himself and cry like a child." In the end, thanks in good measure to Longstaff, Morshead survived with only the loss of the top joints of three fingers on his right hand.

Having left the invalid in the care of his wife, Evie, and the medical authorities in Darjeeling, Longstaff, along with Colonel Strutt and George Finch, pushed on for Calcutta on June 29, arriving in time to take luncheon with Lord Lytton, the governor of Bengal, before boarding the night train for Bombay. A slow passage to Aden brought them to Suez on July 10, and from there the gentle sea carried them past Crete and through the Strait of Messina to the south of France. A problem with customs at Marseille delayed their disembarkation, and it was not until late in the afternoon that they reached the Gare Saint-Charles to catch the overnight train to Calais. Having been away from England for five months almost to the day, they landed at Dover at 8:00 p.m. on Sunday, July 16.

Longstaff's wife, Dora, awaited him in London at the Imperial Hotel. Their reunion was marred by an urgent message from Arthur Hinks, ordering Longstaff, along with Strutt and Finch, to attend a special meeting of the Everest Committee scheduled for the very next morning. Word of the avalanche on Everest and the death of seven Sherpas had broken in the London papers even as the *Macedonia* docked in Marseille. Having left base camp before the disaster occurred, Longstaff, Finch, and Strutt were completely in the dark. Longstaff, in particular, was appalled by the news, for he had strongly opposed a third assault, going as far as to formalize his protest in writing in an official complaint to General Bruce. At Chöbuk, their first stop on the journey home, he had been much relieved to look back at the mountain and see it cloaked in fresh snow. "Everest a snowpack," Longstaff noted in his diary on the evening of June 6, "will take 3–4 days sun to clear. Impossible now." He had turned his thoughts to the slow climb to the Pang La and the road to Shegar, certain that conditions on the North Col would force Mallory to abort the ill-conceived attempt.

It infuriated him now to read Bruce's front-page story in the *Times*, a delayed dispatch from Rongbuk written on June 11, four days after the accident, in which the general glossed over accountability with a turn of phrase: "Everest is a terrible enemy, and the chances against those attacking it very great." In truth, as Longstaff recognized with regret, there had been a failure of leadership on the part of his old friend. General Bruce acknowledged in his dispatch that the monsoon had begun, and that even as he'd authorized Mallory to have a final go at the mountain, he had ordered, for reasons of safety, the evacuation of the upper camps on the East Rongbuk Glacier. The climbing party had left base camp on June 3 in "threatening weather." How they had been permitted to proceed by Bruce, and why Mallory, at Camp III, had persisted when there was no conceivable chance of success and every possibility of disaster, was beyond Longstaff's comprehension.

Their differences aside, Longstaff deeply admired Bruce, and believed that the general had been unduly pressured for results by Hinks and Younghusband, a conviction that was only reinforced by the tone of the meeting with the Everest Committee that following morning, Monday, July 17. Younghusband held the chair. Hinks played the inquisitor, and all three climbers felt as if on trial. Longstaff responded aggressively, ridiculing Hinks's assertion that he and the others had abandoned the expedition when they had, in fact, hastened across Tibet to save Henry Morshead's life. Longstaff later expressed his outrage in a letter to Sandy Wollaston, veteran of 1921, a member of the Everest Committee and the sole voice of moderation during the morning's heated discussions. The general, as expedition leader, had performed brilliantly, Longstaff noted, as had John Morris and Geoffrey Bruce as transport officers. Teddy Norton was a great success, as indeed was Finch, a brilliant climber, who had overcome any number of impediments to establish a new record on the mountain. "With any reasonable conditions he would have stood on the final ridge," Longstaff noted. "With luck he would have got to the top."

Longstaff reserved his wrath for the climbers who, as far as he was concerned, had led the innocent Sherpas to their deaths. "Mallory is a very good stout hearted baby," he wrote Wollaston, "but quite unfit to be in charge of anything, including himself. Somervell is the most urbanely conceited youth I have ever struck—and quite the toughest . . . He was honestly prepared to chuck his life away on the most remote chance of success . . . Mallory cannot even observe the conditions in front of him. To attempt such a passage in the Himalaya after new snow is idiotic. What the hell did they think they could do *on Everest* in such conditions even if they did get up to the North Col? By their ignorance and unwillingness to take advice Mallory and Somervell have brought discredit on old Bruce—and that's why we were so savage the other day."

Longstaff had every reason to be angry. His authority as medical officer had been undermined at base camp on Rongbuk, his advice as a seasoned Himalayan mountaineer ignored with mortal consequences, his honor challenged by an insinuation of desertion, even his homecoming to his beloved wife compromised by what he viewed as Hinks's hysteria. Still, the intensity of his response, his defensiveness, suggests a man trying a little too hard to set the record straight. Longstaff dismissed Arthur Wakefield as a man "who could not face the altitude at all, rather worse than I was and is ignorant of the arts of mountaineering." This was both ungenerous and untrue, and it suggests an aging climber coming to terms with his own limitations, the shame of personal failure, and the "disgrace," as Longstaff himself saw it, of having physically collapsed and been carried down the mountain by Tibetan porters. It was an embarrassing outcome for a man who in his prime had climbed 6,000 feet in a day to reach the summit of Trisul in 1907. In 1922 Trisul remained the highest mountain ever climbed, but at 23,360 feet its peak was nearly 4,000 feet lower than the highest point achieved by the Everest climbers, including Geoffrey Bruce, who had never before been on a mountain. For Longstaff, incapacitated at the lowest camp, their success must have been bittersweet.

A cloud nevertheless hung over Mallory and Somervell, both still in Tibet and unable to mount their own defense. On July 21, Hinks sent a note to Norman Collie, president of the Alpine Club and a member of the Everest Committee, saying, "All who have come back think Mallory's judgment in purely alpine matters was bad and inferior to Norton of whom everyone speaks very highly."

Privately, as his letters to his wife and close friends reveal, Mallory was deeply disturbed by the accident, as indeed was Somervell. "Do you know that sickening feeling that one can't go back and have it undone and that nothing will make it good?" he wrote to Geoffrey Young. "I don't much care what the world says, but I care very much what you and a few others think." In a letter that reached Mallory within days of his return to England in August, his old mentor urged him to set aside any thought of being responsible for the tragedy: "You made all the allowance for the safety of the party that your experience suggested . . . You took your full share, a leading share, in the risk. In the war we had to do worse: we had to order men into danger at times when we could not share it. And surely we learned then that to take on ourselves afterwards the responsibility for their deaths, to debate with ourselves the 'might-have-beens,' was the road to madness."

Within a fortnight of his return, Mallory had a chance to present his side of the story in a September 4 lead article on the front page of the *Times*, "Mount Everest Risks: Why the Last Climb Was Attempted." It was not a spirited defense as much as a muted statement of the obvious. Climbers in the moment make choices, and they take calculated risks. The weather was visibly breaking, and the general was of the opinion that a "succession of fine days would follow the first snow." After all they had endured, retreat from a "mountain so nearly conquered" was too bitter a prospect to accept. They had proceeded carefully, testing the snow. Despite all precautions, the accident had happened. Good men had died, and the survivors had lived on to bury the grievous loss in memory.

That was the end of it. Within the Everest Committee, Younghusband rallied to Mallory's support, as did Hinks, who was not about to allow the death of seven porters to tarnish the reputation of the man who had become the public face of the entire enterprise. While formally bemoaning the tragic loss of life, Hinks recognized an opportunity when he saw one. As Strutt cynically reminded Mallory in a letter of August 2, the "British Public, the middle classes, shop-keepers, gillies, etc., who alone show a real interest in the expedition, these rather welcome the accident (dead bodies always appeal to them), and think us real heroes in consequence."

Hinks, with the ongoing support of John Buchan, continued to use the press to build interest in Everest. The *Times* alone published some sixty articles between April and September 1922, with many making the front page. These, in turn, were echoed by the other London dailies and picked up by scores of local papers throughout Britain. Given the competition for headlines, it was no mean achievement. In Russia, Soviet policies since the revolution had provoked famine. Throughout the country, the *Times* reported, people were reduced to eating grass and acorns; five million perished in 1921 alone. In Italy, Mussolini came to power even as Italian troops ravaged Libya. Egypt secured its independence from Britain; Morocco rose up against Spain; while in Ireland the assassination of Michael Collins sparked civil war. In Germany all was chaos, with hyperinflation forcing housewives to use wheelbarrows to carry money for the purchase of a single loaf of bread. In London T. S. Eliot published *The Waste Land*. In Paris *Ulysses* appeared and James Joyce famously dined with Pablo Picasso, Marcel Proust, and Igor Stravinsky at the Majestic Hotel, their first and only encounter. King George V visited, for the first time, the trenches of the Western Front, which had become one of France's most popular tourist attractions. In a speech to his constituents on November 11, Winston Churchill distilled the somber mood of the nation: "What a disappointment the twentieth century has been. How terrible and melancholy is the long series of disastrous events, which have darkened its first twenty years. We have seen in every country a dissolution, a weakening of bonds, a challenge to those principles, a decay of faith, an abridgement of hope, on which the structure and ultimate existence of civilized society depends."

Hinks and Buchan worked to position the Everest story as an antidote and distraction for the nation. Above all they sought to build a momentum that could not be denied. Within two days of Mallory's article in the *Times*, the September issue of the *Geographical Journal* announced that planning had begun for a third Everest expedition. At the end of the month, Hinks sent a reporter to meet General Bruce as his ship, the *Malva*, docked in Marseille. "Nature still has secrets which she cannot be forced to reveal," General Bruce told the man from the *Times* who boarded his northbound train on October 1. "When one seeks to penetrate the mysteries of the world, their guardian rises in one form or another to forbid our approach. Here it is the ice, there the heat. On Everest it was the wind, a capricious wind. Sometimes it blew in icy squalls. Sometimes in warm gusts that melted the ice and caused unlooked for catastrophes. Nothing could be foreseen. I have never encountered a worse enemy."

Asked whether the effort to conquer the mountain would be renewed, the general replied, "Yes, perhaps in two years." The journalist made a remark about British tenacity. General Bruce replied with a laugh and a single word: "Shackleton."

The interview ran the following morning, October 2, in the same edition that carried a dispatch from John Noel in Gyantse. The photographer had lingered in Tibet to document what the article's title called the "gruesome customs of the lamas," local color for his Everest film. Along with "devil dances" featuring lamas wearing aprons of human bones, playing drums made from skulls and trumpets from thighbones, Noel had witnessed a sky burial. He wrote, "After a lama has said prayers and incantations over the naked corpse the professional butchers sliced the body up with knives, cutting off separately the legs and arms and lastly the head. They hack and smash each member into pulp on a rock with hatchets, and throw it to the vultures who stand waiting only 5 feet away. The birds consume every particle of flesh and the crushed bone . . . Although I had my cinematograph with me when I saw this burial I refrained from photographing the custom. The thing was simply too awful and soul stirring to photograph."

Seven dead on the slopes of the mountain, an ordeal of survival worthy of Shackleton, lurid rituals, macabre and mesmerizing, and the promise of a third expedition, a final gesture of heroic redemption—what more could the newspapers want? The challenge for the Everest Committee was to make it happen. Any number of impediments had to be overcome before another expedition could be launched. Younghusband's wildly impractical proposal that an advance team be sent out immediately in the fall of 1922 to establish camps and ready the way for a climbing party in the spring of 1923 was mercifully allowed to die by Bruce when the general took over as chair of the Everest Committee, even as Percy Farrar, to the delight of Hinks, resigned his place at the table. Hinks and Bruce clearly had 1924 in mind.

Their first challenge was money. The 1921 reconnaissance had cost £4,241, but donations and the sale of various rights had yielded a net profit of £7,845, which had been placed in reserve for 1922. This considerable sum had only partially funded Bruce's expedition, which, better supplied and indulged by the general's extravagances, had cost a staggering £12,548. In time, revenues from lectures, photographs, publications, and ticket sales to Noel's first film would also generate a surplus, but only of £2,474. In the fall of 1922, however, the Everest Committee faced a short-term deficit of several thousand pounds. Bruce insisted that a budget of £1,000 per Englishman was required, an arbitrary figure but one given authority by the general's prestige and reputation, not to mention his place as chair of the Everest Committee and, as of early 1923, president of the Alpine Club.

Not only was the Everest Committee broke, it had serious liabilities and had suffered unanticipated reverses. Arthur Hinks had been promised £250 for his tireless efforts, a well-deserved yet costly bonus. A less legitimate charge was a bill for £360 sent by the India high commissioner for the useless government mules that had given Howard-Bury such trouble in 1921. More bad news came with the failure of the Alliance Bank of Simla, which took down another £700 of reserves. But the worst crisis came in the fall of 1922 when it emerged that a twenty-eight-year-old accounts clerk hired by Hinks at the Royal Geographical Society, Charles Eric Thompson, had embezzled over £700.

Married with two children, Thompson was arrested at Chelmsford, living with a woman who was not his wife, and ultimately sentenced to twelve months' imprisonment with hard labor. What made the case particularly embarrassing was the fact that Thompson, a profoundly disturbed young man, had written to Hinks, essentially admitting to the crime, and it was this confession alone that revealed the extent of the graft, which might not otherwise have come to light. Edward Somers-Cock, the treasurer of the Everest Committee, was so mortified that he personally offered to repay £350, provided the matter be kept quiet. It was for a while, but eventually the scandal slipped into the *Times*, in a brief notice on February 7, 1923, that incorrectly doubled the size of the loss to £1,400. It was not the sort of news to encourage donations.

Aside from financial matters, there remained the question of personnel. The collapse of Longstaff and the failure of Wakefield as a climber, together with the loss of Raeburn and Kellas in 1921, had finally convinced even the most recalcitrant of the old guard that Everest was a young man's game. But this, in turn, illuminated a growing divide between those who still considered climbing to be a sport of gentlemen and those of a new generation, who played in an altogether different league. The former used the language of war to describe their efforts and intentions on a mountain; the latter had lived through a war that allowed them to walk with grace and commitment at the very edge of death. These were climbers prepared to do almost anything to succeed. George Finch, as much as Mallory and Somervell, exemplified the new breed. In his contribution to the official account of the 1922 effort, Finch argued that the "margin of safety must be narrowed down, if necessary to the vanishing point." A climber on Everest must drive himself beyond exhaustion, "even to destruction if need be."

Such convictions stunned and horrified many fellows of the Royal Geographical Society and the Alpine Club, most especially desk-bound bureaucrats such as Hinks and those too old to have known the war firsthand. That the oxygen debate remained unresolved was yet another measure of this generational rift. Invoking outdated notions of fair play to challenge the use of oxygen recalled General Haig's attachment to the horse and his refusal to acknowledge the utility and effectiveness of the machine gun on the Western Front. It was not as if gas lifted one to the summit. As Finch wrote, "Oxygen renders available [to the climber] more of his store of energy and hastens his steps, but it does not, alas! fit the wings of Mercury on his feet."

THAT THE Tibetan government had formally sanctioned a third expedition to Everest was announced on the evening of Monday, October 16, 1922, at a joint meeting of the Royal Geographical Society and the Alpine Club at Central Hall, Westminster. The evening was a triumph for Hinks. Central Hall was as grand a venue as could be found in London, a great Edwardian monument to progress, built just before the war but in a baroque style evocative of the great works of the architect Christopher Wren. Above the theater hovered one of the largest domed ceilings ever constructed.

Lord Ronaldshay, president of the RGS, opened the proceedings, moving to center stage to introduce General Bruce, who presented a brief overview of the 1922 expedition. Bruce ended his remarks by quoting a wandering holy man encountered on the road back to Darjeeling: "I hear you have climbed the Himal by means of thread," said the sadhu, "no doubt the thread of life." Mallory came next, and spoke in subdued terms of the challenges of wind and cold. "It is not impossible for men to reach the summit of Everest," he said, "but unless the weather can mend the habit we observed this year, their chances of reaching it and getting down in safety are all too small." Finch followed and recalled how he and Geoffrey Bruce had survived the night by using oxygen. To the amusement of all, he ended his brief remarks by quoting Geoffrey's last vow to the mountain: "Just you wait, old thing, you'll be for it soon."

Notably absent were the other members of the 1922 expedition. Morshead was convalescing in Darjeeling. Geoffrey Bruce had returned to his regiment on the North-West Frontier, as had Morris. John Noel remained in Tibet. Somervell was in southern India. Longstaff, sick with phlebitis, rested at his country house in the New Forest, while Wakefield had returned to his home in Cumberland without so much as stopping in London. Norton, who wanted no part of public spectacles, had happily returned to military life and a posting in Constantinople. That left available only Mallory and Finch, precisely as Hinks had hoped. Gerald Christy, the agent handling all lecture bookings, had insisted that only the two star climbers be asked to speak.

On the morning of October 17, a notice in the *Times* announced that Mallory and Finch would be returning to Central Hall on Friday, three days hence, and again the following Wednesday, October 25. Mallory would speak at 3:00 p.m., Finch at 8:30. The order would be reversed at their second appearance, with Mallory delivering the evening performance, and Finch the matinee. Thus was set in motion a whirlwind of public engagements, fifty appearances alone by the end of December, that would keep both men away from their families for many weeks, and in the end tear apart the one climbing partnership that was the nation's best hope for success on Everest.

The problem began with money. On the first two expeditions, Longstaff, Wollaston, Strutt, and Howard-Bury had paid their own way to India; each was a wealthy man. Soldiers and survey officers such as Geoffrey Bruce, Morris, Norton, Wheeler, and Morshead took leave and after the expeditions returned to their regiments or, in the case of the surveyors, to their positions at the Survey of India. Guy Bullock by the spring of 1922 was secure in a diplomatic posting in Le Havre, soon to be transferred and promoted to Addis Ababa. Wakefield and Somervell were both highly trained and accomplished physicians and surgeons.

Mallory, by contrast, the son of a vicar, returned from Everest unemployed, just one of 2.5 million Englishmen without work in 1922. With the help of his father-in-law, a prominent architect who provided an annual stipend of £750, he and Ruth maintained their home and social position. But he was not a man of means. Nor was his companion on the lecture circuit. Finch had an academic post at the Imperial College of Science and Technology, but the compensation was meager. He had no inheritance, a family of his own to support, and a number of other obligations, not the least being alimony payments of £100 a year to his second wife. The five months on Everest had cost him half a year's salary, even as he spent £200 of his own money on film stock. As Hinks conceded, the two men singled out to bring the story of Everest to the public were those least able to shoulder the financial burden and sacrifice.

As he had in 1921, Hinks offered each speaker a percentage of the lecture revenues, a third of the proceeds after expenses. Mallory, with a grueling schedule that kept him traveling throughout the fall, actually made out rather well, earning £75 in November, £225 in December, and an additional £100 in January, far more than he'd ever been paid as a schoolmaster at Charterhouse, where his annual salary was but £270. Finch, who by the spring of 1923 had delivered eighty-three lectures in Britain and abroad, remained dissatisfied. Unlike Mallory, he had already established himself as a professional lecturer before the Everest expedition and it had been his primary source of income. After suffering through a number of poorly attended events, he asked that the Everest Committee, in addition to covering travel expenses and offering a percentage of the net proceeds, guarantee a minimum fee of £25 a lecture. Hinks and Younghusband refused, setting in motion an inevitable confrontation.

Every member of the Everest expeditions had been obliged to sign a confidentiality agreement, pledging loyalty to the chain of command in the field and agreeing to forgo any communication with the public or media, save contacts directly sanctioned by the Everest Committee. The contract further specified that any collections, photographs, or "observation" made by any of the climbers be "handed over" to the committee. The story, in other words, from start to finish belonged to no one climber but to the collective enterprise. In the short term, these provisions made sense. Aside from its legal obligations to specific news outlets—the exclusivity agreement with the *Times* being just one such arrangement—controlling the message was clearly in the interests of the Everest Committee. It was consistent with everything John Buchan had mastered as a propagandist during the war, and it gave Hinks the formal authority to secure and monopolize to the greatest extent possible every conceivable revenue stream. None of the climbers had been keen on the document, but they had no choice in the matter if they wanted to go to Everest.

George Finch had reluctantly signed the agreement, but in a letter to Hinks on December 21, 1921, he had qualified his position: "I take it that I am not to be the official photographer of the expedition and that any snap shots I take, or sketches and paintings I make, remain my property subject to the control of the Committee as before." Finch's caveat was as imprecise and ambiguous as Hinks's response. In a return letter the following day, the secretary split hairs by agreeing that any images taken for private use ultimately belonged to the photographer, even as he insisted that as long as the Everest Committee wished to retain rights to such photographs they could not be used privately. So the matter rested as Finch made his preparations for Everest.

The situation came to a head in the fall of 1922, prompted by a casual request from Mallory to borrow a number of Finch's glass negatives to augment his lecture. Both Hinks and Mallory were taken aback when Finch refused. His position was firm. At considerable personal expense he had secured arguably the best portfolio in 1922, altogether some two thousand images worth printing, and he was not about to relinquish control or allow Mallory to benefit from his efforts. In similar circumstances at the end of the 1921 reconnaissance, Guy Bullock had declined to lend Mallory his diary. Clearly there was tension. When Howard-Bury, at a meeting of the RGS, twice referred to Mallory as "the most distinguished climber" on the 1922 expedition, Finch took personal offense and complained in writing to Hinks. As far as lending his images, he stood his ground, writing to Mallory on October 5, "I have carefully considered this question and hold the opinion that it would not be in the interests of the Everest Committee, but also contrary in the extreme to my own interests for slides of my photographs to be shown in the public other than by myself. My style of lecturing is, as you perhaps know, essentially different from yours and is, amongst other things, chosen to set off my slides to their best advantage. Any other than my own lecturing methods would not only fail to let them be seen to proper advantage but would plagiarize them in the eyes of the public; that I cannot permit, as I wish to use these slides later when free to lecture on my own behalf."

Mallory almost certainly shared the contents of this letter with Hinks. The final line was the red flag. Finch would honor his obligations through the weeks and months following his debut at Central Hall, but as his note to Mallory indicated, he had every intention of returning to his private speaking career as soon as possible. As far as Finch was concerned, his commitment to the Everest Committee was limited to one lecture season following the return of the 1922 expedition. Hinks, by contrast, considered the agreement binding until the mountain was successfully climbed. Finch viewed this as preposterous, given that the summit of Everest might never be achieved. Still, he kept his side of the bargain, lecturing under the auspices of the Everest Committee through the spring of 1923, even as he contributed, without compensation, three chapters for the official account, *The Assault on Mount Everest*, which also featured many of his photographs.

In the early summer of 1923 Finch, who had grown up on the Continent and spoke fluent German, was asked by friends to deliver a series of lectures in Switzerland. Demand for him as a speaker had fallen off in Britain and, as always, he needed money. Precisely what transpired remains unclear. Finch's son-in-law and biographer, Scott Russell, maintains that permission was sought from Hinks, who categorically refused, even though Finch offered to share the proceeds with the committee. Other Everest historians suggest that Finch accepted the assignment on his own initiative, only to refuse a subsequent demand from Hinks for a share of the revenues. Whatever the truth, the conflict provoked Finch to seek legal counsel. Not surprisingly, given the ambiguous language of the original document, his solicitors advised that the agreement was in no way legally binding, a conclusion that Finch conveyed to Hinks in a letter of June 28, 1923. With Hinks away from London, the letter was forwarded to the joint secretary, Sydney Spencer at the Alpine Club, who immediately passed it on to General Bruce, who shared the contents with Younghusband. They consulted their own lawyer, J. J. Withers, a member of the Alpine Club, who essentially agreed with Finch's legal position. This did nothing to quell their outrage. Finch's transgression was not a matter of law; it was a violation of social convention.

A threat of legal action in 1923 was a most serious matter. Gentlemen did not go to court; men of character did not expose their colleagues to such humiliation and shame. General Bruce viewed Finch's letter as a form of blackmail. Finch surely knew, Bruce surmised, that the Everest Committee could never allow such a scandal to surface in a courtroom, in full view of the public and the press. All the key players—Bruce and Hinks, Younghusband, Spencer, even Percy Farrar, Finch's most loyal supporter—not to mention the climbers, from Howard-Bury to Mallory, essentially viewed the document in question as an agreement among peers to be interpreted, as Hinks maintained, "in the broadest grounds of honourable understanding and certainly not by process of law." To exploit a legal loophole for personal gain, as Finch appeared to be doing, was "prideful vulgarity," the action of a "barrack room lawyer" intended only to sully the glory of the entire endeavor.

As early as October 1922 it had been decided that General Bruce would lead the third expedition, which would indeed be put off until the spring of 1924. Colonel Norton would serve as second-in-command and climbing leader. On March 1, 1923, the general wrote Sydney Spencer with a preliminary list of suggested climbers: "Somervell,

Mallory, Norton, Finch (I am sorry to say) and Bruce." It was a less than ringing endorsement of the man who had set the height record the previous year. In a follow-up letter of March 16, the roster had changed and Finch was not mentioned.

Three weeks later the Everest Committee announced the formation of a selection panel, which included among others General Bruce, Spencer, Collie, and Farrar of the Alpine Club; Everest veterans Strutt, Longstaff, and Mallory; as well as Noel Odell, a geologist with considerable expeditionary experience in the Arctic. The final climbing team would not be determined until late 1923, and it is unclear up to what point Finch remained in the running. He may well have been eliminated from consideration as early as March. Certainly Farrar's resignation from the Everest Committee at the end of May, ostensibly due to work pressures, was driven by the committee's attitude toward Finch, whom Farrar considered the finest climber in Britain. Finch's fate was most assuredly sealed the moment the contents of his June 28 letter became known. Even Farrar was appalled. He immediately urged Finch to withdraw the letter, which he did, but to no avail. The die was cast. In London, General Bruce wrote to Spencer on June 30, saying, "Well at any rate he's torn it now. There are compensations for everything and I think this action on his part definitely rules him out of the next expedition. What an absolute swine the man is."

That summer, acting on the advice of his lawyers, Finch defied Hinks and delivered the lectures in Switzerland as an independent scholar and mountaineer. In three months he earned £225. His agent pocketed £33. A belated letter to Finch from the Everest Committee requesting 50 percent of the profits went unanswered. By that point, the rupture was complete.

In a final exchange of letters in September 1923, Finch confirmed his independence, even as he closed the door on Everest. He wrote to Hinks from Zurich, "If I am to understand that the 3rd paragraph of page 2 of your letter in reply sets me free of any further obligation to the Committee I am content. I understand indirectly that for reasons doubtless sufficient to the Committee I am not to be asked to join the next expedition, notwithstanding the relative success gained by my own party, and my subsequent very willing services in connection with the improvements of the oxygen apparatus."

George Finch was the finest ice and snow climber in Britain and the world's leading scientific authority on the use of oxygen in mountaineering. As late as June 16, 1923, the members of the Everest Committee had invited him to brief them on the latest developments, even as they chose to deny him a place on the expedition because of concerns about his personal character. With no rest for two nights and a day, no food and little drink, cursed by the worst weather encountered to that date on the mountain, Finch had reached far higher and closer to the top of Everest than any climber alive. He may well have conquered the mountain, had he not instead chosen the very path of decency and humanity to save the life of his climbing companion. This may well have been lost on General Bruce during the deliberations in London in the spring of 1923, but his nephew Geoffrey never forgot. Geoffrey wrote to Finch on May 31, "I can never thank you enough for electing to take me with you on that climb, or for the perfectly astonishing way you pulled me through it all. It was wonderful."

GEORGE MALLORY would go to Everest in 1924 convinced that Finch had been treated unjustly. On the eve of his departure he would arrange for Ruth to invite Finch and his wife for an overnight visit on the first weekend after his return. It was a generous gesture, for if the climbers came home triumphant, Finch would not be forgotten. But in the months leading up to Finch's dismissal, Mallory kept his distance from the entire affair. "*La question Finch m'ennuie,*" he wrote to Hinks on November 2, 1922, calling the Finch question boring. "It may interest you," he added, "to hear that a cheque of his drawn to me for a sum of 2 pounds was returned through my bank with the ominous letters R.D. However, he has since made good by postal orders . . . But this explains part of his conduct."

Hinks no doubt relished this bit of gossip. To bounce a check was not trivial in their social circle, and it was commonly known that Finch had taken considerable time to repay a small loan from General Bruce. Hinks's conflict with Finch had become personal. The experience of 1922 made it almost certain that the party destined to reach the summit of Everest would do so with oxygen. Even Longstaff had come around to accept the inevitable. Finch was the strongest advocate of oxygen, and the climber with the greatest experience with the apparatus. This gave him a considerable advantage. Hinks might tolerate the use of oxygen, but he could not bear the thought of Finch becoming the first man to reach the summit of the world. Under the guise of defending the integrity of the Everest Committee, he was prepared to compromise the strength of the climbing team, and thus its safety and chances of success.

Mallory, by contrast, felt no malice toward Finch, nor any particular affection. If he remained disengaged, neither coming to Finch's defense nor joining the chorus of critics, it was simply because he was caught in his own whirlwind of obligations. In eight years of marriage he and Ruth had been apart as much as they had been together. His oldest daughter, Clare, was only six, yet she had watched her father go away for months at a time on five occasions in her short life. Following his return from Everest in 1922, the painful pattern continued. He had but six weeks at home before beginning a lecture swing that took him from London to Leeds, Birmingham to Bristol, Chester to Cambridge, a different city every two days for seven weeks. After little more than a fortnight at home over Christmas, he embarked alone for a three-month tour of the United States and Canada, countries he had never visited.

It all began with great promise. Hinks booked passage on the *Olympic*, a luxury liner of the White Star fleet, the sister ship of the *Titanic*. The American agent arranged for a posh landing, reserving rooms in New York at the Waldorf-Astoria. On the way over, Mallory tried his best to prepare himself for the challenge. He struggled to understand his dinner companions—returning American tourists for the most part, many from the Midwest. Their table manners appalled him. One man, he wrote to Ruth, was so vulgar that he "often forks things off his wife's plate." Uncertain what awaited him, he spent hours alone in his stateroom practicing an American accent, thinking that it might help with servants and railroad porters. When the ship docked, on January 17, 1923, he got his first look at modern skyscrapers, which he described to Ruth as "immense silhouettes against the sky . . . all playing a part in a grotesque world of toy giants." The city seemed unreal: great canyons of towering buildings above cross streets narrow and blackened by rain, the broad avenues with their trolley lines and rivers of cars. "New York gives the impression," he wrote on his third day in America, "of a splendid gesture against a background of emptiness."

Mallory found his agent, Lee Keedick, a pleasant man, but he was surprised to learn that his first lecture was not scheduled for ten days. He used the time well, writing two long chapters for the official expedition account, a total of thirty thousand words, before leaving New York on January 25 for Washington, D.C. His debut the following afternoon was less than successful. Not a laugh, nor a clap—altogether the most unresponsive audience he had ever encountered as a speaker. The evening performance, fortunately, was seamless; Mallory felt he had never done better. The day grossed $1,000, a considerable sum in 1923. Philadelphia came next: two different halls, each sold out, a total audience of some 3000. Everything boded well for the most important date on the tour, the Broadhurst Theatre in New York on February 4. A decent audience filled half of the 1,100 seats, but unfortunately the critics did not appear. The lecture series went largely unnoticed in the press and actually lost money.

Swallowing his pride, Mallory headed for Canada, only to discover that the Toronto event had been canceled. Montreal grossed a mere $48. He did better in Detroit, had a raucous reception at Harvard, in Cambridge, and then set off for a brief swing through the Midwest that took him to Toledo and Iowa City, before he returned east to Rochester and finally Hanover, New Hampshire. It was not exactly the A-list of American cultural centers. Keedick dropped the minimum fee to $250 and still failed to secure additional dates. After a month in the country, they had only three firm bookings ahead of them. "Mallory is a fine fellow and gives a good lecture," Keedick confessed in a letter to the Everest Committee. But "the American people don't seem to be interested in the subject."

Mallory returned to New York in a restless mood, anxious to get home. A failed attempt to climb a mountain evidently could not capture an American imagination fired by more splendid news, such as the discovery in Egypt of the treasure of King Tutankhamen, a story that broke in the New York papers on February 17, or the Tibetan adventures of William Montgomery McGovern, a Buddhist scholar who sneaked into Lhasa disguised as a monk, his skin and hair blackened with dye, only to be imprisoned and forced to make a harrowing escape. The only thing about Everest that seemed of interest to the American press was the fact that Mallory had taken a swig of brandy at 27,000 feet. Booze was a local hook. Prohibition was just beginning to convulse the country.

Oddly enough, the most memorable note to turn up in the American papers was a casual remark Mallory made at the end of one of his lectures. Asked why he wanted to climb Everest, no doubt for the umpteenth time, Mallory reportedly replied, "Because it's there." This simple retort hit a nerve, and took on an almost metaphysical resonance, as if Mallory had somehow in his wisdom distilled the perfect notion of emptiness and pure purpose. It was first quoted in the Sunday *New York Times* on March 18, in the opening paragraph of a half-page feature, "Climbing Mount Everest Is Work for Supermen." In time, it would be inscribed on memorials, quoted in sermons, cited by princes and presidents. But those who knew Mallory best, including two of his biographers, his close friend David Pye and his son-in-law David

Robertson, interpreted the comment rather more casually. To them it was simply a flippant response by an exhausted and frustrated man who famously did not suffer fools. Or as Arnold Lunn remarked, Mallory, no stranger to New York speakeasies, just said it to get rid of "a bore who stood between him and a much needed drink."

Whatever its genesis, the phrase caught on because it did in fact capture something essential. "Everest is the highest mountain in the world," Mallory later wrote, "and no man has reached its summit. Its existence is a challenge. The answer is instinctive, a part, I suppose of man's desire to conquer the universe." Elsewhere he added, "I suppose we go to Mount Everest, granted the opportunity, because—in a word—we can't help it. Or to state the matter rather differently, because we are mountaineers."

Mallory did not regret his time in America. He had been warmly received, most especially by a great cadre of new friends in the American Alpine Club, and in his quiet hours even managed to slip away to the Morgan Library to study some of Boswell's letters. At the University Club, which made him an honorary member, he took tea and read the *Guardian Weekly*, catching up on news from London. Mostly he wandered the streets of the city, enjoying all the fresh, new sounds of America: jazz and unfettered classless laughter, the shouts of newspaper boys, all the strange accents and immigrant gestures, along with the screech and cacophony of snarled traffic, still a novelty for an Englishman in 1923. When finally, on March 31, he boarded the *Saxonia* for the journey home, he had only one serious concern. Financially, the tour had been a failure, and his earnings were hardly sufficient to warrant the time abroad. He returned to his family just as he had left, unemployed and with no immediate prospects, as insolvent, in fact, as the Everest Committee to which he had hinged his fate.

Mallory's fortunes happily turned within days of his reaching his spring garden at the Holt, the old stone house near the river Wey purchased for Ruth by her father as a wedding gift. While Mallory had been in America, Arthur Hinks had run into an old friend, Reverend David Cranage, who told him of a teaching position being advertised by the Board of Extra-Mural Studies at Cambridge. It was all rather unorthodox, Cranage explained to Hinks. They were looking for a historian who could design a curriculum suitable for workingmen and -women, and who was willing to travel from village to village in the greater Cambridge area, reaching out to those who had never had an opportunity to attend proper and decent schools. The lectures would run in collaboration with the Workers' Educational Association.

It was not exactly Charterhouse, which was precisely why it appealed to Mallory. It played to his strengths as a lecturer, his passion for new forms of learning, and his progressive values, first embraced at Cambridge, where he had flirted with Fabian socialism. Mallory submitted his application on April 20, scarcely a week after returning to the country. There were twenty-five other candidates for the post, many with far more extensive teaching experience, but he made up for it with a flood of reference letters. Arthur Benson wrote from Cambridge, Younghusband and George Trevelyan from London. Strong support came from the headmasters of both Winchester and Charterhouse. Mallory made the short list of five, and then sealed the deal with a brilliant interview on May 8. Ten days later the job was his. It came with an annual salary of £350, which, augmented by lecture fees, would give him a very respectable income of at least £500, a sum certain to please his father-in-law, who continued to provide Ruth with a yearly allowance.

There was, unfortunately, a downside. In the short term, it implied yet another extended separation from his family. He had to be in Cambridge by the end of June. Ruth would stay behind in Surrey until they managed to sell the Holt. Even once she and the children joined him in October, his schedule of meetings and night classes precluded a normal family life. He left home each day at 4:00 p.m. and rarely returned before midnight. They had all the challenges typical of young married couples. Renovations to Herschel House, their new home in Cambridge, proved more costly than anticipated, and they frequently overdrew their accounts at the bank. Mallory's old friends at Cambridge were delighted to have him back, but some were not especially pleased that he had come with a wife. For all the difficulties, in the fall of 1923 George and Ruth, for the first time in their marriage, faced a stable and secure future. Their three young children, Clare, Beridge, and John, delighted in the presence of their father, at last a constant in their midst.

Into this domestic calm inevitably roared the winds of Everest. John Noel's first film, *Climbing Mount Everest*, had a disappointing premiere, and only modest success when it toured the country. Although it ultimately grossed £10,000 at the box office, net profits for the Everest Committee were but £500. This setback did not for a moment deter the filmmaker. In June 1923, even as Mallory was settling into his new job, Noel made an unexpected and unprecedented offer to the Everest Committee. In exchange for all photographic and film rights to the upcoming 1924 expedition, he pledged to raise £8,000, an extraordinary sum in 1923. The terms of the deal were very specific. He would pay £1,000 upon signature, an additional £5,000 by December 31, the end of the year, and a final installment of £2,000 by March 31, 1924. The Everest Committee, for its part, would guarantee diplomatic access to Tibet, facilitate his work in the field provided it was not in conflict with the goals and safety of the expedition, and provide equipment: three tents at Camp III, two on the North Col, as well as one oxygen apparatus and five thousand liters of oxygen. The Everest Committee would have access to the photographs for promotional purposes and various publications, including the anticipated expedition account. But ownership would rest with Explorer Films, the company established by Noel to make all of this possible. Among Noel's private investors were the Aga Khan and Sir Francis Younghusband, who also served as chairman of the board of the new enterprise.

It was an odd fulcrum of mountaineering history. The quest for the highest summit slipped from imperial venture to commercial opportunity. The Everest Committee had no choice but to accept. The cash infusion transformed its bottom line. Noel's offer implied not only an investment of £8,000 but also a savings of £2,000, as the committee would no longer be responsible for paying for film and photographic costs. In a single gesture Noel shouldered all financial risks, even as he liberated the committee to move ahead aggressively with plans for a third expedition to the mountain.

THE CHOICE of General Bruce as expedition leader had been a foregone conclusion. The avalanche controversy notwithstanding, he remained universally admired, a figure larger than life. Mindful of his well-being, never venturing higher than base camp, he had returned from Everest in 1922 having shed a good part of his belly and some ten years in appearance. Of all the men on the expedition, he alone had not once been sick or ill disposed, a fact he shared with any doctor who would listen. His charismatic authority in the field and the uncanny ease with which he inspired and motivated the native porters made him the inevitable choice, despite lingering and, indeed, growing concerns about his true state of health.

The same Harley Street physicians who had turned a blind eye in 1922 felt compelled to come clean when they examined him again in late 1923. Bruce's bluster aside, his blood pressure was dangerously high, his heart dilated on the left side, and the mitral murmur had increased in severity. There were also indications of kidney disease.

Anderson authorized him to go, provided he not climb higher than 15,000 feet, a condition that alone precluded his participation. Larkins, to his credit, did not gloss over problems in his diagnosis, reporting, "I passed him for the expedition [in 1922] because in spite of his defects I felt he was fit for the job, but this time I honestly do not feel comfortable about passing him."

Bruce's response was to ignore the Harley Street experts and seek the advice of his personal physician, Dr. Claude Wilson. On November 9 Wilson, a general practitioner, wrote to Larkins from Tunbridge Wells: "I don't want General Bruce to see a modern heart specialist. His electro-cardiogram would probably not be ideal, and they would, almost to a man, turn him down on this, or on his blood pressure. I don't want him frightened and I don't want him turned down. I am willing to take full responsibility." Wilson, not surprisingly, authorized Bruce to go, with the minor caveat that he agree to undergo a further medical examination before setting off for Tibet from Darjeeling. Notified of the decision, Larkins and Anderson, convinced that the general's life was at risk, "washed their hands of the entire affair."

The Everest Committee did not share their dire concerns, but it hedged its bets with the selection of Colonel Norton as second-in-command. Should the general falter, it would be essential to have a subordinate ready to take his place, one accustomed to command and capable of orchestrating the complex logistical and diplomatic arrangements of what was increasingly perceived as a military campaign, a battle with a mountain. Mallory, despite his prominent role in 1921 and 1922, was never a contender. He could scarcely keep track of his own kit, let alone manage an expedition, and he was most certainly not a professional soldier. The Everest expeditions, inspiring to the country, had touched a particular nerve in the army. When, in the late spring of 1923, Colonel Strutt, following an audience with the king and queen of Belgium, visited the Rhine Army of Occupation at Cologne, more than four thousand British officers attended his lecture. The following day, June 20, another three thousand officers and enlisted men crammed a zeppelin shed at Wahn to listen to the same talk. The conquest of Everest had transcended sport and become a national mission. That the final assault might be led by anyone other than a military officer was inconceivable.

In 1922 Norton had proved exceptional in every way. Calm in a crisis, stoic in the face of adversity, he was a confident leader whose measured orders were embraced readily by those under his command. Norton's mind—unlike that of so many senior officers they had known during the war—did not run on rails. He was open to discussion, tolerant of debate, and had a way of making each man feel a part of what were ultimately his decisions alone. As a personality and a mountaineer, he quite literally stood out from the pack. Mallory, Somervell, Geoffrey Bruce, and indeed most of the alpine climbers were of remarkably similar stature. Each was an inch shy of six feet and weighed roughly 160 pounds fully clothed. Norton, by contrast, was six foot four, exceedingly tall and thin, approximating, as he quipped, "Euclid's definition of a straight line." Heralded by all, and most especially by Mallory, Norton's unofficial appointment in October 1922 took on particular significance when only a month later General Bruce, finally exhausted by the trials of the past six months, did indeed take seriously ill, leading even Hinks to question the wisdom of sending him back out to Everest in 1924.

Recruiting the rest of the 1924 expedition would ultimately consume the better part of a year. Various names were bantered about as early as the autumn of 1922, but it was only with Noel's funding in place in late June 1923 that serious attention turned to the makeup of the climbing party that seemed destined to place a man on the top of the world. By then, of course, Finch was out. Kellas was dead. Raeburn had lost his mind, and would be gone within three years. Longstaff, Wakefield, Crawford, and Strutt were nonstarters, even had they been interested, which they were not. Sandy Wollaston, Howard-Bury's confidant in 1921, volunteered to serve as naturalist and medical officer but was disqualified due to age. Guy Bullock, ensconced as consul at Le Havre, was not about to forfeit his diplomatic career. Howard-Bury had turned his passions and considerable wealth to Tory politics, gaining election to Parliament in 1922. In the summer of 1923 his thoughts were on Ireland and India and the troublesome agitations of Gandhi, whose cause he strongly condemned in a bitter parliamentary debate in late July. Oliver Wheeler, back in India after an extended leave in Canada, reluctantly sent General Bruce his regrets; the Survey of India was unable to spare a single officer for the 1924 expedition. Colonel Ryder offered instead to dispatch an accomplished Indian topographer, one Hari Singh Thapa, No. 2304, a naik, or corporal, in the 2nd Battalion, 5th Gurkha Regiment. Ryder's order excluded not only Wheeler but also the indefatigable Henry Morshead, who was keen to have another go despite the severity of his injuries. John Morris, granted eight months' leave in the spring of 1923, spent much of the summer scrambling around Switzerland with General Bruce. He, too, was eager to return to Everest, and the general wanted to have him. Unfortunately, his regimental commander deemed it inconvenient. Thus, aside from General Bruce, Colonel Norton, and the photographer John Noel, of the twenty veterans of the first two expeditions, only Geoffrey Bruce, Howard Somervell, and George Mallory remained viable candidates for the third campaign.

Somervell, after three months in India, had returned to London in mid-November 1922 and immediately flung himself into the daunting task of completing, in a matter of weeks, the score for Noel's film. It was a considerable challenge. To save money Hinks insisted that the orchestra be small, no more than nine players. Undeterred, Somervell forged ahead, driven in part by his growing conviction that all of the world's music had been born in Tibet. Modern jazz, only just reaching the West End clubs of London, he interpreted as but a wild return to the root sounds and arrangements of the primordial musical impulse of the Himalaya. General Bruce dismissed Somervell's musical theories as poppycock, but he admired his energy, just as he had admired his strength, courage, and commitment on Everest.

In the summer of 1923 the general encouraged Somervell to travel to the Dolomites and assess two prospective candidates for the third expedition. One was Frank Smythe, a promising but as yet untested climber of just twenty-four. The other was Bentley Beetham, whose name had been floated by the general for several months. Age thirty-eight, Beetham had a passion for birds and had traveled once to the Arctic, in 1911. In six weeks Somervell led thirty-two successful climbs. He was struck by lightning, nearly killed by a massive boulder, and, after fracturing his fibula, climbed through the pain until the bone healed. His record on the mountains was remarkable, but his final report to the general was an astonishing miscalculation. He scored Beetham well, securing for his old friend a journey to Everest, where the man would break down completely and offer in the end nothing. Beetham, for forty years a teacher at the same institution he had attended as a boy, the Barnard Castle School in county Durham, would end his climbing career at Raven Crag in the Lake District, with a fall that would crack his skull in six places. On Everest in 1924 he would walk with the gait of the lame, and never reach higher than Camp III.

Frank Smythe, by contrast, overlooked by Somervell perhaps because of his youth, would go on to extraordinary acclaim. A member of the three British Everest expeditions of the 1930s, frightful attempts inspired directly by Mallory's legacy, he would in June 1933 reach higher than any man before him, following the path of his mentors, the ghosts of 1924. After two nights in the death zone, emaciated after weeks at altitude, he would turn his back on the summit and upon his descent begin to hallucinate, convinced that someone was at his side, a companion who hovered above, pulsating like a spirit in the mist. Just days before, he had come upon an "inexpressibly desolate and pathetic scene": Mallory's last camp. "Where were they?" he desperately wanted to know. Would Everest yield its secret? As he gazed aloft from those dreadful heights, he felt only anguish. He cared less about whether Mallory had reached the top than he did about his own deliverance, the peace that comes over the climber who has failed but survived. In his journal he wrote of the "relief of not having to go on." The last 1,000 feet of Everest, he said, "are not for mere flesh and blood." In time Smythe would triumph, not on Everest but on scores of other Himalayan peaks, becoming one the finest climbers and arguably the greatest mountaineering writer of his century. Unfortunately, his spirit and sublime gifts as an alpinist were lost to the men of 1924.

So Beetham was in and Frank Smythe out. It was a considerable blunder, but not by any means the gravest mistake made by the selection committee. Richard Graham, like Beetham a schoolmaster, was another child of the Lake District, a keen hill walker as a boy, an accomplished rock climber in his teens, and a veteran of all the great summits of Europe before his thirtieth birthday, in 1923. A graduate of Magdalen College, Oxford, he was at the top of everyone's list for Everest, well known to the entire climbing fraternity as a cheerful and generous companion, a natural leader with a great eye for a route, and a fine strategist and tactician who was particularly strong on snow and ice. He was the obvious replacement for George Finch. On March 16, 1923, General Bruce put Graham's name forward in a letter to Sydney Spencer at the Alpine Club, but an official announcement would not be made until November 6, at a general meeting of the club.

Graham's elation upon hearing the news was matched in its intensity only by his disappointment when, scarcely a month after the announcement, the offer from the Everest Committee was formally rescinded. Graham was a Quaker; his father was a leading member of the Society of Friends. Both were pacifists by religious conviction. Following his graduation from Oxford, in 1915, Richard had registered successfully as a conscientious objector, a status not casually granted by the military authorities. He'd served throughout the war as a schoolmaster at Bishop's Stortford College, a contribution that satisfied the army but not, as it turned out, a shadowy member of the Everest endeavor who refused to participate in 1924 unless the "conchie" was tossed off the expedition. General Bruce and Younghusband, Hinks, Spencer, and Collie, in a gesture of rank cowardice, acquiesced. Graham, shaken by the rebuke, decided to offer his resignation rather than risk disrupting the harmony of the climbing party. His humiliation was complete when word of his dismissal appeared in the press.

Graham sent a note of explanation to Mallory, who came immediately to his defense in a furious letter that reached General Bruce on December 17, 1923. If the man was good enough, Mallory fumed, to pass muster with the senior members of the selection committee, who surely knew of his war record, he must certainly be good enough for any member of the expedition. To force Graham to resign after his nomination had been approved and made public in the newspapers was "simply a thing which is not done." The suggestion that the majority of the climbing party was "very strongly against him," Mallory continued, was patently untrue. He warned Bruce in no uncertain terms that whoever was "agitating to turn down Graham" would feel his wrath and become his enemy. Mallory had no idea of the identity of the culprit, he said. But whoever it was, he declared, "I hereby agitate against him!" It was without doubt one of Mallory's finest moments.

And he was not alone. Upon learning of the scandal, Howard Somervell, who by this late date had returned to his medical mission at Neyyoor, in southern India, immediately wrote to Sydney Spencer, threatening to resign from the Alpine Club. The "caddish treatment" of Graham, "a dirty piece of work," as he put it, was surely a deliberate attempt by someone who "being outside the expedition is hoping for a place therein. I personally served throughout the war and don't hold with conscientious objectors; but if something connected with the Alpine Club [has brought this about] I feel I ought not remain a member of the club."

All protests aside, the decision stood. Both Spencer and Younghusband explained away the controversy with the claim that Graham had proactively tendered his resignation for personal reasons that were beyond the discretion of the Everest Committee to reveal. In a letter to General Bruce on February 22, 1924, Hinks went as far as to say that Graham's wartime status had played no role whatsoever in the committee's deliberations. This was a blatant falsehood. As it turned out, the man who had assaulted Graham's reputation and destroyed his dream of Everest was none other than Bentley Beetham, the one member of the 1924 Everest party, aside from Sandy Irvine (who was too young for the call-up), who had not actually served in the war. Like

Graham, Beetham had escaped the front, spending all those terrible years as a schoolmaster, motivated, no doubt, by a raw emotion other than religious conviction.

Having rejected George Finch, Frank Smythe, and now Richard Graham, three of the finest climbers of their era, not to mention two other future Everest climbers, Hugh Ruttledge and George Wood-Johnson, the Everest Committee inexplicably turned to John de Vars Hazard, a dour thirty-six-year-old engineer who had spent much of his professional life in West Africa building bridges, pontoon wharfs, jetties, and seawalls. Born in Nigeria, raised in France, educated in Geneva, he had hovered around the mountaineering scene for some time, nursing a plan to escape postwar London for India, where he hoped to live for several years. As early as December 4, 1919, he had written to Hinks, expressing a keen interest in going to Everest. Though never a member of the Alpine Club, he was an acquaintance of Noel Odell's, and in 1920 had been invited to join Kellas's expedition to Kamet. His closest friend among the Everest men was Henry Morshead, who had been his commanding officer in the Royal Engineers during the war, where together they had endured some of the worst of the fighting. Hazard, awarded the Military Cross for gallantry in action, had been wounded twice. Shrapnel had torn open his back, machine gun fire his thigh and hips. This left him with a slight problem that the Everest Committee either by choice or by negligence overlooked: Hazard's wounds had never healed. In the midst of the greatest crisis of the 1924 expedition, he would find himself helplessly debilitated. Ridiculed later as a misfit, Hazard would quite unjustly become the scapegoat of 1924. In truth, if there was fault to assign, it lay with the Everest Committee, which had banished Richard Graham, a highly accomplished and proven climber known for his great stamina, and chosen in his stead a man intrepid and brave but half crippled by the war.

THE LOSS of George Finch, with his scientific mind and technical acumen, left a gaping hole that the Everest Committee attempted to fill with one of its own: Noel Odell, like Mallory an official member of the selection committee. Hinks, woefully ignorant and openly disdainful of science, assumed that Odell, a geologist with the Anglo-Persian Oil Company, would be a natural candidate to take on all the duties associated with oxygen and the redesign of the apparatus. He wasn't, and indeed had little interest in the challenge, but he would nevertheless prove an invaluable addition to the expedition. For once, and almost in spite of itself, the Everest Committee got it right. Two years previously Odell, already committed to an exploration of Spitsbergen, had been obliged to turn down an invitation to join the 1921 reconnaissance. In 1924, on Everest, he would secure his place in mountaineering history.

Born the son of a vicar on Christmas Day 1890 on the Isle of Wight, Odell first made his mark as a climber in the Lake District at the age of thirteen. Three years later, already a member of the Alpine Club, he moved on to northern Wales, honing his craft on the smooth slabs of Cwm Idwal before heading to the Mont Blanc massif, where he climbed Aiguille du Tour at eighteen. Having discovered a love of ice and snow, he spent twelve seasons in the Alps, developing skills that would allow him, in 1936, to become the first to reach the Himalayan summit of Nanda Devi (25,645 feet), for fourteen years the highest peak ever climbed. Two years later, in 1938, he would be back on Everest, climbing to within 1,500 feet of the summit before being turned back by deep powder snow impossible to negotiate. A spare figure, with a kind and genial nature, Odell strode through life possessed of infinite reserves of energy, a seemingly limitless well of stamina that would have him attempting serious peaks at the age of eighty-seven and traversing glaciers at ninety-three. In time, mountain features on three continents would bear his name, as would a distant star in the constellation Lyra. In a climbing career that spanned three-quarters of a century, he inspired generations of young British climbers. In old age he was known to them as Noah, a nickname he adored.

In 1923, all of this, of course, lay in the distant future. The war had been Odell's seminal experience, as it had been for most of his generation. Attached to the 59th Field Company of the Royal Engineers, he first reached France in July 1916. His baptism of fire was the Battle of the Somme. His younger brother Eric, just twenty-two and a lieutenant in the 8th Black Watch, served in the same theater and was killed near Arras, just before Christmas. In his war diary, Noel scarcely mentions his brother's death. The entire entry for Monday, December 18, 1916, reads: "Stayed in hut till tea time, when went across to mess until bedtime. Tonsillitis better. Eric wounded by trench mortar bomb. Died 20th."

It is impossible to know what this cryptic note implies, if indeed anything. Odell's journal entries both during the war and on Everest were notoriously curt. But there is one curious uncertainty. Noel Odell went to his death convinced that he had been wounded three times; the fact is noted prominently in several obituaries, as well as in his official profile in the *Dictionary of National Biography*. The War Office records, however, indicate but a single incident, an accident behind the lines at Allouagne on April 14, 1917, when Odell inadvertently struck a buried bomb with a pickax. The concussion from the detonation reputedly blinded him for two days, but according to the medical board his injuries were minor: one small fragment of steel was removed from his left temple; a second minute bit of metal remained lodged subcutaneously in his nose. It was the type of wound men at the front dreamed of getting, a ticket out of the war. After a lengthy recuperation, which included time for climbing and trekking in the Scottish Highlands, Odell entered the Home Service in a training capacity, which even allowed him to be close to his wife and infant son. Like Wakefield, he lost track of his Christian faith. Both his father and his father-in-law were clergymen, and there were vitriolic family arguments when, in the last year of the war, Odell and his wife, Gwladys Mona, showed little interest in christening their only son.

Odell's response to the horror, which he certainly experienced during his months at the front, was to float above conflict, cultivating an air of detachment—an attribute that served him exceedingly well on Everest. One of his companions in 1924, E. O. Shebbeare, hired in Darjeeling as transport officer by General Bruce, would write, "Odell, a wonder on the mountain, is quite useless in the ordinary affairs of life." But his great quality, Shebbeare continued, was his refusal to worry about anything: "In an emergency, and we had plenty of emergencies on our trip, he never offered fatuous advice. Instead he would sit placidly on a rock and read the *Times Literary Supplement*, a copy of which, by that time many months old, he always carried in his rucksack, and so he would wait for the situation to clear. It made you ashamed to worry and at the same time heartened you to get something done to justify such implicit confidence."

Noel Odell brought to Everest one other remarkable asset, in the form of a second-year engineering student from Merton College at Oxford, twenty-one-year-old Andrew Comyn Irvine. Known as Sandy to his friends, he was an extremely good-looking lad, with a bright smile and a great shock of blond hair. A superb athlete, he rowed for the Oxford Eight, gaining his blue letter even as a freshman, and there is little doubt that his place at the university was secured in good measure by his physical prowess. Intellectually, he lagged. He wrote poorly, was a dreadful speller, and today might well be diagnosed with some learning disability, quite possibly dyslexia. In truth, he had the brilliant mind of an inventor, precise, analytical, and methodical. At the age of fifteen he independently devised from scratch an interrupter gear that would allow a machine gun to fire through a propeller, thus offering a solution to a strategically vital technical challenge of the war effort. When he submitted his unsolicited sketches to the War Office, along with a second invention, a design for a gyroscopic stabilizer for airplanes, the response was stunned disbelief. More than a tinkerer, he was a mechanical savant. There was nothing engineered by man that he could not take apart and put back together. His most prized possession was a 1914 Clyno 750cc motorcycle and sidecar, the same V-Twin model the army mounted with Vickers machine guns at the front. At sixteen, while holidaying in the Welsh mountains of Snowdonia, he went off-road in the Carneddau range and just kept driving. Approaching the 3,205-foot summit of Foel Grach, he ran into none other than Noel Odell, and casually asked the astonished climber for directions.

Their paths crossed again in the spring of 1923 at Putney on the Thames, where Irvine and his crew were training for the annual Oxford-Cambridge boat race. Sandy's close friend George Binney, then in the process of putting together a second Oxford exploratory expedition to Spitsbergen for the summer of 1923, had recruited to the effort Odell as geologist and Tom Longstaff as doctor. Sandy had signed on for the adventure formally known as the Merton College Arctic Expedition. By then Odell was committed to Everest for 1924, and very much on the lookout for young talent. From their first training climbs in Wales, at Great Gully on Craig yr Ysfa, Irvine stood out from the rest. He was invariably in high spirits, remarkably resourceful, ferociously strong, and exceedingly personable. Odell took him under his wing. During one outing on Spitsbergen, he and Irvine alone traversed the Lomme Bay Glacier to reach a series of formidable peaks that soared out of the ice. Sandy had no experience as a climber, but he fearlessly followed Odell up 3,000 feet of hard metamorphic rock, reaching the southeast ridge of a summit in the Stubendorff Mountains that Odell would later name Mount Irvine. On that day a mountaineer was born.

Odell was more than impressed. If Geoffrey Bruce, a soldier who had never been on a mountain, could climb with Finch and establish a height record, surely Irvine was fit for Everest. They needed youth, and Sandy's mechanical skills would be a godsend. Odell, assigned oxygen duties, dreaded the prospect, and was thrilled to be able to pass along the responsibility to one far more suited to the task. Upon their return to London in September 1923, Odell immediately floated

Irvine's name. A month later, on October 24, the formal invitation came, along with a letter from Merton College granting the undergraduate two semesters of leave. As Mallory explained in a note to Geoffrey Winthrop Young, "Irvine represents our attempt to get one superman, though lack of experience is against him." Soon after, Sandy got hold of a sample oxygen apparatus from 1922, which he took home to his workshop to strip down into parts. Within the week, and without bothering to seek authorization from the Everest Committee, he sent the manufacturer, Siebe Gorman, a list of improvements for what amounted to a total redesign of the equipment.

The inclusion of young Irvine in 1924, given the tragic destiny that awaited him on the mountain, has always provoked controversy. But in the circumstances he was a logical and, indeed, ideal choice. The criticism that he had never been on a mountain is unfounded. Odell tested him in Wales and on Spitsbergen and had been astonished by his natural abilities. His raw strength and physical agility alone made him easily the match of any number of more experienced mountaineers, especially on Everest, where endurance counted far more than technical skills with a rope. The prurient notion that Mallory had designs on the young man—a theory put forth seriously by some Everest historians—suggests a complete misunderstanding of both Mallory's sexuality and Irvine's libido. Mallory's emotional bonds to men, even his physical attractions, were a reflection of his times and the experimental culture of Cambridge before the war; they had little to do with homosexuality as we know it today. At thirty-seven, he was a devoted father and husband. Sandy Irvine, by all accounts, was wildly and devilishly heterosexual.

If these older men—Mallory and Odell and, in due course, Norton and Somervell—appear to have been especially keen on Irvine, and not merely for the skills he brought to the expedition, the explanation may lie in another realm of unspoken emotion. Sandy, born in 1902, never served in the army, the war having mercifully ended before, at sixteen, he would have been eligible for the fight. But he was not untouched by the conflict. His cousin Edward was killed in France. And his brother Hugh, nearby when a German shell landed in a gas dump, was splattered all over with mustard gas, which etched burns deep into his neck and back. The open wounds would never heal; they would have to be dressed twice a day every day until he died, in 1965. Odell and Norton had both lost brothers at the front. Somervell had struggled through acres of dying boys at the Somme. Mallory and all of them had borne witness to the carnage, in many cases for years. If they were all powerfully drawn to young Irvine, it was perhaps because in some small way he embodied, with his vitality, innocence, and limitless possibilities, the reason they had all fought and the future for which so many of their friends had died.

TWO DAYS after Irvine received his formal invitation from the Everest Committee, a brief note appeared in the *Times* officially announcing that a third expedition, under the command of General Bruce, would be going out to Everest in 1924. There was no list of names, but it was assumed by all that George Mallory would be leading the alpine assault. Indeed, perhaps the only person in Britain who had any doubts was Mallory himself. Formally offered a place on the expedition as early as May 1923, he had yet to tender a reply. When, on October 16, at a meeting of the selection committee, he was asked to draw up a final list of candidates, he scratched down his name but added beside it a question mark. He did much the same in a letter to his old friend and mentor Geoffrey Young.

In truth he was deeply conflicted, torn between his family and his fellow climbers, haunted by the specter of a mountain that laid claim to his every thought, even as it summoned him back, he feared, to his doom. Indecision tormented him through the fall of 1923, shaking even the tranquillity of his marriage to Ruth. His closest friends became deeply concerned. Geoffrey Young's brother Hilton had married Kathleen Scott, the widow of Captain Robert Falcon Scott, whose quest for the South Pole had ended in agony and death. At Mallory's request, he and Geoffrey, along with Young's wife, Len, paid a visit to Kathleen. When they left in a taxi, according to Len, Mallory "confessed to us that he did not want to return to Everest again." Geoffrey Keynes came away from a meeting with his old friend with very much the same impression. Keynes recalled, "He said to me that what he would have to face would be more like war than adventure, and that he did not believe he would return alive. He knew that no one would criticize him if he refused to go, but he felt it a compulsion. The situation has its literary counterpart in Melville's Captain Ahab and his pursuit of the White Whale, Moby Dick."

Young and Mallory's sister Mary both urged him not to go. His wife, Ruth, had premonitions of disaster. Mallory himself hoped that circumstances would resolve his dilemma. He had scarcely begun his teaching obligations at Cambridge. Surely, he hoped, Reverend David Cranage would refuse to allow him to abandon his post. Cranage, of course, came under intense pressure from Hinks and the Everest Committee to do precisely the opposite, and in the end granted him six months' leave at half pay, a generous offer that placed the burden of decision directly back on Mallory. Hinks and Younghusband lobbied hard, appealing to his patriotism, but their rhetoric meant little to him. Mallory wrote to his father, seeking his advice. "It is an awful tug," he noted, "to contemplate going away from here instead of settling down to make a new life here with Ruth . . . [But] I have to look at it from the point of view of loyalty to the expedition and of carrying through a task begun."

On December 15 the front page of the *Times* led with a big story, "Mount Everest Third Expedition Next Spring." Three and a half weeks later, on January 10, 1924, a follow-up article listed by name the members of the expedition. Prominent among them was Mallory, though in truth even then he remained undecided. In the end, however, Everest fever proved too powerful to resist. At the world's first Winter Olympics, which opened in Chamonix on January 25, Colonel Strutt accepted fifteen silver medals on behalf of the 1922 expedition, described in the citation as "the greatest feat of alpinism in the preceding four years." Not to be outdone, the Vatican sent a letter through its secretary of state, Cardinal Gasparri, indicating that Pope Pius XI, a keen climber in his youth, would also be awarding a gold medal to the expedition. Throughout Britain, every manufacturer and commercial enterprise hit up by Hinks for free services now reaped their rewards; images of Everest and heroic climbers helped sell everything from playing cards and cigarettes to newspapers, Kodak film, mint candies, gabardine jackets, work boots, jams and jellies, butter, and bully beef. When the British Empire Exhibition, a two-year extravaganza, opened at Wembley in the spring of 1924, the key attraction of the India pavilion was a large-scale model of Everest. Some twenty-seven million visitors took in the celebration, the largest event of its kind ever staged.

On January 28 a lead editorial in the *Times* heralded the upcoming expedition as not just an inspiration to the nation but as the very embodiment of British values and spirit, the essence of the race. "Whether the result be victory or defeat," the piece noted, "the third attempt to conquer Everest will mean like the two before it an inspiring display of the resolution and endurance and indifference to discomfort and danger that all through the ages and to the uttermost ends of the earth, have made the people of these islands, above all a race of pioneers. When General Bruce says that the great adventure of Everest has now become almost a pilgrimage, he touches upon a profound truth."

After all he had endured and invested in the quest, it was inconceivable that Mallory would not be there at the end. On February 13, just two weeks before he was scheduled to sail to India, he finally signed the official contract, committing himself to the expedition. Seldom had a more ambivalent man set out on a more perilous mission.

In 1924, the climbers converged on Darjeeling from all corners of the empire. Noel Odell traveled east from the oil fields of Persia. Howard Somervell came north by train from his mission in Travancore, crossing the length of India. The new medical officer, Major Richard Hingston, took leave from his post at the RAF hospital in Baghdad and sailed from Basra on February 15.

From England, Norton and General Bruce went out first, arriving by mail steamer in Bombay on February 16. They traveled immediately to Delhi to meet with Lord Rawlinson, the commander in chief of the Indian Army, who had personally intervened on Bruce's behalf to secure Hingston's respite from the air force. The thirty-six-year-old Irish doctor was a veteran of the 5th Gurkha Regiment and well known to the general. Hingston had fought throughout the war; like Somervell and Wakefield, he had dealt with wounds never before imagined by surgeons and had borne witness to the death of hundreds, even while saving the lives of countless more. Serving in Mesopotamia in 1916, he won the Military Cross for the rescue under close and constant enemy fire of a wounded sepoy, an act of heroism that inspired enlisted men throughout the Gurkha regiments. It was no wonder that eight years later General Bruce was prepared to go right to the top to secure Hingston leave to join the Everest expedition. One could not find a better man, or one more certain to stand firm in a crisis. For Hingston, the general's intervention was a godsend. After years of heat, cholera, and sandstorms, he longed for the mountains of India. "What we all hunger for," read the last lines of his war diary, "are hills and valleys, the green fields and shady woods, the rivers, the torrents, the glaciers and the snows. I see visions of the Himalaya and all its wondrous beauty."

General Bruce, having paid his respects to the high command in Delhi and thanked Lord Rawlinson for help in the Hingston affair, ordered Norton on to Calcutta and then headed for the North-West Frontier to rendezvous with his nephew Geoffrey and three of the Gurkha NCOs seconded to the expedition: Umar Gurung, Hurke Gurung, and Tejbir Bura, all of the 2nd Battalion, 6th Gurkha Rifles. He had an ulterior motive as well: to drop by a favorite shop in Abbott-

abad and purchase a supply of a particularly esteemed brand of fine
woolen puttees from Kashmir, which he considered an essential article
of clothing for mountain travel. Bruce had notoriously strong opinions
on such matters. When, as a young officer, he had found his Frontier
Scouts struggling on steep terrain in their regulation trousers, he'd
ordered them to cut their pants at the knee, thus introducing shorts
to the British Army. In time, the garment became standard issue for
service in the tropics.

In Calcutta, meanwhile, Norton arranged for the bulk of the expedition supplies and equipment—close to a thousand cases, according
to the logs of the Army and Navy Stores—to be dispatched by rail
directly to Kalimpong. The personal kits of the expedition members
went through Siliguri to Darjeeling, where John Morris's replacement,
Edward Oswald Shebbeare of the Indian Forest Service, another most
remarkable character, would take charge.

The son of a Yorkshire vicar, educated at Charterhouse, Shebbeare had fled England at the age of twenty and, since arriving in
India in 1906, had devoted his life to the study of elephants, both tame
and wild—preferably the latter. He was also the recognized authority on the birds and fishes of North Bengal. Fluent in Hindustani,
Bengali, and a number of regional dialects, he was, at thirty-nine, a
rough-and-tumble naturalist who most assuredly did not stand on ceremony. Detailed late in life to accompany the governor of Bengal on a
tiger hunt, he famously turned up in a bush shirt and tattered shorts,
his bare feet thrust into boots commandeered from a Japanese guard in
the prison camp that had held him for three years after his capture at
Singapore in 1941. On the day of the shoot, he wore the same ragged
outfit but had added a pair of socks. "Well, you know," he explained to
a companion, "on these occasions you have to cut a bit of dash." His
one published book was an elephant's life story, told from the point
of view of the animal. Everything about Shebbeare was conceived to
endear him to Bruce. "He was, is, and ever will be," the general wrote,
"a glutton for work, and with him discomforts count not."

In the last days of February, General Bruce and Geoffrey joined
Norton and Shebbeare in Darjeeling. Hingston arrived on March 7
and Noel Odell two days later. The general's plan was to have the
bulk of the stores organized and ready to go before the remainder of
the party arrived in the third week of March. With this goal in mind,
he ordered Norton and Shebbeare down to Kalimpong on March 13
to deal with the baggage and supplies that had been sent there, altogether three thousand pounds of food, tents, and equipment destined

for the mountain. Among the supplies were sixty tins of quail in foie gras and forty-eight bottles of champagne, Montebello 1915, the general's favorite vintage.

Noel Odell remained in Darjeeling, apparently to have fun. His diary chronicles a veritable social whirlwind: squash at the Gymkhana Club followed by tea at the Rendezvous, dinner and dancing for 150 at the Planters' Club, lawn tennis with a young lady followed by billiards and then more dancing, evenings that rarely ended before two in the morning. On Thursday, March 20, the day Somervell finally reached Darjeeling, Odell spent the afternoon looking at stuffed birds at the Natural History Museum, the evening dancing at the Gymkhana Club.

While Odell frolicked, General Bruce and Hingston set out to recruit the porters, interviewing and inspecting some three hundred, of whom seventy would be chosen. Hingston, who had done scientific investigations of the physiological effects of oxygen deprivation at altitude, and who expected to continue the work begun with pilots by monitoring the Everest climbers, did his best to evaluate the porters objectively, using measurements and performance tests. General Bruce scoffed at the notion, hiring men on instinct and reputation. Karma Paul would go out again as translator, and Gyalzen as sirdar. Old Poo the cook signed on for his third expedition. The melancholy cobbler Moti brought along his brother. Hingston hired as his assistant a Lepcha naturalist by the name of Rhombu. Among the Sherpas hired for the high camps was Angtarkay, one of the two survivors of the avalanche in 1922. Bruce also made a last-minute attempt to draft both John Morris and Henry Morshead to the cause. Neither could secure leave, however, and Morris, Bruce informed Younghusband and Hinks in his first progress report, suffered, in addition, from some strain in his foot that would require surgery—"tennis elbow of the heel," as it was described.

The photographer John Noel, General Bruce was pleased to note, had arrived in Darjeeling and was up to his old tricks. His latest scheme involved every schoolchild in the empire. With him at the Everest Hotel was his wife, Sybille, a folklorist with a keen interest in mythology, and their friend Francis Helps, an artist who had designed for Noel a commemorative postcard with a swastika, an ancient symbol of the Hindu faith, and a photograph of Mount Everest taken from base camp. For a slight fee children could write in with their return address and request that a card be mailed to them from the foot of the mountain. For the youth of Britain at the time, it was as exciting a prospect as receiving a letter postmarked on the Moon. Noel arranged for thousands of these cards to be carried across Tibet, and then dispatched home from Everest on the backs of porters through arrangements with the Indian postal service.

Noel had a number of more serious challenges to overcome during the few days available to him in Darjeeling. His attempt to develop and process film in the field in 1922 had proven to be extremely difficult. Dust and sand ruined the emulsions. Water and even chemical developers froze overnight. The air inside his lightproof tent became toxic to breathe. For 1924 he decided to concentrate all the work in Darjeeling. Using funds from his investors, he bought a piece of land and ordered the construction of a photographic laboratory, fully equipped with developing trays, chemical supplies, and an electric generator for power. To run the lab Noel hired a local photographer, Arthur Pereira, who with one assistant would work seven days a week for four months. The film itself would travel to Darjeeling in relays of porters and horsemen, carried in air- and watertight containers that had been custom-built in London. Altogether Noel had fourteen cameras, including one small pocket-sized model designed to carry but two minutes of film, for the men to take on the summit attempt.

Noel's technical innovations were startling. Obliged to use black-and-white film, he recorded the colors of every still photograph by reference to a standard chart, such that once converted to glass negatives, the images could be accurately tinted by hand. His film cameras had special features that mitigated the effect of static electricity, and electric motors that allowed both time-lapse and slow-motion exposures, both novelties at the time. Clipped to his camera was a six-power telescope, which was synchronized with the optimal axis of the lens such that the image in the telescope was also in the aperture of the lens. With a twenty-inch Cooke telephoto lens he would capture still images at three thousand yards, a greater distance than had ever been achieved in the history of photography. From a perch above Camp III, at an altitude of about 22,000 feet, he would be able to film the ascents from a distance of three miles with almost perfect clarity. To transport his cameras, he bought mules, and had saddles specially designed. With the aid of two trained porters, he found that with practice he could have his camera out of its box and mounted on a tripod in thirty seconds or less. The footage that eventually found its way back to *Pathé News* and to theaters all over Britain would be of a quality rarely before seen in newsreels.

·   ·   ·

MALLORY SAILED from Liverpool on February 29 on SS *California*, a new ship out of Glasgow of ten thousand tons, bristling with tourists. Many recognized him by sight and pestered him for photographs and stories of Everest. He hid away in his stateroom, reading Maurois's *Ariel* and practicing his Hindustani, even as he worked through every detail of supply and organization for the upcoming climb, the high camps where his word would carry such weight. There would be no height records for their own sake this year. All that mattered was the summit. He shared his cabin with Hazard but took most of his meals with young Irvine, whom he described to Ruth as "sensible and not at all highly strung," adding that "he'll be one to depend on for everything perhaps except conversation." Beetham was also on board, bunking with Irvine. They passed the time working out in the gym, tossing about a medicine ball, and running laps of the deck—whatever they could manage to do to stay fit.

Mallory was haunted by memories of the previous months: the tensions and difficulties at home, the foolishness of it all. He had been on the road lecturing as late as February 27, two days before his departure. "I fear I don't make you very happy," he wrote to Ruth on March 8, the day before the *California* reached Port Said. The day of his departure a powerful westerly wind had pressed the ship against the quay where Ruth stood waving farewell. It took the tugboats so long to drag the vessel out to sea that she gave up and simply went home. His last image of her was of her back as she slowly walked away.

The *California* reached Bombay on March 17. When a journalist asked Sandy Irvine about the prospects of the climb, he replied, "It is the duty of the Alpine Club to climb as near as it can to heaven!" Mallory felt far less ebullient in the torrid heat. During the five-day rail journey across India, the thermometer did not once drop below one hundred degrees until the tracks finally rose from Siliguri into the mists of Darjeeling. They arrived at the Everest Hotel on March 22, just three days before the expedition was scheduled to depart for Tibet.

Mallory's spirits lifted the moment he met the other members of the expedition. He deeply admired Norton, felt a strong bond with Somervell, took an immediate liking to Hingston, and in Odell recognized "one of the best." He always got a great kick out of John Noel, whom he found "more than ever" up to his old schemes. From their long sea journey together, he knew both Beetham and Hazard to be unselfish and personable. Irvine was a delight, not only a mechanical wizard but also a very fine and enthusiastic photographer. The last-minute recruitment of John Macdonald to supervise the mails promised great improvements. And perhaps the most uplifting news of all came from the medical officer. "The General," Hingston reported rather hastily, for he had yet to examine Bruce, "is in exuberant spirits and looks the picture of health." At the welcoming dinner hosted that night by Lady Lytton, wife of the governor of Bengal, toasts were many and heartfelt. "We couldn't be a nicer party," Mallory wrote to Ruth. Norton was especially confident: "I don't believe a stronger party will ever be got together for Everest."

The following day, Mallory and Irvine scrambled to arrange their kits. Each man was allotted two mules, each capable of carrying 160 pounds. A Whymper tent weighed 60, leaving Irvine 260 pounds to divide among three suitcases, one large valise, one ice ax case with four axes, each wrapped in maps of the mountain, and one small case for cameras and delicate equipment such as binoculars. None of them traveled light. Taking a break to play a last-minute game of tennis with Lady Lytton, Irvine did not have his gear finally packed until the early hours of March 24. They would leave the following day, the entire expedition coming together in Kalimpong, where Norton and Shebbeare, as well as Noel, had been based for some days.

THE MARCH to Tibet began in earnest on March 26, with the men once again dividing into two parties so as not to overwhelm the capacity of the *dak* bungalows. General Bruce, Somervell, Hazard, Beetham, Noel, and Geoffrey Bruce headed out first, followed by Norton, Hingston, Mallory, Odell, Irvine, and Shebbeare. Between them they drove ten mules laden only with money. The previous year, the Tibetan authorities had recalled all of the silver in the country, forcing the expedition to rely on copper currency, seventy-five thousand coins altogether.

The most interesting impressions came from those making the journey for the first time. Hingston was much taken by the Buddhist prayer flags, "tall and narrow, fixed to high poles," inscribed with "mystic words" and incessantly in motion. "At every quiver," he wrote after the initial day's march to Ghoom, "a thousand prayers were given to the mountain breeze." Six days later, as he struggled up the heights of the Jelep La, exhaustion turned his tone to contempt: "The summit of the pass was decked with flags. Our porters added their contribution to the streamers, piled a few more stones on the existing heap, and uttered their monotonous prayer *Om mani padme hum.* But how feeble did this religious ceremony seem amidst such a world of snowy mountains. Round about them was the monument of universal power, while they worshipped a mere cluster of flags."

Sandy Irvine, when not admiring butterflies, taking pictures, sampling new foods, or pestering Shebbeare about the curious habits of the local people, flung himself into his role as mobile repair shop, fixing Odell's tripod and tinkering with his own wristwatch. At Kalimpong he first attacked the oxygen stores, repacking the frames and the cylinders for the long journey ahead. To his horror, he discovered that Siebe Gorman had utterly ignored his instructions. In a letter written to a friend from Pedong on March 28, he complained, "They haven't taken my design, but what they have sent is hopeless, breaks if you touch it, leaks, is ridiculously clumsy and heavy." Out of ninety cylinders, he found that fifteen were empty and twenty-four had leaked badly even before getting to Calcutta. "Ye Gods!" he exclaimed. "I broke one today taking it out of its packing case." Three days later he reported to the general that all but one of the oxygen frames had been damaged in shipping.

With limited tools at hand, Irvine set out to salvage what could be recycled into a new design, which in the end would prove to be both lighter and far more functional than the dubious product of the Siebe Gorman lab. Indeed, in a month Irvine accomplished more than the company engineers had achieved in two years. That he was able to do so while marching across Tibet, fighting off the bitter winds of early spring, was remarkable. That the task was even necessary was a disturbing sign of just how much George Finch's presence would be missed in 1924.

Irvine's submission to Siebe Gorman had been disregarded chiefly because at twenty-one he lacked gravitas and authority. The Everest Committee, following the break with Finch, largely ignored the oxygen problem. Not one of the new climbers chosen for the 1924 expedition had any experience with the apparatus. Six months passed before the Everest Committee even assigned responsibility for oxygen to Noel Odell, who had no interest in the challenge, being personally opposed to the entire idea of using supplemental gas. Had it not been for Sandy Irvine—both his last-minute selection and his unique mechanical gifts—the expedition would have been without the one experimental innovation that had made all the difference in 1922. Given what had been learned, such casual disregard on the part of the committee was almost criminal. Douglas Freshfield compared the stubborn resistance to oxygen to Scott's rejection of dogs for polar exploration: "So long as the summit of Everest is reached who cares whether it is with or without oxygen. One might as well claim merit for going up the Matterhorn without a rope or ice axe, in dress shoes or in shirtsleeves. A more tragic parallel could be found in the unfortunate prejudice against the use of sledge dogs in the Antarctic." Captain Scott's folly famously had resulted in the death of his entire party.

AS THE EXPEDITION gathered at Yatung on April 2, there was a more immediate and pressing concern. Having promised the Everest Committee that he would undergo a medical examination before leaving Darjeeling, General Bruce finally made time on the tenth day of the journey. In his second progress report to London, dictated to John Noel, who had taken Morris's place as expedition typist, the general was decidedly upbeat. "Subject to directions received, I duly submitted myself to the tender mercies of Hingston and his countless and innumerable instruments were applied to every square inch of my body. Hingston came to the conclusion that Larkins had treated me with extraordinary ferocity and that I might be allowed to proceed. All is well."

Actually, it was not. Hingston, who had been with the second party, was in fact profoundly disturbed by Bruce's condition at Yatung. "Unfortunately," he reported, "I found the General not too fit. He had a chill in crossing the pass and will have to take it easy on the march across Tibet." The same day Irvine wrote in his journal that Bruce was a "little seedy." Somervell noted that the general clearly was "not feeling up to the mark; fever, and he doesn't look fit." Mallory, in a letter to Ruth, voiced concern that Hingston had described Bruce's pulse as "irregular."

A cloud hung over the expedition as it moved up the Chumbi Valley, arriving in Phari on April 6. Odell and Shebbeare were both ill; Beetham was weak from chronic diarrhea. The general put on a good face on the night of his fifty-eighth birthday, as he cracked open a bottle of his family's prized 150-year-old rum. But the mood was grim, and not about to be lifted by the dreary streets of Phari. Shebbeare wrote of "gutters knee deep in filth, dark houses, smoky rabbit warrens, people black with grime." Hingston, no stranger to urban hovels after months in Baghdad, was nevertheless appalled by what he saw: piles of manure scattered about, yak dung heaped against walls and on rooftops, great rotting piles of refuse, yak bones and carcasses. "Phari," he wrote, "was little else than a place of indescribable filth. The ravens and the lammergeiers were its only scavengers and the people were in keeping with the place they lived."

Even the ebullient Sandy Irvine was downcast; word reached him by telegraph on April 6 that the Cambridge Eight had crushed Oxford in the 1924 boat race. He was still trying to digest the news two days later. "I still can't get over Oxford being beaten," he confided in his diary, "by four and a half lengths!" He drowned his disappointment in work, fixing one of the pressure cookers, reducing the weight of his toolbox, repairing Mallory's camp bed and ice ax.

Geoffrey Bruce and the ailing Shebbeare, meanwhile, saw to the transport, hiring some 250 yaks and 80 mules to carry them into Tibet as they headed west, abandoning the main trade route to Gyantse and Lhasa. When the general learned that prices had risen by 25 percent since 1922, he furiously and very publicly threatened to wire a protest to the prime minister of Tibet. After the local authorities yielded to his bluster, he dramatically tore up the telegram and tossed the fragments into the air. It was his last theatrical gesture of the campaign. Noel Odell, who shared a tent with Bruce, reported to Hingston that all through the night the general had been "wheezing and coughing and shaking like an earthquake."

By morning the general was so weak that Hingston proposed that the expedition split: while the main party would head directly over the high passes for Kampa Dzong, as planned, he and John Macdonald would escort the general on the longer route through Tuna, around Dochen Lake and Tatsang, a six-day journey as opposed to four. With clouds gathering, Hingston, Macdonald, and Bruce finally got away just after noon, with twenty-two miles to ride. Hingston, who stayed by Bruce the entire time, was surprised by the harshness of the land, the utter sterility and destitution: "Remove the stones that littered the surface, cut away the hills on either side, and the prospect before us might be the desert in Iraq."

They made camp late, at 14,500 feet, in the frost and winds of Tuna. Hingston went birding at first light and returned to find the general "dressed, but shivering with a violent attack of ague. It was clear he could not proceed today. We got him in bed, covered him in blankets, made hot water bottles out of double soap-dishes and dosed him with Dovers powder, aspirin and quinine." To make matters worse, John Macdonald was down with mountain sickness. A message was dispatched to the main party: "General seedy, Hingston broken all thermometers."

By the following morning, April 9, a Wednesday, the diagnosis was certain. General Bruce had gone on a tiger hunt just before the start of the expedition. As Odell remarked, "He bagged his tiger, but also picked up malaria." The only option was evacuation. Bruce's spleen was dangerously enlarged, and his body so racked with fever that he would lose nearly thirty pounds in a week.

Hingston sent a runner to Phari, with a note to be dispatched by telegraph requesting that a stretcher be brought in all haste from Gyantse. It arrived on April 11, having been carried on horseback, night and day: six stages in less than twenty-four hours. More bad news came from the main party. Beetham had virtually collapsed with severe dysentery, and Mallory was down with what was feared to be appendicitis, a life-threatening ailment in 1924; Somervell was making plans for emergency surgery. There was nothing for Hingston to do save rally the porters for the difficult and immediate task ahead. He selected eighteen of the strongest men, and they set off for the safety of Yatung on the morning of April 12. "I had the General in his stretcher by 9 a.m. and away we marched across the plain to Phari. In a sense it was a mournful procession; the stretcher being hoisted on the shoulders of six men who changed with others when they became tired. But we moved along at a fair pace, and the Tibetan porters relieved the monotony with a lively rhythmical chant."

The air trembled before Hingston's eyes. Exhausted with tension, no doubt with thoughts of Kellas's fate in mind, he rode as if into a mirage or hallucination, with the entire horizon constantly changing shape and color before his gaze. "On the ground," he wrote, "the air seems to dance in a shimmering layer or spreads itself into a watery sheet. Imaginary lakes conceal the plateau or rest beneath a rounded hill. In these we see the reflections from the mountains and their draperies of ice and snow. When the fierce winds blow we see the haze in motion; the mirage seems then to sweep across the plateau in circling waves of foam. We observe the usual distortion of objects, the irregular outlines, the confused shapes, the fantasies of the trembling air."

In a day they reached Phari, white beneath a blanket of fresh snow. As they traveled farther down the valley, their procession seemed to Hingston to become less mournful. Their spirits rose as they entered the gorges and moved into forests sheltered from the harsh winds of the plateau. The Tibetans continued to chant. "Though monotonous," Hingston recalled, "it was a pleasing tune and seemed to blend with the rumble of the stream. The General's health should now quickly improve."

And it did, presenting Hingston with yet another dilemma once they had reached the comfort of Yatung on Easter Monday. He looked first to the men, rewarding them generously for their extraordinary feat; in two days they had carried Bruce, an enormous man, more than fifty miles down off the Tibetan Plateau, thereby no doubt saving his life. Hingston then turned to his new challenge: the general, despite the severity of the attack, insisted on returning to the expedition. Hingston dispatched a telegram to the Everest Committee: "Bruce returned Yatung malaria convalescent Norton commanding. Hingston." Then he wrote a more severe note to be delivered by post: "General Bruce is anxious to rejoin the expedition. But this I consider to be most unwise. He is still very weak; his spleen is enlarged, the malarial infection still exists in his system and is liable to become active at anytime if he is exposed to the cold and wind of Tibet. Should this occur in some part of the plateau where he could not quickly be transferred to a lower altitude the most serious consequences might occur. I have, therefore, advised General Bruce that it would be most dangerous for him to rejoin the expedition, and that, if he does so, I cannot be responsible for the consequences that may occur."

The pressure on Hingston was considerable. A letter from Norton delivered by postal runner urged him, as medical officer, to return to the main party with all haste. Beetham was so severely disabled that Norton was considering sending him back to the Swedish missionaries at Lachen. Mallory's abdominal pain had worsened. Somervell was filling in as medical officer, but was desperately needed for the climbing party, especially if Mallory was forced to withdraw. Hingston's plan was to accompany General Bruce as far as Gangtok, where he might recover at the residency of the British political officer, F. M. Bailey, Morshead's old companion in exploration and a veteran of Rawling's expedition of 1904. Hingston would then return posthaste across the Serpo La to rejoin the expedition at Rongbuk, perhaps by as early as May 15.

Unhelpfully, Hinks sent a telegram suggesting that the final decision on the course of action be left to Bruce. By their third night at Yatung, the general was decidedly restless. He diagnosed the attack as a recurrence of the Banna fever he and his wife had contracted in 1916, which had not flared up since May 1919, save a brief episode in 1921. His heart, he boasted to Hingston, had never been better. His weight loss could only be for the good.

For all his bravado, however, the general knew he was through. As early as April 12, at the height of the crisis, he had ordered John Macdonald to forward a particular shipment from Yatung to the men at Kampa Dzong: his most valued asset, twelve bottles of his family's vintage whiskey. That was his moment of surrender. The final blow came on April 22, as Hingston made his plans for his return journey to Tibet. He had hired nine mules, two Tibetan muleteers, a cook by the name of Tenchadder, a pony wrangler named Dabla, a pony, and a Tibetan dog. He was ready to set out for a monthlong journey through lands he had never seen. "My partnership with the General is over," he wrote. "This morning I walked with him and Bailey as far as the Rajah's palace. At the entrance I bade him farewell. The General, I think felt the severance; it must have seemed to him the cutting of the last link with the party."

NEWS OF the general's collapse reached Kampa Dzong on April 13, with the arrival of John Macdonald. The gift of whiskey was most welcome; most of the champagne had frozen, shattering the bottles. The main party had experienced such cold coming up from Phari that ink froze and Somervell had abandoned an attempt to sketch Chomolhari; even his paints were rock hard with cold. Though Finch's eiderdown designs had not caught on, most of the men at least wore windproof clothing rather than tweed, felt hats instead of topees. Each also had a Whymper tent, a welcome bit of privacy. Norton had designed a large and comfortable mess tent. Sent well ahead of the party on a pair of mules dubbed Jack and Jill, it was a welcome sight at the end of long and bitter marches. Still, with the temperatures hovering around four degrees Fahrenheit, the passage remained most difficult, especially for Beetham, who had foolishly drunk from every stream during the long march from the lowlands.

Even as Norton took over as expedition leader, he had to decide whether to allow Beetham to continue. Seven days of dysentery had taken a dreadful toll, and there was no end in sight. Odell and Irvine were also not well. Mallory's brush with appendicitis had turned out to be a false alarm, but he was still weak. During the four days they spent at Kampa Dzong awaiting new transport and word of the general, Mallory passed much of the time in bed, reading the letters of Keats and passages from *The Spirit of Man*. A letter from his sister Mary, in Colombo, suggesting that the monsoon might break a fortnight earlier than usual, only added to a general unease in the camp.

In Hingston's absence, Somervell had taken over sick parade, and it was his word alone that caused Norton to allow Beetham to continue, a decision not made until the morning of their departure from Kampa Dzong. "Beetham came on with us," Mallory wrote to Ruth. "At present [he] looks years older, in much the same way that Raeburn did in '21, only at a younger stage and has quite lost all kick, and there was no one more energetic earlier." Beetham would never fully recover. His shameful treatment of Graham notwithstanding, he was a highly accomplished and experienced climber, and his collapse left a void in a team that was already far weaker than it might have been.

The loss of General Bruce, as it turned out, was far less problematic. As Mallory said in a letter to Younghusband, the general would be missed "a good deal in the mess, and we shall miss his moral force behind the porters later on and the absence of his genial chaff." But his departure would be of little consequence once the men were on the mountain. Shebbeare and Geoffrey Bruce, both fluent in the local languages, were perfectly capable of handling the transport and porters. John Macdonald was also available as a translator. Not one of the men regretted the appointment of Norton, who was in any number of ways a more serious, methodical, and dependable leader. His promotion freed Mallory to take on the official role as head of the climbing party, a position he cherished and fully deserved. Despite the setbacks and loss of personnel, the expedition that left Kampa Dzong on April 15 was arguably stronger and more focused than the one that had left Darjeeling but three weeks before. By the evening of the following day, as they reached Tinki Dzong and celebrated Somervell's thirty-fourth birthday with a dessert of plum pudding washed down by absolute alcohol, they had resolved any number of conflicting ideas and at last settled on a plan for the conquest of the mountain.

HOVERING OVER the expedition from the very start was the ghost of 1922. That year they had marched on the mountain brimming with confidence; now they approached with even higher expectations, yet greater uncertainty. On Everest, they had learned, little could be predicted save the inevitability of the unexpected. General Bruce's final dispatch of 1922, written at Shegar Dzong on July 24, ended, as he put it, with a "little aphorism . . . There is only one motto for the Himalaya: When in doubt, don't."

For more than a year each of the key players—Mallory and Norton, certainly Somervell and Geoffrey Bruce—had looked back on what had gone wrong, even as they'd anticipated what needed to be done for things to go right. Each returned to the field intent and focused on success, with strong opinions that had to be reconciled into a single strategy. As early as Christmas 1923 Norton had circulated a proposal, prompting a critique and counterproposal from Mallory, with no final decision reached even as the men sailed for India. The discussions continued at Darjeeling and Phari, with pressure growing to resolve any differences before the expedition left Kampa Dzong. A deadline loomed for the British press: the makeup of the climbing teams would have to be announced, at the very least, by the time the expedition reached Rongbuk. And for their morale, the men needed clarity.

From the start, it was assumed that attempts would be made with and without oxygen, and it was fully understood by all that the climbers at the highest camps would require a complex scaffolding of support, both of men and of equipment. The logistics of supplying and maintaining the highest camps demanded precision. Mallory's fundamental disagreement with Norton concerned the number of camps required above the North Col. Norton's initial scheme called for two men without oxygen to try for the summit from a Camp V at 26,500 feet. Mallory rightly suggested that a second and perhaps a third camp above the col would be necessary, most especially for a party without gas. Mallory, in truth, had concluded that any attempt without oxygen was quixotic. Irvine, a witness to the deliberations, noted on the evening of April 14, "We all had a long discussion about the method to adopt to climb the mountain. Norton suggests non-oxygen followed by oxygen attempt one day apart. Mallory wants two oxygen attempts one day apart, and both agree to have third attempt some days later."

The solution came to Mallory on the road from Kampa Dzong to Tinki, a flash of insight he eagerly shared with his wife. "I've had a brain-wave," he wrote on the evening of April 17, a Thursday. "No other word will describe the process by which I have arrived at another plan for climbing the mountain."

His idea called for two simultaneous attacks on the summit, one with oxygen starting from a Camp VI, and one without gas from a Camp VII, situated an appropriate distance higher on the mountain. The goal would be a rendezvous on the summit. Norton immediately saw the wisdom of the plan and signed off. In his first formal report since assuming command of the expedition, written on April 19 in Chiblung, en route for Shegar Dzong, he laid out the details.

On day one, leaving Camp IV, at 23,000 feet on the North Col, two climbers with fifteen porters would establish Camp V at 25,500 feet and partially stock it with oxygen before returning to the col. The next day, the party climbing without gas would head up to Camp V, again with fifteen porters, to complete its cache of supplies and oxygen. Sending seven porters down, keeping eight, they would spend the night. The following morning, day three, they would climb to 27,300 feet and establish Camp VII. Sending their porters down to Camp V—

or, should conditions permit, all the way to the North Col—the two climbers would sleep alone at VII. On that same day three, the oxygen party with unburdened porters would head up from Camp IV to V, and then transport that camp with its equipment and oxygen supplies to 26,500 feet to establish a Camp VI, before again sending its porters back to the col.

Thus by the night of the third day, four climbers would be perched high on the mountain: the oxygen party at Camp VI, and those climbing without gas at Camp VII, some 800 feet higher but within visual sight of the lower camp. The following morning, day four, the two parties would set out separately, each ready to support the other should something go wrong, but with the ultimate goal of meeting on the summit of the world. Should the first attempt fail, the other four climbers waiting in reserve would be standing by at Camp III or IV, ready for a second attack, with the flow of men, oxygen, and equipment already determined by the original plan and readily replicated.

As for the team members, it was agreed that Mallory and Somervell would take the two lead roles. Somervell's remarkable performance in 1922 made him the obvious choice to head the party climbing without oxygen. Should it fail, he would recover quickly and, if the previous expedition was any indication, be ready for another attempt with gas. Climbing with Somervell would be Norton. Mallory, convinced that only oxygen could carry a man above 26,000 feet, eagerly accepted the lead of the oxygen party. As his second he chose Sandy Irvine, again for quite logical reasons. Beetham was down, Hazard of questionable strength, and Geoffrey Bruce, scarcely more experienced than Irvine, lacked Sandy's knowledge of the oxygen apparatus. Noel Odell, the only other serious possibility, though a far more experienced climber, had not performed well on the march across Tibet. His lassitude in the mornings had driven his companions to distraction, particularly Shebbeare, who, as the transport officer, was responsible for breaking camp. All that concerned Mallory was success. Committed to oxygen, responsible for the safety of both climbing parties on their descent from the summit, he was not about to leave behind Irvine, the physically strongest member of the expedition and the only one who knew enough about the oxygen apparatus to improvise in a crisis.

So it was decided. Geoffrey Bruce and Noel Odell would establish Camp V. Somervell and Norton, climbing without oxygen, would head for the summit from Camp VII; Mallory and Irvine would strike out on the same day from Camp VI, 800 feet lower but with the advantage of "English air." A second wave, if necessary, would consist of

Odell and Geoffrey Bruce with oxygen, Hazard and Beetham, if fit, without it. Norton dispatched the official announcement on April 21 from Shiling; on that same day Mallory and Irvine climbed above their encampment and young Sandy had his first view of Everest. Though thrilled to climb with Mallory, he was quietly disappointed to have been chosen for the oxygen party.

Mallory felt only relief that the key decisions had been made. Everything was falling into place. Karma Paul, rejoining the main party at Chiblung, had brought the post, with a number of letters from General Bruce, confirming that he was safe and well in India. A kind and generous letter from Ruth, written just days after Mallory's departure from Liverpool, swept away any lingering worries about their love, freeing Mallory, with her blessing, to focus solely on the challenge at hand. As he wrote to the Everest Committee, he had total confidence in Norton, an inspired leader, knowledgeable about every detail, a tremendous adventurer "dead keen to have a dash with the non-oxygen party," yet humble enough to yield any decision-making authority concerning his own involvement to Mallory and Somervell. "Isn't that the right spirit to bring to Mount Everest?" Mallory asked. Somervell, too, was a wonder, whether transcribing music, extracting a decayed wisdom tooth from a Tibetan porter with an improvised pair of pincers, or discussing modern art, as he did with Mallory over the course of a six-mile march to Kyishong on the morning of April 22.

Mallory's confidence grew with each passing day, as they came nearer to their goal. Even the prospect of an early monsoon, predicted yet again and with greater certitude in another note from his sister in Colombo, could not faze him. Writing to Tom Longstaff, he dismissed the dire forecast of the "meteorological people" with a flash of bravado: "But what does it all mean? We're going to sail to the top this time, and God with us, or stamp to the top with our teeth in the wind."

"The conquest of the mountain is the great thing," he wrote to Ruth on April 24 from Shegar Dzong, "and the whole plan is mine and my part will be a sufficiently interesting one and will give me, perhaps, the best chance of all of getting to the top. It is almost unthinkable with this plan that I shan't get to the top; I can't see myself coming down defeated. And I have very good hopes that the gasless party will get up; I want all four of us to get there, and I believe it can be done."

Shegar Dzong, as always, held them for three days, as Norton paid respects to the various authorities and Bruce and Shebbeare arranged for new transport to carry them across the Pang La to Rongbuk and the mountain. Irvine spent his days at a bench set up outside his tent, tinkering with the oxygen equipment. He had managed to salvage several sets, reducing their weight by five pounds. Mallory tested the new model against the original, climbing high to the fortress summit of the *dzong*. He returned, favorably impressed, though the device (with two cylinders) still weighed thirty pounds—a "manageable load" provided one carried no more than two cylinders for the final summit assault. That this might imply insufficient oxygen supplies at the most critical moment of need was for the moment overlooked as Irvine, to the delight of all, played a trick on the onlookers. As he told it, "I chased a crowd of Tibetans with a loudly hissing cylinder of oxygen. I've never seen men run so fast—they must have thought it a devil coming out."

The following morning, Irvine spent three hours at the monastery, enchanted by everything he saw. He gave two half-filled oxygen cylinders to the lama to be used as gongs, explaining that within each was a devil whose breath would kindle a spark. He demonstrated on a glowing bit of incense. At one point John Noel observed Irvine intently examining a massive prayer wheel. "What's he doing?" Noel asked. "I expect," replied Somervell, "he is trying to work out how to mechanize it for them."

On April 24, the eve of their departure from Shegar and the day King George V opened the British Empire Exhibition in London, Mallory hastily finished a letter to Ruth: "Only four marches, starting tomorrow morning, to the Rongbuk monastery! We're getting very near now. On May 3rd four of us will leave the Base Camp and begin the upward trek, and on May 17th or thereabouts we should reach the summit . . . The telegram announcing our success, if we succeed, will precede this letter, I suppose; but it will mention no names. How you will hope that I was one of the conquerors! And I don't think you will be disappointed."

CHAPTER 13

The Price of Life Is Death

THE EXPEDITION CROSSED the Pang La on Saturday, April 26, and reached Chöbuk, the last village on their way to Everest, the following evening. At the pass, huddled close to the ground, they hesitated for some time, glassing with binoculars and a telescope the upper slopes of Everest, some thirty-five miles distant, searching in vain for anything resembling level ground between 25,000 and 28,000 feet where high camps might be established. Coming down out of the Pang La, they leaned into winds so fierce that small stones caught up in the gusts lacerated their skin. The land, Sandy Irvine noted, "looked for all the world like the moon, with hardly a sign of vegetation." A garden of willows at Chöbuk offered relief for the night, but the following day, as they trekked up the valley of the Rongbuk Chu, they returned to country so spartan it evoked for Norton memories of the Western Front. "The stage from Chöbuk to Rongbuk," he wrote, "bears to the wide plains behind and the big glaciers ahead somewhat the same relation as, in an approach march of the Great War, the ruined areas bore to the fertile fields of France behind and the stricken battlefield ahead. For it is a cheerless, desolate valley suggestive at every turn of the greater desolation to which it leads."

Their small army, some three hundred pack animals and 150 native porters, along with the ten sahibs and their ponies, arrived at Rongbuk just after 3:00 p.m. on Monday, April 28, and made camp for the night on a stony shelf just before the monastery. Colonel Norton learned to his regret that the abbot, Dzatrul Rinpoche, was ill and could not "carry out the ceremony of blessing the whole expedition, on which, on behalf of our porters, we set considerable store." A small delegation nevertheless visited the monks, delivering a number of gifts for the lama, including a yakload of portland cement needed to repair the monastery's dominant chorten. While Hazard, a sapper in the Royal Engineers during the war, showed the monks how to mix the cement with gravel and sand, the rest of the men toured the temples and prayer halls.

John Noel was the first to notice an unsettling mural evidently painted since the 1922 expedition. As he later recounted, "An old man with a gnarled face and only two teeth in his head, shuffled over the courtyard wrapped in his maroon gown, and led me to the temple entrance, where on an inner wall, so dark that I could not at first distinguish it, he showed me a freshly executed painting." The mural, a most "curious picture," Noel wrote, depicted cloven-hoofed devils armed with pitchforks casting a party of climbers into a vortex that spun ever deeper into a cold abyss, a hell zone that for Tibetans is not a place of fire but a realm of ice, snow, and murderous winds. Ferocious dogs guarded the flanks of Everest, while at its base lay prostrate a single white body, speared and ravaged by horned demons.

Noel took a tracing and photographed the image; his wife later added a commentary, allegedly a quotation from Dzatrul Rinpoche: "Chomolungma, the awful and mighty Goddess Mother, will never allow any white man to climb her sacred heights. The demons of the snow will destroy you utterly." It is doubtful that the lama spoke these words. For Tibetans, Everest was the domain of Miyolangsangma, one of the Five Sisters of Long Life. These minor mountain deities were long ago subdued by Guru Rinpoche and transformed into acolytes of the Buddha, generous benefactors who showered the dharma community with wealth and good fortune. The benevolent reputation of Miyolangsangma was, in fact, one reason the local porters were prepared to work for the British, despite the physical and spiritual dangers associated with the mountain.

The inspiration for the mural, as the porters of 1924 learned to their dismay, was not so much the death of the seven Sherpas by avalanche but, rather, a terrifying encounter that occurred after the departure of the 1922 expedition. In their retreat the British had abandoned at the higher camps large quantities of *tsampa* (roasted barley flour), rice, oil, and other goods. Naturally the local herders and villagers were keen to salvage the supplies; Dzatrul Rinpoche, knowing the mood of the deities, cautioned against it. Defying the lama, twenty youths from a low-lying hamlet slipped past the monastery in the darkness. They slowly made their way up the East Rongbuk Glacier, braving, over a matter of days, the impossible ice. When they finally reached the base of the North Col, one of them saw seven yetis spring from the snow. Fearing for their lives, the boys raced down the valley, hardly stopping until they gained the monastery, where they desperately sought the lama's forgiveness and blessings. The apparition of demons, Dzatrul Rinpoche told them, was a certain sign that the "hidden land's protectors are unhappy." He then instructed the wayward youths to perform "Fulfillment and Purification practice" in homage to all the mountain deities, which they fervently did over the next many days.

In 1922, Dzatrul Rinpoche had received the British with compassion and curiosity, offering prayers that General Bruce, for example, might be reborn a "trainable being of the Buddha Dharma field." In 1924, he reacted to their arrival with compassion tinged with bewilderment. Having endured such hardships, why had they returned for more? The Tibetans pitied the British for their folly, and Dzatrul Rinpoche, writing in the Water-Dog year, 1922, went to some lengths to account for their delusions. The return expedition of 1924, by contrast, occurring in the Wood-Bird year, the fifty-eighth year of the lama's incarnation, did not warrant a single remark in his autobiography.

The motivations of the climbers remained a mystery for the Tibetans. They made offerings to the mountains, and every day, with their rituals, assuaged the wrath of the deities. But the idea of risking one's life, this vital incarnation, in order to crawl over ice and rock into nothingness was for them the epitome of ignorance and delusion. On the Tibetan Plateau death was already near; it stalked every nomadic encampment, found a place in every hamlet. To court annihilation deliberately in the frozen wastes of a mountain was inconceivable. In Tibetan, there is no word for a mountain summit; the very place the British so avidly sought, their highest goal, did not even exist in the language of their Sherpa porters. Among the "Tigers," men handpicked by Norton and Bruce for the most difficult work at the highest elevations, there were many who believed that the British were actually searching for treasure, a golden statue of a cow, perhaps a yak, rumored to reside at the highest point, which they would pillage and melt down into coins. In their mercantile zeal, inspired by generations of trans-Himalayan traders, their own forefathers, the Tibetans assumed that the British sought wealth, which in a certain sense was true. Fame and fortune most certainly awaited the first victors on Everest, rewards and ambitions that lure climbers to its flanks to this day.

ALL OF THIS, of course, was lost on the British climbers who left the monastery that first evening, content with gifts of *tsampa* and dried meat, and returned to their tents, even as night fell and a cold wind unlike any they had ever known swept from the glaciers to the base of the mountain. The following morning, Norton wasted no time pushing the expedition farther up the valley to base camp. "We walked over five rough miles of tumbled moraine and a frozen watercourse to the camp just under the snout of the Rongbuk glacier, in the teeth of a bitter wind," he reported. His goals were precise, the timetable exacting. In 1922 the monsoon had broken on June 1. Norton wanted all camps as far as the base of the North Col fully established and provisioned by May 17, at which time the assault on the summit would begin in earnest. Each man had his duties. Mallory and Beetham were responsible for the alpine equipment and the provisioning of the high camps beyond the col. Shebbeare was in charge of all supplies and stores, save the oxygen apparatus, which was detailed to Odell and Irvine. Hazard would run the mess.

Geoffrey Bruce organized the transport, with the goal of conserving the strength of those destined for the highest camps. The locations of the first three camps would be as in 1922, at elevations of roughly 17,800, 19,800, and 21,000 feet. Establishing Camps I and II would be supervised not by the climbers, as had been the case in 1922, but by the Gurkha NCOs Hurke Gurung and Tejbir Bura, both veterans of that earlier expedition. To spare the elite Sherpas, those expected to establish Camps V, VI, and VII, Bruce recruited 150 locals to carry as far as the North Col. Each earned twelve *annas* a day, less than a rupee at a time when a woodcutter made ten rupees a week. It was not a wage certain to hold the loyalty of men and women being asked to heft eighty-pound loads across ice fields that were the domain of demons.

On Wednesday, April 30, with the sky clear and the ground blanketed by fresh snow, Bruce dispatched 151 loads to Camp I. Half the porters would stay overnight, ready to move up to Camp II in the morning. The others were expected to return the same day to base, which they did, but fifty-two deserted the expedition altogether. This forced Bruce reluctantly to use his high-altitude Sherpas, a setback that would prove significant. On May 1, with Shebbeare and Norton, he pushed another seventy-five loads to Camp I, and by the end of the following day, Camps I and II were fully established. Bruce then dismissed all of the local porters as undependable and provisioned Camp III with fifty-two Sherpas—two assault groups of twenty, as he put it, with a reserve of twelve.

Mallory, still at base camp, was enthralled by the military discipline of Norton and Geoffrey Bruce. "I can't tell you how full of hope I am this year," he wrote to his sister Mary on May 2. "It is all so different from '22 when one was always subconsciously dissatisfied because we had no proper plan of climbing the mountain . . . On May 17th the four of us should join up somewhere about the base of the final pyramid; and, whether we get up or not, it will be my job to get the party off the mountain in safety . . . No one, climber or porter, is going to get killed if I can help it. That would spoil all."

With Mallory was Irvine, whose first days on the mountain were not his best. He had felt "pretty seedy" for some time. At Rongbuk, while the others visited the monks, he had remained in his tent, mending his sleeping bag and repairing Mallory's saddle. That night he took four castor oil pills, which had "the reverse of the expected result." The walk up the valley from the monastery had been exhausting, and he had found the setting of their base camp unexpectedly harsh and "very uninviting," despite the wonderful birds, the scores of rock doves and ravens and alpine choughs. His first journal entry from there began: "Bloody morning, light driving snow, very cold and felt rather rotten."

Weakened by illness and suffering from the altitude, Irvine nevertheless got right to work, struggling against time to ready the oxygen equipment. It was no easy task. Parts were missing or damaged. Drills, taps, and hacksaw blades snapped in the cold. The conditions were so bleak that he had no choice but to seek shelter. Though often nauseated from the solder fumes, he managed to retrofit in two days six complete sets of the oxygen apparatus. He also found time to work on Beetham's camera, even as he repaired the expedition's forty-pound roarer cooker, which he then used as a forge to shorten the spikes on both of Mallory's crampons by two inches. In doing so, he badly spiked one hand and scorched the other in two places. On top of everything, even as his thoughts on the first of the month turned wistfully to Oxford and the traditional celebrations of May morning, a highlight of the university year, he came down with a "tummy ache from eating Beetham's birthday cake."

Young Irvine's mood improved dramatically when he learned the results of the hemoglobin tests conducted by Somervell on the morning of May 3. Of all the men, Irvine had by far the highest percentage of red blood cells, a strong indication of fitness and acclimatization. His mentor, Noel Odell, was a distant second. "Hope this is a really good sign," Sandy wrote as he prepared his kit for a fortnight on the mountain. That afternoon, shortly after lunch, he and Mallory, with Odell and Hazard, headed up for Camp I, overtaking en route the twenty porters dispatched earlier that morning. The porters were not a happy lot, and several complained about the weight of their loads, which included several sets of the oxygen apparatus. Irvine later confessed in his diary, "I'm glad that I didn't have to carry any of their loads 100 yards," let alone several miles up the East Rongbuk Glacier. Camp I, protected from the wind and in the sun for long hours was, as Odell wrote that evening, "an awfully comfy camp." With a good meal, the porters found their balance, and all troubles and complaints were for the moment forgotten.

The immediate goal was to get Mallory and Irvine to Camp III, where they might test the oxygen equipment and acclimatize in preparation for the main assault. Odell and Hazard, meanwhile, would scout the route up the North Col and make Camp IV ready. John Noel would be there to film. Thus, on the morning of May 4, even as the Gurkha NCO Umar Gurung escorted the second group of twenty porters up from base camp, Mallory and the men made their move to Camp II, arriving shortly after noon. It was the first time Sandy Irvine witnessed Mallory's storming of a mountain. "A devil must have got into Mallory," he later wrote, "for he ran down all the little bits of downhill and paced all out up the moraine. It was as bad as a boat race trying to keep up with him." They set up two Whymper tents, and then, while Mallory and Odell searched for a new and better route up to Camp III, Irvine supervised the building of a two-room shelter, low stone walls that could be covered with a tent fly. He worked for nearly three hours, moving heavy boulders, "trying to set an example to the coolies," until blood began to flow freely from his nose. That evening the temperature dropped to zero Fahrenheit, and the weather turned.

They awoke to the sound of a Tibetan bellows blowing over the coals of a yak-dung fire. The cook was up, but the porters remained in their shelter, immobilized by the cold. One was apparently seriously ill. Tensions rose as Mallory shook them out of their lassitude; he threatened one with a fist to the face. They were not off until nearly noon, with Irvine on one rope with six, Hazard leading a long line of eleven, and Odell on a third rope with another six. Mallory walked alone, breaking trail. At one point Irvine grew so frustrated with one porter's pace that he offered to carry his load. Mallory intervened and stopped him. Irvine then let the man off the rope, cursing him with the threat of ice devils and demons. From that moment things began to deteriorate badly.

They reached Camp III at 6:00 p.m. in bitter cold. "My boots were frozen hard on my feet," Mallory wrote, "and I knew we could do nothing now to make a comfortable camp." They quickly erected two Meade tents, and Kami the cook somehow managed to produce a hot meal, mutton and vegetable stew washed down by cool coffee, their first food since morning. There was no soup to be found, and the cheese and jam were frozen solid. Thirsty and still hungry, Irvine turned in at 8:30 p.m., but had trouble sleeping on the stony ground. "The sleeping bag," he wrote, "seemed to shrink to half its normal size . . . and I kept turning over into patches of frozen breath."

Mallory lay awake, haunted by other thoughts. He noted, "It was a queer sensation reviving memories of that scene, with the dud oxygen cylinders piled against the cairn which was built to commemorate the seven porters killed two years ago. The whole place had changed less than I could have believed possible." His more immediate concern was the impossible cold. In packing the loads for Camp III, they had made the oxygen apparatus a priority, and inexplicably had failed to bring sufficient bedding for the porters. The high-altitude sleeping bags, intended strictly for the highest camps, were at Camp II, but he had specifically ordered that they not be brought up to Camp III the following day with the second wave of porters. Clearly, in this cold they would be needed. His only option was to get down to Camp II the following morning early enough to stop the men and reconfigure the loads. He assumed that, given the conditions, the convoy would not set off from the lower camp until at least 9:00 a.m.

On Tuesday, May 6, Mallory rose early, eager to set off down the valley. "Energetic beggar," Irvine noted. "I feebly asked if I could be of any help, without the slightest intention of moving from my warm sleeping bag. He gallantly refused my offer." While Irvine slept, rising only at 9:00 a.m. for a meager breakfast of tinned milk and a sausage, Mallory embarked on what would be one of the more fateful days of the entire expedition. As it turned out, the porters at Camp II had left early, and by the time Mallory reached them they were well advanced, moving up the snow of the glacier in the face of what by early afternoon would be a full-out blizzard. All bore heavy packs. One struggled with the cooker, itself a forty-pound load. Some had brought blankets, fully expecting to sleep at Camp III, which was the last thing Mallory desired. He had no choice but to escort them up the valley, with the hope of reaching Camp III in time to dispatch them all back down the mountain to Camp II. In the snow and howling wind it proved impossible, and they had to dump their loads on the glacier in a cache well below Camp III. As it was, they barely made it back to Camp II before the storm obliterated every feature in the valley.

Mallory returned to Camp III, where all was lethargy and collapse. The porters had endured a dreadful night, with little food and no proper bedding. Of the twenty-three, only four were fit for duty.

Most were already incapacitated with mountain sickness. In the late afternoon Odell and Irvine, with the able porters, returned a mile down the glacier to bring up six loads from Mallory's cache. Irvine hoisted a sixty-pound Whymper tent on his back and set a fast pace that got them back to Camp III just before dark. Unfortunately, what they most needed was not shelter but bedding and supplies. The temperature that night dropped to minus twenty-one degrees Fahrenheit, fifty-three degrees of frost, and none of the porters had any protection save the clothes on their backs and a blanket apiece. For food, they had nothing but uncooked barley, no more than a handful for each man. At any rate, most were too sick to eat and by morning were comatose. Those still capable of movement were vomiting. "One of them," Mallory noted, "who was absolutely without a spark of life to help himself, had swollen feet, and we had to pull on his boots without socks. He was almost incapable of walking; I supported him with my arm for some distances and then told a porter to do that."

With Odell "distinctly unfit" and Irvine suffering from a severe headache, Mallory, on the morning of Wednesday, May 7, ordered Hazard down to the glacier cache to meet ten porters expected around noon from Camp II. Not one of the porters at Camp III was capable of carrying a load. Most could barely walk and required support as they hobbled off the mountain. Mallory escorted them halfway down to Camp II, then returned to join Hazard at the cache. When Irvine arrived with hot food and drink, he found a desolate scene: a forlorn Hazard, three exhausted porters from Camp II, and a thoroughly bedraggled Mallory. With Sandy hoisting a bundle of eight high-altitude sleeping bags, they managed to get seven loads up the glacier, and mercifully, on the night of May 7, those few porters still at Camp III slept in warmth and reasonable comfort. On the following morning, even as Odell and Hazard set out to scout a route up the North Col, Mallory dropped down to Camp II to confer with Norton and Geoffrey Bruce.

QUITE UNAWARE of the crisis at Camp III, Norton, Somervell, and a reinvigorated Bentley Beetham had headed up the East Rongbuk on the morning of Tuesday, May 6, leaving Shebbeare in charge at base camp. The following day, while Shebbeare was off tracking three bharal near a hermit's cave just above their camp, Geoffrey Bruce set out with twelve porters, their last reserves. The full extent of the debacle did not become clear until Norton and Somervell reached Camp II that afternoon. By then many of the debilitated Sherpas had stumbled into camp, overwhelming its capacity and forcing the British to break open supply boxes carefully packed and intended only for the final assault on the summit.

The situation deteriorated further the following day, when Bruce, expecting to find Camp II empty, arrived with yet another twelve men to feed and shelter. By then, as John Noel recalled, the entire transport and supply system lay in ruins. In but two days, Mallory wrote to Ruth, "the morale of the porters had gone to blazes." As Norton and Somervell watched the last of the wasted porters come down the ice, Norton was reminded of his worst moment in the war as a British soldier. He wrote in his May 13 dispatch to the *Times* that the men coming off the mountain looked "all the world like the stragglers of the British army I once saw blocking the roads south of Le Cateau on August 27, 1914 . . . As at St Quentin, Chauny and Noyen in 1914, there is now no time to count the cost nor look far ahead."

The crisis, in other words, called not for reflection or recriminations but for action. Norton immediately ordered Somervell to head up with every available fit porter to complete the supply of Camp III. With Camp II effectively becoming the base of the expedition, he needed men fluent in the native languages. Hazard therefore was recalled from Camp III and sent to base camp to relieve Shebbeare, who was brought forward and posted to Camp II with orders to remedy the supply situation. Shebbeare was dumbfounded to learn that Mallory had given priority to the oxygen equipment, leaving behind the sleeping bags, and had from the very start expected his porters to stay at least one night at Camp III, with only blankets for warmth.

Conditions at Camp III worsened dramatically over the next forty-eight hours. Friday, May 9, was a "perfectly bloody day," Irvine wrote; "nothing else will describe it." Hunkered down in their tents were Odell, who with Hazard had been unable to reach the North Col, and Somervell, who had arrived the previous day. Three Sherpas remained at the camp, and the cook. There was no hot food or drink. The wind blew so fiercely that even Irvine, risking frostbite, could not get the stoves to ignite.

That morning Norton and Geoffrey Bruce, along with Mallory and twenty-six Sherpas, set out from Camp II to relieve the higher camp. They met Hazard on his way down, but in the wind exchanged hardly a word. The storm grew with such furious intensity that Norton was forced to let most of the porters dump their loads on the glacier and return to Camp II. With eight of the strongest, the rest of the party struggled on, reaching Camp III just after 1:00 p.m. It was a desolate scene, as Geoffrey Bruce recalled: "No one moved about the camp; it seemed utterly lifeless. The porters there were wretched, and this terrible blizzard, coming immediately on top of their hardships of a few days ago, completely dampened their spirits and energy... The fierceness of the wind made movement outside a tent almost impossible."

Mallory crawled into a Whymper shared by Odell, Somervell, and Irvine. To Somervell's bemusement, he removed his boots and knickers, put on his favorite footless stockings knitted by Ruth, and then pulled from his pack a set of playing cards and his well-worn copy of *The Spirit of Man*. Irvine alone was unfamiliar with the book. "I began reading one thing or another," Mallory later wrote to Ruth. "Howard reminded me that I was reproducing on the same spot a scene which occurred two years ago when he and I lay in a tent together. We all agreed that 'Kubla Khan' was a good sort of poem. Irvine was rather poetry shy but seemed impressed by the Epitaph to Gray's 'Elegy.' Odell was much inclined to be interested and like the last lines of 'Prometheus Unbound.' Somervell, who knows quite a lot of English literature, had never read a poem of Emily Bronte's and was happily introduced."

As they passed the afternoon reading aloud from the anthology of verse first compiled as a propaganda tool during the bleakest days of the war, the storm outside, as Geoffrey Bruce wrote, "continued with unabating violence." Mercifully, they had hot soup; Irvine had managed to start the Haddock cooker. But as Mallory recalled in a letter to Ruth on May 10, "tremendous gusts" tormented them through a sleepless night. "I don't know how the tent stood it," he added. Through the long hours of darkness the snow "drifted into our tents covering everything to a depth of an inch or two. The discomfort in the night was acute. Morning came, and the snow stopped falling, but fallen snow was being driven along the surface of the glacier, producing the same effect as a blizzard."

By Saturday morning they were running out of food. Mallory and Irvine, both showing signs of strain, were ordered down the mountain to Camp II. Norton and Somervell, with seventeen of the porters, accompanied them as far as the supply dump on the glacier, where they managed to retrieve nineteen loads, though the effort completely shattered the Sherpas. When they reached Camp III, Bruce recalled, they "simply flopped into their tents and lay there. We forced them to eat and drink, took off their boots, and saw them safely tucked into their sleeping sacks. I do not think that I have ever seen men so tired, and it was not to be wondered at, for the majority of them had carried loads through wind and snow on five successive days."

That night the temperature dropped to minus thirty-nine degrees Fahrenheit. The wind, as Norton wrote in his dispatch, "appeared to be shot high in the air over the North Col, Rapiu and Lhakpa La, the three passes surrounding us and, from some point high in the zenith descended on the camp like a terrier on a rat-pit, and shook our little tents like rats . . . Sleep was an impossibility with the noise of the wind and the wild flapping of the tents." By morning, snow had drifted into every shelter. The porters "huddled in their tents, not caring whether they lived or died," Norton related. The North Col was out of the question, and as Bruce and Norton determined, "there was nothing for it but retreat."

The decision made, it fell to Geoffrey Bruce to get the men moving. As Norton reported, Bruce stood tall in the middle of the camp "in the teeth of the gale. How he got the men to work, only he can tell. Perhaps his stinging words cut more than the wind, but it is on record that he found time and opportunity to give exactly the right amount of sympathy to the really sick." The evacuation took the broken men down what Norton described as a Via Dolorosa, traversing the length of the glacier to Camp II, "then the rough miles of tumbled moraine, withdrawing every man to Base Camp, with a melancholy procession of snow-blind, sick, and frost bitten men, being shepherded down by their comrades."

By the evening of May 11, Mallory, Beetham, Hazard, Irvine, and Noel were at base camp, twelve miles down from the North Col. Norton and Bruce, with half the porters, were at Camp II, while Odell and Somervell, with the remainder of the expedition, had reached Camp I. By extreme good fortune Major Hingston, the expedition's medical officer, having escorted General Bruce to safety in Sikkim, had arrived at base camp at 4:00 p.m.

At Camp I Howard Somervell had been dealing with the injured for much of the day. One of the Gurkhas, Lance Corporal Shamsher-pun, lay comatose with what was believed to be a blood clot on his brain. The feet of the Darjeeling cobbler Manbahadur were frozen solid to the ankles; if he lived, they would have to be amputated. Several porters were down with severe pneumonia and bronchitis, including Sanglar, Kellas's man in 1921, who had attached himself to Noel in 1922. Finally there was Tamding, Somervell's servant on the march across Tibet, who had stumbled and broken his leg just below the knee during the retreat. Noel, Beetham, Mallory, and Irvine had rushed to his aid with a stretcher improvised from a carrying frame with strips of canvas ripped from a tent fly, only to find him being carried down the moraine by Dorjee Pasang. What sympathy his injury elicited was somewhat quelled once the British found him wearing clothes that had been stolen from Somervell. Irvine, in particular, was appalled by the way the Sherpas treated the injured. On his way down the mountain he had found Manbahadur at Camp I "lying out in the cold making no attempt to keep warm or look after himself. The three porters that had carried him down from II took absolutely damn all notice of him. I'm afraid both his feet are lost from frost-bite."

Hingston, having traveled for twenty days to rejoin the expedition, headed immediately for Camp I on May 12, to assist Somervell. "On the way I met our porters coming down from the mountain," he wrote that night in his journal. "They were a sorry lot. Worst of all I fear that their morale may be sapped. The only thing to do was to evacuate the mountain and rest until the weather changed." Returning to the base that afternoon, Hingston spent the rest of the day treating the sick and injured.

On the morning of May 13 Norton sent Karma Paul to the Rongbuk Monastery with a request that the lama bless all of the members of the expedition at a ceremony in two days' time. Geoffrey Bruce and Hingston, meanwhile, returned to Camp I, with the hope of moving Shamsherpun down to base camp. They found him, Hingston reported, "even worse than when we had left him. However we had to try and get him down. We improvised a stretcher out of blankets and tent-poles, got six Tibetans to act as carriers, and marched him as comfortable as conditions allowed. It was a long and difficult carry. They got him down to near the Base Camp where he suddenly died." His body was brought into camp just after sunset and buried the following morning, in a shallow grave later marked by a memorial stone.

Of the other casualties, all would survive save the cobbler Manbahadur. Hingston did his best, but the man's legs were dead to the hips, his feet black and putrid with rot. He hung on for a fortnight before finally dying on May 25, a victim, in some sense, of Mallory's obsession with the summit, or at least his failure to supply the porters at Camp III properly. It is difficult to know what impact these deaths had on the British, whose attentions turned quickly to the task at hand. Hingston considered it "unfortunate that the casualties should have occurred at this time. They will tie me down to the Base Camp. I am anxious to get at least as far as Camp III." In their various journals and diaries, there is little mention of the deaths that had occurred but no shortage of remarks about the delights and comforts of base camp: hot food and lots of it, spacious and warm tents, camp beds and chairs.

On May 11, the initial day of the evacuation, they gathered, as Irvine recalled, for

> a very amusing dinner with a couple of bottles of champagne. A very dirty and bedraggled company. Hingston clean-shaven and proper sitting opposite Shebbeare with a face like a villain and a balaclava inside out on the back of his head. Hazard in a flying helmet with a bristly chin sticking out even further. Beetham sat silent most of the time, round and black like a mixture of Judas Iscariot and an apple dumpling. George sitting on a very low chair could hardly be seen above the table except for a cloth hat pinned up on one side with a huge safety pin and covered in candle grease. Noel as usual, leaning back with his chin down and cloth hat over his eyes, grinning to himself. Everyone was very happy to be back in a Christian mess hut eating decent food.

THE RETREAT stretched into a hiatus of six days. Irvine tinkered the entire time, while Mallory, for the most part, fretted. "He seemed ill at ease," wrote Noel, who invited him to bunk in his tent, "always scheming and planning. It was obvious to me he felt this setback more acutely than any of us." If idleness drove Mallory to distraction, Norton's decision to rest and regroup proved uncannily prescient. By bringing his men to altitude, then leading them off the mountain for an extended period before returning them to the heights, he had inadvertently anticipated what in time would become standard mountaineering procedure for optimizing acclimatization at extreme elevations. It was a good bit of serendipitous luck on an expedition that would need a great deal of it.

On Thursday, May 15, the entire party, save Somervell and Beetham, walked down from base camp to the Rongbuk Monastery for the audience with Dzatrul Rinpoche, arranged successfully by Karma Paul. No one knew what to expect. While the porters waited in the outer court, the climbing party shared a long meal of minced meat and macaroni, radishes and hot peppers, before finally being ushered into a smaller courtyard lined on all sides with elaborate embroidered benches and sheltered at one end by an overhanging wooden roof. There, beneath the veranda, was the high lama, seated on a red throne and flanked by attendants. "He was an imposing person," Hingston recalled, "with a striking face full of character and humour, and quite different from the ordinary Lama type. He is considered a person of extreme sanctity, an equal even to the Dalai Lama. He is said to have spent twelve years incarcerated in a hermit's cell. His dress was of the usual dark red material, but in addition he wore a yellow hat elegantly adorned with gold. Round him were the assistant functionaries, other lamas who held various sacred implements."

One by one the British sahibs silently went forward. According to Hingston, "He pressed a silver prayer-wheel against our heads. The interior of the wheel held some sacred objects, probably a collection of Buddhist prayers. The porters then were blessed in turn. Each prostrated himself three times before the Lama and then came forward to receive the touch of the wheel. Each porter made an offering and also presented a white scarf. Geoff made an offering for all the Sahibs, and Norton presented the sacred gentleman with a roll of embroidery and a watch."

Norton asked the rinpoche for a few words of encouragement for the men. The lama instructed the porters to obey the British and work hard on the mountain; he assured them that he would pray for their well-being. "This," Hingston wrote, "from our point of view, was the main object of the ceremony, since the porters are naturally somewhat disheartened after the severe trials through which they have passed. Then the Lama proceeded to prayers. The men were very reverent and impressed. It ended up with many repetitions of *Om mani padme hum*, which we all followed in a chorus in the same way as one does in a church at home. The Ceremony seemed to have an excellent influence on the porters, and we left satisfied with the day's business and impressed with the whole affair."

Not all of the climbers were similarly touched. Mallory made no mention of the event in the letters he wrote the following day to his wife and mother. Odell scratched a quick note in his diary: "Typical Thibetan tiffin with chop-sticks, before interesting and solemn blessing by the dignified yet genial lama who touched our head with a silver prayer-wheel and gave very sensible exhortation to coolies." John Noel, who filmed the entire proceedings from the rooftop of the courtyard, rather fancifully claimed that the lama had uttered an ominous and dire warning: "Your turning back brings pleasures to the demons. They have forced you back, and will force you back again."

Young Irvine was intrigued yet bewildered by the entire scene, and he had serious misgivings about Tibetan cuisine. "After being blessed and having our heads touched," he wrote, "with a white metal pepper pot (at least it looked like that) we sat down while the whole damn lot of coolies came in doing three salaams—head right to the ground—then presented their offerings and were similarly blessed. The Lama addressed the coolies in a few well-chosen words and then said a prayer or prayers—it all sounded the same—ending on a wonderfully deep note. We got back to camp about 3 p.m. My Tibetan food recurred rather often on the way back." Norton and Bruce cared only that the event had fortified the porters, which clearly it had. "His prayers and blessings put fresh heart into them," Bruce recalled, "and on the return journey to the Base Camp they were very nearly their cheery normal selves once more."

Beneath all, however, ran an undercurrent of uncertainty. No amount of ritual or prayer could alter physiological reality. Just seven terrible days at Camp III, as Somervell later acknowledged, had "reduced our strength and made us thin and weak and almost invalided, instead of being fit and strong as we had been during the 1922 ascent."

Mallory remained almost frenetically optimistic, as he always was on the eve of a mountain adventure, once decisions had been made and everything given over to the summit quest. "I must tell you, with immense physical pride," he wrote to Ruth the morning after the visit to Rongbuk, "I look upon myself as the strongest of the lot, the most likely to get to the top, with or without gas. I may be wrong, but I'm pretty sure Norton thinks the same. He and I were agreeing yesterday that none of the new members, with the possible exception of Irvine can touch the veterans, and that the old gang are bearing everything on their shoulders."

This was precisely the problem. The expedition was too thin. Odell and Hazard had been slow to acclimatize. Beetham, having more or less recovered from dysentery, remained weak. Hazard was also a problem for the group. He and Beetham did not get along. Indeed, of all the men, only the unflappable Odell could endure the temperamental Hazard, who, Somervell wrote, had since the war "built a psychological wall round himself inside of which he lives. Occasionally he bursts out with a 'By gad, this is fine!' for he enjoys, inside the wall, every minute of Tibetan travel, and even hardship. Then the shell closes, to let nothing in."

If Somervell had his doubts about Hazard, Mallory had his private concerns about his closest friends on the expedition. "Somervell seems to me a bit below his form of two years ago," he wrote to Ruth on

May 16, "and Norton is not particularly strong, I fancy, at the moment. Still they're sure to turn up a tough pair. I hope to carry all through now with a great bound." Increasingly, his allegiance and hopes turned to young Sandy Irvine, "the star of the new members," he told his mother, "a very fine fellow . . . very decent with the porters . . . full of common sense, mild but strong, yet with high ideals." Of all the men, he wrote to Ruth, "Irvine has much more the winning spirit, he has been wonderfully hard working and brilliantly skillful about the oxygen; against him is his youth (though this is very much for him in some ways) hard things seem to hit him harder—and his lack of mountaineering training and practice, which must tell to some extent when it comes to climbing rocks or even to saving energy on the easiest ground. However he'll be an ideal campaigning companion and with as stout a heart as you could wish to find."

Friday dawned a crystal morning, just as the lama had predicted. "The weather has made a great change for the better," Hingston wrote. "Norton seems pleased with the turn of affairs. He intends to start the new offensive tomorrow." Saturday was even finer, "a perfect day," Irvine noted in his diary. "No wind early. What a pity!" The date, May 17, originally designated for the assault on the summit, now marked simply a return, a new beginning, with all its potential for triumph or tragedy, transcendence or devastation. "This retreat is only a temporary set back," Mallory had written. "Action is only suspended. The issue must shortly be decided. The next time we walk up the Rongbuk Glacier will be the last. We will gather up our resources and advance to the last assault."

LINGERING OVER everything was the specter of the monsoon. In 1922 it had arrived two weeks early, a "soft breath of the south-east wind," as Norton recalled, that swept over the face of the North Col and lured seven men to their death on June 7, a black Wednesday. If what they had endured to date in 1924 was any indication, the first stage of the monsoon was already upon them. On May 17 they thus launched the second phase of their campaign, "obsessed," as Norton wrote, "by the fear that we were already too late and that its full force would be on us before we had even established ourselves on the North Col." There was little to do but persevere with the original plan, with the understanding that the final attack from Camps VI and VII would be launched on May 29, precisely two weeks later than originally scheduled.

Geoffrey Bruce worked miracles; his was the strongest voice in camp and, according to Somervell, the most essential in the crisis. "Some people know naturally what is the right thing to do," Somervell later wrote, "others have the ability to make others do what they think ought to be done. Geoffrey is one of the few people I know who combines these two qualities. He knows exactly how to get the best out of the porters, and does it with strength combined with kindness." Mallory had similar regard for Norton. "I'm glad the first blow lies with me," he wrote in one of his last letters home. "We're not going to be easily stopped with an organization behind us this time." Norton, he added, deserved all the credit. If they were to get up the mountain, it would be on the backs of the soldiers, Bruce and Norton.

The weather on Saturday, May 17, was glorious. After a light lunch, Norton, Odell, Somervell, Shebbeare, and Mallory, along with eleven porters, started up for Camp I, intent on reaching Camp II by Sunday evening. Irvine, down with dysentery, took a heroic dose of lead and opium and managed to join Hazard and Noel the following morning, leaving only Hingston at base to look after the invalids, including Bentley Beetham, crippled with sciatica. By Monday evening Noel and Bruce were at Camp I, en route directly the next day for Camp III; Irvine and Hazard were at Camp II ready to push on for Camp III; and Shebbeare had returned to Camp II from Camp III, having secured at the high camp the four strongest and most experienced climbers on the expedition: Norton, Somervell, Mallory, and Odell. After all the setbacks, in but forty-eight hours Norton had gotten the expedition once again poised at the base of the North Col.

On the morning of May 20, even as Irvine and Hazard rose to Camp III, Mallory and the others set out to fix a route up the North Col. As they trudged up the lateral moraine above camp, struggling to catch their breaths at 21,000 feet, the sky opened and for the first time they had a chance to glass the upper reaches of the col. As expected, everything had changed. In 1922 there had been a narrow crevasse just a few feet wide running across the col just below where Camp IV had been. In just two years the entire lower side of this crevasse had fallen hundreds of feet away from the face; what had been the upper side was now exposed as a formidable cliff of blue ice, dark and brittle.

Mallory and Norton took a line somewhat to the north of the 1922 route, and rather than traverse, they went straight up, more difficult but ultimately safer. Somervell fell out within the hour, weak with fever. Mallory took the lead, followed by Norton and eventually by Odell and Lhakpa Tsering, a veteran of 1922 who carried wooden pickets and coils of rope to fix lines. In short order they came to a formidable obstacle, a narrow chimney that could not be turned, rising 200 feet up the sheer face of the ice cliff. The wall was manageable, but the narrow chimney, smooth on both sides, with not a sign of a toehold and with a base that fell away into the darkness of a bottomless crack, was, as Norton put it, "the deuce." He glanced at his companion. "Confronted with a formidable climbing obstacle," he later wrote, "Mallory's behavior was always characteristic. You could positively see his nerves tighten like fiddle strings. Metaphorically he girt his loins, and his first instinct was to jump into the lead. Up the wall and chimney he led here, carefully, neatly and in that beautiful style that was all his own." It was less a climb, Norton added, than a gymnastic exercise, "and one is little fitted for gymnastics above 22,000 feet. I suppose the whole 200-foot climb to a most welcome little platform at the top took us an hour of exertion as severe as anything I have experienced."

Odell suffered terribly, and Mallory took note of it, but eventually he and Lhakpa joined the others, and they continued on, traversing the face and straddling, at one point, a narrow ridge of ice that fell away on one side to the blackness of a fathomless crevasse and on the other to open space and the head of the glacier, thousands of feet below. Finally, at 2:30 p.m., some seven hours after starting out, they reached the high shelf where their camp had been in 1922. There was no sign of it. The configuration of the snow and ice was completely different. Though still protected from the winds of the col by a high wall, what had been a broad platform was now a narrow band at no point more than thirty feet wide, a "hog-backed ridge of untrodden, glistening snow," Norton recalled, "barely affording level space for our proposed row of little 6-foot square tents."

While Norton held back, enjoying the shelter from the wind and the wide sweep of the sun, Odell and Mallory pushed on, tracking a route through the maze of snow ridges and crevasses that separated the shelf from the surface of the col. For Mallory, who had done the lion's share of the step cutting on the way up, the subsequent hour was, Norton recalled, "cruel work for a tired man." Odell led the way, finding an ice bridge across the most perilous of crevasses, an arch that would hold and carry them to the higher camps for the duration of the expedition. At 3:45 p.m., having rendezvoused with Norton and Lhakpa at the new site of Camp IV, they hastened down the mountain to Camp III with the careless abandon of men exhausted beyond the reach of reason. "The less said about the descent," Norton later quipped, "the better."

In truth, they were lucky to survive. Against all caution, they had followed the line of 1922, the very route that had ended in disaster. Norton and Mallory were unroped; Lhakpa brought up the rear, tethered to Odell. None had crampons. Norton slipped and momentarily lost control, as did Lhakpa, who plunged dangerously down the slope before coming to a halt in a patch of soft snow. Inexplicably, Odell had allowed him to tie in with a simple reef knot, which had not held. At one point Mallory simply disappeared. He wrote, "The snow gave way and in I went with the snow tumbling all round me, down luckily only about ten feet before I fetched up half-blind and breathless to find myself most precariously supported only by my ice axe, somehow caught across the crevasse and still in my right hand—and below was a very unpleasant black hole. I had some nasty moments before I got comfortably wedged and began to yell for help up through the round hole I had come through, where the blue sky showed." He shouted for help, but the others were down the slope, well out of earshot. Eventually he had to cut through the side of the crevasse, knowing that his every move risked dislodging his precarious hold and plunging him farther into the dark and unknown depths beneath him, almost certainly to his death.

It was a chastened party that finally reached Camp III that night, shortly after 6:30 p.m. There was no warm homecoming. The site was miserably cold; the dark stones that in 1922 had captured the sun and radiated heat in the chill of evening were now all covered in snow. The streams were ice, and with the elevation it was impossible to make a hot meal, let alone a proper cup of tea. Norton wrote of the "hatefulness of the evening meal, with the camp in cold shadow and one's feet like stones." The food tasted of kerosene, and with the cold air, the lining of the men's throats became so raw as to make eating painful. Along with chronic headaches, they were all, to one degree or another, tormented by hacking coughs so violent as to render sleep impossible.

Despite his exhaustion, Mallory lay awake much of the night, "distressed," he wrote to Ruth, "with bursts of coughing fit to tear one's guts." Norton, who shared a tent with Mallory, also failed to sleep, preoccupied with concerns about the coming monsoon and the imposing challenge of the ice chimney, most especially for porters laden with loads. At first light he scribbled some notes: "Indifferent night—head too full of the very apparent difficulties and dangers of the whole business; overcast and warm, light snow in early a.m. Don't like the look of weather much. Pray Heaven it's not the beginning of monsoon, as no power on earth can make parts of North Col route safe under monsoon conditions."

The following morning, Wednesday, May 21, even as the snowfall grew more severe, Hazard, Irvine, and Somervell led a dozen porters up to the North Col to provision Camp IV. The conditions were terrible, Irvine recalled, the "going perfectly bloody." Hazard and the porters "sweated blood," Somervell wrote, to cut a trail through the heavy snow. For Hazard, it was literally true: the war wound on his right hip had opened, and beneath his kit he bled profusely for a good part of the day.

Somervell led up the ice chimney, followed by Irvine. Hazard, from below, tied on the loads, and over the course of two and a half hours, Irvine and Somervell hauled them up, one by one. "Young Irvine," Norton reported, "was a perfect tower of strength, and his splendid physique never stood him in better stead." Still, it was long and exhausting work, and in order to return, as planned, to Camp III before dark, Irvine and Somervell left Hazard and the porters just 150 feet below the shelf of the col, at the site of Camp IV. Mist and snow reduced the visibility to a hundred yards; Irvine had "one nasty slip on the way down." Tired and parched, they reached Camp III just as dusk settled over the glacier.

The plan was for Hazard and his porters to remain at Camp IV for a single night before returning to Camp III. While Somervell and Irvine, at Camp III, prepared for their first attempt at the summit, Odell and Geoffrey Bruce, with another twelve porters, would proceed to Camp IV on Thursday morning, spend the night, and then continue up the Northeast Shoulder to establish Camp V at 25,500 feet. But, fatefully, the snowfall that had practically blinded Somervell and Irvine on their descent from the col continued through the night and well into Thursday, confining everyone to camp. "Awful day," Somervell wrote. "The party we hoped to bring up to the North Col to complete its equipment couldn't even start. Camp 3 was hell. I think the 13 of them on the North Col are more comfortable than we are. But this snow is making the way up very dangerous. We hope to send another party up tomorrow, but it's not too safe on the slopes of the Col." That night the temperature dropped to minus twenty-four Fahrenheit, a record cold on Everest, according to Odell. "Snowed hard all day until 3 p.m.," Norton wrote in the Camp III diary. "Impossible to do anything but lie in flea bags with feet like stones and worry about Hazard and his faithful 12."

Friday, May 23, dawned clear and bright, with the air as "keen as a knife." Bruce and Odell were off by 9:30 a.m. Their goal was Camp IV, but in the heavy snow their party soon bogged down. Odell required oxygen, as eventually did Bruce. By 3:00 p.m. they'd managed to reach only as far as the foot of the ice chimney. Forced to retreat, they were stunned to see, above them, Hazard and a small party of porters, struggling down the face. Though the sky was bright, the spindrift obscured their vision; the white winds absorbed every sound. They shouted but were not heard, and had little choice but to turn their backs on the mountain and lead their exhausted party back down to Camp III.

Hazard, meanwhile, made his way down, arriving at Camp III at 5:00 with a terrible story to tell. Having endured a dreadful night of cold, and assuming that Bruce and Odell and their party would reach Camp IV that day, Hazard had left the cook, old dependable Poo, alone at the North Col and led his twelve porters back to Camp III. But en route three lost their nerve, and in a panic returned to the shelter of their tents at Camp IV. In the chaos and exhaustion Hazard had apparently not noticed their departure. So he was now back at Camp III with only eight of his men, having left the other four stranded for a second night on the North Col. Their one bag of rations had dropped over a cliff, and all they had to eat was barley flour; the only other provisions at Camp IV were tinned goods for the sahibs, impossible for the Tibetans to open. The other British climbers at Camp III were dumbfounded by Hazard's folly. "It is difficult to make out how it exactly happened," Mallory wrote, "but evidently he didn't shepherd his party properly at all, and in the end four stayed up, and one of these badly frost bitten."

The situation presented the ultimate test of Norton as a leader. With the monsoon winds growing, conditions on the North Col could only worsen. If the porters were not rescued within a day, at most two, they would surely die. Yet his climbers were exhausted, and their ordeal, the quest that had drawn them halfway around the world, had scarcely begun. Mallory and Somervell had bronchitis and terrible coughs from the altitude and cold. Irvine was down with diarrhea. Odell had not slept in days, and Hazard, with his seeping wound, was a nonstarter. Saving the Tibetans would require the skills and endurance of the strongest of the climbers—Mallory, Somervell, Irvine, and Norton himself—putting at risk the very men who had the best chances of reaching the summit of Everest.

Norton did not waver for an instant. "The only thing that mattered," he wrote, "was to get the men down alive." There would be no repeat of 1922 on his watch. It would, however, be a precarious operation. Movement up the col would be exceedingly slow and difficult. The danger of avalanche was acute, the snow conditions horrendous. Norton put the odds at two to one in favor of success. Mallory, in a letter home to Ruth, thought ten to one in failure's favor a better bet. That night they gathered by candlelight in the mess tent and made plans for the morning. "It was a gloomy little conference; we could not but recognize that to turn our backs once more on the mountain at this date might well mean the abandonment of all hope of success for the year."

Before going to bed they gathered, as was their habit, between their two tents, stomping feet on the flat stones for warmth. They called their tents Balmoral and Sandringham, after the estates of the royal family. Odell and Somervell slept in one; Norton and Mallory shared the other. Little was said. "As we lay in our tent that night and listened to the soft pattering of snow on its walls," they knew their chances were slim, recalled Norton, "although at the time we kept such pessimistic views to ourselves. About midnight the snow stopped falling and the moon came out."

SATURDAY, MAY 24, Empire Day, dawned bright, even as shadows hung over the expedition and the marooned porters on the North Col. Sandy Irvine, scheduled to participate in the rescue attempt, woke with such a severe headache and stomach troubles that he had to return down the mountain with Geoffrey Bruce and Hazard, who had been ordered by Norton to evacuate Camp III. Their goal was Camp I, but Irvine was so weak he had to be left in Shebbeare's care at Camp II, while Hazard pushed on for base camp. Beetham, in defiance of Hingston's orders, had struggled up to Camp II, but he remained too feeble to assist in any meaningful way. Hingston, at base camp, had just learned of his father's death, which had occurred three months before, even as he nursed the ailing cobbler Manbahadur, who had contracted pneumonia and lay in critical condition. "Hingston daren't leave the base," Irvine noted in his journal, "as the frostbite waller may die any day. Good night, but face very sore." Irvine's fair skin, blistered by the sun, wind, and cold, was so raw that every time he touched his face, burnt bits came off in his hands.

At Camp III, Mallory, Somervell, and Norton set out at 7:30 a.m., trudging waist-deep through fresh snow that blanketed the ground to and beyond the base of the North Col. Mallory led as far as he could before yielding to Somervell, who struggled to the snow gulley where Bruce and Odell had abandoned their loads the previous day. Norton then took over; he alone wore crampons. He climbed until he could do no more, and passed the lead back to Mallory. And so it went;

each man climbed to the point of exhaustion. At no time during the seven-hour ascent to the North Col did they not have to plow through snow to the knee; often it reached their thighs or higher. When finally, utterly spent, they approached the ledge of Camp IV, the four porters appeared, stumbling and leaning each upon another. Norton shouted, demanding to know whether they could walk. "Up or down?" came the reply from the stalwart Sherpas, even though two of them, Nam-gya and Uchung, were severely frostbitten. "Down, you fool!" Norton cried, stunned to realize that the men had no idea of the danger they were in.

Separating the four from the rescue party was a steep and severely exposed slope, a precarious traverse across deep snow in what were clearly avalanche conditions. Belayed by Norton and Mallory, Somervell, with 200 feet of rope, slowly made his way toward the men. He got to within 30 feet before reaching the end of his tether. It was already 4:00 p.m. There was no time to go down for another rope. The men would have to come to him. The first reached Somervell safely, and was quickly passed along to Norton's anchor. The second did equally well, but as he was just within reach of Mallory, the other two rashly decided to come down together. Somervell screamed at them to halt, but it was too late. Their combined weight cut loose a great sheet of snow, and they plunged down the slope, seemingly to their doom.

The slide suddenly stopped, the snow compacting not ten yards from the edge of ice cliffs that fell away 200 feet. The two men stood, quivering in fear, too frightened to move. Somervell ordered them to sit. He then untied his belay, drove his ice ax into the snow as an anchor, and passed the rope around it. He glanced back at Norton and Mallory, saw that they were secure, and then slowly lowered himself, with one hand on the rope and the other free to grasp the victims. It was as unnerving as swimming up to a drowning man at sea: in their panic they might do anything. He had barely enough slack to grab each by the scruff of the neck, and with numbing authority lead them, one at a time, to safety.

It was now 4:30, and they still had to make their way down the North Col with four trembling wards, two suffering from severe frost-bite, all weak with hunger and fear. Mallory led, trailing one of the porters on a rope. Somervell followed, shepherding two others. Nor-ton brought up the rear, leading Namgya, whose useless hands were swollen grotesquely from the frost. They negotiated the ice chimney and stumbled on in the fading light, reaching the glacier at the base of the col at dusk. There Namgya broke down completely. Norton took him by the shoulder, like a wounded soldier at the front. At 7:30 p.m., as they finally reached the moraine that ran for a mile above Camp III, two shadowy figures approached out of the dark. It was Odell and John Noel with food and a thermos flask of hot soup. Noel, who had been filming the rescue all afternoon, later described the moment they encountered the returning men:

> We had toiled through the darkness for about one and a half hours when, in reply to our frequent call, we heard answering shouts. When we met, the whole lot of them sank down in the snow. They were absolutely done. The porters were like drunken men, not knowing what was happening. Norton, Somervell and Mallory hardly spoke. We got out our hot food to give them. One of the porters vomited as quickly as he took the stuff into his mouth and the other we had to prop up with our knees. They were not fit for another stroke of work for the rest of the expedition. In fact, during the next few days there was a general exodus from Snowfield Camp [Camp III] of everybody who was not up to the mark.

Unfortunately, this meant everyone. With every day counting, and the rising monsoon winds constantly tormenting his thoughts, Norton, to his intense disappointment, had no choice but to order a second full retreat from the flank of the North Col. "Next morning," he wrote, "we thankfully turned our backs on Camp III and escorting a miserable little convoy of the halt, the lame and the blind, reached Camp II in due course in the teeth of a northeast wind and with snow falling again."

By Sunday evening, May 25, Norton, Somervell, Odell, and Shebbeare were at Camp II, with Norton and Somervell ready to head farther down the mountain the following day. Mallory had continued all the way to Camp I to join Irvine and Bruce. Hazard and Beetham were at base camp, where that morning the cobbler Manbahadur, in his agony, had finally succumbed. "Ill fortune besets the expedition," Hingston wrote.

> Manbahadur, whose feet were badly frostbitten, died this morning of pneumonia. It was better that he should do so, for both feet would have to be amputated later. But far worse than this is the change of weather. Today there was no fierce wind from Everest, but a strong wind from the opposite direction. More-

over it is a warm wind and accompanied by white of cloud. Can it be that the monsoon has come? This would be a very serious blow. It would mean that the mountain had become impossible; and none has yet been above the North Col. It really is unthinkable that the Expedition will fail. But we have met with weather conditions far more severe than anyone anticipated. Shebbeare sent me a note from Camp II. He said there is going to be a revision of plans. Norton has come down to Camp I. Probably some new scheme is under consideration. The Expedition can never return after having reached only the North Col.

The following day Norton summoned Hingston to Camp I for "a council of war." The fate of the expedition clearly hung in the balance. The rescue of the four marooned Tibetans had been a very close call. When Tom Longstaff read of it in the Indian papers, he famously exclaimed, "Talk about pulling the whiskers of death—these folk crawled in through the chinks between the closed teeth!" It was later acknowledged that Geoffrey Bruce had been excluded from the rescue party because Norton, convinced that there was a good chance that all three of them would die, did not want to expose Bruce to the risk, knowing that his knowledge and skills would be needed to lead the survivors home to India.

There is no indication in the official camp diaries, in the private journals of Shebbeare, Hingston, Odell, or Irvine, in the letters of Mallory or Beetham, or in any of the subsequent accounts and memoirs to suggest that any member of the expedition questioned Norton's decision to risk all to save the lives of the stranded Tibetans. At the same time, everyone understood what the rescue effort implied. As Shebbeare, the transport officer, reflected, "This was the most daring and the most strenuous effort of the whole expedition and the resulting loss of condition by three of the strongest climbers may have cost us the mountain."

THE EXPEDITION was in desperate straits. Norton and Mallory, and certainly Odell, Somervell, and Bruce, were acutely aware that the expectations of a nation—indeed, an empire—called for nothing but success, for victory, whatever that term had come to mean. On May 26, the very day that Norton was bringing together his war council at Camp I, the fellows of the Royal Geographical Society gathered in London for their anniversary meeting and dinner, a thousand men in black tie and tails, trading stories of Everest and the supreme announcement they so eagerly anticipated. Most knew nothing of the mountain and could not have imagined the fate that had befallen the men.

A month had passed since the climbers' arrival at Rongbuk, and despite their refined plans, little had been accomplished. At Camp IV, on the col, they had only four tents in place, and sufficient sleeping bags for twelve porters and one climber. Food and supplies for the higher camps lay scattered the length of the East Rongbuk Glacier. Of the fifty-five Tigers, the Sherpa elite so dramatically elevated by General Bruce at the outset of the expedition in Darjeeling, only twelve (according to Shebbeare; as many as fifteen by Bruce's estimate) remained fit and capable of returning to Camp III and the North Col. The oxygen equipment was the one thing ready to go, thanks to young Sandy Irvine. But with its weight and the complete breakdown of the supply train, it seemed in the moment less an asset than a liability. At Norton's war council, Geoffrey Bruce pushed to eliminate oxygen altogether, in order to free the few fit porters to carry more essential goods: food, fuel, tents, and gear.

Norton, for his part, was desperately concerned about the weather. They were but a week shy of the date in 1922 when the monsoon broke in full fury, and there was every indication that the season might already be upon them. There were, of course, no meteorological records and no precedent save what the two previous expeditions had observed. The mountaineers had no way of knowing that the conditions they had experienced, so unusual for the early weeks of May, had nothing to do with the annual monsoon. In 1924 a trough of low pressure, a depression in western Afghanistan, flung a series of powerful storms across the length of northern India, bringing cold and severe weather to the entire Himalaya. This information, even had it been available, would have brought little comfort to the men. It explained why they had suffered, but it also implied they had yet to confront the monsoon and, with it, the full wrath of Everest.

The council of May 26, which began at midday, stretched into the evening, with all of them—Norton, Mallory, Somervell, Irvine, Bruce, and Hingston—dining together in Irvine's tent. "The scheme has to be recast," Hingston wrote that night. "The original intention was to have a camp seven; at best only six can be established now. It is possible that the use of oxygen will have to be abandoned. Different schemes were discussed and opinions taken; but the definite decision is postponed till the morning. Certainly another attempt will be made, that is if the weather at all permits. But it will have to be an attempt on a more slender scale; and this, of course, both increases risks and diminishes the chance of success."

This rather casual journal entry, written with the calm detachment that made Hingston such a valuable member of the expedition, in fact suggests a most fateful turning point. Until May 26 the very strength of the endeavor had been the discipline imposed by a plan based on two sound and fundamental convictions. Finch's dramatic results in 1922, and everything that had been learned since, had left little doubt that oxygen would play an essential role, if the summit were to be reached and the climbers safely return. Mallory, though a late convert to gas, had come so far as to believe that any attempt without oxygen would be little more than a gesture, an act of nostalgia. Second, the experience of 1922 had left Mallory, in particular, convinced that only a second and properly supplied camp above the col, established at least as high as 27,300 feet, would allow a climber a chance to get up and back in a day. This was key, an essential element of his scheme, his "brain-wave" that Norton and the others had enthusiastically endorsed at Shegar Dzong. To abandon both oxygen and the scaffolding that might realistically position a summit attempt implied a loss of both focus and reason, and the embrace of desperation. But on May 27, as Norton ordered Odell, Shebbeare, and John Noel down from Camp II to join in the deliberations, this is precisely what the expedition elected to do.

"We decided," Norton later wrote, "to scrap oxygen altogether." They would rest and regroup for two or three days, and then six climbers and all available Sherpas would reposition to Camp III. On two successive days, two teams of two men would set out from Camp IV. The first would establish a Camp V at 25,500 feet, and then the following day continue to a higher Camp VI at 27,200 feet—in the circumstances essentially a light bivouac—and from there set out for the summit. The second team, quite independent of the first, would try to do the same, should the first attempt fail. A third team of two would be held in reserve at Camp IV.

As for the configuration of the climbing parties, it was a simple determination. Shebbeare, thinking of Geoffrey Bruce in 1922, volunteered, but "Norton put his foot down very firmly on this suggestion." Beetham, of course, was out, still suffering from sciatica. Hazard, having lost the confidence of the men, would remain at Camp III. Irvine was strong but young, and thus would form the reserve with Odell, who, despite his considerable experience, "apparently suffers much from the altitude," noted Hingston's medical report of May 26. Thus the lead climbers would be, as if by process of elimination, Geoffrey Bruce and Mallory, Somervell and Norton.

Mallory recognized the scheme for what it was: less a plan than an act of folly and compulsion. Three days before, on the eve of abandoning Camp III for the second time, he had written to Ruth, expressing his sympathy for Norton's dilemma: "Poor old Norton was very hard hit altogether, hating the thoughts of such a bad muddle." Now, on the eve of their return to Camp III, he wrote bitterly to his old friend from Cambridge, David Pye: "We are on the point of moving up again, and the adventure appears more desperate than ever . . . All sound plans are now abandoned for two consecutive dashes without gas. Geoffrey Bruce and I in the first party provided I'm fit, and Norton and Somervell in the second, old gangers first, but in fact nothing but a consideration of what is likely to succeed has come in. If the monsoon lets us start from Camp IV, it will almost certainly catch us on one of the three days from there. Bright prospects!"

Mallory concealed his private concerns in the last public pronouncement he would make, an uplifting quotation that went out in the May 26 dispatch to the *Times*, the final word to reach the British public as the fate of the expedition still hung in the balance: "Action is only suspended before the more intense action of the climax. The issue will shortly be decided. The third time we walk up East Rongbuk glacier will be the last, for better or worse. We have counted our wounded and know, roughly, how much to strike off the strength of our little army as we plan the next act of battle . . . We expect no mercy from Everest."

His true feelings and deepest fears he saved for his beloved Ruth, in a letter written on the evening of May 27. "Dear Girl, this has been a bad time altogether—I look back on tremendous efforts and exhaustion . . . looking out of a tent door onto a world of snow and vanishing hopes . . . The physique of the whole party has gone down sadly . . . The only plum fit man is Geoffrey Bruce. Norton has made me responsible for choosing the parties of attack, [after] himself first choosing me into the first party if I like. But I'm quite doubtful if I shall be fit enough . . . We shall be going up again the day after tomorrow—six days to the top from this camp!"

As he lay in his sleeping bag, writing that letter destined to reach Ruth long after the issue had been decided, his thoughts turned to home and all the small things of family and life. He fretted that their car had been giving her such trouble, shared his delight to have received a lovely poem from their daughter Clare, passed along the happy news that his mother was well and in great spirits, on holiday in Aix-en-Provence. He asked in particular that Ruth send a note to David Pye, who had written from Pen y Pass, the mountain getaway in Wales where their lives had found such expression before the war. Then he ended what would be his last letter home, his final written words: "The candle is burning out and I must stop. Darling I wish you the best I can—that your anxiety will be at an end before you get this—with the best news, which will also be the quickest. It is 50 to 1 against us but we'll have a whack yet and do ourselves proud. Great love to you, Ever your loving, George."

THE FOLLOWING DAY, Wednesday, May 28, dawned clear, but all was not well. Mallory looked ill and was spending much of his time alone resting in his tent. His strength seemed gone, according to John Noel. Their finest climber, as the filmmaker recalled, was "running on nerves." Cautioned by Noel, Norton kept Mallory back for the day, along with Somervell and Geoffrey Bruce.

Sandy Irvine was dispatched forward to join Odell and Shebbeare, who had returned to Camp II. Their task over the next forty-eight hours would be the creation of a rope ladder that would solve the challenge of the ice chimney. It was Irvine's idea and, naturally, his design. Every third rung would be a large wooden tent peg, with the rest of it being made of hemp rope, spliced by hand—an exacting and difficult challenge for hands numb from the cold. With Irvine, Norton sent up to Camp II the only Sherpas fit for the mountain, fifteen men altogether, each one of them a "Tiger." The simple numbers—ten English, fifteen Sherpas—created a certain balance, an equilibrium that challenged two hundred years of British decorum in India.

The British climbers admired the Sherpas, but made little effort to understand their world. Younghusband famously said that there were hundreds of Tibetans living at the base of Everest who could have reached the "summit any year they liked. Yet the fact remains they don't. They have not even the desire to. They have not spirit." Beetham believed, too, that there was something fundamentally missing in the Sherpa character. He stated, "It has been said that these men could easily reach the top if they themselves really wished to do so. I do not believe it for one moment . . . they have acclimatized bodies but lack the right mentality."

Norton wrote that the Sherpas were "singularly like a childish edition of the British soldier. They have the same high spirit for a tough and dangerous job; the same ready response to quip and jest. As with the British soldier the rough character often comes out strongest when up against it in circumstances where the milder man fails." From Norton this was high praise. He was not a nuanced man when it came to culture, but he recognized courage and authenticity when he saw it.

Of all the men, it was the good doctor Hingston who came closest to sensing something sublime in the Tibetan way of being. Even as Sandy Irvine and the Sherpas made their way up the corridor of the East Rongbuk for the final assault, Hingston, back at base camp, had a remarkable encounter. He recalled in his journal on the evening of May 28:

> This morning I explored a narrow gorge in which a hermit had taken up his abode. I did not approach his cell too closely; but it appeared to consist of a natural cave partially closed in by a stone wall. He was literally buried in the mountains, surrounded only by cliffs and stones and a frozen torrent, which rushed through the gorge. He has been in his cell for three years and intends to stay there for another two. Once a month food supplies are sent him from the monastery; but beyond this he never sees a human being. It is a genuine and I imagine a miserable hermitage in cold and barren mountains at 17,000 feet. Of course he will earn great merit by it and will be considered an especially saintly lama when he returns to monastic life. No doubt he regards our attempt to climb Mount Everest in much the same light as we look on his incarceration. Each to the other must seem futile and ridiculous; yet each in its own way earns merit, and each is no doubt of equal value, the gain being purely moral and spiritual and of little, if any, practical use.

THE FOLLOWING morning, Ascension Day, May 29, Mallory, Somervell, Norton, and Geoffrey Bruce made their way to Camp II, arriving just in time for a light midday meal. Beetham and Noel were already there, along with Irvine, Odell, and Shebbeare. Hazard began the day at base camp, but had orders to go to Camp III. "A third attempt is to be launched tomorrow," Hingston noted. "Two parties will attempt to reach the summit. Mallory and Bruce are the first party; Norton and Somervell compose the second. It is not altogether a forlorn hope, but it will be the last attempt. There is a chance if the weather holds, but the difficulties are indeed great." At Camp II they all enjoyed a "beautiful evening and a great deal of noise on the glacier all night."

Friday was a perfect day, and spirits rose as the climbers made for Camp III. Mallory and Irvine went together, arriving well ahead of Bruce and Norton, Somervell and Odell. To the astonishment of all, Beetham, having defied Hingston, hobbled into camp in the early afternoon. He had apparently told the doctor to go to hell, that after his efforts he was not about to miss all the action. Norton considered it an act of mutiny and promptly ordered Beetham back to base camp, with instructions to dispatch Hingston up the mountain. His medical skills, Norton suggested, would be needed. That afternoon the weather broke completely in their favor, though there were signs of clouds by nightfall. Irvine had never felt stronger. "Feel very fit tonight. I wish I was in the first party instead of a bloody reserve." He was not alone with this sentiment. Mallory clearly would have preferred Irvine to Bruce, but the die was cast.

May 31, Saturday, and the stars faded to a turquoise dawn. Hazard left Shebbeare at Camp II and headed up to Camp III. Mallory and Bruce, with Odell and Irvine in support, left Camp III at 8:45 a.m. with nine porters. A sharp crust of over two feet of snow made the going difficult, and they traded off the lead, even as the Sherpas trudged behind, burdened by especially heavy loads. When they reached the ice chimney, Mallory and Odell went ahead, fixing the rope ladder, which made all the difference. The porters climbed readily, without having to shed their loads. Above the chimney young Irvine led, and as they approached the shelf, Odell cut the final steps. To the extent possible, they tried to spare Mallory and Bruce for the challenge that surely awaited them above the col. By 3:00 p.m. they were all secure at Camp IV. Irvine made a "fine meal of cocoa, pea soup and tongue." Mallory's eye had been touched somewhat by the sun; it was irritated, slightly raw, but not a serious concern. The night bode well, with all the heavens illuminated by the silence of the stars. "Lovely calm evening," Odell wrote. "Magnificent situation." Only one of the porters had collapsed.

Irvine was up at 4:30 a.m. to cook breakfast for the climbers. He found it, not surprisingly, a "very cold and disagreeable job. Thank God my profession is not to be a cook! Sun struck the camp about 5:10 a.m." In a flush of optimism, Mallory and Bruce and eight porters managed to be off at 6:10, escorted as far as the surface of the col by Irvine and Odell, who led the way. Then they met the wind. Nothing like it had been experienced in 1922. It was a bitter return to

1921, when Wheeler, Bullock, and Mallory had nearly frozen to death, ghostlike in an instant. Odell and Irvine were not unhappy to retreat, even as Mallory, Bruce, and the porters leaned into the gusts; like mere shadows they were obliterated from view within moments by the spindrift rising off the snow.

The entire morning of June 1, as they struggled up the Northeast Shoulder along a track Mallory had come to know so well in 1922, they fought against the cold and the wind, with each step forcing the full weight of their bodies forward as they climbed a slope of forty-five degrees. Their brows were often lower than their knees, and yet the wind held them off the ground. At 25,000 feet, well below the goal for Camp V, four of the porters balked and dumped their loads. Like men waiting to die, they just sat, refusing to do more. Mallory, Bruce, and the four other porters, led by the indomitable Lobsang Sherpa, struggled up another 300 feet and cleared two pads for their tents. Bruce and Lobsang then returned to the miserable men below, shaming them by doing not one but two carries forward with the gear. The packs were light, a mere twenty pounds, but to scramble up and down that slope twice after climbing to 25,300 feet was a supreme effort, and one so wrenching that it dangerously strained Bruce's heart, though he had no way of knowing at the time.

Mallory sent the five spent porters down to the North Col, keeping only the three he deemed fit to carry farther up the mountain to Camp VI—at 27,000 feet or more, the intended springboard for the summit attempt. That night, Mallory and Bruce shared one of the two light Meade tents; the three porters crammed into the other. These flimsy shelters—ten pounds of canvas and little more—were perched on the east flank of the ridge, partially sheltered from the wind but still dangerously exposed. Two hundred feet below them the tattered remnants of Mallory's 1922 high camp lay scattered among the stones.

In the morning the weather held, a glorious day, but not the men. Not one of the porters stirred, and no amount of shame, including every cussword Bruce could harness, could bring them courage to do anything but retreat. Mallory, though furious with the Sherpas, at least according to Odell's recollection, scratched out a note for Norton and sent it down with Dorjee Pasang. "Show's crashed," it read, "wind took the heart out of our porters yesterday." He and Bruce would remain at Camp V just long enough to clear off a third tent site and then return to the col. With the porters down, the summit attempt was off.

It is curious that Mallory chose to abandon the mountain, rather than continuing higher with Bruce alone, if only to prepare a Camp VI for Somervell and Norton, who were on this very day on their way up from the col, precisely as planned. Mallory's decision to pull back may in fact have saved Bruce's life, but as he knew nothing at the time of the younger man's weakened heart, this was clearly not his motivation.

Mallory was not interested in Camp VI. His goal was the summit, and had there been a chance he would have happily gone on with Bruce. But once the porters were out, and the summit beyond reach, his only thought was to get down that he might live to have another go. Indeed, it is not clear that he ever put much faith into this attempt without oxygen. That he had abstained from assisting Lobsang and Bruce the previous afternoon as they heaved up the loads was quite unlike him, and it suggests that the moment he knew the game was off, the majority of the porters down, he deliberately marshaled his strength for a second assault, with oxygen and with Irvine, which had been his intention from the very beginning.

Even as Mallory awoke to desolation at their miserable bivouac at Camp V that morning, Irvine was down at Camp IV on the North Col making breakfast for Norton and Somervell, who had arrived the previous afternoon. Odell, meanwhile, had gone to Camp III for supplies, reaching there in ninety minutes, where he dined with Hazard and Noel and spent a delightful night in thirty-nine degrees of frost. No one noticed, but something mysterious was coming over Odell, a wave of newfound strength and endurance. The following morning, carrying a considerable load, he popped back up to Camp IV with Hazard.

At Camp IV, Monday, June 2, was another day of absolute perfection. Irvine was out of his tent by 5:00 a.m., and Norton and Somervell, with six porters, got off by 6:45. They had one light Meade tent, two sleeping bags, and food and fuel for three nights. Each had a rucksack, with a compass, an electric torch, a change of socks, and some extra woolen clothes. Norton described in some detail what he looked like that morning, dressed against the wind:

> Personally I wore thick woolen vest and drawers, a thick flannel shirt and two sweaters under a lightish knickerbocker suit of windproof gaberdine the knickers of which were lined with light flannel, a pair of soft elastic Kashmir putties and a pair of boots of felt bound and soled with leather and lightly nailed with the usual Alpine nails. Over all I wore a very light pajama suit of Messrs Burberry's "Shackleton" windproof gabardine. On my hands I wore a pair of long fingerless woolen mits inside a similar pair made of gaberdine . . . On my head I wore a fur-lined

motor-cycling helmet, and my eyes and nose were protected by a pair of goggles of Crooke's glass, which were sewn into a leather mask that came well over the nose and covered any part of my face which was not naturally protected by my beard. A huge woolen muffler completed my costume.

Somervell was similarly dressed, as were the porters, all in layers of wool, leather, canvas, and gabardine. They were all bundled like "gollywogs," Norton admitted, absurd in appearance but at least ready for the wind. Or so they thought. The instant they crested the height of the col, the full wrath of Everest made a mockery of their preparations. "The wind even at this early hour," Norton later wrote, "took our breath away like a plunge into the icy waters of a mountain lake, and in a minute or two our well protected hands lost all sensation as they grasped the frozen rocks to steady us." When Somervell tried to take a photograph, he could expose his bare fingers for only a second or two before they became too cold and numb even to press the shutter.

As had Mallory and Bruce the day before, they leaned into the gusts, making their way from the wind-ravaged funnel of the col to the base of the Northeast Shoulder. There the sun offered some relief from the cold, and Norton led the way up the rocks, along the same direct route they had followed in 1922. At midmorning they reached a familiar spot, and Norton smiled to recall knocking over his pack in '22, and watching as all his warm clothes tumbled off the mountain. As they continued up the ridge, they were startled to see Dorjee Pasang, Mallory and Bruce's lead porter, coming down the mountain. The man was wasted, and simply handed Norton Mallory's note indicating the failure of the first attempt. A few minutes later, roughly halfway to Camp V, they crossed paths with Mallory and Bruce coming down. Scarcely a word was exchanged. Mallory merely cautioned Norton to watch for small strips of cloth, indicating where they should abandon the ridge and make a short ascending traverse to reach Camp V. They wished one another good luck and shuffled on, one party going up, expectant and hopeful, the other down in muted disappointment.

Mallory lingered at Camp IV, on the col, just long enough to confide in Odell that only oxygen would allow the summit to go. Leaving Odell and Hazard in support of the men up the mountain, Norton and Somervell, he continued directly down to Camp III with Bruce, conscripting Irvine on the way, who without orders from Norton followed them down. They arrived at 4:30 p.m. Mallory immediately instructed Bruce to find a cadre of fit porters, should it be possible. Of Irvine he demanded an inspection of the oxygen apparatus, until the two most dependable sets had been identified. Irvine did as he was told, though he was in considerable pain, his face, as he wrote in his diary, "badly cut by the sun and wind on the Col," his lips so "cracked to bits" that he found it agonizing to eat. Mallory, though exhausted, was content. There would be a third attempt by him with oxygen, as originally planned. With him—again, as originally intended—would be Irvine. He had no more confidence in Odell than he did in Hazard or Beetham. "None of these three," he had confided in his last letter to Ruth, "has any real guts." This was both unfair and untrue, but it certainly indicates that Mallory never wavered in his choice of Irvine for his last climb.

NORTON AND SOMERVELL, meanwhile, had continued up the mountain, reaching Camp V just after 1:00 p.m. In six and a half hours they had gained 2,500 feet. If such a rate could be maintained and all obstacles overcome, they could conceivably reach the summit in another ten to twelve hours of steady climbing. With the weather at last on their side, as it seemed to be, there was every hope, and one might have expected a certain elation, given all that they had endured.

Instead the mood was dour, muted by exhaustion. Mallory's two tents still stood, pitched on crude stone platforms piled up in the lee of the ridge. Norton sent his two weakest men back to Camp IV, leaving him four to cram into a single tent. Norbu Yishé he compared to an old soldier: undependable in daily life but a rock in a crisis, when things mattered. Llakpa Chédé was outwardly a small man, quiet and diffident, whose discretion veiled a fierce inner strength. He was, Norton wrote, "a brilliant man on a mountain." Semchumbi was a rogue, a cadger around the officers' mess, dismissed by Bruce but recognized by Norton as a force to be reckoned with in battle. Lobsang Tashi was a "simple good natured giant from the eastern borders of Tibet," which actually meant he was Khampa, a people who to this day fight fiercely for their freedom and independence.

They stood about in the late afternoon light, shuffling and stamping in the cold, not yet ready to surrender to their tents, where there would be neither warmth nor sleep. Norton and Somervell struggled to prepare dinner. The "most hateful part of the process," Norton later wrote, "is that some of the resultant mess must be eaten, and this is only achieved by will power; there is but little desire to eat—

sometimes indeed a sense of nausea at the bare idea—though of drink one cannot have enough." In the end they went to bed with only pemmican, bully beef, coffee, and biscuits in their bellies.

Norton and Somervell lay in the upper tent, cold and damp, unable to sleep. The Sherpas squeezed together down below. As the early midnight hours waned, the wind suddenly revealed its power. Nothing else could account for the stones that rained down, slashing the canvas, slicing open Semchumbi's knee, cracking Lobsang's skull, leaving pools of blood that by dawn froze all along the bottom of their tent. Unaware of their suffering, Norton stumbled out into the morning cold and took measure of his men. He found them, he recalled, "packed like sardines" in their tent. Then he saw the blood, and immediately knew that Lobsang was finished. Semchumbi was half lame. He tried to rally the other two, Norbu and Llakpa, with promises that if the summit was achieved, their names would be inscribed for all time in a book of gold.

This meant nothing to them, but honor did. Three, including the wounded Semchumbi, were ready to continue. Each was given a twenty-pound pack. The five men left Camp V at 9:00 a.m. and walked until 1:30 p.m., reaching 26,800 feet. Somervell stayed by the wounded Semchumbi the entire day, coaxing him aloft, just as he had lifted the lives of so many in the war. Shortly after midday they passed the highest point they had reached with Mallory in 1922. At 2:30 p.m. the porters went down, all of them, including Semchumbi; they had 4,000 feet to descend to the North Col before dark.

As the sun fell on the evening of Tuesday, June 3, Somervell and Norton were alone at what they grandly called Camp VI. Far below they could see their old camp from 1922, and they wondered how they had managed to reach so much higher. They gazed as if from another dimension at a sunset that, Somervell later wrote, was seen "all over the world, with all the mountains black against a red sky." They would sleep that night at an elevation where no man had reached without oxygen. Only Finch and Bruce in 1922 had managed to climb as high. They went to their tents content and optimistic. "With a clear day ahead of us," Norton wrote, "and given favourable conditions, what might we not achieve!"

Norton rested well, failing to waken even as the cork of one of his two thermos flasks popped off, soaking his bedding with the hot tea he had intended to carry with him on their summit bid. This caused a delay in the morning, as they waited to melt snow for drinking water. The sky was bright, the air bitterly cold. They were off at 6:40 a.m., just two men, moving light, as Norton wrote: "cardigans, a thermos flask of coffee and a vest-pocket Kodak; nothing else save ice axes and a short rope."

The day was fine and nearly without wind, a "perfect day for our task," Norton observed. Rather than continue directly up the shoulder to its junction with Northeast Ridge, Norton and Somervell stayed well below the skyline, climbing on the diagonal toward the Yellow Band, which they reached in an hour. Their pace was dreadfully slow: twenty steps followed by a pause, as if moving across the bottom of a sea with all the weight of the ocean on their back. Five minutes of agony, then a minute or two of rest. Norton shook so violently from the cold he thought he was suffering from an attack of malaria. He took his pulse and found it to be 64, 20 beats above his norm. He stumbled dangerously as he moved across the sandstone slabs and broad ledges, all bare of snow. His goggles impeded his sight. He removed them, a critical mistake.

After six hours they approached their immediate goal: a broad couloir, a gully that cleft the entire face of the mountain, running from the Rongbuk Glacier far below all the way to the base of the summit pyramid. From the start Norton's plan had been to avoid the Northeast Ridge, the skyline with its impossible winds and unknown obstacles. He had an uncanny eye for mountain approaches, intuitions honed by his very first outings with his grandfather in the Alps. A band of rock guarded the final pyramid of Everest, encircling its base. Where the cliff met the skyline of the Northeast Ridge, it formed a formidable escarpment, what Norton and the men of 1922 had identified as the First Step. Beyond this on the same ridge was another even more challenging barrier, dubbed by the men the Second Step. From a distance it was impossible to ascertain the severity of either pitch. Which is precisely why Norton, not by nature a ridge walker, had chosen to go along the side of the hill, aiming to hit the couloir, with the hope that it might be ascended. This would leave him and Somervell above the last of the obstacles of the Northeast Ridge, spat out at the foot of the final pyramid, which even from a distance was transparently a go.

It was noon. They were but a thousand feet below and a quarter of a mile in distance from the summit of the world. In the Lake District these figures might have implied an hour of easy climbing. At 28,000 feet on Everest, such distances invoked infinity.

Somervell's body was the first to fail. During the rescue of the porters at Camp IV, he had strained every fiber of his being; his throat was burnt raw from the effort, seared by frost. Now he found it increasingly difficult to breathe. He sat down on a stone in shelter from the sun, and urged Norton to go on alone.

With a nod Norton continued, following the upper edge of the Yellow Band until it met a pronounced buttress, geologically the same strip of rock that erupted on the Northeast Ridge as the Second Step. He dropped down until he found a cut that led through to the gully itself, the great couloir that in time would bear his name. This was the opening to the summit. The exposures were desperate. A simple slip like any one of the many they had endured would mean disaster, a violent glissade into the void of the glacier many thousands of feet below. The footing was terrible, the deep snow impossible. The Yellow Band had been manageable, a "whole face composed of slabs like tiles on a roof and all sloped at much the same angle as tiles," he noted. But the couloir was ice lightning, with not a handhold or any chance of a reprieve, most especially for a blind man.

And that was precisely what Norton was becoming with every step, each moment. He'd first sensed trouble as low as 27,500 feet, long before he reached the couloir; his eyes dripped fluid, which froze upon his cheeks. By 28,000 feet he was seeing double. Still he moved into the couloir, even as the going got steadily worse. The snow reached to his waist; it was too soft to cut steps. He stepped, he recalled, half blind from "tile to tile, as it were, each tile sloping smoothly and steeply downward; I began to feel that I was too much dependent on the mere friction of a boot nail on the slabs. It was not exactly difficult going, but it was a dangerous place for a single, unroped climber, as one slip would have sent me in all probability to the bottom of the mountain."

In another hour he gained but 100 feet in elevation, perhaps in distance 300 yards. "The strain of climbing so carefully was beginning to tell and I was getting exhausted," he later wrote. "In addition my eye trouble was getting worse and was by now a severe handicap. I had perhaps 200 feet more of this nasty going to surmount before I emerged on the north face of the final pyramid and, I believe, safety and an easy route to the summit. It was now 1 p.m. and a brief calculation showed that I had no chance of climbing the remaining 800 or 900 feet if I was to return in safety."

Snow-blind, suffering from double vision, which was madly disorienting and excruciatingly painful, he went on until he could do no more, turning back finally at 28,126 feet, less than 1,000 feet from the summit. Then things became dangerous. His nerves cracked from exhaustion. In one moment he had been fearlessly pressing on, climbing in waist-deep snow up a chute that exposed him to death with every step. Then the instant he gave up the chase, a world of fear and intimidation closed in on him. Merely to turn about was a daunting challenge. He came to a patch of snow—a trivial impediment given what he had faced all day—but in the moment he froze and desperately called out to Somervell for help. Somervell rose quickly to the call, offering a rope and a belay. A moment later, with Norton once again at ease, Somervell accidentally dropped his ice ax, and they both watched in horror as it careened off the mountain, end over end, dropping several thousand feet into the void. Norton followed the clinging and clanging as the steel struck rock all the way down. He felt Somervell tie a rope to his waist.

They stumbled down to Camp VI, pausing only long enough to anchor the tents with stones and salvage a tent pole for Somervell to use in place of his ice ax. He brought up the rear, knowing that Norton was slipping into the realm of the blind. At Camp V they foolishly unroped. The ground was easy; sunset was unfolding, and all seemed well with the world. Norton unexpectedly left Somervell behind, slipping off the ridge in a series of bold glissades. He was soon so far ahead that he assumed his companion had stopped deliberately, perhaps to sketch or take pictures, as was his habit. In fact, Somervell was fighting for his life. Somervell later wrote, "I sat in the snow to die whilst Norton walked on, little knowing that his companion was awaiting the end a few yards behind him."

All day and indeed for several days he had been troubled by a burning sensation in his throat, which made both eating and speaking impossibly painful. While Norton walked ahead, Somervell had suddenly collapsed, quite unable to breathe. A coughing fit on the way down the mountain, not unlike the many he had endured over the past week, had dislodged the mucous lining of his larynx. Frostbite had scorched all of his airways, leaving every surface raw. "I made one or two attempts to breathe but nothing happened. Finally I pressed my chest with both hands, gave one last almighty push and the obstruction came up. What a relief! Coughing up a little blood I once more breathed really freely—more freely than I had done in some days." Though still suffering intense pain, Somervell was able to increase his pace and finally catch up with Norton.

It was small relief, for darkness was coming on and they were nowhere near the safety of Camp IV. Odell and Mallory, who had returned to Camp IV, spotted torch lights on the mountain just after 8:00 p.m., but it was another hour and a half before Norton and Somervell reached the base of the Northeast Shoulder and the broad surface of the col. They shouted for help, but as Norton later recalled,

"My own throat and voice were in none too good a case, and my feeble wail seemed to be swallowed up in the dim white expanse below glimmering in the starlight." They might both have readily died. They had been exposed to the wind and the agony of the heights for more than fifteen hours, with nothing to eat and precious little to drink. Out of the darkness of the col emerged two shadowy figures, Mallory and Odell, saviors save for one thing: they brought to the rescue not soup and hot tea but bottles of oxygen. Norton erupted in rage, the only time during the entire expedition when he lost his military discipline and composure. "We were parched and famished with thirst," he later wrote, still furious in recollection. "I remember shouting again and again, 'We don't want the damn oxygen we want drink.' "

ON JUNE 3, even as Norton and Somervell moved up with their porters to Camp VI, Hingston arrived at Camp III, astonished to find Mallory and Bruce there and not somewhere higher up the mountain. Odell and Hazard, in support at the North Col, that same day decided to climb to Camp V, both to resupply it and simply to pass the time. Hazard wanted to stretch his legs; Odell, to study the geology of the mountain. After feeble beginnings, both had acclimatized unexpectedly well, and with little effort they scrambled to heights that only two years before had been considered by science beyond reach of any human without supplemental oxygen. At Camp III, meanwhile, Mallory brooded, concerned about Irvine, who'd awoken that morning in agony. "A most unpleasant night," he noted, "when everything on earth seemed to rub against my face . . . which made me nearly scream in pain."

The following morning, Wednesday, June 4, shortly after breakfast a porter arrived from the North Col, bringing word that Norton and Somervell had reached 27,000 feet the previous afternoon, poised for a summit attempt. From his perch above Camp III John Noel trained his telephoto lens on the summit. Everyone stirred, the entire camp expectant and hopeful. "This is great progress," Hingston wrote, "and must have been a splendid achievement. If they are not completely exhausted, they may have a chance today of climbing the remaining 2,000 feet. But our field glasses and telescopes could detect nothing. Noel has had his camera trained all day on the peak. This, however, does not mean that they have been unsuccessful. It is extraordinarily difficult to pick up people at such a distance against a background of rock."

By midday on June 4, Mallory could no longer bear the uncertainty and tension. Hazard that morning had inexplicably abandoned his post and returned to Camp III, leaving Odell alone in support at Camp IV. Concerned about the plight of Norton and Somervell, and desperately keen to position himself for a third attempt, Mallory, with Irvine, set out shortly after lunch for the North Col. Climbing with oxygen, they reached Camp IV in less than three hours, arriving at 5:10 p.m. feeling, in Mallory's words, "very surprisingly fresh."

Odell, at Camp IV with two Sherpa companions, Nema and Dasno, had spent the afternoon glassing the upper slopes, watching to no avail for Norton and Somervell. "I hope they've got to the top," Irvine wrote that evening, "but by God, I'd like to have a whack at it myself." After dark Mallory and Odell moved up the col with electric torches, hoping to draw the attention of Norton and Somervell. Irvine remained behind, preparing food and tea. The second team finally stumbled into camp at 9:30 p.m., supported by Mallory and Odell.

That night Mallory and Norton shared a tent, and Mallory laid out the rationale for a third attempt. It was the first Norton had heard of the plan. "I entirely agreed with this decision," he later wrote, "and was full of admiration for the indomitable spirit of the man, determined, in spite of his already excessive exertions, not to admit defeat while any chance remained, and I must admit—such was his will power and nervous energy—he still seemed entirely adequate for the task." Noble words, to be sure, but composed long after the fact.

Norton, at the moment, was utterly spent. He questioned Mallory's choice of Irvine, but it was a pointless query, for the die was cast. Mallory was not concerned about mountaineering experience; he needed someone with limitless strength who could manage the oxygen apparatus, upon which the entire venture depended. Norton was in no condition to argue. As he dozed off, his body aching with cold and fatigue, he was startled awake by a sharp agonizing pain in his eyes. He could not see. By morning, after a sleepless night, he was totally blind from the sun; he would not fully recover his sight for three days. At this most critical of junctures, the expedition had no leader. Mallory had taken over. "It was not time to think of altering existing arrangements," Norton later acknowledged, "especially as Mallory was leader of the climbing party and organizing his own show, while I was a blind crock."

On Thursday, June 5, the weather remained clear. Unbeknownst to the men at Camp IV, it was the onset of the ten days of fair skies that typically precede the monsoon. The previous day a telegram forwarded by runner had reached Geoffrey Bruce at Camp III: "Monsoon has appeared on Malabar Coast but extension into Bengal likely to be later than usual." All of their concerns had been for naught. There had been no need to abandon their carefully crafted plans, no need for Norton's mad dash at the mountain, no need to abandon oxygen as an option.

Somervell, exhausted and sleepless, headed down for Camp III. Norton was so severely snow-blinded that he could not be moved; they piled sleeping bags over his tent to keep out the light. Occasionally he poked his head out of his tent to say something to the porters; of the English at Camp IV, he alone could speak their language. But mostly he hid away in the dark, the long length of his narrow body curled up in pain. Irvine reported that the temperature in the sun that day soared to 120 degrees, though the air in the shadows remained below freezing. "My face a perfect agony," read the last lines of his last journal entry. "Have prepared two oxygen apparatus for our start tomorrow morning." With a prearranged signal—blankets placed out in the snow—Odell sent a message to Camp III that brought up Hazard to replace Irvine in reserve.

The morning of Friday, June 6, dawned clear. Hazard and Odell made the climbers a breakfast of fried sardines, biscuits, chocolate, and tea. Mallory did not overdress: cotton and silk underwear, a flannel shirt, a brown long-sleeved pullover, and a woolen waistcoat that had been a gift from his wife. For the wind he wore a gabardine Shackleton jacket. He had two pairs of goggles, a fur-lined helmet, woolen mittens, and a scarf. Crammed into the pockets of his jacket and in two pouches worn around his neck were several miscellaneous small items: nail scissors and a penknife, a box of Swan Vesta matches, extra laces and straps, a tube of petroleum jelly, and two handkerchiefs, one burgundy, green, and blue, the other red, blue, and yellow, each monogrammed GLM. He had a list of supplies, scratched out on a bit of paper, and three letters. One was from his brother, Trafford, in London, dated April 2. A second had come from Mary, his sister in Colombo, written on April 12. The third was from a woman he had met in New York, Stella Cobden-Sanderson. No scandal here: he had often mentioned her to his wife, and the contents of the letter were frivolous, innocent gossip, nothing romantic or significant. On the back of the envelope he had written information about the pressure levels of the oxygen cylinders, which is the only reason he carried her letter with him on the fateful day.

Sandy Irvine wore similar gear, but with breeches and puttees beneath his Shackleton jacket. He had a felt hat, which he pulled down low over his face for protection from the sun. They had eight porters, each carrying twenty-five-pound loads: sleeping bags, meta fuel to melt snow, and several spare gas cylinders. For food they packed lightly, high-energy snacks mostly: chocolate, ginger nuts, macaroni, sliced ham and tongue, Kendal mint cakes, and tea. Mallory and Irvine each carried an apparatus, but because of a shortage of gas cylinders, they planned not to use oxygen until they reached Camp VI, which meant they would climb for two days encumbered by twenty-five pounds of deadweight on their backs.

Norton, still in pain and unable to see, waved them off from the flap of his tent. He recalled the time as 7:30 a.m. Odell wrote in his diary that they set out more than an hour later, at 8:40 a.m. "The party moved off in silence," Odell recalled, "as we bid them adieu and they were soon lost to view." Norton felt decidedly uneasy.

Hingston arrived an hour later, up from Camp III with two porters, Nema Tundrup and Chutin. He "bathed Norton's eyes" and with the help of Hazard, at least as far as the ice chimney, escorted the blind invalid away from the white glare of the shelf and down the face of the North Col. Norton could walk, but he could not see a single footstep. Hingston, by reputation no mountaineer, stayed by his side the entire descent, 1,500 feet of ice and snow, guiding his companion's feet to every rung of Irvine's rope ladder, placing each of his crampons one at a time into steps cut into the snow. At the base of the col, six porters met them with a one-man carrier. The going was rough, "boulders, ice and frozen scree," and it took them until 5:00 p.m. to sling the expedition leader down the moraine to the safety of Camp III, where John Noel and Geoffrey Bruce waited anxiously. Norton shared with them his hopes for Mallory and Irvine; however desperate the attempt, there was not a man among them who anticipated disaster.

"We said good-bye to Mallory and Irvine," Norton later wrote. "My last impression of my friends was a handshake and a word of blessing, for it was only in my imagination that I could see the little party winding its way amid the snow humps and ice crevasses leading to the Col."

The following morning, Norton's sight began to improve, though he would remain in pain for another two days. He elected to stay with Bruce, Hingston, and Noel at Camp III while awaiting the outcome of the final climb. "During the next four days," he wrote, "we were to pass through every successive stage of suspense and anxiety from high hope to hopelessness, and the memory of them is such that Camp III must remain to all of us the most hateful place in the world."

. . .

MALLORY AND IRVINE evidently made good progress on the first day of their climb; at 5:00 p.m. that evening, four of their eight porters returned from Camp V to the North Col with a note for Odell: "There is no wind here, and things look hopeful." The following day, Friday, June 7, was the calm before the storm. In the absence of further news, Hingston enjoyed a quiet day at Camp III, content that their ordeal on Everest would soon be over. "Personally I have not much hope of their success," he wrote, "unless the oxygen is of greater value than we expect. This will be the last of the attempts. Already arrangements are on hand for the evacuation of the camps. The monsoon will be on us any time. The party is exhausted by fatigue and exposure. Within a week we should all be off the mountain. And no one will regret it. All have had a grueling this year and need a rest at lower elevations."

John Noel carried his cameras to the North Col, along with instructions from Norton as to the blanket signals to use to communicate success or failure on the mountain. He returned that afternoon at 5:30 to Camp III. Odell, meanwhile, with Sherpa Nema, one of two fit porters at hand, left the col and climbed up the Northeast Shoulder to Camp V, again in support for Mallory and Irvine, who that day had pressed on to Camp VI. Odell and Nema reached Camp V, soon to be joined by the last four of Mallory's porters heading back down to the North Col. They lingered only long enough to give Odell two additional notes from Mallory, one addressed to him and a second to John Noel.

"Dear Odell," began the first, "We're awfully sorry to have left things in such a mess—our Unna cooker rolled down the slope at the last moment. Be sure of getting back to IV tomorrow in time to evacuate before dark, as I hope to. In the tent I must have left a compass—for the Lord's sake rescue it: we are here without. To here on 90 atmospheres for the two days—so we'll probably go on two cylinders—but it's a bloody load for climbing. Perfect weather for the job! Yours ever, George Mallory."

The note for Noel was far more significant. It read: "Dear Noel, We'll probably start early tomorrow (8th) in order to have clear weather. It won't be too early to start looking out for us either crossing the rock band under the pyramid or going up the skyline at 8.0 p.m. Yours G Mallory." The reference to a start time of 8:00 p.m. was an obvious mistake; Odell knew to watch for them in the morning. The rock band was not the Yellow Band, which Norton and Somervell had traversed; it referred to a dark rim of rock at the very base of the summit pyramid. Mallory left no doubt that he intended to follow the Northeast Ridge, despite the impediments of the First and Second Steps. He was by nature a ridge walker, and a climber not easily intimidated by cliffs of rock, even at 28,000 feet. From the elevation and location of Camp VI, Odell surmised, it might well be possible to attain the skyline in two hours.

Odell sent the ailing Nema down the mountain with the others—they would descend 6,000 feet in a day—and settled in to spend the night at Camp V. As Mallory's note had indicated, there was no stove at Camp V. Odell could neither heat food nor melt snow for water, and yet he was quite comfortable and utterly content. "Wonderful time alone at V," he enthused in his diary. He ate a dinner of jam, macaroni, and tomatoes, and then lay back to enjoy the "most gorgeous cloud effects" of the night sky. The weather was hopeful, the view spectacular. "Westward," he wrote, "there was a savage, wild jumble of peaks, culminating in Cho Uyo [sic] bathed in pinks and yellows of most exquisite tints. Right opposite were the gaunt cliffs of Everest, the north peak, intercepting a portion of the wide northern horizon, of a brilliant opalescence, which threw into prominence the outline of a mighty peak far away in Central Tibet. Eastward floating in the thin air, the snowy top of Kangchenjunga appeared and at last the beautifully varied outlying Gyangkar range. Sunset and after at that altitude were a transcendent experience never to be forgotten."

Thus on the eve of the last climb, the men were spread the length of the high camps: Shebbeare was, as always, stationed in logistical support at Camp II; Norton, Bruce, John Noel, and Hingston were at Camp III; Hazard was alone on the North Col at Camp IV; Odell was up the Northeast Shoulder at Camp V; and Mallory and Irvine slept somewhere close to 27,000 feet at their Camp VI.

That night Irvine must have asked Mallory to do a final check on the pressure levels of their oxygen cylinders; Mallory sketched the notations on the back of the envelope of the letter from Stella Cobden-Sanderson. Four were up to 110, a fifth just at 100. They clearly aimed for an early departure on the following morning; Mallory's note to Noel anticipated getting to the skyline or even reaching the rock band at the base of the summit pyramid by 8:00 a.m. This would imply breaking camp as early as 6:00 a.m., possible but unlikely at 27,000 feet. As always with Mallory, there would have been a certain amount of chaos. He had left behind his compass at Camp V. At Camp VI it would be his torch—an extraordinary oversight given his experience in 1922 when he, Norton, Morshead, and Somervell had very nearly perished stumbling down the mountain in the dark. Had it been anyone other than Mallory, such a blunder would have been highly worrisome, indicative perhaps of a loss of mental focus at elevation. But for him it was just typical behavior, suggestive only of his absentmindedness and impatience to get on the move.

Leaving camp, Mallory and Irvine would have donned masks and communicated in hand signals. The oxygen mask would have painfully irritated Sandy's face. Their route would have carried them on a long diagonal ascent to just below the crest of the Northeast Ridge; at 27,760 feet they rested and dropped a gas cylinder. From this point they could have traversed to follow Norton's route up the couloir or continued up to the ridge. Mallory naturally chose the skyline.

To reach the Northeast Ridge from Camp VI, Mallory and Irvine would have moved up and through angled sandstone slabs on a slow ascending traverse that would have brought them to the top of the Yellow Band and left them on the ridge at the foot of a distinctive face of darker rock, which itself was the base of a higher strata of black stone, much steeper than the Yellow Band, that ran across the North Face. Beyond this tower, the First Step, the Northeast Ridge continues upward until challenged by the Second Step, an even more formidable barrier, a vertical cliff 100 feet high. Once these hazards are overcome, the way to the summit is free and open, with no serious obstacles, save exhaustion, elevation, and exposure.

ODELL HAD SLEPT WELL at Camp V. He woke at 6:00 a.m. and was off two hours later up the mountain, carrying a light pack—mostly food and drink for Mallory and Irvine, but no oxygen. The dawn had been clear, but as he rose up the Northeast Shoulder, mist rolled in from the west. The sky beyond was luminous, leaving him hopeful that the summit remained free of clouds. He assumed that Mallory and Irvine were well on their way, perhaps even climbing the final pyramid. If so, it implied they had found a way up or around the two daunting impediments that had intimidated Norton and kept him and Somervell away from the skyline.

Supremely confident in Irvine's strength and endurance and Mallory's ability as a rock climber, Odell lingered in support, in no particular hurry to go anywhere. Feeling wonderfully fit despite his many days at altitude, he left the Northeast Shoulder and drifted across the North Face, examining the geology of the mountain, the great "variety of gneisses," as he reported, "highly altered limestones and igneous intrusions of light granitoid rocks." At nearly 26,000 feet he came upon a small crag perhaps a hundred feet high, easily avoided but nevertheless tempting—a chance, he thought, to test his conditioning. Just as he reached the top, the sky lifted, the mist dissipated, and he had an unexpected glimpse of the Northeast Ridge. What he saw, or claimed to see, would be challenged for the rest of his life, to a point of such madness that he himself in time would equivocate, qualify, and reimagine the vision that unfolded before his eyes.

In his diary, there is no indication of doubt: "At 12:50 saw M & I on ridge nearing base of final pyramid." Writing only days later in a formal dispatch from the mountain, again with the clarity of immediate and unimpeded memory, Odell reported, "There was a sudden clearing of the atmosphere, and the entire summit ridge and final peak of Everest were unveiled. My eyes became fixed on one tiny black spot silhouetted on a small snow crest beneath a rock step in the ridge; the black spot moved. Another black spot became apparent and moved up the snow to join the other on the crest. The first then approached the great rock step and shortly emerged on top; the second did likewise. Then the whole fascinating vision vanished, enveloped in cloud once more.

"There was but one explanation." Odell continued. "It was Mallory and his companion moving, as I could see even at that great distance, with considerable alacrity, realizing doubtless that they had none too many hours of daylight to reach the summit from their present position and return to Camp VI by nightfall. The place on the ridge referred to is the prominent rock step at a very short distance from the base of the final pyramid, and it is remarkable that they were so late in reaching this place. According to Mallory's schedule, they should have reached it several hours earlier if they had started from the high camp as anticipated."

Odell dropped off his isolated rocky crag, elated yet still confused. Clearly, according to his ocular testimony, what he saw and believed in the moment was that Mallory and Irvine had reached the top of the Second Step and were still moving upward on the mountain. They were unexpectedly, even dangerously, behind schedule. What might have held them back was anyone's guess. But if they were indeed beyond the Second Step, as Odell reported, though the hour was late, they would still have had time to reach the summit, assuming they could gain roughly 650 feet in elevation in the remaining hours of daylight.

Coming down would be another matter, and that was the immediate concern that propelled Odell farther up the mountain. The weather had closed in with a vengeance, a drop of pressure so sudden as to squeeze the breath out of stones. Odell climbed into the teeth of a squall that became ever more violent the higher he went. After an hour he managed to find Mallory and Irvine's highest camp, Camp VI, even as the visibility dropped to nil. He entered their tent, searching for a sign, a note or clue that might indicate Mallory's intentions or suggest why they had been so slow getting off in the morning. He found only some food and an oxygen cylinder. Perhaps, he thought, they had used gas to sleep; otherwise the equipment would have been left outside the tent. Discarded parts of a regulator scattered haphazardly about the floor suggested a repair; possibly Irvine had brought the apparatus into the tent to make adjustments, again delaying their advance.

The wind pounded the canvas; the flaps beat like gunfire. He waited an hour. Then, fearing that Mallory and Irvine might be unable to find their camp, Odell went back into the storm and climbed another 200 feet up toward the ridge. He cried out and yodeled, but the driving sleet swept away his voice. He took shelter behind a rock and waited. After another hour, he had no choice but to retreat. It was now late afternoon. Just as he reached the tent, the wind abated. The squall passed, and in the wake of the storm a golden light swept the entire upper face of Everest. He scanned the summit ridge, the dark face and the Yellow Band below. All he could see was freshly fallen snow evaporating before his eyes, a gossamer veil rising off the body of the mountain.

Odell faced an agonizing decision. His every climber's instinct urged him to stay, ready to help the men upon their return. If only he had carried with him a small tent; he readily could have managed the ten-pound weight. But now he had no option but to abandon their camp. There was no room in a small Meade for three men. The thought that Mallory and Irvine might not return was too terrible to contemplate; Odell did not even consider the possibility.

At 4:30 p.m., having placed Mallory's compass conspicuously in a corner of the tent, he closed the flaps and made his way down the crest of the ridge. Frequently, upon his descent, he glanced back in bright sun without once seeing a hint of a man following behind. Reaching Camp V at 6:15 p.m., he could find no reason to linger. There was no food or fuel, no stove. He hurried off the mountain in a series of glissades that brought him in thirty minutes all the way to the North Col.

At Camp IV Hazard waited with tea and hot soup. Odell, famished and parched, shared only good news. The weather had come and gone, and there had been delays, but he was convinced that Mallory and Irvine had made the top and would soon be seen coming down triumphantly to Camp VI. He and Hazard stayed up throughout the night, keeping watch, straining their eyes for a sign—the light of a torch, a candle, one of the magnesium flares that each climber normally carried. "The feeble glow that after sunset pervaded the great dark mountain face above us was later lost in filtered moonlight reflected from the high summits of the West Rongbuk," Odell wrote. Perhaps, he thought, the moonlight would help them, if by chance some unforeseen event had occurred.

ON THE MORNING of June 8, the day of Mallory and Irvine's last ascent, John Noel sat on a promontory just above Camp III, his long telephoto lens focused on the summit pyramid three miles away, as Mallory's note had instructed. Eight o'clock came and went without a sign. By 10:00 a.m. clouds and mist had rolled over the mountain, enshrouding the Northeast Ridge and obscuring all but a faint luminous shadow of the summit itself. By noon it was hopeless. Noel, stiff with cold, crawled out of his eagle's nest, as he called his favorite perch, and made his way back to Camp III. In the mess tent he found Norton dictating a dispatch for the *Times* to Geoffrey Bruce. At Norton's request Somervell later added a personal note: "We now await news of Mallory and Irvine who today are making another attempt hoping that they may reinforce the feeble summit air by artificially provided oxygen, and by that means be enabled to conquer the chief difficulty of reaching the summit. May the Genie of the Steel Bottle aid them! All of us are hoping that he may, for nobody deserves the summit more than Mallory, the only one of our number who has been at it for three years."

These were generous words, and hardly the sentiments of one concerned for the plight of a close friend. Outwardly, the men at Camp III remained sanguine; few dared contemplate disaster. "Eyes glued to the mountain," Hingston wrote. "There is just a chance of Mallory and Irvine getting to the summit. But the clouds today have been very thick. Only on occasions and for momentary intervals do we happen to see the final pyramid through the mist. We have, therefore, seen nothing of the climb and can only hope for the best. There is no sign of their having returned as yet to Camp IV. Whatever happens this must be the last attempt and in a few days we shall be leaving these high camps."

Norton was the exception. Throughout the day, as John Noel recalled, the expedition leader "paced backwards and forwards in front of his tent, speaking little, visibly affected and I think already resigned to the worst." At midday Norton ordered Hingston to ready all medical supplies and be prepared to launch a relief effort to the col. He dictated a furious reprimand for Hazard, still at Camp IV. "I am writing this for Norton," Bruce wrote, "whose eyes are still bad. He cannot understand why you sent down all except one man yesterday evening, as it is hard to see what good you can be with one man if there is trouble up the mountain. You are to keep these two men and the one you already have with you until the last Sahib is off the mountain; as in the case of snowblindness, frostbite, broken leg etc. it takes at least 3 men to get a casualty off the N. Col. Re: Evacuation. Not one single stitch of anything need be brought down from Camp IV. The whole thing is to get away safe and quick."

By the morning of Monday, June 9, there had been no sign of either Mallory or Irvine since Odell's fleeting glimpse at 12:50 p.m. the previous day. The only hope was that somehow they had slipped back unseen to Camp VI; the chances of surviving a bivouac higher on the mountain were slim to nil. At 11:00 a.m. Norton dispatched a second note to the North Col, addressed to Odell, saying, "The absence of a signal from you spells disaster I fear." He instructed Odell to keep watch on the mountain, most especially the Northeast Ridge up to Camp VI, throughout the day, posting a sentry for two hours after dark. No one, he stressed, should climb toward the rescue unless fully capable of returning to Camp IV the same day. Odell was to remain in support until 4:00 p.m. the following day. "I send you this principally to give you a definite time limit," he wrote, "and for you to clearly understand that the guiding principle must be not to risk a single other life English or Tibetan on the remote chance of retrieving the inevitable. You are the man on the spot and within these limits must use your own discretion. Your position is a most trying one old boy and I fully sympathize with you. Excuse writing as my thumb is frostbitten."

Noel, meanwhile, had erected his telescope in the middle of camp, with men posted in shifts to scan the upper slopes during every daylight moment. No sooner had the porter carrying Norton's second note reached the base of the North Col than three figures were spotted above Camp IV, heading up the mountain.

Odell and Hazard had been up since before first light, glassing the summit approaches with Irvine's binoculars. They'd begun to fear the worst. They'd improvised a series of signals: a code of flashes if by night, a spread of sleeping bags by day. Without awaiting instructions from Norton, Odell and two porters, Nima Tundrup and Mingma, had headed up for Camp V at 12:10 p.m., arriving at 3:25 p.m., an extraordinary rate of climb of 600 feet an hour. The camp was precisely as Odell had left it. Everything now depended on what would come with the dawn. "Nothing further of Mallory and Irvine," Odell scratched in his diary. "One's sole hopes rested," he later wrote, "on Camp VI though in the absence of any signal from here earlier in the day, the prospects could not but be black."

Hingston described the tension that night at Camp III: "A most anxious day. Not a sign of Mallory and Irvine. At the latest they should have been at Camp IV this morning, but there is no trace of them as yet. The condition of the mountain has changed for the worse. For most of the day it has been in cloud with every indication of a bitter wind. Everything points to a fatality, which would be a disastrous ending to the affair. Norton is of the same opinion. He has sent instructions to Odell on the North Col to do what is possible in the way of a search. But he is loath to involve more people in the mountain especially as there is indication of the approach of the monsoon."

Norton, Bruce, Hingston, and Noel huddled near the Whymper tent that served as their mess. Noel wrote, "Now and then we called over to the watchers on the telescope, 'Kutch Dekta?' Do you see anything? The men turned and shook their heads each time: Kutch Nahin, Sahib. Nothing at all, Sir. Two whole days and nights had now gone, with hope fading at every hour." That afternoon Shebbeare arrived from Camp II with a team of Sherpas, ready to begin the evacuation of the mountain.

At Camp V the weather closed in. "The cold was intense," Odell recalled, "aggravated by high wind." Though inside a tent, fully dressed, dry, and covered in two sleeping bags, he shivered through a miserable night, too chilled to sleep. He shuddered to think of men alone, exposed to the elements. By morning, Nima and Mingma were useless; he sent them down to Camp IV with a note for Hazard, indicating that he would proceed up to Camp VI, returning to the North Col by dark. He reached the higher camp shortly after 11:00 a.m. and, to his despair, found it precisely as he had left it: strewn with a small assortment of provisions, bits and pieces of the oxygen apparatus, a single cylinder, and, in the corner, Mallory's compass, just where he had placed it. Some part of him knew his companions were gone, but he pushed farther up the mountain and waited for two hours, his shouts echoing off the stones.

"The upper part of Everest," he later reflected, "must be indeed the remotest and least hospitable place on earth, but at no time more emphatically and impressively so than when a darkened atmosphere hides its features and a gale races over its cruel face. And how and when more cruel could it ever seem than when balking one's every step to find one's friends. After struggling on for nearly two hours looking in vain for some indication or clue, I realized that the chances of finding the missing ones were indeed small on such a vast expanse of crags and broken slabs and that for any more extensive search toward the final pyramid a further party would have to be organized."

Odell turned his back on the summit ridge and slowly walked back to Camp VI. "With a great effort," he reported, "I dragged the two sleeping bags from the tent and up the precipitous rocks behind to a steep snow-patch plastered on a bluff of rocks above . . . It needed all my efforts to cut steps out over the steep snow slope and then fix the sleeping bags in position, so boisterous was the wind." At 2:10 p.m., 4,000 feet below on the North Col, Hazard saw the signal, a dark T against the snow; this meant "No trace can be found, given up hope, awaiting orders." Five minutes later Hazard relayed the message to Camp III, using six blankets in the form of a cross, placed on the surface of the snow; it was the message of death. Noel, at his telescope, spotted it first. Geoffrey Bruce asked him what he had seen. Noel could not bring himself to speak. They both looked again "and tried," Noel recollected, "to make the signal different, but we couldn't." Finally they told Norton, who hesitated for ten empty and endless minutes before ordering three rows of blankets to be arranged in response: "Abandon search. Return as soon as possible." Hazard acknowledged receipt of the order by removing the blankets he had laid in the snow. He then signaled Odell: "All right. Return."

ODELL TOOK Mallory's compass and the oxygen apparatus from Camp VI, proof that his young protégé Sandy Irvine had remained devoted to his mission until the last, and then closed the flaps of the tent. His final diary entry for the day reads: "No trace found. Left some provisions in tent, closed it up & came down ridge in violent wind & didn't call at V."

Odell later wrote of his long, mournful descent to the North Col: "I glanced up at the mighty summit above me, which ever and anon deigned to reveal its cloud-wreathed features. It seemed to look down with cold indifference on me, mere puny man, and howl derision in wind gusts at my petition to yield up its secret—this mystery of my friends. What right had we to venture thus far into the holy presence of the Supreme Goddess? If it were indeed the sacred ground of Cho-molungma, had we violated it, was I now violating it?"

But then he sensed a shift:

And yet, as I gazed again another mood appeared to creep over her haunting features. There seemed to be something alluring in that towering presence. I was almost fascinated. I realized that no mere mountaineer alone could but be fascinated, that he who approaches close must ever be led on, and oblivious of all obstacles seek to reach that most sacred and highest place of all. It seemed that my friends must have been thus enchanted also; for why else should they tarry? In an effort to suppress my feelings, I turned my gaze downwards to the North Col far below, and I remembered that other of my companions would be anxiously awaiting my return eager to hear what tidings I car-ried. How then could I justify my wish, in face of such anxiety, to remain here the night, and prolong my search the next day? And what hope, if I did, of finding them alive? Alone and in medita-tion I slowly commenced my long descent.

Odell reached Camp IV safely just after 5:00 p.m., finding only Hazard and the Sherpas Nima and Mingma. The following morn-ing, June 11, leaving behind tents and all equipment, they abandoned Camp IV, bringing down from the North Col only their exhausted selves and the personal effects of the two missing climbers. The tem-perature, Hazard remembered, in the sun was eighty-seven degrees Fahrenheit; the clouds were light, with high winds above, the moun-tain smoking all along the ridge.

Norton had ordered the immediate evacuation of Camp III. He, Bruce, and Noel had left the previous afternoon, as soon as the fate of Mallory and Irvine was certain. No one would be tempted out of sentiment to search for the bodies or launch a quixotic and dangerous rescue effort. Somervell was already down at base camp, along with Beetham. Hingston alone awaited Odell and Hazard at Camp III. As medical officer he wanted them all off the mountain. "They all badly need a rest," Hingston wrote, "and are no longer needed at Camp III. I shall not be sorry to leave this spot. If only we abandoned it under hap-pier conditions. Everest is a most dangerous mountain. In three expe-ditions it has claimed twelve victims. It is just possible that Mallory and Irvine may have climbed it. Odell last saw them at about 800 feet from the summit and going strong for the top. We are all heartily sick of the business by now. No one is fit to stay here any longer, much less to make another attempt. Everyone has lost a great deal of weight. We must get down to lower altitudes and recuperate in some green spot."

Even as Odell and Hazard were heading down from Camp IV, Shebbeare arrived at Camp III with twenty-eight porters and orders to destroy the camp. At 1:00 p.m., carrying only essentials, the convoy headed down the East Rongbuk Glacier. "It was a fine descent," Hingston wrote, "through the fantastic iceberg scenery, which I have already described. The porters care little for the weight of their loads since they are now on the downhill path."

Odell's diary entry for Thursday, June 12, but two days removed from the final acknowledgment of their loss, reads in its entirety: "Lovely a.m. Left Camp II 9:30 with Hingston and Shebbeare, glorious walk down good moraine track; had tiffin at Camp I and continued to Base Camp via upper moraine and visited stone polygons with Hingston; lovely spring alpine flowers here and there from Camp I."

Odell's performance had been nothing less than heroic. Since May 31, when Norton had rallied the men for a third series of attacks on the summit, the final campaign, Odell had climbed from the base of the North Col to Camp IV, at 23,000 feet, three times. From Camp IV he had gone once to Camp V (25,300 feet) and from Camp IV to Camp VI (26,800 feet) twice over four consecutive days. In twelve days he had slept only one night below 23,000 feet. For nearly a fortnight he had thus lived at elevations higher than science had believed possible. His reward, as Norton would write in a final dispatch, was to have been the last to see their friends, "going strong for the top." He was convinced, according to Hingston, that Mallory and Irvine had reached the summit, only to die from exposure upon their return. It was pure speculation, Hingston acknowledged, but it satisfied Odell, who never wavered in his conviction that they had achieved their highest goal. They were dead, and as he walked off the mountain, there was nothing more to say, think, or feel.

At base camp, Somervell found the news hard to accept, writing, "My friend and fellow-climber, Mallory, one in spirit with me, dead? I found it difficult to believe." There were only two possibilities, he later added: "accident or benightedment. It is terrible. But there are few better deaths than to die in high endeavor, and Everest is the finest cenotaph in the world."

Odell was relieved to be back at base camp, as was Hingston. "It was a luxury," the doctor wrote on June 12, "to have a chair to sit on and a camp bed on which to sleep at night." The following morning,

Norton asked Odell to sort through the personal effects of the dead, selecting what should be returned to family in England and what left to burn. Odell's diary entry reads, again in its entirety: "Had lovely night in camp bed and first bath in a month. Lovely day. Sorted out Mallory and Irvine's kit most of the day. Others prepared memorial for the casualties of the three expeditions. Noel took our photos as ever."

As Somervell and Beetham worked on the memorial, a great cairn of stones with the names of all the dead chiseled with screwdrivers into the rock, Norton busied himself with dispatches. The most urgent went out in code, by runner for the distant telegraph lines at Phari: "Obterras London—Mallory Irvine Nove Remainder Alcedo—Norton Rongbuk." It would be wired from Phari on June 19 at 4:50 p.m. By Saturday morning, June 21, all of London would know that George Mallory had died on June 8, ten days before his thirty-eighth birthday, along with his young companion, Andrew Irvine.

At base camp Norton ordered Hingston to examine all of the survivors. Their condition was as expected. "There was no question of any further resumption of hostilities on the mountain," Norton later wrote. "At my request Hingston examined the whole party and reported that without exception all those who had been above Camp IV had their hearts distended . . . he warned us that further exertions at high altitudes would be liable to cause serious and permanent disability."

Norton sent two additional reports by telegraph for London on June 13. First to the Everest Committee: "Our attempts for the year are definitely finished. I enclose a medical report on the six remaining climbers. All are entirely hors de combat for high climbing, and the same applies to the porters." The second wire was addressed personally to Younghusband and Hinks: "I am afraid I can report success in no respect; for not only have we failed to establish a definite claim to have climbed the mountain—the point must always remain in doubt—but Mallory and Irvine have been killed and two of our native establishment have died." On the very day he dispatched these reports, a new post arrived by runner. Among the mail was a packet of letters addressed to Norton wishing the expedition all success on their last climb.

On Sunday, June 15, Norton ordered all surplus supplies and equipment to be burned. Late in the day the climbers and all the porters gathered around the memorial cairn. It was an extraordinary monument, a square plinth of stones three feet high, with a pyramid of small boulders rising higher than a man, and all the names of the dead inscribed: 1921 Kellas, 1922 Thankay, Sangay, Temba, Lhakpa, Pasang Namgyn, Norbu, and Pema, 1924 Mallory and Irvine, Shamsherpun and Manbahadur. It stood on an open moraine against the backdrop of Everest, the North Face.

That evening several of the men visited the Rongbuk Monastery, slipping into the prayer hall in the middle of a service. Beetham later wrote,

> Hitherto we had felt nothing but repulsion for the lamas: their mode of life and everything that pertained to them. We were therefore hardly in a mood to be prepossessed. Yet it must be admitted that that was one of the most impressive, the most moving services I, for one, have ever attended. Perhaps it was the unexpectedness of the whole thing, and especially of the worshippers' profound devotion. In any case it must have been only an appeal to eye and ear, and not to the conscious mind, for we could not understand one word of what was said. It was an instinctive acquiescence in their earnest consecration. The building was in such darkness that at first we could see nothing, but as the eyes grew accustomed to the gloom, row upon row of lamas were revealed seated motionless as images upon the floor. Only the unimpassioned faces of the lamas chanting the deep guttural prayers appeared, their crouching bodies, swathed in dark togas, remained unseen. Such light as entered illuminated the faces of the idol-buddhas and filtered down between a maze of old silken banners reaching from the roof nearly to the worshippers. The music was supplied by a large number of deep drums, cymbals and some reed instruments, and as it rose and fell the air vibrated as with an organ. At intervals the worship ceased, and tea was brought round by little boys; then the service was resumed.

On Monday, June 16, the expedition departed Rongbuk. "We were a sad little party," Norton later wrote. "From the first we accepted the loss of our comrades in that rational spirit which all our generation had learnt in the Great War, and there was never any tendency to a morbid harping on the irrevocable. But the tragedy was very near. As so constantly in the war, so here in our mimic campaign Death had taken his toll from the best."

THAT NIGHT, in the wake of their march away from the mountain, they camped high by the Dzakar Chu, on a hill at 18,000 feet overlooking the Rongbuk Valley and all of the glory of Everest. One of the men gazed out from his tent and spoke for all when he later recalled:

I could see the whole of the historic ground, the scene of the protracted adventure, spread out like a map and bathed in soft full moonlight. And what a strange impelling light it is! By daylight we view matters in an eminently earthly, worldly aspect; moonlight seems to bring us face to face with greater and more lasting ideas; it lends a touch of the supernatural to our vision. That night and with that scene in front of one, it was quite easy to realize that the price of life is death, and that, so long as the payment be made promptly, it matters little to the individual when the payment is made. Somewhere up there, in that vast wilderness of ice and rock, were two still forms. Yesterday, with all the vigour and will of perfect manhood, they were playing a great game—their life's desire. Today it is over, and they had gone, without their ever knowing the beginnings of decay. Could any man desire a better end?

Epilogue

COLONEL NORTON'S MESSAGE acknowledging the death of Mallory and Irvine took eight days to pass by runner overland to Phari and eight hours to circle the globe by telegraph to London. The cable reached Arthur Hinks at the Royal Geographical Society on the afternoon of Thursday, June 19, just as he returned to his office from a late lunch at his club. Nothing had been heard from the expedition since Norton's dispatch of May 26, written on the eve of the final campaign. Hinks eagerly tore open the telegram, keenly anticipating the phrase "Voiceful Lud benighted Charles," prearranged code indicating that the summit of Everest had been achieved. His eyes fell instead on nine words. He knew from the length of the text alone that the expedition had ended in disaster.

The secretary informed the *Times*, but kept the news from the families for nearly twenty-four hours. Sandy Irvine's mother and his two youngest brothers were on holiday at their cottage in Wales; his father was home in Birkenhead. The telegram from Hinks arrived just after 7:00 p.m. on Friday evening. It read: "Committee deeply regret receive bad news Everest Expedition today Norton cables your Son and Mallory killed last climb remainder return safe President and Committee offer heartfelt sympathy Hinks."

The wording of Hinks's telegram to Ruth Mallory was the same, save for a shift in the order of names; he concealed from her, too, that he had known of the deaths since the previous day. His wire reached Herschel House, in Cambridge, at 7:45 p.m. A journalist from the *Times* got there first. The editors wanted to spare Ruth the shock and indignity of learning of her husband's death in the morning paper. She went out for a walk with old friends, and then returned home to gather her three children into her bed. She told them what had happened. Curled under the covers, they "all cried together."

Despite the efforts of the RGS, Hinks, and the *Times* to embargo the news, the story broke that night in the *Westminster Gazette*. The following morning, Saturday, the *Times* rushed into print its world exclusive: "Mt. Everest Tragedy, Two Climbers Killed, Fate of Mr. Mallory and Mr. Irvine." By afternoon the language of war once again dominated headlines throughout the country. "Mallory and Irvine Killed in the Final Assault," proclaimed the *Daily Graphic*. "The Grim Tragedy," read the *Sphere*. "The Fight with Everest," "Triumph Frustrated by Death," "The Battle with Everest: The Mountain's Heavy Toll," declared others. Obituaries ran alongside the news; they had been prepared well in advance. "I knew long ago that this was going to happen," wrote Geoffrey Keynes in a mournful letter to Ruth, "but that doesn't make the fact any easier to bear."

A formal message from the king appeared in the *Times* on Monday, June 23, expressing support for the families and heralding the heroic efforts of the "two gallant explorers." On Tuesday students and teachers at Cambridge gathered at Magdalene College Chapel. Younghusband went up from London for the memorial, as did Hinks and Spencer. Two days later, the bishop of Chester addressed a service at St. John's Church in Birkenhead, attended by both the Mallory and the Irvine families. Throughout the country the outpouring of concern and grief was intense and beyond all expectations. "We have been overwhelmed," Hinks wrote to Norton on June 26, "with telegrams and messages of sympathy from the King, from many geographical societies and climbing clubs all over the world and from numbers of individuals in this country. The papers have vied with one another in paying their respect to the glorious memory of Mallory and Irvine."

Attention soon turned to the question on everyone's mind. Had Mallory and Irvine died on their way up the mountain or upon their descent? Had they achieved their highest goal or slipped into the void having failed to reach what Mallory had long called the "summit of our desires"?

In the immediate wake of the tragedy, Norton had moved to forestall idle speculation. At a conference at base camp on June 12, he, along with Somervell and Bruce, Hazard, Beetham, Noel, and Shebbeare, had agreed to hold firm to the opinion that the two climbers, roped together, had suffered a fatal fall. Odell alone maintained that Mallory and Irvine had died of exposure, trapped in a bivouac somewhere above Camp VI. This was unlikely yet, for Odell, reassuring. He felt responsible for Irvine's fate. Upon his return to London in September, he would stay with his own wife and child for little more than a day before traveling to Birkenhead to visit and console Sandy's parents. It was comforting to believe that his young protégé did not lie broken and bloody on the rocks of Rongbuk, but rather had died a painless death, his unblemished body wrapped and numbed by the cold, his older companion silent by his side. In Odell's grief, mercy did not demand truth.

As for the summit, it was anybody's guess. Norton and Somervell had deliberately stayed well below the Northeast Ridge, traversing the entire breadth of the Yellow Band to reach the couloir and avoid the Second Step. Odell had been at least 2,000 feet below the skyline when he had last seen Mallory and Irvine alive. They had vanished in a world known only to them.

AND SO, as in war, the survivors simply moved on; Noel headed directly to Darjeeling to work on his second Everest film, Hazard back up the West Rongbuk to complete mapping work with the Gurkha surveyor Hari Singh Thapa, Norton and the others to the Rongshar Valley for rest and recuperation before beginning the long journey home to Darjeeling. "I feel the loss of Mallory and Irvine very much," Norton wrote to Sydney Spencer on June 28. "I wish one could know whether they succeeded or not before the end."

In London, where Spencer received Norton's letter at the Alpine Club, such uncertainty was unbearable, given the nobility of the effort and the agony of the loss. On July 5 the *Times* published Norton and Odell's dispatch of June 14, the first account sent from Rongbuk in the wake of the tragedy. "We leave here with heavy hearts," Norton wrote. "We failed to establish success, for who will ever know whether the lost climbers reached the summit before the accident which caused their death." Just this hint of doubt gave editors at the *Times* license to run the story under the headline "Everest: The Last Climb: Hopes That Summit Was Reached." Odell went much further than Norton. "Has Everest been climbed?" he asked with deliberate flourish. "It will ever be a mystery." He then added, "Considering all the circumstances and the position they had reached on the mountain I personally am of the opinion that Mallory and Irvine must have reached the summit."

Odell gave people what they wanted to hear, but his choice of language was curious. He did not state directly that the climbers had reached the summit; he expressed his conviction that they *must* have done so. This wishful sentiment matched the mood of the nation. "In this country," declared an editorial in the *Times*, "which owes its very existence and its vast Empire to the adventurous spirit of its sons, there should be no room for feeble reflections." Mallory and Irvine had clearly stood "above everything in the world," with a "glimpse almost of god's view of things." Mallory, as Norton himself acknowledged, was no mere mortal. "It was the spirit of the man," the colonel said, "that made him the great mountaineer he was; a fire burnt in him and caused his willing spirit to rise superior to the weakness of the flesh; he lived on his nerves . . . The conquest of the mountain became an obsession with him, and for weeks and months he devoted his whole time and energy to it." That he and Irvine had perished without final victory was simply inconceivable.

Even as the expedition's survivors slowly made their way back to India, the men exhausted and beyond reach, their full stories yet to have been told, the leading figures of British mountaineering rallied in defense of Mallory's honor, convinced that the summit had indeed been conquered. Writing from Darjeeling on July 11, General Bruce endorsed Odell's "very reasonable opinion that the top was reached and that M and I were overtaken on their way back, probably by dark . . . It's dreadful, heartbreaking but wonderful." A week later Martin Conway argued in the *Times* that their failure to return safely was itself proof that they had reached the summit; otherwise they would have retreated in time to get back to their highest camp.

"It's obvious to any climber that they got up," Tom Longstaff told Hinks. "You cannot expect of that pair to weigh the chances of return . . . Nothing could have stopped these two with the goal well in their grasp." Francis Younghusband invoked the metaphysical. Everest, he declared, was the embodiment of the physical forces of the world. Against it the climbers had only, as Norton had suggested, "the spirit of man." But this, he implied, was enough. "Of the two alternatives, to turn back a third time, or to die, the latter was for Mallory probably the easier. The agony of the first would be more than he as a man, as a mountaineer, and as an artist, could endure." Geoffrey Young, in France when the news broke in London, spoke with unique authority: "Difficult as it would have been for any mountaineer to turn back with the only difficulty past—to Mallory it would have been an impossibility . . . my own opinion [is] that the accident occurred on the way down and that if that is so, the peak was first climbed, because Mallory was Mallory."

In an obituary that ran in the *Nation and Athenaeum* on July 5, Young elevated Mallory into the realm of myth, writing,

> From boyhood he belonged to mountains, as flame belongs to fire . . . In that final magnificent venture against the unknown,

we are thrilled by the knightly purpose, by the evident joyousness of the attempt, as much as by the audacity and endurance. It is the burning spirit of chivalrous, youthful adventure, flaming at the close, higher than the highest summit of the known world. However the end of that great contest came . . . that flame, we know, burned radiantly to the last. George Mallory—Sir Galahad always to his early friends—gave back to the hills their life of inspiration, content. The greatest mountain upon earth is the monument to his clean and selfless use of his rare manhood. While there are hearts to quicken still at tales of heroism, merciless Everest—terrible to us—will remain for them a mountain of beautiful remembrance.

Ruth Mallory was touched by such sentiments, coming from their oldest and closest friend, a man she and George deeply loved and admired. But obituaries and personal letters of condolence did little to soften her pain. Hers was a private grief, fathomless and cruel. All of the climbers on Everest, "every one of them," she noted in a gracious letter to Hinks, had been "heroic beyond words." But she had little interest in public talk of conquest and sacrifice, of nobility and honor in death. Her generation of women had seen too much of it. As one of her well-known contemporaries, Nancy Cooper, had wearily remarked, "By the end of 1916, every boy I had ever danced with was dead."

On July 1, the anniversary of the Somme, Ruth received a letter from Geoffrey Young, his first since learning of the tragedy. He spoke of a "long numbness of pain" even as he acknowledged that his sadness could be "but a shadow of yours, for indeed one cannot think of you separately." He meant, of course, separately from her lover and husband, the boy-man he had described in his eulogy as the "magical and adventurous spirit of youth personified."

"It is not difficult for me to believe," Ruth replied, "that George's spirit was ready for another life and his way of going to it was very beautiful. I do not think this pain matters at all. I have had far more than my share of joy and always shall have had. Isn't it queer how all the time what matters most is to get hold of the rightness of things? Then some sort of peace comes."

Later in the week she sent Young a more anguished note. "I know George did not mean to be killed," she wrote. "I don't think I do feel that his death makes me the least more proud of him. It is his life that I loved and love . . . Whether he got to the top of the mountain or did not, whether he lived or died, makes no difference to my admiration for him . . . Oh Geoffrey, if only it hadn't happened! It so easily might not have."

In later years, long after she had happily remarried, Ruth would slip into her garden alone with a copy of *The Spirit of Man* and read the poems that George had whispered on Everest on cold nights when all thoughts turned to home. She raised her three children not in the shadow of a lost and mythic father but in the spirit in which he had lived: free, unfettered, and open to all the possibilities of life. She succumbed to cancer in 1942, even as George's younger brother, Trafford, commander in chief of Fighter Command, orchestrated the aerial attack that would finally, a generation late, bring Germany to its knees. Like Ruth, Trafford would not survive Hitler's war. En route to India in 1944, his plane crashed in a blizzard in the French Alps. He was buried at Le Rivier d'Allemont, in the shadow of the very peaks that so enchanted George in the innocent years of their youth, before the wars.

PRIVATE GRIEF gave way to national catharsis on October 17, 1924, when King George V and the Prince of Wales, the Duke of York, and the Duke of Connaught joined a sea of mourners at St. Paul's Cathedral for a service in memory of Mallory and Irvine. It was the first and only time in British history that mountaineers had been so honored. The bishop of Chester delivered the eulogy, drawing all eyes to Odell's final sighting, as if it were a collective vision: "That is the last you see of them, and the question as to their reaching the summit is still unanswered; it will be solved some day. The merciless mountain gives no reply. But that last ascent, with the beautiful mystery of its great enigma, stands for more than an heroic effort to climb a mountain, even though it be the highest in the world."

That evening Lord Ronaldshay presided over a joint meeting of the Royal Geographical Society and the Alpine Club, held as a memorial at the Royal Albert Hall. All the leading figures in the Everest adventure were there: Francis Younghusband, Arthur Hinks and General Bruce, Douglas Freshfield, Norman Collie and Sydney Spencer of the Alpine Club, as well as Wollaston and Heron from the 1921 reconnaissance; Longstaff, Strutt, Norton, Geoffrey Bruce, and Finch from 1922; and Hingston, Beetham, Hazard, and Odell from the expedition of 1924.

Norton said of Mallory: "His death leaves us the poorer by a loyal friend, a great mountaineer and a gallant gentleman." Odell remembered the mountain's cold indifference, the wind howling in wild derision as he stumbled down to the North Col, certain at last that his friends were dead. The monsoon, he recalled, broke on the very day they retreated from the Rongbuk Valley. The shadow of Everest's North Face, Hingston had written that night, "never looked larger, more magnificent or more impregnable than when we turned our backs on it today . . . I wonder when the next attack will be made on the mountain."

This was very much an open question. Initially the Everest Committee proceeded as it had in the wake of the two earlier expeditions. Within a week of the memorial service at St. Paul's, Odell spoke at Queen's Hall. Somervell, identified by Hinks and John Buchan as another rising star, was soon delivering as many as three lectures a day, first in London and later at venues throughout the country; he would personally earn some £700, which he later used to purchase an X-ray machine for his Indian mission. The great hope, of course, was commercial success for John Noel's film of the climb, *The Epic of Everest: The Immortal Film Record of This Historic Expedition*, scheduled to debut at the New Scala Theatre in London on December 8.

Since the inception of Explorer Films, incorporated on Christmas Eve 1923, John Noel had been running on nerves. From an initial offering of just two hundred shares at £1 each, the company had grown dramatically, fueled by the promise of the third expedition; by February 1924 Noel's stake alone consisted of 350 preferred and 5,142 deferred shares. His goal, as he wrote to General Bruce, was to produce a film that could compete head-to-head with any movie "in the cinematograph trade," meaning any dramatic feature coming out of Hollywood. It was a bold ambition. His 1922 effort, *Climbing Mount Everest*, had enjoyed only modest success. In 1924 he and his investors had put up £8,000, a small fortune. Much could go wrong. Noel fretted about Somervell's score for the new film, the absence of footage from the higher camps, even the lack of a female star. He considered making two new films: a climbing saga of Everest and a grand travelogue of exotic Tibet. These very different themes morphed into one, somewhat awkwardly, and the pressure mounted. As Noel acknowledged from the start, only something on a scale previously unimagined in the documentary field would "obtain a large enough scope to repay the cost of producing the film. Success will depend virtually on whether the mountain is conquered."

The death of Mallory and Irvine forced Noel to reconfigure the film from heroic triumph to sublime tragedy. As if to distract the audience from the expedition's ultimate failure, he set out to create a total theatrical experience. Hiring a noted set designer, he transformed the stage of the New Scala into a Tibetan courtyard, with painted backdrops of Himalayan peaks illuminated in the haunting half shimmer of dusk. As the picture began, the lights would fade, the temple doors open, and the curtain rise to reveal the flickering drama of another world. For an added touch of authenticity, Noel arranged for John Macdonald to bring from Gyantse seven Tibetan monks, along with full ritual regalia: cymbals, copper horns, handbells and swords, trumpets made from thighbones, and drums crafted from human skulls. The monks, according to Noel's plans, would tour with the film, performing before every screening an overture of religious music and dances, setting the mood, as he put it, with "large doses of local colour."

The arrival of the "seven lamas" from India prompted newspaper coverage not likely to please the Tibetan authorities. Among the headlines in the *Daily Sketch:* "High Dignitaries of Tibetan Church Reach London; Bishop to Dance on Stage; Music from Skulls." On the film's opening night, a dreary Monday, a fog bank swept the length of Tottenham and Charlotte streets, seeping into the theater and disrupting the debut. Returning to their flat following the premiere, John Noel and his wife, Sybille, rather inauspiciously came within fifteen minutes of dying from a gas leak in their kitchen.

Their fortunes improved in the coming days as positive reviews rolled in, not only from *Kinematograph Weekly* and the *Bioscope,* the industry rags of record, but from all the daily papers. Noel's concern about the lack of a female love interest proved unwarranted. The *Weekly Dispatch* identified the mountain itself as the "leading lady," with the film being the story of "man's passionate struggle to conquer the dreadful virgin of the snows." In time *The Epic of Everest* would tour Britain and Germany and crisscross North America seven times; in Canada and the United States alone, more than a million people would see it. Noel's financial gamble paid off, at least in the short term, but the very success of the film doomed any hope for an immediate return to Everest.

Inevitably the production came to the attention of the Tibetan government, which lodged an official diplomatic protest. Ostensibly the offenses were cultural and religious. Aristocratic Lhasa did not take kindly to scenes of local men and women delousing their children and eating the lice. That seven monks had traveled abroad without the permission of their abbot, only to perform rituals onstage like some carnival show, provoked outrage, especially among the conservative monastic factions then ascendant in the Tibetan capital. Noel promoted his film as if it had emerged from a quaint and timeless void. In truth, Lhasa in 1924 teetered on the brink of revolution, with the fate of the nation in the balance.

At the center of the diplomatic firestorm was Morshead's old companion in exploration F. M. Bailey, warrior, diplomat, and spy, who had succeeded Charles Bell as political officer in Sikkim in 1921. If Bell had tolerated the Everest expeditions, Bailey dismissed them as pointless provocations that compromised the key British diplomatic initiative in Tibet, the modernization of the country as a foil to the aspirations of both China and Soviet Russia. The Thirteenth Dalai Lama, personally committed to the path of modernity, was actively opposed by the monastic orders, which wanted no European presence in Lhasa, and certainly no British expeditions marching across the southern frontier of the nation, disturbing the deities and corrupting the people. Tensions in the capital were high, and there was even talk of overthrowing the Dalai Lama, an outcome certain to be disastrous for British interests.

In June 1924, even as Norton and Mallory had made their final plans for Everest, Bailey had traveled to Lhasa, officially to promote trade but with the actual goal of fomenting an uprising against the traditional religious orders. The key players were Tsarong Shapé, commander in chief of the army, and Laden La, the Darjeeling police inspector Bailey had sent to Lhasa some months before with the task of recruiting a two-hundred-man cadre to serve as the core of the rebel force. In the summer of 1924 Bailey himself remained in Lhasa for four weeks, meeting repeatedly with both Tsarong Shapé and the Dalai Lama. It is not clear what transpired, but in the end there would be no revolt. When Bailey returned to Sikkim, Tsarong Shapé joined him in exile, soon to be followed by Laden La. The traditionalists retained power, and a pronounced chill came over diplomatic relations between Tibet and the Raj.

With the Dalai Lama and the liberal factions in the army already on the defensive, Noel's film could not have come at a worse time. The maharaja of Sikkim found the scenes of Tibetans eating lice so insulting that he banned John Noel from his kingdom. The Dalai Lama considered the entire extravaganza an affront to the Buddhist religion and called for the immediate arrest of the seven Gyantse monks who had gone abroad. The prime minister of Tibet sent a formal note to Bailey, demanding their immediate return; he ended his reprimand with a phrase the Everest Committee had hoped never to read: "For the future, we cannot give permission to go to Tibet."

There would be no return to Everest in 1925. Within a year Explorer Films would be out of business. When, in 1926, the Everest Committee again sought permission to mount an expedition, Bailey did not deem it necessary even to forward the request to the Tibetan authorities. What became known as the "Affair of the Dancing Lamas" had profound and lasting political consequences. Reinforcing the strength of the traditionalists, it undercut the reforms of the Thirteenth Dalai Lama, policies that no doubt would have placed Tibet in a much stronger position to cope politically and militarily with the Chinese onslaught of 1949 and the subsequent invasion that led, a decade later, to the death of a free nation.

As for Everest, it would not be until 1933, nine years after the disappearance of Mallory and Irvine, that another British climbing party would reach the base of the North Col. Two of the old veterans went along as transport officers—Colin Crawford from 1922 and E. O. Shebbeare from 1924—but the climbers were of a new generation, Eric Shipton and Percy Wyn-Harris, Bill Wager, Frank Smythe, and Jack Longland, all too young to have known the war. Only the expedition leader, Hugh Ruttledge, might have served, had not a hunting accident kept him on administrative duty in India for the duration of the conflict.

On the mountain that year three men went high: first Harris and Wager, and then Frank Smythe climbing alone the following day. Avoiding Mallory's route along the crest of the Northeast Ridge, they all traversed to the couloir, each managing to ascend just high enough to equal but not surpass Norton's height record of 1924. Nothing so grand would be achieved by subsequent British efforts. The reconnaissance of 1935 barely reached the North Col. An early onset of the monsoon repulsed the 1936 expedition, much to the chagrin of John Morris, who went along to organize transport. In 1938 heavy snow limited all movement; no one climbed higher than 27,300 feet. That Noel Odell, at the age of forty-eight, struggled to within a day of the summit was remarkable, but hardly enough to inspire a nation grown tired of the entire endeavor.

Britain in 1938 was no longer a land of grand imperial gestures. After a decade of stunned silence, scores of novels, memoirs, books of poetry, letters, and diaries had flooded popular culture, redefining the narrative of the war, laying waste to any remaining illusions of glory. The war to end all wars had ended nothing, save certainty, confidence, and hope. The Great Depression had brought such misery that even those financially secure questioned the legitimacy of costly mountaineering expeditions, increasingly viewed as sport, that invariably resulted in failure. If achieving the summit of Everest had at one point been a symbol of imperial redemption, the record of seven unsuccessful attempts was a reminder of national impotence.

The Everest Committee met for the last time on June 14, 1939, eleven weeks before Hitler's invasion of Poland. Arthur Hinks, who had dedicated twenty years of his life to the quest, resigned that day. There was talk of returning to the mountain, and permission was formally sought to launch expeditions in 1940, 1941, and 1942. Hitler's war buried such dreams, and by the time it was over, the Chinese Maoists were poised to take over Tibet and shut down all access to Everest from the north. In 1950, succumbing to pressure from Britain and the United States, Nepal opened its borders. British and Swiss expeditions probed the mountain from the south, along the axis that Mallory and Bullock had scoped in 1921, when they peered down from the heights of the West Rongbuk Glacier to the Khumbu Icefall and the Western Cwm.

In 1953 victory came at last. Arthur Hinks had not lived to see the headlines, made not by Englishmen but by a beekeeper from New Zealand, Edmund Hillary, a farmer from the ultimate frontier of empire, and a bold Nepali Sherpa, Tenzing Norgay, a man not simply ready for history but destined to invert history itself, transforming in a single athletic accomplishment the very definition of what it meant to rule and to be ruled. When Hillary and Norgay first returned to base camp from their triumph, Hillary motioned to Wilfrid Noyce, one of the other British climbers, and said simply, "Wouldn't Mallory be pleased if he knew about this?" A telegram celebrating their success reached London on the eve of the coronation of Queen Elizabeth II. Lest it overshadow the royal pageantry, the announcement was held back from the press for twenty-four hours. Only two people outside of a small inner circle were immediately told the news: the queen mother and Lieutenant Colonel Charles Howard-Bury, whose leadership during the 1921 reconnaissance had set the stage for the ultimate success.

As attention shifted to Nepal and the southern approaches, with Swiss and American expeditions reaching the summit in 1956 and 1963, the story of Mallory and Irvine faded into legend, their fate obscured on the northern side of the mountain, behind a veil of physical and political isolation. Certain clues had emerged, though. In 1933 Wyn-Harris came upon Sandy Irvine's undamaged ice ax some sixty feet below the crest of Northeast Ridge, roughly two hundred yards east of the First Step. The 1933 expedition also located Mallory and Irvine's Camp VI and found inside the tattered remnants of their tent a perfectly functioning electric torch, which Odell had apparently overlooked. If Mallory and Irvine had died of exposure stranded on the mountain at night, Norton had argued, there would surely have been some sign of a light. Evidently the notoriously forgetful Mallory had neglected to carry a torch on the fateful day, just as he had failed to bring his compass or flares.

Everything depended on the accuracy of Odell's last sighting. Had he seen Mallory and Irvine mounting the Second Step, as he'd claimed, or cresting some other rise? The young cadre of British climbers on Everest in the 1930s examined the 100-foot face of the Second Step and dismissed scaling it as impossible. Such opinion hardly deterred Odell. He had climbed with Wyn-Harris, Shipton, and Wager in 1938. Though twenty years their senior, he had outpaced them with little effort. They, on the other hand, as Odell was wont to remind them, had never walked with Mallory, "a man with whom few could live uphill," as Norton had written, "a knight amongst mountaineers and the greatest antagonist that Everest has had—or is likely to have."

So the matter stood for more than half a century. There was every hope but little evidence that Mallory and Irvine had reached the summit before meeting their end. As Sir Edmund Hillary so patiently explained whenever asked his opinion, a good measure of success in mountaineering is surely returning from the adventure alive.

Then, in 1979, a curious report emerged from the north side of the mountain. Ryoten Hasegawa, a member of a Sino-Japanese expedition, casually asked a Chinese climber, Wang Hongbao, whether he had ever seen the body of Maurice Wilson, whose corpse mountaineers sometimes spotted at the foot of the North Col, where he had died in 1934 in his bizarre attempt to climb the mountain alone. Wang spoke no Japanese but through sign language managed to convey that during the Chinese expedition of 1975, he had indeed encountered a dead European dressed in vintage clothing—only not on the North Col but above 26,500 feet, just below the Northeast Ridge, a twenty-minute walk from the Chinese expedition's highest camp. If this was true, the body could only have been that of either Mallory or Irvine. Before Hasegawa could learn more, however, Wang and two other Chinese climbers died the very next day in an avalanche on the North Col.

Over subsequent years dozens of expeditions would attempt Everest, and the mountain would become an open graveyard, littered with more than three hundred corpses, a dead climber for every ten who successfully returned from the summit. Many who went to Everest were familiar with the story of Mallory and Irvine, but few were inclined to exhaust precious resources in a search for evidence of their fate. The first dedicated research expedition was not launched until 1986, when noted Everest historians Tom Holzel and Audrey Salkeld, inspired by Hasegawa's account, joined forces with David Breashears, a veteran of eight Everest expeditions, including five successful summit attempts, in a systematic attempt to locate the site of Wang's reputed discovery. It was known that Howard Somervell had lent Mallory a small Kodak Vest Pocket camera. Technicians had assured Holzel that film frozen even for decades might still be processed. The goal was to find the camera. Unfortunately, weather and the death of one of the expedition's members on the North Col cut short the 1986 expedition before it could examine the rock terrace where the body of the "English dead" was said to lie.

The thread of the mystery was not taken up until 1999, when a young German geologist, Jochen Hemmleb, an acolyte of Salkeld and Holzel's, organized a second search, to mark the seventy-fifth anniversary of the disappearance of the climbers. Known formally as the Mallory and Irvine Research Expedition, the team was composed largely of American climbers under the lead of noted Himalayan guide Eric Simonson, along with filmmakers from the BBC and PBS. Among those recruited for high altitude was Conrad Anker, arguably the finest climber of his generation—indeed, the Mallory of his era, in spirit, character, and deed. At 11:45 a.m. on May 1 Anker would make mountaineering history.

While Jochen Hemmleb, by radio and telescope from base camp, directed the systematic search of a grid determined by the careful study of maps and photographs, Anker drifted out of the zone, following his own intuitions as he studied the lay of the mountain. He looked up to the Northeast Ridge, south toward the Norton Couloir, and moved toward where he believed a body would end up, should a climber fall from the height of the Yellow Band. Between where he was, at roughly 27,000 feet on the north side of the mountain, and the summit there were known to be no fewer than seventeen dead. He soon came upon not one but two corpses, broken and shattered, and in the macabre way of Everest, the clothing and gear alone told him the decade in which each had died. Both were of the modern era, with plastic boots and down parkas.

Then his eye fell upon something white that was not snow, and as he approached more closely he recognized the frozen body of a man, facedown, arms extended as if clinging for survival. The left arm was exposed, the right buried in ice and rock, as was the head. A shock of brown hair stuck out of a leather-flapped helmet. The right leg was badly broken, both the tibia and the fibula. The left leg lay over the right, as if to protect the injury—which, along with the outstretched arms, suggested that the man had still been alive when his body had come to rest. A hobnailed boot on the right foot and the tattered remnants of silk and wool, eight layers altogether, clearly dated the corpse to early British expeditions. The man's buttocks had been eaten away by goraks, Himalayan ravens, and the birds had eviscerated the gut. But the musculature of the back was firm and the skin, though tough as leather, covered a body perfect in form and as white as an Elgin marble.

By prearranged code, Anker radioed news of the find to the other climbers, who as swiftly as possible at such heights converged on the discovery. Initially they assumed the body to be that of Irvine, and they were surprised to find a clothing label marked with Mallory's name. Then it dawned on them that they were in fact at the final resting place of a legend. Wrapped around the midsection of the cadaver was a braided cord of cotton rope, altogether ten feet in length. The frayed end revealed that Mallory and Irvine had not separated on that fateful day, as some theories had suggested, or succumbed to the elements, as Odell had so hopefully maintained, but, rather, had fallen together, each to die violently. It was also possible, of course, that the rope had broken as Irvine belayed Mallory, perhaps down the slabs of the Yellow Band in the dark. Nothing was certain.

What transpired next is a matter of controversy. The expedition maintained that Mallory's body was treated with the utmost dignity, and several of the climbers later confessed to having been emotionally and spiritually overwhelmed by the moment. But the subsequent dissemination of photographs of the corpse to media outlets throughout the world caused considerable offense. Sir Edmund Hillary was appalled that "expedition members should flog off the photograph of this heroic figure." Sir Chris Bonington, himself an Everest legend, told the *Observer*: "Words can't express how disgusted I am. These people don't deserve to be called climbers." Mallory's own grandson remarked, "Frankly it makes me bloody angry. It's like digging for diamonds without having to do any of the digging."

Part of the conflict was a matter of culture. No one really had expected to find Mallory's body, and in retrospect the discovery was due to a combination of luck, Anker's rare sensibilities as a mountaineer, and the fact that snowfall on Everest that year had been unusually slight. Few of the American climbers—young mountain guides such as Jake Norton and Tap Richards, both in their mid-twenties—were media-savvy, and all were thrust overnight into the spotlight. For the British it was one thing that the body of a national hero had been found and, in the eyes of some, exploited by a party of Americans; it was quite another to endure online commentary that was singularly inarticulate and dominated by words such as "awesome." Eric Simonson, an exceptionally fine expedition leader, did not help when, having sold images of Mallory's corpse, he told a magazine reporter, "We all think this is a totally cool picture . . . We were kind of surprised people were bummed." Nor did it soothe British sentiments when, during the May 2 webcast announcing the discovery, he acknowledged his many commercial sponsors in the United States but failed to recognize his British partners on the expedition, including Graham Hoyland, the grandnephew of Howard Somervell, who had been instrumental in securing the participation of the BBC.

Footage shot in the moment of discovery reveals a more complicated scenario than the sanitized version conveyed to the media at the time. No one can expect exhausted climbers in bitter winds at 26,700 feet to perform precision high-altitude archaeology. But the suggestion that the body was handled with deference is a matter of interpretation. For several hours the search party hacked and gouged the frozen ground with ice axes and knives, prying up the limbs, crudely tearing at the clothing, creating the very cloth fragments later so carefully cataloged as rare specimens at base camp. At one point a climber is seen standing on Mallory's left leg as he struggles to prop up the torso of the cadaver. "He's almost free, let's go ahead and free him," says one voice. "There's still some more shit here," comments another. "This is something . . . I think it's frozen fucking closed" ends another exchange.

Clearly, the immediate priority of the team was the excavation of the corpse and the recovery of artifacts. A number of items were found: a broken altimeter, a pair of scissors, a tin of beef lozenges, a box of matches, and a tube of zinc oxide. A pair of goggles tucked into a pocket suggested that the accident had occurred after dark—unless, of course, Mallory, acutely aware of what had happened to Norton the previous day, had elected to carry a spare pair. The climbers found a batch of letters, silk scarves, a pocketknife, but in the end no camera. Cutting away a piece of the skin for DNA analysis, with prior permission from the Mallory descendants, they then in true solemnity and at considerable effort dug stones from the frozen ground and covered the body, committing it with an Anglican prayer and a recitation of the 103rd Psalm, as the family had requested.

On May 16, a fortnight after the news of the discovery had flashed around the world, two members of the expedition, Thom Pollard and Andy Politz, returned to the burial site equipped with a metal detector. Bidding wars in the media had by then increased the price of a single photograph of the corpse to as much as $40,000. Stone by stone they exhumed the grave. Politz removed the hobnailed boot from Mallory's right foot and found a watch in one of his pockets. The hour hand pointed to two. This could imply night or day, or even the possibility that the timepiece had ceased to function and been stashed in the pocket for safekeeping. Perhaps it had survived the fall and wound down after his death. Thom Pollard decided to examine Mallory's face. They pried up the cadaver like a frozen log, and Pollard slithered on his back until his body lay supine beneath that of the corpse. The face, he reported, had been somewhat distorted by the weight of snow over the years but was otherwise perfectly preserved. Mallory's eyes were closed, and a stubble of whiskers covered his chin. Over his left eye was a hole, with two pieces of the skull protruding. Blood could still be seen.

That same day Conrad Anker and Dave Hahn set out for the summit of Everest. Anker had never before been on the mountain and he had already resolved that should he reach the top of the world, he would touch it with his hand but, in deference to Buddhist tradition, not set foot upon the peak. Like any mountaineer, he was drawn inexorably to the highest point, but his quiet purpose was to ascertain whether, before their death, Mallory and Irvine could possibly have traversed the major impediments on the Northeast Ridge, especially the Second Step.

In the days since the discovery of the body, the entire expedition had become charged with speculation. The young climbers, Tap Richards and Jake Norton in particular, identified with Mallory and could not help but imagine that he had made it to the top before dying. Norton proclaimed with 90 percent certainty that the summit had been climbed; Richards suggested somewhat lower but still generous odds. Expedition historian Jochen Hemmleb, who never went above base camp, placed Mallory's chances at fifty-fifty. As he studied, through his telescope, climbers moving up the Northeast Ridge, he determined his angle of sight to be very close to Odell's in 1924. What he saw, albeit from a distance of thousands of feet, led him to believe that Mallory and Irvine had been observed by Odell not overcoming the Second Step but scrambling beyond the Third Step to the actual base of the summit pyramid. Andy Politz, posted far higher on the mountain, scaled the same rocky crag where Odell had stood the last time he'd seen Mallory and Irvine alive. Politz independently came to the same conclusion. If they were right, that would place Mallory and Irvine at 12:50 p.m. on June 8, 1924, within hours of the summit, with little but exhaustion and exposure to impede their progress.

It was of course in the interests of the expedition, which had already electrified the world with one stunning discovery, to prove that Mallory and Irvine had reached the summit of Everest. In all the excitement, it was only natural for the team members to envision success. Anker, by contrast, and to his credit, withheld judgment until he could study the route and know the actual ground as a climber. He had found Mallory's body. He alone would carry the memory of that moment to the summit of the mountain. No climber on Everest in 1999 had a greater desire to learn the truth. His conclusions, carefully crafted and drawn from direct personal experience, resonate with authenticity. Unless and until further discoveries are made, they must surely be considered definitive.

Anker's reservations are several. First, there is the matter of clothing and equipment. Mallory and Irvine had primitive crampons, but they could not use them at high elevation, as the leather straps impaired their circulation and increased the risk of frostbite. On his summit climb Anker found crampons essential; he never removed them, even on the rock face of the Second Step. He and his companion, Dave Hahn, also had the advantage of fixed ropes, which greatly facilitated route finding and the speed, ease, and safety of descent. All of their climbing ropes were made of nylon, with a breaking strength seven times that of the cotton weaves used by the British in the 1920s. Anker had modern climbing aids, a rack of cams and stoppers; Mallory lacked even metal pitons. Both teams climbed with oxygen, but Anker's apparatus weighed fourteen pounds, Mallory's over thirty. Mallory wore seven, perhaps eight, layers of thin silk and wool. Anker had double fleece, a wind parka, and a full down suit with four inches of insulation. In place of leather and hobnails, he had thick nylon boots insulated with closed-cell foam. Mallory covered his head with a leather helmet snitched from the Royal Air Force. Anker had a wool knit hat and a thick down hood engineered into his parka. Despite all of this protection, Anker still suffered from the cold, unless he was moving; he found it difficult to imagine how Mallory had managed.

From the accounts of 1924 it is clear that Mallory and Irvine began their last climb physically depleted. They had lost their stove. Limited in their ability to melt snow, they set out for the summit already severely dehydrated. Irvine suffered terribly from the sun; his entire face was blistered and raw. That they left a torch in their tent suggests that they began their day after sunrise; Anker and Hahn, by contrast, set out in the early hours of the morning, at 2:00 a.m., and returned from their successful summit attempt only at 9:15 p.m., well after dark. They both found the route up the Northeast Ridge daunting, a knife edge of ice and rock, exposed on one side to the Kangshung Face, a drop of 10,000 feet, and on the other, after a fall of a mere 9,000 feet, to the North Face. Hahn, a highly accomplished mountaineer and in time a veteran of no fewer than twelve successful Everest summit attempts, by his own admission struggled much of the day, becoming both mentally and physically exhausted. Casting no judgment, neither he nor Anker could imagine what it must have been like for Sandy Irvine, whose experience was so limited.

But the final proof lay in the severity of the Second Step. In 1975 a Chinese expedition had secured an aluminum ladder over the steepest and most perilous pitch. Anker's goal was to climb without making use of this artificial aid, facing the challenge just as Mallory would have done in 1924. The initial ascent of some 45 feet he rated as moderately difficult but not extreme: no trouble for Mallory, though possibly beyond Irvine's abilities. But the next pitch, including the crack crossed by the ladder, was vertical rock, formidably difficult. Anker tried but was unable to free-climb it; the position of the ladder obliged him to set one foot on a rung. He later graded it a "solid 5.10," a technical rating implying a rock challenge far more difficult than anything being attempted by British climbers in Wales or elsewhere in the 1920s. That Mallory and Irvine might have overcome such a pitch, a climb made doubly perilous by an exposure of 8,000 feet, defied belief. And even had they done so, it was not clear how they could have returned. Conrad and Hahn, like all modern climbers on the Northeast Ridge, counted on rappelling down the Second Step, their rope anchored to a large and prominent boulder at the top of the final pitch. The climbing ropes available to Mallory and Irvine were neither strong nor long enough for such a rappel. Had they surmounted the Second Step, Mallory and Irvine would have been forced, upon their return, to down-climb, an imposing challenge readily acknowledged by Anker, among the top technical rock climbers of the modern era, as being at the limit of his capabilities.

As Anker and Hahn crested the Second Step and began the long and still dangerous climb toward the summit of Everest, they had answered many of the essential questions. Mallory and Irvine had certainly reached the First Step; this would later be confirmed with the discovery in situ of a discarded oxygen cylinder, which Jochem Hemmleb dated positively to 1924. In all likelihood they overcame the First Step but then turned back either at the foot of the Second Step or somewhere along the ridge between the two. Perhaps in failing light, or blinded by the squall that swept the mountain that afternoon, Mallory removed his goggles as he attempted to find a route down through the slabs of the Yellow Band. Tied as one, perhaps with Mallory on belay, they fell together, not from the height of the Northeast Ridge but from far lower on the North Face, quite possibly within easy reach of their highest camp. Indeed, later expeditions would determine that Mallory had come to rest not three hundred yards from the safety of his Camp VI.

Mallory and Irvine may not have reached the summit of Mount Everest, but they did, on that fateful day, climb higher than any human being before them, reaching heights that would not be attained again for nearly thirty years. That they were able to do so, given all they had endured, is surely achievement enough. "To tell the truth," Dave Hahn remarked, "I have trouble believing they were as high as we know that they were." And as Conrad Anker noted, there is still one possibility, one scenario by which they might have indeed surmounted the Second Step. Had the very storms that so battered the 1924 expedition, burying the high camps and causing Norton to retreat not once but twice from the North Col, brought heavy snows of similar magnitude to the Northeast Ridge, it is possible that a drift accumulated, large enough, if not to bury the cliffs of the Second Step, at least to create a cone covering the most difficult pitches of rock. Such a scenario did in fact unfold in 1985, albeit in the autumn. Had this been the case, Mallory and Irvine might simply have walked up the snow, traversing the barrier with the very speed and ease that Odell so famously reported. Had this occurred, surely nothing could have held Mallory back. He would have walked on, even to his end, because for him, as for all of his generation, death was but "a frail barrier" that men crossed, "smiling and gallant, every day." They had seen so much of death that life mattered less than the moments of being alive.

Acknowledgments

I WOULD LIKE TO THANK Daniel Taylor, who introduced me to Tibet and the spacious silence of the Kama Valley, where we first spoke of George Mallory and the British expeditions of 1921–24. For an understanding of the story from the Tibetan perspective, I am indebted to Barbara Nimri Aziz, Hildegard Diemberger, Thinley Dondrup, Carroll Dunham, Glenn Mullin, Kalden Norbu, Charles Ramble, Matthieu Ricard, Hamid Sardar-Afkhani, Akhu Sherap, Robert Thurman, Tsering Tsamchu, Lama Urgyen, Joshua Waldman, Lama Wangdu, and Jamyang Wangmo. I would like especially to thank Helen and Michael Schmidt, as well as Trulshig Rinpoche and the monks, nuns, and laity of Thubten Chöling, who welcomed us so generously on several visits to their spiritual community.

For financial support and companionship in the field, my thanks go to Darlene and Jeff Anderson; Sherab Barma; Bob Fleming; Andrew Gregg; Thomas Kelly; Ian MacKenzie; Terry and Mike Matkins; Pat and Baiba Morrow; Chris Rainier; Daniel Taylor and his children, Luke, Tara, and Jesse-Oake; Andrew Wong; and, especially, Dorjee Lhatoo and his gracious wife, Sonam Doma. At a critical point in the research, Dorjee, as a mountaineer, teacher, and guide, was a great inspiration.

In Britain I found many friends. My thanks to Daphne and Micky Astor, Gerry Bodeker, Arabella Cecil, Robin Hanbury-Tenison, Chili Hawes and the October Gallery, John and Sukie Hemming, Richard House, Stephen and Christine Hugh-Jones, Bea Kayser, Christina Lamb, Leander and Stephanie McCormick-Goodhart, Andrew Nurnberg, Carol O'Brien, and Tristram and Louisa Riley-Smith. Among scholars I thank Grant Guyer, as well as Richard Blurton, David Fieldhouse, John Keegan, Andrew Porter, Glyn Williams, Jay Winter, and, especially, Patrick French, Alex McKay, and Audrey Salkeld. My thanks in America go to Broughton Coburn, George Martin, Thom Pollard, Peter Steele, and Dale Vrabec. For assistance in sourcing photographs my thanks to Trevor Frost, Susan Hare, Kate Holiday, Thomas Laird, Sandra Noel, Peter Odell, Jamie Owen, Peter Smith, Charles Wakefield, Ed Webster, Joy Wheeler, and Cathleen Wright.

It was a privilege to meet and come to know climbers who understand Everest in ways the rest of us only imagine. Reinhold Messner and the late Sir Edmund Hillary were both insightful and generous with their time, but my true guides along the way were Conrad Anker, Pete Athans, David Breashears, Ed Douglas, Tom Hornbein, Dorjee Lhatoo, and Ed Webster, all giants in their own ways.

The family members of the British climbers of 1921–24, in both Canada and the United Kingdom, were exceedingly helpful. My thanks to Ronald Bayne, Sheila and Richard Hingston, Jill Hingston, Graham Hoyland, Sally Izod, Sandra Noel, Richard Norton, Bill Norton, Susan Robertson, Anne Russell, and, especially, to Peter Odell, Julie Summers, Charles and Donna Wakefield, Robert Wakefield, and John Wheeler. Without the letters, diaries, photographs, and personal insights shared so openly, this account of their fathers, granduncles, and grandfathers could not have been written.

Several friends and colleagues read all or parts of the manuscript. Thanks to Caroline Alexander, Roger Barrington, Keith Bellows, Ed Bernbaum, Tom Buri, George Butler, Andrew Cockburn, Leslie Cockburn, Lavinia Currier, Carroll Dunham, Karen Davis, Simon and Cindy Davies, Terry Garcia, Andrew Gregg, Dan Jantzen, Peter Matson, Joel McCleary, Scott and Corky McIntyre, Gail Percy, Travis Price, Johan Reinhard, Daniel Taylor, Robert Thurman, Chuck Savitt, Tim Ward, and Jann Wenner.

The real heroes of this project, however, are the curators, librarians, archivists, and keepers at some fifty institutions in Canada, Germany, the United States, Ireland, and the United Kingdom. My thanks to Greta Connell, Gerald Davies, Lucy Dillistone, Margaret Ecclestone, Susanah Farmer, Mary Farrell, Aude Fitzsimmons, Rita Gardner, Livia Gollancz, Francis Herbert, Michael Holland, Beverley Hutchinson, Marian Keaney, Bob Lawford, Sheila MacKenzie, Sharon Martins, Carol Morgan, Roger Nixon, Helen Pye-Smith, Paula Rodino, Maggie Roxburgh, Joanna Scadden, Yvonne Sibbald, William Spencer, Sarah Strong, Andrew Tatum, Tim Thomas, Julia Walworth, Anne Wheeler, and Nigel de Winser. I would especially like to thank the Board of Trinity College Dublin and to acknowledge Marian Keaney for her scholarly devotion to the memory of Charles Howard-Bury.

My thanks to all those who offered assistance at: the National Archives of Canada, Ottawa; the Whyte Museum, Banff, Alberta;

the Berg Collection, New York Public Library, New York; Deutscher Alpenverein, Munich; Trinity College Dublin; the Custodians of Belvedere and Westmeath County Library, Mullingar, Ireland; University College Library and Archives, Cork, Ireland; the Ministry of Defense, Army Personnel Centre, Historic Disclosures, Glasgow; the University of Glasgow Archives, Glasgow; the Regimental Museum of the Royal Scots (the Royal Regiment), Edinburgh; the National Library of Scotland, Manuscripts Collection, Edinburgh; the Welch Regiment Museum, Cardiff; the Royal Welch Fusiliers Museum, Caernarfon Castle, Wales; the Royal Leicestershire Regiment Museum Collection, Leicestershire; the Fell and Rock Climbing Club Archives, Cumbria Records Office, Kendal; the Kendal Local Studies Library, Kendal; the Gurkha Museum, Peninsula Barracks, Winchester; the Royal Green Jackets Museum, Peninsula Barracks, Winchester; the National Army Museum, Chelsea; the Royal Artillery Museum, Woolwich; the Royal Engineers Corps Library and Museum, Chatham; the Winchester College Archives, Winchester; the Charterhouse School Archives, Godalming; the Eton College Library, Windsor; the Magdalene College Archives, Cambridge; the King's College Archive Centre, Cambridge; the Scott Research Institute, Cambridge; the Rhodes House Library, Oxford; the Merton College Archives, Oxford; the Liddell Hart Centre for Military Studies, King's College London; the Institution of Civil Engineers Library, London; the Theatre Museum Archives, London; the Principal Probate Registry Reading Room, High Holborn, London; the Imperial War Museum, Department of Documents, London; the Institution of Civil Engineers, London; the Wellcome Library for the History of Medicine, London; the BBC Archives, London; the Natural History Museum Archives, London; the National Trust; the British Library, Manuscript Collection, and India Office Records, Asia, Pacific and Africa Collections, London; the Oriental and India Office Library, London; the National Archives, Kew; the Alpine Club Library and Archives, London; the Royal Geographical Society Archives, Foyle Reading Room, London.

In London I would like to thank Will Sulkin, Tom Drake-Lee, and Suzanne Dean at the Bodley Head, and, especially, Michael Sissons, a former soldier, who understood this book from the start. At our first meeting Michael recited a litany of his family members who had been killed in the First and Second World Wars. Only toward the end of his military career, he added, did it dawn on him that he and his peers would not have to die for their country, as had their fathers and grandfathers.

At Knopf Canada I would like to thank Louise Dennys, executive publisher, and Deirdre Molina and Amanda Betts. And at Knopf in New York: Maria Massey, Gabrielle Brooks, Erica Hinsley, and, especially, Andrew Miller, a wonderful editor who was unfailing in his support. David Lindroth created the maps. Editorial help came from many quarters, and I would like as well to acknowledge my friend Keith Bellows, editor in chief of *National Geographic Traveler* magazine, who worked through the entire manuscript as we traveled together for a month to a dozen countries. I also had the invaluable editorial insights of Jonathan Cobb, an old-school editor if ever there was one. Finally, I cannot express strongly enough my thanks to Ash Green and Sonny Mehta, who never lost confidence in the book, even as the years piled up to a decade. I don't know of another editor or publisher who would have stood by a writer as they did. The same must be said of my agent and friend at Sterling Lord, Peter Matson.

Roger Barrington worked with me as a research partner for virtually the duration of the project. Unfailingly upbeat and thoughtful, he made this effort his own, and his wizardly ability to source primary documents never ceased to amaze me. In Nepal, Carroll Dunham introduced all the key Tibetan players, even as she showered me with books and suggested readings, translations of sacred texts, massive tomes and small prayers. Carroll's mind, as all who know her attest, is dazzling, but what makes her such a beloved figure in Nepal is her bodhisattva heart.

Finally, of course, there is my family, my sister, Karen, a constant light of love, and Gail and our daughters, Tara and Raina, for whom the saga of this book has shadowed half of their lives. Gail helped in so many ways, with research in the early years in London, and with editing and advice on each draft of the manuscript. For her love and support, and for the beautiful and kind young women that Tara and Raina have become, I am so very grateful.

Washington, D.C.
February 12, 2011

Annotated Bibliography

My interest in this story began in the spring of 1996 as I completed a four-thousand-mile overland journey from Chengdu, in western China, through southeastern Tibet to Lhasa and on to Kathmandu. Leading that ecological survey was a good friend, Daniel Taylor. Raised in the Himalaya, the son and grandson of medical missionaries, Daniel was a veteran of some forty-five expeditions to Tibet and had been largely responsible for the creation of the QNP, the 14,000-square-mile nature preserve that encompasses the approaches to Everest.

As it happened, we passed by the mountain just as events unfolded that were later chronicled in two remarkable books: *Into Thin Air*, by Jon Krakauer (New York: Villard Books, 1997); and *The Climb*, written by Anatoli Boukreev and G. Weston DeWalt (New York: St. Martin's Press, 1997). Like many in the climbing community, Daniel was deeply disturbed that the commercial transformation of Everest had resulted in such loss of life. In 1949, his father was a member of the first expedition officially sanctioned to enter Nepal. By 1996, thousands of foreigners were flocking to Everest each year—and those with the means to pay as much as $65,000 to be guided aloft, often with fatal results.

In the late fall of 1997, Daniel and I returned to Tibet, intent on photographing clouded leopards, among the most elusive of the great cats. Our journey took us from Kharta south into the Kama Valley along the same trails traveled by the British expeditions of the 1920s. Daniel had grown up with tales of George Mallory; his father was a close friend of Howard Somervell's. The British climbers were his heroes and role models when he was a boy, intrepid men who had walked off the map for hundreds of miles just to find a mountain that no European had encountered at close quarters. Their Everest was the mountain of Daniel's imaginings, not the ignoble scene of today.

Compared to the British expeditions of the 1920s, our monthlong sojourn in the Kama Valley was a trivial undertaking. Nevertheless, the extremes of altitude took a toll, as did the blizzards and the cold. From our camp at Pethang Ringmo, at the base of the Kangshung Face, we stared up at a mountain that has killed one climber for every ten that have reached the summit. It is a formidable sight. Though we were standing on ground higher than any in North America, the mountain rose two miles above, with fluted ribs and ridges, gleaming balconies and seracs of blue-green ice, shimmering formations ready to collapse in an instant. The thought of those early British climbers, "dressed in tweeds," as Daniel put it, and "reading Shakespeare in the snow" as they confronted such hazards, filled me with admiration, curiosity, and awe. Who were these men, and what was the spirit that drew them on?

On my return to Canada I dropped by a bookstore owned by an acquaintance in Vancouver. As we chatted, I noticed directly behind him on a shelf of rare books first editions of the three official accounts of the early Everest expeditions: C. K. Howard-Bury's *Mount Everest: The Reconnaissance, 1921* (London: Edward Arnold, 1922); C. G. Bruce's *The Assault on Mount Everest, 1922* (London: Edward Arnold, 1923), and E. F. Norton's *The Fight for Everest, 1924* (London: Edward Arnold, 1925). These became the first acquisitions in a research collection for this book; it would grow to include more than six hundred volumes.

After reading the early accounts, I turned to classic biographies of Mallory, one written by his son-in-law, David Robertson's *George Mallory* (London: Faber and Faber, 1969), and a second by a close friend of the climber's: David Pye's *George Leigh Mallory* (London: Oxford University Press, 1927). Those interested should see also Dudley Green, *Mallory of Everest* (Roughlee: Faust, 1990), reissued as *Because It's There: The Life of George Mallory* (Brimscombe: Tempus, 2005), and Showell Styles, *Mallory of Everest* (New York: MacMillan, 1967).

Next came three fundamental sources: Tom Holzel and Audrey Salkeld, *The Mystery of Mallory and Irvine* (London: Jonathan Cape, 1986); Kenneth Mason, *Abode of Snow* (New York: Dutton, 1955); and Walt Unsworth, *Everest* (London: Oxford Illustrated Press, 1989). See also: Ian Cameron, *Mountains of the Gods* (New York: Facts on File Publications, 1984); Ronald Clark, *Men, Myths and Mountains* (New York: Thomas Crowell, 1976); Howard Marshall, *Men Against Everest* (London: Country Life, 1954); Micheline Morin, *Everest* (New York: John Day, 1955); W. H. Murray, *The Story of Everest* (Letchworth: J. M. Dent, 1953); Stanley Snaith, *At Grips with Everest* (London: Oxford University Press, 1938); James R. Ullman, *Kingdom of Adventure: Everest* (New York: William Sloane, 1947); and Walt Unsworth, *Hold the Heights* (London: Hodder & Stoughton, 1994). For three more recent books on the history of climbing and Everest, all grand in scale and insight, see: Maurice Isserman and Stewart Weaver, *Fallen Giants* (New Haven: Yale University Press, 2008); Robert Macfarlane, *Mountains of the Mind* (New York: Pantheon, 2003); and Michael Ward, *Everest: A Thousand Years of Exploration* (Glasgow: Ernest Press, 2003).

Many of the men on or associated with the expeditions published personal memoirs, which became my next level of engagement. See especially: F. M. Bailey, *Mission to Tashkent* (London: Jonathan Cape, 1946) and *No Passport to Tibet* (London: Travel Book Club, 1957); Charles G. Bruce, *Himalayan Wanderer* (London: Alexander Maclehose, 1934); Norman Collie, *Climbing on the Himalaya* (New York: Charles Scribner's Sons, 1902); George Ingle Finch, *The Making of a Mountaineer* (London: Arrowsmith, 1924); Tom Longstaff, *This My Voyage* (London: John Murray, 1950); David Macdonald, *Twenty Years in Tibet* (London: Seeley, Service, 1932); John Morris, *Hired to Kill* (London: Rupert Hart-Davis/Cresset, 1960); John Noel, *The Story of Everest* (New York: Little, Brown, 1927), later reprinted as *Through Tibet to Everest* (London: Hodder & Stoughton, 1989); and T. Howard Somervell, *After Everest* (London: Hodder & Stoughton, 1936).

Ian Morshead and Nicholas Wollaston wrote fascinating and deeply moving biographies of their fathers. See: Ian Morshead, *The Life and Murder of Henry Morshead* (Cambridge: Oleander, 1982); and Nicholas Wollaston, *My Father, Sandy* (London: Short Books, 2003). Among his many books, Francis Younghusband wrote two specifically about the Everest adventure: *The Epic of Mount Everest* (London: Edward Arnold, 1926) and *Everest: The Challenge* (London: Thomas Nelson and Sons, 1936). Obituaries of all of the key players in the Everest adventure appeared in both the *Alpine Club Journal* and the *Geographic Journal*, the official publications of the Alpine Club and the Royal Geographical Society. Another fundamental source is: the *Oxford Dictionary of National Biography* (Oxford: Oxford University Press, 2004).

I first wrote about Mallory in *Shadows in the Sun*, a collection of essays published by Island Press in 1998. In February 1999 I wrote a letter to my agent and friend, Peter Matson, outlining thoughts for a book. It provoked considerable interest, which led to a wonderful editor, Ash Green, and a contract with Knopf. What interested me from the start was not whether Mallory reached the summit but, rather, why on that fateful day he kept going, quite possibly aware that he was walking to his death. I knew that most of the men on the three expeditions had gone through the fire of the Great War. As I wrote in that letter more than ten years ago: "There was indeed something Homeric about Mallory and his companions. After the war, when so many had died, life was precious but effervescent. Perhaps this explains his willingness to climb on, accepting a degree of risk that might have been unimaginable before the war. They were not cavalier, but death was no stranger. They had seen so much that it had no hold on them. What mattered was how one lived."

In May 1999, just as my research was getting under way, the discovery by Conrad Anker of Mallory's body transformed the field of play. By chance I had a profile of Mallory in press at the time, which became the first feature magazine article heralding the discovery ("Everest's First Hero," *Men's Journal*, June–July 1999, pp. 132–36, 183–84). This was simple luck, and it drew little attention in a whirlwind of international media coverage celebrating a truly remarkable event in mountaineering history. Within a year no fewer than eight books would appear, many of them splendid. Audrey Salkeld, the preeminent historian of Everest, and Tom Holzel reissued their classic account with revisions and a new foreword by Eric Simonson, the leader of the expedition that found Mallory's corpse: *The Mystery of Mallory and Irvine* (Seattle: Mountaineers, 1999). Audrey also brought out an illustrated book with David Breashears, *Last Climb* (Washington, D.C.: National Geographic Books, 1999). The expedition that found the body published two accounts: Jochen Hemmleb, Larry Johnson, and Eric Simonson, *Ghosts of Everest* (Seattle: Mountaineers, 1999); and Jochen Hemmleb and Eric Simonson, *Detectives on Everest* (Seattle: Mountaineers, 2002). From the BBC, contingent on the expedition, came Peter Firstbrook's *Lost on Everest* (Chicago: Contemporary Books, 1999). Conrad Anker collaborated with David Roberts to produce *The Lost Explorer* (New York: Simon & Schuster, 1999). Inspired by the discovery, Reinhold Messner published *The Second Death of Mallory* (New York: St. Martin's, 2000). Peter and Leni Gillman wrote a fine and updated Mallory biography: *The Wildest Dream* (London: Headline Book Publishing, 2000). This was followed by the first biography of Sandy Irvine, written by his grandniece; this essential contribution had been in the works long before the sensational events of the spring of 1999: Julie Summers, *Fearless on Everest* (London: Weidenfeld & Nicolson, 2000).

These publications presented something of a quandary. What possibly remained to be said about a story that had been covered by so many writers? Assuming that Knopf might be wondering the same thing, I offered to return the advance. Ash Green generously replied that he had not offered me a contract because he wanted another book on Mallory but, rather, because he wanted a book by me on Mallory. I casually remarked that it might take ten years to complete—which, I am afraid to say, turned out to be true.

The challenge from the start was to go beyond the iconic figure of George Mallory and take the research to new levels of depth and scope. I began with several visits to London to work through basic archival sources, most especially the forty-one boxes of files containing reports, correspondence, and miscellaneous documents of the Mount Everest Committee housed at the Royal Geographical Society, which also has the most complete visual record of the expeditions in its photographic collections.

The archive of the Alpine Club was equally rich, yielding a number of key diaries and reports, as well as a complete collection of press clippings from the era. The letters of George Mallory are for the most part at Magdalene College, Cambridge. Thanks to the generous cooperation of these institutions, I was able to secure copies of all documents pertinent to the research, a collection that itself fills six file-cabinet drawers in my office. While in London on those early visits I was also able to contact some family members, descendants of many of the key figures in the story. All were exceedingly helpful: Colonel Norton's sons, Richard and Bill; Geoffrey Bruce's niece, Sally Izod; John Noel's daughter Sandra; Peter Odell, grandson of Noel; Graham Hoyland, grandnephew of Howard Somervell; and Julie Summers, grandniece of Sandy Irvine.

Julie Summers was especially gracious and provided a connection to a brilliant historical researcher, Roger Barrington. My goal from the start was to learn as much as possible about the lives of all twenty-six men who went to Everest in 1921–24. I was especially interested in their experiences during the war, and my own preliminary efforts at the National Archives (TNA; formerly the Public Record Office), the Imperial War Museum, the British Library, and other repositories had convinced me that I needed the help of a professional researcher living in Britain who was familiar with the complex distribution of military records, many of which are housed in regimental archives scattered throughout the nation. Suffice it to say that without Roger's partnership over several years, this book could not have been written. Some of the expedition members escaped the war; Arthur Kellas and Harold Raeburn were too old; Sandy Irvine, too young; Tom Longstaff served in India; Guy Bullock, in the diplomatic corps; Bentley Beetham remained at home, a schoolmaster. But the other twenty men most assuredly did see the fighting, and thanks in good measure to Roger's research, we were able to determine, with some notable gaps, where each was posted on virtually every day of the entire war.

Once I knew the military unit and the location in both time and space of each protagonist throughout the war, my next research challenge was to ascertain, to the extent possible, what each man might have endured. It was famously said of both Passchendaele and the Somme that the army lacked the clerk power to tabulate the dead. If so, it recorded just about everything else. The Great War was so thoroughly documented that one wonders how the men found time to fight. Every unit maintained a war diary, with the task of reporting on operations, intelligence, casualties, and any other pertinent information rotating among the junior officers. These diaries, together with letters, personal journals, and trench maps made it possible to track each of our men through the war with a level of specificity I would not have imagined possible at the outset.

The British war zone in France was relatively small, the number of men engaged enormous, and the outpouring of literature after the war so vast that virtually every corner of the battlefield at every point in the war has been described by multiple voices, by enlisted men and officers, in poetry and prose, in tones as brash and confident as a fearless Yorkshire sergeant's and as haunted as the wail of a young subaltern in a well of despair. As long as I knew that one of our key figures was present at an action, I could extrapolate from other sources what had transpired. Mallory, for example, may not have described the black night when his unit moved south to the Somme, but Ramsay, his commanding officer's batman, did. Typical of these secondary sources that proved so useful are: Anonymous, *Four Years on the Western Front* (London: Odhams, 1922); William Andrews, *Haunting Years* (London: Hutchinson, 1930); A. F. Becke, *History of the Great War: Order of Battle of Divisions* (London: His Majesty's Stationery Office, 1945); J. C. Dunn, *The War the Infantry Knew* (London: P. S. King, 1938); Rowland

Feilding, *War Letters to a Wife* (London: Medici Society, 1929); J. D. Hills, *The Fifth Leicester* (Loughborough: Echo, 1919); E. A. James and Hugh Jeudwine, *A Record of the Battles and Engagements of the British Armies in France and Flanders, 1914–1918* (London: London Stamp Exchange, 1990); Christopher Moore, *Trench Fever* (London: Little, Brown, 1998); E. W. C. Sandes, *The Military Engineer in India* (Chatham: Institute of Royal Engineers, 1933); and E. A. Tandy, *The War Record 1914–20*, Records of the Survey of India, vol. 20 (Dehra Dun, 1925).

In addition to personal memoirs, a number of books and anthologies give voice to individual soldiers, poignant testimonies that read like notes in a great musical score of madness. See: Max Arthur, *Forgotten Voices of the Great War* (Guilford, Conn.: Lyons, 2002); Malcolm Brown, *The Western Front* (London: Sidgwick & Jackson, 1996); John Ellis, *Eye-Deep in Hell* (Baltimore: Johns Hopkins University Press, 1976); Laurence Houseman, ed., *War Letters of Fallen Englishmen* (London: Dutton, 1930); John Laffin, *British Butchers and Bunglers of World War One* (Thrup: Sutton, 1989); Lyn Macdonald, ed., *Voices and Images of the Great War* (London: Penguin, 1991); Anne Powell, ed., *The Fierce Light* (Aberporth: Palladour, 1996); and David Robert, *Minds at War* (Burgess Hill: Saxon, 1996).

"The war," Duncan Grant wrote to Mallory, "is simply undermining my life so the less said about it the better." But it could not be ignored. On October 25, 1914, Robert Graves wrote to Cyril Hartman, an old friend from school, "You have probably seen the Charterhouse casualty list; awful . . . I am in the special reserves which feed out two battalions in France. The 1st has been annihilated—except for two officers and a few men . . . The chance against returning whole-skinned if we go out now is about 2–1 and I have consequently resigned myself." The odds of dying only got worse as the war went on.

In his war memoir, *Good-bye to All That* (London: Jonathan Cape, 1929), Robert Graves estimated the life expectancy of a young subaltern to be about three months, after which time he would be either wounded or dead. There were roughly four wounded for every fatality, and of these one would be hurt so severely as to never return. The three lightly wounded recovered only to face the same odds again and again, until in the end those who survived the war had been wounded more times than they could remember. Such a cycle of morbidity and death, and its impact on the mind and the imagination, was not readily curtailed by the Armistice, which was seen by many as arbitrary in nature, meaningless in content, a mere truce that simply postponed the inevitability of another conflict.

If the war shattered the last vestiges of the old order, making a mockery of notions of glory, honor, and valor, peace heralded the birth of modern times, a new century stained, as Winston Churchill would write, in blood. Caught between worlds, the old and the new, spinning in a whirlwind of psychological and social uncertainty, was an entire Lost Generation, including most of the key players in the Everest adventure. Beyond simply knowing what they had faced in the war, it was essential that I understood what the war had implied for the society and culture in which they lived. For this I turned to two brilliant books: Modris Eksteins, *Rites of Spring: The Great War and the Birth of the Modern Age* (New York: Anchor, 1989), and Paul Fussell, *The Great War and Modern Memory* (Oxford: Oxford University Press, 1975). See also: Joanna Bourke, *Dismembering the Male: Men's Bodies, Britain and the Great War* (Chicago: University of Chicago Press, 1996); Samuel Hynes, *A War Imagined: The First World War and English Culture* (New York: Atheneum, 1991); Eric Leed, *No Man's Land: Combat and Identity in World War I* (Cambridge: Cambridge University Press, 1979); George Mosse, *Fallen Soldiers: Reshaping the Memory of the World Wars* (Oxford: Oxford University Press,

1990); and Jay Winter and Blaine Baggett, *The Great War and the Shaping of the 20th Century* (New York: Penguin, 1996).

Yet another major research challenge took me into the history of the Raj and the complex diplomatic maneuvers of Lord Curzon, Charles Bell, and the frontier cadre engaged in the Great Game. For this I was most fortunate to have the assistance of my cousin Grant Guyer, an authority on British colonial history. Grant very kindly joined me in London on my first visit, introducing me to the ways of research in Britain and to any number of historians, colleagues with whom he had worked while pursuing his doctoral studies at Oxford. The key connection was Alex McKay, the author of the seminal book *Tibet and the British Raj: The Frontier Cadre 1904–1947* (Richmond: Curzon, 1997). See also: Alex McKay, ed., *Pilgrimage in Tibet* (Richmond: Curzon, 1998).

In Canada, two avenues of research proved extremely useful. After Everest, Arthur Wakefield settled in Quebec, where members of his family still live. His son Bob, who passed away at ninety-two in 2007, and his grandson Charles very kindly shared personal insights, as well as Arthur's war diary and Everest journal and the private letters he wrote to his wife, Madge, both from the Western Front and from Everest. These proved invaluable.

E. O. Wheeler grew up climbing in the Canadian Rockies, and his papers are housed at the Whyte Museum, in Banff, Alberta. His son John, after an illustrious career with the Geological Survey of Canada, retired to Vancouver, where I found him, at age seventy-five, living a block away from the house my parents had owned when I was born. It was a wonderful encounter. He and my father had attended the same boarding school at more or less the same time, and I, by chance, had climbed many of the northern peaks that John had been the first to survey. We met for a long afternoon, at the end of which he produced a remarkable treasure. According to Everest historians, only Guy Bullock kept a complete journal during the 1921 expedition, curt notes that were published in two parts in the *Alpine Journal*. See: "The Everest Expedition, 1921, Diary of G. H. Bullock," *Alpine Journal*, vol. 67, no. 304 (1962), pp. 130–49, and no. 305, pp. 291–309. Mallory wrote letters and Howard-Bury official dispatches, but neither kept a daily account. E. O. Wheeler, as it turned out, did—two complete volumes that had never been seen by anyone outside of his immediate family.

I was so astonished that I could not bring myself to ask that they be copied. But as we parted late in the day, John Wheeler handed me the two journals, saying simply that he thought I would find them useful. I have them with me still, and it is my hope that I may be able to repay John his trust by having them, with his permission, published in their entirety. They provide an astonishing perspective on the 1921 reconnaissance, arguably the most interesting of the three expeditions. And they reveal the character and personality of a remarkable man who spent more time alone, higher and closer to the mountain, than anyone—the unheralded Canadian surveyor who mapped the inner core of the Everest massif and solved the puzzle of the North Col, thus opening the doorway to the mountain.

A second major phase of the research entailed several return journeys to Nepal and Tibet. Having delved into the literature, I went back to Everest in 2000 with fresh eyes. Accompanying me was an extraordinarily insightful man and one of the greatest of Himalayan climbers, Dorjee Lhatoo, former head of the Himalayan Mountaineering Institute in Darjeeling, the training ground for all great Indian climbers. Established in the immediate wake of the British conquest of Everest in 1953 by Jawaharlal Nehru, the father of Indian independence, the HMI from inception was inspired by new ways of thinking about mountaineering. Its formal mandate was to train young men and women "not only to climb Himalayan peaks, but also to create in them an urge to climb peaks of human endeavor." Dorjee had been recruited to the HMI as an ideal candidate to realize Nehru's dreams. He was married to Sonam Doma, niece of Tenzing Norgay, who first reached the summit of Everest with Hillary in 1953.

Born at Yatung, in the Chumbi Valley, Dorjee had fled Tibet as a small boy with his widowed mother. They were economic refugees, and his anger at what the Chinese have done to his country was matched in its intensity by his disdain for what the Tibetan theocratic leadership had failed to provide for the Tibetan people before the Chinese invasion. "They offered us prayer wheels," he would say, "when what we needed and wanted were real wheels." A veteran of Everest, not to mention Nanda Devi and Chomolhari, Dorjee had trained generations of Indian climbers, including Bachendri Pal, the first Indian woman to reach the summit of Everest.

For two months, Dorjee and I walked in the footsteps of the British reconnaissance of 1921. We visited Tingri and Nyenyam, climbed to the summit of the ruined fortress at Shegar, retraced the explorers' approach to the Rongbuk Monastery, went up the East Rongbuk Glacier to the North Col, and later crossed from Kharta by way of the Samchung La and the Chog La to the lower Kama Chu and the headwaters of the Arun. From below Sakeding we traversed the length of the Kama Valley to Pethang Ringmo and the Kangshung Face, before returning over the Langma La to explore the upper reaches of the Kharta Chu. Dorjee led me up any number of subsidiary peaks, and was an invaluable source of information not only on the challenges of Himalayan climbing but on the ethnography and history of Kharta, where his wife's family originated.

We did not by any means go everywhere the British went. A plan to reach the Jelep La, visit the village of Dorjee's birth, and then follow the Chumbi Valley to Phari and, beyond, to Kampa Dzong was stymied by Chinese officials who, having promised us a permit to enter borderlands off-limits to foreigners since the 1959 invasion, reneged at the last moment, stranding our party in Tibet, even as they pocketed the $25,000 fee. This setback aside, in those weeks we covered enough ground on foot to leave me only more astonished by what the British had accomplished in a single season. Dorjee and I returned to this theme when I visited him in Darjeeling in 2002. We spent several days touring the town; Dorjee introduced me to a new generation of Sherpa climbers, even as he pointed out what remained of the Darjeeling the British had known in 1921–24.

The more time I spent with Tibetans in the environs of Everest, the more interested I became in what the mountain meant to them, and how their great-grandparents might have viewed the arrival and activities of the British climbers, the first Europeans many of them would have known. A main point of interface, as we have seen, was the Rongbuk Monastery, headed by its charismatic abbot, Ngawang Tenzin Norbu, or Dzatrul Rinpoche. Although several of the British climbers wrote of their impressions of Rongbuk, the only account of the British from a Tibetan perspective is based on a few excerpts from Dzatrul Rinpoche's *namthar*, or spiritual autobiography. This is the encounter between the rinpoche and General Bruce widely quoted in the Everest literature. See: Alexander MacDonald, "The Lama and the General," *Kailash*, vol. 1, no. 3 (1973), pp. 225–33. The autobiography, as far as I could tell, had never been translated in its entirety.

To learn more, I turned to Carroll Dunham, an old friend and a brilliant anthropologist living in Nepal, who became, like Roger Barrington in the United Kingdom, an indispensable partner in the project. Carroll opened the door to the entire Tibetan community in Kathmandu. With her help I was able to secure a copy of the *namthar* and have it translated by a revered Buddhist monk, Lama Urgyen. An extraordinary scholar, Lama Urgyen had worked on no fewer than forty *namthars*. Thus he delivered not only a complete and accurate translation but also great insights into the character of Dzatrul Rinpoche, the intensity of his devotion, and the reverence with which the people of the region embraced him. While in Kathmandu I met Tsering Tsamchu, a ninety-year-old Buddhist nun who had studied with Dzatrul Rinpoche at Rongbuk. I asked her what he had looked like. She replied without hesitation: Shakyamuni, the Buddha.

When Dzatrul Rinpoche passed away, in 1940, his spiritual heir Trulshig Rinpoche became abbot of Rongbuk. In 1959, with the final Chinese conquest of Tibet, the monks and nuns of Rongbuk were forced to flee to Nepal, crossing the Nangpa La. After a time in solitary retreat, Trulshig Rinpoche saw to the construction of a new monastery at Thubten Chöling, which in every way replicated the devotional ambience and ritual rigor of Rongbuk.

Thus, in order to know what life was like at Rongbuk in 1924, Carroll and I had only to travel to Solu Khumbu and Thubten Chöling, home today to some eight hundred Buddhist monks and nuns. To stay at the monastery and be in the presence of Trulshig Rinpoche was from the Tibetan perspective to return spiritually to Rongbuk and the radiance of Dzatrul Rinpoche. In terms of ritual activities, this was quite literally true, for the esoteric rites and purifications delineated in such detail in Dzatrul Rinpoche's *namthar* mark fixed points in a liturgical calendar that does not vary year to year. The "devil dances," for example, that several of the climbers witnessed and that John Noel filmed at the end of the 1922 expedition were elements of a celebration known as Mani Rimdu, an eighteen-day festival that Carroll and I attended at Chiwong Monastery in 2005. See: Luther Jerstad, *Mani-Rimdu: Sherpa Dance Ritual* (Seattle: University of Washington Press, 1969), and Richard Kohn, *Lord of the Dance* (Albany: SUNY Press, 2001). More significantly, our time at Thubten Chöling opened my mind to the power and wonder of the Buddhist path. This new awareness unfolded with even greater insight during the month Carroll and I spent walking close to Everest with Matthieu Ricard, a renowned scholar and monk, as we studied the Buddhist science of the mind.

A final phase of research grew out of these travels. First I needed to learn more about the practice of *chöd*, and for this I turned, in Kathmandu, to Lama Wangdu, one of Carroll's teachers. Second, I wanted to know more about the Shining Crystal Monastery at Shegar; its fortress and temples had captivated, among others, Howard-Bury. In Kathmandu, Carroll learned of two unpublished manuscripts written by Pu Rab Ngawang, a Tibetan who, with his brother, a monk from Shegar, had been imprisoned by the Chinese for twenty years before escaping to Nepal. Despite the risk, his brother had returned to Shegar to smuggle out of the monastery its principal canonical text, the *Ngag Dbang Skal Ldan Rgya Mtsho*. He was caught, imprisoned again, and the text confiscated by Chinese authorities. When Carroll and Pu Rab Ngawang met, he was astonished to see a facsimile of this text on the cover of a book I had left with her, a remarkable translation: Pasang Wangdu and Hildegard Diemberger, *Shel Dkar Chos 'Byung: History of the "White Crystal": Religion and Politics of Southern La Stod* (Vienna: Verlag der Österreichischen Akademie der Wissenschaften, 1996). See also: Maria Antonia Sironi, Hildegard Diemburger, and Pasang Wangdu, *The Story of the White Crystal* (Bergamo, Italy: Ferrari Editrice Clusone, 1995). Pu Rab Ngawang's own writings on the history of Shegar were translated by Thinley Dondrup, a Tibetan scholar from Tribhuvan University and the University of Wisconsin. Thinley also translated the *namthar* of Lingkhor Rinpoche, who was the lama of Shegar at the time of Dzatrul Rinpoche and the British expeditions. Both documents offered curious insights.

Finally, I needed to understand Tibetan notions of sacred geography. I had first learned of hidden valleys and spiritual refugia in the writings of two friends and colleagues, Ed Bernbaum and Johan Reinhard. See: Edwin Bernbaum, *The Way to Shambhala* (Boston: Shambhala, 2001) and *Sacred Mountains of the World* (San Francisco: Sierra Club Books, 1990), and Johan Reinhard, "Khembalung: the Hidden Valley," *Kailash*, vol. 6, no. 1 (1978), pp. 5–36. Their work led me to Hildegard Diemberger, a brilliant scholar and adventurer who had spent much of her life in the Himalaya. Her father was the renowned Himalayan climber Kurt Diemberger. It did not surprise me that the daughter of such a man would turn out to be one of the world authorities on Tibetan ideas of sacred landscape. I found her at the anthropology department at Cambridge University, where she welcomed me warmly even as she opened my mind to the real meaning of mountains. It was Hildegard who showed me that the entire time the British were scrambling across the flanks of Everest, they were walking in mystic space.

1: Great Gable

The memorial gathering at Great Gable was widely reported. See: "A Mountain War Memorial: Ceremony on Great Gable," *Yorkshire Post*, June 9, 1924; "Mountain War Memorial: Unveiling of Tablet on Great Gable," *Times*, June 9, 1924; "Memorial Service in the Clouds," *Daily Mail*, June 10, 1924; and "A Mountain Memorial: Climbers Who Fell in the War," *Advertiser*, June 13, 1924. For the annual FRCC dinner at Coniston where the gift of land was announced, see: "A Mountain Memorial," *Westmoreland Gazette*, October 20, 1923, and "Splendid War Memorial," *Yorkshire Post*, October 23, 1923. For Wakefield's speech at the dinner, see: "Preserving the Heart of Lakeland: 3,000 Acre Gift to the Nation," *Manchester Guardian*, October 15, 1923. Wakefield's climbing record is noted in: Ashley Abraham, "Lake District Fell Walking," *Fell and Rock Climbing Club (FRCC) Journal*, vol. 5, no. 2 (1920), pp. 173–80. Documents regarding the ceremony, including Geoffrey Young's account of the day and Wakefield's correspondence as president of the club, may be found in the Collection of the FRCC at Kendal.

For a fine biography of Geoffrey Young, see: Alan Hankinson, *Geoffrey Winthrop Young* (London: Hodder & Stoughton, 1995). For a sense of the spirit of the Pen y Pass gatherings—along with Young's memorable description of Mallory as a climber: "He swung up rock with a long thigh, a lifted knee, and a ripple of irresistible movement"—see: Geoffrey Winthrop Young, Geoffrey Sutton, and Wilfred Noyce, *Snowdon Biography* (London: J. M. Dent, 1957). For more on Pen y Pass, see: Geoffrey Winthrop Young, "An Impression of Pen y Pass, 1900–1920," in H. R. C. Carr and G. A. Lister, eds., *The Mountains of Snowdonia* (London: Crosby Lockwood, 1948), pp. 75–89.

For Young's harrowing account of the first months of the war, see: Geoffrey Winthrop Young, *From the Trenches* (London: Unwin, 1914). The passage beginning, "In the new army around us" is quoted from p. 226 of his hauntingly beautiful memoir, *The Grace of Forgetting* (London: Country Life, 1953); "the writing of madmen" is from p. 155; "Is that death?," p. 169; "In the half-exposed remnant," p. 245; "for then we still thought all men were human," p. 233.

G. M. Trevelyan, a friend from Cambridge of both Young's and Mallory's, served with Young on the Italian front. For an account of that campaign and the action at Monte San Gabriele that cost Young his leg, see: G. M. Trevelyan, *Scenes from Italy's War* (London: T. C & E. C. Jack, 1919). *The Roof Climber's Guide to Trinity*, published anonymously by W. P. Spalding in 1900, was reissued by Oleander Press in Cambridge in 2009. Young describes Mallory's near disaster on Nesthorn in *On High Hills* (London: Methuen, 1927), p. 178. See also: Geoffrey Winthrop Young, ed., *Mountain Craft* (London: Methuen, 1920), a book dedicated to the memory of fifty "gallant comrades," climbers, for the most part, killed in the war.

The vast literature on the Great War continues to expand by the year. Books encompassing the entire war that I found especially helpful include: Arthur Banks, *A Military Atlas of the First World War* (Barnsley: Leo Cooper, 2004); Niall Ferguson, *The Pity of War* (New York: Basic Books, 1999); Martin Gilbert, *The First World War* (New York: Henry Holt, 1994), and *A History of the Twentieth Century, 1900–1933* (New York: Morrow, 1997); Edward Gleichen, ed., *Chronology of the Great War* (London: Greenhill Books, 2000); B. H. Liddell Hart, *A History of the World War, 1914–1918* (London: Faber and Faber, 1934); Richard Holmes, *The Western Front* (New York: TV Books, 1999); John Keegan, *The First World War* (New York: Knopf, 1999); Hew Strachan, *Oxford Illustrated History of the First World War* (Oxford: Oxford University Press, 1998), and *The First World War: To Arms* (Oxford: Oxford University Press, 2001); and Denis Winter, *Death's Men* (London: Penguin, 1979). See also: Lyn Macdonald, *1915: The Death of Innocence* (New York: Henry Holt, 1995), and *To the Last Man: Spring 1918* (New York: Carroll & Graf, 1998).

Wherever Wakefield traveled as a missionary and a doctor, he sowed the seeds of imperial desire, attracting to the colors the very best men, the brothers, uncles, and fathers of all those whose lives he had affected as a physician and healer. He had begun in 1911 at St. Anthony, at the northernmost tip of Newfoundland, and by 1914 he had established local branches of legionnaires in virtually every settlement in his domain. "It is most encouraging," he would write in a report from Mud Lake, as the winter snows of early 1914 drifted past the second-floor window of his study, "to find so keen a sense of duty to their country, and of love to their King and to the Empire, of which they are citizens, amongst those living in these northern wilds . . . On my northern trip Legion meetings were held at Nain and Hopedale, and the greatest loyalty was displayed, nearly all the able bodied young fellows, and many of the older men also, joining with enthusiasm." Both Wakefield and his wife, Madge, sent accounts of their experiences to *Toilers of the Deep*, the official publication of the Royal National Mission to Deep Sea Fishermen. For accounts of the Grenfell Mission, see: Wilfred Grenfell, *A Labrador Doctor* (Boston: Houghton Mifflin, 1919), and *Forty Years for Labrador* (Boston: Houghton Mifflin, 1932).

Wakefield's World War I service papers dating from December 1916, when he joined the Canadian Expeditionary Force, are found in the database of the Library and Archives Canada (RG 150; Accession 1992–93/166, Box 9990–17). These include records of his service on HMHS *Letitia* beginning on March 12, 1917. See also: War Diary, 2 Canadian Stationary Hospital (TNA: PRO WO95/4109).

Thirty-three letters written by Wakefield to his wife, Madge, between 1914 and 1919 survive (those from 1917 are missing, presumed accidentally destroyed). Several provided particular insights: on the *Florizel* on October 6, 1914; at Salisbury Plain on December 4, 1914; on German atrocities on November 26, 1918, from Pamploux; "I assure you I am doing my best" on December 8, 1918, from Ludendorf.

Two letters proved especially important in the early phase of the research. We knew that Wakefield had left the Newfoundland Regiment just before it embarked for Gallipoli. A letter written to his wife on September 12, 1915, placed him in France with the 29th Casualty Clearing Station. A separate document, a movement order dated September 25, 1915, indicated that Wakefield on that date returned on leave to England. A search in the National Archives, War Office (WO) records, revealed that for inexplicable reasons the war diary of the 29th CCS does not cover the period from August 15 through December 15, 1915. Because of this gap in the war diary, it was uncertain when Wakefield returned to France, and if, when he did, he remained attached to the same medical unit.

All communications from the front were censored, and junior officers, responsible for vetting the letters of their enlisted men, exercised discretion with their own correspondence. On February 3, 1916, Wakefield wrote to his wife, with a postscript that noted his location as being simply "Somewhere in France." But in the letter he mentioned a bronze statue of a virgin, sunk by its own weight at a right angle to the steeple of a ruined church. This was undoubtedly the Madonna of the Basilica of Albert, a mournful image of pity and despair that had over time taken on redemptive, even mythic, significance for the men on both sides of the trenches. It was said that if she fell to earth, the side responsible would be destined to lose the war. Many claimed that blood rained from her body, just as tears fell from the eyes of the Christ child in her arms. This reference indisputably placed Wakefield in Albert, the staging ground for the Somme, in the spring of 1916.

Knowing that the army was not likely to have transferred experienced surgeons out of the sector on the eve of the assault, I was curious whether Wakefield might possibly have been responsible for the medical support for his beloved Newfoundland Regiment, which arrived at the Somme front in April, less than three months before the battle. In the archival records, the unit diary of the 29th CCS resumes on January 1, 1916, which allowed us from that date to track Wakefield's movements.

The first challenge was to determine whether, at the Somme, the 29th CCS received the wounded from the 29th Division, which included the Newfoundland Regiment, attached at the time to the 88th Brigade. The DMS (Director of Medical Services) for the Third Army (TNA: PRO WO 95/381) revealed that as of March 3, 1916, the 29th CCS was transferred to the administration of the Fourth Army, under Rawlinson, which included the 29th Division. The Fourth Army DMS diary (TNA: PRO WO 95/447) confirmed that as of July 1, 1916, the 29th CCS remained attached to it. The next step was to consult the diaries of the field ambulance units (88th Field Ambulance [TNA: PRO WO 95/2296]; 1/1 South Midland Field Ambulance [TNA: PRO WO 95/2752]) responsible for evacuating casualties from the regimental aid posts to the 29th CCS at Gézaincourt and of the ambulance trains that carried the wounded from there to the base hospitals at Boulogne, Étaples, Le Havre, and Rouen. On July 3, 1916, for example, six trains evacuated a total of thirty officers and 4,206 other ranks from the 29th CCS.

The war diary of the DMS for the Fourth Army (TNA: PRO WO 95/447) provides in a single entry a haunting sense of the chaos and agony of July 1. At 10:00 p.m. admissions to the field ambulances totaled 526 officers and 14,146 other ranks. Trains from Acheux carried these to 29th CCS, where the wounded already numbered 528 officers and 7,236 enlisted men, including 1,460 victims of poison gas. The war diary of the 88th Field Ambulance, which supported the 88th Brigade, confirmed that it was based at Acheux, close to Beaumont-Hamel, where the Newfoundland Regiment was annihilated. On the casualty lists were names that confirmed that the handful of Newfoundlanders who survived the debacle at Beaumont-Hamel did indeed pass through Wakefield's 29th CCS.

For the overall medical challenges of the war, see: Lyn Macdonald, *The Roses of No Man's Land* (New York: Atheneum, 1989); T. J. Mitchell and G. M. Smith, *Medical Services: Casualties and Medical Statistics of the Great War* (Nashville: Battery Press, 1997), originally published in 1931; and Ian Whitehead, *Doctors in the Great War* (Barnsley: Leo Cooper, 1999).

Howard Somervell describes his early life in his memoir *After Everest*. For his military record, see: Officer File (TNA: PRO WO 374/64114) and the war diary of the 34th CCs (TNA: PRO WO 95/415). Many medical records from the Great War were destroyed in the German attacks on London in 1940. Fortunately, those of the 34th CCS survived. TNA MH 106/776 contains a complete record of surgical procedures undertaken at 34th CCS between June and August 1918; those performed by Somervell alone take up thirty-three pages. His expertise, forged out of necessity and constant experimentation, resulted in a number of publications both during and after the war. See: T. Howard Somervell, "The Symptoms and Treatment of Trench Foot," *Journal of the Royal Army Medical Corps*, pp. 38–45, and *The Surgery of the Stomach and Duodenum* (London: Edward Arnold, 1948). For Somervell's correspondence with the Everest Committee, see: RGS Box 11, File 6.

For the best account of the opening assault on the Somme, see: Martin Middlebrook, *First Day of the Somme* (New York: Norton, 1972). See also: Malcolm Brown, *Somme* (London: Sidgwick & Jackson, 1996); John Keegan, *The Face of Battle* (New York: Viking, 1976); Gerald Glidden, *When the Barrage Lifts: A Topographical History and Commentary on the Battle of the Somme, 1916* (Barnsley: Leo Cooper, 1990); and Ray Westlake, *British Battalions on the Somme, 1916* (Barnsley: Leo Cooper, 1994). In recent years, a number of books have attempted to exonerate Douglas Haig by suggesting that after 1915, attrition was both a legitimate goal and the lone strategy that could have brought an end to a war that in an unprecedented manner had harnessed the full economic and industrial capacities of nation-states. Denis Winter, in *Haig's Command: A Reassessment* (London: Penguin, 1991), suggests to the contrary that Haig's mind ran on rails and that for four years the field marshal cast away the lives of his troops as if on a mission to reduce the national population.

For Somervell's description of walking through six acres of wounded soldiers at Vecquemont on July 1, 1916, see: *After Everest*, pp. 38–40. The experience transformed him into a pacifist and no doubt led to his decision to devote his life to saving lives in India. See: Howard Somervell, *Knife and Life in India: Being the Story of a Surgical Missionary at Neyyoor, Travancore* (London: Hodder and Stoughton, 1940), and *India Calling* (London: Livingston, 1947). In *After Everest*, he recalled:

> One day I went for a short walk on the battlefield. I sat down to rest on a sandbag. Just in front of me was a lad asleep, looking very ill—sallow skin, quite still. My God he's not breathing! He's dead! I got a real shock. I sat there for half an hour gazing at that dead boy. About eighteen I should say. He lay on his back, not mutilated, perhaps not dead many hours. Strange that, with corpses and bits of them strewing the ground for miles around, I should be so impressed by this one dead body. But so it was. For the moment he personified the madness called War. What did it mean to him? What were diplomacy, national relationships, commercial interests to him? Why should he be cut off before really tasting the joys and hardships and glories of life? And he was just one of tens of thousands.

For the official account of fate of the Newfoundland Regiment, see: General Sir James Edmonds and Major A. F. Becke, eds., *History of the Great War: Military Operations, France and Belgium, 1916* (London: Macmillan, 1932). See also: Richard Cramm, *The First Five Hundred of the Royal Newfoundland Regiment* (Albany: C. F. Williams & Son, 1923).

The wreck of the *Letitia* dominated the front pages of the *Halifax Herald* on August 2 and 4, 1917. The program for the service at Great Gable, preserved in the papers of the FRCC, reads: "War Memorial: Unveiling and Dedication of Bronze

Tablet Great Gable, The Fell & Rock Climbing Club, Whit-Sunday, June 8th, 1924
2.PM." It includes the full text of Young's address, the names of the dead, and the
words to the hymns sung that day. For Wakefield's correspondence with the Mount
Everest Committee, see RGS Box 13, File 5.

2: *Everest Imagined*

George Nathaniel Curzon wrote a dozen books, including *Persia and the Persian Question* (2 vols.; London: Longmans, Green, 1892); *Russia in Central Asia in 1889 and the Anglo-Russian Question* (London: Longmans, Green, 1889); and *British Government in India* (2 vols.; London: Cassell, 1925). For his account of his travels to meet the emir of Afghanistan in 1894 and his explorations of the Pamirs, see: *Tales of Travel* (New York: George Doran, 1923), and *The Pamirs and the Source of the Oxus* (London: Royal Geographical Society, Edward Stanford, 1896). For biographies of Curzon, see: David Gilmour, *Curzon* (London: John Murray, 1994), and Kenneth Rose, *Superior Person: A Portrait of Curzon and His Circle in Late Victorian England* (New York: Sterling, 2001).

For a sense of the spirit and character of what has been called the British century, there is no better source than Jan Morris's astonishing trilogy. See: *Pax Britannica: The Climax of an Empire* (New York: Harcourt, 1968); *Heaven's Command: An Imperial Progress* (New York: Harcourt, 1973); and *Farewell the Trumpets: An Imperial Retreat* (New York: Harcourt Brace Jovanovich, 1978). The wonderful phrase describing India as the "peacock bird in the gilded cage" is hers. See also two fine books by Lawrence James: *The Rise and Fall of the British Empire* (New York: St. Martin's Griffin, 1994), and *Raj: The Making and Unmaking of British India* (New York: St. Martin's Griffin, 1997). See also: Charles Allen, *The Buddha and the Sahibs* (London: John Murray, 2002); David Cannadine, *Ornamentalism: How the British Saw Their Empire* (London: Oxford University Press, 2001); Geoffrey Moorhouse, *India Britannica* (New York: Harper & Row, 1983); and Valerie Pakenham, *Out in the Noonday Sun: Edwardians in the Tropics* (New York: Random House, 1985). For the Great Trigonometrical Survey and the discovery of Everest, see a truly splendid book: John Keay, *The Great Arc* (New York: Harper-Collins, 2000), and J. R. Smith, *Everest: The Man and the Mountain* (Latheronwheel: Whittles, 1999).

For Tibetan history, most especially the complex diplomatic maneuverings between 1880 and 1950, there is no better source in English than Hugh Richardson, who served as British diplomatic representative in Lhasa from 1936 to 1940, and from 1946 to 1950. A brilliant linguist, fluent in Bengali, Richardson spoke, according to the Tibetan historian Tsepon Shakabpa, "impeccable Lhasa Tibetan with a slight Oxford accent." Like Charles Bell, he felt that Britain, the only European power to have treated with an independent Tibet, had betrayed its obligations. He wrote several books, including: *Tibet and Its History* (London: Oxford University Press, 1962), and, with David Snellgrove, *A Cultural History of Tibet* (London: Weidenfeld & Nicolson, 1995). Other writings on Tibetan history and culture appear in an essential collection: Hugh Richardson, *High Peaks, Pure Earth* (London: Serendia, 1998). Included is a vital source: "Tibetan Precis," a book-length summary of the history of British diplomatic relations with Tibet originally submitted in 1945 as a classified report to the government of India.

The Tibetan name of the Buriat monk who so aroused British suspicions was Tsenshab Ngawang Lobzang Dorje. Tsenshab is a title, indicating that he was one of seven spiritual tutors of the Dalai Lama. As Russians could not pronounce "Dorje," it became Dorjev, which in turn became Dorjeiff to Charles Bell and other writers.

Adding to the confusion was the Mongolian transposition of Ngawang to Agwang, and Dorje to Dorj. So in the literature, the man I am calling Agvan Dorzhiev after Alex McKay, *Tibet and the British Raj: The Frontier Cadre, 1904–1947* (Richmond: Curzon, 1977), has been identified by various names, including most commonly, Dorjieff (Charles Bell, *Portrait of a Dalai Lama: The Life and Times of the Great Thirteenth* [London: Collins, 1946]; Glenn H. Mullin, *The Fourteen Dalai Lamas: A Sacred Legacy of Reincarnation* [Santa Fe, N.M.: Clear Light Publishers, 2001]).

Other important sources on Tibetan history include: Charles Allen, *The Search for Shangri-La* (London: Little, Brown, 1999); Melvyn Goldstein, *A History of Modern Tibet, 1913–1951* (Berkeley: University of California Press, 1989); Glenn Mullin, *The Fourteen Dalai Lamas: A Sacred Legacy of Reincarnation* (Santa Fe, N. M.: Clear Light, 2001); Geoffrey Samuel, *Civilized Shamans: Buddhism in Tibetan Societies* (Washington, D.C.: Smithsonian Institution Press, 1995); Tsepon Shakabpa, *Tibet: A Political History* (New York: Potala Publications, 1984); David Snellgrove, *Buddhist Himalaya* (New York: Bruno Cassirer, 1957); Warren Smith, *Tibetan Nation* (Boulder: Westview, 1996); and R. A. Stein, *Tibetan Civilization* (London: Faber and Faber, 1972). To see how these diplomatic maneuvers and betrayals played out, with horrific consequences for Tibet, see: Tsering Shakya, *The Dragon in the Land of Snows* (New York: Columbia University Press, 1999). For extraordinary accounts of espionage and clandestine travel, see: Sarat Chandra Das, *Indian Pandits in the Land of Snow* (Calcutta: Baptist Mission Press, 1893), and *A Journey to Lhasa and Central Tibet*, edited by Phoebe Folger (Delhi: Book Faith India, 1998); as well as Derek Waller, *The Pundits: British Exploration of Tibet and Central Asia* (Lexington: University Press of Kentucky, 1990).

For the Anglo-Russian rivalry, see: Peter Hopkirk, *The Great Game* (London: John Murray, 1990), and Karl Meyer and Shareen Brysac, *Tournament of Shadows* (Washington, D.C.: Counterpoint, 1999). For a wonderful biography of Younghusband, see: Patrick French, *Younghusband: The Last Great Imperial Adventurer* (London: HarperCollins, 1994). The description of Younghusband's wardrobe I owe completely to Patrick, a friend. He captured in these details a portrait of a lost era of imperial travel, when an expedition leader such as Younghusband brought along not only clothing for every diplomatic and social occasion but also several tents for his personal use, a camp bed and chair, folding tables, a deck chair, a tea basket for picnics, several umbrellas, walking sticks, a box of Mannlicher ammunition, three rifles, and two swords. To carry this gear, the British turned to locals, whom they referred to as coolies, using a Hindu word meaning simply "porter." Though not considered a pejorative term at the time, it is now, and thus throughout the text I use the word "porter," though I retain "coolie" if used in a direct quote. Of greater concern ought to be the manner in which Tibetan porters were treated by the invasion force. At a time when union rules in Britain prevented bricklayers from carrying loads of more than fourteen pounds, the expedition porters—Nepali Sherpas, Rais, Limbus, and Lepchas—regularly hefted two hundred pounds, with some men carrying two or three telegraph poles, each weighing ninety pounds.

For two other fine Younghusband biographies, see: George Seaver, *Francis Younghusband: Explorer and Mystic* (London: John Murray, 1952), and Anthony Verrier, *Francis Younghusband and the Great Game* (London: Jonathan Cape, 1991). Younghusband himself wrote many books. The one that first made his reputation was *The Heart of a Continent: A Narrative of Travels in Manchuria, Across the Gobi Desert, Through the Himalayas, the Pamirs, and Chitral, 1884–1894* (London: John Murray, 1904). See also his *The Heart of Nature* (London: John Murray, 1921), *Wonders of the Himalaya* (London: John Murray, 1924), and *The Light of Experience* (Boston: Houghton Mifflin, 1927).

For three very fine accounts of the Younghusband invasion, see: Charles Allen, *Duel in the Snows* (London: John Murray, 2004); Peter Hopkins, *Trespassers on the Roof of the World: The Race for Lhasa* (London: John Murray, 1982); and Peter Fleming, *Bayonets to Lhasa* (London: Rupert Hart-Davis, 1961). Save for what they had gleaned from the accounts of the pundits, in 1904 the British knew very little about Tibet. Among the handful of sources that Younghusband, his officers, and the journalists accompanying the invasion force might have read before the expedition were accounts by intrepid individuals who had slipped into Tibet unauthorized. See: Hamilton Bower, *Diary of a Journey Across Tibet* (New York: Macmillan, 1894); Henry Savage Landor, *In the Forbidden Land* (2 vols.; New York: Harper and Brothers, 1899); Susie Carson Rijnhart, *With the Tibetans in Tent and Temple* (London: Oliphant, Anderson & Ferrier, 1904); William Rockhill, *The Land of the Lamas* (New York: Century, 1891); and Fanny Bullock Workman and William Workman, *In the Ice World of Himalaya* (London: T. Fisher Unwin, 1901).

The first real portrait of Lhasa to reach the West came in the books published in the wake of the expedition. For Younghusband's own account, see: *India and Tibet* (London: John Murray, 1910). See also: Edmund Chandler, *The Unveiling of Lhasa* (London, 1905; reprinted New Delhi: Cosmos, 1981); Perceval Landon, *Lhasa* (2 vols.; London: Hurst and Blackett, 1905; published in New York by Doubleday as *The Opening of Tibet 1905*); and L. Austine Waddell, *Lhasa and Its Mysteries* (London: Methuen, 1906).

The sense of something having been lost in the "unveiling of Lhasa" was captured in a book by John Buchan: *The Last Secrets: The Final Mysteries of Exploration* (London: Thomas Nelson & Sons, 1923). The opening chapter covers the Younghusband invasion, and the last heralds the campaign to conquer Everest. The frontispiece is a classic photograph of Everest taken by Sandy Wollaston in 1921, and the book is dedicated thus: "To the Memory of Brig.-Gen. Cecil Rawling, C.M.G, C.I.E. who fell at the Third Battle of Ypres, An Intrepid Explorer, A Gallant Soldier, and the Best of Friends." During the war Buchan was attached to the War Propaganda Bureau and later served as director of information. Commissioned as a second lieutenant in the Intelligence Corps, he wrote speeches and acted effectively as press secretary for Field Marshal Douglas Haig. He also wrote two best-selling spy thrillers: *The Thirty-Nine Steps* (London: William Blackwood, 1915) and *Greenmantle* (London: Hodder & Stoughton, 1917). In 1935 King George V elevated Buchan to the peerage, and for five years, until his death in 1940, he served as Lord Tweedsmuir, governor-general of Canada. Recruited by the Everest Committee to orchestrate all press relations for the 1921–24 expeditions, Buchan as much as anyone promoted and, indeed, personi-fied the impulse of imperial ambition and redemption that ran from Younghusband's invasion of Tibet, through the cataclysm of the Great War, to the exalted radiance of Everest.

Joanna Bourke, in *Dismembering the Male: Men's Bodies, Britain and the Great War* (Chicago: University of Chicago Press, 1996), argues that after the war the anonym-ity of death in the trenches and the endless images of maimed and broken bodies came to symbolize the emasculation of a nation. The Everest expeditions momentarily returned meaning and virility to words such as "honor" and "sacrifice" and in doing so offered a promise of regeneration. For a fascinating discussion, see also: Peter Bayers, *Imperial Ascent: Mountaineering, Masculinity, and Empire* (Boulder: University Press of Colorado, 2003). For more on Buchan, see: Janet Adam Smith, *John Buchan* (London: Rupert Hart-Davis, 1965).

For Rawling's expedition to the source of the Brahmaputra, see: Charles C. Rawling, *The Great Plateau* (London: Edward Arnold, 1905). Freshfield's most significant books were: *The Exploration of the Caucasus* (2 vols.; London: Edward Arnold, 1902) and *Round Kangchenjunga: A Narrative of Mountain Travel and Exploration* (London: Edward Arnold, 1903). Originally published in 1885, Clinton Dent's *Above the Snowline: Mountaineering Sketches Between 1870 and 1880* was reprinted by Kessinger Publishing in Whitefish in 2007. For Curzon's proposal to Freshfield beginning with "It has always seemed to me a reproach," see the Alpine Club Archives, Minute Book 9.

General Bruce wrote of his upbringing and early days as a soldier in *Himalayan Wanderer.* See also: Michael Underhill, "A Gurkha in Wales," *Country Life,* February 2, 1984. Bluster and laughter aside, Bruce was a battle-scarred warrior. He and his Gurkha soldiers fought with calculated ferocity at Hazara in 1891, in the relief of Chitral in 1895, at Waziristan in 1894–95, and throughout the entire Tirah campaign in 1897–98. As a commander, Bruce was mentioned in despatches on three occasions and awarded six clasps to two frontier medals. Of the Tirah pacification, he wrote in the regimental records:

> The troops under my command have marched everywhere within Orakzai and Afridi limits, and the whole of Tirah has now, for the first time, been accurately surveyed. Our enemies, wherever encountered, have been punished, and their losses are stated on unimpeachable evidence to have been extremely severe. The towers and walls of almost every fortified village in the country have been leveled to the ground, and the winter supply of grain, fodder, and fuel of both tribes has been consumed by the force. The Orakzais have been completely subdued, and have complied with the terms prescribed for them, but the Afridis still hold out, although I have strong hopes that they may before long submit, and thus save their country from a fresh invasion in the spring.

From the start Charles Bruce was drawn to mountains. In 1892, he and Martin Conway climbed to 22,600 feet on Kabru, a peak just south of Kangchenjunga. Three years later, Bruce was on Nanga Parbat, the world's ninth-highest mountain, when Alfred Mummery and two porters, having attained 22,965 feet, were swept to their death while reconnoitering the Rakhiot face. In 1907, he and A. L. Mumm, along with Tom Longstaff, set out for the Nanda Devi massif in the Garhwal Himalaya to attempt Trisul, a 23,360-foot peak revered by the Hindu as the trident of Shiva, the god of destruction and procreation. In thirteen hours Longstaff climbed 6,000 feet, reaching the summit, before descending 7,000 feet to base camp. For more than two decades this would remain the highest mountain ever climbed.

Tom Longstaff was an extraordinary figure in the early days of Himalayan climbing. Born in 1875, nine years after Bruce and eleven years before Mallory, Longstaff was in age a contemporary of Arthur Wakefield and Geoffrey Young's. A physician by training, educated at Eton and Oxford and St. Thomas's Hospital, he famously disdained the practice of medicine. His 1900 nomination for membership in the Alpine Club lists his profession simply as "Gentleman." His grandfather had made a great deal of money as a paint manufacturer, and his father had spent a good portion of it—some £25,000, a fortune in those days—underwriting Scott's first Antarctica expedition. Though independently wealthy, Longstaff himself lived frugally. If Martin Conway and the Duke of Abruzzi established the tradition of enormous expeditions laying siege to a summit, Longstaff set the precedent for what became known as the Alpine approach: small parties unencumbered by elaborate equipment making quick dashes for the heights. He famously lived off the land, eating whatever came his way and sleeping among the stones or on the dirt floor of the most modest of shelters.

In 1905 Longstaff and Charles Sherring, a deputy commissioner in the Indian Civil Service, crossed the Himalaya to reach Kailash and the sacred lake of Manasarowar. On the Gurla Mandhata massif, south of Kailash, Longstaff climbed to 23,000 feet only to be torn off the mountain by an avalanche that left him battered 3,000 feet below. He was forced to bivouac in the open. The following day, rather than retreating to safety, he retrieved his ice ax and headed back up the mountain, spending a second night in an ice cave. The next day he reached within 1,000 feet of the summit before sheer exhaustion forced him to turn back. Altogether Longstaff spent six months in Tibet in 1905, an expedition that cost him, railhead to railhead, less than £100. Four years later, having turned down an invitation to join Scott's fateful Antarctic expedition, Longstaff disappeared into the Karakoram, crossing the Saltero Pass to discover the upper reaches of the Siachen Glacier, just one of a score of journeys that would be recognized in 1928 when he was awarded the Founder's Medal of the Royal Geographical Society. See: Norman Collie, *From the Himalaya to Skye* (Edinburgh: David Douglas, 1902), and Charles Sherring, *Western Tibet and the British Borderland* (London: Edward Arnold, 1906). For Longstaff's correspondence with the Everest Committee, see: RGS Box 11, File 1; Box 28, File 7.

Alexander Kellas played a major role in the initial planning of the 1921 reconnaissance. For his correspondence with the Everest Committee, Hinks, and other members of the 1921 expedition, see: RGS Box 2, File 2. The paper read at the afternoon meeting of the RGS on May 18, 1916, was published as: A. M. Kellas, "A Consideration of the Possibility of Ascending the Loftier Himalaya," *Geographical Journal*, vol. 49 (January 1917), pp. 26–48. A modified version of this paper was submitted to the Alpine Club in March 1920 but not published until 2001. See: "A Consideration of the Possibility of Ascending Mount Everest," *High Altitude Medicine and Biology*, vol. 2, no. 3 (2001), pp. 431–61. See also: A. M. Kellas, "The Possibility of Aerial Reconnaissance in the Himalaya," *Geographical Journal*, vol. 51, no. 5 (May 1918), pp. 374–89, originally presented at the RGS on March 18, 1918. For more on Kellas, see: John B. West, "Alexander M. Kellas and the Physiological Challenge of Mt. Everest," *Journal of Applied Physiology*, vol. 63 (1987), pp. 3–11, and "A. M. Kellas: Pioneer Himalayan Physiologist and Mountaineer," *Alpine Journal*, vol. 94 (1989), pp. 207–13. For correspondence regarding the use of oxygen, see: RGS Box 30, File 5 and, at the National Archives, Kew, FD1/1208, DSIR 36/421, DSIR 36/394 (including reports from the ascent of Kamet and Finch's experience on Everest in 1922), and DSIR 3/254. See also: N. E. Odell, "Hypoxia: Some Experiences on Everest and Elsewhere," in Charles Clarke, Michael Ward, and Edward Williams, eds., *Mountain Medicine and Physiology* (London: Alpine Club, 1975, pp. 67–72).

For John Noel's correspondence with the Everest Committee, see: RGS Box 18, File 3 and Box 31, File 4. For his account of his 1913 journey, the paper read on March 10, 1919, at Aeolian Hall, see: John B. Noel, "A Journey in Southern Tibet and the Eastern Approaches to Mount Everest," *Geographical Journal*, vol. 53, no. 5 (May 1919), pp. 289–308. Accompanying this article are two photographs, captioned "North-East Glacier Flowing from Mount Everest" and "Mountains North of Makalu (27790) to Snout of North-East Mount Everest Glacier." The credit reads, "From photographs lent by Dr. A. M. Kellas." Kellas clearly did not take the photographs; he had been in the mountains beyond Kangchenjunga, but never as far west as Noel reached in 1913. Noel came within forty-five miles of Everest; these images of the Rabkar Glacier were taken within ten miles of the Kangshung Face. Kellas must have trained one of his local native companions and dispatched him with a camera to reconnoiter the eastern approaches to the mountain. For a splendid collection of Noel's photographs, edited by his daughter, see: Sandra Noel, *Everest Pioneer: The Photographs of Captain John Noel* (Thrupp: Sutton, 2003). For biographical material, see Noel's *Through Tibet to Everest*, 1989, and Reuben Ellis, *Vertical Margins: Mountaineering and the Landscape of NeoImperialism* (Madison: University of Wisconsin Press, 2001).

3: The Plan of Attack

The January 1912 article in the *Badminton Magazine* (vol. 34, no. 198, pp. 14–26) was written by George D. Abraham, brother of Ashley, both pioneering figures in British rock climbing. Thomas Holdich was president of the RGS from 1917 to 1919. See: T. H. Holdich, *Tibet the Mysterious* (New York: Frederick Stokes, 1906).

Many important documents concerning the diplomatic efforts to secure permission from both the Tibetans and the government of India are found in the India Office Records (IOR) Mount Everest File, India Office Library (British Library) Asia, Pacific and Africa Collections (formerly Oriental and India Office Library). The file is in four parts, with one devoted exclusively to maps and charts. Part 1 (IOR L/PS/10/777) covers the years up to 1923; Parts 3 and 4 (IOR L/PS/10/778) treat 1924 and beyond. For the minutes of the June 23, 1920, meeting between the RGS delegation and Lord Sinha, undersecretary of state for India, see Part 1 (IOR L/PS/10/777). Also of great interest in this file are various exchanges referring to Howard-Bury's initial mission, including Bell's objections and Viceroy Lord Chelmsford's concurrence that no expedition be authorized until the dispute over the sale of arms was resolved. For correspondence concerning preliminary plans for the expeditions, see also: RGS Box 1, Files 1–7 and 20.

In the aftermath of the attack at Loos on September 25, 1915, "The Roll of Honour" in the *Times* filled four full columns, a litany of the dead. During the battle Robert Graves was ordered to assault a machine gun nest in bright sunlight. His platoon ran twenty yards and, to a man, fell to the ground. He whistled the advance, but nobody stirred. He jumped from a shell hole and cursed them as cowards. "Not cowards, sir," his platoon sergeant shouted over the din and the pain of a shattered shoulder, "willing enough. But they're all fucking dead."

Roland Leighton had graduated from Uppingham on a radiant day in July 1914, a month before the outbreak of the war, a cadet officer dressed in khaki, a star athlete, and the winner of seven of the school's top academic prizes. The headmaster, in his farewell address, invoked patriotic duty and stated that if a man could not be useful to his country, he would be better off dead. Of the sixty-six boys who entered school with Roland, seventeen would, in fact, die in the trenches. Everyone who "goes out there," he wrote to his fiancée, Vera Brittain, returns irrevocably changed after two or three months. He added, "Horror piled on horror till one feels that the world can scarcely go on any longer."

Vera Brittain wrote the most poignant of all the war memoirs, *Testament of Youth* (London: Victor Gollancz, 1934). See also: Alan Bishop, ed., *Chronicle of Youth: Vera Brittain's War Diary, 1913–1917* (New York: William Morrow, 1982); Alan Bishop and Mark Bostridge, eds., *Letters from a Lost Generation* (Boston: Northeastern University Press, 1998); and Paul Berry and Mark Bostridge, *Vera Brittain: A Life* (Boston: Northeastern University Press, 2002).

Robert Bridge's *The Spirit of Man* (London: Longmans, Green, 1916) went through six editions before 1919. For the actual poetry of the war, see: Tonie and Valmai Holt, *Violets from Overseas: Poets of the First World War* (Barnsley: Leo Cooper, 1996); Jon Silkin, ed., *First World War Poetry* (London: Penguin, 1996); and Jon Stallworthy, ed.,

The Oxford Book of War Poetry (Oxford: Oxford University Press, 1984). As late as 1936, William Butler Yeats, then seventy-one and editor of the *Oxford Book of Modern Verse*, excluded from the anthology the work of Wilfred Owen, Siegfried Sassoon, Robert Graves, Ivor Gurney, Herbert Read, and Isaac Rosenberg. Yeats maintained that the passive suffering of war, however nobly expressed, lacked the moral vision essential to poetry. Such a conceit denied both what these men had achieved in their verse and what they had endured in a conflict that had made a mockery of the very notion of morality. Though Sassoon lived until 1967, he would never write of anything that occurred after 1920. His six volumes of autobiography are the stories of a life that died with the war.

For John Noel's record in the opening weeks of the war, see the war diary for 2/KOYLI (the King's Own Yorkshire Light Infantry; TNA: PRO WO 95/1558). His regiment was attached to the 13th Brigade (TNA: PRO WO 95/1548), 5th Division (TNA: PRO WO 95/1510). For documents detailing Noel's two diagnoses of shell shock, see the medical board reports for September 14, 1914; May 3, 1915; August 3, 1915; November 6, 1915; and March 9, 1917. These are referenced in the National Archives (TNA PRO WO 338/14) but housed with Ministry of Defence records in Glasgow (MOD Glasgow P/123705/1).

Howard-Bury served with 9th Battalion KRRC (King's Royal Rifle Corps) until December 10, 1916 (TNA: PRO WO 95/1900). He was then transferred to 7th Battalion KRRC (TNA: PRO WO 95/1897). On May 26, 1917, promoted to lieutenant colonel, he returned to 9th Battalion, where he served as commanding officer until captured on March 21, 1918, during the German Spring Offensive. See also the war diaries of the 42nd Brigade (TNA: PRO WO 95/1897) and the 14th Division (TNA: PRO WO 95/1874), as well as the *King's Royal Rifle Corps Chronicle*, on deposit at the Imperial War Museum.

Howard-Bury's personal papers are found at Trinity College Dublin (TCD). Of particular interest is his POW diary, which includes an account of his dramatic escape attempt (TCD MS 10823). Also on deposit at Trinity are two wartime diaries—one handwritten, from May 29 to September 8, 1916 (TCD MS 10821), and a second, typed as a manuscript, covering November 1, 1916 to September 25, 1917 (TCD MS 10822). Another important collection of Howard-Bury papers and photographs is found at the West Meath County Library at Mullingar, close to his family estate at Belvedere. Marian Keaney, a former librarian at West Meath, has produced two fine books from Howard-Bury's diaries. For his 1920 journey to Tibet to confer with Charles Bell and his literary contribution to the official account of the 1921 expedition, see: Charles Howard-Bury and George Leigh-Mallory, *Everest Reconnaissance*, edited by Marian Keaney (London: Hodder & Stoughton, 1991). For an account of his 1913 explorations of central Asia, see: Charles Howard-Bury, *Mountains of Heaven: Travel in the Tian Shan Mountains*, edited by Marian Keaney (London: Hodder & Stoughton, 1990). For unpublished manuscripts, again edited by Keaney from pre-war diaries, see: Charles Howard-Bury, "Rajahs, Rewals and Tigers: Travels in India 1906–1912," and Charles Howard-Bury, "Jubbulpore to England, 1909–1910," as well as Marian Keaney, "Lt. Col. Charles Howard-Bury: A Biographical Introduction." See also the Howard-Bury papers on deposit at the Liddell Hart Centre for Military Archives, King's College London, and his correspondence with the Everest Committee, RGS Box 13, File 1.

Maurice Wilson has been widely ridiculed for attempting Everest on his own, unprepared and poorly equipped. It was indeed an act of folly, but in a way no more crazy than what the climbers on the official expeditions were attempting to do. His war scars just ran deeper. See: Dennis Roberts, *I'll Climb Mount Everest Alone: The Story of Maurice Wilson* (London: Robert Hale, 1957), and Ruth Hanson, *Maurice Wilson: A Yorkshireman on Everest* (Kirkby Stephen: Hayloft, 2008).

For more on the transition to peace, see: Correlli Barnett, *The Collapse of British Power* (London: Pan Books, 2002); David Cannadine, *The Rise and Fall of Class in Britain* (New York: Columbia University Press, 1999), and *The Decline and Fall of the British Aristocracy* (New York: Vintage, 1999); Hugh Cecil and Peter Liddle, eds., *At the Eleventh Hour: Reflections, Hopes and Anxieties at the Closing of the Great War, 1918* (Barnsley: Leo Cooper, 1998); C. F. G. Masterman, *England After the War* (New York: Harcourt Brace, 1923); Brian Moynahan, *The British Century* (New York: Random House, 1997); Charles Mowat, *Britain Between the Wars, 1918–1940* (London: Methuen, 1955); Alan Palmer, *Victory 1918* (New York: Atlantic Monthly, 1998); and Stanley Weintraub, *A Stillness Heard Round The World: The End of the Great War* (New York: Dutton, 1985). *The Great War and Modern Memory*, by Paul Fussell, is an essential source; see also his *Abroad: British Literary Traveling Between the Wars* (New York: Oxford University Press, 1980).

For Younghusband's May 31, 1920, address to the RGS fellows, see: Francis Younghusband, "Natural Beauty and Geographical Science," *Geographical Journal*, vol. 56, no. 1 (July 1920), pp. 1–13. For Howard-Bury's correspondence from India on his first journey, see: IOR Part 1 (L/PS/10/777) and RGS Box 1, File 8. Howard-Bury and Charles Bell first met at Yatung at the home of David Macdonald, a quaint shingled bungalow of seven rooms with a glassed-in veranda; it was surrounded by lawns and beautiful terraced gardens, which Howard-Bury much admired.

Charles Bell wrote the first books on Tibet that were scholarly in a modern academic sense. See: Charles Bell, *Tibet: Past and Present* (Oxford: Clarendon, 1924); *The People of Tibet* (Oxford: Clarendon, 1928); *The Religion of Tibet* (Oxford: Clarendon, 1931); and *Portrait of a Dalai Lama: The Life and Times of the Great Thirteenth* (London: Collins, 1946). See also Charles Bell, "A Year in Lhasa," *Geographical Journal*, vol. 63, no. 2 (February 1924), pp. 89–105 (read before the RGS on December 3, 1923), as well as his introduction to F. Spencer Chapman, *Lhasa: The Holy City* (London: Readers Union, 1940). The contrast with the bombastic style of Claude White is telling. See: J. Claude White, *Sikhim and Bhutan: Twenty-one Years on the North-East Frontier, 1887–1908* (London: Edward Arnold, 1909). For another perspective on the Chumbi Valley, see: Lawrence John Lumley Dundas, Marquis of Zetland, *Lands of the Thunderbolt: Sikhim, Chumbi and Bhutan* (London: Constable, 1923).

At the outbreak of the war, the Thirteenth Dalai Lama sent a message to the British authorities through an emissary, Lonchen Sholkhang: "Tibet is willing to send one thousand Tibetan troops to India, to the support of your Empire, because we realize that the existence of Tibet depends on the continuance of Great Britain's Empire." The Dalai Lama then entered religious retreat to contemplate Yamantaka, the wrathful form of Manjushri, destroyer of death. He would not emerge until October 1919, close to a year after the cessation of hostilities in France.

4: Hinks's Watch

The Alpine Club Archives has a comprehensive collection of press clippings covering the Everest expeditions from 1921 through 1924. Among the headlines on January 11, 1921: "Where White Man Has Never Trod!," "Mile Higher Than Man Has Ever Been!," and "After Mt. Everest What?" Complete press coverage of the era is found at the Colindale Newspaper Library, an affiliate of the British Library. George Abraham's remarks appeared in the *Daily Mail* on January 14, 1921. To grasp the extent of Arthur Hinks's contribution, one need only peruse the Mount Everest Committee papers at the RGS Archives. His hand is present in virtually each of the 230 files that fill the 41 boxes of documents. For the applicants seeking to join the 1921 reconnaissance, see: RGS Box 5, Files 1–4. The more amusing letters are found in Boxes 14 and 15. For Hinks on photography, publicity, and the sale of magazine rights, see: Box 6, Files 1–6. For photographic equipment, see: Box 7, Files 1–3. Box 9, Files 1–4, contains correspondence related to botanical collecting and the sale of rare seeds. Box 8, Files 1–3, includes an exhaustive inventory of stores and equipment for the 1921 and 1922 expeditions.

On January 10, 1921, Younghusband addressed a meeting of the RGS and formally announced plans for a reconnaissance expedition. He also named the members of the newly formed Everest Committee. At a subsequent meeting on January 24, he named Howard-Bury expedition leader and Harold Raeburn leader of the climbing party. See: "The Mount Everest Expedition," *Geographical Journal*, vol. 57, no. 2 (February 1921), pp. 1–3. Four important preliminary papers appeared in short order: J. N. Collie, "A Short Summary of Mountaineering in the Himalaya, with a Note on the Approaches to Everest," *Alpine Journal*, vol. 33, no. 222 (March 1921), pp. 295–303; C. Howard-Bury, "Some Observations on the Approaches to Mount Everest," *Geographical Journal*, vol. 57, no. 2 (February 1921), pp. 121–24; "Dr. Kellas' Expedition to Kamet, Including His Report to the Oxygen Research Committee," *Geographical Journal*, vol. 57, no. 2 (February 1921), pp. 124–30; and H. T. Morshead, "Report on the Expedition to Kamet, 1920," *Geographical Journal*, vol. 57, no. 3 (March 1921), pp. 213–19. For Harold Raeburn's correspondence with the Everest Committee, see: RGS Box 2, File 1. See also the Geoffrey Winthrop Young Collection, Alpine Club Archives. For Raeburn's book, see: *Mountaineering Art* (London: T. Fisher Unwin, 1920).

For Bruce's November 8, 1920, address to the RGS, see: C. G. Bruce, "Mount Everest," *Geographical Journal*, vol. 57, no. 1 (January 1921), pp. 1–21. For his military service up to May 1914, see: *History of the 5th Gurkha Rifles (Frontier Force), 1858–1928* (London: Naval and Military Press/Imperial War Museum, 2006). For his subsequent service, see: G. C. Strahan, *Historical Record of the 6th Gurkha Rifles*, vol. 1, *1817–1919* (Aldershot: Gale and Polden, 1925). For an account of operations leading up to the assault on June 30, 1915, see: the war diary of the 29th Indian Brigade, May 15, 1915, to July 1, 1915 (TNA: PRO WO 95/4272), and the war diaries of the 29th Divisional HQ (TNA: PRO WO 95/4304, 95/4305). See also: Ian Hamilton, *Gallipoli Diary*, vol. 1 (London: Edward Arnold, 1920). Bruce's personal file (TNA: PRO WO 374/10207) contains the "Proceedings of a Medical Board," September 1, 1915, with a description of his wounds suffered that day. Also of interest is a letter from the India Office dated August 5, 1920, permitting Bruce to retire with the honorary rank of brigadier general, effective July 1, 1920. For Bruce's correspondence with the Everest Committee, see: RGS Box 18, File 1; Box 22, Files 1 and 2; and Box 36, File 2. For Winston Churchill's remarks, see: Martin Gilbert, *Churchill: A Life* (New York: Henry Holt, 1991), p. 362.

For Wollaston's early life, see: Nicholas Wollaston, *My Father, Sandy* (London: Short Books, 2003). For Wollaston's two travel books, see: A. F. R. Wollaston, *From Ruwenzori to the Congo* (New York: Dutton, 1908), and *Pygmies and Papuans* (London: Smith, Elder, 1912). For other perspectives on these expeditions, see: Mirella Tenderino and Michael Shandrick, *The Duke of Abruzzi: An Explorer's Life* (Seattle:

Mountaineers, 1997), and Charles G. Rawling, *The Land of the New Guinea Pygmies* (Philadephia: J. P. Lippincott, 1913). On June 3, 1930, Wollaston was murdered in his chambers at Cambridge by an undergraduate. After his death, his wife compiled a collection of his personal papers; Mary Wollaston, ed., *Letters and Diaries of A. F. R. Wollaston* (Cambridge: Cambridge University Press, 1933). For Wollaston's extensive correspondence with the Everest Committee, see: RGS Box 3, File 1. Additional correspondence is found at the King's College Archives, Cambridge, and in the Geoffrey Young Collection, Alpine Club Archives.

Wollaston described his African experiences in letters to Douglas Freshfield. On the eve of his final assault across the glaciers to the summit of the Ruwenzori, word reached him that natives had attacked his base camp, killing one man and wounding five. Abandoning the climb, Wollaston ordered a retreat that became a rout, a series of deadly encounters fought over three days. "It was impossible to take photographs," he wrote, "for we were dodging spears and arrows all the time. It was rather disconcerting to see one gentleman, not a dozen yards from me, take aim with bow and arrow." The two friends fell out when Freshfield published these letters without permission (*Times*, October 5, 1906). The rift became so complete that Freshfield tried to have Wollaston denied a place on the 1921 reconnaissance. Charles Rothschild, Wollaston's companion and patron, committed suicide in 1923. For Wollaston's naval service, see the Admiralty Archives (ADM171/88, ADM171/81).

For the early family life of George Finch, see: Elaine Dundy, *Finch, Bloody Finch: A Life of Peter Finch* (New York: Holt, Rinehart and Winston, 1980). Also of great interest is a long biographical essay written by Finch's son-in-law as an introduction to the reissue of Finch's classic memoir. See: Scott Russell, "George Finch—the Mountaineer" in G. E. Finch, *The Making of a Mountaineer* (Bristol: J. W. Arrowsmith, 1988), pp. 1–116. For Finch's correspondence with the Everest Committee, see: RGS Box 3, File 3. For additional correspondence, see: Geoffrey Winthrop Young Collection, Alpine Club Archives. For a fascinating correspondence between Scott Russell and Tom Blakeney of the Alpine Club concerning the Finch controversy, see: Ref: P 10 "Correspondence on G.I.'s Obituary and Between TSB and Scott Russell," a folder on deposit along with all of Blakeney's papers at the British Library. See also: J. B. West, "George I. Finch and His Pioneering Use of Oxygen for Climbing at Extreme Altitudes," *Journal of Applied Physiology*, vol. 94, no. 5 (May 1, 2003), pp. 1702–13.

For Finch's army file, including a fitness report, see TNA: PRO WO 339/18080. For his record in Salonika, see: war diary, Director of Ordnance Salonica (TNA: PRO WO95/4787 and TNA: PRO WO 95/4952). Finch's complicated personal life is also on record. The relevant papers are found in Divorce and Matrimonial Causes files, Court for Divorce and Matrimonial Causes and Probate, Divorce and Admiralty Division of the High Court Justice (TNA: PRO J77/1740, TNA: PRO J77/1768, TNA: PRO J77/1410). He married Betty Fisher in June 1915 and remained married at the time of his demobilization in May 1919. A search of the divorce papers index for 1915–21 reveals one divorce for George Ingle-Finch (file no. 3328–1918) and one for George Finch (file no. 04194–1920). These papers include evidence of his marriage to Gladys May on November 6, 1920, and copies of their correspondence from but a month later (December 5) in which she beseeched him to return to her side and he refused.

For the March 7, 1921, meeting of the RGS, see: Francis Younghusband, "The Mount Everest Expedition: Organization and Equipment," *Geographical Journal*, vol. 57, no. 4 (April 1921), pp. 271–82. For medical reports, see: RGS Box 29, File 5. The announcement naming the members of the 1921 expedition, including Finch, appeared in "The Monthly Record: The Society," *Geographical Journal*, vol. 57, no. 5 (May 1921), p. 232.

For Guy Bullock's correspondence with the Everest Committee, see: RGS Box 2, File 3. For records of his diplomatic service and correspondence concerning leave to join the expedition, see: National Archives, Foreign Office records FO 369/635, FO 369/646, FO 369/794, FO 369/752, FO 369/874, FO 369/1500, FO 369/1573, FO 369/1576, FO 369/1785, FO 371/2677, FO 371/24188, FO 382/292, FO 382/392, FO 382/1034, and FO 383/213. See also Bullock's obituary in: *The Foreign Office List and Diplomatic and Consular Year Book, 1957* (London: Harrison and Sons, 1958), p. 492.

For correspondence between Hinks and the Alpine Club (January 1921 to May 1923), see: RGS Box 12. For Collie's correspondence as president of the Alpine Club, see: RGS Box 11, File 5, and Box 25, File 9. For letters of Douglas Freshfield, see: RGS Box 26, File 5. For Sydney Spencer, see: Box 34, File 3. For sale of magazine rights, see: RGS Box 6, Files 2 and 6. For correspondence with the *Times*, see: Box 34, File 8. For fund-raising and accounting, see: RGS Box 21 and Box 16, Files 5 and 6. The pledges of support by King George V and the Prince of Wales, essential to Hinks's fund-raising efforts, were announced in: "The Monthly Record," *Geographical Journal*, vol. 57, no. 5 (May 1921), pp. 394–95.

5: Enter Mallory

George Mallory's papers are housed at the Magdalene College Archives, Cambridge. Among the documents are notes and letters from his time at Charterhouse, as well as a manuscript of "The Book of Geoffrey" and reviews and correspondence concerning his one published book: *Boswell the Biographer* (London: Smith Elder, 1912). Mallory aspired to be a writer, and he was responsible for roughly a third of the content of the official expedition accounts of both 1921 and 1922. In making these contributions, he recycled material from letters sent to friends and family members from the mountain. The 1924 account includes his actual letters, written to Ruth before his death. Mallory is at his best as a writer in such direct and simple exchanges. When he consciously sets out as an essayist, his prose tends to the florid. Mallory's biographer Peter Gillman has compiled a collection of his writings, including the contributions to the official expedition accounts: George Mallory, *Climbing Everest: The Complete Writings of George Mallory* (London: Gibson Square, 2010).

The bulk of the Mallory papers at the Magdalene College Archives consists of letters written to his wife. These are arranged in seven boxes, four of which contain 723 letters written between April 3, 1914, four months before the outbreak of war, and January 1919, two months after the Armistice. The Everest correspondence is limited to eighty-four letters (Box III, 5 Files), with the last dated May 27, 1924. Ruth's letters to George appear to have been lost; the archive contains but one. For Mallory's correspondence with the Everest Committee, see: RGS Box 3, Files 4 and 5.

For Mallory's early life, see the biographies already cited, especially Robertson (1969), Pye (1927), and Gillman and Gillman (2000). For a sense of prewar Britain, see: Simon Nowell-Smith, ed., *Edwardian England, 1901–1914* (London: Oxford University Press, 1964). For the writings of Graham Irving, see: R. L. G. Irving, *Ten Great Mountains* (London: J. M. Dent & Sons, 1940); *A History of British Mountaineering* (London: B. T. Batsford, 1955); and a volume he edited, *The Mountain Way: An Anthology in Prose and Verse* (London: J. M. Dent, 1938).

Having attended a British boarding school, albeit one transplanted to British Columbia, complete with cadet corps, rugby, predatory prefects, and English and Scottish masters hardened by the wars, I was not completely unfamiliar with the ethos of public schools such as Winchester and Charterhouse. Still, to reach back to Edwardian society and venture to understand male sexuality in the context of the times was a task as challenging as deciphering the most obscure cultural practices of Tibet. Among my guides were five fine books: Michael Adams, *The Great Adventure: Male Desire and the Coming of World War I* (Bloomington: Indiana University Press, 1990); Hugh David, *On Queer Street: A Social History of British Homosexuality, 1895–1995* (London: HarperCollins, 1997); H. Montgomery Hyde, *The Other Love* (London: Heinemann, 1970); Alisdare Hickson, *The Poisoned Bowl: Sex and the Public School* (London: Constable, 1995); and Neil McKenna, *The Secret Life of Oscar Wilde* (London: Century, 2003).

To be sure, physical intimacy among men was publicly perceived as something perverse, and it remained, as Oscar Wilde's companion Bosie Douglas wrote, "the love that dare not speak its name." But in Edwardian parlance, sex implied penetration. Other forms of physical contact, such as kissing or mutual fondling, were not necessarily tolerated, but they were anticipated, especially among the cloistered halls of public schools and universities, where women rarely entered. Men who would be appalled to be labeled sodomites expressed homoerotic sentiments reflexively and shamelessly. The term "homosexuality" was coined in Germany only in 1890 and did not come into common usage in England until the turn of the century. Greek love, as the practice was known, was seen as a passing phase, an indulgence that boys would outgrow as they moved into the world and married. As Robert Graves, a student of Mallory's at Charterhouse, wrote, "In the English public schools romance is necessarily homosexual. The opposite sex is despised and treated as something obscene. Many boys never recover from this perversion." In Edwardian discourse, the term "effeminate" referred to a man who spent too much time with his wife.

Mallory attended Cambridge at a time when a man could not remain a don if he elected to marry. Arthur Benson's repressed desires no doubt played on his depression, and he was not alone in his confusion. For a fine biography, see: David Newsome, *On the Edge of Paradise: A. C. Benson, Diarist* (London: John Murray, 1980). For biographies and memoirs of several of the key figures in Mallory's circle, see: Christopher Hassall, *A Biography of Edward Marsh* (New York: Harcourt, Brace, 1959), and *Rupert Brooke* (New York: Harcourt, Brace & World, 1964); Nigel Jones, *Rupert Brooke: Life, Death and Myth* (London: Richard Cohen Books, 1999); Geoffrey Keynes, *The Gates of Memory* (Oxford: Clarendon Press, 1981); Nicholas Mosley, *Julien Grenfell* (New York: Holt Reinhart & Winston, 1976); Mike Read, *Forever England: The Life of Rupert Brooke* (Edinburgh: Mainstream, 1997); and Frances Spalding, *Duncan Grant* (London: Pimlico, 1998). See also: Paul Delany, *The Neo-Pagans: Friendship and Love in the Rupert Brooke Circle* (London: Macmillan, 1987), and S. P. Rosenbaum, ed., *The Bloomsbury Group* (Toronto: University of Toronto Press, 1995).

In the prewar Cambridge scene, sexual license was celebrated as the antidote to Edwardian convention. "Do you understand about loving people of the same sex?" Rupert Brooke asked in a November 30, 1908, letter to Erica Cotterill. "It is the question people here discuss most, in all its aspects, and of course most of the sensible people would permit it." Returning to Cambridge after a sojourn at the India Office, Maynard Keynes put it more bluntly in a letter to an old friend: "The thing has grown in leaps and bounds in my two years of absences and practically everybody in Cambridge is an open and avowed sodomite!"

For a sense of the web of emotional entanglements among these friends, see: Keith

Hale, ed., *Friends and Apostles: The Correspondence of Rupert Brooke and James Strachey, 1905–1914* (New Haven: Yale University Press, 1998). Lytton Strachey was seven years older than his brother James. Duncan Grant, a cousin from India, moved in with the Strachey family in 1902, the year Lytton went off to university, leaving younger brother James at home. When Duncan visited Cambridge, Lytton was smitten. Grant dismissed his overture with a turn of phrase: "Relations we may be; have them, we may not." But in the summer of 1905, they began an affair. In a letter to Maynard Keynes, Lytton described the experience as a glimpse of heaven: "Oh dear, dear, dear, how wild, how violent, and how supreme are the things of this earth! I am cloudy, I fear almost sentimental. But I'll write again. Oh yes it's Duncan."

Maynard Keynes, meanwhile, was in love with Arthur Hobhouse, an undergraduate who had also captured Lytton's heart. When Hobhouse hinted at affection, Strachey advised Keynes not to waste a moment and to proceed directly to rape. Maynard responded to Lytton with kinder advice about Duncan: "You are the only person it would be the least good his being in love with, and he is the only person for you to be in love with. I am in love with your being in love with one another."

Lytton then gave Maynard the lowdown on Duncan: "He's a genius—a colossal portent of fire and glory . . . His feelings transcend all—I have looked into his eyes, and the whole universe has swayed and swam and been abolished, and we have melted into one indescribable embrace. His features were molded by nothing intermediary, but by the hand of God itself; they are plastic like living marble, they clothe a divinity, a quintessential soul."

With his older brother distracted, James Strachey fell for Rupert Brooke, described by Leonard Woolf as "exactly what Adonis must have looked like in the eyes of Aphrodite . . . [his] was the sexual dream face not only for every goddess, but for every sea-girl wreathed with seaweed red and brown." James, seven years younger than Lytton, admitted that his friendship with Rupert was founded in lust. "I have spoken to Rupert again," he wrote to Duncan Grant. "Nowadays three sentences in the street seem incredibly heaven like . . . The whole of my behavior must have seemed to indicate to him that I wanted to bugger him."

Crushed to learn that Brooke was having an affair with Lytton's lover Hobhouse, who was also sleeping with Duncan Grant, James was diverted by a new face in the crowd. To Vanessa Bell's news that Rupert had twice bedded Hobhouse, Virginia Woolf responded with an "equally thrilling piece of gossip . . . a divine undergraduate with a head like a Greek God . . . George Mallory."

Mallory fell for James Strachey, though Lytton remained keenly interested, at one point describing Mallory's body as "vast, pink, unbelievable . . . a thing to melt into and die." Lytton pursued Mallory to Charterhouse.

"Lytton seems to have had a hot time of it with George," James reported in an October 19, 1910, letter to Rupert Brooke. "I gather that on Sunday he only didn't go right through with it out of terror that someone would come in—as there was no key to the door. "The copulation never came," Lytton admitted to Duncan Grant, "though there were singular moments."

Lytton suggested that Grant use Mallory as a model. Mallory was charmed by the idea. "I am profoundly interested in the nude me," he responded in a note to Duncan. Grant, at the time in love with and living with Adrian Stephen, visited Mallory at the school and they agreed to collaborate on a series of portraits, both photographs and paintings. Grant left Charterhouse in a whirlwind of emotions. "I did not mean to suggest that I was in love with you," he wrote to Mallory. "I am far too fond of somebody else I think to fall in love. But I cannot help wanting to express my feelings for people to them and mine are so complicated towards you that I was somehow conscious that a kiss would somehow do it. When I say complicated I mean difficult to explain in words . . . I think you beautiful for one thing . . ."

More than anyone, Cottie Sanders understood what lay at the heart of the "Cambridge School of Friendship." For her remarks and her description of meeting Mallory at Zermatt, see David Robertson's biography, *George Mallory*, pp. 37, 59. Mallory's breathless correspondence with James Strachey, including his December 20, 1909, letter from France, is deposited at the British Library, Additional Manuscripts Collection (ADD 63119, 63119–63126 Blakeney Collection, vols. XLI–XLVIII Papers and Correspondence Relating to Mountaineering: 1861–1971; ADD 60679 Strachey Papers [20th Century Series], vol. XXV [ff. 181]. 2. ff. 4–40, George Herbert Leigh Mallory, Mountaineer). For Robert Graves on Mallory, see: *Good-bye to All That*, pp. 61–66. Additional correspondence between these Cambridge friends and lovers is on deposit at King's College Archives, Cambridge. The Geoffrey Winthrop Young Collection, Alpine Club Archives, contains twenty-five letters from Mallory to Young, as well as three from Mallory's daughters to Young, their godfather.

For the "Dreadnought hoax," see Frances Spalding's *Duncan Grant*, pp. 85–89. For Bloomsbury's reaction to the war, see: Jonathan Atkim, *A War of Individuals: Bloomsbury Attitudes to the Great War* (Manchester: Manchester University Press, 2002). The highlight of Mallory's school career at Winchester was the day his 1904 shooting team, competing against all the other public schools, won the coveted Ashburton Shield, securing a victory with a bull's-eye on the final shot. "It was simply glorious," he wrote to his sister Avie. "We won the Public Schools Racquets last holidays, we badly beat Eton at cricket, and now we have won the Public Schools shooting, which is really the best of the lot, because every decent school goes in for it, and it comes to the public notice much more than anything else." The entire school had welcomed home the winners, hoisting them aloft and carrying them through the gates of the school. Ten years later, skill at shooting had taken on a new significance. In 1914, 383 boys from 43 schools competed for the Ashburton Shield. Of these 66 would die in the war, and 79 others would be wounded, many severely. For a haunting sense of the role these schools played in the war, see: Peter Parker, *The Old Lie: The Great War and the Public School Ethos* (London: Constable, 1987). For Mallory's popularity as a lecturer, see back issues of the *Carthusian*, 1912–14, Charterhouse School Archives. Also to be found is a list of his students in two forms of Under VI Modern History; cross-referenced against casualty lists, these provided a sense of rates of morbidity and mortality among the students he had taught and sent off to war.

During the war Mallory was attached to the 40th Siege Battery, and invalided home. Upon his return to France in September 1918, he served with the 515th Siege Battery. Having consulted seven relevant war diaries, we found no record of Mallory. In a more promising avenue of research, we tracked the service record of James Lithgow, Mallory's commanding officer in the 40th Siege Battery in the University of Glasgow Archives and at the National Library of Scotland, in Edinburgh. Among the documents were the reminiscences of Lithgow's batman Ramsey, which included an account of the deaths of the Port Glasgow lads, Craig and Forrest, as they accompanied Mallory back from a forward observation post. In tracking the movements of the 40th Siege Battery through the war diary of the 2nd Corps commander of artillery (TNA: PRO WO 95/689–691), we found it evident that Mallory's battery was part of the 30th H.A.G. (Heavy Artillery Group), attached to the 8th Division. The war diary for the commander of artillery of the 8th Division (TNA: PRO WO 95/1684) revealed that 30th H.A.G. was put at the disposal of the commander of artillery of the

8th Division at 9:45 a.m. on July 1, 1916, the morning of the Somme assault. Hence it became possible to follow the movements of the 40th Siege Battery at a crucial period of Mallory's service.

Mallory's correspondence with Eddie Marsh (thirteen letters, seven postcards) may be found at the Berg Collection of English and American Literature, New York Public Library. Also in this collection are 128 letters from Robert Graves to Marsh, including one (October 10, 1916) noting that Mallory had not had leave for six months, and another (December 29, 1917) that looks ahead to his marriage to Nancy Nicholson: "George Mallory as my oldest surviving friend who first introduced me to mountains and through you to modern poetry, my greatest interests next to Nancy and my regiment, is going to be my best man on the 23rd." Also of great interest in this collection are 128 letters and three postcards written by Graves to Siegfried Sassoon. It was fascinating to discover that Mallory had met Wilfred Owen, and through Graves had become familiar with not only the two finest poets to emerge from the war, but arguably two of the bravest soldiers.

Siegfried Sassoon was with Graves at the Somme, where he fought with the savagery of the doomed, making a specialty of murderous forays into enemy trenches at night. Wounded by a sniper's bullet through the chest, and later shot accidentally in the head by his own men, Sassoon received the Military Cross and the DSO, medals he would one day toss into the Mersey. A graduate of Marlborough and Cambridge, a published poet and a son of the landed gentry, he was deemed a hero, which made it especially awkward when he stunned the British establishment by coming out against the war in the summer of 1917 with a powerful manifesto published in the *Times*. "I am making this statement as an act of willful defiance of military authority," it began,

> because I believe the war is being deliberately prolonged by those who have the power to end it. I am a soldier, convinced that I am acting on behalf of soldiers. I believe that this war, upon which I entered as a war of defense and liberation, has now become a war of aggression and conquest . . . I have seen and endured the suffering of the troops, and I can no longer be a party to prolong these sufferings for ends which I believe to be evil and unjust . . . On behalf of those who are suffering now I make this protest against the deception that is being practiced on them; also I believe that I may help destroy the callous complacence with which the majority of those at home regard the continuance of agonies which they do not share, and which they have not sufficient imagination to realize.

For a serving officer to publish such a tract was tantamount to treason. To avoid the embarrassment of a military court-martial, the government agreed to a compromise suggested by Graves. Sassoon would be declared mentally unfit and dispatched to Craiglockhart, a military hospital in Edinburgh that specialized in the treatment of officers suffering from neurasthenia, or shell shock. Graves made this arrangement not to compromise his friend but, rather, to save him. At the medical review board, Graves acknowledged that Sassoon suffered from hallucinations, visions of the dead rising from the corpse-strewn soils of Picardy. Three times during his testimony he burst into tears, recalling the ground where he, too, had been abandoned to die. Only one who had lived through the insanity of the trenches, he said, could understand that Sassoon's statement was no mere protest. It was the agonized cry of a soldier doomed never to be free from the horror.

At Craiglockhart Sassoon met Wilfred Owen. Owen had joined the 2nd Manches-

ters in December 1916 and within a week had been at the front, "marooned on a frozen desert," lying beside the stiff bodies of friends dead from the cold. For twelve days
he did not sleep, wash, or remove his boots. Under constant gas and artillery attack,
with shells bursting within yards of his position, burying comrades alive, Owen shattered. It was not about courage or cowardice. Later in the war he would win the Military Cross by single-handedly seizing a German machine gun and using it to kill more
of the enemy than he wished to remember. He would die seven days before the end of
the war, leading his men in an attack across the Sambre River and the Oise Canal. Shell
shock was not due to personal weakness; it was a state of being that afflicted, to one
degree or another, a majority of the men who actually knew the reality of the front. In
1916 it accounted for 40 percent of the casualties in combat zones. More than 80,000
men were formally diagnosed, and these were the ones who came out of the line not
just dazed but rabid, incapable of speech, incontinent, their eyes bulging in rage, their
fingers clawing at their mouths, drooling with the livid faces of the half dead. Owen
endured for three months, until, shaking and tremulous, his memory vacant, he was
evacuated from the front.

At the hospital Owen showed some of his unpublished poetry to Sassoon, who
encouraged him to write about the war. Through Sassoon, Owen became friendly with
Graves. By the same post that brought Owen an invitation to Graves's wedding came a
letter from the *Nation* accepting for publication the "Miners," his first poem to appear
in a national magazine. Owen must have felt some elation as he traveled to London
and St. James's Church in Piccadilly for Graves's wedding on January 23, 1918. He no
doubt shared his good news with Graves and perhaps with Mallory, himself an aspiring writer. Graves and Owen had first met at Craiglockhart in early October 1917,
an encounter so inspirational to Owen that he had within the week composed six
new poems. Among them was "Dulce et Decorum Est," arguably the greatest anti-
war poem ever written. The title comes from Horace, from a line that had been
inscribed in public school minds for generations: "It is sweet and proper to die for
one's country."

> Bent double, like old beggars under sacks,
> Knock-kneed, coughing like hags, we cursed through sludge,
> Till on the haunting flares we turned our backs
> And towards our distant rest began to trudge.
> Men marched asleep. Many had lost their boots
> But limped on, blood-shod. All went lame; all blind;
> Drunk with fatigue; deaf even to the hoots
> Of tired, outstripped Five-Nines that dropped behind.
>
> Gas! GAS! Quick, boys!—An ecstasy of fumbling,
> Fitting the clumsy helmets just in time,
> But someone still was yelling out and stumbling,
> And flound'ring like a man in fire or lime . . .
> Dim, through the misty panes and thick green light,
> As under a green sea, I saw him drowning.
>
> In all my dreams, before my helpless sight,
> He plunges at me, guttering, choking, drowning.
>
> If in some smothering dreams you too could pace
> Behind the wagon that we flung him in,
> And watch the white eyes writhing in his face,

His hanging face, like a devil's sick of sin;
If you could hear, at every jolt, the blood
Come gargling from the froth-corrupted lungs,
Obscene as cancer, bitter as the cud
Of vile, incurable sores on innocent tongues,—
My friend, you would not tell with such high zest
To children ardent for some desperate glory,
The old Lie: *Dulce et decorum est*
Pro patria mori.

For more on Owen and Sassoon, see: Dominic Hibberd, *Wilfred Owen* (Chicago: Ivan R. Dee, 2003); John Stallworthy, *Wilfred Owen* (Oxford: Oxford University Press, 1974) and (as editor) *The Poems of Wilfred Owen* (New York: Norton, 1986); Max Egremont, *Siegfried Sassoon* (New York: Farrar, Straus and Giroux, 2005); and Jean Wilson, *Siegfried Sassoon: The Making of a War Poet* (New York: Routledge, 1999).

For a sense of the scale of the industrial war effort, consider that for four years and four months, gunners fired as many as a million shells a day. Behind the narrow British front, engineers laid 6,879 miles of railroad, along which rolled millions of tons of supplies: food, weapons, bandages, bullets, timber, petrol for the tanks and trucks, and hay by the trainload for tens of thousands of horses. The army requisitioned more than thirty thousand miles of flannelette to clean rifles, six million rabbit skins for winter vests, fifty-one thousand rubber stamps, ten million shovels, and 137,224,141 pairs of socks.

Mallory's final break with Charterhouse came at a memorial service for the school's dead. The headmaster sat proudly as Field Marshal Lord Plumer remembered the war as "a complete vindication of the English Public-School training in enabling inexperienced soldiers to take responsible posts successfully." Mallory knew the poetry of Siegfried Sassoon, and Plumer's remark brought to mind the final verse of "Suicide in the Trenches":

You smug-faced crowd with kindling eye
Who cheer when soldier lads march by,
Sneak home and pray you'll never know
The hell where youth and laughter go

When Mallory went to Ireland, Desmond Fitzgerald, head of propaganda at the Dáil, the provisional Irish assembly, personally authenticated his documents, writing, "Mr. G Mallory is anxious to have first hand information as to acts of oppression and terror. I shall be glad if he can be assisted."

6: The Doorway to the Mountain

For a sense of Darjeeling and its railroad circa 1921–24, I consulted contemporary guidebooks, including one written by David Macdonald, the British trade agent at Yatung. See: *Darjeeling and Its Mountain Railway* (Calcutta: Caledonia, 1921); K. C. Bhanja, *Darjeeling at a Glance* (Darjeeling: Oxford Book & Stationery, 1941), and *Lure of the Himalaya Embodying Accounts of Mount Everest Expeditions by Land and Air* (Darjeeling: Gilbert, 1944), *History of Darjeeling and the Sikkim Himalaya* (New Delhi: Gyan, 1993; originally published in 1948); E. C. Dozey, *A Concise History of the Darjeeling*

District Since 1835 (Calcutta: Jetsun, 1989; originally published in 1922); David Mac-donald, *Touring in Sikkim and Tibet* (New Delhi: Asian Educational Services, 1999; first published by the author in Kalimpong in 1930); and Jahar Sen, *Darjeeling: A Favoured Retreat* (New Delhi: Indus, 1989). For the breakdown of the mules, see: "Mount Ever-est Expedition," *Geographical Journal*, vol. 58, no. 1 (July 1921), pp. 56–59.

In September 1920, Kellas, accompanied by Morshead, reached 23,600 feet on Kamet in the Garhwal Himalaya. Even as Raeburn and Howard-Bury arrived in Darjeeling, he climbed Narsing (19,930 feet) and reached 21,000 feet on Kabru, a peak just south of Kangchenjunga, to photograph the Everest group from the Kang La, some sixty to eighty miles, he estimated, from the face of the mountain. After nearly a year in the field, he was spent and exhausted before even beginning the Everest reconnaissance. The telegram announcing his death read: "Younghusband. Geographical London Deeply regret report death of Kellas from sudden heart failure at Kampadzong on June Fifth." It was wired from Calcutta at 12:50 p.m. (7:20 a.m. GMT on June 8). Sent as urgent three times, at three times the normal expense, it was received in London on the afternoon of June 8, exactly eight and a half hours after having been sent from Calcutta. For the formal announcement of the loss, see: "Mount Everest Expedition," *Geographical Journal*, vol. 58, no. 2 (August 1921), pp. 136–37.

For Morshead's early life, see Ian Morshead's biography *The Life and Murder of Henry Morshead*. For the Lohit and Dibang expeditions, see: E. W. C. Sandes, *The Military Engineer in India*, and *The Indian Sappers and Miners* (Chatham: Institute of Royal Engineers, 1948). For the exploration of the Tsangpo, see: Bailey, *No Passport to Tibet*, and H. T. Morshead, "An Exploration in Southeast Tibet," *Royal Engineers Journal* (January 1921), pp. 21–40. During the war Morshead commanded the 212th Field Company Royal Engineers (TNA: PRO WO 95/2414), 33rd Division (TNA: PRO WO 95/2411). His second-in-command was John de Vars Hazard. According to the war diary, Lieutenant Hazard was severely wounded at 11:00 p.m., May 15, 1916, while supervising the construction of an observation post on the Somme front. On June 1, 1918, Morshead's command shifted to the 46th Division (TNA: PRO WO 95/2672) after his predecessor and his adjutant were struck by a shell and killed instantly. Morshead himself was badly wounded by rifle fire on September 25, 1918. In May 1919 Morshead was transferred to India and placed in charge of the Waziristan Survey Force; see *History of the Corps of Royal Engineers*, vol. 5 (Chatham: Institution of Royal Engineers, 1952). For his correspondence with the Everest Committee, see: RGS Box 31, File 2, and Box 11, File 3. Setting out from Darjeeling, Morshead's team included the surveyors Lalbir Singh, Gujjar Singh, and Torabaz Khan, the photogra-pher Abdul Jali, and fifty porters. For his account of the 1921 expedition, see: H. T. Morshead, *Royal Engineers Journal* (September 1923), pp. 353–70. See also: "Report on the Operations of the Mt. Everest Survey Detachment 1921," Royal Engineers Library, 30/34 1921 (97206), ms. 16 pages. Of interest as well is a comprehensive obituary published in the *Royal Engineers Journal* (December 1931), pp. 718–23.

For the early life of E. O. Wheeler, see: Esther Fraser, *Wheeler* (Banff: Summer-thought, 1978). For his record as a cadet at RMC, see National Archives of Canada, II-K-7, vol 7. Both Wakefield and Longstaff climbed with Wheeler and his father. See: A. W. Wakefield, "A Canadian Alpine Club Camp," *FRCC Journal*, vol. 5, no. 3 (1921), pp. 261–73. Wheeler's papers (M169) at the Whyte Museum include a diary for 1911–12 and two scrapbooks, one spanning 1914 to 1924 and a second with per-sonal papers from 1910 through 1933. Of note are newspaper clippings tracking his military honors, first the Military Cross in February 1915, and in December the cross of the Légion d'honneur (Chevalier 5th Class), awarded personally by General Haig.

From August 16, 1914, Wheeler served in the 1st King George V's Own Bengal Sappers and Miners, No. 3 Company. The war diary (TNA: PRO WO 95/3938) indicates that the unit embarked for France on September 9, reached Marseille on October 14, and was entrenched at the front on October 31, where its soldiers served through the worst of the fighting until November 1915, when the unit was shipped out to Mesopotamia. In the subsequent campaign Wheeler was mentioned in despatches five times in three months, before being invalided to India with typhoid fever (TNA: PRO WO 95/5134). As of April 17, 1917, Wheeler was attached to the 8th Field Company KGO Sappers and Miners (TNA: PRO WO 95/5222); he ended the war at the 55th Infantry Brigade headquarters (TNA: PRO WO 95/5229) and was later transferred to the 51st Brigade, 17th Division, the occupying army (TNA: PRO WO 95/5210). See: J. W. B. Merewether and Frederick Smither, *The Indian Corps in France* (London: John Murray, 1918).

Wheeler called his wife Dolly; her full name was Dorothea Sophie Danielsen. She was from Birmingham but had made her way to London during the war. They were engaged five days after first meeting. She sailed for India before either knew that Wheeler would be offered a place on the Everest expedition. Married at the Bombay cathedral on March 15, they had but a month together before heading to Darjeeling. Wheeler wrote eighty-three letters to Dolly during the expedition, the first from Rongli on May 21 and the last from "Toong Bungalow" on October 16, three days before they were reunited. These letters complemented Wheeler's journal and provided a fascinating lens on the 1921 expedition. For Wheeler's correspondence with the Everest Committee, see: RGS Box 4, File 4. For his account of the 1921 reconnaissance, see: E. O. Wheeler, "The Mount Everest Expedition, 1921," *Canadian Alpine Journal*, vol. 13 (1923), pp. 1–25.

The modern Western fascination with Tibet arguably began with the theosophists. See Annie Besant, *The Ancient Wisdom* (London: Theosophical Publishing, 1899); Helena Petrovna Blavatsky, *The Secret Doctrine* (2 vols.; London: Theosophical Publishing, 1888); and Sylvia Cranston, *Helena Blavatsky* (New York: Jeremy Tarcher, 1993). In the late 1920s and early '30s, just as scores of war memoirs broke the silence of a decade, a number of books appeared heralding the mystical wonders of Tibet and riding the wave of interest in the occult and all things metaphysical that followed the war. See: Alexander David-Neel's *My Journey to Lhasa* (New York: Harper & Brothers, 1927), *Initiations and Initiates in Tibet* (London: Rider, 1931), and *Magic and Mystery in Tibet* (New York: Claude Kendall, 1932); Barbara Foster and Michael Foster, *The Secret Lives of Alexandra David-Neel* (New York: Overlook, 1998); James Hilton, *Lost Horizon* (London: Macmillan, 1933); and Nicholas Roerich, *Altai-Himalaya* (New York: Frederick Stokes, 1929), and *Heart of Asia* (New York: Roerich Museum Press, 1930). These books influence perceptions of Tibet to this day. Walter Evans-Wentz published a translation of *The Tibetan Book of the Dead* (Oxford: Oxford University Press, 1927); forty years later it would provide the lyrics for a song by John Lennon and the Beatles, "Tomorrow Never Knows," from the album *Revolver*, released in 1966.

In recent years, a number of excellent books have examined this cult of the sacred, particularly in the context of contemporary Tibet and the politics of the exile community and the West. See: Peter Bishop, *The Myth of Shangri-La: Tibet, Travel Writing and the Western Creation of Sacred Landscape* (Berkeley: University of California Press, 1989), and *Dreams of Power: Tibetan Buddhism and the Western Imagination* (London: Athlone Press, 1993); Thierry Dodin and Heinz Räther, eds., *Imagining Tibet: Perceptions, Projections and Fantasies* (Somervell: Wisdom, 2001); Lee Feigon, *Demystifying Tibet* (Chicago: Ivan R. Dee, 1996); and Donald Lopez, *Prisoners of Shangri-La: Tibetan Buddhism and the West* (Chicago: University of Chicago Press, 1998).

7: *The Blindness of Birds*

There has been much discussion and controversy concerning Tibetan names for Everest. The Swedish explorer Sven Hedin first proposed the name Tchoumou Lancma, and suggested that it had been noted by French Jesuits in China as early as 1717. See: Sven Hedin, *Mount Everest* (Leipzig: Verlag Brockhaus, 1923). Charles Bell disagreed, suggesting that the name was not Chomolungma but Cha-ma-lung, a prosaic reference to a southern region of snows where Tibetan kings delighted in feeding birds. See: Sydney Burrard, "Mount Everest and Its Tibetan Names," *Survey of India*, Prof. Paper 26 (1931). In 1930 David Macdonald, the British trade agent at Yatung, was told by Tibetan officials that the proper name was Mi-ti Gu-ti Cha-pu Long-nga, the full meaning of which was, according to Charles Bell, more or less, "the mountain whose summit was invisible to those nearby, but seen from all nine directions, and so high that birds flying over its peak go blind." One thing is clear: the popular translation of Chomolungma as "Goddess Mother of the World," commonly cited in the Everest literature, is a romantic projection with little connection to ethnographic or historical reality. See: Edwin Bernbaum, "A Note on the Tibetan and Nepali Names of Mount Everest," *American Alpine News*, vol. 8, no. 227 (1999), pp. 25–26; Ed Douglas, *Chomolungma Sings the Blues* (London: Constable, 1997); Johan Reinhard, "The Sacred Himalaya," *Alpine Journal*, vol. 29, no. 61 (1987), pp. 123–32; J. R. Smith, *Everest: The Man and the Mountain*, pp. 211–24; T. S. Blakeney, "A Tibetan Name for Everest," *Alpine Journal*, vol. 70, no. 311 (1965), pp. 304–10.

For an understanding of Tingri as a trading nexus, with routes reaching east to Shegar and Shigatse, west to Nyenyam, and south across the Himalayan passes to Nepal, see: Barbara Nimri Aziz, *Tibetan Frontier Families: Reflections of Three Generations from D'ing-ri* (New Delhi: Vkas, 1978); and "Tibetan Manuscript Maps of Dingri Valley," *The Canadian Cartographer*, vol. 12, no. 1 (1975), pp. 28–38. For an introduction to the Buddhist dharma, see: Keith Dowman, *The Sacred Life of Tibet* (London: Thorsons, 1997); Thomas Laird, *The Story of Tibet: Conversations with the Dalai Lama* (New York: Grove, 2006); Jean-François Revel and Matthieu Ricard, *The Monk and the Philosopher* (London: Thorsons, 1998); and Robert Thurman, *Essential Tibetan Buddhism* (New York: HarperSanFrancisco, 1995).

For hidden valleys and sacred geography, see the writings of Hildegard Diemberger: "Beyul Khenbalung, the Hidden Valley of the Artemisia: On Himalayan Communitites and Their Sacred Landscape," in A. W. MacDonald, ed., *Mandala and Landscape* (New Delhi: D.K. Printworld, 1997), pp. 286–334; "Political and Religious Aspects of Mountain Cults in the Hidden Valley of Khenbalung-Tradition, Decline and Revitalization," in Anne Marie Blondeau and Ernst Steinkeller, eds., *Reflections of the Mountain* (Vienna: Verlag der Österreichischen Akademie der Wissenschaften, 1996), pp. 219–32; "Pilgrimage to Hidden Valleys, Sacred Mountains and Springs of Life Water in Southern Tibet and Eastern Nepal," in Charles Ramble and Martin Brauen, eds., *Anthropology of Tibet and the Himalaya* (Ethnological Museum of the University of Zurich, 1993), pp. 60–72; "Mountain Deities, Ancestral Bones and Sacred Weapons," in P. Kvaerne, ed., *Tibetan Studies* (Oslo: Institute for Comparative Research in Human Culture, 1994), pp. 144–53; and "The Hidden Valley of the Artemisia," dissertation, University of Vienna, 1992. See also: Toni Huber, ed., *Sacred Spaces and Powerful Places in Tibetan Culture* (Dharamsala: Library of Tibetan Works and Archives, 1999); *The Cult of Pure Crystal Mountain: Popular Pilgrimage and Visionary Landscape in Southeast Tibet* (Oxford: Oxford University Press, 1999); Franz-Karl Ehrhard, " 'A Hidden

Land' in the Tibetan-Nepalese Borderlands" in A. W. MacDonald, ed., *Mandala and Landscape* (New Delhi: D.K. Printworld, 1997), pp. 335–64; Hamid Sardar-Afkhani, "The Buddha's Secret Gardens: End Times and Hidden Lands in Tibetan Imagination," dissertation, Department of Sanskrit and Indian Studies, Harvard University, 2001; and Ngawang Zangpo, *Sacred Ground* (Ithaca: Snow Lion, 2001). For the *chöd* tradition, see: Jérôme Edou, *Machig Labdrön and the Foundations of Chöd* (Ithaca: Snow Lion, 1996); Sarah Harding, ed., *Machik's Complete Explanation: Clarifying the Meaning of Chöd* (Ithaca: Snow Lion, 2003); and Joshua Waldman, Lama Wangdu: "Chod Tradition," thesis, University of Wisconsin, Madison.

For insights concerning the charismatic lama of Rongbuk, Dzatrul Rinpoche, I had both his spiritual autobiography, the *namthar* translated by Lama Urgyen, and Barbara Aziz's superb book *Tibetan Frontier Families*, which grew out of extensive interviews with Tibetans from Tingri and the Everest region living in exile in Kathmandu. Also of great interest is the work of Sherry Ortner. See: *Sherpas Through Their Rituals* (Cambridge: Cambridge University Press, 1978), *High Religion: A Cultural and Political History of Sherpa Buddhism* (Princeton: Princeton University Press, 1989), and *Life and Death on Mt. Everest* (Princeton: Princeton University Press, 1999). For a lovely book of reflection, evocative of the spiritual life in the monasteries founded by Dzatrul Rinpoche, see: Hugh Downs, *Rhythms of a Himalayan Village* (San Francisco: Harper and Row, 1980).

For E. O. Wheeler and the Canadian photographic survey technique, see: Don Thomson, *Men and Meridians: The History of Surveying and Mapping in Canada*, vol. 2, *1867–1917* (Ottawa: Queen's Printer, 1967); A. O. Wheeler, "The Application of Photography to the Mapping of the Canadian Rocky Mountains," *Canadian Alpine Journal*, vol. 11 (1920), pp. 76–96; E. O. Wheeler, "The Canadian Photo-Topographical Method of Survey," *Royal Engineers Journal* (April 1922), pp. 177–85; "Report on the Trial of the Canadian Report on Photo-Topographical Method of Survey," unpublished manuscript Royal Engineer Library, Mt Everest Operations of the Survey Dept, 1921 (97206); and *The Survey of India During War and Early Reconstruction, 1939–1946* (Dehra Dun: Survey of India, 1955).

8: Eastern Approaches

For the unraveling of the Raj between the wars, see: Arthur Herman, *Gandhi & Churchill* (New York: Bantam, 2008). For the natural history and geology of the Everest region, with special reference to the Arun drainage and the eastern approaches to the mountain, see: Edward Cronin, *The Arun* (Boston: Houghton Mifflin, 1979); and Toni Hagen, G. O. Dyhrenfurth, C. H. von Fürer-Haimendorf, and Erwin Schneider, *Mount Everest* (London: Oxford University Press, 1963). For the culture of the Sherpas and the cross-border trade between Tibet and Nepal, see: Christoph von Fürer-Haimendorf, *The Sherpas of Nepal* (London: John Murray, 1964), *Himalayan Traders* (New York: St. Martin's Press, 1975), and *The Sherpas Transformed* (New Delhi: Sterling, 1984). If the British introduction of the potato brought new wealth to the Sherpas of Solu Khumbu, the rise of international mountaineering transformed their identity, for better and for worse. See: Vincanne Adams, *Tigers of the Snow* (Princeton: Princeton University Press, 1996); Jonathan Neale, *Tigers of the Snow* (New York: Thomas Dunne, 2002); and Tashi Tenzing, *Tenzing Norgay and the Sherpas of Everest* (New York: McGraw-Hill, 2001).

9: The North Col

For a complete account of Morshead and Wollaston's journey to Nyenyam, see Wollaston's "An Excursion to Nyenyam and Lapche Kang," in *Mount Everest: The Reconnaissance 1921*, pp. 281–89. For more on Lapche, see: Keith Dowman, *The Sacred Life of Tibet* (London: Thorsons, 1997), and Lobsang Lhalungpa, *The Life of Milarepa* (New York: Dutton, 1977). For progress reports on the expedition, see: "Mount Everest Expedition," *Geographical Journal*, vol. 58, no. 3 (September 1921), pp. 225–26, and "Mount Everest Expedition," *Geographical Journal*, vol. 58, no. 6 (December 1921), pp. 446–54. For publication of the first photographs sent from the mountain, see: "Mount Everest Expedition," *Geographical Journal*, vol. 58, no. 4 (October 1921), pp. 276–83.

Mallory and Howard-Bury were as oil and water. "Frankly I was quite glad Bury was away," Mallory wrote after Howard-Bury left Kharta for the Kama Valley. "I can't get over my dislike of him." Mallory cared only for the climb. Howard-Bury's proudest achievement, as he wrote to Younghusband, was the discovery in the valley of the fourteen lakes of a "deep claret coloured meconopsis," a species of poppy, quite possibly new, "growing from two to two and a half feet high and covered with fifteen to twenty flowers growing up the stem."

As the expedition finally came to grips with the mountain, reaching the heights of the Lhakpa La and facing the ordeal of the North Col, the men were exposed to brutal cold and winds as violent as any experienced by polar explorers. Everest folklore suggests that they endured these conditions pathetically underequipped, dressed in tweeds, as the story goes. In fact, they had the very latest gear, and it was not insubstantial. For a fascinating review of the development of mountaineering equipment and clothing, with a discussion of what was available in 1921–24, see: Mike Parsons and Mary Rose, *Invisible on Everest* (Philadelphia: Northern Liberties Press, 2003).

When Mallory recalled first seeing the Kangshung, or East Face, of Everest, two vertical miles of hanging ice, he famously wrote, "Other men, less wise, might attempt this way if they would, but, emphatically, it was not for us." The East Face would not be climbed until 1983, thirty years after Hillary and Tenzing's ascent. That successful climb, by an American expedition led by James Morrissay, was followed in 1988 by a four-man American-British team that pioneered a route up the South Buttress to the South Col. Among the climbers were Stephen Venables and Ed Webster, who lost several fingers to the frost. Both have written wonderful books, and Venables, in particular, has emerged as one of the finest mountaineering writers. See: Stephen Venables, *Everest: Kangshung Face* (London: Hodder & Stoughton, 1989), *Everest: Alone at the Summit* (New York: Thunder's Mouth Press, 2000), and *Everest: Summit of Achievement* (New York: Simon & Schuster, 2003); and Ed Webster, *Snow in the Kingdom* (Eldorado Springs: Mountain Imagery, 2000).

Reaching the summit of Everest today virtually implies that a book celebrating the effort will follow. Most of these recall why the anthropologist Claude Lévi-Strauss dismissed travel books as "grocery lists and lost dog stories." But among the scores of mountaineering books on Everest and the high Himalaya are some that are truly memorable. For the wonderful writings of Frank Smythe, see: *The Kangchenjunga Adventure* (London: Victor Gollancz, 1930), *Kamet Conquered* (London: Hodder & Stoughton, 1932), *The Spirit of the Hills* (London: Hodder & Stoughton, 1935), *Camp Six* (London: Adam & Charles Black, 1937), *The Adventures of a Mountaineer* (London: J. M. Dent & Sons, 1940), and *The Mountain Vision* (London: Hodder & Stoughton,

1941). For the first successful aerial reconnaissance, see: P. F. M. Fellowes, L. V. S. Blacker, and P. T. Etherton, *First Over Everest: The Houston–Mount Everest Expedition, 1933* (New York: Robert McBride, 1934). For the 1963 American success, see: *Americans on Everest* (Philadelphia: J. B. Lippincott, 1964). For classic accounts by three of the greatest Everest climbers of the modern era, see: Chris Bonington and Charles Clarke, *Everest: The Unclimbed Ridge* (London: Hodder & Stoughton, 1983); Chris Bonington, *The Everest Years* (London: Hodder & Stoughton, 1986), and *Everest* (London: Weidenfeld & Nicolson, 2002); Thomas Hornbein, *Everest: The West Ridge* (Seattle: Mountaineers, 1989); Reinhold Messner, *Everest: Expedition to the Ultimate* (London: Random House, 1979), and *The Crystal Horizon* (Ramsbury: Crowood Press, 1989).

Harold Raeburn could not get a break. That he had walked across the flooded landscape of Tibet to rejoin the party counted for little; his failure to bring the mail invoked the wrath of all. "Raeburn's capacity for being tiresome is unlimited," wrote Mallory to Geoffrey Young. "Raeburn like a mug didn't bring the mail on," noted Wheeler in his journal, "much to everyone's disgust." Bullock lamented, "Raeburn, who looks very grizzled, passed our mails and stores at Chushar, but did nothing to bring them on!" The missing mail had become an obsession. On September 8, 1921, Wheeler noticed a familiar figure climbing up the slope on the far side of the river, across from his camp in the upper Kharta Valley. He shouted but could not be heard. The man turned and gestured. It was Morshead's colleague from the survey party, Gujjar Singh, who had been mapping the country north of Kharta. They were all old soldiers, so Wheeler wrapped a white towel around his ice ax and for more than thirty minutes communicated with Singh, signaling in Morse code. "Our hopes were raised when he started 'mail,'" Wheeler later wrote his wife, "but they fell when the next word was 'not' and continued 'arrived at Kharta yet.'"

For Heron's correspondence with the Mount Everest Committee, see: RGS Box 11, File 4, and Box 27, File 3. For formal acknowledgment of Wheeler's discovery of the East Rongbuk route to the North Col, see: "Mount Everest Expedition," *Geographical Journal*, vol. 58, no. 5 (November 1921), pp. 371–78. See also: J. N. Collie, "The Mount Everest Expedition," *Alpine Journal*, vol. 34, no. 223 (November 1921), pp. 114–17. The return of the last of the party to Britain and the formal end to the 1921 reconnaissance was announced in "Mount Everest Expedition," *Geographical Journal*, vol. 59, no. 1 (January 1922), pp. 50–51.

10: The Summit of Their Desires

John Morris served with the 1st Battalion of the 5th Leicester Regiment in 1915–18 and then with the 3rd Battalion of the 9th Gurkhas. For his early life and his war experience, see *Hired to Kill*, as well as Christopher Moore's *Trench Fever*, a haunting account of his grandfather's frontline experiences in the same regiment in which Morris served. See also: J. D. Hills, *The Fifth Leicester* (Loughborough: Echo, 1919), and the war diaries of the 1st Battalion of the 5th Leicester Regiment (TNA: PRO WO 95/2690). Morris's impressive military record, on deposit at the British Library Asia, Pacific, and Africa Collections, India Office Records (IOR), belies the self-deprecating style of his memoir (IOR: Service Record L/MIL/14/16968). Commissioned into the Indian Army on July 29, 1918, Morris served with the 9th Gurkhas until October 27, on which date he reported for duty with the 2nd Battalion of the 3rd Gurkhas, then stationed in Haifa (TNA: PRO WO 95/4689). For his active service as part of the

Waziristan Field Force in 1921, including an account of the ambush that resulted in the slaughter of his force, see the 2nd Battallion, 3rd Gurkha Rifles War Diary (TNA: PRO WO 95/5399). Morris, the only more or less openly homosexual member of the Everest expeditions, was very close to E. M. Forster. Their letters, from the early 1930s to the late 1960s, are in the E. M. Forster Collection, King's College Archives, Cambridge University. For Morris's correspondence with the Everest Committee, see: RGS Box 31, File 3. For his ethnographic work, see: John Morris, *Living with Lepchas* (London: Heinemann, 1938). See also: John Morris, *A Winter in Nepal* (London: Rupert Hart, 1964), and W. Brooke Northey and John Morris, *The Gurkhas* (London: John Lane, 1928).

For the formal announcement of those selected for the 1922 expedition, see: "The Mount Everest Expedition," *Geographical Journal*, vol. 59, no. 3 (March 1922), p. 207. With the men en route for India, the RGS and the Alpine Club published the results of the 1921 effort. See: C. K. Howard-Bury, "The Mount Everest Expedition," *Geographical Journal*, vol. 59, no. 2 (February 1922), pp. 81–99; George Leigh Mallory, "Mount Everest Expedition: The Reconnaissance," *Geographical Journal*, vol. 59, no. 2 (February 1922), pp. 100–11, and "The Mount Everest Maps and Photographs," *Geographical Journal*, vol. 59, no. 2 (February 1922), pp. 131–36. For papers read at the joint meeting of the RGS and at Queen's Hall December 20, 1921, see: C. K. Howard-Bury, "The 1921 Mount Everest Expedition," *Alpine Journal*, vol. 34, no. 224 (May 1922), pp. 195–214; and George Leigh Mallory, "Mount Everest: The Reconnaissance," *Alpine Journal* vol. 34, no. 224 (May 1922), pp. 215–27.

The discussion concerning the use of oxygen was ongoing. See: "The Mount Everest Expedition," *Geographical Journal*, vol. 59, no. 5 (May 1922), pp. 379–83; and P. J. H. Unna, "The Oxygen Equipment of the 1922 Everest Expedition," *Alpine Journal*, vol. 34, no. 224 (May 1922), pp. 235–50. See also: Arthur Hinks, "The Mount Everest Maps and Photographs," *Alpine Journal*, vol. 34, no. 224 (May 1922), pp. 228–35; A. M. Heron, "Geological Results of the Mount Everest Expedition, 1921," *Geographical Journal*, vol. 59, no. 6 (June 1922), pp. 418–36, and A. F. R. Wollaston, "The Natural History of Southwest Tibet," *Geographical Journal*, vol. 60, no. 1 (July 1922), pp. 5–20.

Colin Crawford was commissioned as second lieutenant on March 26, 1915, and from November 27, 1916, he was in Mesopotamia with the 2nd Battalion, 5th Gurkhas. His medical officer was Richard Hingston, who would later serve in the same capacity on the 1924 Everest expedition. The men were together in the field for several months, until Hingston took ill and was invalided out of the war zone. On March 10, 1917, Crawford was sent to reinforce the 1st Battalion, 2nd Gurkhas, and after June 1, 1917, to the 1st Battalion, 6th Gurkhas at Aziziya. For war diaries, see: 2/5 Gurkhas (TNA: PRO WO 95/5197); 1/2 Gurkhas (TNA: PRO WO 95/5180); 1/6 Gurkhas (TNA: PRO WO 95/5020, TNA: PRO WO 95/5024). See also: F. J. Moberly, *Official History of the Great War: The Campaign in Mesopotamia, 1914–1918*, vol. 3 (London: HMSO, 1925). In 1940, with Britain under siege, Crawford as a schoolmaster and member of the Home Guard led night patrols of boys, searching for German saboteurs. In place of a revolver, he carried a "villainous looking kukri," the stealth weapon of choice of the Gurkha regiments. For Crawford's correspondence with the Everest Committee, see: RGS Box 13, File 4.

Geoffrey Bruce, commissioned in August 1914, served alongside his father, Lieutenant Colonel G. T. Bruce, the brother of General Charles Bruce of Everest fame, in the Glamorgan Yeomanry. For his army record, see TNA: PRO WO 374/10236. His unit reached Egypt on March 3, 1916; on October 5, 1916, his father became commanding officer (TNA: PRO WO 95/4427). On February 2, 1917, the Glamorgan

Yeomanry was absorbed as part of the 24th Battalion, Welsh Regiment. Bruce served in Egypt and Palestine until he joined the 6th Gurkha Rifles in July 1917, destined for deployment to the North-West Frontier. For accounts of skirmishes, pitched battles, and British pacification efforts led by Bruce, see: D. G. J. Ryan, *History Record of the 6th Gurkha Regiment*, vol.1, *1817–1919* (Aldershot: Gale and Polden, 1925), and H. R. K. Gibbs, *History Record of the 6th Gurkha Regiment*, vol. 2, *1919–1948* (Aldershot: Gale and Polden, 1955).

For Bruce's record in the Indian Army, see: IOR L/MIL/14/607. His annual performance review for 1920 describes a soldier not "decidedly above or below average in any respect as to call for special notice." He was not recommended for accelerated promotion, and his name did not make the "Selected List" for the Staff College. In 1923, by contrast, in the wake of his great success on Everest, the Annual Confidential Report describes Bruce as "an exceptionally brilliant officer . . . His record as a member of the Mount Everest Expedition last year, marks him as a born leader and as possessed of the greatest determination, endurance and self reliance." Recommended immediately for the Staff College, Bruce would in time attain the rank of major general and serve as deputy chief of staff of the Indian Army. For him, as for many, Everest had indeed been a good career move. For his correspondence with the Everest Committee, see: Box 36, File 3, and Box 22, File 3.

Many documents pertaining to Tom Longstaff are preserved at the Alpine Club Archives. See especially: P44 Longstaff Papers; Geoffrey Winthrop Young Correspondence; B49 Miscellaneous Correspondence. D57 contains a set of personal diaries, including the one he kept from February 16 through July 18, 1922. It begins on the eve of his departure for India and ends when finally, suffering from phlebitis, he reaches home, having endured Hinks's tirade at the RGS in London on the morning of July 17. Longstaff's journal is really a series of short notes, with as many as three days covered on a page. It is not nearly as comprehensive as the diary of George Finch (National Library of Scotland, Manuscripts Collection), which begins on March 3, as he leaves Victoria Station, and ends in Bombay on July 1, as he embarks on the P&O *Macedonia* for home. But together with Wakefield's journal, these diaries provide a fascinating lens on the 1922 expedition.

Colonel Strutt, a career officer, has a large army file (TNA: PRO WO 339/12240); it includes correspondence concerning his rescue of the Austrian royal family. For more on the controversy and the wrath of Curzon, see: TNA: PRO WO 371/6102. Strutt sailed for France on September 9, 1914. In command of the 2nd Battalion, Royal Scots, 8th Brigade, 3rd Division, he was wounded at Vieille-Chapelle on October 15, during the retreat from Mons. For the war diary of the 2nd Royal Scots, including a report of Strutt being wounded, see: TNA: PRO WO 95/1423. For his medical board proceedings on October 26, see: TNA: PRO WO 339/12240. For his correspondence with the Everest Committee, see: RGS Box 18, File 2. For additional correspondence, see: Alpine Club Archives, Geoffrey Winthrop Young Collection and F7 Strutt Papers.

Arthur Wakefield's 1922 Everest diary begins on Sunday, February 26, and ends on Saturday, September 30, 1922. It is a record of a man far more active and engaged than the disparaging remarks by General Bruce and Finch after the expedition would suggest. With Longstaff hors du combat, Wakefield stepped in as an effective and hardworking medical officer. For a fascinating review, see: Ronald Bayne, "Dr. Arthur Wakefield on Mount Everest in 1922: 'This Has Not Been by Any Manner of Means a Picnic,' " *Journal of Medical Biography*, vol. 11 (2003), pp. 150–55. For Wakefield on the death of the Sherpas in 1922, see: "The Everest Disaster: Dr. Wakefield's Experience," *Times*, January 22, 1923.

For documents, reports, and correspondence concerning the challenge of oxygen, see TNA: PRO DSIR (Department of Scientific and Industrial Research) Records Bureau Files. For Kellas on Kamet, Haldane's experiments at Oxford, Finch's report regarding the performance of the 1922 oxygen apparatus, and correspondence among Bruce, Farrar, and Professors Unna, Dreyer, and Hill, see: TNA: PRO DSIR 36/394 and TNA: PRO DSIR 3/254. For minutes of the Oxygen Research Committee, 1918–21, see: TNA: PRO DSIR 3/248. For additional Kellas correspondence about oxygen, see: TNA: PRO FD 1/1208.

As a key player in 1922 and expedition leader in 1924, Teddy Norton had an extensive correspondence with the Everest Committee. See RGS Box 11, File 2; Box 26, File 3; Box 31, File 5; and Box 36, File 7. Within twelve days of the British declaration of war on August 4, 1914, Lieutenant Norton arrived in France from Ireland with the 3rd Cavalry Brigade, Royal Horse Artillery. He was awarded the Mons Star (TNA: PRO WO 329/2509) and, serving in D Battery (TNA: PRO WO 95/1133), was promoted to captain in October. On January 22, 1915, Norton was transferred to the 6th Divisional Ammunition Column (TNA: PRO WO 95/1588). In February 1915 he was mentioned in despatches and awarded the Military Cross. He joined the 53rd Battery, 2nd Brigade RFA in March (TNA: PRO WO 95/1596). Three months later he was at Ypres, assigned to the 1st Canadian Artillery Division (TNA: PRO WO 95/3740, 95/3733), Canadian Corps (TNA: PRO WO 95/1059). Mentioned for a second time in despatches in June, he served with the Canadians at the Somme, was promoted to major in September, and returned to D Battery, RHA, in February 1917 (TNA: PRO WO 95/1133). In 1917 he saw action at Arras, Loos, and Cambrai. His brother, Lieutenant Richard C. Norton, E Battery, RHA, was killed on March 23, 1918, the same month Norton was awarded the Distinguished Service Order (DSO) for "conspicuous gallantry and devotion to duty" during the retreat of the Fifth Army after the German Spring Offensive. Richard, thirteen years younger than Teddy, was just twenty when he died.

For Somervell on Tibetan music, see: "Tibetan Culture," chapter 14 of *The Assault on Mount Everest, 1922*, pp. 313–318. See also: "The Mount Everest Film: Examples of Tibetan Music," *Times*, January 16, 1923.

Dzatrul Rinpoche's autobiography is replete with references to his spiritual life and practice. In the third month of the year, for example, he offered a fire *puja*, fervent prayers that cast him into a dream state. A single cymbal-like sound spun into being three circles of light, the clear bliss light of his teacher, Trulshig Rinpoche, whose radiant face emerged from the void, the embodiment of loving compassion and wisdom. In the fourth month, even as the British marched on the mountain, a messenger arrived from Lhasa with sacred treasures, the long-life offerings of the Thirteenth Dalai Lama, and other blessings for Dzatrul Rinpoche. In the sixth month, as was tradition, the lama entered summer retreat, giving his life over to the recitation of the Kangyur, the great canon of the Buddhist dharma. These devotions and many others are described in detail in the *namthar*. Of the arrival of the British climbers in 1924, there appears scarcely a word.

11: Finch's Triumph

For Finch's ongoing tussle for respect, see a book of his first published in German in 1925: George W. Rodway, ed., *George Ingle Finch's The Struggle for Everest* (Ross-on-Wye: Carreg, 2008). That Wakefield and Crawford were serious about making their own attempt is evident in Wakefield's diary entry for Friday, May 26, 1922: "Finch and Bruce return and go down to 3. Crawford and I alone plan ascent tomorrow. Wind W, sun and mist." For the announcement of Finch and Bruce's record climb, see: "The Mount Everest Expedition, 1922," *Geographical Journal*, vol. 60, no. 1 (July 1922), pp. 67–71. For the death of the Sherpas on the North Col, see: "The Mount Everest Expedition, 1922," *Geographical Journal*, vol. 60, no. 2 (August 1922), pp. 141–44. For a summary of achievements and notice of Morshead's injuries, see: "The Mount Everest Expedition, 1922," *Geographical Journal*, vol. 60, no. 3 (September 1922), p. 218.

12: *The Thread of Life*

For the first extensive set of images from the 1922 expedition, see: "Photographs from the Mount Everest Expedition," *Geographical Journal*, vol. 60, no. 4 (October 1922), pp. 228–91. For the papers read at the October 16, 1922, joint meeting of the Alpine Club and the Royal Geographical Society, see: C. G. Bruce, "The Mount Everest Expedition of 1922: I. Darjeeling to the Rongbuk Base Camp," *Geographical Journal*, vol. 60, no. 6 (December 1922), pp. 385–424; George Leigh Mallory, "The Second Mt. Everest Expedition," *Alpine Journal*, vol. 34, no. 225 (November 1922), pp. 425–39; and George Finch, "The Second Attempt on Mt. Everest," *Alpine Journal*, vol. 34, no. 225 (November 1922), pp. 439–50. For Noel's first film, see: "The Mount Everest Kinematograph Film," *Geographical Journal*, vol. 61, no. 1 (January 1923), pp. 48–50. Throughout the fall of 1922 Finch remained committed to the Everest project, and loyal to the Everest Committee. On November 20 he addressed the technical challenges in a paper read before an afternoon meeting of the RGS. See: George I. Finch, "Equipment for High Altitude Mountaineering, with Special Reference to Climbing Mount Everest," *Geographical Journal*, vol. 61, no. 3 (March 1923), pp. 194–206. Finch also made a significant contribution to the official expedition account. See: "The Attempt with Oxygen," in C. G. Bruce, *The Assault on Everest 1922* (New York: Longmans, Green, 1923), pp. 227–72. Correspondence tracking the conflict that led to his being denied a place on the 1924 expedition is found in the archives of both the Alpine Club and the RGS. For the formal announcement of the members of the 1924 expedition, see: "The Mount Everest Expedition of 1924," *Geographical Journal*, vol. 63, no. 4 (April 1924), pp. 340–42. The failure in 1922 prompted a number of reassessments by leading figures in British mountaineering. See: Tom Longstaff, "Some Aspects of the Everest Problem," *Alpine Journal*, vol. 35, no. 226 (May 1923), pp. 57–74, and Douglas Freshfield, "The Conquest of Everest," *Geographical Journal*, vol. 63, no. 3 (March 1924), pp. 229–37. Somervell recalled that the snow at Camp III had been of a thick consistency "not previously seen in the Himalaya." Plowing through "snow of an unpleasant texture," it took them two hours merely to reach the base of the North Col from the upper camp. Longstaff was quite right in suggesting that the attempt ought never to have been made.

For the adventures of William McGovern, see: *To Lhasa in Disguise* (New York: Grosset & Dunlap, 1924). Among those at Cambridge less than welcoming to Ruth Mallory was Arthur Benson. In his diary he described her as "beautiful, self-conscious, brusque and extremely inattentive. She believes herself to be a suggestive and humourous talker, but she is a thin and truculent performer." Benson, of course, neurotic and obsessive, destined to be dead within two years, wrote unpleasant things about everyone and could be readily ignored.

Bentley Beetham went to Barnard Castle School as a boy and remained for forty years, living out his life as a schoolmaster, with a special interest in ornithology and climbing. His books include: *Among Our Banished Birds* (London: Edward Arnold, 1927), *The Home-Life of the Spoonbill* (London: Witherby, 1910), and *Photography for Bird Lovers* (London: Witherby, 1911). His main contribution to the 1924 expedition was as a still photographer. He secured by far the finest images during the expedition, thus allowing Noel to concentrate on his film. For samples of his work, see: Bentley Beetham, "An Everest Portfolio," *FRCC Journal*, vol. 7, no. 1 (1925), p. 69. For Beetham's correspondence with the Everest Committee, see: RGS Box 24, File 4.

John de Vars Hazard served with the 212th Field Company, Royal Engineers (TNA: PRO WO 95/2414), which was attached to the 33rd Division (TNA: PRO WO 95/2411). Hazard was wounded twice, most severely on May 15, 1916, on the Somme front, and again in 1918 while serving in Italy with 529th Field Company, Royal Engineers (TNA: PRO WO 95/4221). For his correspondence with the Everest Committee, see RGS Box Hazard 27, File 2. Hazard was largely responsible for the debacle that stranded porters on the North Col, leading to the rescue effort that may well have fatally weakened Mallory, Somervell, and Norton on the eve of their summit attempts. But it was not completely Hazard's fault. He had been left alone in dire conditions on the North Col with porters who shivered with fear, as Geoffrey Bruce discerned, certain that the sounds they heard by night were the fierce howls and barks of watchdogs guarding the goddess's abode. That Hazard could perform in any capacity at 23,000 feet was remarkable. As he explained in a letter to Eric Shipton, "On my part a severe war wound of the right hip had opened up for the second time since reaching the mountain, causing worry which, added to the stress at the loss of Mallory and Irvine would not have found me at my best." Clearly a man in Hazard's condition ought not to have been on the expedition from its inception.

Noel Odell, the last to see Mallory and Irvine alive, is a pivotal figure in the Everest story. For his correspondence with the Everest Committee, see RGS Box 30, Files 1 and 2. Additional papers, publications, and correspondence may be found at the Alpine Club Archives. See especially the Geoffrey Winthrop Young Collection, as well as Ref: C138, B74, B75 Misc. Papers, F13/1, F13/2, F13/3. Ref: D98 contains a partial copy of Odell's 1924 Everest diary, May 25 to June 21. The complete diary begins in earnest on March 9, with his arrival in Darjeeling, and runs through September 6, the day his ship docked at Dover on his return to England.

During the war Odell served in the 59th Field Company, Royal Engineers (TNA: PRO WO 95/1535). The Medal Card Index indicates that he first entered a theater of war in July 1916, the summer of the Somme; the unit diary records that he reached Mametz on July 27. On April 14, 1917, he was wounded at Allouagne in an accident, as his pick struck buried ordnance. Following his accident, according to Odell's personal war diary, spanning 1915–18, he did not return to France until January 18, 1918, when he was dispatched on a training assignment. For three weeks he gave and endured lectures well behind the lines, until he returned to England on Friday, February 8, where he remained for the duration of the war.

Odell began his military service as a subaltern. During the entire war he received but a single promotion, to first lieutenant, a rank that, given his class and education, was virtually a birthright in the British wartime army. His name does not appear among the Medal Lists, nor was he ever mentioned in despatches. He was, of course, exposed to the suffering; he lost his brother Eric, of the 8th Black Watch, who died of wounds inflicted at Arras on December 18, 1918. And he no doubt shared his sister-in-law's agony as she wrote letter after letter to Eric's commanding officer, a Captain Wil-

liamson, seeking details of his death, anything that might give meaning to the sacrifice (TNA: PRO WO 339/27163). Nevertheless, every indication suggests that Noel
Odell himself had a relatively easy war, and an exhaustive search of the archival records
found evidence of only the one minor injury while on active duty. Exaggerating one's
war record was no crime and not uncommon, especially among those who had not
faced the worst of the fighting. Men had any number of reasons for doing so, and
there is nothing in this small mystery that would challenge Odell's character, integrity,
or honor. He was by all accounts an exemplary and beloved individual. Still, his insistence that he had been wounded three times during the war, if indeed untrue, does
suggest something about his sense of personal narrative, which in this instance would
be important, given that the entire mystery of Mallory and Irvine hinges on his eyewitness account of their disappearance.

For Andrew "Sandy" Irvine, there is no better source than the biography written
by his grandniece Julie Summers, *Fearless on Everest.* For his correspondence with the
Everest Committee, see: RGS Box 28, File 1. For Irvine's 1924 Everest journal, see:
Herbert Carr, ed., *The Irvine Diaries: Andrew Irvine and the Enigma of Everest 1924*
(Reading: Gastons-West Col, 1979). Edward Shebbeare's most significant contribution to the Everest legacy is a very fine diary from the 1924 expedition, the only one of
his notebooks to survive his imprisonment during the Japanese occupation of Malaya.
It is on deposit at the Alpine Club Archives, D101. For Shebbeare's correspondence
with the Everest Committee, see: RGS Box 33, File 11.

Though Richard Hingston came late to the Everest adventure, he was without
doubt one of the most compelling characters. An old Asia hand, he had been a member
of the 1913 Russian Pamir triangulation expedition and served with distinction for
many years in the Indian Army, where he met Charles Bruce. Hingston's papers are on
deposit at Trinity College Dublin, which has both a forty-nine-page Everest notebook
(TCD MS 10473 Everest 1924) and his complete Everest diary (TCD MS 10474);
the diary begins on March 7 in Darjeeling and ends on August 1, again in Darjeeling,
with a local band playing, the town bedecked in flags, and Lady Lytton waiting at the
crossroads for the returning heroes. Also at Trinity and of great interest are Hingston's
personal war diaries. The first begins on September 16, 1914, at Abbottabad and runs
for 128 pages through February 22, 1915 (TCD MS 10514 Diary East Africa 1914).
The second starts on January 22, 1916, again in Abbottabad, and ends on May 19,
1918, in Bombay after the long campaign in Mesopotamia. The last lines read: "What
we all hunger for are hills and valleys, the green fields and shady woods, the rivers, the
torrents, the glaciers and the snows. I see visions of the Himalaya and all its wondrous
beauty." See also: TCD MS 10472 "Notes on Baghdad."

For his military service record, see: British Library Asia, Pacific, and Africa Collections, India Office Records IOR L/MIL/9/425 f.535–43 and L/MIL/14/15501.
Hingston began the war as medical officer to the 2nd Battalion of the 5 Gurkha Rifles
and soon joined Indian General Hospital No. 6 in support of Expeditionary Force B,
slated to make the ill-fated invasion of German East Africa. The armada sailed from
Bombay in the third month of the war. The forces landed at a forgotten place called
Tanga, where machine guns waited in the jungle and British officers watched as the
army they had built over years crumbled to pieces within minutes. In desperation they
beat their soldiers with swords and shot them dead with their revolvers, but nothing
could rally troops bled white with fear.

Hingston's task was to dress the wounded in a rubber planter's bungalow, on a
veranda stained red with blood, overlooking fields where the "dying and dead strewed
the ground in all directions." The wounded groaned and cried through the night.

Some walked about waving the stumps of amputated limbs, insisting in their delirium that they remained unharmed. "Bones shattered, fingers blown away; faces mangled out of recognition," Hingston wrote, "formed a never to be forgotten sight. The most horrible wounds were those which entered the back of the head and travelled forward until the bullet blew away the palate and the jaws."

When the order to withdraw finally came, men panicked in their rush for the open boats, trampling and drowning those among the wounded who stumbled in the sand. On the skiff that carried him away, Hingston encountered a man whose arm he had removed the previous day, and another with a hole in his back the size of a fist. "Scarce a word was uttered," he wrote. "Men looked as though they had aged as many years as they had spent days in that country."

Thus began four years of fighting that took Hingston from East Africa to the North-West Frontier and, ultimately, to Mesopotamia and the relief of Kut. On September 17, 1916, he was awarded the Military Cross for a heroic act that he later described almost as an afterthought. During a search-and-destroy mission near Nasiriyah on September 11, 1916, his troops were ambushed by an Arab force that soon grew to over 8,000. In the chaos Hingston and two orderlies, including his old friend Harkadhoy Rai, braved a hail of bullets to reach a soldier shot through the shoulder and chest. To evacuate him by stretcher across that "bullet-swept plain" was suicidal. The only option was for Hingston to lift the man onto his shoulder and make a run for it. As soon as they stood up, the air all around hissed with bullets. "One went crashing through Harkadhoy's head, blowing a huge piece out of his skull. He uttered a faint, broken gasp, and fell dead, with the wounded man and myself, in the same heap."

Hingston's journal entry for the day continues with a curious digression, almost as if in the midst of the battle he had stepped back to observe the moment with clinical precision, as if the words might somehow insulate him from the terrible reality of his friend's death: "A bullet passing through the skull makes a sharp smashing sound, extremely unpleasant to hear, resembling, as nearly as I can compare it, to the flat blade of an oar striking the surface of the water. This must be due to the instantaneous shattering of so much bone; certainly this man's head was so blown to pieces that I could have put my fist into his brains."

Hingston gathered three riflemen and placed the wounded soldier on the stretcher. Then, crawling on hands and knees, with Arab fire coming from three sides, they wriggled back toward their lines, a foot at a time, hoisting the limp burden, pushing it forward a few inches, and then collapsing from exhaustion before having another go. Under constant fire they covered but ten yards in thirty minutes. The Arabs pressed their attack. As he lay prostrate in the sand, Hingston recalled, "I used to peep above the camel thorn from time to time to watch them rushing forward singly or in small groups. They were picturesque in their white flowing garments; on they came waving their rifles wildly over their heads, shrieking aloud in their enthusiasm, madly gesticulating, leaping like lunatics into the air; one almost expected to see them cutting themselves with knives like the howling fanatics at the Altar of Baal. But they were receiving lead in exchange for their fervour; our rearguard was hammering them at every rush."

Hingston's deed did not go unnoticed, and he was awarded the Military Cross within six days, a remarkably short interval. The citation acknowledged his "gallantry and devotion to duty in treating the wounded continuously under heavy fire at close range regardless of his personal safety."

For Hingston's correspondence with the Everest Committee, see: RGS Box 27, File 4. Like all medical officers on the Everest expeditions, in 1924 Hingston also served as naturalist, and he fulfilled these duties with a zeal matched only by that of Wollaston in 1921. He collected 500 distinct species of plants, and more than 10,000 additional specimens, including 211 bird skins, 387 spiders, 439 mollusks, and 8,554 insects. For a summary of this work, see his contribution to the official expedition account: "Natural History," *The Fight for Everest, 1924*, pp. 261–88. See also: Richard Hingston, *A Naturalist in Himalaya* (Boston: Small, Maynard, 1920).

John Noel and his first wife, Sybille Moore Graham, had been married since November 14, 1914. Sybille accompanied her husband to Darjeeling in 1924 and embarked on a study of Tibetan folklore, which led to a forgotten but curious book, *The Magic Bird of Chomo-Lung-Ma: Tales of Mount Everest, the Turquoise Peak* (New York: Doubleday, Doran, 1931). For news of General Bruce's collapse, see: "The Mount Everest Expedition," *Geographical Journal*, vol. 63, no. 6 (June 1924), pp. 525–27. For the comings and goings at base camp, and between Camps I, II, III, and IV, see the typed copies of the individual camp diaries: RGS Box 41, File 3. As for the final retreat from the mountain, Bentley Beetham wrote a stirring account that included the phrase that serves as an epitaph for the entire effort: "The price of life is death." See: "The Return Journey," *The Fight for Everest, 1924*, pp. 155–92.

13: *The Price of Life Is Death*

In the final month leading to the last climb, Norton sent four dispatches from the mountain, all destined for the *Times*, according to the arrangement worked out by Hinks. On May 13 he wrote from the base camp on Rongbuk, the sixth dispatch of the expedition; it was published in London on May 31. Norton left a memorable account of the horrific conditions at Camp III encountered on May 10: "The wind appeared to be shot high in the air over the North Col, the Rapiu-La and the Lhakpa La, the three passes surrounding us, and, from some high point in the zenith, descended on our camp like a terrier on a rat-pit, and shook our little tents like rats."

Mallory and Norton worked together on the next dispatch, sent on May 26 from "East Rongbuk Glacier"; anticipating the final assault, it sparked considerable interest when it appeared in print on June 16. By then, of course, Mallory and Irvine were dead. Their fate was the subject of Norton's eighth dispatch, begun on the East Rongbuk on June 8, the day of their final effort, and completed with a contribution from Somervell on June 11 at base camp. News of the disaster reached Hinks in London on June 19 and was published in the *Times* on June 21. Norton's dispatch of June 11 appeared in the newspaper on June 26. On June 14, he sent his final dispatch from the Rongbuk base camp. Published in London on July 5, it included Odell's account of what he had last seen of Mallory and Irvine on the mountain.

All of these reports, together with four subsequent dispatches written from Kyetrak, the Rongshar Valley, Tingri Dzong, and Yatung, were published as: "The Mount Everest Dispatches," *Alpine Journal*, vol. 36, no. 229 (November 1924), pp. 196–241. In this same number of the journal appeared the papers read at the joint meeting of the RGS and the Alpine Club held at the Royal Albert Hall on October 17, 1924. See: Charles Bruce, "The Organisation and Start of the Expedition," pp. 241–44; Geoffrey Bruce, "The Journey through Tibet and the Establishment of the High Camps," pp. 251–60; Norton, "The Personnel of the Expedition," pp. 244–51, and "The Climb with Mr. Somervell to 28,000 Feet," pp. 260–65; and Odell, "The Last Climb," pp. 265–72. Odell recalled his excitement upon discovering fossils in a limestone band at 25,500 feet, even as he sought out the fate of his lost companions. Norton remembered Mallory: "A fire burnt in him, and it made him one of the two most formidable antagonists Everest has ever had. He was absolutely determined to conquer the mountain."

The RGS formally acknowledged the loss of Mallory and Irvine in: "The Mount

Everest Expedition," *Geographical Journal*, vol. 64, no. 1 (July 1924), pp. 56–58. The RGS also published the proceedings of the October 17 meeting. See: C. G. Bruce, Geoffrey Bruce, E. F. Norton, and N. E. Odell, "The Mount Everest Expedition of 1924," *Geographical Journal*, vol. 64, no. 6 (December 1924), pp. 433–69.

In his last dispatch, sent from Yatung, Norton wrote: "In the piping time of peace, how else than by such undertakings as Polar and Everest expeditions is the last flicker of the old spirit of adventure and enterprise which made the British Empire to be kept alive?"

Epilogue

For the memorial service at St. Paul's, see: Right Reverend Henry Luke Paget, Lord Bishop of Chester, "Memorial Services in Memory of Men Killed on Mt. Everest," *Alpine Journal*, vol. 36, no. 229 (November 1924), pp. 273–77. For Odell's moving obituary of Sandy Irvine, see: Noel Odell, "Andrew Comyn Irvine, 1902–1924," *Alpine Journal*, vol. 36, no. 229 (November 1924), pp. 386–89. Graham Irving, the schoolmaster who first introduced Mallory to the Alps, wrote his obituary. See: R. L. G. Irving, "George Herbert Leigh Mallory, 1886–1924," *Alpine Journal*, vol. 36, no. 229 (November 1924), pp. 381–85. The tribute from the king, received by Sir Francis Younghusband, was printed in that same issue of the *Alpine Journal*, p. 195.

For a time there remained a sense that another expedition would be imminent—if not in 1925, then certainly the following year. On December 15, 1924, Norton summed up the challenge in a paper read before the members of the Alpine Club. See: E. F. Norton, "The Problem of Mt. Everest," *Alpine Journal*, vol. 37, no. 230 (May 1925), pp. 1–21. Hingston reviewed the challenges of acclimatization. See: R. W. G. Hingston, "Physiological Difficulties in the Ascent of Mount Everest," *Geographical Journal*, vol. 65, no. 1 (January 1925), pp. 4–23. Odell presented his findings as a geologist. See: Noel Odell, "Observations on the Rocks and Glaciers of Mount Everest," *Geographical Journal*, vol. 66, no. 4 (July–December 1925), pp. 289–315.

For documents concerning the "Affair of the Dancing Lamas," see Indian Office Records (IOR) Mount Everest File Parts 3 and 4 (IOR L/PS/10/778), and correspondence between the India Office and the Everest Committee (RGS Box 27, Files 6 and 7). The controversy was widely covered in the press, and records may be found in the clippings file of the Alpine Club Archives and in the collections of the Colindale Newspaper Library. See, for example, General Bruce's article "Lamas of Tibet: From Monastic Cell to London Stage," *Times*, January 21, 1925, p. 17, and "Seven Tibetan Lamas Arrive in London," *Sphere*, December 6, 1924. On December 27, the *Sphere* published photos and a brief review under the headline "Tibetan Music at the Scala Theatre." The interlude, the paper reported, "is one of the strangest and most bizarre things in London at the present moment . . . Giant horns send their thunderous notes pulsating through the theatre. At first the music seems to picture Chaos, but in a second or two one seems to visualize the birth of the world."

For Bailey's opposition to further Everest expeditions, see: India Office Records (IOR) Mount Everest File Part 1 (IOR L/PS/10/777) and Parts 3 and 4 (IOR L/PS/10/778) 1924. For his correspondence with the Everest Committee, see: RGS Box 24, File 2, and Box 1, File 20.

For the British Everest expeditions of the 1930s, see: Tony Astill, *Mount Everest: The Reconnaissance 1935*, published by the author, 2005; Hugh Ruttledge, *Everest 1933* (London: Hodder & Stoughton, 1934; published in the United States as *Attack on Everest* [New York: Robert McBride, 1935]) and *Everest: The Unfinished Adventure* (London: Hodder & Stoughton, 1937); and H. W. Tilman, *Mount Everest 1938* (Cambridge: Cambridge University Press, 1948).

In 1950 Teddy Norton, at the age of sixty-eight and by then retired, reviewed these failed attempts, even as he sought to rekindle interest in another assault from the North Col. He was certain that the couloir that by then bore his name could be successfully climbed, assuming the weather cooperated and the porters proved to be as stouthearted as the men he had come to know in 1922 and 1924. "The rest," he wrote, "is on the knees of the Gods." See E. F. Norton, "Mount Everest: The Last Lap," *Alpine Journal*, vol. 57, no. 280 (May 1950), pp. 285–92.

For the Swiss attempt from Nepal in 1952 that came so close to success, see: R. Dittert, G. Chevalley, and R. Lambert, *Forerunners to Everest* (London: George Allen & Unwin, 1954). For Hillary and Tenzing's historic climb in 1953, see: John Hunt, *The Ascent of Everest* (London: Hodder & Stoughton, 1953), and Jan Morris, *Coronation Everest* (London: Faber and Faber, 1958). For the life of Tenzing Norgay, see: Ed Douglas, *Tenzing: Hero of Everest* (Washington, D.C.: National Geographic Books, 2003); Tenzing Norgay and James Ramsey Ullman, *Man of Everest: The Autobiography of Tenzing* (London: George Harrap, 1955); and Tenzing Norgay and Malcolm Barnes, *After Everest: An Autobiography* (London: Allen & Unwin, 1977). For a beautiful book that acknowledges the heroism of a father, even as a son seeks to forge his own identity on this mountain of all desires, see: Jamling Tenzing Norgay and Broughton Coburn, *Touching My Father's Soul* (New York: HarperCollins, 2001).

For the Chinese expeditions with photographs that capture the ideological thrust of their efforts, see: *Another Ascent of the World's Highest Peak—Qomolangma* (Peking: Foreign Languages Press, 1975), and *A Photographic Record of the Mount Jolmo Lungma Scientific Expedition (1966–1968)* (Peking: Science Press, 1977).

For the three letters found on Mallory's body, as well as twenty-seven letters of condolence written to Ruth at the time of his death, see: Mallory Papers, Box 7, Magdalene College Archives, Cambridge. For Conrad Anker's insights, see: *The Lost Explorer* (New York: Simon & Schuster, 1999).

In a letter home, Billy Grenfell, age twenty-five, tried to explain life on the Western Front. "Death is such a frail barrier out here," he wrote, "that we cross it, smiling and gallant, every day." Billy was killed on July 30, 1915, leading a suicidal charge at Hooge, within a mile of where his brother Julian, age twenty-seven, had fallen on May 13, struck in the head by a shell fragment. Julian, a poet, died of his wounds four weeks later, his mother at his side. In the carnage of the Ypres Salient, Billy was buried in haste, his body lost, never to be recovered.

Index

abominable snowman, 353

Abors, 208–9

Above the Snowline (Dent), 69

Abraham, Ashley, 157–8

Abraham, George, 126

Abruzzi, Duke of, 70, 75, 78, 125, 138, 391, 428

acclimatization, 69, 78, 126, 510

"Affair of the Dancing Lamas," 562–4

Afghanistan, 40, 47, 51, 72, 294, 375–6, 523

Aga Khan, 468

airplanes: in mountaineering, 100, 108, 112, 140; in warfare, 15, 16, 93, 126

Allen, Lancelot, 187

Alliance Bank of Simla, 456

Alpine Club, 77, 137, 143, 148, 155, 167, 168, 176, 183, 371, 473, 485; Bruce as president of, 456; first Everest expedition and, 68–9, 70–1, 73–5, 83, 100, 101, 109, 126, 156; generational rift among climbers and, 457; joint meeting of RGS and (1922), 457–8; Mallory and Irvine memorialized at joint meeting of RGS and, 560–1

Alpine Club of America, 466

Alpine Club of Canada, 217

Alpine Journal, 68, 69, 168

Alps, 76–7, 130, 143, 144, 147–8, 155, 168–9, 176, 177, 203, 261, 283, 346, 370, 371, 377, 380, 475, 534; glaciers as easiest routes of approach in, 274; Mallory's ascents in, 8–9, 168–9, 177–8, 183–4; Mallory's honeymoon plans in, 184–5

Amarkantak, India, 103

Amo Chu, 116, 218, 219

Ampthill, Lord, 61

Amritsar Massacre (1919), 294–5, 296, 390

Anderson, Graeme, 145–6, 148, 152, 370, 413, 468–9

Angdanel, 350

Anglo-Chinese Treaty (1893), 52

Anglo-Chinese Treaty (1906), 118

Anglo-Russian Boundary Commission (1885), 51

Anglo-Russian Convention (1907), 74, 118

Ang Pasang, 327, 355, 356, 358

Angtarkay, 483

Ang Tenze, 323

Anker, Conrad, 567–9, 570, 571–3

Antarctica expeditions, 110, 383, 487, 488; applications for first Everest expedition from veterans of, 128–30

anthropology, 46

Apostles (secret society), 173–4

Araguaya, 37

Ari, 214, 215

Armstrong, John, 45

Army and Navy Stores, 157, 394, 482

Arnold, Edward, 380

Arras, Battle of (1917), 105, 193, 194, 195, 211

Arun, 82, 238, 258, 259, 282, 297–8, 338; crossing of, 80, 83, 242; great gorge of, 83, 250, 257, 308, 326, 447; headwater tributaries of, 224, 239, 298 (*see also* Phung Chu)

Asghar Khan, 260, 264, 285

Asquith, Herbert, 183

Asquith, Raymond, 196

Asquith, Violet, 188

Assam, 63, 208, 209, 210

Assault on Mount Everest, The (Bruce), 460

A NOTE ABOUT THE AUTHOR

WADE DAVIS is the best-selling author of fifteen books, including *The Serpent and the Rainbow, One River,* and *The Wayfinders,* and is an award-winning anthropologist. He currently holds the post of National Geographic explorer-in-residence, and divides his time between Washington, D.C., and northern British Columbia.

A NOTE ON THE TYPE

THIS BOOK was set in Janson, a typeface long thought to have been made by the Dutchman Anton Janson, who was a practicing typefounder in Leipzig during the years 1668–1687. However, it has been conclusively demonstrated that these types are actually the work of Nicholas Kis (1650–1702), a Hungarian, who most probably learned his trade from the master Dutch typefounder Dirk Voskens. The type is an excellent example of the influential and sturdy Dutch types that prevailed in England up to the time William Caslon (1692–1766) developed his own incomparable designs from them.

Composed by North Market Street Graphics,
Lancaster, Pennsylvania
Printed and bound by Berryville Graphics,
Berryville, Virginia
Designed by Virginia Tan

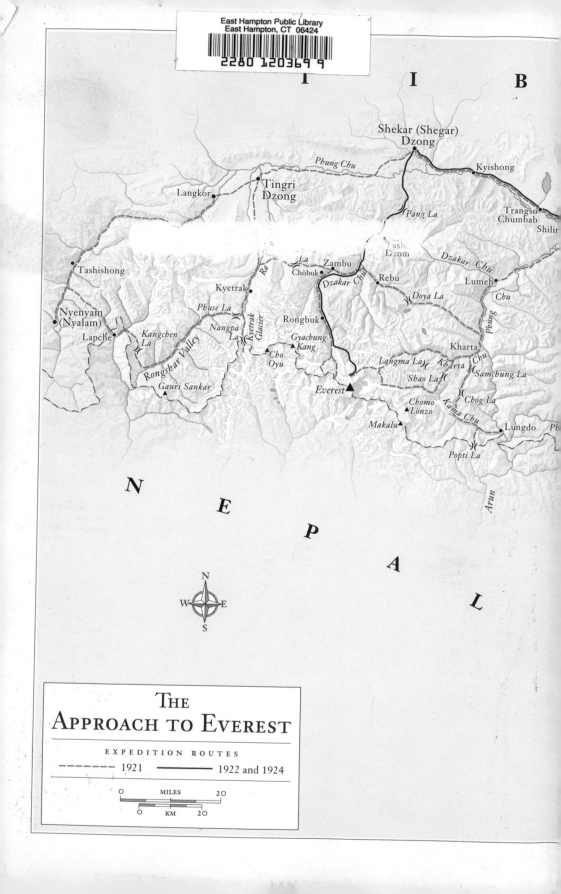

I   I   B

Shekar (Shegar)
Dzong

Phung Chu

Kyishong

Langkor

Tingri
Dzong

Pang La

Trangso
Chumbab

Shilir

Tashi
Dzom

Dzakar Chu

Tashishong

La

Zambu

Chöbuk

Dzakar Chu

Rebu

Lumeh

Chu

Kyetrak

Doya La

Phuse La

Ra

Kyetrak Glacier

Rongbuk

Phung

Nyenyam
(Nyalam)

Nangpa La

Gyachung Kang

Kharta

Lapche

Kangchen La

Cho
Oyu

Langma La

Kharta Chu

Samchung La

Rongshar Valley

Shao La

Chog La

Gauri Sankar

Everest

Chomo Lönzo

Kama Chu

Lungdo

Makalu

Popti La

Arun

N   E   P   A   L

N
W   E
S

THE
APPROACH TO EVEREST

EXPEDITION ROUTES
- - - - - 1921 ———— 1922 and 1924

MILES
0   20
0   KM   20